Understanding and Managing Model Risk

For other titles in the Wiley Finance series
please see www.wiley.com/finance

Understanding and Managing Model Risk

A Practical Guide for Quants, Traders and Validators

Massimo Morini

WILEY

A John Wiley & Sons, Ltd., Publication

This edition first published 2011

Registered Office
John Wiley & Sons Ltd, The Atrium, Southern Gate, Chichester, West Sussex, PO19 8SQ, United Kingdom

For details of our global editorial offices, for customer services and for information about how to apply for permission to reuse the copyright material in this book please see our website at www.wiley.com.

Library of Congress Cataloging-in-Publication Data:

Understanding and managing model risk : a practical guide for quants, traders and validators / [edited by] Massimo Morini. – 1st ed.
p. cm. – (Wiley finance series)
Includes bibliographical references and index.
ISBN 978-0-470-97761-3 (hardback)
1. Risk management. 2. Risk management–Mathematical models. I. Morini, Massimo.
HD61.U53 2011
332.64′5–dc23 2011031397

ISBN 978-0-470-97761-3 (hbk), ISBN 978-1-119-96085-0 (ebk),
ISBN 978-0-470-97774-3 (ebk), ISBN 978-0-470-97775-0 (ebk)

A catalogue record for this book is available from the British Library.

Set in 10/12pt Times by Aptara Inc., New Delhi, India
Printed and bound by CPI Group (UK) Ltd, Croyden, CRO 4YY

Contents

Preface

One fundamental reason for writing this book is that I do not think that models can 'kill Wall Street', as someone was heard to say during the credit crunch. Shortsighted policies and regulations, and bad incentives for market players, are much more likely killers (see Chapter 1 for some precise results regarding the role they can play in fuelling a crisis). And yet I am perplexed when I hear some fellow modellers deny any responsibility, saying 'Models were not a problem. The problem was in the data and the parameters! The problem was in the application!'. As a researcher and bank quant, I find these disclaimers paradoxical. Models in finance are tools to quantify prices or risks. This includes mathematical relations, a way to use data or judgement to compute the parameters, and indications on how to apply them to practical issues. Only by taking all these things together can we talk of 'a model'. Modellers should stay away from the temptation to reduce models to a set of mathematical functions that can be thought of separately from the way they are specified and from the way they are applied. If this were the case, models would really be only blank mathematical boxes and people would be right to consider them useless, when not outright dangerous.

This is not the definition of models considered in this book. I think that mathematical models are magnificent tools that can take our understanding of markets, and our capability to act in markets, to levels impossible to reach without quantitative aids. For this to be true, we must understand the interaction between mathematics and the reality of markets, data, regulations and human behaviour, and control for this in our management of model risk.

The fact that thousands of technical papers speak of very advanced models, and just a handful focus on model risk and how to manage it, is one of our problems. Too often models have been used to create a false sense of confidence rather than to improve our understanding. Increasing the complexity of the mathematical details to hide our ignorance of the underlying system is an abuse of the beauty and power of mathematics.

At the same time we have relegated model validation and risk management to become a formal and boring topic for bureaucrats. So I do not find it strange that this book has been written not by a risk manager or a validator, but by a front office quant who has spent the last ten years inventing new models, implementing them, and helping practitioners to use them for buying, selling and hedging derivatives. No one has seen how many unexpected consequences the practical use of models can have more often than a front office quant. This forces us to think of model robustness and of the effect of different calibrations or estimations of parameters. While risk managers and validators can at times afford to take a formal approach to model risk, front office quants must go deeper into the mathematical aspects of models for their implementation, and are also those who then have to deal with the most practical side of model risk.

I have also been helped by the fact that I am a researcher and trainer in the field of quantitative finance, am up-to-date with the variety of models developed by quants and enjoy the benefit of many discussions with my fellow researchers and students about the use and misuse of models. Another important element is the role I have been allowed to play in the study of the foundations of modelling at my bank, and the close collaboration with a wise and far-sighted risk management and validation group team during my last years at Intesa Sanpaolo.

In this book I have tried to avoid the two opposite extremes that I have seen too often. On one hand, training material on risk management often gives a lot of details on formal compliance or simple techniques to produce numbers that are acceptable to put in reports, but lacks the quantitative approach that would be needed to understand models deeply, and the practical examples on how real risks can arise from the use of models and hit the business of your bank or institution. Now a consensus is growing, even among regulators, that we need something different. On the other hand, many papers on financial models are weighed down with mathematics and numerics, but just a few focus on the consequences that different modelling choices can have on enterprise-wide risk and on the analysis of financial conditions and practical misuses that can lead to model losses. It is also rare to find papers that show how many alternative models are possible giving you the same good fit and efficient calibration but leading to completely different pricing and risk assessment for complex products. Before the crisis models did not play the role of allowing as transparent as possible a translation of assumptions into numbers. They have often hidden poor and oversimplified assumptions under a lot of numerical and mathematical details.

In this book you will find the rigorous mathematical foundations and the most recent developments in financial modelling, but they are analyzed taking into account the regulatory and accountancy framework, and they are explained through a wide range of practical market cases on different models and different financial products, to display where model risk hides and how it can be managed. The consequences of model assumptions when applied in the business, including explanation of model errors and misunderstandings, the comparison of different models and the analysis of model uncertainty are a focus of this book, to build up a practical guide for reducing the likelihood of model losses.

Those who like mathematics, will find as much of it as they can desire, especially in the second part of the book. But in the first part of the book there are also hundreds of pages of explanations in plain words, without formulas, that I strongly advise should not be ignored. They are sometimes the only way to think about the real purposes for which formulas are developed, and they are often the only way to explain models to many who will use them. Those who do not really like mathematics will be happy to see that in these pages all concepts are also explained without formulas. But please, do make an effort to engage with the mathematics. Here it is explained, often from the foundations, and always put in relation to practice, you may be surprised to find just how useful it can be. This also makes the book suitable for students that want to see financial models within the context of their application, and for users that have to choose different models and want to explore their hidden consequences.

Some of the mathematical complexities we have seen in models in the past decade are probably useless or even disturbing. But financial problems are seriously complex, and very often a high level of mathematical ability is really needed. I do think, however, that the high level of theoretical complexity reached by models must be balanced by a practical and not-too-complex approach to model risk management. In what follows you will find all the mathematics needed to understand models, but you will not find complex theoretical and mathematical frameworks for how to perform model risk management or validation. We want to reduce model risk, not to compound the risk of complex models with the risk of complex model validation. We keep our distance from fascinating but overcomplex frameworks that are often inapplicable and inhibit fresh thinking.

My aim is to help regulators, senior management, traders, students, and also quants themselves to a deeper understanding and awareness of the financial implications of quantitative models. Even more importantly, I want to provide quants, risk managers and validators with tools for investigating and displaying effectively the reasons for choosing one model and rejecting another, and for understanding and explaining why in many cases model uncertainty is unavoidable and models must not be used to create a false sense of confidence or as a shield for dangerous business decisions. Before the recent crisis, this analysis and this explanation failed too often and the consequences have been harsh.

In any case: if the book fails to fulfil this role, at least it has reached such a size that it can be used by quants and technical traders to stop physically any dangerous model misuse or misunderstanding. The sheer weight of its pages will force the errants to stop and think about what they are doing, without, one hopes, leaving any permanent physical consequences.

A final remark is in order. No book should even try to be a definitive work on model risk. If this were the case, we might feel entitled to stop thinking about and doubting our model tools, and a crisis worse than the one we have just seen would be forthcoming. In spite of the range of models and markets considered, this search for risks, errors and misunderstanding in the development and use of models is necessarily very partial and incomplete. But I am confident that coming with me on this quest will make you a better hunter.

One of the exercises for the reader is to spot the model risks that managed to escape the nets of this book, or survive defiantly among its pages, and propose solutions. I have even set up a website: www.managingmodelrisk.com.

HOW WE PROCEED

The book is divided into two parts. In the first, I want to build solid knowledge of the theory and the empirical evidence underlying the best practice of model risk management, constructing a practical scheme for model choice and model validation. I want the reader to not just accept each step passively, but to gain a thorough understanding of why it is useful and of how it must be applied in different situations. Since the different possible situations in financial markets are a continuous infinity of a high order, the only way to gain confidence is to explore each step deeply through market examples. I have tried in the examples to keep a practical and 'teaching' approach, as confirmed by the number of 'handwritten' figures that come from my courses for practitioners.

This book covers a wide range of asset classes. The lion's share is probably played by interest rates and credit, which is not surprising because in almost all banks model risk management has a special focus on these asset classes. The most natural examples in the first part of the book, that deals with errors in model assumptions and model application, come from credit, where these issues have emerged most often, particularly in the recent credit crunch. The second part of this book deals with more technical errors, particularly in computational methods, hedging, and mathematical techniques. Here, most of the examples come from interest rates, because it is here that the most advanced techniques were developed and applied. These two asset classes are also those that are experiencing the most changes in modelling approach now. However, equity modelling is mentioned very often throughout the book, and actually the majority of the issues dealt with in the book can have an application within complex equity models, as I often point out. We also speak of cross-currency, and liquidity and hybrid modelling have sections devoted to them.

Below is an extended summary of the contents

In Chapter 1 we want to understand what Model Risk really means in practice. To achieve this goal:

- We study the foundations of quantitative pricing and their relationship with the actual workings of the markets.
- We see the most relevant analyses of model risk given in the literature, and we test them on the reality of the past crises, from the stock market crash of 1987 to the LTCM collapse, and the Russian default, up to the credit crunch, to see which model errors really led to large losses and how this risk could be managed.
- We investigate the links between the way we use models and the accounting standards, in particular the concepts of fair value, mark-to-market and levels 1, 2 and 3 for pricing.
- We describe the prescriptions of regulators to see which constraints they set on modelling and which indications they give on model risk management.

In Chapter 2 we consider three market examples, so as to apply the scheme for Model Validation and Model Risk Management developed at the end of Chapter 1.

- We consider three asset classes: credit, equity and interest rates.
- For each asset class we consider a few payoffs, and apply to them a range of different models, including the most popular modelling alternatives in the market. One goal of this chapter is to understand how to perform model comparison and model choice.
- We show how to deal with model uncertainty with provisions such as Reserves and Model Lines or Limits to Exposure. We perform market intelligence and show how to interpret the results of it with reverse engineering.
- The first example is introduced here for the first time, for the other two we analyze the existing literature and then go beyond it.

In Chapter 3 we look at stress-testing to understand the core risk of a payoff by using models, an issue already tackled in the previous chapter, and we look at the stress-testing of models to understand their weaknesses, an issue resumed later in Chapter 6.

- We devote particular attention to avoiding the pitfalls that are most likely to occur when performing stress-testing.
- We investigate what cases of stress one should consider (market conditions, payoff features, characteristics of the counterparties...) and we see a few examples of how to use historical and cross-section market information to design stress scenarios.
- As a playground we display here, via stress-testing, the errors in the practice of credit derivatives that were at the center of the crisis, including the still widespread copula and mapping methods, and present alternatives to these.

In Chapter 4 we consider the most painful event in terms of model losses: when a model consensus in the market suddenly breaks down and is replaced by a radically different standard.

- We carry the study on with the purpose of understanding the mechanisms of consensus change, already considered in the first chapter, so as to be not fully unprepared for the changes that will happen in the future.
- The first example of the death of a model, and the birth of a new one, regards the changes that happened recently to the pricing of even the simplest interest rate derivatives: the separation of discounting and forwarding, the multiplication of term-structures and the explosion of basis spreads. In this analysis we investigate the hidden assumptions of a modelling framework, by seeing how the traditional mathematical representation of interest rates taught in books must be replaced by a different approach.
- The second example, related to the first one, deals with the inclusion of liquidity and funding in pricing. Since we are still in the middle of this transformation of pricing foundations, we can now study the risks to which we would be exposed depending on the direction the market takes.

The second part of this book is devoted to those aspects of the practice in the financial markets where model risk management is most crucial.

In Chapter 5 we focus on hedging, an activity based on models but dangerously overlooked by the research in quantitative finance, or addressed in a theoretical way unrelated to practice. We take a different approach.

- We study how models are used in real hedging, and how this differs from their use in pricing. These differences must be studied and the intrinsic risks understood and managed. The principal example is on local and stochastic volatility models for equity options.
- We look at how to perform a P&L-Explain test, where one tests the hedging performance of a model. We want to understand the limitations of this technique but also what it can actually tell us about the appropriateness of a model.

In Chapter 6 we focus on computational methods, in order to understand how they must be assessed, stress-tested, and their efficiency monitored.

- We focus on approximations since these can hide the sneakiest model risk. In fact when market conditions change approximations often break down, but the market may take some time to react.
- The examples we see regard mostly the approximations used in the interest rate market, for example convexity adjustment, BGM-model approximations or the SABR formula. In testing them we also show the problems they are having in the current market conditions.
- We see how an approximation can be tested against an exact method or against a more precise numerical procedure. We also show examples and exercises of the risks in simulation and numerical integration.

In Chapter 7 we analyze the risks associated with two common operations: interpolation and extrapolation. We show two approaches:

- How to use non-trivial market information in order to minimize the need for extrapolation. We see this in particular for the volatility smile.
- How to use the mathematical properties of some quantities in order to make interpolation more consistent and avoid the use of extrapolation. Here we focus on the correlation skew.

In Chapter 8 we tackle the risk involved in correlation modelling from two different perspectives:

- We present useful technical solutions for modelling and parameterizing correlations, with examples from different asset classes where correlations need to have different properties.
- We explore the most common errors made when devising assumptions about correlation, such as assuming rigid relations for factors that have a degree of independence (the 1-correlation risk) and conversely the risk of taking as unrelated those things that have structural links (the 0-correlation risk). Two market cases are observed.

In Chapter 9 we complete the treatment of a topic that is covered in almost all other chapters: calibration. We look at exposing the residual mode uncertainty that remains after a calibration, and minimizing this uncertainty by enrichment of the calibration set.

- Introducing some model risk management tools needed to perform diagnostics of a calibration procedure, such as assessing the stability of the resulting model.

Chapter 10 is devoted to an issue that at times is not included in a narrow definition of model risk, but has high relevance: the risk of errors in the description of the payoff.

- We consider the case when the errors arise from a superficial interpretation of the termsheet or of the legal prescriptions. We see an example that has a strong impact on the pricing of counterparty risk.
- We consider the errors that arise from simplifications introduced to ease the mathematical representation of a payoff. The example is on Index options.

Chapter 11 considers an application of models which is typical of hedge funds or proprietary trading desks: using models for statistical or model arbitrage, exploiting temporary inconsistencies among related products. We see in practice two classic examples:

- Capital-structure arbitrage, based on equity and bonds/CDS, and here addressed with a recent structural model.
  Cap-swaption arbitrage in a Libor market model.
- We show by looking at empirical results how "arbitrage trades" can be easier to risk manage as directional trades on market uncertainty.

WHAT ELSE YOU WILL FIND IN THIS BOOK

In explaining model risk and model validation, we describe in detail practical examples where we cover a number of relevant topics for today's finance, not mentioned, or only hinted at, in the above summary:

- Correlation modelling for equity with stochastic volatility, interest rates, FX rates, default events.
- The comparison of local vs stochastic volatility models both in terms of hedging and in terms of pricing path-dependent/forward-start derivatives.
- The most dangerous correlation errors in the computation of wrong-way counterparty risk.
- The modern pricing of interest rate derivatives with multiple curves for basis swaps and alternative discounting curves.
- The up-to-date treatment of the impact of funding liquidity in pricing.

- The impact of market illiquidity on the way we compute prices, and its relation to model uncertainty.
- How to set quantitative triggers to detect when a market formula is going to break down.
- Bubbles, arbitrage and market completeness in practice.
- A detailed account of the development of the credit crunch and its relationship with model choices and model errors.
- Diagnostic tools used on the behaviour of a model, such as the way to compute the model-implied evolution of volatilities and smiles.
- What is really explained by P&L-Explain tests.
- Different examples of reverse-engineering to understand which models can have generated observable prices.
- The analysis of the most relevant problems when using copulas for default events, the impossibility to control the timing of related events, and a solution to this.
- The analysis of gap risk using different models that treat information differently.
- The meaning, advantages and risks of taking into account the default of our institution in pricing (DVA).
- Detailed examples from asset classes including credit, interest rates, equity, cross-currency and funding.
- The analysis of the behaviour of the SABR model and the limits of its pricing formulas.
- The large number of changes to modelling standards which are required by the post-crisis market patterns.
- The risks hidden within the pricing procedures for plain vanilla derivatives.
- An alternative way to model correlations that can explain the correlation skew.
- Counterparty risk adjustment and the indetermination associated with an unclear legal definition of default payments.
- The reality of the lack of fundamental information in markets and the role this plays in derivatives marketing and trading.
- Dealing with funding liquidity and credit simultaneously and the risks of double-counting, loss of competitiveness or excessively aggressive behaviour.
- New analysis on the pricing of Bermudan swaptions and CMS derivatives.
- We explore the popular issue of calibrating a model to European options and then applying it to early exercise American/Bermudan derivatives.
- The explanation via liquidity and counterparty risk of the presence of basis swaps, and the hedging consequences of multiple curves.
- The explanation and a non-standard analysis of a range of models that include local and stochastic volatility models, jump models, the Libor market model for interest rate derivatives, structural models, copulas, mapping methods, reduced form credit models.
- Two analyses of correlation risk in hedging, for equity and for rates.
- And much more... but not inflation, nor the variance-gamma model!

Acknowledgements

The author acknowledges fruitful conversations with Bruno Dupire, Riccardo Rebonato, Marco Avellaneda, Emanuel Derman, Igor Smirnov, Umberto Cherubini, Jon Gregory, Vladimir Piterbarg, Paul Wilmott, Emilio Barucci, Josh Danzinger, Antonio Castagna, Claudio Albanese, Ziggy Johnsson, Christian Fries, Marc Henrard, Rama Cont, Alberto Elizalde, Pierpaolo Montana, Andrej Lyashenko, Vladimir Chorny, Lorenzo Bergomi, Alex Lipton, John Crosby, Gianluca Fusai, Pat Hagan, Francesco Corielli, Lane Houghston, Stewart Hodges, Francesca Minucci, Wim Schoutens, Nicola Pede. All of the participants who attended my workshops and courses are deeply thanked (some of them are actually mentioned in the body of the book).

I am also grateful to my colleagues in the Financial Engineering of Banca IMI, for the discussions on the foundations and the details of modelling. Some of them must be named individually: Nicola Moreni for his rigour, Daniele Perini for his precision, Giulio Sartorelli for the extraordinary depth, Mario Pucci for always mixing wit with fun, Federico Targetti for his eclecticism, Gianvittorio Mauri and Ferdinando Ametrano for their experience, Paola Mosconi and Alessio Calvelli for bringing clever fresh thinking (and adding Roman wisdom to our Nordic strictness). A thank you also goes to Andrea Bugin, our boss, for always favouring deep reasoning and discussion, and to Alberto Mina, for his endless hard work while we were reasoning and discussing (waiting for your own book, Alberto). Last but not least I thank Giorgio Facchinetti, whose intellectual honesty and technical solidity has proven the best test for any new original idea. Among the other colleagues I need to mention (and I am surely forgetting many) Luigi Cefis, Pietro Virgili, Cristina Duminuco, Francesco Fede, Sebastiano Chirigoni, Salvatore Crescenzi, Giuseppe Fortunati, Fabio Perdichizzi, Cristiana Corno, Francesco Natale, Federico Veronesi, Luca Dominici, Stefano Santoro, Pierluigi D'Orazio, Raffaele Giura, Michele Lanza, Roberto Paolelli, Luca Brusadelli, Biagio Giacalone, Marcello Terraneo, Massimo Baldi, Francesco Lago, Stefano Martina, Alessandro Ravogli, Cristiano Maffi, Valeria Anzoino, Emiliano Carchen, Raffaele Lovero. Marco Bianchetti and Andrea Prampolini are thanked for the insight they gave me on many occasions, but even more for being so close to what a trader and a validator should be in the dreams of a quant. A special thank you in the quant community goes to my masters of old Damiano Brigo, Fabio Mercurio, my brother Maurizio, Nick Webber, Pietro Muliere and my late professors Umberto Magnani and Carlo Giannini.

Among those that made this book physically possible I thank Pete Baker, Aimee Dibbens, Tessa Allen, Lori Boulton, Mariangela Palazzi-Williams and all the Wiley team. The advice of Raul Montanari is gratefully acknowledged.

I thank my son Vittorio, for showing me, even too often, that the desire to understand how things really work comes before all the theory and the books, and my daughter Giulia, for teaching me regularly, at the age of three, how things should be properly explained. A thank you to Enzo and Mirella, for their principles have proven as good in the global financial markets as they were in a village in the Italian countryside. No thanks will ever be sufficient for Elena.

"The wide world is all about you; you can fence yourselves in, but you cannot forever fence it out."

Gildor in 'The Lord of the Rings', by J.R.R Tolkien

"There was no way, without full understanding, that one could have confidence that conditions the next time might not produce erosion three times more severe than the time before. Nevertheless, officials fooled themselves into thinking they had such understanding and confidence, in spite of the peculiar variations from case to case. A mathematical model was made to calculate erosion. This was a model based not on physical understanding but on empirical curve fitting ... Similar uncertainties surrounded the other constants in the formula. When using a mathematical model careful attention must be given to uncertainties in the model."

Richard Feynman, from 'Rogers' Commission Report into the Challenger Crash Appendix F – Personal Observations on Reliability of Shuttle'

"It does not do to leave a live dragon out of your calculations, if you live near him."

'The Hobbit', by J.R.R Tolkien

"Official management, on the other hand, claims to believe the probability of failure is a thousand times less. One reason for this may be an attempt to assure the government of NASA perfection and success in order to ensure the supply of funds. The other may be that they sincerely believed it to be true, demonstrating an almost incredible lack of communication between themselves and their working engineers."

Richard Feynman, from 'Rogers' Commission Report into the Challenger Crash Appendix F – Personal Observations on Reliability of Shuttle'

"Now, therefore, things shall be openly spoken that have been hidden from all but a few until this day ... And I will begin that tale, though others shall end it ... You may tarry, or come back, or turn aside into other paths, as chance allows. The further you go, the less easy will it be to withdraw."

Elrond in 'The Lord of the Rings', by J.R.R Tolkien

Part I

Theory and Practice of Model Risk Management

1 Understanding Model Risk

1.1 WHAT IS MODEL RISK?

In the last years, during and after the credit crunch, we have often read in the financial press that errors on 'models' and lack of management of 'model risk' were among the main causes of the crisis. A fair amount of attacks regarded mathematical or quantitative models, like the notorious Gaussian copula, that were accused to be wrong and give wrong prices for complex derivative, in particular credit and mortgage-related derivatives. These criticisms to valuation models have been shared also by bank executives and people that are not unexperienced on the reality of financial markets. In spite of this it is not very clear when a model must be considered *wrong*, and as a consequence it is not clear what model risk is.

We can probably all agree that *model risk is the possibility that a financial institution suffers losses due to mistakes in the development and application of valuation models*, but we need to understand which mistakes we are talking about.

In the past, model validation and risk management focused mainly on detecting and avoiding errors in the mathematical passages, the computational techniques and the software implementation that we have to perform to move from model assumptions to the quantification of prices. These sources of errors are an important part of model risk, and it is natural that model risk management devotes a large amount of effort to avoid them. We will devote a share of the second part of this book to related issues. However, they regard that part of model risk that partially overlaps with a narrow definition of operational risk: the risk associated to lack of due diligence in tasks for which it is not very difficult to define what should be the right execution. Is this what model validation is all about? In natural science, the attempt to eliminate this kind of error is not even part of model validation. It is called *model verification*, since it corresponds to verifying that model assumptions are turned correctly into numbers. The name model validation is instead reserved to the activity of assessing if *the assumptions of the model are valid*. Model assumptions, not computational errors, were the focus of the most common criticisms against quantitative models in the crisis, such as 'default correlations were too low'.

The errors that we can make in the assumptions underlying our models are the other crucial part of model risk, probably underestimated in the past practice of model risk management. They are the most relevant errors in terms of impact on the reputation of a financial institution that works with models. A clear example is what happened with rating agencies when the subprime crisis burst. When they were under the harshest attacks, rating agencies tried to shield themselves from the worst criticisms by claiming that the now evident underestimation of the risk of credit derivatives was not due to wrong models, but to mistakes made in the software implementation of the models. Many market operators, that knew the models used by rating agencies, did not believe this justification, and it had no other effect than increasing the perception that wrong models were the real problem. What is interesting to notice is that admitting wrong software appeared to them less devastating for their reputation than admitting wrong models.

Unfortunately, errors in mathematics, software or computational methods are easy to define and relatively easy to detect, although this requires experience and skills, as we will see in the second part of the book. Errors in model assumptions, instead, are very difficult to detect. It is even difficult to define them. How can we, as the result of some analysis, conclude that a model, intended as a set of assumptions, has to be considered wrong? We need to understand when a valuation model must be called wrong in order to answer to our first crucial question, *what is model risk?*

In this section we look for the answer. The first sources we use to clarify this issue are the words of a few legendary quants that in the past have tried to say when models are right or wrong in order to give a definition of model risk. You will see that not even among quants there is consensus about what model risk is. But then, when we apply these approaches to past crises to understand how they could have protected us from the worst model losses, we will see that the different approaches can lead to similar practical prescriptions.

1.1.1 The Value Approach

As early as 1996, before both the LTCM collapse and the credit crunch, the two events that put most critical pressure on the risk involved in using mathematical pricing models, one of living legends of quantitative finance, Emanuel Derman, wrote a paper titled *Model Risk*. This is a natural starting point to define our subject, also because it can be seen as the foundation of one of the two main schools of thought about model risk. The views of the author on the subject are further specified by a later paper written in 2001 that addresses model validation prescriptions, under the title *The Principles and Practice of Verifying Derivatives Prices*.

Derman notices first that the previous years had seen the emergence of an *'astonishingly theoretical approach to valuation of risky products. The reliance on models to handle risk'*, he points out, *'carries its own risk'*. Derman does not give a definition of model risk, but he indicates some crucial questions that a model validator should have in mind:

1. Is the payoff accurately described?
2. Is the software reliable?
3. Has the model been appropriately calibrated to the prices of the simpler, liquid constituents that comprise the derivative?
4. *'Does the model provides a realistic (or at least plausible) description of the factors that affect the derivative's value?'*

Can we deduce a definition of model risk from these points? The first two points are not trivial. When speaking of approximations and numerics in Chapter 6 we will talk of errors to avoid in implementation, and we even devote the entire Chapter 10 to the errors that can be made in the description of a payoff. However, these points do not add to our understanding of Derman's ideas about the nature of the errors we can make in model assumptions.

The third point instead underlines a feature that models must have: the capability to price consistently with the market the simpler instruments related to a derivative, namely to perform the so-called *calibration*. This is an important issue, on which we will focus later on. But not even this point clarifies what model risk is. All banks, now, calibrate their models to liquid market prices. For any asset class or financial product there are many models which are different from each other and yet can all be calibrated very well to the market. Once we have satisfied this calibration constraint, are we sure that model risk has been eliminated, or instead the core of model risk is crucially linked to the fact that we have *different* models allowing for good calibration, so that calibration does not solve our model uncertainty?

A better clarification is given in the fourth point. From this we can deduce a definition of model risk. Once we are sure that we have correctly implemented payoff and software, and our model appears calibrated to the liquid underlying products, we have a residual risk that seems to be the core of model risk:

> *Model risk is the risk that the model is not a realistic/plausible representation of the factors affecting the derivative's value*

This is confirmed when Derman says that for less liquid or more exotic derivatives one must verify the *'reasonableness of the model itself'*. There is more. Derman (1996) gives an account of the things that can go wrong in model development, and he starts from some examples where lack of realism is surely the crucial problem:

> *'You may have not taken into account all the factors that affect valuation ... You may have incorrectly assumed certain stochastic variables can be approximated as deterministic .... You may have assumed incorrect dynamics ... You may have made incorrect assumptions about relationships'*. E. Derman, Model Risk.

So, is Derman saying that we should try to find out what the *true model* is? No, in fact he never uses those somewhat exoteric concepts like the *true model* or *right model*. He states, and it is hard to disagree, that a model is always an *'attempted simplification of a reality'*, and as such there can be no true or perfectly realistic model. But realism and reasonableness, coupled with simplicity, must remain crucial goals of a modeller, and their lack creates model risk.

Is Derman saying that we must look for realism and reasonableness in all aspects of the model? Not either. We must care for those aspect that have a relevant impact, limiting the analysis to *'the factors that affect the derivative's value'*.

This approach to model risk is probably the one shared by most practitioners of finance and beyond, and does not appear too far away from the views expressed more recently by Derman. For example, in the 'Financial Modeler's Manifesto', written with Paul Wilmott, another legend of quant finance, we read among the principles that a modeler should follow *'I will never sacrifice reality for elegance without explaining why I have done so. Nor I will give the people who use my model false comfort about its accuracy'*. We refer to this, and to Derman's recent book 'Models Behaving Badly – Why Confusing Illusion with Reality Can Lead to Disaster, on Wall Street and in Life', whose title is already very telling, for more about Derman's views.

It is clear to everyone that knows finance and does not confuse it with mathematics and not even with physics, that there is not such a thing as the 'true value' of a derivative that the model should be able to compute. However realism and capability to describe the actual behaviour of the relevant risk-factors are crucial principles to judge a model, and more realistic models should be preferred. Somewhat, we can say that the right model and the right value do not exist in practice, but wrong models and wrong values do exist, they can be detected and we should commit ourselves to find models giving values as 'little wrong' as possible, and then manage the residual unavoidable risk. This is the reason why we talk of 'Value approach'.

There are cases where we can all agree that the price given by some models does not correspond to the value of a derivative. Most of these cases are trivial. If we are selling an out-of-the money option on a liquid volatile underlying, the model we use must incorporate some potential future movement of the underlying. We cannot use a deterministic model, assuming no volatility. Otherwise we would be selling the option for nothing, based on an assumption that can be disproved just waiting a bit and seeing the price of the underlying move in the market.

We will see other examples which are less trivial and yet we can easily spot that some assumptions are not realistic. To give an example regarding the infamous credit models, you will see in Chapter 2 the case of default predicted exactly by spreads going to infinity according to standard structural models or in Chapter 3, speaking of Gaussian copula, again a default predicted exactly, and some years in advance, by the default of another company. These assumptions are unrealistic and yet they are hidden in two very common models. When they do not impact in a relevant way the value of a derivative, we can consider them harmless simplifications. When, like in the examples we will analyze, we can show that they impact strongly the value of a derivative, we should raise a warning. At times it is more difficult to say when a relevant feature of a model is realistic or not; in this case we will have to use our judgement, collect as much information as possible and try to make the best possible choice.

You may at first think that everyone must agree with such a reasonable and no-nonsense approach, and with the definition of model risk it implies. It is not like that. A view on Model Risk that starts from completely different foundations is analyzed in the next section.

1.1.2 The Price Approach

If Derman has been one of the fathers of quantitative modelling between the end of the eighties and the nineties, Riccardo Rebonato marked the development of interest rate models – the field where the most dramatic quantitative developments have been done – between the end of the nineties and the subsequent decade. He has been a master in bridging the gap between complex mathematics and market practice. After the turn of the century Rebonato wrote a paper titled *Theory and Practice of Model Risk Management* that presents a view on the subject strongly different, at first sight, from the classic view explained above.

Rebonato (2003) takes the point of view of a financial institution, which is worried not only of the material losses associated to model risk, but even more of the effect that evidence of model risk mismanagement can have on the reputation of a financial institution and its perceived ability to control its business. Under this point of view, this classic definition of model risk and model validation are misplaced. In fact derivatives need to be marked-to-market, as we will see in Section 1.3, and this means that the balance-sheet value of a derivative must come as much as possible from market prices.

If this is the situation, what should the main concern of a model validation procedure be? Should we worry so much that '*the model provides a realistic (or at least plausible) description of the factors that affect the derivative's value*'? Well . . . at least this is not the first concern we must have, since, to use the words of Rebonato, '*Requiring that a product should be marked to market using a more sophisticated model (ie, a model which makes more realistic assumptions) can be equally misguided if . . . the market has not embraced the "superior" approach.*'

These considerations lead Rebonato to an alternative definition of model risk, that has become so popular that we can consider it the motto of a different approach to model risk, the Price approach:

> '*Model risk is the risk of occurrence of a significant difference between the mark-to-model value of a complex and/or illiquid instrument, and the* price *at which the same instrument is revealed to have traded in the market*'. Rebonato R., *Theory and Practice of Model Risk Management*

Rebonato (2003) justifies this view pointing out that the real losses that hit an institution's balance sheet usually do not appear '*because of a discrepancy between the model value and the "true" value of an instrument'*, but through the mark-to-market process, because of a discrepancy between the model value and the market price.

Fair enough. It is hard to disagree with such statements. As long as the market agrees with our model valuation, we do not have large losses due to models. When we evaluate with a model which is the same one used to reach market prices, we do not have model losses arising from mark-to-market thus we have no accounting losses. More interestingly, we can also avoid material losses, because, if the market agrees with our valuation model, we can always sell an asset or extinguish a liability at the price at which we have booked. This is true even if the market model is, to use the words of Rebonato, *'unreasonable, counterintuitive, perhaps even arbitrageable'*.[1]

This has another implication. When the market price can be observed quite frequently, there is little time during which the model price and market price of a derivative can diverge, so that big model risk is unlikely to be generated. If a bank notices a mispricing, this will be controlled by provisions such as stop-losses and will not generate losses so big to worry an institution, although they can worry a single trader. The problem arises with very complex or illiquid products, for which market prices are not observed frequently. Then the model price of a derivative and its market price can diverge a lot, and when eventually the market price gets observed a large and sudden loss needs to be written in the balance-sheet, with effects on a bank which are also reputational.

The different definition of model risk given by Rebonato (2003) requires, at least at first sight, a different approach to model validation. Large losses with reputational damage emerge when a sudden gap opens between market price and model booking. This can happen for three reason:

1. The reason can be that we were using a model different from the market consensus, and when we are forced to compare ourselves with the market – because of a transaction or because the market consensus has become visible – this difference turns into a loss. From this comes the first prescription of the Price approach, given strongly in Rebonato (2003), to gather as much information as possible on the approach currently used by the majority of the market players. This can be done through different channels. We follow Rebonato (2003) and we add some more of our own, which have become more important after Rebonato's paper was written.
   A. Some channels are based on the idea that if we can observe prices from counterparties, then we can perform *reverse-engineering* of these prices, namely we can understand which models were used to generate them. Examples of how this can be performed are in Chapter 2, in Section 4.1 and throughout the book. How can we collect counterparty prices when the market is not liquid?
      - getting as much information as possible about the deals which are struck in the market or other closeout prices such as those for unwindings and novations.
      - analyzing the collateral regulations with counterparties. Collateral is the amount of guarantees (usually cash) exchanged between banks in order to protect the reciprocal

[1] Some could argue that losses may arise, even if we use the same model used by the market, from the fact that we are hedging with an unreasonable model. We discuss similar issues in Chapter 5, where we will see that the above argument has some solid foundations, but also that real hedging strategies do not follow strictly model assumptions, so that it can be difficult to quantify the hedging losses due to unreasonableness of a valuation model. According to Rebonato (2003), in any case, losses incurred because of an 'incorrect' hedging strategy are unlikely to be of such magnitude to have a major impact, and thus should not be the focus of model risk management. More recently, Nawalkha and Rebonato (2011) points out that when a derivative is hedged, losses due to model errors may cancel out, at least in part, between the derivative and the hedge.

exposures from counterparty risk. The amount of collateral must be kept equal to the expected discounted exposure, that corresponds approximately to the price of all deals existing between two counterparties. We can observe this frequent repricing from our counterparties, in some cases also specifically for a single deal, to get information on the models they use.

- monitoring broker quotes (that usually do not have the same relevance as prices of closed deals) and consensus pricing systems such as Mark-it Totem. This is a service that collects quotes from market operators on a range of different over-the-counter derivatives, eliminates the quotes that appear not in line with the majority, and then computes an average of the accepted quotations. The market operators whose quotes were accepted get informed about the average. There are derivatives for which this service provides a very relevant indication of market consensus. Today, this is considered an important source of market information.

B. A few channels suggested by Rebonato (2003) regard gathering *market intelligence* by
- attending conferences and other technical events where practitioners present their methodologies for evaluating derivatives.
- asking the salesforce for any information they have about counterparty valuations. Additionally, salespeople can inform us if the prices computed with our models appear particularly competitive in the market (are we underestimating risk?) or are regularly beaten by competitors' prices (are we being too conservative?).
- Rebonato (2003) says finally that 'contacts with members of the trader community at other institutions are invaluable'. We can rephrase it, less formally, as follows: keep in touch with your college mates that work in other banks and make them speak out about the model they use at the third pint of beer at the pub.

2. If, thanks to any of the above channels, we are confident that we are using the same model prevailing in the market and this model is not changing, the only cause for large gaps between our booking and market prices can be the model/operational errors like software bugs or errors in describing the payoff. Therefore these errors must be avoided.
3. The two points above do not appear to help us in the past examples of big market losses. In 1987 there appeared to be a market consensus on the use of something similar to the Black and Scholes formula to price equity derivatives. After the market crash in October 1987 the pricing approach changed dramatically, with a clear appearance of the smile. The market consensus had moved from a lognormal model to some approximation of a model with fat-tails, may it be a stochastic volatility model or a model admitting jumps, and this was a big source of losses. Those that had sold out-of-the-money puts for nothing had to book a loss not only because of the fall of the underlying, but also because the volatility used by market player to evaluate them became much higher than the one used for at-the-money options. Even following the above points 1) and 2) of the Price approach, we would have been completely exposed to such losses. Similar market shifts in the pricing approach to interest rate derivatives characterized the aftermath of the LTCM crisis in 1998. And we have recently experienced the most dramatic event of this type with the subprime crisis and the fall of the Gaussian copula based pricing framework for CDOs. This gives the third way in which we can have a large gap between the way we were pricing and the market price: even if we are using the market consensus model, the market consensus can suddenly change. This issue is taken into account by Rebonato (2003) that, after presenting knowledge of the market approach as the first task of a model risk manager, adds that *'the next important task of the risk manager is to surmise how today's accepted pricing methodology might change in the future.'*

There is actually one fourth case that I have to add, but that we can resume in the third one. It is the case when our market intelligence research reveals that there is no model consensus in the market, a case that we analyze in Chapter 2. Also in this case the diligent risk manager will try 'to surmise' which future consensus will emerge. Some other indications on how to behave in this case are given in Chapter 2.

Now the crucial question that a model risk manager surely will ask is: how the hell can we surmise or anticipate how the market model is going to change? Can we devise some patterns in the dramatic changes in model consensus that have led to big model losses? It is unavoidable to start our analysis of this point from the recent, still hurting credit crunch crisis. In the following account I do not minimally try to be exhaustive in describing the reasons and the mechanism of the crisis; with the amount of books and papers written on this that would be indubitably redundant. I will try instead to focus only on the modelling aspect of what happened in 2007, and in doing this I will try to single out what I find are the most relevant elements.

1.1.3 A Quant Story of the Crisis

Let us recall what was the situation before the subprime crisis burst. An efficient market intelligence would have revealed that there existed a consensus, agreed upon at least among the most active market participants, over the pricing of those credit derivatives where the crisis burst first.

Rating agencies and banks used the Gaussian copula, that we resume here and analyze in detail in Chapter 3, for computing the prices of bespoke CDO's. For the few that, during the crisis, were not able to learn what CDOs are, see the next section. We call 'bespoke' those CDO's which are written on a portfolio of credit risks whose correlations are not liquidly traded. The predominant mass of CDO's, including mortgage-backed CDO's, were bespoke. While the Gaussian copula was used by the majority of players, there were differences in the computation of correlations. Rating agencies computed correlations historically while banks had a mixed approach. On one hand they kept an approach consistent with rating agencies since they needed ratings to market their products, on the other hand they often performed mark-to-market of CDO's by a Gaussian copula with a correlation smile given by some mapping approach that will be explained in Section 3.5.

The modelling frameworks used made it almost always possible to extract from a portfolio of defaultable mortgages a good size of senior and mezzanine CDO tranches (explained below) whose risk was evaluated to be quite low, allowing in particular to give high ratings to these tranches. Senior and mezzanine tranches had been at the heart of the expansion of portfolio credit derivatives before the crisis, and then they were the first market where the crisis burst. The optimistic judgement on the riskiness of these products was crucial to fuel the growth of their market. In fact, the underlying mortgages generated a high level of returns, which kept the spread paid by these products much higher than a risk-free return (even 200bp over Libor for AAA securities) in spite of the low risk certificated by high ratings. This correspondence of high returns and low certified risk made the products very attractive.

In the following Section 1.2.1 we explain better how the demand and supply markets for CDOs were composed, which provides an even better understanding as to why rating was a crucial element for the investment choices of funds and also banks. There we tackle also another issue that you may have already heard of: did rating agencies and banks really believe the above picture? The issue is tricky. It may be that the modelling framework we are going to present was so much liked in the market because, by minimizing the risk of CDO's, it matched well the distorted perception of risk of some operators with an artificially short-term investment horizon, like those we will see in Section 1.2.1. More likely, there were surely bona-fide players that truly believed the optimistic picture (I have met some of them), there were some others that were bending models to their purposes, and a large mass of operators that did not have elements to make an informed judgement and followed someone else's advice.

Here this is of limited relevance to us, because what counts was that there was a consensus on the modelling assumptions for valuation. This model consensus was followed by the active operators and as such it protected those using it from model losses, as noticed by the Price approach to model risk, no matter if the model was right or wrong, believed by all players or not. The losses arose when the model consensus fell, and the causes of this fall we are going to study, to understand how the market consensus on a model can suddenly change.

The pre-crisis market model

CDO's are derivatives where one party buys protection from the losses that can arise from a portfolio of investments, for example mortgages, while the other party sells protection on these portfolio losses. What makes them special is that here *the loss is tranched.* What does it mean? If we buy protection on the tranche with *attachment point A* (for example 3% of the total notional) and *detachment B* (for example 6%) we only receive the part of the loss that exceeds A and does not exceed B.

For a portfolio with 100 mortgages in it, all for the same notional and with zero recovery in case of a default, the situation of a buyer of the above 3%–6% tranche is as follows (notice that the buyer of a tranche is the protection seller). Until the first three defaults in the portfolio, he suffers no losses. At the fourth loss, namely when total losses have just exceeded its 3% attachment point, he loses $\frac{1}{3}$ of the nominal of its tranche. He will lose another third at the fifth loss, and the last third at the sixth loss, when its 6% detachment point is touched. From the seventh default on, he will lose nothing more. He has already lost everything. For him the best situation is when there are either 1 or 2 or 3 defaults, because he loses nothing, and the worst situation is any in which there are 6 or more defaults, because in this case, irrespective of the precise number of defaults, he has lost everything.

Such a tranche was often called 'mezzanine', since it has intermediate position in the capital structure. A tranche $0\% - X\%$, that suffers the first losses, is called an equity tranche for any $X\%$, while a tranche positioned at the opposite end, $X\% - 100\%$, of the capital structure is called a senior tranche. Also tranches that were intermediate but with sufficiently high attachment and detachment were usually called senior.

The expected loss for an investor depends on the correlation assumed among the default events. Let us consider an investor that has sold protection for a nominal of 100, first on the most equity tranche possible, the $0\% - 1\%$, with maturity of 5 years. We suppose that all the mortgages have a $20\% = 0.2$ probability to default within 5 years, and they have a 1, or 100%, default correlation ρ. In the market standard, that will be fully understood (including its tricky and misleading aspects) in Chapter 3, a 100% default correlation means, in this case, that all mortgages will default together. What is the distribution of the loss in 5 years?

$$Loss_{0\%,1\%} = \begin{cases} 0 & \text{with 0.8 probability} \\ 100 & \text{with 0.2 probability} \end{cases},$$

so that the expected loss

$$\mathbb{E}[Loss_{0\%,1\%}|\rho = 1] = 20.$$

If instead we say there is zero default correlation, then the one-hundred default events for the one-hundred mortgages are independent. Now the probability of having zero defaults is $0.8^{100} \approx 0$, so that

$$Loss_{0\%,1\%} = \begin{cases} 0 & \text{with 0 probability} \\ 100 & \text{with 1 probability} \end{cases},$$

leading to

$$\mathbb{E}[Loss_{0\%,1\%}|\rho = 0] = 100.$$

Take instead a protection sale on the most senior tranche, 99% – 100%. Under correlation 100%, the distribution of the loss is

$$Loss_{99\%,100\%} = \begin{cases} 0 & \text{with 0.8 probability} \\ 100 & \text{with 0.2 probability} \end{cases},$$

so that

$$\mathbb{E}[Loss_{99\%,100\%}|\rho = 1] = 20.$$

If instead we say there is zero default correlation, now the probability of having 100 defaults is $0.2^{100} \approx 0$, so

$$Loss_{99\%,100\%} = \begin{cases} 0 & \text{with 1 probability} \\ 100 & \text{with 0 probability} \end{cases},$$

$$\mathbb{E}[Loss_{99\%,100\%}|\rho = 0] = 0.$$

We can notice first that an equity tranche is more risky than a senior tranche. They are the same for 100% correlation, but for all lower levels of correlation the senior tranche is less risky. Then we notice that for equity tranches risk decreases with correlation, while for senior tranches risk is increasing with correlation from almost no risk at 0 correlation up to maximum risk at unit correlation.

Now we give a rough description (improved in Chapter 3) of the market model for these derivatives, trying in particular to explain how this modelling framework allowed regularly to extract from a bunch of mortgages a number of tranches with low risk.

The market model was made up, following the approach of a Gaussian copula, by default probabilities and correlations. The historical approach, favoured by rating agencies, based the correlations on observing past data and extrapolating some conclusions from it. The mapping approach, often used by banks and funds, was based on a modification of today correlations from some reference markets which are very different from and much less risky than the bespoke CDOs to which it was then applied. We will show in 3.5 that this approach, which was supported by mathematical considerations with very little financial justifications, was biased towards underestimating the correlations of subprime CDOs and in general of all CDOs more risky than the reference markets. This bias was not immediate to detect, probably because of the lack of transparency and intuitiveness of the methodology. We have included the unveiling of this model error in Chapter 3 devoted to stress testing of models.

In this section we focus instead on the historical estimation approach, because it was this approach, used by rating agencies, that led to those favourable ratings which were the crucial driver of the market growth. And it was the break-down of this historical approach that then ignited the crisis. The users of this approach took as an input the historical default rates of mortgages, divided into the national rate and the regional rates, which were often rather different from the national one. From these data they could compute the correlation among the default events of the different borrowers. The historical evidence was that subprime borrowers, that are known for being unreliable, defaulted most often for their personal financial problems, with a low dependence on the regional trend of the economy and an even lower one on the national trend. The historical evidence on the default of subprime mortgagers, formally organized as in Remark 1, was the foundation of the tendency to give low correlation to subprime mortgagers, reducing the riskiness of senior tranches in subprime CDO.

In the years preceding the crisis, someone suspected that this model may not be anymore reasonable for the current times. In fact during the first decade of this century the number of subprime mortgages had been increasing, while the losses on them had been low, and this was due to a fact not taken into account by historical data. During the entire decade house prices had been increasing, and the evolution of the financial system had made it easy to perform *equity withdrawals*, which means the mortgager getting cash from an increase in the price of his house, without selling it. The simplest way for a mortgager to get this is to refinance his debt. If I bought a house for \$100.000, using a \$100.000 mortgage guaranteed by my house, but after one year my house is worth \$150.000, I can go to another bank and get a \$150.000 mortgage guaranteed by my house. I can use \$100.000 to extinguish the previous mortgage and spend the remaining \$50.000, including paying regularly the interest on my mortgage. Clearly at the same time I have also increased my total indebtment, increasing in the long or medium run my risk of default.

Why were banks or mortgage companies happy about this? Again, because of the increasing house prices: mortgage lenders that, with a default, became proprietors of a house with a price higher than the value of the mortgage, and easy to sell, can have a gain and not a loss from the default. This led to an expansion of mortgages, that in turn sustained the increase of house prices on which the mortgage expansion itself was based.

It is clear that the picture was changed by the new situation: now the fact of having losses on mortgages depended crucially on the trend of house prices, since as long as the trend is increasing losses are less likely. This should alter also our reasoning on correlation, since the dependence on a common trend creates stronger correlation. If the real reason that made the market function is the one we described above, a generalized decrease in house prices should first of all create problems to refinance the debt for all mortgagers, increasing the probability that they default together, and secondly, after a default, it increases the probability that these defaults generate losses due to lower house prices. Rating agencies knew this somewhat, but this did not change dramatically their correlation assumptions: the large number of AAA ratings remained. This is justified as follows by Brunnermeier (2009):

'Many professional investors' statistical models provided overly optimistic forecasts about structured mortgage products for a couple of reasons: 1) they were based on historically low mortgage default and delinquency rates that arose in a credit environment with tighter credit standards, and 2) *past data suggested that housing downturns are primarily regional phenomena—the U.S. had never experienced a nation-wide housing slowdown. The seemingly low cross-regional correlation of house prices generated a perceived diversification benefit that especially boosted the evaluations of AAA-rated tranches.*'

The rating agencies followed again historical observations, and they noticed that, at least in the recent past considered, 'the U.S. had never experienced a nation-wide housing slowdown'.

This is the crucial observation, together with the other 'housing downturns are primarily regional'. House prices had gone down in single states, but then, when looking at the national numbers, the house prices had never decreased during the historical period used for evaluating CDO's. Thanks to this evidence, the correlation was increased only for mortgagers belonging to the same state, but not for mortgagers living in different states. Since the CDO's designed by banks tried to pool together names coming as much as possible from different states, the rating agency models gave low correlation to the names in the pool, making senior tranches deserve a high rating.

Thus for the first approach that rating agencies had used in the past correlation of subprime was low since subprime are based mainly on idiosyncratic risk. For the more up-to-date model, that took into account the link between subprime losses and house prices, the crucial implicit assumption justifying low correlation was in assuming that the national house trend can only be increasing, what Oyama (2010) calls the system of *loans with real estate collateral based on the myth of ever-increasing prices.*[2]

What happened to this myth in 2007? If you want a more detailed technical account of the modelling framework used by agencies, banks and funds to compute correlations, you can read the following remark. Otherwise, you can get directly to the answer in the next section.

Remark 1. ***Technical Remark on Factor Models.*** *Rating agencies were using factor models, where the default time τ of a mortgager happens before the mortgage maturity* T *in case a standardized Gaussian random variable*

$$X \sim \mathbb{N}(0, 1)$$

is lower than a threshold H,

$$\Pr(\tau \leq T) = \Pr(X \leq H) = \Phi(H),$$

where Φ is the cumulative probability function of a standardized Gaussian distribution, so that once $\Pr(\tau \leq T)$ *has been estimated we can say that default happens before maturity when*

$$X \leq \Phi^{-1}(\Pr(\tau \leq T)).$$

This model lacks in any real dynamics, in the sense that with such a model one can find only silly answers to questions such as: given that the mortgager has survived until a date T_1 in the future, what is the likelihood that he will survive until $T_2 > T_1$? But we will leave this aspect to Chapter 3, when we analyze the liquidity problems that followed the subprime crisis and the difficulties to deal with them using this model. For the time being, we focus on the fact that the variable X *is the one through which these models can capture the dependency, and therefore the correlation, between the default times of different mortgagers. They assume that for the mortgager* 'i' *of the state* 'a' *we have a factor* X *shaped as follows*

$$X_i = \gamma_{US} Y_{US} + \gamma_a Y_a + \gamma_i Y_i$$

where γ_{US} is the factor which is common to all mortgagers in the US, γ_a is a term common to only the mortgagers in state a *and independent of the US factor, and Y_i is an idiosyncratic*

[2] Once, during a workshop on the crisis, when we arrived at this point one guy, anticipating that this low correlation was what in the end turned out wrong, told me: 'You see? The problem were not wrong models, but wrong data!'. I have already expressed what I think in the preface: I find this comment paradoxical, particularly when coming from a modeller. The data in this case were historical data about house prices, and they were actually right. What was wrong was the choice to extrapolate the recent past trend to the future, without introducing in the model the likelihood of an important deviation from it. This was absolutely a modelling choice!

factor that takes into account the probability that mortgager i *defaults independently of the trend of the national or regional economy. The loadings* γ_{US}, γ_a *and* γ_i *are the weights of the three different terms. If we believe that the dependency on the national factor* γ_{US} *is the crucial one, we are going to have*

$$\gamma_{US} \geq \gamma_a, \gamma_i,$$

if instead we believe that the mortgagers usually default for their personal reasons, we are going to set

$$\gamma_i \geq \gamma_{US}, \gamma_a.$$

It is logic to take these three factors independently. In fact if there are links between the different states in the US, this will be captured by a higher weight γ_{US}, *while if there is a link between mortgagers in the same state* a, *this will be captured via a higher weight* γ_a. *Notice that if we take the three factors* Y_{US}, Y_{a} *and* Y_{i} *to be all standardized Gaussians* $\mathbb{N}(0, 1)$, *and we set*

$$\gamma_{US}^2 + \gamma_a^2 + \gamma_i^2 = 1$$

we have kept the property that X_{i} *is* $\mathbb{N}(0, 1)$, *in fact*

$$\mathbb{E}[X_i] = \gamma_{US}\mathbb{E}[Y_{US}] + \gamma_a\mathbb{E}[Y_a] + \gamma_i\mathbb{E}[Y_i] = 0$$

and

$$Var[X_i] = \gamma_{US}^2 Var[Y_{US}] + \gamma_a^2 Var[Y_a^2] + \gamma_i^2 Var[Y_i^2] = 1.$$

The interesting thing for us is that this factor model also determines the correlation between the default risk of different mortgagers. In fact for two mortgagers i *and* j *belonging to the same state* a *we have*

$$\begin{aligned} Corr[X_i X_j] &= \mathbb{E}[X_i X_j] \\ &= \mathbb{E}\left[(\gamma_{US}Y_{US} + \gamma_a Y_a + \gamma_i Y_i)\left(\gamma_{US}Y_{US} + \gamma_a Y_a + \gamma_j Y_j\right)\right] \\ &= \gamma_{US}^2\mathbb{E}[Y_{US}^2] + \gamma_a^2\mathbb{E}[Y_{US}^2] = \gamma_{US}^2 + \gamma_a^2. \end{aligned}$$

while if the two mortgagers belong to two different states a *and* b *we have*

$$\begin{aligned} Corr[X_i X_j] &= \mathbb{E}[X_i X_j] \\ &= \mathbb{E}\left[(\gamma_{US}Y_{US} + \gamma_a Y_a + \gamma_i Y_i)\left(\gamma_{US}Y_{US} + \gamma_b Y_b + \gamma_j Y_j\right)\right] = \gamma_{US}^2. \end{aligned}$$

The historical evidence was that subprime borrowers had a low dependence on the regional trend of the economy and an even lower one on the national trend. Thus γ_{US} *and* γ_a *were low, leading to low default correlation. Then the importance of the trend of house prices became more important: the effect of the national economy on the probability of default of a mortgager was through the possibility that national house prices went down; the effect of the regional economy was through the possibility that house prices in a given state went down. Then there was the residual factor* Y_{i} *associated to the classic default risk of a subprime: he loses his job and after his default it is difficult to sell his house, independently of the trend of the housing market. Inspired by the above historical evidence, analysts took* γ_{US} *to be very low, since the national housing trend had always been increasing and could not be a reason for defaults. The* *dominant factor was the state factor γ_a, since state housing trends can turn from increasing to decreasing and a decreasing trend can lead to default. Thus they had a very low correlation for names belonging to different states, and a higher one for names belonging to the same state, getting low correlations for CDOs diversified across states, as most CDOs were. We are back to the crucial question: what happened to the myth of ever-increasing national house prices in 2007?*

The strike of reality

We follow Brunnermeier (2009), an early but very accurate account of the preparation and burst of the crisis, along with some other sources, to describe those seemingly minor events in 2007 that had such a strong impact on the future of finance.

An increase in mortgage subprime defaults was registered as early as February 2007, but it seemed a temporary slow-down with no consequences. However, something else happened in March. From the *Washington Post* on 25 April 2007, we read that sales of homes in March fell 8.4 percent from February, the largest one-month drop since January 1989, when the country was in a recession. Operators tried to play down the relevance of such figures. David Lereah, chief economist for the Realtors group, attributed the downturn partly to bad weather in parts of the country in February that carried over to transactions closed in March.

But there was something more relevant. The median sales price fell to \$217,000 in March, from \$217,600 in March 2006. It is a very small decrease. But in light of the above analysis it is easy to see just how disquieting it must have appeared to operators in the CDO market. The situation became even worse later, and did not only concern 'houses', but real estate in general. Figure 1.1 illustrates the dramatic reversal of the price trend in the crucial sector of commercial property, that also happened around the summer of 2007, with some early signs in the preceding months.

Many operators in those days seemed to change their minds about the prospects of the market. UBS shut down their hedge fund focused on subprime investments. Moodys put a number of tranches on downgrade review: while not yet a downgrade, it usually anticipates one. Others tried to carry on as normal. Bear Sterns in mid June injected liquidity to save one of their funds investing in subprime mortgages, that was experiencing liquidity troubles. It is interesting to note that Bear Sterns had no contractual obligation to do this, but acted to save its reputation.

From 25 to 26 July 2007 the CDX 5-year maturity index, a good measure of the average credit risk of US senior corporations, jumped by 19% from 57bp to 68bp. Nor was the reaction limited to the US. The i-Traxx 5-year maturity spreads, an indicator of the confidence of market operators on the credit perspectives of the European economy, jumped from 36bp to 44bp, a 22% increase that was by far the largest one day-jump in its history to date. For the financials sub-index, the situation was even more dramatic: the jumps was from 23bp to 33bp, a jump of 43%. From Monday, 22 July to Friday, 27 July, just one working week, the spread of financials almost tripled, from 23bp to 59bp.

It seems market operators had put two and two together. If house prices go down, mortgage equity withdrawals become difficult and defaults in the subprime markets are doomed to rise. This will result in banks and mutual funds becoming proprietors of the houses of the defaulted mortgages. In a context of falling house sales and falling house prices, this will turn into material losses.

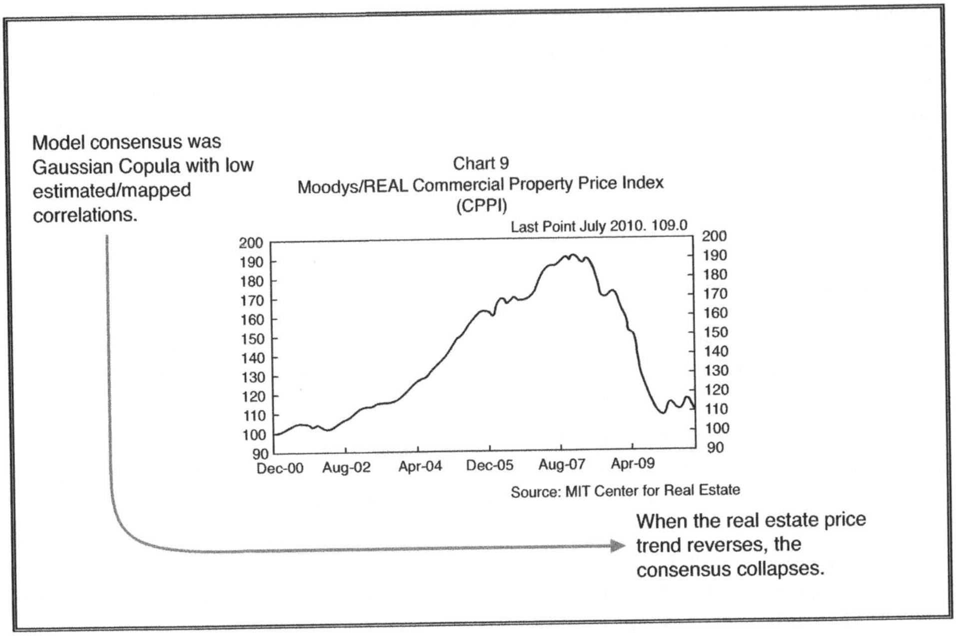

Figure 1.1 The credit crunch is the first example of model consensus collapse that we analyze

If banks can suffer losses from the default of mortgages, all the mortgage-based derivatives that were sold as virtually risk-free AAA assets will soon become junk. There are so many of them around that the whole financial system will suddenly be in big trouble, banks will have to reduce their lending and this will turn into an increased risk of default for all economic players worldwide. The decrease in national house prices shattered the foundations of a splendid, if fragile, edifice: the economic system built in the first decade of the 21st century.

The first wave of this tide hit the CDS and CDO market. On 31 July American Home Mortgage Investment Corporation announced it was unable to meet its obligations, and it defaulted officially on 6 August. Everything that followed has been recounted in hundreds of books, and we will not reprise it here. We will mention the topic again in Section 3.4, where we explain that after the subprime crisis burst and the initial clustered credit losses, these losses generated liquidity stress and a panic that exacerbated the liquidity stress. There we will show why the Gaussian copula market model is particularly unfit too for the management of the risk of clustered losses, an element that certainly did not help anticipate the real risks associated with CDO investments, nor did it help ease the panic and the liquidity crunch once the crisis had burst. But that's another story and one told in Chapter 3.[3]

[3] After this recap, one might wonder: are we simplifying how things actually went, thanks to the benefit of insight? That's for sure. But not that much: the crisis was really triggered by such a simple event as a decrease in real estate prices. There has been a lot of talk of Black Swans in the aftermath of the crisis, but the swan that hit us was a plain white swan, already seen in the not-too-recent past. What we had forgotten is that swans can migrate and stay away for some time . . . but they usually come back. Such delusions are not uncommon in finance. The 'new paradigm' of economy at the end of the 1990s predicted that we were not going to see recessions or crises again, but that also was belied by reality.

1.1.4 A Synthetic View on Model Risk

Let us go back to our initial question. What can trigger the market suddenly to abandon a consensus pricing methodology, as happened with the subprime crisis? The analysis of the crisis shows what happened in that case: *an event related to the fundamentals was observed*. There was a decrease in house prices at national level. This reminded market operators that the model used was crucially based on a hypothesis extremely biased towards an aggressive scenario, that of ever-increasing house prices, *that could be macroscopically disproved by evidence*. The solidity of the market could be destroyed by a generalized decrease in house prices, a scenario that had previously been considered impossible. Now this scenario was becoming a reality in the housing market. We can say that the crisis burst when *an element of unrealism of the model was exposed to be more relevant than previously thought*.

Clearly, we are speaking with the benefit of recent hindsight, but the *death of a model* seen in this crisis is a typical pattern of crisis in regard both to quantitative and qualitative models. The losses in the derivatives world in 1987 were driven in part by the appearance of the skew (a decreasing pattern of implied volatilities when plotted against the option strike), that corresponds to abandoning a Gaussian distribution of returns and replacing it with a distribution where there is more likelihood of large downwards movements of the underlying stock prices. This was clearly driven by the fact that such a large downward movement *had just happened in reality*, in the stock market crash of Black Monday, as we can see in Figure 1.2. The model change was effected without any sophistication, but simply by moving implied volatilities to patterns inconsistent with the previous Gaussian model, and it was done very fast.

Even the dot com bubble of the '90s was sustained by a sort of model, mainly qualitative but with some quantitative implications on simple financial indicators, that predicted a *change of*

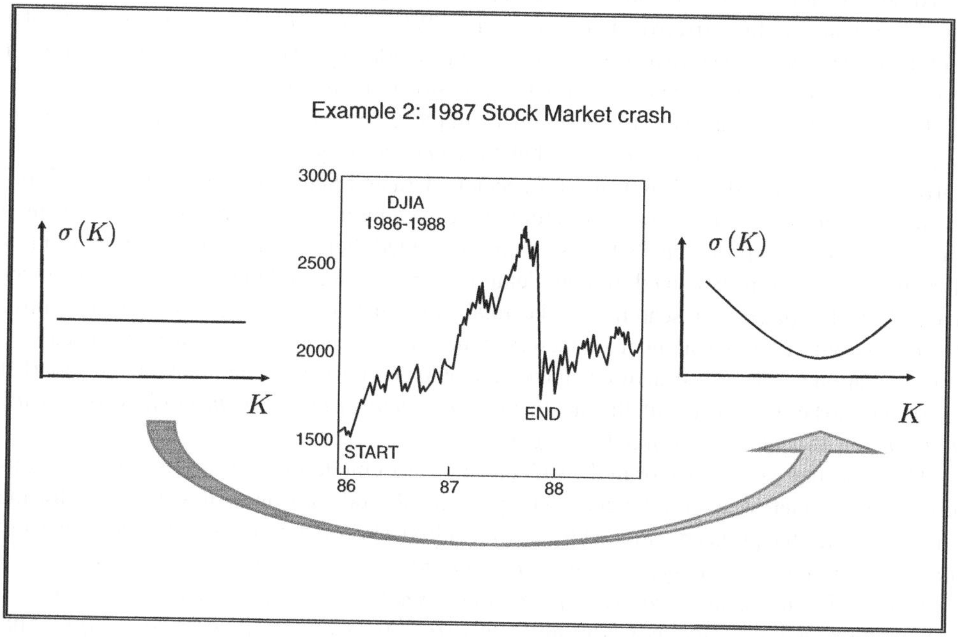

Figure 1.2 Another example of model shift is the 1987 Stock Market crash

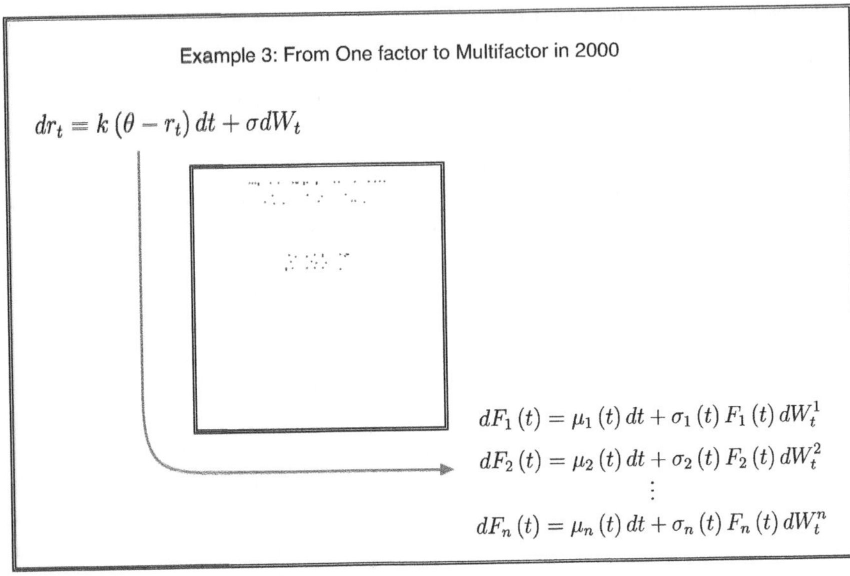

Figure 1.3 An example of a model shift triggered also by a piece of research

paradigm in the economy that should sustain *all* internet companies in obtaining performances never seen before. When the model was disproved by the reality that internet companies had started to default, the bubble burst.

Another example is the hypothesis of deterministic recovery, usually set at 40%, that was used in pricing credit derivatives before the crisis. When the credit crunch and, in particular Lehman's default, showed that recoveries with one single digit were quite likely in a time of crisis, there was a move by many players towards stochastic recovery models.

These conclusions are confirmed by an example given by Rebonato (2003) where the consensus was not changed by a crisis, but *by a new piece of research*. The paper 'How to throw away a billion dollar' by Longstaff, Santa-Clara and Schwartz, around the year 2000, pointed out that if the market term structure was driven by more than one factor, then using a one-factor model exposed banks to losses and prevented them from exploiting opportunities for profit (the issue is explained in more detail in Section 2.8.2 and in Chapter 9). The outcry caused by this piece of research was the final blow that made a majority of banks move to models with a higher number of factors. Since the number of factors driving a realistic representation of the term structure behaviour should certainly be higher than one, this market shift can also be associated with the fact that *an element of unrealism of the model was exposed to be more relevant than previously thought.*

The importance of this factor in the sudden changes of modelling consensus in the previous crises has an interesting consequence. The patterns of model changes show that also for the Price approach the points mentioned by Derman (1996) become important *'You may have not taken into account all the factors that affect valuation ... You may have incorrectly assumed certain stochastic variables can be approximated as deterministic ... You may have assumed incorrect dynamics ... You may have made incorrect assumptions about relationships'*. This means that in the Price approach we also need to understand if a model is sufficiently *realistic*, or at least if it is sufficiently *reasonable* and *robust* to changes in market reality not to expose users to sudden losses as soon as a not particularly unlikely scenario turns out to be true.

This reduces the practical difference between the Price approach and Value approach. The fundamental requirement of the Value approach, that models should give *'a realistic (or at least plausible) description of the factors that affect the derivative's value'*, is also important in the Price approach. Additionally, if an institution is particularly worried about the reputational side of model losses, losses which are revealed to be based on an unrealistic model are particularly difficult to justify. This is true even when the unrealistic model has been used by the majority of players, as shown by the example on rating agencies set out at the beginning of this chapter.

The Price approach makes the fundamental contribution of pointing out an element that appeared to have been overlooked in classic approaches: the importance of understanding the modelling consensus in the market, which we cannot afford to overlook since derivatives are regularly marked to market. However, notice that this could have been done relatively easily for the CDO market before the crisis, by finding out about Gaussian copula, historical correlations and mapping, and yet if the approach had stopped there, assuming that as long as we are consistent with the market consensus we have no model risk, it would still have led to big losses. Avoiding this requires the second step of the approach, surmising how the model consensus can change, and this makes realism relevant also to the Price approach, as the main element whose lack can trigger a sudden change in the model, and as a blueprint that allows us to make an informed guess about which new model may in due course replace the old one.

On the other hand, classic approaches to model validation, focused only on using realistic rather than consensus models, would make the life of a bank rather difficult. For example, if a more realistic model had been used for credit derivatives before the credit crunch, this model would probably have been more pessimistic about the risk of CDOs. The bank using the realistic model would have waited for many years before seeing the predictions of its model come true. In the meantime, the bank would have gone against the market, accumulating mark-to-market losses.

But is it true that the Value approach would have led to such silly behaviour? Only on a superficial interpretation. The Value approach does not underline the importance of consistency with the market as clearly as the Price approach, but it does not overlook it. First of all, the requirement for good calibration is not as trivial as may appear at first sight. Remember that model validation is mainly for complex derivatives that do not have liquid observable price. What Derman says at point 3 of his prescription is that, although the price of the derivative is not observable, we observe the market prices for the simplest derivative that represent the constituent parts of that derivative, and we must be able to calibrate these prices well. For that part of the market that is observable, we must be consistent with the market at least in terms of price fitting. This is not enough to control model risk, as we show with a number of examples in Chapter 2, but it is a basic element of consistency with the market.

There is more about this in Derman (1996). Among the factors that a realistic model should consider is 'market sentiment':

> *'A model may be "correct in principle" but the market may disagree in the short run. This is really another way of saying the model is limited, in the sense that it didn't take other short-term factors into account (including market sentiment) which can influence price.'*

Thus market sentiment is a factor that should influence our choice of the model. This is logical, since it is certainly one of 'the factors that affect the derivative's value'. Additionally, we see that Derman (1996) says it is a short-term factor, that can easily change in the future.

This does not sound very different from the Price approach suggestion of taking into account the market's modelling consensus but being ready for sudden changes in this consensus.

We can now start to draw together a number of points which, according to both approaches, form the backbone of a model validation practice.

- Both approaches require a *price verification* where the mathematics and the implementation of the model are validated, together with the description of the payoff. This is explicit in the Value approach, while in the Price approach is a consequence of the need to remain in line with market prices.
- The Price approach focuses on collecting information about the market consensus, and points out for the first time the importance of this aspect. This is not, however, in contrast to the Value approach, which requires calibration to liquid market prices and takes into account market sentiment.
- Both approaches require consideration the realism and robustness of the model in different financial scenarios. For the Value approach this is the fundamental requirement. For the Price approach it is a consequence of the need to anticipate changes in market consensus.

What should happen when, as in the case we analyze in Chapter 2, we find no market consensus at the second step? In this case we have to guess which model consensus may form in the future, since if a consensus forms we may have to mark the derivative to that consensus. In this case, a model with some features of realism and some simplicity of application is the best choice we can make. It may not predict correctly the model that will emerge, but we have no elements to make any different reasonable guess. When there is no market consensus and we expect it will never form, and we also think we are going to keep the derivative until maturity (albeit this is quite a strong assumption), the focus will be especially on the realism, since what matters in such a case are physical cashflows (a default or a survival, an option ending in or out of the money, a loan prepaid or not).

Remark 2 ***Buy-side vs Sell-side.*** *The analysis of Nawalkha and Rebonato (2011) bears some relation to the trade-off between consistency with the market and realism considered here. One implication of their analysis is that this trade-off can be viewed differently by banks on the sell-side of derivatives and funds or bank treasuries or institutions on the buy-side. On the sell-side we have players who regularly hedge most of their derivatives. In this case, there will be more focus on consistency with the market consensus model – in particular the model consensus for the pricing of the hedging instrument – and on computational efficiency, since these two features allow an efficient hedging. Such efficient hedging will allow in turn some partial cancellation of a model's unrealistic features between derivative and hedges. This corresponds to the requirement for calibration that we will see in our scheme for model validation and risk-management in Section 1.5. On the other hand, as pointed out in Nawalkha and Rebonato (2011), these unrealistic features still generate model risk due to the 'basis' between hedges and derivative, which they say is associated with issues such as correlations or time-dependencies of parameters, at least in interest rate derivatives. We will add to this later in this chapter where we see that some apparently efficient hedges break down when model consensus collapses due usually to its unrealistic features, exposing also the sell-side to large model losses, and in Chapter 5 where we discuss correlation risk in hedging, and in Chapter 9 where we consider time-dependency of parameters.*

Those who do not perform very active hedging, either because they are on the buy-side or simply because, as happens for many complex derivatives, efficient hedging is not possible, will have an even higher focus on the realism of model features, such as volatility mean-reversion in Nawalkha and Rebonato's example.

Remark 3 ***Is a realistic model always a sophisticated model?*** *There is one more interesting comment by Rebonato (2003). It regards what happened at the end of the 1998 Russian crisis* 'Anecdotal evidence suggests that, for instance, after the liquidity crunch associated with the Russia crisis, traders reverted to pricing Bermudan swaptions with cruder and more conservative models, such as the Black-Derman-and-Toy, rather than with the indubitably more sophisticated and realistic Libor Market Models'. *Is this a case where there was a shift in the market consensus towards a* less realistic *model? Not quite, for at least two reasons. First, this example does not appear a change in the 'market consensus model'. When the Russian crisis burst only a minority of advanced banks had already adopted the Libor Market Model, while the models used by the majority of the players for Bermudans were still short-rate models like Black-Derman-and-Toy. In fact the Russian default/restructuring was announced on 17 August 1998. As Rebonato (2003) recalls, one crucial driver of the generalized shift towards the Libor Market Model is the aforementioned paper* 'How to throw away a billion dollars' *by Longstaff et al., whose first version appeared in January 1999. This is after the Russian crisis. The same paper pictures the situation as it was at that time:* 'extensive conversations with numerous brokers and dealers indicate that most Wall Street firms use some form of a single-factor Black-Derman-Toy model in valuing their swaption positions and making exercise decisions. For example, the Black-Derman-Toy model is the default valuation model for American-style swaptions in the widely-used Bloomberg system'.

What happened in the aftermath of the crisis was not a reversal of a market consensus about LMM, a consensus that did not exist yet, but rather the retreat of some sophisticated banks that had decided to go 'against the market', adopting early the LMM and betting that the market would soon be forced to follow them. The bet failed and the retreat was towards the low-factor models that had remained the market consensus. The market consensus actually shifted some time later, and it was towards the more realistic LMM, as confirmed by Rebonato (2002a), who also associates this shift with the introduction of advances in Monte Carlo simulation for Bermudans, whose most popular example is the Least Squares Monte Carlo that only became known to most banks around 2000.

It is now time to note that, when the market shifts consensus in a crisis, the move is rarely towards more sophisticated and realistic *models, but rather towards* less sophisticated and more realistic *models! These models underlie assumptions that appear more realistic in the light of recent events, but the implementation needs to be simple: in a tempest one shelters on a rough but solid rock rather than wasting time trying to build a light hypermodern yacht. There are a number of examples: the appearance of the smile in 1987 disrupted the Black and Scholes model with no additional model complication, the abandonment of the CDO market model in 2008 was only carried out by a change in the way of computing the parameters (correlation and recovery).*

It is interesting to recall also the most relevant example related to the aftermath of the Russian crisis. We follow again Rebonato (2002) who notices, 'the Russia default and the near-collapse of LTCM in 1998 brought about unprecedented dislocations in several markets. The interest rate volatility surfaces were not immune from these upheavals'. *The events illustrated dramatically how unrealistic a deterministic volatility model can be, and the smile made a clear appearance in the interest rates market. Players clearly desired models incorporating stochastic volatility, but when did the market really introduce, even simply for quotations, a stochastic volatility model that became part of market consensus? It was only a few years after the crisis, when a tractable stochastic volatility model was developed, the SABR model introduced by Hagan et al. (2002). The shift happened with little increase in implementation complexity, since the SABR model is just an elaborate way of computing a strike-dependent implied volatility to be put in a Black formula, as we will see in Chapter 6 and Chapter 7.*[4] *This is a perfect example of how a model can evolve towards a more realistic model that allows better understanding of the market without excessive computational complications. The most likely model towards which the market will turn is the one which is more realistic without dramatically increasing computational complexity.*

1.2 FOUNDATIONS OF MODELLING AND THE REALITY OF MARKETS

After this introduction into the concept of model risk, we will go into the details of model risk management and provide a number of examples. In order to do so, we now need to review the foundations of the mathematical models used for pricing, and to define precisely the different components of the standard way to compute prices. In the meantime, we will see the relation between the standard pricing procedure and the reality of financial markets.

1.2.1 The Classic Framework

Consider a financial product that pays X_T at time T. The price of this derivative is formally written as

$$\Pi_t = \mathbb{E}^{\mathcal{Q}}\left[D(t,T)X_T \,|\, \mathcal{F}_t\right] \tag{1.1}$$

There are a number of symbols to describe here.

Risk-free discounting

First, $D(t,T)$. This is the discount factor, so that

$$D(t,T)X_T$$

is the discounted payoff. Usually $D(t,T)$ is written mathematically as

$$D(t,T) = e^{-\int_t^T r(s)ds} = \frac{B(t)}{B(T)}.$$

The quantity $B(t)$ is the value at t of the *money market account*, the mathematical representation of a bank account. We assume that the amount of money in a bank account grows every instant with continuous compounding at a rate of interest $r(t)$ called *instantaneous spot rate* or *short rate*. Formally, the equation for its evolution is then

$$dB(t) = r(t)B(t)dt \tag{1.2}$$

[4] Where, incidentally, we will also see how, many years later, SABR, by then a consolidated market consensus, was shaken by new market evidence.

so that, by solving the very simple *deterministic* equation (1.2), we find out that if we invest 1 at time 0 we have at t

$$B(t) = e^{\int_0^t r(s)\,ds}.$$

We say that the equation (1.2) is deterministic since we do not have, as happens for example with the equation for the value of a stock in the Black and Scholes model, a term like

$$\ldots + \sigma B_t dW_t.$$

We have no dependence on the instantaneous movement of a random process dW_t. Although interest rates can be stochastic in our models, in which case $B(t)$ is not already known at time 0, its movement in the next instant, given by (1.2), is deterministic. We do not expect it to be modified by some sudden arrival of financial news, that would be represented by a dW_t. This is the reason why the money market account is also called the *locally risk-free asset* ('locally' means: over the next instant). It does not have a volatility σ.

This is a relatively realistic representation of a real-world bank account. Real interest is not paid or accrued instantaneously, but in any case quite frequently. And we do not expect such sudden variations in the value of a bank account as we would with a stock price. For simplicity, in the following reasoning suppose that interest rates are deterministic.

We assume that with this bank account we can both invest the money we earn and fund ourselves by withdrawing from the account. We invest and borrow at the same rate $r(t)$, which may be unrealistic for a household, but less so for a trading desk in a bank. Since all the money that we save for some time, or that we borrow for a period, goes into this account, the way its value changes over time tells us what for us is the *time-value* of money. When we know the time-value of money, we can build a discount factor, that expresses the quantity X_T received at T in the equivalent amount of today t money. The discount factor is given by the ratio between the value of the bank account at t, and its value at T, so, as we wrote above

$$D(t, T) = \frac{B(t)}{B(t)} = e^{-\int_t^T r(s)\,ds}.$$

This representation does not take into account the reality of credit risk and liquidity risk that can affect money lent by one bank to another bank, as we will see in Chapter 4, but these two risks can be more or less neglected in times far from crisis, making this representation of discounting sufficiently realistic to be viable for many years. Even in the aftermath of the credit crunch this representation is still valid for derivatives that are collateralized through a CSA agreement with collateral paying overnight interest, that we consider in Chapter 4.

Risk-neutral expectation

Now let us analyze the other unusual terms in the above expression. You are probably already familiar with all of them, but before proceeding to an in-depth analysis of our models and their application, it is best that we agree on the fundamental definitions. The symbol

$$\mathbb{E}^Q[\cdot|\mathcal{F}_t]$$

indicates *expectation*, using the available *information at t*, indicated as $\mathcal{F}_t$, under a *risk-neutral* or *risk-adjusted probability measure Q*.

Usually the formal framework is a triplet called a probability space

$$(\Omega, \mathcal{F}, Q)$$

where Ω is the set of all possible future scenarios or states of the world ω, $\mathcal{F}$ is the set of all possible claims that we can make about the state of the world – called events – and Q is the probability measure used to give a probability to such events. Thus Q is a set of probability distributions for the different objects in the market, a specification of their rates of growth, volatilities, dependencies, possibly probability of jumps etc. Namely, Q is the hero, or the villain, of this book: it is *the model.*

We will talk about *it* at length so now let us concentrate on the other word we have used to define Q. Q is not only a probability measure. We have said it is a *risk-neutral* or *risk-adjusted* probability measure. You may well know a lot about it, but I have read so many misconceptions on the subject, particularly after the subprime crisis, that I think it useful to go over this concept, albeit in a simple way.

Why on earth should we consider a risk-neutral probability measure? The intuition is dramatically simple. In the above expression we have written that a price is an expectation. This should set alarm bells ringing because if the expectation was taken under the *real-world probability measure* P – the probability measure that we consider when we express our usual probabilistic views, such as 'there is 1 in 6 probability that a roll of a dice gives you a 6' – this way of computing prices would be completely wrong. In fact, it would mean evaluating a security based only on its expected rate of return, and this leaves out something relevant. What?

Say, for example that X_T is the return promised by an internet start-up at the end of the '90s. We may have been told that according to analysts the expected return is 50%. The market expected very high returns from such companies at the time of the dot com bubble of the late '90s and in some Google-style cases they were right. But this 50% expected return may come out of two equally likely scenarios; in one scenario the return will be 125%, in the other it will be −25% (better in any case than most realized returns on internet companies other than Google). The expectation is

$$\frac{1}{2}125\% - \frac{1}{2}25\% = 50\%,$$

as in a fixed-return investment paying you 50% guaranteed, but the two investments are not the same.

In the first case there is a *risk*, and you should take it into account, because, unless you are a very special investor, you will prefer a 50% return guaranteed to the internet company. A normal investor in the financial market is averse to risk, and demands a premium for every risk it takes. Standard expectations do not take risk into account, since for a standard expectation the internet company and the fixed investment are exactly the same. In order to avoid this we consider a special expectation, the risk-adjusted or risk-neutral one.

There may be different ways of taking risk into account, for example we could use a higher discount rate $r^{Risk} > r$ for risky products, or we could compute an expectation and then subtract some term that expresses risk. Quants preferred instead to keep the simplicity of an expectation with no modified discounting and no additional terms, but they understood that they had to correct somehow the real world distribution P to take into account risk; in particular they understood that, due to risk aversion, they had to *reduce* expected rates of return compared to those in the real world. This is the meaning of setting up a risk neutral probability measure. Far from being a way to 'neglect risk', as I once read in the financial press, risk neutral valuation is a way of taking risk fully into account, to *reduce* the value of securities, and certainly not to inflate it.

In the standard simplified approach, risk is usually measured by the *volatility* of an asset. How much should we reduce rates of return to take volatility into account such that an expectation is correctly reduced by the consideration of risk? First answer this question: what is the only security whose distribution is not affected by this change of probability to take risk into account?

The bank account $B(t)$ of (1.2), because it has no volatility and thus no risk. If you try to modify its rate of return to take into account its own risk, you realize that there is nothing to modify, because its risk is zero. It evolves at the spot rate $r(t)$ under the real world probability measure and also under the risk-adjusted probability measure.

Now, if we want this fact to tell us something about the general features of the risk-neutral distributions, we have to add two subtle assumptions, that we will discuss below.

No-arbitrage pricing

The first assumption is *absence of arbitrage opportunities*. The intuition is that an arbitrage is a free lunch, an investment strategy that costs nothing, has no possibility of generating losses, and a positive possibility of generating gains. To give a simple example, we have an arbitrage opportunity when two *tradable* payoffs which are exactly the same have two different prices. This inconsistency can always be transformed into a free lunch: we buy it where it costs less and immediately sell it where it costs more. If the market is arbitrage-free, this must be impossible. In the simplified market representation of standard quantitative finance, where assets can be described only based on their expected rate of return and their risk, when two *tradable* investments have the same risk and different returns we have an arbitrage. If the market is arbitrage-free, this too must be impossible.

Under a risk-neutral probability measure, returns have already been diminished to neutralize risk, so all assets can be treated as if they have zero risk. But if the risk is zero for all tradable assets and the market is arbitrage-free, then the expected rate of return must be the same for all tradable assets. We know that one of them, the locally riskless bank account, has an expected rate of return equal to $r(t)$. The other assets must have the same expected rate of return, therefore they also must have a rate equal to $r(t)$.

Above we have used two assumptions: the first assumption has been stressed explicitly, and it is absence of arbitrage. The second assumption was more covert: for the absence of arbitrage to have an effect on the securities, we have required that the securities be *tradable*. If they are not tradable, they cannot be used to build an arbitrage opportunity, therefore they are not forced to be consistent with the locally riskless asset. We analyze arbitrage first, and will return later to the other assumption of tradability, that with a term more common among practitioners that we may call liquidity while academics often call it completeness.

Is assumption of absence of arbitrage opportunities a reasonable assumption? Lack of arbitrage opportunity should be expected if all operators in the market were rational, well informed and committed to exploit all opportunities for profit. Experience tells us that many investors are not rational in this way, use very partial information and are guided by emotions. As a consequence, standard mathematical finance has been based on less heroic assumptions: the existence of a reduced number of rational and well informed professional players who are committed to exploiting every opportunity for profit, and can act as efficient arbitrageurs eliminating arbitrage opportunities. When an arbitrage opportunity arises, they will take advantage of it by buying assets that are underpriced and selling assets that are overpriced, eliminating underpricing and overpricing.

This assumption sounds more reasonable than the previous one. First, on intuitive grounds, anyone who claims that arbitrage opportunities are abundant in the market should always be asked if he is fabulously rich. If he is not, it is not clear why he knows of so many free lunches and yet, rather than exploiting them, goes around passing preposterous judgements about market functioning. But there is something more. Notice that, if the principles of risk-neutral valuation had been taken into account by market operators in the years before the crisis, such things as subprime credit derivatives with AAA rating and paying 200bps over treasury bonds would have appeared at least awkward, or even suspicious. In fact, for such assets the rating was taken by many market operators as the only measure of risk. AAA rating means negligible risk; in an arbitrage-free market an almost zero risk should be associated with a return similar to the one of treasury bonds, not 200bps over that. Thus, far from being a reason behind the existence of such derivatives, as someone claimed in the financial press, the risk-neutral pricing approach tells us that, if the market is arbitrage-free, there must have been something wrong with such derivatives, in particular the risk of these products could not really have been negligible.

But then, is the existence of such derivatives a proof that arbitrage opportunities do exist in real markets? On the one hand, the answer can be a resounding *no*. In fact, time has shown even too well that the risk was non-negligible and the return was risky, so a spread over the risk-free one was fully justified! *In the long term*, what appeared to be a blatant arbitrage opportunity for protection sellers, receiving a high fee in return for no risk, as was indicated by the ratings, was completely belied by the explosion of the subprime crisis. The problem was with the ratings, not with the market extra-return.

But the devil stays in this detail. *In the long term* ... the apparent arbitrage opportunity detectable before the crisis has been revealed to be no such thing. But in the *short/medium term*, many of the valuations made by the market appeared very far from a rational reality of fundamentals for excess of *optimism*. And later, someone has argued that immediately after the crisis burst the quotes were far from the reality of fundamentals for excess of *pessimism*.

In the end, the no-arbitrage principle seems to have been confirmed over the long term, and banks appear to believe in it by continuously trading in derivatives and hedging them with the underlyings: the practice of hedging, and even the name 'derivative' securities, would be meaningless lacking no-arbitrage, which is in the end just the principle of consistency between different securities. Some market evidence that strikingly supports the idea of consistency between the prices of different securities is given later in the book, like the replications in Chapter 4, or the cross-asset calibrations of Chapter 11. But the idea that the no-arbitrage mechanism works perfectly and instantaneously, always and in all markets, as claimed by dogmatic theorists, appears just a practical simplification. It would require a perfection in the market and in the working of professional operators that does not appear realistic, so we always have to treat it with a generous pinch of salt.

We may add that in some very liquid markets, like the interest rate derivatives market that is split into only a few macro markets (dollar, euro, yen etc) with very strong pressure from a very large number of professional traders on the very same products, traders really believe in fundamental market efficiency. This is confirmed by the importance given in the last few years to model developments only intended to make advanced models fully arbitrage-free, at times thanks to what may appear as minor details (the no-arbitrage drifts of BGM, the issue of convexity adjustments, that we will see in Chapter 6). On the other hand in the credit market, which is more opaque and split among hundreds of issues and thousands of portfolios, longer lasting arbitrages appear much more likely and mathematical details to enforce precise no-arbitrage are much less important than more fundamental considerations.

Bubbles and cheaters

There is something more to say here. A crucial element of market reality that is not sufficiently considered in the analysis of market behaviour is that, even if operators are perfectly rational, informed and committed, in some situations, usually generated by external distortions, they have incentives to act in a way that, for an external observer, may not appear in line with the reality of fundamentals. Here are some simplified but quantitatively precise examples of how this can happen; all the examples have a connection to events observed in the recent credit crunch.

Example 4 ***Examples of rational cheat pricers.*** *After the crisis there was a wave of criticisms against the practice of linking the remuneration of market operators only to short-term gains rather than to long-term risks. Leaving aside any moral considerations, we show below that this can have a mathematical effect on the way prices are computed. Let us consider a protection seller in some credit derivative, who has a loss at some default time τ if this happens before the maturity T of the product. The expected value of their loss is*

$$ELoss(0) = \mathbb{E}\left[e^{-r\tau}1_{\{\tau<T\}}\right] LGD$$

where LGD is the Loss Given Default. From now on, you can consider $\mathbb{E}$ as indicating an expectation under a risk-adjusted pricing measure, unless differently specified. We model τ as the time of the first jump of a Poisson process (see Appendix and Chapter 2), getting

$$\begin{aligned} ELoss(0) &= \int_0^T e^{-r\tau}\lambda e^{-\lambda\tau}d\tau LGD = \lambda\int_0^T e^{-(r+\lambda)\tau}d\tau LGD \\ &= \frac{\lambda}{r+\lambda}\left(1-e^{-(r+\lambda)T}\right) LGD. \end{aligned}$$

Now suppose that the person who has to take the decision about selling protection or not is a bank's salesperson or a fund-manager who will get, if the deal is closed, a fantastic bonus at the end of the year sufficient to retire for the rest of his life. This is the perfect 'short-termist'. Why should he care about those cashflows, maybe negative, that will happen after the end of the year? He has no incentive to do so, thus his real maturity will not be the product maturity T, say 5 years, but his personal horizon αT, say 1 year with $\alpha = 0.2$. For him

$$ELoss^{Short}(0) = \frac{\lambda}{r+\lambda}\left(1-e^{-(r+\lambda)\alpha T}\right) LGD.$$

His expected loss will definitely be lower compared to other market players that will not get such a bonus, and this will make him more aggressive. It's even funnier if we take $r = 0$,

$$ELoss(0) = \left(1-e^{-\lambda T}\right) LGD, \qquad ELoss^{Short}(0) = \left(1-e^{-\lambda\boxed{\alpha T}}\right) LGD$$

For the other market players who do not know he is a 'short-termist', this will appear a model disagreement, since they may not understand that the disagreement is between T and αT, but *may think that the disagreement is between λ and λα,*

$$ELoss^{Short}(0) = \left(1 - e^{-\boxed{\lambda\alpha}T}\right) LGD.$$

By the way, the decisions of our short-termist may be underpinned by a model with default probability λα that actually fits correctly the risk appetite of this investor by misrepresenting the default probability. This can easily distort the market.

The presence of many such investors can easily distort a market even when the other market players have understood they are dealing with short-termists. In fact, they may decide to exploit the existence of such a bubble by selling to a cheater just before αT. The expected loss becomes:

$$\begin{aligned} ELoss^{Opportunist}(0) &= \mathbb{E}\left[1_{\{\tau<\alpha T\}}\right] LGD + \mathbb{E}\left[1_{\{\tau>\alpha T\}} ELoss^{Short}(\alpha T)\right] \\ &= \mathbb{E}\left[1_{\{\tau<\alpha T\}} LGD\right] = \left(1 - e^{-\lambda\boxed{\alpha T}}\right) LGD. \end{aligned}$$

So that the non-short-termist price would also coincide with the short-termist's one until the bubble bursts.

Another such 'price cheater' may be the manager of a bank who has invested so much on an asset class X that he knows the bank's default or survival will depend crucially on the future price X_T of this asset class (suppose for simplicity that T is the maturity of its investments). He does not care if the bank defaults, because in any case he will not be affected by any subsequent loss, and it may also be that the bank is bailed out by the government. How does he regard an additional simple investment on X, a forward agreement with payoff $X_T - K$? The value of this investment for an investor can be written as

$$\Pi(0) = \mathbb{E}\left[e^{-rT}(X_T - K)\right]$$

but, if the investor does not care what happens after its own default time τ^{Inv} it should possibly be written as

$$\Pi^{Survival}(0) = \mathbb{E}\left[e^{-rT} 1_{\{\tau^{Inv}>T\}}(X_T - K)\right].$$

Our initial investor strongly exposed to X may know that his bank's default corresponds to the case where this investment has a negative return, $X_T < K$. This means

$$\left\{\tau^{Inv} > T\right\} = \{X_T > K\}$$

and the value of the payoff becomes

$$\begin{aligned} \Pi^{Survival}(0) &= \mathbb{E}\left[e^{-rT} 1_{\{X_T>K\}}(X_T - K)\right] \\ &= \mathbb{E}\left[e^{-rT}(X_T - K)^+\right]. \end{aligned}$$

A forward contract has been transformed into an option contract, that under any model yields

$$\Pi^{Survival}(0) \geq \Pi(0).$$

The price-cheater is eager to pay a much higher price for this contract, distorting the market. The other players will see a price that, incidentally, is consistent with the hypothesis that the prices of X cannot be below K at the maturity T. This fits pretty well with the case of the ever-increasing house prices that many of the most aggressive and active operators appeared to assume in their pricing of mortgage-backed derivatives. Perhaps they really believed in this aggressive hypothesis, but it may also be that they were aware to have such an exposure to this market that a decrease in the prices of the ultimate underlying real estates, would have triggered their own default. A normal investor may be confused by this pricing, until the hypothesis of ever-increasing house prices is revealed to be totally unrealistic. Going beyond the quite sterile debate about market efficiency, this is an issue that has a lot to do with model risk.

Back to the crisis. Banks, funds and ratings

There are other examples that we can take, less simplified and even more relevant to the crisis. In the market of CDOs and similar credit derivatives at the heart of the crisis, demand and supply were often driven by different forces. The demand was represented by those willing to sell protection on CDO tranches (buyers of risk), the supply was made up of those willing to structure CDOs and buy protection on their tranches (sellers of risk). Among the risk-buyers we have institutional investors such as pension funds. The decisions about the investment of such funds are not made by the households that put their money in the fund. They are made by the fund manager.

This can be a perfect example of an operator that does not always have clear incentives to act in a way which in the end is rational for the people who put their money in the fund. The manager has one obvious goal: maximizing the return from the investment. Clearly the investors also have the goal of keeping the risk minimized, but often this goal is pursued by setting very precise restraints on the manager's mandate. For example, some funds can only invest in securities with very high rating. The rating is a measure of the probability of default of a security. High rating meant an extremely low probability of default. For securities like bonds or tranches bought by institutions, such as funds, that often keep them on banking books, namely do not perform mark-to-market, the default probability is the crucial measure of risk, so this appeared an efficient way of controlling risk.

However, the rating is based on a limited set of information, strongly biased towards the use of historical data, and just gives qualitative information. More importantly, the rating agency is not the entity that suffers the loss in case of default. The agency may have negative impacts if its estimations are proven wrong, but it may also have incentives to make over-optimistic estimations, for example because it is paid by the issuers themselves.

Even without assuming unfair behaviour on the part of rating agencies that had behaved quite fairly for decades in giving ratings to *issuers*, we have to recognize that the approach to ratings for *issuances* had some weaknesses, which is interesting to mention in a book on model risk. Ratings were based on one model. The issuers could propose an issuance, see the rating and, if that rating did not satisfy the issuer, they could change at almost no cost some features of the issuance, in an attempt to exploit all the unavoidable simplifications that were in the rating model (like increasing the maturity to take advantage of some mean-reversion features, see Barucci and Morini (2009)). The rating model was in fact, in the end, very well known to issuers. Thus many derivatives were *overfit* to the details of the model behaviour, making the rating hardly robust in the face of serious discrepancies between model and reality. This was not possible when the ratings were given to issuer companies. A company cannot be changed overnight to adapt to a model, a derivative can.

But let us go back to our fund manager. Once the rating constraints are satisfied, he can say to investors that risk is under control and he will just concentrate on finding the highest returns. So if ratings are biased, his investment behaviour will be biased, even if everyone is rational.

In the crisis this was probably one important factor inflating the demand of CDOs. Banks could easily match this demand by securitizing their high return and high risk exposures at a cost that was probably cheaper than it would have been without the rating-sustained demand. We can add that the high ratings made selling protection on senior and mezzanine tranches attractive not only for funds but also for banks themselves, because of the capital charges dictated by the Basel Accords, that were much lower for securities with high rating. It may even be convenient for a bank to take its own mortgages, securitize them, and then buy them back.

It was difficult for non-distorted traders to bring this situation back to equilibrium. Betting against the market exposes one to mark-to-market losses in the short to medium term. A bank trader will find it difficult to make them acceptable to the risk managers monitoring the VAR of their books. A fund trader usually receives the money to invest from investors who may withdraw their support in the face of mark-to-market losses. This risk makes the trades against the mispricing less appealing, as explained in Rebonato (2003).

We have already seen that these bubbles usually burst, like in the subprime crisis example. But this is not the consequence of a dogmatic assumption of perfectly efficient markets with perfectly rational and undistorted operators who know the 'true values'. It happens when the fog really clears, and the models justifying the bubble are exposed as unrealistic in an incontrovertible way, as we have seen in the analysis of the kind of events that, in market practice, trigger model evolution in the most dramatic and relevant cases. But in the meantime distortions can influence the market for non-negligible periods.

A synthetic view of model risk that takes into account both the reality of fundamentals and the deviations from it that we can see in the market price, is confirmed to be a reasonable approach. Moreover, the different forces we have seen so far, some driving models to change to incorporate evidence in the reality, others drifting them away from our perception of the reality of the fundamentals, are confirmation that we crucially need a dynamic management of model risk. Consider also that in many real world cases we cannot distinguish, just by observing market quotes and using our no-arbitrage models, if a market is 'distorted/arbitrageable' or 'realistic'. We devote Chapter 11 to this topic. When, however, we believe there is a divergence between what we think is a realistic model and the model the market is using, only the tools of model risk management – for example the model reserves and the limits to exposures subject to model risk that we will mention later – allow us to take into account the market model and at the same time manage the risk that its unrealism is exposed, driving a painful shift in market consensus. These tools are what we need for dealing with cases where we have *uncertainty* about the right model to use, which is the topic of the next section.

1.2.2 Uncertainty and Illiquidity

The first section, starting from the analysis of Derman and Rebonato, has tried to better understand model risk by analyzing which features, such as realism or consistency with market consensus, a model should have. But even when the goal is clearer, a lot of uncertainty can remain about which model to use. In fact it can be by no means obvious which one is most realistic among different representations of reality. There can be no consensus in the market, where there may also be the presence of distorted operators. One more reason for uncertainty that we will see later on in this section, relates to the different risk aversions of the different operators. Thus we need to define more precisely what *model uncertainty* is in order to understand how to deal with that.

Formalizing Uncertainty

Uncertainty is what finance is all about. Investment decisions are choices between different uncertain returns. Pricing is computing the properly adjusted expectation of an uncertain future payoff. As a consequence, our first thought may be that model uncertainty is just an element that adds uncertainty to our payoff, so that we may deal with model uncertainty as we normally do with the uncertain quantities that appear in a payoff . . . we can take expectation of all that is uncertain and this is the price, with no uncertainty left.

However, if we think a bit more deeply, we realize that this is not the only way, and probably it is not the best way, to deal with model uncertainty. Being uncertain about which model we should use is very different from using a model that assumes that a payoff is uncertain, since it is stochastic according to a specific law.

A very instructive example of this difference can be built starting from a class of models that had a moment of popularity shortly after 2000. They are probably the simplest extension of Black and Scholes.

A model with random parameters

Following Brigo et al. (2004), in such models one assumes that, under the pricing measure, the underlying of an option looks like a standard lognormal diffusion

$$dS(t) = r(t)S(t)dt + \sigma^I(t)S(t)dW(t)$$

but has in fact a crucial difference: here the volatility is uncertain, in the sense that it is a random variable, independent of $dW(t)$, with distribution

$$\sigma^I(t) = \begin{cases} \sigma^1(t) \text{ with prob } p_1 \\ \sigma^2(t) \text{ with prob } p_2 \end{cases}. \tag{1.3}$$

Brigo et al. (2004) say that the intuition underlying this model is that 'the asset volatility is unknown and one assumes different scenarios for it'. In our examples we consider only two scenarios so we have two possible deterministic volatility functions. The greatest advantage of this model is the pricing formula for a call option with strike K and maturity T. We have as usual that the option price is

$$\Pi(K, 0, T) = P(0, T)\mathbb{E}\left[(S(T) - K)^+\right],$$

where $P(t, T)$ is the t price of a risk-free bond with maturity T, with

$$P(t, T) = D(t, T)$$

when interest rates are deterministic as they are in this example, and

$$P(t, T) = \mathbb{E}_t\left[D(t, T)\right]$$

when they are not ($\mathbb{E}_t[\cdot]$ is a shorthand for $\mathbb{E}[\cdot|\mathcal{F}_t]$). We can use the law of iterated expectations (see Appendix) and write

$$\Pi(K, 0, T) = P(0, T)\mathbb{E}\left[\mathbb{E}\left[(S(T) - K)^+ |\sigma^I\right]\right].$$

Notice that the external expectation regards a random variable that can take only discrete values, so the expectation is given by a weighted average of these values, where the weights are the probabilities of the different volatility scenarios:

$$\Pi(K,0,T) = P(0,T)\sum_{i=1}^{2} p_i \mathbb{E}\left[(S(t)-K)^+ | \sigma^I(t) = \sigma^i(t)\right].$$

Now look at the inner expectation. Taking into account that $\sigma^I(t)$ is independent of $dW(t)$, we have that, conditional to $\sigma^I(t) = \sigma^i(t)$, $S(t)$ is just a geometric brownian motion with volatility $\sigma^i(t)$. Therefore the option price is just the average of two Black and Scholes prices.

$$p_1 B\&S\left(S(0), K, rT, \int_0^T \left[\sigma^1(t)\right]^2 dt\right) + p_2 B\&S\left(S(0), K, rT, \int_0^T \left[\sigma^2(t)\right]^2 dt\right). \quad (1.4)$$

This pricing formula for a call option is as simple as Black and Scholes itself, but it is consistent with the presence of some form of smile in the market.

If instead we need to compute a price with Monte Carlo, that we describe in Section 6.2.3, we must simulate different paths. For simulating up to T *we must know the values of all model quantities for all t* with $0 < t \leq T$. This is a fundamental feature for calling something *a model*, but at times we revisit it only when we have to perform Monte Carlo simulation. And here an issue arises with the above model. *When do we get to know* $\sigma^i(t)$*?* When is this variable observed? It seems that we need to observe it very soon, since we need to know it for all $t > 0$. This is exactly what Brigo et al. (2004) do: 'The volatility uncertainty applies to an infinitesimal initial time interval with length ε, at the end of which the future volatility value is drawn'.

This specification should help us understand better the nature of the above model. The intuition about it of Brigo et al. (2004) is that we are uncertain about the volatility, in fact the model is called 'uncertain volatility model'. But is this a real representation of *model uncertainty*? If the answer were yes, we might conclude that the correct approach to model uncertainty is taking an average of the prices under each model, as done in (1.4).

Unfortunately, here there is no model uncertainty because the model is only one. In a simulation we first – at an infinitesimal time ε – draw σ^I, then once we know that on this scenario $\sigma^I = \sigma^i$, with $i = 1$ or $i = 2$, we use this volatility function until maturity. This is *one specific model* with random volatility, it is not a representation of model uncertainty.

Uncertainty on model parameters

The situation most similar to the one above but involving model uncertainty would be a situation where we know for certain that the underlying is lognormal but we have model uncertainty about the true value of the asset volatility. In this case:

1. at ε we will *not* know the right volatility. There is no precise moment when the volatility will be revealed. In models with uncertain parameters there is essentially a jump of the volatility in ε, regulated by the distribution of (1.3), in model uncertainty there is only our ignorance.
2. the probabilities p_1 and p_2 are part of no model, they are only a representation of our ignorance. We have no way of estimating them historically, for example, and fixing them can be extremely difficult.
3. other market players may know the real value of σ, or have in any case a different degree of uncertainty about it and therefore they give different probabilities to the scenarios. A market

player with more information than us may actually not even include σ^2 in his pricing since he knows the right volatility is σ^1, while a player with less information than us may also have included a value σ^3 to which we have implicitly given 0 probability.

This alters the picture. How are we to deal with this? Cont (2006) analyzes model uncertainty and says that in reality market operators work with a multiplicity of models, or triplets

$$(\Omega, \mathcal{F}, Q_i),$$
$$Q_i = Q_1, Q_2, \ldots Q_N$$

and calls the uncertainty on the right probability measure – the right model – a kind of Knightian uncertainty, from Knight (1921), who first described that type of uncertainty *where we are unable to give a distribution to the future events*, as opposed to cases of uncertainty *where we do not know the future outcome but we know its probability distribution*. The latter is what we usually call 'risk'.[5] Hoeting et al. (1999) suggests using in a Bayesian framework, an approach similar to the averaging of formula (1.4) also for model uncertainty. But this makes no sense in our context, since it makes uncertainty *on* the model indistinguishable from uncertainty *in* the model.

The distinction between the two forms of uncertainty is crucially based on knowledge vs ignorance of the probability distribution. Model risk is a case where we have uncertainty on the distributions. This case is completely different from the typical examples of risk to be found in finance books, which are almost always examples where there is no uncertainty about the distribution. In my opinion the best such example is a bet on a fair roulette. The outcome of the roulette is uncertain, but the probabilities are known precisely.[6]

The irony is that, while most books about risk focus on how to deal with roulette-type problems, the majority of problems in financial markets belong to the other category, where we do not know the distribution, and model risk is a central problem.

Understanding that finance belongs to the second category has some dramatic consequences. In my opinion the most crucial difference, particularly relevant in trading, between the models with random parameters (that still belong to the roulette case) and uncertainty on model parameters (model risk) is that in the first case the probabilities p_1 and p_2 *are assumed to be the same for all players*, while in the second case, even if we can guess them, *the probabilities will be different for different players*, and some players will have higher variance (more uncertainty) while others may have minimum variance because they know better what the best model is. This clearly shows that the approach that works reasonably in the first category, averaging across scenarios, may be dramatically inappropriate in the second situation.

Cont (2006) notices that the typical approach of banks when faced with model uncertainty is not to average across models but rather to adopt a worst case approach. Suppose that we were a bank with model uncertainty about σ^1 or σ^2, where we take $\sigma^2 > \sigma^1$. There is only one way to make sure that we will not suffer losses from any model error mispricing: we must use σ^1 to price when we are option buyers, and σ^2 when we are option sellers. This would

[5] So, according to Rama Cont, this book should be called 'Understanding and Managing Model Knightian Uncertainty' rather than 'Understanding and Managing Model Risk'. I agree, but there was not enough room on the cover.

[6] By the way, notice a curiosity. Roulette is a good example of standard risk, with no model uncertainty, for an ordinary casino player. For a sophisticated cheater who uses sophisticated laser scanners and computers to predict the roulette outcome, like those that won more than £1 million at the Ritz Hotel in London in 2004, then model uncertainty can be relevant. When we speak of roulette, we do not refer to this quite special case.

imply for a call option:

$$p^{ask} = B\&S\left(S(0), K, rT, \left(\sigma^2\right)^2 T\right), \quad p^{bid} = B\&S\left(S(0), K, rT, \left(\sigma^1\right)^2 T\right).$$

This is the old 'conservative approach' so popular with many banks. If the above bid-ask is too large, the bank will not be very competitive in this option market and will probably remain quite out of it, focusing on markets where they do not have such uncertainty. Gibdoa and Schmeider (1989) explain that one can even formalize this conservative or worst case approach, showing that it corresponds to maximization of utility when we are faced with total ignorance on the probabilities. A relevant reference is in Avellaneda et al., (1995) and Avellaneda and Paras (1996) that, in an analysis where the uncertainty is centred on the volatility, similarly to this example, take a worst-case approach.

Following this line, Cont (2006) proposes two measures of model uncertainty: one is essentially the conservative one, where we use the model that maximizes the price when we have to sell the derivative, and the model that minimizes the price when we have to buy it, so that model uncertainty is quantified as

$$\max_{Q_{i=1,\ldots,N}} \text{Price} - \min_{Q_{i=1,\ldots,N}} \text{Price},$$

while in the second approach the investor should weight more or less models depending on their higher or lower capability to price liquid market instruments.

The first approach appears oversimplified. The second one is more elaborate, but probably it does not add much in practice because model uncertainty is usually among models that all have the same fitting capability, since in current market practice models with bad fit would have been excluded from the start, as we will see in Chapter 2.

Another interesting consideration on Cont (2006), that in my opinion remains the best paper on the formalization of model uncertainty, is in respect of the links between model uncertainty and liquidity, and model uncertainty and static hedging. According to Cont, there is no model uncertainty when:

1. the market is liquid (model uncertainty is always lower than bid-ask spread!)
2. we can set up a model-independent static hedge

These two points appear correct for a theoretical definition of model uncertainty, but in Section 1.3.4 we will see some examples that diminish their relevance when we move from theoretical model uncertainty to practical model risk management. We provide a case where the disruption of a modelling standard exploded all of a sudden exactly in a liquid market, the interbank interest rates market. This broke down the standard practices for discounting cashflows, scrambled the hedging strategies for the liquid products traded in the interbank market, and also soon made the market illiquid. In reality we should never be complacent about model risk and model losses even if today the market appears liquid.

We will also see that what was considered a 'model-independent static hedge' suddenly broke down when the market consensus on the modelling framework changed. This example shows that in practice we must be very careful to define a hedge as model-independent and static, since there can be crucial modelling assumptions behind such hedges that are usually hidden but can be exposed in times of model shifts.

The above section also sought to clarify the strong link between model risk and illiquid markets, namely markets traded at low frequency with high bid-ask spreads. Model uncertainty is an important element that drives the existence of large bid-ask spreads. The two things also tend to shrink together: when a market become more liquid, bid-ask spreads naturally reduce, and at the same time we get to know more of what a market thinks of a price, reducing part of model uncertainty. One final consideration regards a topic that, if you ever took any Master's courses in finance, may have appeared rather theoretical, but can have dramatically practical consequence, as we shall see in abstract in the following section and then with a very practical example in Chapter 2. We are speaking of *market completeness*.

Illiquid markets, ignorance and completeness

It was pointed out that there is another hidden assumption in the standard pricing framework where securities are priced as expected values of their payoffs after the drifts of the underlyings have been reduced to r in order to take risk into account. The assumption is that all the underlyings must be traded. If they were not traded, there would not be any arbitrage trades to bring the drift in their dynamics to r after the risk is taken into account. The assumption of an arbitrage-free market does not justify the above pricing framework if it is not coupled with the possibility for arbitrageurs to trade the underlyings to eliminate arbitrage opportunities.

A market where there are non-traded underlyings is called incomplete. Another way to define it is as a market where not all derivatives can be perfectly hedged. The link between lack of completeness and price uncertainty or model risk is quite strong: when a derivative can be perfectly hedged, it means it can be perfectly replicated with liquid products, namely I can 'build up' the derivative based on simpler, visible products, which suggests that a unique visible price should exist in an arbitrage-free market. The idea of perfect replicability is strongly linked to the two fundamental assumptions of Black and Scholes: continuous price processes in continuous time, that allow me to hedge out the infinitesimal changes in price in an infinitesimal time. Unfortunately these are features that we lose easily when moving to real markets. In the following we investigate more thoroughly the link between the theoretical framework of incomplete markets and the reality of model risk.

Even if with non-traded underlyings the basic pricing framework of mathematical finance does not work, when pricing we should in any case consider that the drift μ we observe in the real world must be reduced to take risk into account. We will use our own assessment of the *price of risk*, mainly of how many units of return we have to take away from μ to take all risk into account. The typical parameterization given to this implicit operation carried out by a market investor is based on the concept of a linear price of risk, a quantity γ such that, if an asset has a volatility σ, we must reduce its drift by

$$\sigma_t \gamma_t.$$

For the above stock price the dynamics to use in the risk-adjusted pricing measure would be

$$dS(t) = (\mu_t - \sigma_t \gamma_t)\, S(t)dt + \sigma_t S(t)dW(t).$$

When the asset is traded the working of the arbitrageurs will act so that the risk adjusted return is the same as the return of the riskless asset, namely

$$\mu_t - \sigma_t \gamma_t = r, \tag{1.5}$$

which has the important consequence that the price of risk

$$\gamma_t = \frac{\mu_t - r}{\sigma_t} \tag{1.6}$$

is fixed by the market that determines μ_t, and we can speak of the *market price of risk*. In particular, a market price of risk will emerge for any source of risk like $dW(t)$, so we should more explicitly indicate (1.6) by γ_t^W.

But when the underlying is not traded, we do not have (1.5) and the market does not tell us what is the agreement on γ_t^W. We can use our personal market price of risk, depending on our risk aversion, without creating any arbitrage opportunity in the market, as long as we always use the same γ_t^W every time we consider the risk of $W(t)$.

So, even if all market players knew exactly the parameter μ_t of the real-world probability distribution, we would not know which drift the other players will use in pricing, since the pricing drift has to be $\mu_t - \sigma_t \gamma_t$ and γ_t can differ for different market players. This is not so different from the model uncertainty case we have seen just above, so this element also adds to our final model uncertainty.

When a bank structures a complex derivative, it usually prefers to make it dependent on a source of risk which is not liquidly traded. The availability of a liquidly traded market for such underlying risks, from which anyone could easily extract the price of the derivative, would make the derivative less attractive for banks, eliminating many opportunities for profit. A bank that considers itself more sophisticated than most counterparties finds it more attractive if there is no full consensus on how to price the crucial risk on which a derivative depends. In the end the majority of complex derivatives in the reality of financial markets, if not all of them, have underlyings that also depend on risks which are not liquidly traded.

Now we have a better understanding of how in this context uncertainty on the price comes from at least three distinct yet interconnected elements:

1. If the market for the underlying risk is illiquid, we do not see prices giving information on the risk neutral dynamics and it is more difficult to estimate the parameters of its real-world dynamics.[7]
2. If the market for the underlying risk is illiquid, we are also in the context of incomplete markets, and therefore the price can be affected by risk preferences and the uncertainty on them.
3. Where there is so little consensus, it is more likely that distorted prices like those seen in 1.2.1 emerge and prosper for some time, adding to the total uncertainty.

So, in the reality of complex derivatives we usually know exactly neither the parameters under the real-world probability measure nor the market price of risk, as in the main example in Chapter 2. In the above simplified example, this would mean that we do not know neither

$$\mu_t, \gamma_t, \sigma_t.$$

and our uncertainty on the parameters under the real-world probability measure compounds with the uncertainty on the right price of risk to use.

The theory of incomplete markets gives an organic theoretical explanation of the second form of uncertainty. It explains that in an incomplete market the price for each player depends on its own risk aversion. For the first type of uncertainty, linked to uncertainty on the real-world underlying dynamics, we do not have such an established and organic explanation, but the

[7] Notice that if a risk factor is not traded but is anyway observable, one may in any case consider using historical estimations. This is unlikely to solve our uncertainty on models and model parameters. For example, observing the history of the underlying we can estimate historically the parameters but if they are time-dependent this is irrelevant. There are even cases, like credit, where the real underlying is the default indicator $1_{\{\tau<T\}}$ – but this quantity is zero until default and observing its history tells us absolutely nothing about the parameters to model it.

above analysis based on Cont (2003), with its focus on a worst-case approach, suggests that even in this situation risk aversion plays a role in determining how different models will be used by different players. In market practice different operators ponder models considering their realism and the market opinions on them, but in the end they are influenced in model choice by their risk appetite and their side in the deal. This is one analogy between model uncertainty and the choice of the appropriate risk adjustment. A second analogy is that there is uncertainty also in the choice of the risk adjustment. An institution has to estimate its own risk aversion, and at the same time find out about the risk aversion of its competitors, since it may have to deal with them in the future.

In the end the two forms of uncertainty do not appear very different to deal with in practice. And since when a bank designs a pricing model it usually does not distinguish between the real-world dynamics and price of risk that expresses risk aversion, these two forms of risk will be indistinguishable in the market. But it is important that a model risk manager does not forget the presence of these two components.

Remark 5 ***Incompleteness in advanced (realistic) models.*** *In the above example the interaction between risk preferences and uncertainty on real world dynamics only took into account the drift parameters, while the volatility parameter is not affected. Volatility in Black and Scholes can be affected by model uncertainty, but not by the change of 'pricing measure' that we have to make in order to take risk preferences into account. This is what Girsanov's Theorem says and is also a consequence of the intuition we gave about risk-neutral pricing: we modify drifts to take volatility into account, not the other way around.*

In practice this interplay can be more relevant. In fact, the separation between preference-sensitive parameters and preference-independent parameters exists also in other models, but with very different implications. For example, in the Heston model the drift of the stochastic volatility depends on the risk-preferences if the market is not complete for this volatility risk factor. Thus the risk preferences enter also the diffusion coefficient of the stock dynamics through the stochastic volatility. And in a model with jumps the parameters related to the frequency and size of the jumps are preference-sensitive. For example, if we consider a jump model where the jump can have an infinite number of possible sizes, we cannot think of any practical market which is complete, because this would require an infinity of traded instruments (each possible jumps size works as a risk-factor and therefore we would need an infinity of liquid markets to have the market price of risk for all of them). See Andersen and Andreasen (2001) and Cont and Tankov (2004) on jump models.

We know that the Black and Scholes model bears only a faint relation to reality. When we move towards more realistic models, we have to add features like stochastic volatility and jumps. Thus we move towards models where market incompleteness is very likely, and where very many parameters are affected by it becoming preference-dependent. And even when we are forced by practical constraints to use simplified versions of these models, they can at best be seen as approximations, reasonable projections, one hopes, of realistic models on the space of simpler and more tractable models. In this case their parameters, like the 'volatility' of the Black and Scholes model, summarize in some way the stochastic volatilities and jumps of the real world, and it is arguable whether to consider them preference-independent. All the elements of our uncertainty are likely to compound there too.

We conclude that in the practice of markets the problem of market incompleteness and the problem of model uncertainty interact dramatically. In reality we will have an uncertainty on the pricing model – which is under the risk-adjusted measure Q – that compounds our uncertainty on the parameters of the 'real' P dynamics and our uncertainty on how to quantify the risk aversion.

1.3 ACCOUNTING FOR MODELLERS

Usually modellers do not care much about accountancy matters. However, there are some accountancy issues that strongly affect our job. In fact, models are not only used to give a value to a derivative the day the derivative is bought or sold to a counterparty. Models are used along the life of a derivative, from inception to maturity, to update its value for accountancy purposes. It is in this accountancy process, and not in real money, that most profits and losses emerge for banks. The famous crises of the past, from the LTCM debacle to the credit crunch, were not generated by actual losses incurred by banks as money outflows, but by losses that emerged from the daily updates of the accountancy values of derivatives. For most financial crises the feared money outflows were anticipated by the balance-sheet accountancy losses, and these balance-sheet losses were enough to force funds like LTCM or banks like Lehman into liquidation, generating plunges in confidence and liquidity shortages. Thus, the part they have in determining accountancy values is one crucial role of models, if not the most crucial. Although we do not need to be experts in accounting details, the fundamental prescriptions and first principles given by national or international accountancy boards on how a derivative should be evaluated for accountancy purposes must not be ignored.

1.3.1 Fair Value

The principles to be followed for the valuation of financial assets and liabilities are given by international organizations such as the International Accounting Standards Board (IASB) or the Financial Accounting Standards Board (FASB). The IASB is an international body which since 1973 has tried to standardize accountancy rules at global level. In the past it published the International Accounting Standards (IAS) and more recently the International Financial Reporting Standards (IFRS). The IASB meets in London and its recommendations have a strong relevance, for example in the countries of the European Union, although they are reformulated by European and national bodies before becoming binding rules. In almost every country there are autonomous local bodies; the most important example is the above-mentioned FASB, the body designated by the SEC (Securities and Exchange Commission) to formulate generally accepted accounting principles (GAAP) valid for the US. When an accountant or auditor speaks to a quant and, after being hushed by talks of martingales and *cadlag* processes, tries to have his own moment of superiority by mentioning dozens of strange acronyms, he probably refers to the main sources of accountancy principles.

In what follows the FASB prescriptions will be taken as the main source when describing the accountancy principles driving the valuation of derivatives. In fact, IASB prescriptions are general and not directly binding in any country, thus for our purposes it is better to look at the rules that apply in one specific country, since they have a direct validity. The US is the most relevant possible example, also due to the feedback that FASB decisions have also on IASB (see below for what happened between September and October 2008). In any case, since 2002 the FASB has undertaken the convergence project with the IASB to keep their prescriptions consistent.

According to both IASB and FASB, derivatives and all financial assets or liabilities which are not held for an investment until maturity (banking book products) but can be bought and sold (trading book products) *should be evaluated following the principle of fair value*.

'Fair valuation' is similar to what traders call *mark-to-market*, and actually is not a principle imposed by accountants on financial market operators but, on the contrary, is an approach that developed in financial markets and then spread to the accountancy practices of the rest of the economy. Mark-to-market as an accounting device first developed among futures traders in the Chicago Mercantile Exchange, prior to 1980. Then it was adopted by big banks and is now an important principle for all corporations.

The IAS 39 document, first issued in 1998 and regularly revised, gives the IASB definition of fair value as

> *'the amount for which an asset could be exchanged, or a liability settled, between knowledgeable, willing parties in an arm's length transaction'*(IAS 39)

while the FAS 157 document issued in September 2006 by the FASB states that

> *'Fair value is the price that would be received to sell an asset or paid to transfer a liability in an orderly transaction'* (FAS 157)

Let us point out a few relevant and non-trivial implications of the above definitions, in particular the one in FAS 157.

1. The idea underlying fair value is that the market is the ultimate reference to give a value to a derivative. If a banks internal model indicates that a derivative has a value different from the one that prevails in the market, the market should win when it comes to accountancy. This principle, however, must be balanced with the considerations below at point 4.
2. Fair value is not a mid-price. In the case of an asset it must be the sell price, with the implication that a radical application of this approach in a market with a relevant bid-ask price may lead, one instant after an asset has been bought, to the buyer marking a loss as wide as the entire difference between ask price and bid price. In the case of a liability, we must consider the price required to extinguish it. Fair value is an *exit value*.
3. It seems that everything that would enter the exit price must be considered. For example, if the product is not collateralized, we should consider the default risk of our counterparty (*credit value adjustment, CVA*) and possibly our default risk (*debt value adjustment, DVA*). The introduction of counterparty specific elements, however, is not dealt with in the same way in all countries. It is a non-trivial issue in any case, since default risk of the counterparty makes equal payoffs have different fair values, while the introduction of our default risk can, according to some market operators and some regulators, induce a form of moral hazard. We investigate this issue in Section 4.2.
4. The expression *'arm's length transaction'* is a conventional legal phrase indicating that the two counterparties to the transaction must be on an equal footing, without one having a contractual power much stronger than the other one. It must not be, for example, a transaction between a parent company and one of its subsidiaries. A similar concept is expressed by FAS 157, which says that fair value must refer to the price in an *'orderly transaction'*. This is easy to understand for financial markets: we must not consider distressed conditions, for example when the seller is forced to sell due to a funding liquidity shortage. The transaction must happen under normal market conditions.

When looking at the first point above, the accountancy view appears more in line with the Price approach to model risk, which puts discrepancies between market price and model price as the first cause of model-driven losses, rather than the difference between true or at least realistic value and model price. But some questions remain unanswered. What should we do when a market does not exist? What if such market is illiquid? Such considerations have been addressed since the issuance of the above documents, in particular through the definition of a three-level hierarchy, which we describe in Section 1.3.3 following FAS 157.

One question remains open in spite of this, and it is a crucial one: what should we do if we have reason to think the market prices *are wrong* ? This question was fully addressed by boards of accountants only after the credit crunch, and the answer they gave is so relevant to an understanding of the current interpretation of fair value that we address it first.

1.3.2 The Liquidity Bubble and the Accountancy Boards

The issue that market prices can be wrong and irrational, and therefore can in some cases not be a good foundation for giving a balance-sheet value to derivatives, was raised very often after the subprime crisis burst, when products like CDOs, that had previously been treated as almost default-free, started to be evaluated in the market as if all the underlying debt were on the verge of default, even when a rational analysis suggested that this was not the case. This process peaked after Lehman's default, when many banks complained that the market was dramatically undervaluing assets and overestimating liabilities, they were creating the risk that banks following market prices for fair valuation could also be led to default even if not affected by big material losses.

Accountancy boards and regulators answered complaints on 30 September 2008, when the SEC and the FASB issued a joint clarification in which they pointed out that fair value definition speaks of market prices in *'orderly transactions'*, as we noted in point 4. From this it follows that when a market is affected by illiquidity and panic there cannot be orderly transactions, thus market prices may not constitute fair value – and thus can be corrected by personal judgement.

These statements by the accountancy board may appear surprising, since they seem to say that we should account at market prices only when market prices are deemed to be right. When the markets are instead deemed to be wrong, we should account at what we think is the correct price. What is a correct price, in the view of accountants and regulators? In their joint clarification, called 'Sec Office of the chief accountants and FASB Staff Clarification on Fair Value Accounting', the SEC and FASB state that reliable prices need to come out of *reasonable risk-adjusted, liquidity-adjusted and credit-adjusted 'expected cash flows'.*

Only a fortnight later the international board, the IASB, issued a similar paper, in which they claim that a firm should *not* 'automatically conclude that any observed price is determinative of fair value', and that if necessary it can make 'adjustments to the transactions price that are necessary to measure the fair value'. Even the Accounting Standard Board of Japan published a paper on 5 December along the same lines.

These clarifications say that fair prices should be descriptive of expected future cashflows, and therefore they need to coincide with market prices only when market prices can be broadly believed to be already such realistic descriptions. This sounds closer to the Value approach to model risk than to the Price approach, while at first sight the latter appeared closer to accounting principles. This debate in the field of accountancy rules really mirrors the debate we have already seen from a quant's perspective in Section 1.1. And, similarly to the conclusions reached there, in the current view of the boards market consistency is still treated as the first benchmark to take into account in valuation, but they clarify that this can and must be mitigated by considerations that take account of the reasonableness of market prices.

1.3.3 Level 1, 2, 3 . . . go?

There is another similarity between the accountancy prescriptions and the ideas about model risk that we have seen in Sections 1.1 and 1.2. It is the principle that there is a link between model risk and a shortage of liquid market information. There exists in fact a three-level hierarchy in accounting principles that classifies the prices based on the inputs that enter the valuation procedure: prices based only on objective inputs, coming from liquid markets considered surely appropriate for the product to price, rank 1; while prices based on inputs computed making use of a plainly high amount of personal judgement rank 3. We present this hierarchy, then provide a few examples to show why it must be taken with a pinch of salt from the point of view of model risk management.

1. Level 1 (Liquid specific quotes). The valuation of a derivative falls into this category when it is based on the price coming from a *liquid* market where products *identical* to the derivative to price are traded. When such a market is available, we must give our derivative the price that we read in this market at the valuation moment. We have one single input taken directly from a liquid market, and no transformation of the input is required
2. Level 2 (Comparable quotes or Illiquid quotes). These fair value prices come from either:
   A. a *liquid* market where products *similar* (but not identical) to the derivative to evaluate are traded. Here we apply judgement in the application of the input to the derivative to value.
   B. a market where products *identical* to the derivative to evaluate are traded but the market is rather *illiquid*. Here there is judgement in assuming that I could readily sell the derivative at that price.

   In some cases Level 2 prices require an adjustment to be applied to the derivative under evaluation. This often requires interpolations or even extrapolations (see Chapter 7 for the risk involved in these operations, and how to minimize it) that are often carried out via models and can involve personal judgement.
3. Level 3 (Model with non-quoted parameters). These fair value prices come from the use of a valuation technique that requires inputs which involve a crucial amount of personal judgement of the institution computing the price.

The above description is only a summary of the details on how to classify prices into the three categories given by accountancy boards. For example, the FASB explains that Level 2 prices can also make use of valuation techniques, but differently from Level 3 the inputs of these valuation techniques must be available – at least in illiquid markets or for comparables. The valuation techniques used should always be consistent with the definition of fair value, *assumptions that an unrelated party would use* (thus pricing involves making assumptions about someone else's assumptions).

The general wisdom, also contained in some official documents, is that Level 3 prices are 'marked-to-model' and therefore should involve a lot of model risk, while Level 2 prices involve a more limited amount of model risk, and there is no model risk at all in respect to Level 1 prices, which only involve 'market risk'. This formal scheme does not always coincide with the actual distribution of model risk on different deals.

Consider, for example, the distinction between Level 2 and Level 3 prices. They may both involve the use of models, but Level 3 prices are considered less reliable because they involve models that require some input which is not readily available in a market, but must be chosen by the user's judgement or by procedures such as historical estimations. Such a distinction risks fuelling distorted choices about models. If a realistic model recognizes the existence of two different actual risk factors, and allows for a relation to exist between them, it may require a correlation input to be estimated historically. In this case the product will certainly be classified as Level 3, which usually means that the trader will have some penalization compared to a Level 2 price, in the form, for example, of a recognition of his profit that will be diluted in time. This can make sense, but the problem is that another less realistic model may not recognize that two distinct risks exist, treating them as a single one (always perfect correlation), or may recognize the two separate risks but may assume by construction that they are independent (always zero correlations). This model will not require a correlation to be fixed exogenously, thus the prices generated by this model can be recognized as Level 2 and involve less penalization for the trader! The trader will have a clear incentive to choose this second model, which actually involves much more model risk.

In Chapter 8 we show examples of models that make mistakes about correlations which are misinterpreted as perfect dependencies or independencies, and we will see that such models can be dangerous. Another interesting case are the mapping methods described in Chapter 3. Such methods were used before the crisis to evaluate illiquid products based on the quotes of scarcely related liquid products. The relation between liquid and illiquid products was based, as you will see, on very abstract and rigid mathematical relations that created a high model risk. Their rigidity and abstraction did not involve any exogenous parameter choice, which instead would probably have been beneficial to adapt them to the different market situations. But in a shortsighted interpretation of the above accountancy principles, their main flaw may have played in their favour, making them Level 2 rather than Level 3.

Now consider Level 1 prices. Since these come from a market where products are traded identical to the derivative under analysis, they should involve no model risk at all. Here too, the classification can be more formal than substantial, and does not recognize correctly the presence of model risk in a broad sense. In fact, in deciding that a price is Level 1, there is a clear amount of personal judgement, it is the *judgement required to decide that two assets are 'identical'*. One such decision is often based on some assumptions that may be so hidden and rooted in market practice that they are no longer recognizable as essentially 'modelling' assumptions . . . until they become unrealistic and are rejected by market consensus, at times in the blink of an eye. To illustrate how strongly model assumptions can enter into the evaluation of even simple vanilla derivatives, we show some hidden assumptions that enter the valuation of the simplest plain vanilla swap. By the way, these assumptions were generally agreed upon for decades, but were discarded in a day, and we know which day: 9 August 2007.

1.3.4 The Hidden Model Assumptions in 'vanilla' Derivatives

Suppose we have available a liquid interbank market for a few maturities. In this market we can observe the quotes for loans from bank to bank. Banks will agree on the rate at which such loans must happen: this rate has been called Libor for many years. For the maturity T, the market prevailing rate at time t is $L(t, T)$. Which means that if the notional of the loan is

Replicating a FRA

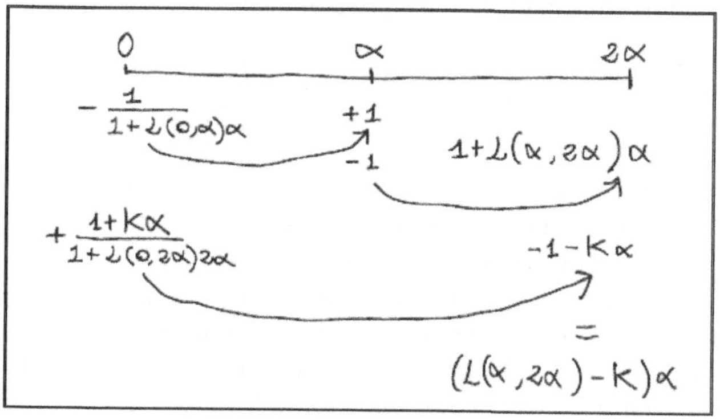

Figure 1.4 FRA standard replication scheme

\$1, the lender gives 1 at t, and the borrower must give back

$$1 + L(t, T)(T - t)$$

at T. But also, if the loan has a notional of $\frac{1}{1+L(t,T)(T-t)}$, the lender gives $\frac{1}{1+L(t,T)(T-t)}$ at t, and the borrower must give back 1 at T. Thus we see that this market, at least for the maturity T, gives directly the spot rate and also the value of a contract that pays 1 at T.

Suppose the rates that we see quoted in the market at t include $L(t, \alpha)$ and $L\,(t, 2\alpha)$. Now we are a bank that has to price, at time $t = 0$, a forward rate agreement with expiry (or fixing) at α and payment at 2α, a product which is the simplest one-period, fixed for floating swap where at 2α one party has a payment indexed to a fixed rate and the counterparty instead pays a floating rate that fixed at α. If the agreed fixed rate is K, the payoff for the payer of the fixed rate is simply at 2α

$$(L(\alpha, 2\alpha) - K)\,\alpha. \tag{1.7}$$

If we are the payer of the fixed rate, we can trivially price it with the following replication, summarized in Figure 1.4. Lend $\frac{1}{1+L(0,\alpha)\alpha}$ to your counterparty for maturity α. You will receive 1 at α. At α lend this 1 for a time α, namely from α to 2α, and you will receive at 2α

$$1 + L(\alpha, 2\alpha)\alpha.$$

This contains part of the payoff of the FRA, $L(\alpha, 2\alpha)\alpha$, but also 1, that does not appear in the FRA payoff (1.7), and on the other hand it does not contain K. In fact at time 0 one must also borrow $\frac{1+K\alpha}{1+L(0,2\alpha)\alpha}$ from the counterparty until 2α. We will pay at 2α

$$-\frac{1 + K\alpha}{1 + L\,(0, 2\alpha)\,\alpha}\,(1 + L\,(0, 2\alpha)\,\alpha) = -1 - K\alpha.$$

Put together with what we receive and get

$$L(\alpha, 2\alpha)\alpha - K\alpha,$$

which is exactly the same payoff from the FRA given in (1.7). Thus the price of the FRA must be equal, in an arbitrage-free market, to the price of the replication strategy:

$$\frac{1}{1+L(0,\alpha)\alpha} - \frac{1+K\alpha}{1+L(0,2\alpha)\alpha}.$$

Is this pricing Level 1, 2 or 3? Well, we are working on liquid markets, we are not using any comparable, but only things that ought to be the same in any arbitrage-free market, and we are using no evaluation model. Thus it looks like Level 1.

One may say: no, wait a second. You are using one modelling assumption: you are assuming absence of arbitrage. This is true, in fact all replication arguments like those above work only if there is no arbitrage, since it is absence of arbitrage which dictates that things which have the same payoff ought to have the same price. But the whole Level 1,2,3 classification is based on the assumption that absence of arbitrage does hold. Otherwise the definition of Level 1 would not make sense. An option on the Microsoft stock with maturity 1 year is Level 1 because we can see in the market the price of other options on the Microsoft stock with same strike and same maturity, and use this price to evaluate my option. But this strategy yields a reliable price only if there is absence of arbitrage, otherwise there would be no reason for two options with the same payoff to have the same price. Thus absence of arbitrage is not an additional assumption, but is rather a foundation of the Level 1,2,3 classification, and my pricing of the FRA above involves no other assumption and no illiquid product so it ought to be Level 1.

Usually an FRA is not Level 1 but Level 2 because the evaluation goes through a bootstrap of the term structure that always involves at least interpolation between maturities, but here we assumed rates and thus discounts for exactly the maturities of the FRA. The FRA appears identical to the portfolio of loans; the payoffs are the same.

And yet, in contrast to usual market wisdom, this price comes from some strong model assumptions, and as such it is subject to a fair amount of model risk since the underlying assumptions, like all model assumptions, can be rejected by the market in the future. This happened in this case at the beginning of the credit crunch, precisely on 9 August 2007. We see in Figure 1.5 that the correspondence between FRA prices and the price of their replication strategy held with surprising precision for many years, before breaking down at the beginning of the subprime crisis.

We will analyse this issue in Section 4.1, since this is of particular interest to us as an example of how a market can change its modelling paradigm. But here we anticipate one point: where are the hidden model assumptions in FRA pricing?

First of all, it is clear that the FRA above is treated as default-free. The first thing we have to consider, therefore, is what happens when we introduce risk of default. We may think that this breaks down the above pricing because a default event spoils the identity between the payoff of the FRA and the replication strategy. We will see in Section 4.1 that this is not necessarily the case because the payoff and the replication strategy may be affected by risk of default in the same way. What default risk really breaks in the replication, even for collateralized FRAs, is that with this additional risk *we have no more guarantee that our counterparty in the replication has the same risk of default which is expressed by the market rate $L(\alpha, 2\alpha)$ that appears in the payoff*.

It is in this detail, and not so much in the possibility of a default event, that the devil hides. As we see in Figure 1.6, the presence of default risk means that my counterparty C will have a fair lending rate $L^C(\alpha, 2\alpha)$ which is not necessarily the same as the rate $L(\alpha, 2\alpha)$ that appears in

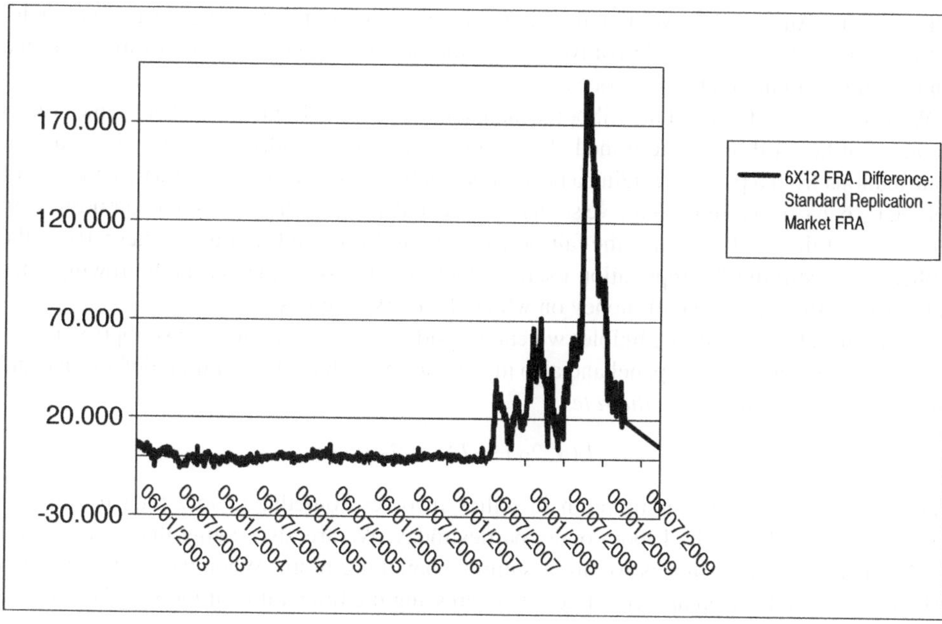

Figure 1.5 Standard replication – Market FRA (6*m* fixing, 12*m* payment)

the FRA payoff, potentially breaking down the above replication, that required this condition to have a payoff really equal to (1.7).

And suddenly this reveals the extreme imprecision of the above payoff description: what does it mean that the FRA will pay a floating rate $L(\alpha, 2\alpha)$ at 2α? What is that rate precisely and how will it be computed at 2α? Here we find out the truth. As long as the market is an idealized market, first and foremost free of risk of default, all interest rates are the same since they simply express the market consensus about the time value of money. But when we introduce further elements of realism, we are forced to analyze precisely which rates we are

Replicating a FRA after the credit crunch

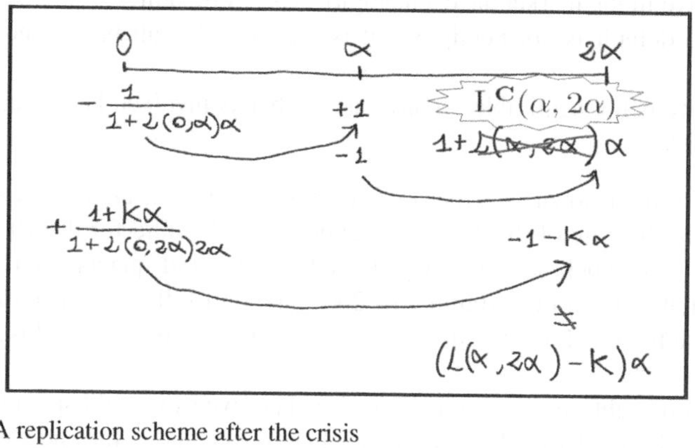

Figure 1.6 FRA replication scheme after the crisis

talking about. And we discover that the FRA is not at all as simple a derivative as we thought, but is more akin to a basket derivative. In fact the rate $L(\alpha, 2\alpha)$ is usually a Libor rate that comes out of a rather elaborate process.

We will give full details of the Libor mechanism in Section 4.1, but we see here some crucial elements of how Libor is determined. The level of Libor is provided by a special average of contributions from a panel including a peculiar set of banks. Only in a market where the risk of default by banks is negligible can we safely assume that all banks have the same fair borrowing rate, and that this is always also the fair borrowing rate for us and for our counterparty in the replication, justifying the replication itself. In fact, in a risk-free market the borrowing rates only express the time-value of money on which the market agrees.

If risk of default is not negligible, we can consider the replication at least approximately valid only if all banks in the panel and also my counterparty have very similar default risk and *this will be expressed at α by the rate*

$$L(\alpha, 2\alpha) = L^C(\alpha, 2\alpha).$$

But notice that the latter assumption in italics involves something more than having our counterparty similar to the Libor counterparties today. We are also saying that this will last until α, but this clearly means we are assuming something more. When we allow for credit risk, all rates can be seen as a risk-free rate expressing the time-value of money *plus a credit spread*,

$$L(\alpha, 2\alpha) = L_{rf}(\alpha, 2\alpha) + Spread^{Libor}(\alpha, 2\alpha),$$
$$L^C(\alpha, 2\alpha) = L_{rf}(\alpha, 2\alpha) + Spread^C(\alpha, 2\alpha).$$

What is the volatility of these spreads? What is their correlation? If the volatility is assumed to be zero, then it is true that similar spreads today imply similar spreads at α. The replication can still be approximately satisfactory. But if the volatility is not nil, then we have to worry about the correlation. Is the correlation between $Spread^{Libor}$ and $Spread^C$ equal to 1? Then again we can still use the above replication, but notice that this implies a unit correlation of C with all 16 banks in the Libor panel (even more for Euribor). If *any* of this assumptions does not hold in a relevant way, the above price obtained by the replication can be absolutely wrong. Thus the above price, which by the way all pre-crisis books on interest rates describe as *The price* of a FRA, actually hangs on either:

1. All banks active in the market have a negligible risk of default.
2. If this risk of default is not negligible, it is the same for all banks and its volatility is negligible.
3. If this volatility is not negligible, in any case all banks involved have their risk of default perfectly correlated.

Seeing them written down, we realize that these are not at all light assumptions, they look pretty strong. In spite of this they were approximately valid for the 10 years preceding the credit crunch, so much so that many market players and quants even forgot that they were used implicitly. But in the summer of 2007, they all fell down, from first to last, like dominos, because traders did not believe them to be valid anymore, and this changed market patterns.

The traders were right: in fact, about 12 months later we saw credit spreads sky-rocketing, some banks being hit harder by the credit crisis than others, and in the end we even saw a big,

Libor panel bank like Lehman default. As soon as traders adopted the new view, for the first time FRA prices went out of line with (1.7). This shows that even with apparently 'Level 1' or, at worst, 'Level 2' prices there are important modelling assumptions, and additionally they can change quite suddenly so that there is also model risk in such Level 1 or Level 2 prices. In Section 4.1 we will analyze the situation in detail, and we will provide technical tools for dealing with it. We will dig deeper showing, for example, that the replication above implies that not only the counterparty but also we who make the replication must have the same risk of default as Libor. More interestingly, we will see that even for a collateralized FRA, as most FRAs in the market are, the above standard replication failed at the credit crunch, even if there is no risk of default in the FRA. In fact, risk of default is in any case included in the Libor rate L. Finally, we show a replication alternative to the one above, one based on more general assumptions and approximately consistent also with the market prices of FRA after the credit crunch.

So far, what matters to us in this example is to show that model risk can actually arise in liquid markets. If the market remains liquid it is formally exposed only to 'market risk'. But this is only a formal distinction. There are variations in the patterns of a liquid market that can be expressed as 'market risk' because we observe them as variation of quoted prices, but can only be understood and anticipated as changes in the *model* consensus by the market. The loss can be lower when this shift happens in a liquid market, because in liquid markets a bank is more likely to have both long and short positions.

However, we must also consider hedging risk, an aspect often overlooked, or treated in a simplified way, in accountancy principles. The change of the model consensus in a liquid market can break down the fundamental hedging strategies. The change in interest rate modelling assumptions triggered by the subprime crisis emerged as market risk for quoted FRAs; but since it was associated with a change in the model consensus it broke down the hedging strategies of FRAs and swaps, both liquid and illiquid, that were based on the model consensus itself.

We see something similar in one of the examples in Chapter 11: even if one were convinced that there is no model risk in the pricing of liquid caps and swaptions, there is certainly model risk if you hedge cap exposure with swaptions, or the other way around, based on the fact that in standard terms structure models they depend on the same risk factors. This risk became painfully evident as early as the Russian crisis of 1998. Even when we find it convenient to talk about 'market risk' when looking at losses in a single FRA or a single Cap, if we want to explain losses like those of 1998 or 2007 *at a portfolio level* we cannot overlook the fact that at those points in time a modelling paradigm broke down.

Moreover, the change in interest rate modelling assumptions of August 2007 also disrupted the pricing of all swaps that were not liquid, and the foundations of the construction of the discounting curve for derivatives of any asset class. All these hinged on the model assumptions whose change was revealed by changes in liquid market price. Liquid markets are often what we need to observe in order to understand the changes in the pricing of illiquid products. Fundamental model assumptions are certainly more stable in liquid markets, but they can change suddenly even there. An investor will find it very difficult to go against the model consensus of a liquid market, so in a strict sense here we have no 'model uncertainty' because if we want to participate in this market we can only do so at the market's consensus. But also in this case, if the model consensus appear unrealistic or if we detect a possibility that it will change in the near future, tools of model risk management such as limits to the exposures like those given at 2.7.3 can prove useful.

Even what happens in liquid markets is strongly related to model risk. Not to mention the fact that with the subprime crisis the interbank market and the FRA market suddenly became illiquid. The fact that the liquidity of a liquid market can dry up confirms what we said in Section 1.2.2: liquid and illiquid markets are affected by model risk in different ways, but setting too sharp a divide between them in terms of model risk management can be dangerous.

1.4 WHAT REGULATORS SAID AFTER THE CRISIS

If this book had been written before the financial crisis of 2007–2009, I am not sure that it would–have included a section on what regulators have to say. Regulators have strongly influenced the world of finance in the past few years, but their role has not always been positive. We have seen in Sections 1.1.3 and 1.2.1 how the importance given to ratings was among the factors that encouraged lax practice in relation to risk management. Some regulators seemed to think that model validation was a formal procedure, and that model risk was minimized if banks were forced to use the same simple, standardized models. The main effects of this approach were: to fuel the so-called regulatory arbitrage, where banks exploit the weaknesses and the rigidities of regulations; to favour procyclicality, making all banks herd together during bubbles and crises; and, most dangerously, to prompt many institutions to commit to following the formal rules given by regulators and then to use this formal compliance as a justification for being particularly lax in terms of substantial model risk management. However, after the crisis regulators issued many documents and uttered numerous words analyzing the mistakes made by banks and those made by the regulators themselves. I think that we should pay attention to what they said for at least two reasons:

1. The guidelines they give about model risk management, in terms of banks' governance, of organization of a risk management unit, and of principles to follow in model validation should become, along the lines of Basel's Pillar II, the benchmark for determining the amount of capital to be held by banks against model risk. Banks that stray too far from these principles will be required to keep more capital.
2. The approach they adopt post-crisis is different from the formal and schematic approaches suggested before the crisis. There is more attention to the substance of model risk, and more awareness that regulators can lay down principles for model risk management but cannot give recipes that work for all banks in all market situations. It seems more evident that model risk management is not an issue of legal compliance but rather a strategic issue that requires a commitment by management tailored specifically to the characteristics of a financial institution and of the markets where the institution operates. Many suggestions are reasonable and should be considered by modellers.

The most important document issued by regulators after the subprime crisis with a strong relevance for model risk is the Basel Committee's 'Supervisory guidance for assessing banks' financial instrument fair value practices', published on 6 February 2009. This is by far the most frequently quoted document by managers and experts at conferences on model risk and validation, and in my opinion it is the best summary of up-to-date regulator views on modelling, as expressed in documents issued by the SEC, FSA, Central Banks and other institutions. The paper 'Supervisory Guidance on Model Risk Management', published by the FED while I was completing this book deserves special mention. Its definition of models is particularly interesting: 'a model is composed of three parts'. They are 'a component which delivers assumptions and data to the model' together with 'a component which transforms inputs into estimates' and, finally, 'a component which translates the estimates into useful business information'. This is a very reasonable assessment to make, as we pointed out in the preface. There are many more similarities between the framework it designs and the approach followed in this book.

Going back to the 'Supervisory guidance for assessing banks' financial instrument fair value practices', we see that it gives 10 principles divided into two groups, 'Valuation Governance and Control' and 'Risk management and Reporting for Valuation'. For the purposes of a technical book such as this, with a focus on model risk management, I have not found it useful to follow the structure of the document. I have skipped those principles I found mainly formal or of little relevance to model risk management and validation, while from the remaining principles I have selected three groups of recommendations which I consider a good summary of the most relevant and innovative elements.

The first group relates mainly to the process of model validation and model management, with specific focus on the role of an institution's management in the process, the use that must be made of the conclusions of the process, and the general principles that should inspire it.

The second group is more specific and relates to how model validation must be adapted to the market and to the specific product under analysis.

The third group of recommendations is really a list of operative steps that should not be omitted in a model validation process.

The second and third groups of recommendations have a real impact on the daily work of a practitioner, and they contain suggestions which are reasonable and in line with the analysis and examples given in this book.

1.4.1 Basel New Principles: The Management Process

1. *'Management must understand the basis of any valuation techniques used by outside parties ... to determine the appropriateness of the techniques used, the underlying assumptions.' 'Reporting to senior management and to the board should be on a regular basis in an appropriately aggregated and understandable form'*
2. *'Bank valuation methodologies are expected not to place undue reliance on a single information source (eg external ratings) especially when valuing complex or illiquid products'*
3. *'Articulating the bank's tolerance for exposures subject to valuation uncertainty ... Analysis should be commensurate with the importance of the specific exposure for the overall solvency of the institution'*
4. *'Fair value measurements may involve a significant amount of judgement'*

After the crisis, when sharp criticism was levelled at the senior management of financial institutions, many senior people in banks claimed to be unaware of the valuation techniques used by the institution they managed, and often laid the blame on technical experts. But it was the senior management of financial institutions who decided the strategies and the risk appetite that eventually led to the crisis, and it was they who received the large part of the revenues from it. It was senior management who knew the amount of exposures built towards the different sources of risk.

The excuse that management did not know or understand the valuation techniques used is unacceptable. Either the senior management, who take the investment decisions, claims to understand at least the fundamental practical aspects of the valuations carried out by the technical experts, or the technical experts should be the ones who take investment decisions and get the revenues from them! If things go on as they did before the crisis, the technical experts will decide nothing and eventually will be held to blame for all losses, while the senior management will get all the revenues from risky investment strategies but will not be held responsible when these strategies lead the bank to default or to be bailed out by government.

The first principle above lays the foundations for senior management to be held responsible also for investment decisions taken using valuation models. They are required to understand *the basis* of the valuation techniques used, and to judge on the underlying assumptions. There is no need for them to understand the technical details, but they must take responsibility for the most relevant underlying assumptions. Only they have sufficient information on the bank's business to judge which assumptions are acceptable and which ones should instead be considered too risky. This should mean that the discharge of responsibilities onto models and modellers carried out by some executives during the crisis will no longer be acceptable.

On the other hand, this also requires a commitment on the part of the technical experts. This is the subject of the second sentence in point 1. The choice of a valuation model cannot fall entirely to a quant (who may be completely unaware of market dynamics and the bank's exposures) downloading from the web a popular paper (perhaps one that simply focuses on the details of the derivation of a closed-form formula) and implementing it, with just some generic hints from a trader or salesman and with the underpinning of a purely formal model validation.

The choice of a valuation model must be based on an analysis about its appropriateness and its implications, and this analysis must be reported to senior management, in an *aggregated and understandable form*. The communication must necessarily be aggregate, because senior management get easily lost in the detail and even more importantly, it must be understandable. Many quants, traders and other technically strong practitioners will find this aspect one of the most difficult. How to make things which are usually expressed in a technical language comprehensible for senior management? A way must be found, if technical people do not want to be held responsible again for the misuse of models. And it is not impossible. This book is devoted also to help quants with this. The first point is that we must be sure to have fully understood the model ourselves, not only in its technical details but also in its fundamental assumptions and financial implications, with a practical focus. At times this point is overlooked by quants, who concentrate on mathematical and implementation aspects, therefore we cover this aspect thoroughly in these pages. We hope this will help also communication between those who understand models and those who take decisions based on them. Without this we have the worst model risk.

The document stresses that management must understand the basis of a valuation technique even when it is provided by an external party, such as a rating agency. This is a recognition that excessive reliance on ratings, partly fuelled by regulations, was one of the causes of the crisis. Ratings are explicitly mentioned in the second point, when it is recommended not to use just one source of information.

The third point is simply common sense but is often lost in model validation. Model risk is not linear with respect to exposure. The last crisis was not generated by a bank using a wrong model, in the sense of a model that was liable to be suddenly discarded for lack of realism. This is exactly what the market model for CDOs was, but banks use many models which are even less realistic. It is unavoidable that some models used are like that, but this does not necessarily generate a crisis. The problem before the credit crunch was that an enormous exposure was built on a source of risk that was assessed with a model subject to strong valuation uncertainty and high likelihood of model revision. It was the unfortunate marriage between large exposure and valuation uncertainty that put the world on the verge of disaster.

The third point recalls the steps to be taken to avoid this scenario. A bank must introduce a link between valuation uncertainty in assessing a risk and the size of the exposure to that risk. The higher the valuation uncertainty, the lower should be the exposure. This can be done in different ways, for example by the institution of 'model lines', similar to the credit lines already used by banks, which are discussed in the next section. All effective tools of model risk management, such as model reserves, have in the end this purpose. The goal of model reserves is not to stop a salesperson or a trader from closing a deal, but to reduce the seeming convenience of the deal when we fear that this convenience can be due to misvaluation. This should prevent exposure to this model risk from growing too much and too fast. When standard reserves are not enough, we can think of reserves linked to coefficients that grow when the bank's total exposure grows. It is in the end the very old principle of diversification applied to model risk. Clearly, this requires a firm-wide approach to model risk management, and confirms that those who conduct validation must work closely with those who have a global view of a bank's business.

The second part of the point serves as a reminder that the effort in model validation must be commensurate with the exposure: when a small exposure is started towards a new risk, a limited effort for model validation is acceptable. A bank cannot expend big resources for a small exposure; and additionally banks and traders learn by trial and error, a new model needs to be tested for a while in order to really know its risks. When the exposure starts growing, a previous model validation must not automatically be considered valid: a surplus of effort can be spent on the model used, an effort that was not economically meaningful in the past but is crucial in the face of an increased exposure. This seems redundant, common sense. However, in practice it can happen that risk managers focus a lot on the validation of a new model for a very small deal. Then, when the model is validated, the model is forgotten even if at some future date the sheer survival of the bank hangs on the validity of that model.

The last point, 4, may also sound like trivial common sense to many practitioners. But it is a minor revolution to see it underlined so clearly in so many official documents. The objectivity of valuation, the idea that there must be one single right model that all banks should use, haunted many regulators. It would be good if they were to abandon this dangerous delusion, and the same applies to those managers or salespeople who expect quants to 'tell them the right model'... and to the quants who think they have the answer because they have just downloaded a popular paper. Model choice is really a choice, and at times personal judgement is the most important ingredient of all. Recognizing this is a good first step for a better understanding of model risk.

1.4.2 Basel New Principles: The Model, The Market and The Product

1. *'Uncertainty is specific to the instrument and to the point in time the valuation is effected'*
2. *'A bank is expected to consider all relevant market information likely to have a material effect on an instrument's fair value when selecting the appropriate inputs'*
3. *'However, observable inputs or transactions may not be relevant. In such cases, the observable data should be considered, but may not be determinative'*

These three points do not relate to the process of model risk management, but they set precise boundaries on its scope. The first point recalls that uncertainty is specific to one instrument.

We cannot automatically extend to a new instrument the validation that was performed to allow a different application. It makes no sense to think of a model separate from a specific application; the validation cannot state that a model is valid for all computations that can be performed with it.

This is a consequence of the old principle, recognized also by Derman, that 'all models are wrong, but some are useful', as the statistician George Box said in the 20th century. A model is a tool that can be useful to solve a problem, but also inapt when solving a related but different problem. Models always make mistakes, and a serious validation is mainly the job of judging if these mistakes are negligible for the product at hand. This makes the scope of validation unavoidably narrow. We will see often in the next chapters, and in particular when discussing stress testing in Chapter 3, that a slight change in the payoff can change, in a dramatic and surprising way, the behaviour of a model. This is clear to most practitioners, but not to everyone. We can still hear old-style risk managers make comments such as 'we have validated the model for interest rate derivatives', as if the set of interest rate derivatives was so limited in its potential expansions that it is easy to find a model appropriate for all of them. The only model with such a property would be the 'true model of interest rate dynamics', but unfortunately such a model does not exist. At times it may be acceptable to gain efficiency by validating models for 'categories of products' rather than single products, as some banks do. But we must be careful in extending the scope of a validation in terms of products. The main risk is the temptation to use this approach in a 'Lego' way. The fact that a model has been considered valid for *spread* options as well as *American* options, for example, does not imply it is appropriate for *American spread* options.

The second part of this point reprises that uncertainty also changes with time, so that a validation performed years ago, or in a more recent but different market situation, is not necessarily still valid today. We have already touched on this point, which implies that rules for the revisions of validation are necessary.

The last two points state that the information to use in valuation is all and only the information relevant to the instrument under analysis. All market information must be collected, but irrelevant market information should be excluded. The document explains that they refer mainly to the cases considered by accountants, such as distressed sale. One element to add here is that even liquid and not distressed market information can be irrelevant. There was, particularly before the crisis, a tendency to overextend the calibration set of models, under the illusion that the more market information included, the better. In principle this is not wrong, but it is useless when market information is not relevant to the risk we want to assess. We will see an example of this kind in the next chapter which describes gap risk and option calibration. The risk of this overcalibration approach is that it creates a false sense of confidence. Apparently it increases the robustness of the model, but often it only makes the model less stable and hides the presence of remaining uncertainty on model features that are calibrated to no liquid market but may be crucial for the complex bespoke derivative under evaluation.

1.4.3 Basel New Principles: Operative Recommendations

1. *'Validation includes evaluations of the model's theoretical soundness and mathematical integrity and the appropriateness of model assumptions, including consistency with market'*
2. *'Bank processes should emphasize the importance of assessing fair value using a diversity of approaches and having in place a range of mechanisms to cross-check valuations'*

3. *'A bank is expected to test and review the performance of its valuation models under possible stress conditions, so that it understands the limitations of the models' 'assess the impact of variations in model parameters on fair value, including under stress conditions'*
4. *'Policies should also identify specific triggers (eg indications of deterioration in model performance or quality) that will cause the review'*

These four points give a precise indication of a few crucial steps that should not be omitted in model validation. They include the appropriateness of model assumptions. The considerations contained in the document make this appropriateness of model assumptions very akin to the model realism at the centre of the Value approach. Further, the consistency with the market, central to the Price approach, is explicitly mentioned as an element to be included. It also recalls the need for model verifications, that includes control of the mathematical correctness.

The second point recalls the need for a diversity of approaches when assessing fair values. This seems in striking contrast to some previous regulatory approaches that emphasized the use of simplified models to be taken as the unique reference, also to guarantee homogeneity across banks. This fuelled regulatory arbitrage and pro-cyclicality. Now not only is this sort of homogeneity not required across banks, but it is not needed even internally. This makes sense: only the comparison of really different models gives us a clear view of our model uncertainty, and outlines the advantages and the disadvantages of each single model. We will focus on this in the next chapter.

The third point is stress testing, the topic of Chapters 3 and 6. Stress testing has been heavily emphasized by regulators in the last few years, with a double meaning that appears also in the recommendations of this document. On the one hand we should test the performance of models under stress conditions, to understand model limitations. This is what in the following we will call 'model stress testing'; the focus in these tests is on what can 'break' the model. On the other hand, we should stress the parameters to see how fair value changes. In this case the focus is on understanding, using a model, how the value of a derivative or a portfolio can change. This helps us understand which risk factors are crucial for our valuation, and which model parameters are associated with maximum risk. This is what in the following we will call 'portfolio stress testing'.

Stress testing often allows us to understand market conditions that, should they become material, would require a revision of our model validation. This helps set precise quantitative indications on when this should be done. The quantitative triggers that warn us that the model reliability is deteriorating are the focus of point 4. We will see examples of this for the rates market in 2007, for correlation models, and in the analysis of approximations.

1.5 MODEL VALIDATION AND RISK MANAGEMENT: PRACTICAL STEPS

We have seen the different approaches to model risk, the foundations of our modelling framework, the role of fair value and accountancy in modelling, and the latest prescriptions by regulators. From this we can deduce a practical scheme with the steps to follow, first in model validation and then in model risk management. These steps will be the topics of the next chapters. Here we give only a synthetic description of them, since a deeper understanding can be reached only through a detailed description and examples. Bullet points are used to indicate the steps in the process, ★ are indications that relate to more than one step, and ■ are the provisions to be put in place to implement the process.

Model Validation and Model Risk Management

1 Model Verification
- Mathematics
- Implementation
- Computational Methods
- Payoff Description

2 Model Validation
- Calibration
- Reasonableness
- Market Intelligence
- Reality Check

★Model Comparison

- ■ Accept/Reject
- ■ Improvements
- ■ Provisions
- ■ Periodic Revisions

3 Stress Testing
- Stressability
- Computational methods
  - A Payoff features
  - B Market conditions
- Model assumptions
  - A Payoff features
  - B Market conditions

- ■ Improvements
- ■ Provisions
- ■ Triggered Revisions
- ■ Payoff Limitations

★ Model Evolution

- ■ Provisions
- ■ Triggered Revisions

Figure 1.7 A scheme for Model Validation and Model Risk Management

1.5.1 A Scheme for Model Validation

1. **Model Verification (check of the internal consistency)**
   The Value approach recommends checking the mathematics and the implementation of a model. The alternative Price approach requires mathematical and numerical correctness in order to get prices similar to those of the other players. The regulators speak of assessing 'mathematical integrity'. In the natural sciences this is called Model Verification: checking that model assumptions are turned correctly into prices and sensitivities. We can distinguish three verifications:
   - **Mathematics**
     Often, a model starts by assuming a dynamics for a financial variable. Then the model developer solves a stochastic differential equation to see which distributions are produced from this dynamics, and from the distributions a number of useful formulas are computed. Examples of this type of model development are short rate models like Vasicek or CIR. In other cases the model starts from a distribution and then derives a consistent dynamics. This is the case for most local volatility models. When a model is used for the first time the passages from dynamics to closed-form formulas or the other way around should be verified. This should be the case for any new model developed by a front office quant, also for any new model that simply appears on the internet – or in a journal. There are errors even in published literature, never be too trusty.
   - **Implementation**
     Verifying a model implementation is not just a boring job where thousands of lines of code must be checked out. Instead, for a quant or a trader, it is an art. There are a number of clever tests that can be performed with a software to ensure that the software is consistent with the underlying modelling assumptions. Although, this book is not

about debugging, it is about understanding the consequences of model assumptions and the special cases that reveal the differences between models. Thus everything that follows here can be of some use in verifying the correctness of an implementation.

- **Computational Methods**
  When a price or a sensitivity cannot be computed exactly in closed form, alternative computational methods have to be used. These have to be validated. The most relevant case, from the point of view of model risk, are approximations. They must be tested in a special case scenario when exact methods are available, or against alternative methods like Monte Carlo simulation, which is not exact but can be made very precise at the cost of high computational effort. Moreover, the implementation of Monte Carlo simulation and other numerical methods such as binomial trees must be verified, usually in special cases where exact methods are available. The first verification of approximations and numerical methods is done under normal conditions, namely with the parameters we find in calibrating the model to today's market conditions. The analysis under extreme conditions is part of stress testing (although it can often be practically anticipated here). Both the analysis under normal conditions and the one under stressed conditions are described in Chapter 6.
- **Payoff Description**
  Next we have to verify that the implementation gives a correct description of the payoff. It is recommended explicitly by Derman, and it is a prerequisite for the Rebonato's goal to price derivatives consistency with market consensus (if the payoff was wrongly described, the price would be different even if we are using the consensus model). The errors made in the representation of the payoff are of two sorts. First there are 'the delta-one trader errors': wrong day-count conventions (actual/360 rather than actual/actual...), errors in the start date (it is today+2 days, not today...) and so on. These errors are important, particularly for traders in rather linear payoffs where money is made out of little spreads on large notionals. But for complex derivatives, they are usually not the core risk, and they have little to do with model risk. Second, there are errors in the interpretation of the payoff which are more sneaky. Spotting them requires a minimum experience of legal issues, documentation and market practice, and also the intuition of a modeller. Chapter 10 describes some potential errors in the representation of a payoff.

2. **Model Validation**
   Here we move from a check of internal consistency and correct description of the payoff to the analysis of model assumptions. This is proper Model Validation, and is described in detail in the examples in Chapter 2 where we compare different models applied to the same payoff. Having a plurality of models is crucial here.

   First, all models under analysis must be assessed on the following two points:

   - **Calibration:** Calibrate with acceptable precision the relevant market information. The topic of calibration is covered specifically in Chapter 9, with a focus on the model uncertainty that can remain after calibrations, and on enriching a calibration procedure to reduce this indetermination. The topic of calibration, however, is so crucial that it is covered in the next two chapters, then again in Chapter 5 where we see the links between calibration and hedging, and in Chapter 11 where the goodness of calibration to two markets jointly is used to spot arbitrage opportunities. In Chapter 7.1 we see how a clever calibration can avoid an extrapolation. Here we must also discuss *computational efficiency*. Due to the standard of calibrating models to a large number of derivatives, and of refreshing this calibration as often as possible, efficiency in pricing the calibration products becomes a prerequisite of a model, even for models that we allow to be time-consuming when pricing non-calibration products. The topic is important for users and should not be completely dismissed by validators: alternative models with very inefficient calibration will be difficult to apply regularly, although they can be used to compute reserves.

- **Reasonableness:** The models must not be plainly unrealistic on elements of market behaviour which are crucial to the value of the derivative under analysis. We know that there exist no perfectly realistic assumptions, all models involve simplifications. However, we must make sure that the model is not senseless for the product at hand. Examples are given in the next chapter, where we will also see that some models do not pass the calibration or reasonableness tests when they are in their standard form, but that they can often be improved so as to pass these preliminary tests.

With the models that have passed the previous two tests, we move to model selection and assessment of model uncertainty through the following analysis.

- **Market Intelligence.** Knowledge of the market consensus on the pricing of a payoff, if there is one, is crucial given todays' practice of marking derivatives to market. A good calibration to simpler derivatives does not always imply that we are using the consensus model for the complex derivative of interest. The tools to use in order to perform market intelligence have already been explained in Section 1.1.2, and here we just revisit them:
  (a) Visible deals, novations, unwindings
  (b) Collateral regulation
  (c) Broker quotes and consensus platforms
  (d) Conferences
  (e) Salesforce information
  (f) Contacts at other institutions

  a, b and c are useful if we are able to perform *reverse engineering* of market quotes in order to understand which models may have produced them. There are a number of examples in the following where we perform reverse engineering. For instance, we explicitly perform reverse engineering of counterparty quotes in 2.6.2, but we also do it to understand how the market consensus changed in Chapter 4. It is an issue so intrinsic to model risk management that it surfaces throughout the book.
- **Reality Check.** We have seen in Section 1.1.4 that realism in the end is important for all model approaches, and even the fair value principle can deviate from consistency with observable prices when they are plainly unrealistic. We must understand which are the crucial risks that affect a payoff, and then use historical analysis, knowledge of the underlying market or plain common sense to understand which models give a reasonable description of these crucial risks (we can neglect those elements of unrealism that do not affect pricing in a crucial way). The issue is touched upon again when speaking of copulas applied to the risk of concentrated losses, when validating mapping against historical scenarios, when discussing the so-called P&L analysis, and also in relation to various other topics.

★ **Model Comparison.** The last two steps can be performed even on a single model, but they make more sense if applied to a family of models. In fact, it is unlikely that the first model analyzed will appear entirely satisfactory from both points of view, thus the task is usually to compare different models in order to understand which one is 'more realistic' or 'more consistent with market consensus'. Derman says explicitly that the use of a battery of models, is crucial, while Rebonato (2003) says 'In order to carry out this task the risk manager will need a variety of properly calibrated valuation models'. In fact, a battery of models is needed to compare the model prices with the market quotes and to understand, via reverse engineering, which model is more consistent with the market quotes. Regulators suggest the use of '*a diversity of approaches*' and '*a range of mechanisms to cross-check valuations*'.

- **Accept/Reject – Improvements – Provisions.** At this point we have to make a first choice about the model to be used for our payoff. We can reject a model, if any serious problems emerged at any of the previous steps, and we can suggest another route, possibly towards one of the models considered at the Model Comparison step. We can suggest improvements in the direction of increasing realism or making the model more consistent with the market standard consensus. We can also accept the model but establish some provisions to control model risk: **Model Reserves**, usually based on some model that emerged in the Model Comparison step, or a **Model Limit** based on exposure if elements emerged in the Reality Check or Market Intelligence step that require caution. See Section 2.7 for more information about provisions.
- **Periodic Revisions.** Specify dates at which the validation must be revised. At this stage we will set periodic revisions, which are scheduled regularly, for example yearly. After one year both the experience in the use of the model and the knowledge of the market where it is applied will have increased, allowing for real improvements. Also market evidence, or the bank's exposure, may have changed.

3. **Stress Testing**

The topic of stress testing, crucial for regulators as we saw in 1.4, is covered partially in Chapter 2, where we see how the use of alternative models can be exploited as stress testing and at length in Chapter 3, where we show different aspects of stress testing and finally in Chapter 6 which covers the testing of computational methods.

- **Stressability.** Verify that it is possible, and relatively easy, within the model, to represent alternative financial scenarios, including extreme scenarios. Lack of this feature should set alarm bells ringing. It means that the model is of no use for understanding the risks of the payoff under stressed conditions, and that we have difficulties in understanding how the model will behave in future market events.
- **Testing computational methods.** Here the analysis done above to validate the non-exact methods is extended to stressed configurations. This point is very important because the precision of non-exact methods such as approximations usually relies on features of the market that are not necessarily permanent, or on specific features of a given payoff such as a short maturity. In part, the same applies to Monte Carlo simulation. The goal is to find out which are the potential conditions that can reduce the precision of our computational methods. There are two types of stress we want to test for:
  A. **Stress payoff features:** maturity, start date (try it forward), strike ... Stress the features of the counterparty, of the issuer or the reference entity if applicable; stress the number of components if we are speaking of a portfolio derivative.
  B. **Stress market conditions:** design market conditions that you can translate into stressed values for the main parameters: volatilities, correlations, smile-related parameters. Try to understand what happens if you explicitly assume one parameter to be stochastic or, more simply, uncertain (see Chapter 11). Notice one important thing: it is usually better to start from market scenarios and derive parameters from them. This is not always easy. For example, changes in the ATM swaption matrix may correspond for the Libor market model of Chapters 6 and 9 to either correlation moves or volatility moves. In these cases it is more revealing to stress the parameters directly.

- **Testing model assumptions** This step involves stress testing to see if the model, which we have judged reasonable at the previous steps, remains such for stressed conditions. The focus is to check that the model does not start giving answers that contradict logic or market experience, and continues to take into account the main risks affecting the payoff. If the model was today judged to be in line with market consensus but problems arise in this part of stress tests, we have to take into account that market consensus is likely to abandon the model under those conditions which make the model appear unreasonable. Here we have the usual two types of stress to perform, but from a different perspective.
  - A. **Stress payoff features**
  - B. **Stress market conditions**
- ■ **Improvements-Provisions** Usually, a model is not rejected as a consequence of a stress test. When a problem emerges under stressed conditions, the most typical intervention is to improve the model to deal with the problematic condition or to introduce provisions to mitigate this risk. Of particular importance is the following provision:
- ■ **Triggered Revisions** Now we have enough information to specify a different sort of revision, not scheduled regularly but contingent on the occurrence of specific events. When a model has an undesirable behaviour under stressed conditions, we must set thresholds or triggers on calibrated parameters or on market values so that we recognize if we are approaching the critical condition. When this happens a revision of the validation is in order. Many banks include unexpected difficulties in calibration among the events that may trigger a revision of model validation. The revision will probably involve the whole validation process if we have detected a problem in relation to model assumptions; if instead the problem has emerged when stressing computational methods, only the validation of the computational method must be revised.
- ■ **Payoff Limitations** When instead a model exhibits undesirable behaviour for variations of the payoff, or for particular issuers/reference entities, or for a particular range of underlying products, this must be reported so that validation is not extended to these cases, or provisions are set.

★ **Model Evolution**

The Reality Check or the Stress Test may already have revealed that a model, perhaps consistent with today's market consensus, has some problems that future market conditions could render intolerable, triggering a consensus shift. This final point is to make sure that when a model has been chosen and validated we make an explicit analysis of the conditions that could make it inadequate in the future, for us and for the market in general. I consider this step important and devote Chapter 4 to recent examples of changes in market consensus. For example, risk is very high, although it may be hidden under the surface, when there is a market consensus but we have judged this consensus to be based on unrealistic assumptions.

- ■ **Provisions** Such a situation can be managed with provisions like limits to exposure or reserves based on a model more robust than the market approach. One should also take into account the considerations of Remark 3 about the limited sophistication of the models that usually emerge immediately after a crisis, and the possibility that we are in a model bubble as described in Section 1.2.1.
- ■ **Triggered Revisions** Once the conditions that could lead to a shift in the market consensus have been exposed, a quantitative measure of the distance from these conditions must be monitored, and when the distance is reduced, a revision of validation is advisable.

1.5.2 Special Points in Model Risk Management

The following points should be given particular attention in model risk management, within the above scheme or separately, because they cover cases where model risk is particularly high, and appears in peculiar ways. Each of these cases is dealt with in a dedicated chapter in the second part of the book.

- **Hedging**
  Valuation models are not used only for valuation at a point in time, but also for dynamic hedging. Hedging is related to model risk management in a double way. First, the assessment of the hedging behaviour of a model, the so-called P&L analysis, can give relevant indications about the behaviour of the model, supplementing the above consideration about the quality of calibration or the realism of the model. However, in order to be useful in model validation, the P&L analysis must be performed under conditions which are often not those under which a trader will really operate, in particular in real hedging a trader will not use the pricing model consistently, but will introduce various adjustments.
  This leads to the other aspect that links hedging to model risk management: the trading strategy implemented using a validated valuation model is not automatically validated, since the model-implied hedging strategy is usually different from the one really implemented, so the latter may deserve a separate validation. Both aspects are covered in Chapter 5.
- **Extrapolation**
  Extrapolations and interpolations are often used in modelling. There are even those who say, as we pointed out in Chapter 7, that modelling in financial markets is only about interpolating and extrapolating a few points that can now be observed in the market. However, in some cases the use of interpolations and in particular of extrapolations, is very explicit. Extrapolation is often used to supplement calibration. When we are using a model, we calibrate it to a narrow area of liquid quotes, and then we use it to create the information corresponding to an artificial market outside this area. This artificial market carries more model risk than the liquid one. At other times, when we are using a quotation system or some parameterization, we even have to fix parameters that we cannot calibrate, and we often do this via extrapolation. Here the risk is even higher. The use of extrapolation can be avoided or minimized, as we show in the examples in Chapter 7.
- **Correlation**
  The modelling of correlation, and more generally the modelling of interdependence among financial variables, should not in principle differ from the modelling of individual financial variables. Instead, it involves more model risk, since correlation is technically more difficult to model than other parameters. Just consider the fact that it is a matrix rather than a single number like volatility. Moreover, correlations are usually observable only historically since there are much fewer quotes giving implied correlations than there are quotes giving implied volatilities. Add to this that correlations tend to be very unstable parameters, so that historical estimation tells us very little about the likely future. This is the reason to single correlation modelling out. We cover it in Chapter 8, treating both the technical difficulties in modelling and risk of making wrong assumptions about interdependency.
- **Arbitrage**
  Arbitrage here is the attempt to secure a profit emerging from the inconsistencies that a model can detect in a market. This is very different from the standard use of models to price financial products. In pricing we start by implicitly assuming that all parts of the market are consistent in the way dictated by our models. Then we calibrate to observable information

and we find a consistent price for a less liquid derivative. The alternative way to use models typical of statistical arbitrage or model arbitrage carries a different model risk, and requires us to manage it differently. The topic is developed, based on two examples, in Chapter 11.

1.5.3 The Importance of Understanding Models

I hope the practical steps we have looked at will help you in the process of model development, model validation, and then in the use of models in practice. But I stressed in the Preface that this book is not about strict rules and bureaucratic checklists, therefore there is an important disclaimer that goes here. It is not the fact of fulfilling the above points, or any other list of points, that can make us effective model developers, validators or users. Checklists are mainly useful for giving some structure to the analysis of a model, and give us hints to look at a model and its application from different perspectives. This is useful since it helps build a deep understanding of how a model works and how it can operate in applications, which is in the end the crucial element allowing good management of model risk. In the previous analysis and in the examples that follow, the crucial part of any achievement in detecting and managing model risk is an understanding of the model behaviour in financial reality, from how the model is built to how it is applied.

The recent credit crunch crisis has further revealed the importance of understanding the models we are using. As for the Gaussian copula, we have seen errors in the way data were used to feed the model, and errors in the way the model was applied, which suggests little understanding of how the model was starting from formal hypothesis to generate numbers, prices and ratings. A deeper stress analysis would have probably helped. The formal correctness of the model, fed with data coming from historical estimations, seemed reassuring to many players. In fact, mathematics and numerics played the negative role of hiding what the model was really doing, namely extrapolating to the future the reality of the previous decade, in a simplified way that minimized the likelihood of a crisis.

In Section 3.3 we will see that reasoning about the nature of correlations in a Gaussian copula suggests a parameterization that introduces the possibility of a systemic crisis, without changing the model but just through an alternative design of correlations. This would have led to a still simplified but more sensible market practice that would have increased the understanding of model implications. In the same chapter we see two more analysis. The first one reveals that the Gaussian copula model chosen for CDOs was badly specified for capturing one of the risks that instead was most relevant at the burst of the crisis, the risk of loss concentration in short time. The second analysis shows that the methods that were used to give parameters to the Gaussian copula for pricing bespoke CDOs, as an alternative to historical analysis, were also biased towards an underestimation of risk for many CDOs. The problem was a poor understanding of the implications of the mathematical model chosen.

Derman (1996) says that *'Having a valuation model doesn't absolve the model user from thinking about the value of a security. Instead, it makes the security value a dependent variable, and requires the user to think about and estimate the values of other independent variables that are easier to grasp and quantify'*. This is the best job a model can do: to improve the understanding of the value of a security, making it easier to reason about it. If the model itself is poorly understood it cannot play this crucial role.

In all parts of this book, understanding the models we use is the primary task. In the next chapter, for example, we will see that only a deep comprehension of the model allows us to understand if it has unrealistic features, and it is also the only way to say, through reverse engineering, if a market quote can come from this model.

My view is that the most dangerous part of model risk is not that the model 'is wrong', but that *the model is not understood*. In Section 1.4 we reported the popular quote 'all models are wrong but some are useful'. Only if we have understood a model deeply will we be able to tell its unavoidable weaknesses from its useful part, and exploit the latter in the best possible way. *Model misunderstanding is the core of model risk*, and it is also that part of model risk that we can really commit to avoid. For the rest, we know that there can be parameters and assumptions in our model that will turn out wrong. If we understand the model properly, however, this will be recognized sooner and our reaction will be more effective.

2

Model Validation and Model Comparison: Case Studies

2.1 THE PRACTICAL STEPS OF MODEL COMPARISON

In this chapter we examine the practical application of the core part of Model Validation, with a specific focus on how we can use different models to study the model risk that affects a payoff. This analysis also works as a stress test on the value of the payoff and allows us to understand better the different assumptions that different models make about it. The analysis will give useful elements to make a choice on the model we want to use and then to quantify the residual risk, and to set a knowledgeable reserve or a model limit line as described in 2.7.3.

In the main example we consider a simple credit-linked note where the only complexity is the assessment of a gap risk. We also limit ourselves to two modelling approaches which are both popular and widely used in the market. We will see that even in such a simple context there is model uncertainty with heavy consequences in terms of pricing and risk management. Finally, we will consider two more examples, one on an equity application with local and stochastic volatility models and one on interest rate derivatives with short rate vs multifactor BGM models. These are actually three of the most debated model alternatives in the literature for the three main asset classes, as recalled in Figure 2.1.

In the first example on credit risk we describe the two most popular credit modelling frameworks, structural and reduced-form, and then we explain the payoff. The application of alternative models can be useful to quantify model risk affecting a payoff, since if two *equally sound* but *different* models give two prices for the same product that differ by, say, one million, we can consider this figure as a first minimal quantification of our model risk. The first tricky aspect of this approach is that we have to understand if the two models are really 'equally sound'.

Such a conclusion requires at least two baseline assessments:

1. Reasonableness: the models must not be plainly unrealistic on elements of market behaviour which are crucial to the value of the derivative under analysis. We know that there exist no perfectly realistic assumptions, all models involve simplifications, thus we need to verify that the simplifications in our models are not excessive on *relevant* factors. This requires first an understanding of the macroscopic risk factors that are relevant to the payoff, and then verification that the models make acceptable assumptions on them. As we will see in the practical examples, it may be difficult to say when an assumption is realistic, but it is not so difficult to say when it is plainly unrealistic. Therefore this step is not too complicated.
2. Calibration: once we have understood at 1) what the macroscopic risk factors are that affect the payoff, we can also judge what the main liquid markets are that surely contain *relevant* information for pricing the payoff. The models we compare must have a similar capability to calibrate these reference markets, otherwise comparing them is meaningless: in general a model that is able to calibrate much better will be preferred. Usually, however, this step does not eliminate our valuation uncertainty, since there are different models that calibrate well the main reference market and yet give different prices to more complex derivatives.

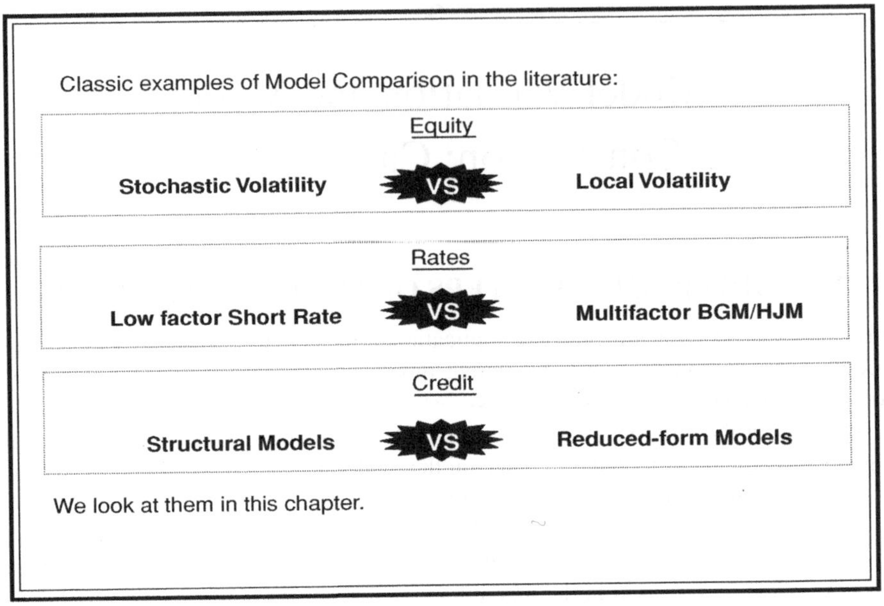

Figure 2.1 The three examples we look at in this chapter

Realism of the model assumptions and consistency with market practice are the two most crucial aspects in all the different views about model risk that we have considered so far (Value approach, Price approach, accounting, regulators). These points 1) and 2) make the first, basic assessment that neither of these two aspects is radically neglected.

Should one of the modelling approaches fail this initial assessment, this does not necessarily mean that we have to discard it straightaway. First, we have to try to *improve* it, searching the literature, and using our experience and quantitative intuition, to see if the modelling approach can be upgraded to a similar version that passes this preliminary test. Only if this is impossible should the model approach be discarded. We will see in the next chapter that both structural and intensity models as they are popularly known in the market fail 1) or 2) with reference to a credit-linked note, but they both can be upgraded with little effort to pass 1) and 2).

Now we can, at a first approximation, consider the two models 'equally sound'. The next tricky point is to understand if they really are 'different'. As we did with the concept of 'equally sound', the concept of 'different' must also be assessed not in general terms but with respect to the payoff at hand. We have to understand which ones are the *crucial risks* that make this payoff different from the reference markets that both models can calibrate well. This is different from the previous analysis, which was aimed at understanding the *relevant risks* that affect the payoff to decide the reference calibration set. This is of no help now. The fact that both models calibrate the reference markets well means that, after calibration, they give the same price to the reference securities. Now we want to see if they give *different prices* to our more complex derivative. If this is the case, the different models really do treat the crucial risks of the complex derivative differently. If we are able to understand why this happens, we will be able to detect the core of our model risk.

In the example below we will discover that the two popular models for credit risk represent the two opposite extremes in terms of assumptions about the crucial risk of the payoff under consideration. One model assumes a market behaviour that minimizes this risk, the other model assumes a behaviour that maximizes it.

The difference between these values will be our first assessment of model uncertainty, but not the end of our efforts. We will have to tackle again the two main principles of model validation:

A. Reality check: analyzing the historical evidence and the financial reality underlying the crucial risk to decide which one of the two approaches has more likelihood of turning out realistic in the future. If we think of the derivative as something that we want to keep until maturity, and for which a liquid market is unlikely to emerge before maturity, this will be the fundamental step, but in any case we will also have to perform step B.

B. Market Intelligence: analyzing our information on the models used by market players and performing reverse engineering of the prices we can observe, in order to decide which of the two approaches is closer to the opinion of the majority of other players. For a classic trading-book derivative this will be the most important step, but we have seen clearly that we can never neglect completely the issue of realism considered in A.

It is possible that this analysis will lead us to select a preferred modelling approach. However, we can also decide that there is not enough historical evidence, and that there does not seem to be sufficient market consensus to make an indisputable choice. This is what we show happening in the example below, in spite of the simplicity of the payoff and the models considered: neither A nor B allows us to choose one of two approaches, and the valuation unavoidably depends on judgement.

In this case we will perform one final fundamental step: developing a family of models that are intermediate among the two different approaches we have analyzed, and that represent two limit cases for the risk in the product. This way we will have the possibility to choose an intermediate model that best fits our goals, and to have a range of models around it to be used for the management of model uncertainty.

2.2 FIRST EXAMPLE: THE MODELS

The first approach to modelling credit risk are **structural models**, one that dates back to some parts of the Black and Scholes (1973) paper, and was then made popular by Merton (1974). In the structural modelling approach, one tries to give a synthetic but explicit economic representation of the default event and of the causes leading to default. Since the aim is an economic description of default, the fundamental modelling quantities are those we can read from the balance sheets of a company: the value of the company's assets and the level of its liabilities. The fundamental intuition is that when the value of the assets is not sufficient for facing the servicing of the company's liabilities, a company enters a default, either forced by a legal action of the bondholders or by the impossibility of fulfilling its obligations. Given this assumption, and a model for asset value and liabilities, one can both describe the default event and derive the dynamics of default probabilities while the company is still alive. The structural approach has been of central importance in fundamental assessment of the default risk. When there is no liquid market for corporate bonds of a given issuer, or a market for default protection, this approach based on balance-sheet companies is often seen as a natural choice.

On the other hand, structural models are considered intrinsically not very flexible and tractable for credit spread modelling or derivatives pricing. In fact, the requirement to describe explicitly the events leading to default constrains the model features, so that standard structural models have quite a rigid structure. But there is more. The realism of the default representation typical of structural models has also been questioned. This is based on observing that in standard structural models the default event is generated by the behaviour of equity and liabilities, treated as observable modelling variables, so that default is somewhat predictable. On the other hand, in reality, market operators can usually understand if a company has a higher or lower probability of default, but, in particular in the most dangerous default cases, the time of default comes as a surprise. The observable information on the financial situation of a company, typically coming from balance sheets and reports, can be unreliable and give a misleading representation of the true value of the assets and level of liabilities, such that market operators cannot anticipate default. Typical examples are the defaults of Enron in 2001 and Parmalat in 2003.

There are some solutions for overcoming these flaws in standard structural models, while maintaining a structural representation of default. However, the radical solution to the weakness of structural models is to stop demanding that they describe the economic causes determining default. Default can be alternatively modelled as a sudden, exogenous event. In this alternative approach we can model the default probability so as to match market implied information, such as the information contained in CDS quotations, but the moment of default is a non-predictable discontinuity. In probability terms, this is best represented using jump processes. The simplest jump process used in financial modelling is the Poisson process, a model for rare events where the fundamental parameter, representing the instantaneous probability of having one event, is called intensity. When default is modelled as the first jump of a Poisson process we have **intensity or reduced-form models**, where the economic determinants of default are not explicitly considered but implicit in modelling default intensity. For this reason, this modelling approach is also known as Reduced-form default modelling. In this approach one models default probability (the intensity) directly, without bothering about describing default. For the mathematical representation of intensity one can choose a functional form flexible enough easily to accommodate market prices, easing calibration. When we are interested in the volatility of credit spreads, modelling intensity with a deterministic function of time is not acceptable, one needs a stochastic process for the intensity. This reduces the model tractability. However, the setting is mathematically similar to long-established short interest rate modelling, so that results can be borrowed from interest rate modelling.

Credit models have the fundamental application of representing default and survival probabilities. Before looking in detail at the different representations given by the two most common families of models, we describe briefly the product which is their most typical application, at least for calibration: the CDS (credit default swaps).

2.2.1 The Credit Default Swap

Two parties, called the Protection Buyer (PB) and the Protection Seller (PS), agree that if a third company, called the Reference Entity (RE), defaults at time τ, $T_a < \tau < T_b$, then PS pays to PB the Loss Given Default $LGD = 1 - R$, where R is the recovery in case of default. In exchange PB pays at regular times T_i, usually every three months, a spread S, interrupting payments in case of default of RE. The discounted payoff to PB, with unit notional, is at $t \leq T_a$

$$\mathbf{1}_{\{T_a<\tau\leq T_b\}}P(t,\tau)LGD - \sum_{i=a+1}^{b} P(t,T_i)\alpha_i S\mathbf{1}_{\{\tau>T_i\}} - P(t,\tau)(\tau - T_{\beta(\tau)-1})S\mathbf{1}_{\{T_a<\tau<T_b\}}$$

where $T_{\beta(\tau)}$ is the first of the T_i's following τ. Modifications to this basic structure are then possible, for example the protection buyer can pay an upfront fee.

For presentation purposes, in the following we simplify the payoff as

$$LGD \sum_{i=a+1}^{b} P(t, T_i)\mathbf{1}_{\{T_{i-1}<\tau\le T_i\}} - \sum_{i=a+1}^{b} P(t, T_i)\alpha_i \mathbf{1}_{\{\tau>T_i\}} S,$$

where we have neglected the accrual payment at default, and have discretized the default event. O'Kane and Turnbull (2003) quantify the effect of these approximations, and consider them small. We advise greater caution: during the credit crunch, some of these approximations were relevant. But for the purpose of understanding the relation between CDS spreads and credit risk, this is enough.

The CDS is priced as usual as an expectation of its discounted payoff:

$$CDS_t^{a,b} = LGD \sum_{i=a+1}^{b} \Pr_t\left(T_{i-1} < \tau \le T_i\right) P(t, T_i) - S \sum_{i=a+1}^{b} P(t, T_i)\alpha_i \Pr_t\left(\tau > T_i\right), \tag{2.1}$$

where $\Pr_t$ indicates probability based on t-information. The traditional CDS quotation is through the equilibrium spread,

$$S_{a,b}(t) = \frac{LGD \sum_{i=a+1}^{b} \Pr_t(T_{i-1} < \tau \le T_i) P(t, T_i)}{\sum_{i=a+1}^{b} P(t, T_i)\alpha_i \Pr_t(\tau > T_i)}, \tag{2.2}$$

where we can see the crucial dependence of CDS spreads from default and survival probabilities. The first requirement we will impose on our credit models will be consistency with the default probabilities bootstrapped from the CDS market.

2.2.2 Structural First-Passage Models

In the earliest structural model, known as the Merton model, the default probability arises from modelling the value of the firm, which is the only stochastic variable and follows under the risk-neutral measure a geometric Brownian motion

$$dV_t = (r - q)V_t + \sigma V_t dW_t, \tag{2.3}$$

where q is the firm payout ratio. The distribution of V_T is lognormal. The debt of the firm is represented as a zero-coupon debt with maturity T and notional L. In this model T is a sort of expiry date for the company: at T the company has to pay back the entire notional debt L. Default can happen only at T, if the company has insufficient resources to pay the outstanding L, namely in case

$$V_T < L.$$

The default time τ of the company is

$$\tau = \begin{cases} T & \text{if} \quad V_T < L \\ \infty & \text{if} \quad V_T \ge L \end{cases}.$$

At maturity T the firm value is used first to pay the debt, and then what is left is given to the equity holders. If $V_T < L$ the firm defaults and all firm value must be given to repay partially the creditors. The equity holders get nothing. Otherwise $V_T - L$, if positive, is the payoff of the equity holders. This description of the firm life and death also provides an easy valuation for the equity of the company. In fact, the payoff of equity holders is

$$S_T = \max(V_T - L, 0),$$

which is the payoff of a call option with underlying V, strike L, and maturity T. Under the assumption that V is lognormal, today equity is priced via the Black and Scholes formula:

$$S_t = B\&S\left(V_t, L, rT, \sigma^2 T\right).$$

The Merton model was successful because introduction of the Black and Scholes formula provided the mathematics for dealing with this model through closed-form formulas. Default probability can also be easily computed here, as the probability that a lognormal variable is below L, available through the tables for Gaussian random variables.

The most unrealistic hypothesis of this model is that default can happen only at a single time. The probability of default before t is zero for all $t < T$. Credit spreads are meaningful only for the single maturity T, for lower maturities credit spreads would be zero and for higher maturities they would be the same as for T. In reality default can happen at any time. The debt of a company has many maturities and payments, and missing any of them can cause a default. Additionally, when a company enters a crisis either the company's management can decide to file for Chapter 11, or the creditors can force the company to default, at any unpredictable time. How to model such a situation?

The solution found by Black and Cox (1976) is to introduce a barrier which represents a level such that if the firm value falls below that barrier, there is default. Default can happen at any time. We still have as fundamental variable the firm value, still a geometric Brownian motion with constant parameters as at (2.3), and now also a default barrier H, such that

$$\tau = \inf\{t | V_t \leq H\}.$$

The difference between Merton's model and this First Passage model is summarized in Figure 2.2.

Assuming a fixed barrier H the situation is similar to a 'down and out' barrier option. The mathematics for pricing barrier options, using the so-called reflection principle, provides formulas for the probability of hitting/not hitting a barrier before a certain time, as long as the barrier is flat and the underlying is a geometric Brownian motion with flat parameters. Such formulas can be used here to compute default/survival probability, and yield

$$\Pr(\tau > T) = \Phi\left(\frac{\ln\frac{V_0}{H} + (r - q - \frac{\sigma^2}{2})T}{\sigma\sqrt{T}}\right)$$
$$- e^{\frac{2(r-q-\frac{\sigma^2}{2})}{\sigma^2}\ln\frac{V_0}{H}}\,\Phi\left(\frac{-\ln\frac{V_0}{H} + (r - q - \frac{\sigma^2}{2})T}{\sigma\sqrt{T}}\right).$$

A closed-form formula makes the computation of survival probabilities simple, and should ease calibration of the model to market credit spreads, in particular CDS spreads. Unfortunately, we need flat parameters in order to have the closed-form formula, and with flat parameters we can calibrate credit spreads for one maturity, but we can hardly extend calibration to a term-structure of credit spreads like the one we see for liquid CDS.

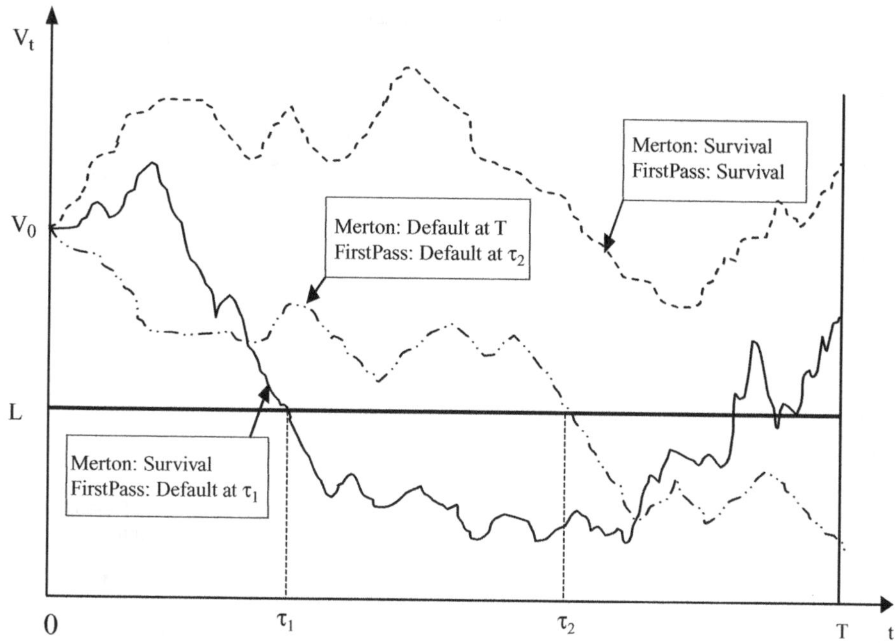

Figure 2.2 Merton and first-passage structural models

2.2.3 Reduced-Form Intensity Models

The radical solution which was proposed in the market was to stop demanding that our models describe the causes determining default, but model default as a sudden, exogenous, unpredictable event using a jump process like the one represented in Figure 2.3.

One can see that, compared to the situation where an observable continuous process must hit a barrier, here there is much more unpredictability, and more parametric freedom since we are not constrained to be consistent with a fundamental explanation.

The jump process usually considered for modelling default is the Poisson process, a model for rare events which is provided in the Appendix.

Poisson for default

The fundamental idea of intensity models is to take the time of the first jump of a Poisson process $N(t)$ as default time τ. We can give the distribution of default time since we know that $Pr(N(T) = 0) = e^{-\lambda T}$. This corresponds to the survival probability up to T,

$$\Pr(\tau > T) = e^{-\lambda T},$$
$$F_\tau(T) = \Pr(\tau \leq T) = 1 - e^{-\lambda T},$$

This is the distribution of a negative exponential random variable that has density

$$f(x) = \lambda e^{-\vartheta x}, \quad E(x) = \frac{1}{\lambda}, \quad V(x) = \frac{1}{\lambda^2}.$$

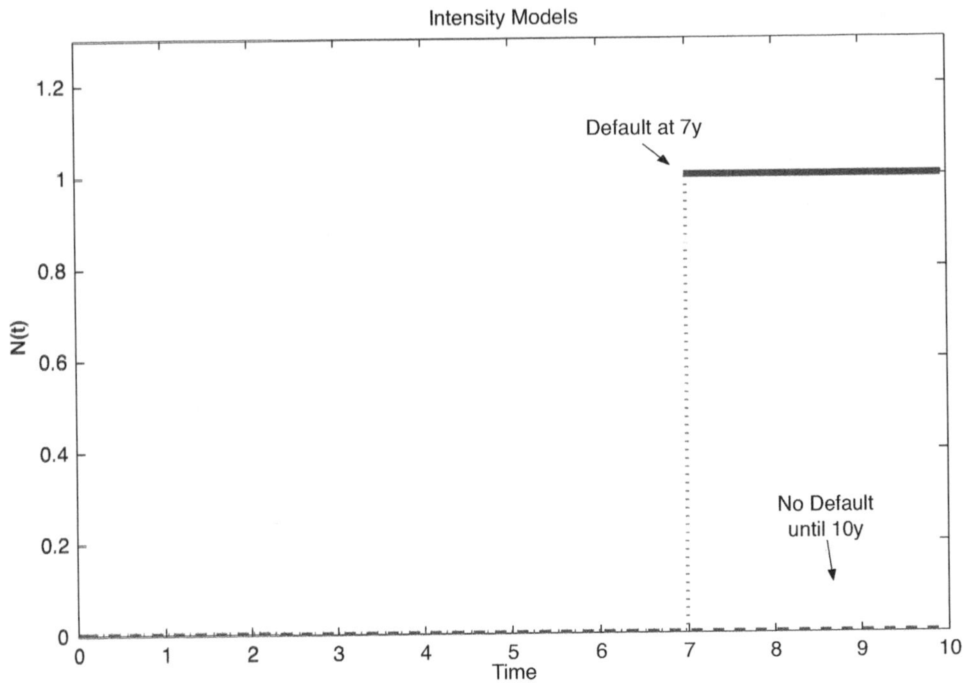

Figure 2.3 Jump process for default in intensity models

Notice that, when we move from time 0 to a general time t, the probability

$$\Pr[N(T) - N(t) = 0] = e^{-\lambda(T-t)}$$

coincides with the probability of survival from t to T but only provided that we did not default before, so we have

$$\Pr(\tau > T | \tau > t) = e^{-\lambda(T-t)}.$$

There are some very useful results for intensity models. First of all, we can represent default in terms of more elementary random variables. In the Appendix we recall that if a variable X has distribution $F_X(x)$ then $F_X^{-1}(U)$ has the same distribution as X when U is *Uniform* [0, 1]. If u is a draw from a uniform, $x = F_X^{-1}(u)$ is a draw from the distribution of the random variable X. This is what all random number generators, used for example for Monte Carlo simulation, actually do: they start from uniformly distributed draws and then transform them to find all possible distributions. For the default time τ,

$$F_\tau(T) = 1 - e^{-\lambda T} \Longrightarrow \tau = F_\tau^{-1}(U) = -\frac{1}{\lambda}\ln(1 - U). \tag{2.4}$$

Notice too that, if we set $\tau\lambda = \varepsilon$, then ε is a unit exponential random variable (which means it has parameter 1), since $F_\varepsilon(z) = F_\tau\left(\frac{z}{\lambda}\right) = 1 - e^{-z}$. So we can also write

$$\tau = \frac{\varepsilon}{\lambda}$$

where ε is a unit exponential random variable.

A simple relation between intensity and spreads

Now we see a result that experienced credit traders never fail to use to impress junior quants. It is a simple, approximate link between credit spreads and default intensity that works under flat intensity. Since assumption C says that jumps in disjoint intervals are independent, then the probability of having default in $(t, t+dt]$ is

$$\begin{aligned}\Pr(\tau \in (t, t+dt]) &= \Pr(1 \text{ jump in } (t, t+dt]) \times \Pr(\text{no jump in } [0, t]) \\ &= \lambda dt \times \Pr(\tau > t) = \lambda dt \times e^{-\lambda t}.\end{aligned}$$

Now consider a CDS where the premium spread S is paid continuously. Every instant t in the life of the contract, the protection buyer pays $S\ dt\ \mathbf{1}_{\{\tau>t\}}$ so, with deterministic interest rates, its discounted expected payment is

$$S\ dt\ \Pr(\tau > t)\ P(0, t).$$

At the same time the protection seller pays $LGD\,\mathbf{1}_{\{\tau\in(t-dt,t]\}}$ so its discounted expected payment is

$$LGD\ \Pr(\tau \in (t-dt, t])\ P(0,t) = LGD\ \lambda dt\ \Pr(\tau > t)\ P(0,t)$$

The equilibrium spread S^* can be chosen to equal the value of the two instantaneous payments at any time:

$$\begin{aligned}S^*\ dt\ \Pr(\tau > t)\ P(0,t) &= LGD\ \lambda dt\ \Pr(\tau > t)\ P(0,t), \\ S^* &= LGD\ \lambda, \\ \lambda &= \frac{S^*}{LGD}\end{aligned}$$

As we said, this trick only works for flat intensity, and leads to flat credit spreads. In reality, when quoted, credit spreads do vary with maturity. To have a term structure of spreads we need to introduce Poisson processes where the intensity, here a fixed quantity λ, can instead be time-varying. These kinds of Poisson process are called time-inhomogeneous Poisson processes, and they are also given in the Appendix.

Time-dependent intensity

In the case of time-dependent intensity, the survival probability, equal to the probability of no Poisson jumps, is

$$\Pr(\tau > T) = \Pr[N(T) = 0] = e^{-\int_0^T \lambda(s)ds},$$

and

$$\Pr(\tau \le T) = F_\tau(T) = 1 - e^{-\int_0^T \lambda(s)ds}.$$

Set now $\int_0^\tau \lambda(s)ds = \Lambda(\tau) = \varepsilon$. What is the distribution of ε? Since $\varepsilon = \Lambda(\tau)$ is increasing

$$\begin{aligned}F_\varepsilon(Z) &= F_\tau\left(\Lambda^{-1}(Z)\right) = 1 - e^{-\int_0^{\Lambda^{-1}(Z)} \lambda(s)ds} \\ &= 1 - e^{-\Lambda(\Lambda^{-1}(Z))} = 1 - e^{-Z}.\end{aligned}$$

The variable ε has unit exponential distribution, and we can write

$$\tau = \Lambda^{-1}(\varepsilon) \tag{2.5}$$

So if we can have a realization of an exponential random variable we can also have a realization of τ. In practice, τ is computed as

$$\tau = \inf\left\{t : \int_0^t \lambda(s)ds \geq \varepsilon\right\}. \tag{2.6}$$

This model implies that spreads are deterministic functions of time only, therefore already known today for all the future. To have a more realistic model that allows for stochastic credit spreads we must have a stochastic intensity model. Such models are Cox processes.

λ	$\longrightarrow$	$\lambda(t)$	$\longrightarrow$	$\lambda(t,\omega)$
Standard Poisson process	$\longrightarrow$	Inhomogeneous Poisson process	$\longrightarrow$	Cox process.

In order to understand these processes we need to look at a technicality that can have important practical consequences.

2.2.4 Structural vs Intensity: Information

The distinction between the two modelling approaches also relates to the assumptions we make in terms of information. In credit modelling it can be useful to split the total flow of information available in the market (the filtration $\mathcal{F}_t$ for $t \geq 0$) into two subfiltrations, two different flows of information: one giving information about default $\left(\left(\mathcal{F}_t^\tau\right)_{t\geq 0}\right)$, and another subfiltration of $(\mathcal{F}_t)_{t\geq 0}$ called $(\mathcal{H}_t)_{t\geq 0}$ and representing default-free market information:

$$\mathcal{F}_t = \mathcal{H}_t \vee \mathcal{F}_t^\tau$$

- $\mathcal{F}_t$ = all available information up to t
- $\mathcal{F}_t^\tau = \sigma(\{\tau < u\}, u \leq t)$ = information up to t on the default event: if it has already happened or not and, in the former case, the exact time τ of default
- $\mathcal{H}_t$ = information up to t on economic quantities which affect default probability, but, if possible, no specific information on when default might occur.

We can intuitively think of the σ-algebra $\mathcal{F}_t$ as a copy of the *Financial Times* on day t, while $\mathcal{H}_t$ is a copy of the same newspaper where all news items that might have informed the reader about the default or survival of the reference entity have been cut out, and pasted onto a sheet of paper that now represents $\mathcal{F}_t^\tau$. A market operator observing the filtration $\mathcal{H}_t$ (the abridged *Financial Times*) can determine the probability of default of the reference entity, but cannot say exactly when, or even if, default has happened.

Is such a separation of information actually possible, maintaining the meaning of the subfiltrations as described above? It depends on the chosen modelling approach.

In standard **structural models** the distinction is meaningless. We would have: $\mathcal{H}_t = \mathcal{F}_t$ since in a structural setting if a market operator wants information on default probabilities, he must observe those economic quantities (firm value and level of the debt/default barrier) whose level also determines the exact default time. The distance between V_t and H_t gives the default probability; when this distance reaches zero, we have default. There is no way of abridging the *Financial Times* as desired, since there is no way of giving information influencing default probabilities without also telling the market operator if default has already happened or not.

Instead, in standard **reduced form models** the distinction is fundamental: $\mathcal{H}_t \subset \mathcal{F}_t$ since default has a part which is exogenous to economic quantities. The observable economic quantities only affect default probability, namely the intensity (a fact that will become relevant when we introduce stochastic intensity), while the exact time of default is given by a jump process which is unpredictable in the sense that it is not determined by observable market quantities. The variable ε does not belong to M_t information. Roughly, this assumption represents default unpredictability. This apparently very theoretical difference has extremely practical consequences, as we will see.

For intensity models, the above result is useful when introducing Cox processes with stochastic intensity. But before that we will look at another technical result for intensity models related to the above split of information.

Pricing with default-free information

The above representation of information helps us study one feature of intensity models. Remember that after default (when $\tau \le t$) probabilities are not defined through intensities, since when $\tau \le t$

$$\Pr(\tau > T|\mathcal{F}_t) = \mathbb{E}_t\left[\mathbf{1}_{\{\tau>T\}}\right] = 0 \neq e^{-\lambda(T-t)}.$$

So we divide the two cases

$$\mathbb{E}_t\left[\mathbf{1}_{\{\tau>T\}}\right] = \mathbf{1}_{\{\tau\le t\}} * \mathbb{E}_t\left[\mathbf{1}_{\{\tau>T\}}\right] + \mathbf{1}_{\{\tau>t\}} * \mathbb{E}_t\left[\mathbf{1}_{\{\tau>T\}}\right].$$

Now in the two different cases we can use the most convenient information:

$$\begin{aligned}\mathbb{E}_t\left[\mathbf{1}_{\{\tau>T\}}\right] &= \mathbf{1}_{\{\tau\le t\}} \times 0 + \mathbf{1}_{\{\tau>t\}}\mathbb{E}\left[\mathbf{1}_{\{\tau>T\}}|\tau > t, \mathcal{H}_t\right] = \mathbf{1}_{\{\tau>t\}}\Pr(\tau > T|\tau > t, \mathcal{H}_t)\\ &= \mathbf{1}_{\{\tau>t\}}\frac{\Pr(\tau > T, \mathcal{H}_t)}{\Pr(\tau > t, \mathcal{H}_t)}.\end{aligned}$$

Where there is deterministic intensity, the presence of $\mathcal{H}_t$ is irrelevant, and we can also write

$$\mathbb{E}_t\left[\mathbf{1}_{\{\tau>T\}}\right] = \mathbf{1}_{\{\tau>t\}}\frac{\Pr(\tau > T)}{\Pr(\tau > t)} = \mathbf{1}_{\{\tau>t\}}e^{-\lambda(T-t)}.$$

For deterministic intensity, the above analysis only serves to remind us that when we use quantities at $t > 0$ we need a survival indicator $\mathbf{1}_{\{\tau>t\}}$ in front of the usual exponential of the intensity. It will be more useful for stochastic intensity, in the form of the following generalization, by Jeanblanc and Rutkowski (2000): for a defaultable (discounted) payoff $\mathbf{Y} = \mathbf{1}_{\{\tau>t\}}\mathbf{Y}$, we have

$$\mathbb{E}_t[\mathbf{Y}] = \mathbb{E}[\mathbf{Y}|\mathcal{F}_t] = \mathbf{1}_{\{\tau>t\}}\frac{\mathbb{E}\left[\mathbf{Y}|\mathcal{H}_t\right]}{\Pr(\tau > t|\mathcal{H}_t)}.$$

From now on, you can consider Pr as indicating probability under a risk-adjusted pricing measure, unless otherwise specified.

Cox processes with stochastic intensity

The rough definition of Cox processes is:

Definition 6. *A process N_t is a Cox process with stochastic intensity $\lambda(t) = \lambda(\omega, t)$ if, conditional on knowing the path of $\lambda(t)$ from 0 to* T, *called $\lambda[0, T)$, then $(N_t)_{0 \leq t \leq T}$ is an inhomogeneous Poisson process with intensity $\lambda(t)$.*

This definition may appear trivial but it is not. First of all, it gives us a tractable way to compute survival and default probabilities. In fact, it allows us to use the results seen for Poisson processes, for example if $N(t)$ is a Cox process then

$$\Pr(N(T) - N(0) = 0|\lambda(s), 0 \leq s \leq T) = e^{-\int_t^T \lambda(s)ds}$$

At this point, unconditional probabilities can be computed recalling the law of iterated expectations

$$\begin{aligned}\Pr(N(T) - N(0) = 0) &= \mathbb{E}\left[1_{\{N(T)-N(0)=0\}}\right] = \mathbb{E}\left[\mathbb{E}\left[1_{\{N(T)-N(0)=0\}} \middle| \lambda[0, T)\right]\right] \\ &= \mathbb{E}\left[\Pr(N(T) - N(0) = 0|\lambda[0, T))\right] \\ &= \mathbb{E}\left[e^{-\int_0^T \lambda(s)ds}\right].\end{aligned} \tag{2.7}$$

In order to have a closed-form formula for survival probability we need an analytic way to compute the above expectation. Notice that if we replace $\lambda(s)$ with $r(s)$ the above expectation is the price of a bond. If we find a process for $r(t)$ which admits a closed-form formula for the bond, then the same process applied to $\lambda(t)$ will provide a closed-form formula for survival probability. An example is the Cox, Ingersoll and Ross (CIR) process that we use in the next application.

The second thing to notice about Definition 6 is that it sets some constraint on our freedom in modelling $\lambda(t)$. Think of this example: if $\lambda(t)$ was actually defined as a process that starts at 0.1, and then jumps to 0.2 after the first jump of our $N(t)$, the resulting process would have a stochastic intensity, but it would not be a Cox process and we could not use (2.7). In fact, in this example *knowing the path of* $\lambda(s)$ would also mean knowing the time of the first jump of $N(t)$, so $N(t)$ would no longer be a Poisson process. It does not fit into Definition 6. If we want a more formal way to specify what can affect the path of $\lambda(\omega, t)$ for us to have a Cox process, we can make use of the above split of information and write

Definition 7. *A process N_t is a Cox process with intensity $\lambda(t) = \lambda(\omega, t)$ if, conditional on H_T, $(N_t)_{0 \leq t \leq T}$ is a Poisson process with intensity $\lambda(t)$.*

2.3 FIRST EXAMPLE: THE PAYOFF. GAP RISK IN A LEVERAGED NOTE

The payoff we consider is a note issued by a bank to sell leveraged default protection on a reference entity. In the most basic form it is a leveraged CDS. The bank sells the note to the client for its notional value, which for simplicity we can assume to be 1, plus a fee. With a unit notional for the note, the bank will sell protection on the reference entity for a notional

$Lev > 1$ and will return to the client the revenues from this selling of protection, namely

$$Lev \times S_T(0),$$

where $S_T(0)$ is the spread of the reference entity for the maturity of the note T. At maturity the client will receive the notional back if the reference entity survives. Otherwise, if the reference entity defaults, he will receive at default the notional diminished by the leveraged default loss. If the leveraged loss is higher than the note's notional, the client receives nothing.

What should the initial fee paid by the client to the bank include? It will surely include a gap-risk fee. In fact the client is responsible only for an amount of money equal to the note's notional paid at inception. In case of a default, the maximum the client can lose is 1. But the loss in case of default may be higher, since it will be

$$Lev \times Lgd,$$

so whenever

$$Lev \times Lgd > 1, Lev > \frac{1}{Lgd}$$

there will be a gap between the loss and the amount of money provided by the client. This gap

$$Lev \times Lgd - 1$$

is covered by the bank, which therefore suffers a *gap risk*. This corresponds to an expected loss

$$\mathbb{E}\left[1_{\{\tau<T\}}P(0,\tau) \times (Lev \times CDS_T(\tau) - 1)^+\right] = \mathbb{E}\left[1_{\{\tau<T\}}P(0,\tau) \times (Lev \times Lgd - 1)^+\right] \tag{2.8}$$

where τ is the default time of the reference entity, $P(0, t)$ is the discount factor for maturity t, here assumed to be deterministic as in most credit pricing, and $CDS_T(t)$ is the market value at t of a CDS with unit notional and maturity T. In the second passage we have used the fact that the value of a CDS at default of the reference entity, $CDS_T(\tau)$, is just the loss given default Lgd.

The expected loss (2.8) will be compensated for by a gap risk fee that can increase the money paid at inception by the client, or otherwise, in running form, it will reduce the spread paid to the client that will not be $Lev \times S_T(0)$ but something less.

There are different ways of mitigating the gap risk, making the note less expensive for the client and less risky to the bank. One popular way of reducing the likelihood of a gap loss and consequently the gap risk fee paid by the client is to set a *trigger*, namely: *the note is interrupted and settled at market value before maturity not only when*

Event A there is a default event on the reference entity at $\tau < T$
but also when

Event B the equilibrium level $S_T(t)$ of the spread of the CDS of the reference entity with maturity T touches first a level *trigger* (we call the touch time t^{touch}), as shown in Figure 2.4.

Thus the early termination date is now at

$$T^{term} = \min\left(\tau, t^{touch}\right).$$

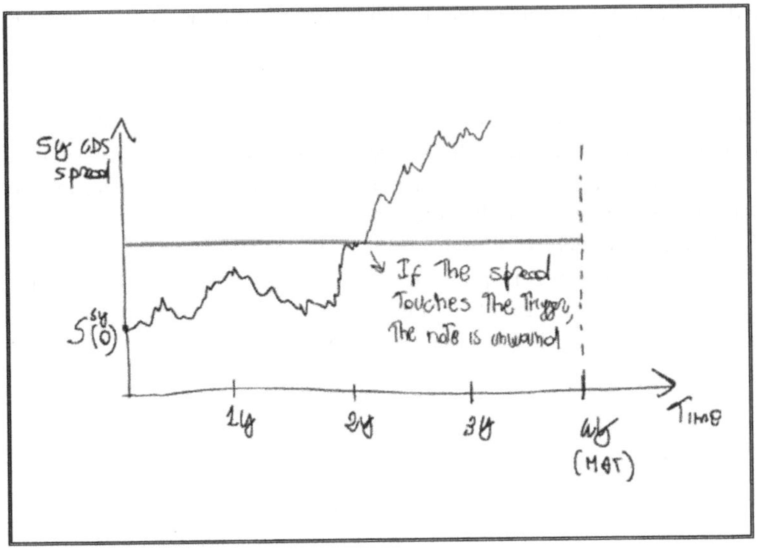

Figure 2.4 Leveraged note with a trigger

The issue now is to quantify the gap risk for this new product. The bank has a gap loss when we jointly have

$$T^{term} < T \quad \textbf{AND} \quad Loss(T^{term}) > 1.$$

Thus the expected discounted loss associated with gap risk is

$$\mathbb{E}\left[1_{\{T^{Term}<T\}} P\left(0, T^{Term}\right) \times \left(Lev \times CDS_T\left(T^{Term}\right) - 1\right)^+\right]. \tag{2.9}$$

Notice that in case $T^{term} = \tau$ (default time) we have $CDS_T(\tau) = Lgd$ and the loss in (2.9) coincides with the loss of the leveraged CDS that we see in (2.8). But there is now also the possibility that $T^{Term} = t^{touch} < \tau$. In this case the loss will surely be lower, since

$$CDS_T\left(t^{touch}\right) \leq CDS_T(\tau) = Lgd.$$

The financial rationale behind the trigger in the note, for the issuing bank, is that in the case of worsening credit conditions, the presence of a trigger should interrupt the note *before* default time, at $t^{touch} < \tau$. Even better, the bank can set the trigger at a level $trigger^*$ such that, when this trigger is touched at t^{touch*} and the note is unwound, we can expect a loss equal to 1, namely the notional of the leveraged note. In this way the loss will be entirely covered by the client and the bank has no gap loss.[1]

How can we find the level $trigger^*$? There is a relation between the value of a CDS at t and the equilibrium market spread $S_T(t)$ of the CDS. For example, using the simple approximation we have seen in Section 2.2.3, we have that for any future date $T > t$ the survival probability

[1] Clearly, a bank with a sensitivity to reputational risk will not like the fact that in this case the client loses everything, and may set the trigger at a different level. But from a mathematical point of view this is the bank's optimum, and we keep this as a reference.

computed at t is

$$\Pr(\tau > T|\tau > t) \approx \exp\left(-\frac{S_T(t)}{Lgd} \times (T-t)\right),$$

and once we have the survival probability we can apply (2.1) and find the CDS value as a function $f(\cdot)$ of the spread,

$$CDS_T(t) = f\left(S_T(t)\right).$$

The 'perfect trigger' $trigger^*$ must give a loss of 1 when it is touched, so we only have to solve in $S_T(t)$ the simple equation

$$\begin{aligned} f\left(S_T(t)\right) &= \frac{1}{Lev}, \\ trigger^* &= f^{-1}\left(\frac{1}{Lev}\right). \end{aligned} \tag{2.10}$$

Since the relation between the value of a CDS and the spread is in general increasing, for any trigger lower than $trigger^*$ the bank has no loss if, when the trigger is touched, the note is immediately interrupted. With a level $trigger^*$, the note is interrupted *as late as possible* for the bank to have no loss from the unwinding. Have we now really eliminated the gap risk for the bank? We will see that this depends crucially on the model we will use to evaluate the expected loss in (2.9). More detail on the analysis that follows can be found in Facchinetti and Morini (2009).

2.4 THE INITIAL ASSESSMENT

There are two fundamental families of credit models that banks use for simple credit derivatives like the one above. As we have seen in Section 2.2, they are structural models, the first approach to credit risk, and reduced-form models where the crucial variable is the default intensity. Which family is more suitable to price this derivative?

2.4.1 First Test: Calibration to Liquid Relevant Products

A first discrimination can be based on the capability to calibrate the relevant financial information. It seems clear that the credit linked note depends on the default probability of the reference entity. If the reference entity has a liquid CDS market, which is typical for notes like this one, the model must be able to calibrate the CDS term structure of the reference entity for all available maturities which are lower than the maturity of the note. In fact, these quotes embed liquid information on the relevant default probabilities.

This seems a point in favour of intensity models, which are preferred by the market exactly because of their greater capability to calibrate CDS term structures compared to traditional structural models. In fact, we have seen in Section 2.2.3 that intensity models are usually implemented with deterministic, time-dependent intensity that allows a good fit to CDS term structures, while, as we said in Section 2.2.2, standard structural models (with flat barrier and flat parameters) cannot calibrate precisely a term structure of default probabilities. Thus we have just ruled out from our set of eligible models the standard structural models, since they cannot calibrate a CDS term structure. We may use these models with time-dependent parameters, but we know that if we do, we lose the closed-form formulas, so the calibration, even if theoretically possible, would become a computational nightmare.

Introducing modern structural models

Ruling out standard structural models does not mean that we have to abandon the structural approach as a whole. We would prefer not to do this, since, as we saw in (2.2), structural models appear to be based on assumptions genuinely different from intensity models, and using them as well can enhance our understanding of model risk. Fortunately there are modern structural models that we can use here. They assume a dynamics for the underlying which is

$$dV(t) = V(t)(r(t) - q(t))\,dt + V(t)\sigma(t)\,dW_t,$$

with time-dependent parameters that allow a calibration to the CDS term structure, coupled with a barrier

$$H(t) = \frac{H}{V(0)}\mathbb{E}[V(t)]\exp\left(-(1+2\beta)\frac{1}{2}\int_0^t \sigma(u)^2 du\right)$$

that, as we explain in 11.2, is financially more meaningful than a flat barrier. In the models we can compute analytically the survival probability $\Pr(\tau > T)$, given by the following formula:

$$\left[\Phi\left(\frac{\log\frac{V_0}{H} + \beta\int_0^T \sigma(t)^2 dt}{\sqrt{\int_0^T \sigma(t)^2 dt}}\right) - \left(\frac{H}{V_0}\right)^{2\beta}\Phi\left(\frac{\log\frac{H}{V_0} + \beta\int_0^T \sigma(t)^2 dt}{\sqrt{\int_0^T \sigma(t)^2 dt}}\right)\right].$$

Coupling this formula with the CDS spread formula (2.2), we can price CDS analytically, so that good or even perfect calibration becomes computationally efficient (for more detail, see Section 11.2 below). What matters is that now, from the point of view of calibration capability, we can compare intensity models in their standard market formulation with these modern structural models with time-dependent parameters and barrier. In fact, both models have passed the first test, CDS calibration.

2.4.2 Second Test: a Minimum Level of Realism

Secondly, there are some basic elements of realism that one would like a model to include when applied to the above derivative. The unwinding of the note above happens when the CDS spread $S_T(t)$, *computed at the future time t*, touches a trigger. This implies that *future* CDS spreads should have a dynamics, and in particular a stochastic dynamics, for the derivative to make sense.

For structural models, both of the standard and of the modern kind, this is not a problem. Even in the simplest case with flat parameters, the value of the firm V_t evolves, under the risk-neutral probability, according to

$$dV_t = rV_t dt + \sigma V_t dW,$$

and the CDS credit spreads at a future date $s > 0$ are functions of the survival probability computed in s (conditional to survival until s):

$$\Pr(\tau > T|\tau > s) = \Phi\left(\frac{\ln\frac{V_s}{H} + \left(r - \frac{\sigma^2}{2}\right)(T - s)}{\sigma\sqrt{(T - s)}}\right) + \\ -\left(\frac{V_s}{H}\right)^{-\frac{2\left(r - \frac{1}{2}\sigma^2\right)}{\sigma^2}} \Phi\left(\frac{-\ln\frac{V_s}{H} + \left(r - \frac{\sigma^2}{2}\right)(T - s)}{\sigma\sqrt{(T - s)}}\right). \tag{2.11}$$

This probability at future time s depends on V_s which is not known at zero but will depend on the stochastic dynamics given above. Thus the entire quantity $\Pr(\tau > T|\tau > S)$ varies stochastically with V_s, and credit spreads vary accordingly.

What about intensity models? In standard intensity models the intensity $\lambda(t)$ is deterministic. The future survival probability

$$\Pr(\tau > T|\tau > s) = e^{-\int_s^T \lambda(s)ds} \tag{2.12}$$

is also deterministic, in fact it coincides with the forward survival probability computed at time 0,

$$\frac{\Pr(\tau > T)}{\Pr(\tau > s)} = e^{-\int_s^T \lambda(s)ds}. \tag{2.13}$$

The future credit spreads are deterministic too. It is possible to know at time 0 if the trigger will be touched or not, and in case it is going to be touched, we know exactly when this will happen.

This is an element of unrealism that strongly affects our valuation, since the moment when we touch the spread is crucial for assessing the gap risk. In these models only the default event, which is one of the two events that can terminate the note in advance, is stochastic and unpredictable. The other crucial event, touching the trigger, is perfectly predictable. Spreads will follow a path which is fully determined by the time-zero term structure of CDS. Unfortunately, this is not the case in reality. Just waiting one day and seeing that spreads actually do move differently from what is predicted by the model will belie this assumption. And it is not an irrelevant assumption: it is an assumption that affects dramatically the value of the payoff. Assuming deterministic spreads here is as meaningless as pricing an option with a model where there is no volatility.

Introducing modern reduced-form models

For the model to be acceptably realistic we need an intensity model with non-null spread volatility. This can be obtained simply by assuming that the default intensity is stochastic, in the framework of Cox processes. We have to choose one specific dynamics for the stochastic intensity. Many researchers have focused on dynamics already used in the literature for the instantaneous spot rate $r(t)$. In fact, the value of a bond when $r(t)$ is stochastic is

$$P(t, T) = \mathbb{E}_t\left[\exp\left(-\int_t^T r(u)du\right)\right]$$

while the survival probability with stochastic $\lambda(t)$ is

$$\Pr(\tau > T | \tau > t) = \mathbb{E}_t \left[\exp\left(- \int_t^T \lambda(u) du \right) \right].$$

The shape of the two quantities is the same, so if we choose a dynamics for $\lambda(t)$ which has already been used for $r(t)$ we may find a ready-made formula in the interest rate literature.

One interesting dynamics with this property is the CIR (Cox, Ingersoll, Ross) dynamics for the intensity

$$d\lambda(t) = k[\theta - \lambda(t)]dt + \sigma \sqrt{\lambda(t)} dW(t),$$

where one can also guarantee positivity of the intensity by imposing the Feller conditions $\sigma^2 < 2k\theta$. Positivity of the intensity is an important element of realism here, since the intensity is akin to an instantaneous default probability.[2] The formula for survival probability is given by

$$\begin{aligned} \Pr(\tau > T | \tau > s) &= \mathbb{E}_t \left[\exp\left(- \int_t^T \lambda(u) du \right) \right] = A(t, T) e^{-B(t,T)\lambda(t)}, \\ A(t, T) &= \left[\frac{2h \exp[(k + h)(T - t)/2]}{2h + (k + h)[\exp((T - t)h) - 1]} \right]^{2k\theta/\sigma^2} \\ B(t, T) &= \frac{2[\exp((T - t)h) - 1]}{2h + (k + h)[\exp((T - t)h) - 1]} \qquad h = \sqrt{k^2 + 2\sigma^2}. \end{aligned} \tag{2.14}$$

The availability of an analytic formula makes calibration to CDS very easy. Since the model has four parameters, $\lambda(0), \theta, k, \sigma$ and a CDS term structure has around five liquid pillars, one can usually calibrate a standard CDS term structure with no indetermination (that arises when there are far fewer market quotes than parameters) and with no need to introduce time-dependent parameters (which may be required when there are far fewer parameters than market quotes). We see in Figure 2.5 the results of the calibration to a Euro market CDS term structure.

The fit is not perfect but it is acceptable for pricing our derivative. Thus this first reality-check suggests that one should get rid of deterministic intensity models and replace them with stochastic intensity models that are based on similar assumptions but allow for stochastic spread. After initial assessment of calibration requirements and basic realism we are left with modern structural models and modern intensity models.

Are we sure this is sufficient? Are there other important elements in the spread behaviour that we have to assess? Is the calibration process concluded with CDS? Are these two families of models now perfectly equivalent in assessing our gap risk, or have we chosen two families of models that really give different answers on this issue?

In order to answer these questions we need to perform a deeper analysis of the payoff.

[2] A brief digression on this choice may be useful here. Models that guarantee non-negative processes are favoured in credit, rates and equity. In my opinion, in credit and equity this must be strictly enforced. Intensities cannot be negative since negative probabilities make no sense for us. We have a mathematical reason to be suspicious of any model that does not satisfy this requirement. Equity prices cannot be negative as long as shares have the 'limited liability' feature: holding a share can never entail a liability beyond the loss of the share value. We have legal reason to think a model allowing for negative equity prices to be fundamentally flawed. In rates, the story is different. Negative rates have been observed, for example in Japan in the 90s. Lenders such as the central bank accepted negative rates to boost depressed investment. And even a household can accept a negative rate on a current account, as long as the money he lost keeping savings in the bank is lower than the costs and the risks of keeping cash at home. The fundamental floor for the level of interest rates is slightly below zero.

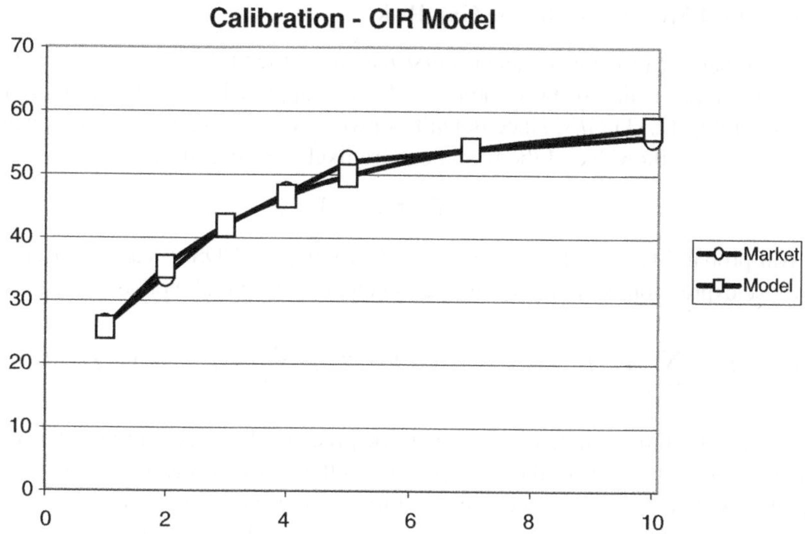

Figure 2.5 CDS calibration – CIR intensity model

2.5 THE CORE RISK IN THE PRODUCT

The gap risk can become a material gap loss when the reference entity defaults. This can be avoided if, before the default, the trigger is touched, even if it is touched just a few days before default. Thus the value of the gap risk crucially depends *on the behaviour of spreads in the time immediately preceding default*: will default be preceded by a significant rally in spread, due to the market anticipating default and retreating from selling protection on the reference entity, or will we have a more abrupt leap to default, with no trigger touch, as may happen when the market does not anticipate the default event and is caught by surprise?

In the first case, the note will be terminated before default at t^{touch*} with an unwinding cost ≈ 1 that should be covered by the note's notional. The only possible loss for the issuer arises when the growth of the spread is so fast that when the actual unwinding takes place at $t > t^{touch*}$ the spread $S_T(t)$ is much higher than $trigger^*$. In such a case the gap risk depends on how often the spread movement is monitored and how easily and fast the bank can unwind the CDS. This is an issue that we will introduce in our pricing by regulating the frequency of the trigger checks and introducing a possible delay between trigger touch and unwinding. What matters to us is that, when the model predicts that default will be preceded by a spread rally, the trigger condition protects the bank from gap risk and, if the unwinding is perfectly timely, we can even eliminate it.

In the second case, which is when default is not preceded by a spread rally, the trigger cannot guarantee protection from losses. The trigger may be touched even if default is not upcoming and, more importantly, default can happen before any trigger touch. In this case the bank will surely suffer a loss, equal to

$$Lev \times CDS_T(\tau) - 1 = Lev \times Lgd - 1.$$

What do our two classes of models, structural and intensity, predict about this issue?

2.5.1 Structural Models: Negligible Gap Risk

We have seen that even the most standard first-passage structural models produce stochastic credit spreads. In particular, if the value of the firm V_t approaches the default barrier H, the survival probability (2.11) *falls*, since default is given by the value of the firm touching the barrier and the lower the value of the firm the more likely this becomes,

$$V_t \downarrow \Longrightarrow \Pr(\tau > T_i | V_t) \downarrow .$$

The survival probability tends to 0 when $V_t \approx H$, driving the CDS spread to extremely high values, whose expression is in fact, from (2.2) adapted to structural models,

$$S_{T_b}(t) = Lgd \sum_{i=a+1}^{b} \Pr(T_{i-1} < \tau \leq T_i | V_t) P(t, T_i) / \sum_{i=a+1}^{b} P(t, T_i)\alpha_i \Pr(\tau > T_i | V_t) .$$

Thus in structural models default will always be preceded by a spread really, since spreads diverge to infinity as the value of the firm approaches the barrier. If the note involves a trigger, at any level, it will be touched before default. If unwinding can be performed timely, the note will be unwound and liquidated before suffering the default loss, and if the trigger has been set lower than or equal to $trigger^*$, then

$$GapRisk \approx 0.$$

This ‘spread to infinity’ prediction of the structural models implies an extreme and very aggressive evaluation of the gap risk.

2.5.2 Reduced-Form Models: Maximum Gap Risk

Let us first recall what happens if $\lambda(t)$ is deterministic. In this case we can predict all future spread levels, that are the forward spreads computed from the forward survival probabilities of (2.12) and (2.13). The trigger is usually set in the market at a threshold higher than any forward spread computed today. In such a case, no doubt the trigger will never be touched. This is so in spite of the fact that, once the models have been calibrated to the same CDS, we have exactly the same default probability as we had with structural models.

The difference is that now the default is absolutely not associated with the spread movements. We are at the opposite end compared to structural models: the trigger is useless, the gap risk is the same as we would have with no triggers and it is the maximum possible gap risk

$$GapRisk = MaxGapRisk = \mathbb{E}\left[1_{\{\tau < T\}} P(0, \tau) \times (Lev \times Lgd - 1)^+\right] \tag{2.15}$$

If we know that $Lev \times Lgd > 1$, this expression simplifies to

$$GapRisk = \mathbb{E}\left[1_{\{\tau < T\}} P(0, \tau) \times (Lev \times Lgd - 1)\right],$$

which can be further simplified if we adopt an approximation where we assume that default will happen at a precise time, for example in the mid point between now and maturity T,

$$GapRisk \approx P\left(0, \frac{T}{2}\right) \times \Pr(\tau < T) \times (Lev \times Lgd - 1).$$

This expression is so simple that all that is required is the knowledge of one discount factor and one default probability.

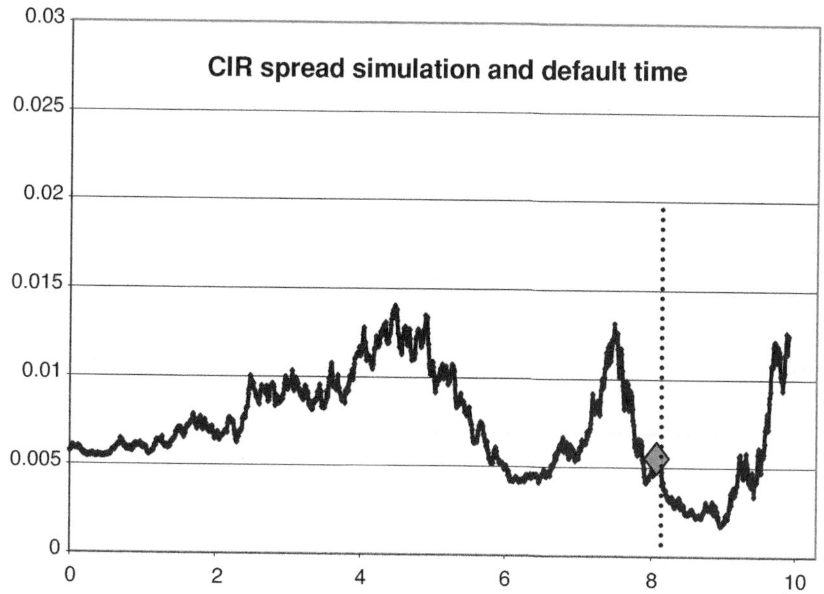

Figure 2.6 Spread and default simulation with CIR intensity

This case, however, has already been ruled out since we have already ruled out deterministic intensity as too unrealistic, even before this deeper analysis of the core risk in this payoff. We have introduced stochastic intensity via a process

$$d\lambda(t) = k[\theta - \lambda(t)]dt + \sigma\sqrt{\lambda(t)}dW(t), \tag{2.16}$$

that gives spreads a non-trivial dynamics. Now the question is: what is the behaviour of the spreads in proximity of default implied by such a model? Let us have a look at Figure 2.6 at one typical path for the spread, computed via Monte Carlo simulation, with the default time indicated by the dotted vertical line.

We see that the default time does not appear to be associated to an increase in spreads. It is the typical *leap to default*, that takes the market by surprise. One may wonder if the above Monte Carlo scenario is not an outlier ... unfortunately it is not. It is just the most common type of path we get when the dynamics we simulate is like (2.16): we see little or no association between spread rallies and default event. In this particular chart, default happens even after a spread decline.

In fact, it is known that intensity models where the intensity is a diffusive process (such that the only stochasticity comes from a continuous process like a Brownian motion), lead to low 'spread-default correlation', namely a scarce relation between spread movements and default time. This generates a high probability of leaps to default, that can be verified by everyone simply by means of Monte Carlo simulation. But this feature can also be explained analytically, as we show in the chart in Figure 2.7.

The dotted line represents intensity simulated with (2.16), while the continuous line is its integral. Notice that, although the intensity goes up and down in time unpredictably, the integral of the intensity, which gives us the cumulated default likelihood, moves rather regularly following a stable increasing path. The discontinuities in the intensity path are too small to

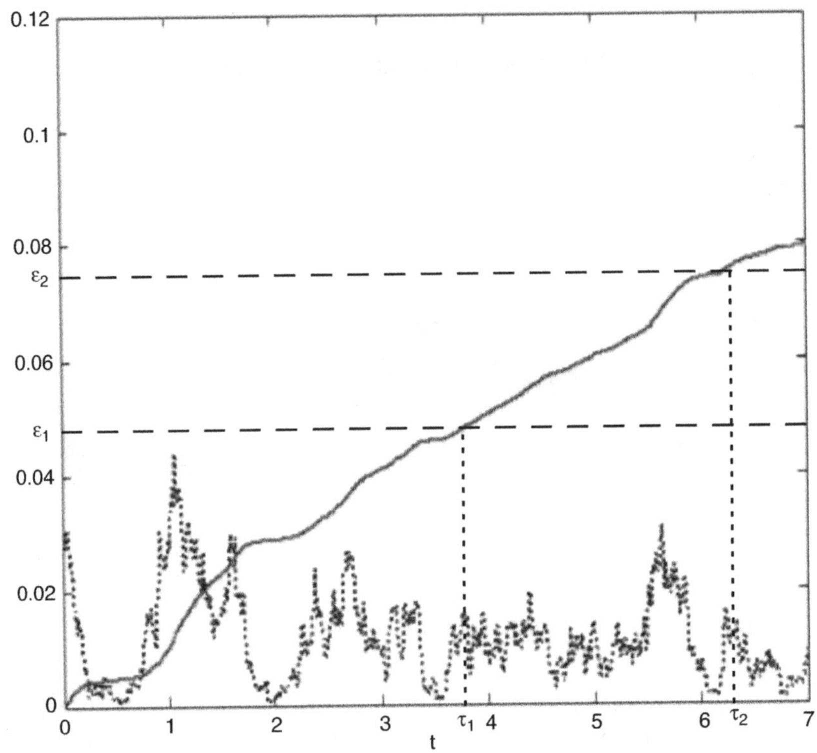

Figure 2.7 Diffusive intensity. The dotted line is a Monte Carlo path, the continuous line is its integral, the dashed lines are the default triggers

generate discontinuities in the integral. We know from (2.6) that default happens when the integral is higher than a random variable ε with standardized exponential distribution. The variable can take all values between zero and plus infinity. If we suppose $\varepsilon = \varepsilon_1$, we have $\tau = \tau_1$, if instead $\varepsilon = \varepsilon_2$, we have $\tau = \tau_2$, which is more than two years later even if ε_1 and ε_2 differ only by around 2%.

It is clear that the random variable which is most important to determine the default time is ε. In fact, as long as the intensity $\lambda(t)$ remains a diffusion with reasonable parameters, even paths of $\lambda(t)$ which appear really different give rise to similar integrals. With such integrals even small variations of ε are crucial to determine τ. Since $\lambda(t)$ is independent of ε, it will be scarcely related to τ. And since the stochastic dynamics of the spreads depends only on $\lambda(t)$, spreads and τ will have a very weak dependency. We say that default is 'unpredictable' in these intensity models, in the sense that the observation of credit spreads gives us only very coarse information about the likelihood of an impending default.

Ultimately, the unpredictability of the default time is one of the reasons why intensity models were often chosen to replace structural models. After cases like Parmalat or Enron where default was the final consequence of a fraud of which most market operators were unaware, they found that the perfect predictability of default in structural models (where you see spreads going to infinity before default) was an element of unrealism.

But now, for this specific product, unpredictability leads us to another extreme result, opposite to structural models. In intensity models with diffusive intensity the gap risk tends to its maximum value:

$$GapRisk \approx MaxGapRisk = \mathbb{E}\left[1_{\{\tau<T\}} P(0,\tau) \times (Lev \times Lgd - 1)^{+}\right].$$

Aren't we making the exact opposite mistake to structural models?

2.6 A DEEPER ANALYSIS: MARKET CONSENSUS AND HISTORICAL EVIDENCE

Under both most common modelling solutions for default risk and credit spreads the evaluation of a leveraged note reduces to a trivial evaluation, for opposite reasons. In order to understand this fact better, let us analyze the payoff in depth.

2.6.1 What to Add to the Calibration Set

Now the first question is: are there any liquid products in the market that allow us to solve this indetermination, giving us an indication on the market assessment of gap risk that could allow us to choose between a structural model and an intensity model?

The optimum would be a liquid market for notes with a similar gap risk; but this market is absent so we have to look somewhere else. For some reference entities it is possible to find relatively liquid markets for CDS options. This derivative is treated in detail in Section 10.3. Here we present only the fundamental elements of it. If a CDS option has expiry T_{ex}, strike K and $T > T_{ex}$ is the maturity of the underlying CDS, the crucial part of the payoff at expiry is given by

$$1_{\{\tau>T_{ex}\}} \left(S_T\left(T_{ex}\right) - K\right)^{+}.$$

The part $(S_T(T_{ex}) - K)^{+}$ of this payoff clearly depends on the volatility and, more generally, on the dynamic behaviour of spread, which affects also the credit-linked note we are considering. Thus it is likely that a trader will suggest calibrating CDS options, where these are available. However, a calibration to spread options cannot solve our model uncertainty because of the other part of the payoff, the indicator $1_{\{\tau>T_{ex}\}}$. The CDS options in the market are knock-out, namely they expire in advance if the company defaults. Thus the information they contain about the dynamic behaviour of the spread is *conditional on having no default during the life of the option*. For the leverage note, on the other hand, our main interest is the dynamic behaviour of the spreads conditional on *being in the proximity of default during the life of the note*.

The two derivatives speak of two different states of the world. We may at first glance think that if an option is more valuable, which entails more spread volatility, it is more likely that the trigger will be touched, protecting us from default losses. But this is not necessarily the case. A reference entity can be characterized by a lot of spread volatility, causing a high price for options, and yet default with no unusual spread movement, without touching the trigger. Analogously, very reliable and transparent companies can have very stable spreads, and yet, in the unlikely case of default, the market can guess it will occur early on and cause an abnormal spread movement. These movements, which have no effect on options, since options are conditional to survival, affect crucially our gap risk.

Options, in the rare case that they are available, can be introduced in calibration when pricing a leveraged note, since they increase our information about the volatility of the spreads. This information impacts, for example, the possibility of touching the trigger even if no default event is near. This is useful information for the client, who would otherwise lose money in that case for no reason, and also for a bank looking after the interests of its client. But it does not give us the crucial information on the bank's gap risk. Calibrating to spread options and then feeling confident that model risk has been minimized is one of the common errors we can make in assessing gap risk.

2.6.2 Performing Market Intelligence

We can try another route to gather market information, suggested by Rebonato (2003). Even in the absence of a market for this note, one can perform market intelligence to find out the modelling approach followed by the majority of the counterparties. This is not, it should be clear by now, mark-to-market, because a proper market does not exist. But it can move us in the right direction of 'fair value', suggesting what would be the market price should a market be born in the future or should we be forced to exit in advance from our position in the note.

In the past, I happened to be informed about quotes for leveraged notes with triggers by two different banks. One was an American bank with a very aggressive stance on credit derivatives (that defaulted some time later, incidentally ...), while the other was a classic European bank, active on the derivatives market but rather conservative on credit derivatives (it emerged from the credit crunch stronger than before).

The American bank was eager to pay, for a leverage note of this kind with a trigger that was a multiple of the current spread level $S_T(0)$, a spread that was around $Lev \times S_T(0)$ with no additional fee. This is consistent with an approach where the gap risk is estimated to be very low. The European bank, for the same note, was available to pay a spread so much lower that it almost included a running remuneration of the maximum gap risk computed in (2.15).

You can consider only the quotation most convenient to you, assuming that, for as long as there is even one single counterparty in the market available to take up a risk for a low price, you will always be able to free yourself from that risk at that price. The problem with this reasoning is that, when the market is thin and there is strong disagreement among players, there is no guarantee that the situation seen today will persist. What we see today may disappear tomorrow. In the example given above, the situation is even ironic, since the most aggressive counterparty disappeared physically from the market in a short time due to default. This is one of those cases where market intelligence does not allow you to eliminate your model uncertainty. If a lot of evidence is collected in performing market intelligence, usually a particular view appears to prevail, but there is nothing like a market consensus.

2.6.3 The Lion and the Turtle. Incompleteness in Practice

Section 1.2.2 showed that even the rigorous theory of financial markets justifies the existence of the disagreement we have seen in the real world case above. It justifies precisely the coexistence of an aggressive price for the American bank and a conservative price for the European one. In fact, the leveraged note, however simple a product, depends crucially on a risk factor, driving the relation between spreads and default time, which is not observable in any market because of the lack of a liquid derivative depending on it. Thus the market is *incomplete*.

In an incomplete market, even if all market participants agree on the real world probabilities of an event (for example on the real world probability of being saved from gap losses by a spread rally that touches the trigger) they can disagree on the compensation they want for this risk. Companies compute prices with *risk-adjusted* probabilities that include compensation for risk.

When the market is incomplete, there is no observable agreement on the right compensation. Thus conservative banks will work with risk-adjusted probabilities for the painful events which are much higher than those used by aggressive counterparties, irrespective of the historical evidence. Here the painful event is the leap-to-default; a conservative bank will increase the likelihood of such an event, an aggressive bank may instead work with its objective estimation of the real world probability (or even a lower probability if it is risk-loving rather than risk-averse . . . a possibility that cannot be excluded for the American bank in this little story). We can't even say if the divergence is based on different views about the default behaviour, or on different risk aversions.

2.6.4 Reality Check: Historical Evidence and Lack of it

After trying to collect as much information as possible on the market implied value of the gap risk, we now look at the real-world behaviour of markets in the past. Do we have clear historical evidence that can give us an indication of what is the most likely possibility, a leap to default or a default preceded by a relatively smooth spread increase? Clearly, the first caveat is that history of past defaults has little to do with future defaults. Moreover, the historical evidence is mixed. A pure leap to default is not common, but the Enron and Parmalat defaults certainly caught the market by surprise, as mentioned above, because their defaults were due to accounting frauds that had been carefully hidden from the market. Argentina's sovereign default, on the other hand, was entirely predictable, with spreads growing steadily until a climax at default. Lehman was mixed. Even Parmalat's default was somewhat anticipated, as we can see in Figure 2.8, but the final one-day spread tally was impossible to exploit in practice.

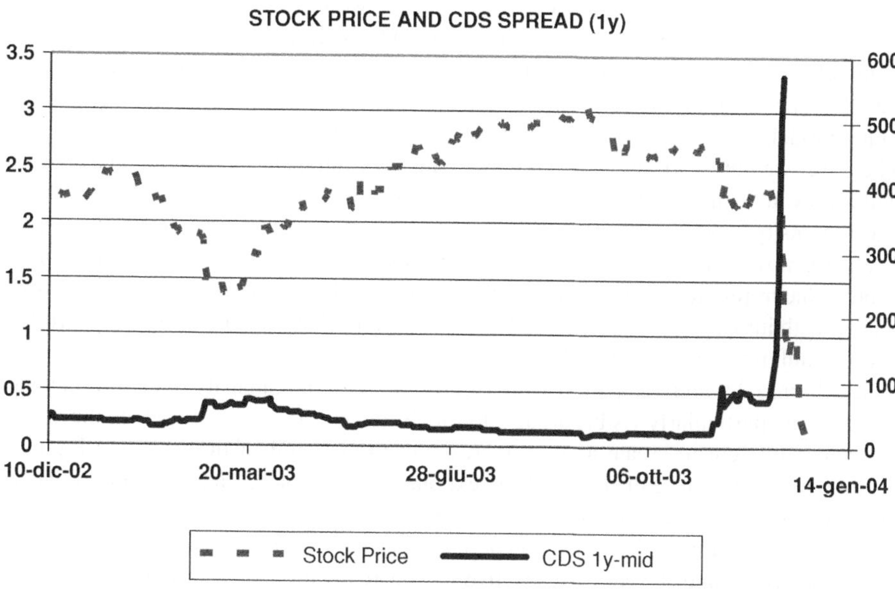

Figure 2.8 Parmalat stock price (in euros, left scale) and 1y-CDS spread (in bps right scale) from Brigo and Tarenghi (2009)

In general, the likelihood of a sudden default is inversely proportional to the transparency of the balance sheet. It is more likely to have predictable defaults with sovereign issuers, and a more abrupt leap to default with companies. With companies it is more usual to have reporting frauds, as in the case of Parmalat and Enron, or, particularly for financial institutions, balance sheets that are objectively difficult to evaluate as in the Lehman case. But there are exceptions such as the Greek accounting fraud revealed after the credit crunch or the anticipation by market operators of the tragic situation of Bear Sterns in March 2008 (although in both cases a default was avoided by bailout). The analysis of the features of the specific counterparty will lead the modeller to form a view, but in any case, as the regulators say, the choice depends on 'judgement'.

And one must not forget that judgement is both on the real world probabilities of a leap to default and on the risk aversion prevailing in the market. Even if the leap to default was considered unlikely in the real world, it may carry a high risk compensation, leading to higher probability under the risk-adjusted pricing measure.

2.7 BUILDING A PARAMETRIC FAMILY OF MODELS

Now we would like to test the effect on gap risk of assumptions less extreme than those represented by either structural or intensity models. Can we find a model where the behaviour is somewhat in-between the null gap risk of structural models and the maximum gap risk of intensity models? There are at least two possibilities.

The first one is to make one further step in increasing the realism of structural models, and take structural models with a default barrier H_t that can move stochastically among different levels. An unpredictable upward jump of the barrier would also create in these models a possibility of a leap to default, and we could play with the parameters to control its probability. A similar effect would be obtained by introducing discontinuities in the asset value dynamics V_t. See Elizalde (2005) for an overview of the many alternatives for increasing the realism of structural models.

Otherwise, we can work on increasing the realism of intensity models, an alternative that we will follow in detail because it is somewhat more original and also more tractable. The idea is to use intensity models with a stochastic intensity *which is no longer a diffusion but can experience jumps*. This introduces into intensity models some predictability of default, and therefore some mitigation of gap risk. The intuition behind it is that jumps in the intensity are associated with jumps both in spreads and in the default probability, increasing the correlation between default time and spread rallies.

Look at Figure 2.9 and compare it with Figure 2.7. Now the intensity dynamics includes a jump behaviour, particularly visible around 4 years from now. The discontinuity in the intensity path is now sufficient to create a sharp increase in the integral of the intensity. Figure 2.7 shows how two different realizations of the exponential variable, ε_1 and ε_2, caused two very different default times, one in less than 4 years from now and the other one in more than 6 years. Now in Figure 2.9 it is the behaviour of the intensity that decides the default time, which in fact is around 4 years irrespective of the realization of ε. Intensity jumps have made default more dependent on the behaviour of the intensity, which is strongly linked to

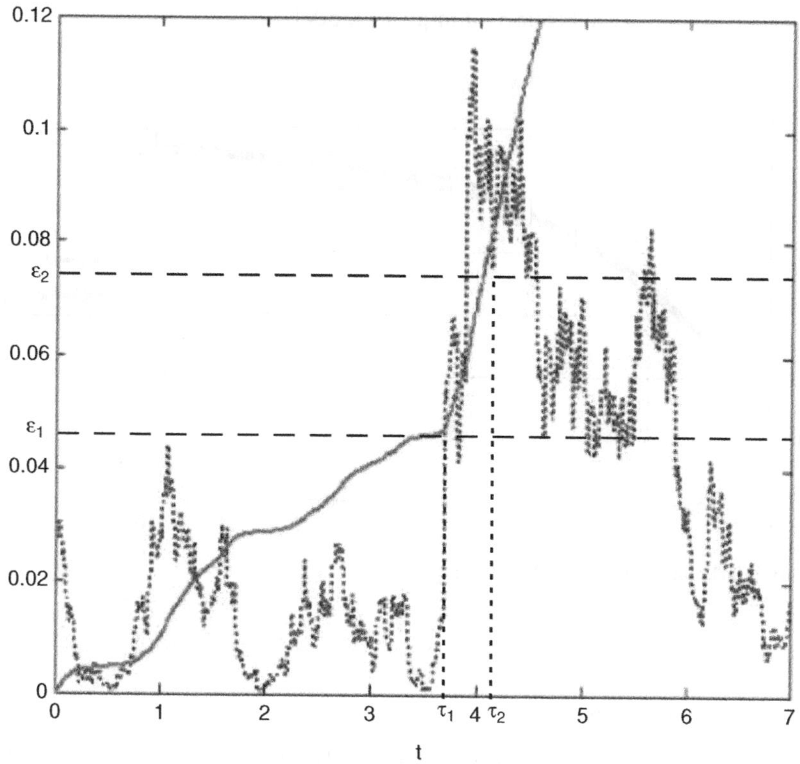

Figure 2.9 Jump-diffusion intensity. The dotted line is a Monte Carlo path, the continuous line is its integral, the dashed lines are the default triggers

the spreads. Here it is more likely that default will be anticipated by a spread rally, and the likelihood depends on the frequency and size of the jumps.

Figure 2.9 is detained from the natural jump extension of our previous CIR model. This is the CIR-exponential Jump model, according to which the intensity dynamics is

$$d\lambda(t) = k[\theta - \lambda(t)]dt + \sigma\sqrt{\lambda(t)}dW(t) + dJ_t^{\alpha,\gamma}. \tag{2.17}$$

where

$$J_t^{\alpha,\gamma} = \sum_{i=1}^{N_t} Y_i$$

with N_t a Poisson process with jump intensity α and $Y_i \sim \exp(1/\gamma)$, being γ the expected jump size. With this choice of jump distribution, survival probability can be computed analytically as

$$\mathbb{E}_t\left[\exp\left(-\int_t^T \lambda(u)du\right)\right] = \bar{A}(t,T)e^{-\bar{B}(t,T)\lambda(t)},$$

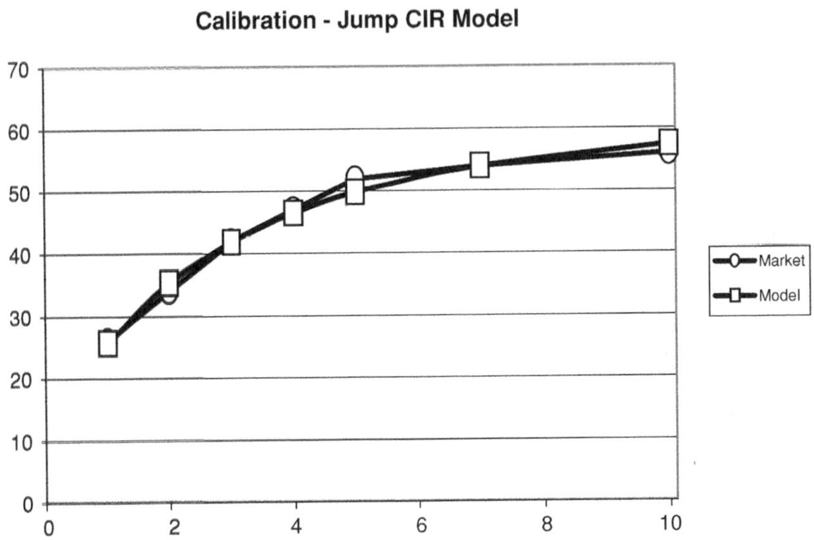

Figure 2.10 CDS calibration – CIR with jumps

where

$$h \neq k + 2\gamma :$$

$$\bar{A}(t,T) = A(t,T)\left[\frac{2h\exp[(k+h+2\gamma)(T-t)/2]}{2h+(k+h+2\gamma)[\exp((T-t)h)-1]}\right]^{\frac{2\alpha\gamma}{\sigma^2-2k\gamma-2\gamma^2}}$$

$$h = k + 2\gamma :$$

$$\bar{A}(t,T) = A(t,T)\exp\left[-2\alpha\gamma\left(\frac{T-t}{k+h+2\gamma}+\frac{\exp((T-t)h)-1}{h(k+h+2\gamma)}\right)\right]$$

$$\bar{B}(t,T) = B(t,T),$$

with $A(t,T)$ and $B(t,T)$ given in (2.14).

The availability of closed-form formulas makes calibration simple. For example, using the same CDS term structure as for the diffusive model, but fixing $\gamma = 100$bps and therefore imposing the presence of a jump that can be very high, we get the calibration in Figure 2.10.

Notice that the calibration quality does not change by adding the jump parameters (although the parameters we get are obviously different). This confirms that, without additional calibration products, both a diffusive and a jump model can be consistent with market CDS. By introducing a new set of risk factors – the jumps – which allow for control of crucial risk affecting the leverage note, we learn that we cannot really determine the model parameters based on the liquid CDS market, since different configurations allow the same CDS fit although they will have different effects on gap risk. This is a further symptom of market illiquidity/incompleteness with respect to this crucial risk that affects the leveraged note.

We see now that, in spite of the analogous fit to CDS, the behaviour of the model including spread jumps is very different, in terms of relations between spread level and default time, from the previous model without jumps. Now we have more correlation between default and spread rallies, as can be seen in the three charts represented in Figures 2.11, 2.12 and 2.13,

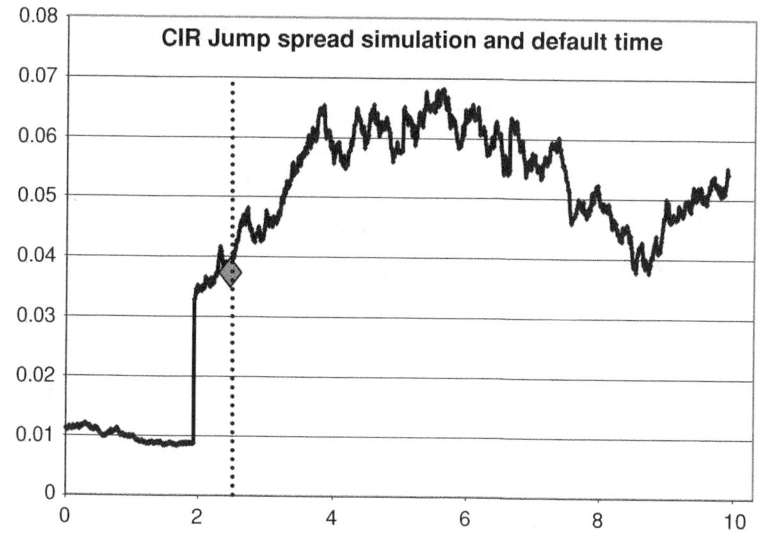

Figure 2.11 Spread and default simulation in case of jumps

which are the first three paths with a default before 10 years which I obtained in a Monte Carlo simulation of (2.17), computing the spreads implied by $\lambda(t)$ at all simulation steps.

In all three cases there is a stronger relation between spread behaviour and default than we had in the diffusive model. This correlation is then reflected in the value of the gap risk. In particular, the level of default-spread correlation, and therefore the level of the gap risk, can be controlled by choosing the average size of the jump γ. Taking for example a note with $T = 5y$ and $trigger = 2.5 \times S_T(0)$, on an underlying with the CDS term structure of Figure 2.10, we

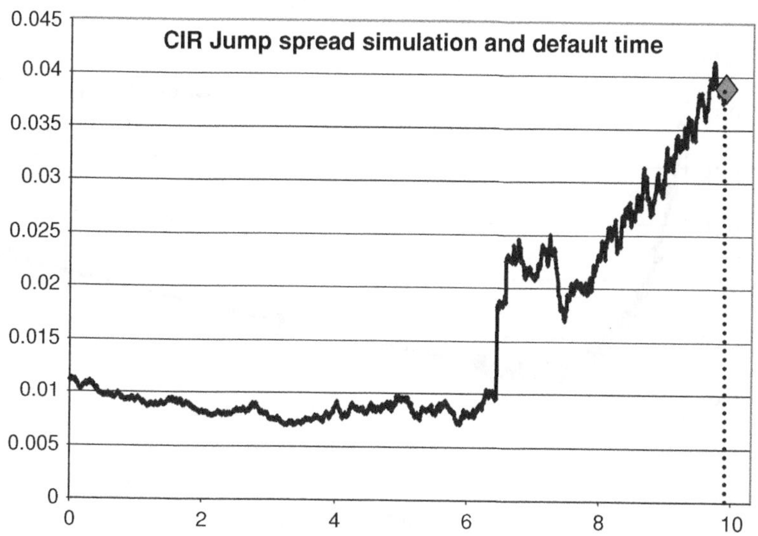

Figure 2.12 Spread and default simulation in case of jumps

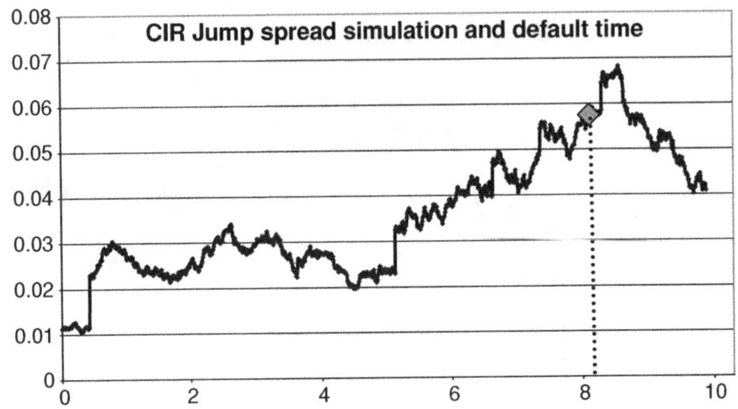

Figure 2.13 Spread and default simulation in case of jumps

have the pattern of Figure 2.14 for the net present value (2.9) of gap risk moving from no jumps to the possibility of very high jumps.

Notice that in all the above cases the model has been calibrated to the same CDS data, and (almost) implies the same default probability. Notice also that the model does not allow us to send the gap risk to zero, the possibility of totally unexpected defaults is not excluded. Additionally, when the spread jump becomes too big, there can be gap losses from the unwinding even before default, since the spreads at the unwinding are already larger than *trigger**.

Note also that one needs an average jump size of almost 1000 bps to minimize the probability of sudden defaults and consequently the gap risk. Such a jump size may appear unrealistic, but

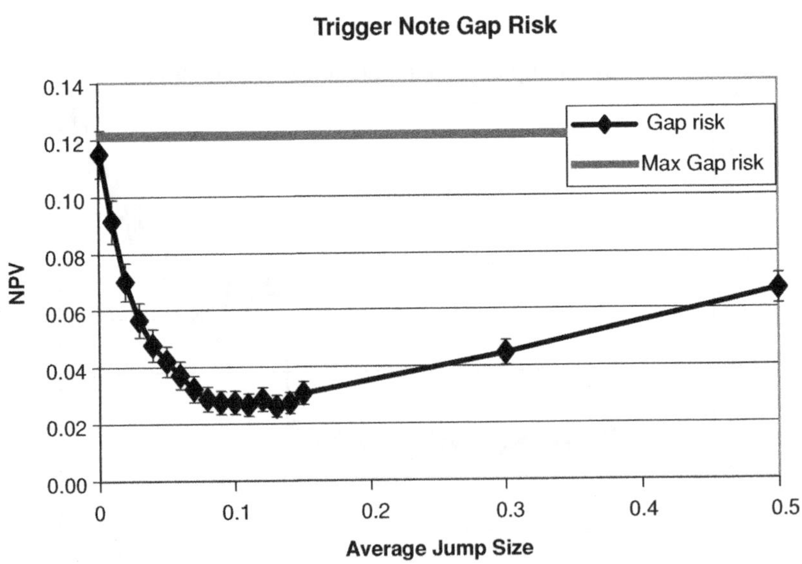

Figure 2.14 Gap risk under different models

it is not necessarily so if we recall what this jump actually means. It must be a very unlikely jump that most times generates a spread rally and then a default. Thus it is not surprising that its average size is larger than the jumps representing the discontinuous behaviour that spreads can have in ordinary trading. By the way, if you look at the behaviour of Parmalat spreads before default as shown in Figure 2.8, you see that there were jumps of hundreds of bps in the weeks preceding default, and even jumps of thousands of bps in the days preceding default.

2.7.1 Understanding Model Implications

The reason for the differences in gap risk for different expected jump sizes appears clearer if we compare two extreme configuration – no jumps vs large jumps with average size ≈1000bps. This can be seen in Figure 2.15. We first show in the top chart that the two models have the same default probability but very different probability of touching the trigger before maturity (Touch Probability). But any model with more spread volatility would produce a higher touch probability. To make sure that jumps really control the probability that the trigger is touched

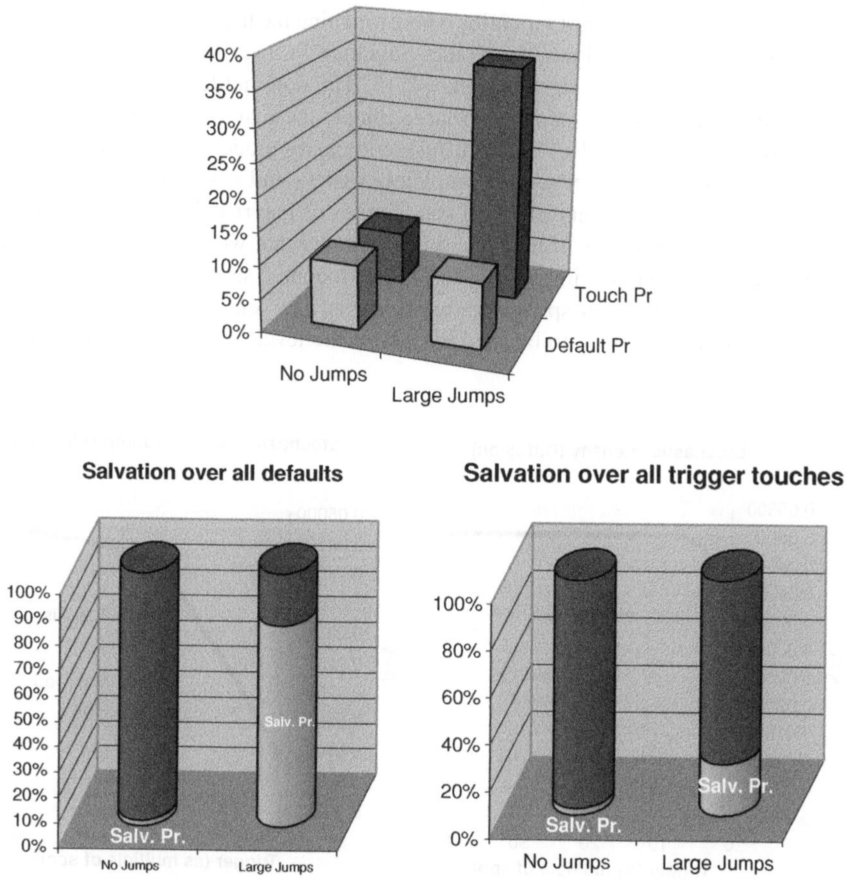

Figure 2.15 Understanding gap risk under different models

when default is upcoming, we show how many defaults that would have led to high gap losses for the bank were actually avoided by touching the trigger. This is shown as 'Salvation Probability' in the chart 'Salvation over all defaults' on the left in Figure 2.15, and it is given by the ratio between the number of Monte Carlo scenarios where $t^{touch} < \tau < T$ and the number of Monte Carlo scenarios where $\tau < T$. We see that here the difference between the two models is much greater than it was when we were simply comparing touch probability. The model with jumps does not lead to touching the trigger more often in a random way, but specifically in scenarios where otherwise there would have been default. This is what is of interest to the banks to understand the effectiveness of the trigger. On the other hand, for a diffusive model, the trigger touches are almost always independent of the actual happening of a default, so that in a very, very large majority of cases the note is unwound but then no default happens.

The holder of the note, on the other hand, is more interested in other, different information. He wants to compare the number of scenarios when the touch actually 'saved' the note from default, with the number of scenarios when the touch stopped the note but then there was no default of the reference name before maturity. The latter is the worst case scenario for the note buyer since he loses money just because of the presence of the trigger, while he would have no losses if the trigger was not there.

The ratio between the number of scenarios where touching the trigger saved from subsequent default, and the number of total touches, is the 'Salvation Probability' of the chart 'Salvation over all trigger touches' on the right in Figure 2.15. The note holder will find this evidence quite disappointing even in the model with large jumps: there are many trigger touches that would not have led to default. But in the diffusive intensity models he would be even more unhappy, because here the trigger seems completely useless and only a loss for him.

Figure 2.16 shows the two very different sensitivities of gap risk to triggers. In a diffusive model, the range of movements of the spread is so limited that we very soon reach levels of the trigger such that it is almost impossible for it to be touched, sending gap risk to maximum value. In case of possible high spread jumps, however, the sensitivity to the trigger has a smooth behaviour, and allows it to be used to control the level of gap risk. If a counterparty

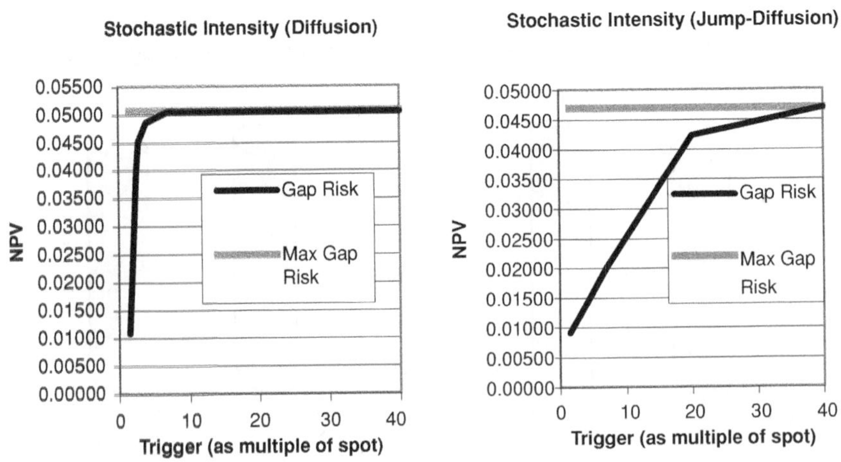

Figure 2.16 The effect of a trigger on gap risk

insists on setting a trigger in such a note, we can already guess something about his model assumptions.

2.8 MANAGING MODEL UNCERTAINTY: RESERVES, LIMITS, REVISIONS

In the above example it is not easy to say, based on historical observation, which price is the most realistic among those included between the two extreme prices, the one minimizing gap risk coming from structural models or the one maximizing it coming from diffusive intensity models. And there is no generally recognized market consensus about the modelling approach to follow. Usually the analysis conducted and the evidence collected allow for the reduction of the reasonable prices to a range smaller than the one included between the two extreme prices, but we definitely remain in a situation of high model uncertainty. This is exactly the case of interest to us.

For dealing with this, we have developed a parametric family of models – intensity models with jumps – that can cover the desired range of prices depending on the value we give to a parameter γ. Cont (2006) points out that the fact that a family of models can be *'embedded in a "single" parametric family is purely conventional and depends on the arbitrary definition of a "parametric family". In fact by embedding all models in Q in a single super-model one can always represent model uncertainty as parameter uncertainty'*. We fully agree in principle, but in practice parametric uncertainty is easier to deal with. In fact, the reduction of model uncertainty to a single parameter γ allows us to find easily models that are intermediate between two extremes. Without this it would have been difficult to find models in-between two approaches as different from each other as structural and intensity models. It also makes a difference if the range of models under consideration requires many radically different implementations or one single implementation where one single parameter changes. The latter case also involves less operational risk.

The parameterization of model uncertainty is useful to compute model reserves, which are a classic tool for the mitigation of model risk. In what follows we describe these and other provisions. We present them considering a deal-by-deal application, focusing on their computation at inception of each deal. In banks this is often not possible, so the application must be done at portfolio level and at some periodic dates, but the principles to follow are the same.

Model reserves

Let us now abstract from the above example. Let us assume that, for the parameter γ that we use to parameterize our class of models, the range which is considered reasonable is $0 \leq \gamma \leq 1$, and that the price $\Pi_t^T(\gamma)$ of some derivative (with maturity T) increases with γ. Suppose that the model validation process reaches the conclusion that $\Pi_t^T(\gamma = 0.5)$ is the 'most reasonable' price and validates the model with $\gamma = 0.5$. At the same time, the validation process recognizes that there is residual uncertainty about the value of γ in the range $0 \leq \gamma \leq 1$. For many banks, this statement about the residual uncertainty in the model validated for a specific product will coincide with the decision about whether this product should be considered Level 1, 2 or 3. This may be acceptable, as long as the bank is aware of the discrepancies between accounting standards and a solid risk assessment pointed out in Section 1.3.

Now the bank finds a counterparty that is eager to pay $\Pi_t^T(\gamma = 0.75)$ to buy the derivative. The difference

$$\mathbb{R} = \Pi_t^T(0.75) - \Pi_t^T(0.5)$$

appears a day-1 profit for the salespeople and the traders who close the deal.

However, since validation has not resolved the uncertainty about the value of the parameter, the model risk managers should decide that $\mathbb{R}$ is not recognized by the trader at day-1, but is used to create a *model capital reserve*. Capital reserves are usually held against unexpected losses rather than against expected losses. As such, a reserve appears the right tool for managing model uncertainty. This reserve will be released to the trader only along the life of the derivative, for example, from time t_1 to time t_2, $t_1 < t_2 < T$ the trader will receive only

$$\mathbb{R}\frac{(t_2 - t_1)}{T} \tag{2.18}$$

What is the rationale behind such a provision? Without it, salesmen and traders would be strongly motivated to sell large notionals of this derivative to counterparties eager to pay $\Pi_t^T(0.75)$, getting an important day-1 profit. However, due to the model uncertainty stated by validation, the management should worry that it is possible that there is no day-1 profit, but that the price $\Pi_t^T(0.5)$ coming from the bank's model is wrong. This may be the only reason why the bank is able to close many deals on this derivative!

With the reserve, the motivation to trade is reduced, because salesmen and traders see no immediate profit. Their P&L will not be increased by all $\mathbb{R}$, and it will generate a reduced end-of-year bonus. In order to get all of this profit, they have to remain in the bank until T. But if they do so, they will see also the potential losses of this derivative in its future life, that can arise from the market becoming more liquid with the emergence of a different price that forces a mark-to-market loss, from an unwinding at a different price, or simply from losses in the settlement of the payoff at maturity. The deferral in the release of the profit forces salesmen and traders to consider these aspects from a personal point of view.

If the bank wants to reduce further the incentive to traders, a rule can be chosen to release the reserve according to a law slower than the linear releasing set in (2.18). The reserve $\mathbb{R}$ may even be released as profit only at maturity T. An even stronger discouragement to trading this derivative at a model risk would be always to compute a reserve based on the most conservative model, thus considering $\Pi_t^T(1)$ when the product is sold, $\Pi_t^T(0)$ when the product is bought, so that the trader would always have a day-1 loss when closing the deal at any intermediate price. Since traders do not like day-1 losses at all, this is a strong action to force them to be prudent and conservative. For many banks, actually, model reserve can only eat out day-1 profit: the day-1 profit is the upper limit of the model reserve.

Remark 8. ***Model Risk* vs *Wrong Models*.** *A different case is when the validation process reveals a clear deficiency of some model used by the front office. For example, it may be a lognormal model that is applied to an option market where there is evidence of a smile. The best choice in this case is clearly to replace the deficient model with an upgraded one able to fit the smile. At times, however, the cost of upgrading the model is considered greater than the benefit. In fact, upgrading the model used by the front office may have massive costs in terms of new implementations, more complex procedures, longer computational times, calibration uncertainty and lack of confidence of the users. Thus at times banks prefer to implement the* *upgraded model only in order to adjust the price of the front office model when a deal is struck. The difference between the price with the upgraded model and the price with the deficient one will be put in a reserve. This approach can bring massive savings of time and resources, because the upgraded model, if not used for the active management of the derivative after inception, does not need any industrial implementation, speed, automation of the calibration or efficient greeks. However, it corrects the distortions of a deficient model only in terms of purchase and sale decisions.*

This use of model reserves does not deal with model uncertainty, but with a clear model deficiency. Its purpose is to force deals to be closed using the upgraded model and not with a deficient model. A model deficiency is not an unexpected loss, like model risk, but an expected cost, *and as such the difference between the price with the upgraded model and the one with the deficient model is a 'correction', to be charged to the counterparty, rather than a reserve. Part of this charge is often resumed in the charge traders make for hedging costs that will be incurred in reality although they are not considered by the model. For example, traders using a lognormal model know that the cost of vega hedging is not included in the model price, since the model does not admit changes to the volatility. Thus they charge this cost to the counterparty, and this partially takes into account the deficiencies of a lognormal model in a world with volatility that changes unpredictably. All these issues will be examined in Chapter 5.*

Model lines or position limits

Another action to mitigate model risk is the introduction of *model position limits* or *model lines* that are analogous to the credit lines used to manage credit risk. In the management of credit risk, for each defaultable counterparty a credit line is established by the management, namely a maximum potential exposure that the bank can reach towards this counterparty. Every time a new deal is struck that increases our exposure to loss in case of default of the counterparty, it eats into a part of the credit line. When the credit line is full, we will not be allowed to take further exposure towards that counterparty.

In our context, if the model for pricing some derivatives is considered subject to high model risk, the bank can validate this model but set a limit to the amount of possible investments in derivatives priced with this model. In other words the bank can set a limit to the exposure that the bank can reach towards this model risk. This way traders and salespeople can use the model for dealing, but the exposure they can build is under control. Often this a reasonable approach: at times, a bank needs to enter a market to gain experience of it and improve its modelling approach. In the meantime, a model with high uncertainty will be used, but the potential exposure is limited. Even if the model turns out to be wrong, the bank will make a loss but will not default.

There are some issues that need to be tackled to enable effective model lines. First, risk managers must have the possibility to monitor completely the use of a model. Secondly, they must recognize if there are models that appear different but are affected by the same model uncertainty, in order to prevent a multiplication of the allowed exposures because multiple models are validated that in the end make the same dubious assumption on the same market factors.

As regulators stipulate, banks should articulate their *'tolerance for exposures subject to valuation uncertainty'*. Thus the first step is to decide the total model line, namely what is the maximum loss they are ready to accept if a model turns out to be wrong. This is a strategic management decision.

Then banks have to compute the specific 'add-on' of a given deal priced with the uncertain model, namely how much a single deal contributes to filling the total line. It amounts to estimating the potential loss on a deal due to model uncertainty. Returning to the example above, an estimation of the potential exposure to model risk (maximum possible model loss) for a product sold at $\Pi_t^T(\bar{\gamma})$ is

$$Notional^* \left[\Pi_t^T(1) - \Pi_t^T(\bar{\gamma})\right]. \tag{2.19}$$

Notice that, as is reasonable, model lines should not be affected by deals sold at the conservative price $\Pi_t^T(1)$, as collateralized deals do not usually affect credit lines.

If the error we expect on γ is no more than $\Delta\gamma$, one can use, as a first order approximation to (2.19), the sensitivity to the uncertain parameter multiplied by $\Delta\gamma$,

$$Notional^* \left.\frac{\partial \Pi_t^T(\gamma)}{\partial\gamma}\right|_{\gamma=\bar{\gamma}} \Delta\gamma. \tag{2.20}$$

The obvious problem with the second option is that we may be dramatically uncertain about the relevance of the point $\bar{\gamma}$ where the sensitivity is computed.

If we use (2.19) or (2.20) the limits to exposures for model risk do not treat the exposure as a future quantity, as is done, for example when setting credit lines. For credit lines the exposure is often a quantile of the future mark-to-market. For a future date $T_i < T$, and a confidence level of 90%, the exposure computed today at t is the level K_i such that

$$K_i(\gamma) = \min\left\{K \,|\, \Pr\left(\Pi_{T_i}^T(\gamma) \le K\right) \ge 90\%\right\}.$$

Then one can take $\hat{K}(\gamma) = \max_i K_i(\gamma)$ and replace the exposures (2.19) and (2.20) with alternative quantities where $\hat{K}(\gamma)$ replaces $\Pi_t^T(\gamma)$. However, notice that model risk is not associated with uncertainty about future values, but about present prices, and this can justify remaining with (2.19) and (2.20). We can also add that, since we have uncertainty on $\bar{\gamma}$, the computation of the quantile increases our exposure to model uncertainty.

Notice that, as it happens with credit lines, a new deal priced with the uncertain model may actually reduce the exposure rather than increase it. This is the case, for example, if the deal is on the other side of the market compared to the majority of existing deals.

Model revisions

Another way to mitigate model risk, which must be used alongside model reserves and model lines, is to specify dates at which the validation must be revised. These revisions can be of two types:

1. **Periodic Revisions.** Periodic revisions are scheduled regularly, for example every year. After one year from the first validation, a lot of new evidence may be available, probably there will be more visibility of traded quotes, and knowledge of the model and its limits will be greater. The market may also have evolved. It is very wise to set periodic revisions, which should be more frequent for models classified as subject to considerable valuation uncertainty.
2. **Triggered Revisions.** The stress testing step of model validation, or the analysis of the most likely consensus changes, may have revealed that under particular market conditions

a model may become unreliable. If one of these market conditions becomes material, the Validation must be redone, and the model may require adjustment as a consequence. The revision dates in this case will be determined by quantitative triggers on market observable, or also on product features. Consider for example the (unlikely, but not impossible) case in which the model has been found faulty only for short maturities: we will be able to schedule the revisions already at inception.

When models are improved after a revision, reserves may be diminished and model lines can be increased. If instead the revision reveals higher model risk and no model improvement is performed, reserves may be increased and model lines diminished. In some realities reserves are recalculated regularly.

2.9 MODEL COMPARISON: EXAMPLES FROM EQUITY AND RATES

The previous sections of this chapter are based on a credit example. Now we see more synthetically two further examples, one from equity and one from interest rates, where we explore model uncertainty and risk between the alternative modelling frameworks which are popular for asset classes other than credit. Both examples relate to issues that fuelled passionate debate both in the market and academia resulting in some important reference papers whose main results we report.

2.9.1 Comparing Local and Stochastic Volatility Models in Pricing Equity Compound and Barrier Options

The example on equity focuses on the comparison between the two most popular modelling approaches in the equity market: stochastic volatility models (SVM) and local volatility models (LVM). Both allow us to solve the main pricing problem in the world of plain vanilla calls and puts: the presence of the smile, ie a Black and Scholes implied volatility that changes when the strike of the options changes, even if the underlying is the same for all options. This is in contrast with Black and Scholes assumptions and requires a model implying fat tails in the distribution of the stock. A way to arrive at this is to make volatility not only time-dependent but also state-dependent (stochastic). Both SVM and LVM feature such a volatility.

The most popular stochastic volatility model is the Heston (1993) model. It assumes the following dynamics for the stock under the risk neutral measure neglecting dividends:

$$\begin{aligned} dS(t) &= r(t)S(t)dt + \sigma(t)\sqrt{V(t)}S(t)dW^s(t) \\ dV(t) &= k(V(t) - \theta)dt + v\sqrt{V(t)}dW^z(t), \\ \mathbb{E}[dW^s(t)dW^z(t)] &= \rho dt \end{aligned} \tag{2.21}$$

where k is the speed of mean reversion and θ is the long-term mean of the volatility. The parameter v is called volatility of volatility, or volvol. The process followed by $V(t)$, which is the 'variance' of the stock price, is analogous to the Cox, Ingersoll and Ross (1985) process also seen for credit. This model allows a tractable pricing formula.

It is not difficult to see what can generate smiles in such a model. If we assume $S(t)$ and $V(t)$ are uncorrelated, the stochastic dynamics of $V(t)$ tends to perturb symmetrically the dynamics of the stock making both large downwards and upwards variations more likely than in a lognormal process, and also generating clusters of very low volatility. This is what is called fat tails (which does not imply only larger downwards and upwards variations, as we will see in Section 3.3, because this can be arrived at just by increasing Black and Scholes volatility) and implies symmetric increases of the Black volatility curve on both sides of the strike range. We can have another effect of stochastic volatility, if we only decide to set a non-zero correlation ρ. In this case the perturbation due to stochastic volatility can, for example, be higher when forward rates are decreasing (case $\rho < 0$). This makes the implied volatility curve decrease when plotted against the strike, a shape which is characteristic of the equity option market and often called skew.

Local volatility models are even more effective in fitting the equity market smile. LVM were introduced in Dupire (1994) and Derman and Kani (1994). The importance of their contribution builds on the results of Breeden and Litzenberger (1978), that show how where we had a continuous and infinite smile σ_K^T, namely a continuum of quoted call options of strikes from zero to infinity, we could get the probability distribution of the underlying at maturity T directly from the market. This hinges on the fact that the price of a call is known when we know the implied volatility (under zero rates, for simplicity) as

$$Call(K,T) = Black\left(S(0), K, \left(\sigma_K^T\right)^2 T\right)$$

and this price can be written as

$$\begin{aligned} Call(K,T) &= \mathbb{E}\left[(S(T)-K)^+\right] \\ &= \int_0^{+\infty} (x-K)^+ f_{0,T}(x)dx, \end{aligned}$$

where $f_{0,T}(x)$ is the probability density, under the pricing measure, of $S(T)$ given information at time 0, namely

$$f_{0,T}(x)dx = \Pr(S(T) \in [x, x+dx)|S(0)).$$

With the necessary regularity conditions, we could find $f_{0,T}(x)$ just taking second derivative of the continuum price curve with respect to the strike, since

$$\begin{aligned} \frac{\partial^2 Call(K,T)}{\partial K^2} &= \frac{\partial^2}{\partial K^2}\int_K^{+\infty} (x-K) f_{0,T}(x)dx \\ &= \frac{\partial^2}{\partial K^2}\int_{+\infty}^{K} (K-x) f_{0,T}(x)dx \\ &= \frac{\partial}{\partial K}\int_{\infty}^{K} f_{0,T}(x)dx \\ &= f_{0,T}(K). \end{aligned} \tag{2.22}$$

By interpolating and extrapolating the quoted options (first model indetermination: strike inter/extra-polation) we can artificially create a continuum of prices and get a density which is consistent with all quoted options. This can be repeated for all quoted maturities T_i, and then a time interpolation and extrapolation can also be computed in order to have a continuum of σ_K^T both in K and in T (second model indetermination: time inter/extra-polation).

And now for Dupire's extraordinary insight. If we model the stock under the risk-neutral measure as

$$dS(t) = r(t)S(t)dt + \Sigma(S(t), t)S(t)dW^s(t),$$

thus as a one-factor diffusion, it is possible to find one function

$$\Sigma(S(t), t)$$

such that $S(T)$ has exactly the distribution $f_{0,T}(K)$ we got from the market smile, for $0 < T < \infty, 0 < K < \infty$. To quote Gatheral (2002), 'given the distribution of final spot prices $S(T)$ for each time T conditional on some starting spot price $S(0)$, Dupire shows that there is a unique risk neutral diffusion process which generates these distributions. That is, given the set of all European option prices, we may determine the functional form of the diffusion parameter (local volatility) of the unique risk neutral diffusion process which generates these prices.' Technically, this is obtained by exploiting the fact that $f_{0,T}(K)$ must satisfy the Fokker-Planck equation

Thus local volatility models have clearly a great calibration power, and can fit any kind of smile/skew shape, even more so than stochastic volatility models. Here a question arises that can prove tricky: if the model is calibrated to all market option prices of all maturities, such that we have fixed the distribution of the underlying at all times, is there any residual model risk or instead our model is completely specified by market quotes and there is nothing we should worry about?

One initial answer is: no, your model is not completely specified by market quotes. The specification of your model comes from arbitrary interpolations and extrapolations both in space and in time, and this carries a high level of model indetermination and uncertainty, and therefore high model risk, as we show in Chapter 7.

This is a good answer. But let us forget it for a moment, and suppose that the market could really provide us with σ_K^T for $0 < T < \infty, 0 < K < \infty$ and therefore with the marginal densities $f_{0,T}(K)$ for any instant from now to infinity. Now for the next question: if we have fixed all the marginal densities, is the model completely specified? Is there a unique model consistent with a set of marginal densities? Have we now eliminated any residual model uncertainty and thus model risk?

Let us look at an example in a simple context that can clarify our ideas from this point of view. I owe this example to Wim Schoutens. Let us set it in the simpler context of discrete time, where there are only a discrete set of business times $t_1, t_2, \ldots t_n$. We have an underlying of which we know the value at current time, $X(0)$. Let us consider two models, A and B, for its future evolution.

Under model A, the underlying $X^A(t)$ has the following dynamics: at time t_1, we draw a standardized Gaussian random variable and we set $X(t_1)$ equal to it, at time t_2 we draw another standardized Gaussian random independent of the first one, and so on, so that

$$\begin{aligned}
&X^A(0) = X(0) \\
&X^A(t_1) \sim \mathbb{N}(0,1) \\
&X^A(t_2) \sim \mathbb{N}(0,1) \perp X^A(t_1) \\
&X^A(t_3) \sim \mathbb{N}(0,1) \perp X^A(t_2) \perp X^A(t_1) \\
&\vdots
\end{aligned}$$

Under model B, the underlying $X^B(t)$ has the following dynamics: at time t_1, we draw a standardized Gaussian random variable and we set $X^B(t_1)$ equal to it, exactly as we did in the model above. Then at time t_2 we just set $X^B(t_2) = X^B(t_1)$. At time t_3 we set $X^B(t_3) = X^B(t_2) = X^B(t_1)\ldots$, and so on, so that

$$\begin{aligned}
&X^B(0) = X(0)\\
&X^B(t_1) \sim \mathbb{N}(0,1)\\
&X^B(t_2) = X^B(t_1)\\
&X^B(t_3) = X^B(t_2) = X^B(t_1)\\
&\vdots
\end{aligned}$$

What are the marginal probability densities of $X(t_i)$ at the different times, seen from time 0, under model A? They are $\mathbb{N}(0, 1)$ at all times.

What are the marginal probability densities of $X(t_i)$ at the different times, seen from time 0, under model B? They are $\mathbb{N}(0, 1)$ at all times.

Are the two models the same? Not at all. Model A involves a lot of stochasticity, an additional independent stochastic factor at all times. The dynamics of X is extremely unpredictable under this model. Model B has instead very little stochasticity, one single stochastic factor at t_1, and after that the dynamics of X is fully predictable. And yet the two models have the same marginals.

Thus the answer to the above question, 'in case we have fixed all the marginal densities, is the model completely specified?' is a resounding no. Once we have fixed the marginals of a model, there are still an infinity of dynamics that can be consistent with these marginals. In fact, fixing the marginal distributions $f_{0,T}(K)$ does not correspond to fixing all the conditional distributions

$$f_{T_1,T_2}(x_2, x_1)\,dx = \Pr(X(T_2) \in [x_2, x_2 + dx)\,|X(T_1) = x_1),$$

namely we have not fixed the probability of a stock having a value around x_2 at time T_2 given it had a value x_1 at time T_1, lower than T_2 but higher than current time. We can see in Wim's simple example that in spite of equal marginals the transition distributions can be radically different: under model A knowing X at T_1 changes nothing in the probability distribution for $X(T_2)$ that remains an independent Gaussian; in model B knowing X at T_1 changes completely the probability distribution for $X(T_2)$, which becomes merely a deterministic, known quantity.

Now we can understand better the local volatility models. What Dupire has found is not the unique model consistent with a continuum of distributions, but the 'unique risk neutral diffusion process which generates these distributions'. There can still be an infinity of models that generate these distributions and yet they are not diffusions. Diffusions are models with one single stochastic factor which is a continuous Brownian motion $dW^s(t)$. Stochastic volatility models, for example, have two factors and therefore they are outside this perimeter, and so are those models that admit jumps.

Therefore there can be model uncertainty even if we have no uncertainty on the marginal distributions. As we understood very well in the above Breeden and Litzenberger example (2.22), knowing the marginals amounts to knowing all the prices of European options, namely calls and puts. Thus the issue becomes: once two equity models perfectly agree on the European option prices, what is the residual model risk? For example LVM can fit the market smile perfectly, and SVM can also obtain a good fit. Are there any products on which they can disagree in spite of analogous calibration to liquid European options, creating model uncertainty and model risk?

Hull and Suo (2002) carry out a test precisely on the model risk involved in using LVM vs SVM. They want to make sure they are using two models with exactly the same calibration power on European options. Since LVM allow perfect fit, they let the European prices be generated by the stochastic volatility model, so that SVM is also perfectly fit by construction. The SVM chosen is similar to the Heston Model. Calibrating the LVM to the surface of quotes for all strikes and maturities generated by the SVM, the two models have exactly the same marginal distributions.

The differences between the two models are now due to the possibility of different transition distributions, as we saw above. Thus Hull and Suo (2002) concentrate on derivatives that have a dependence on transition distributions. They consider two derivatives.

First they take a call-on-call compound option, where the buyer has the right at time T_1 to pay K_1 and obtain a call option to buy the asset for a strike price K_2 at T_2. If we redefine European call prices as

$$Call\,(T_1) := Call_{T_1}\,(K_2, T_2)\,,$$

the pricing problem can be written as

$$\begin{aligned}
&P\,(0,T_1)\,\mathbb{E}\left[(Call\,(T_1)-K_1)^+\right] = P\,(0,T_1)\,\mathbb{E}\left[\left(P(T_1,T_2)\mathbb{E}_{T_1}\left[(S\,(T_2)-K_2)^+\right]-K_1\right)^+\right]\\
&= P\,(0,T_2)\,\mathbb{E}\,[S\,(T_2)\,|S\,(T_2)\geq K_2, Call\,(T_1)\geq K_1]\Pr(S(T_2)\geq K_2, Call(T_1)\geq K_1)\\
&- K_2 P\,(0,T_2)\Pr\,(S\,(T_2)\geq K_2, Call\,(T_1)\geq K_1)\\
&- K_1 P\,(0,T_1)\Pr\,(Call\,(T_1)\geq K_1)\,.
\end{aligned}$$

The product depends on one transition density, the density f_{T_1,T_2} of T_2 variables given T_1 variables.

Some other derivatives depend on more than one transition density. This is the case for the up-and-out barrier call option with strike K and maturity T_M, that pays like a call at T_M only if at the monitor times $T_1, T_2, \ldots T_M$ the stock price remains below the barrier levels $H_1, H_2, \ldots H_M$. Mostly there is a unique level of the barrier $H = H_1 = H_2 = \ldots$ but below we present the pricing problem for the general case where the barrier is not flat:

$$\begin{aligned}
&P\,(0,T_M)\,\mathbb{E}\left[(S\,(T_M)-K)^+\,|S\,(T_1)\leq H_1, S\,(T_2)\leq H_2,\ldots,S\,(T_M)\leq H_M\right]\\
&\quad\times\Pr(S(T_1)\leq H_1, S(T_2)\leq H_2,\ldots,S(T_M)\leq H_M)\\
&= P\,(0,T_M)\,\mathbb{E}\,[S\,(T_M)\,|S\,(T_1)\leq H_1, S\,(T_2)\leq H_2,\ldots,K\leq S\,(T_M)\leq H_M]\\
&\quad\times\Pr(S(T_1)\leq H_1, S(T_2)\leq H_2,\ldots,S(T_M)\leq H_M)\\
&\quad- K\,P\,(0,T_M)\Pr\,(S\,(T_1)\leq H_1, S\,(T_2)\leq H_2,\ldots,K\leq S\,(T_M)\leq H_M)
\end{aligned}$$

In this case the dependence on the transition densities is even more obvious, and they are not simple two dimensional transition densities but general multidimensional transition densities.

Hull and Suo price a call-on-call compound option with $T_1 = 1y$, $T_2 = 2y$, $K_2 = S(0)$ and a range of K_1. They find that in relevant cases the difference between the LVM price and the SVM price is less than 2% of the SVM price. The difference, and thus the model risk, are small, particularly if we compare it with the much bigger error that one would make with a Black and Scholes model calibrated to the at-the-money European options only. The difference between LVM and SVM, additionally, is less than 1% of $S(0)$.

Then Hull and Suo price a barrier option with a range of barriers and $K = 90\%$ or 100% of $S(0)$. In this case the difference between the LVM price and the SVM price can be almost 50% of the SVM price, and this difference can be much higher than the error performed by a simplistic Black and Scholes model calibrated only at ATM. This reveals a much higher model risk.

The result is not completely unexpected. The compound option had a reduced and simple dependence on transition densities, which are where LVM and SVM can differ. The fact of being well calibrated to the skew appears more important than transition distributions in computing this price, so that LVM and SVM give similar prices while Black and Scholes is far away. This is a situation of low residual model risk once we have chosen a model that guarantees good calibration. The barrier option instead has a higher and more complex dependence on transition densities, and this leads to prices that depend much more on these densities than on the calibration, so much so that the choice between LVM and SVM leads to greater price difference than the choice between an SVM perfectly calibrated and a Black and Scholes model with a very loose calibration.

One such analysis is crucial to understand and compare the model risk of different derivatives. In the Hull and Suo (2002) paper the working hypothesis chosen is that stochastic volatility models are the 'true models'. Certainly stochastic volatility models appear a more natural explanation of the skew than LVM. The latter have also been shown by Dumas et al. (1998) to be highly inconsistent with the historical dynamics of the market. However, basing our judgement on model risk just on this issue would amount to limiting ourselves to the 'reality check' part of model validation. On the other hand, Hull and Suo write in their abstract about the local volatility model that 'this a popular model among traders for valuing exotic options'. This is the other aspect to take into account: if everyone uses local volatility models to price barrier options, this is a strong constraint to model choice. It becomes more interesting in this case to understand which aspects of unrealism present in local volatility models that could in the future be exposed so much as to trigger a model change. From this perspective the analysis in the section 'Economic Intuition for Results' in Hull and Suo (2002) is very helpful. They conclude that the main element of unrealism in the LVM is that they do not capture well (in spite of capturing part of it) the effect of the negative correlation that exists between a stock and its volatility, a fact that can be very relevant. The correlation between stocks and their volatilities is actually negative, and it tends to become more negative when during crises prices go down while volatilities go up. One such crisis event is likely to have an effect on the importance that market operators give to the way their models represent this correlation.[3]

One final comment is that, while Hull and Suo (2002) compellingly describe the differences between LVM and SVM, they do not investigate if these give the boundaries to the possible or reasonable values of barrier options. In the simple Wim Schoutens's example it is quite clear that model A makes an extreme assumption on transition distributions ($X^A(t_2) \perp X^A(t_1)$) while model B makes the opposite assumption ($X^A(t_2) = X^A(t_1)$). How much, or how little, LVM and SVM play a similar role? SVM add one single stochastic factor compared to LVM. One interesting aspect to investigate from this point of view is the effect of jumps in the dynamics of the stock. Insights into these issues are contained in Bergomi (2004), (2005) and (2008).

[3] Speaking with hindsight, something similar to a model change actually happened after Hull and Suo (2001) was written. A few facts led to a decline in the enthusiasm for local volatility models. These facts are associated more with 'new pieces of research' rather than market events. One important piece of research was Hull and Suo (2001) itself (an example of the 'reflexivity' of finance often quoted by George Soros?), and the Hagan et al. (2002) paper on the comparison between local and stochastic volatility models that we report in Chapter 5.

2.9.2 Comparing Short Rate and Market Models in Pricing Interest Rate Bermudan Options

When describing the events that can lead to a change in model consensus we mentioned the profound effect on the market of the paper *'How to throw away a billion dollars'* by Longstaff, Santa-Clara and Schwartz (LSS). What did they point out? To understand what they said, we have to anticipate some concepts about interest rate derivatives and models that have already been mentioned in 1.3.4 and will be explained with greater precision in Chapters 6 and 9.

The basics of interest rate derivatives

A swap is a contract in which two parties exchange two flows of payments, called legs. At every instant T_i in a set of scheduled dates $T_{a+1}, \ldots, T_b$, with $T_i - T_{i-1} = \alpha_i$, the fixed leg pays $\alpha_i K$, while the floating leg pays $\alpha_i L(T_{i-1}, T_i)$, the floating Libor rate introduced in 1.3.4. In that section we introduced a payoff, the FRA, which can be seen as a one-period swap. Conversely, a swap can be seen as a collection of FRAs, and therefore can be priced via replication following the procedure for FRAs. Notice that the problems in this replication seen after the credit crunch were years away when LSS wrote their paper in 2000. We know from (4.5) that each exchange of payments

$$\alpha_i(L(T_{i-1}, T_i) - K)$$

can be priced by replication, finding that its value is

$$P(t, T_{i-1}) - P(t, T_i) - P(t, T_i) K\alpha_i,$$

so that the swap has a value given by the sum of the values of all exchanges of payments,

$$\begin{aligned} Swap_t^{a,b}(K) &= \sum_{i=a+1}^{b} [P(t, T_{i-1}) - P(t, T_i) - P(t, T_i) K\alpha_i] \\ &= P(t, T_a) - P(t, T_b) - \sum_{i=a+1}^{b} P(t, T_i)\alpha_i K. \end{aligned}$$

The level of the fixed rate K that makes the above swap have zero value at t is called swap rate $S_{a,b}(t)$, so we have

$$S_{a,b}(t) = \frac{P(t, T_a) - P(t, T_b)}{\sum_{i=a+1}^{b} P(t, T_i)\alpha_i} \tag{2.23}$$

Having defined this rate, the price of a swap with any fixed rate K can be written as

$$Swap_t^{a,b}(K) = \sum_{i=a+1}^{b} P(t, T_i)\alpha_i(S_{a,b}(t) - K).$$

A swaption is an option, with maturity T_a which is the fixing of $L(T_a, T_{a+1})$, giving the right to enter the above swap. Swaptions will be examined in considerable detail in Chapter 6. A Bermudan swaption, instead, is an option giving the right to enter at strike K, at any time T_{ex} in $T_a, \ldots, T_{b-1}$, into the swap starting at the moment T_{ex} of exercise and finishing at T_b, a swap with value

$$Swap_{T_{ex}}^{ex,b}(K) = \sum_{i=ex+1}^{b} P(T_{ex}, T_i)\alpha_i(S_{ex,b}(T_{ex}) - K). \tag{2.24}$$

Bermudan swaptions will be addressed again in Chapter 9 with numerical examples.

The basics of interest rate modelling

Different approaches to the modelling of interest rate derivatives have been proposed since the 1970s. The original approach exploited a clever idea. All rates are defined in terms of bonds. All bonds are defined in terms of the short rate we saw in Section 1.2.1. In fact, if we consider the fundamental equation (1.1) for the pricing of all securities,

$$\Pi_t = \mathbb{E}_t^Q \left[D(t,T)X_T\right]$$

we notice that the bond is the simplest security of all: it has $X_T = 1$, so

$$P(t,T) = \mathbb{E}_t^Q[D(t,T)]. \tag{2.25}$$

It is nothing other than the expectation of a function of the short rate, the discount factor

$$D(t,T) = e^{-\int_t^T r(s)ds}.$$

If rates were assumed to be deterministic, these two quantities $P(t,T)$ and $D(t,T)$ would even coincide, but clearly interest rates must be assumed stochastic in interest rate modelling, where the goal is pricing interest rate derivatives, whose value driver is interest rate risk.

First Vasicek (1977) showed how if we give a no-arbitrage dynamics to the short rate $r(t)$ under the pricing measure, and we provide an easy way to compute the expectation (2.25) at any time s, then we can price, at least by numerical methods, any interest rate derivative. Vasicek proposes the dynamics

$$dr_t = k(\theta - r_t)dt + \sigma dW_t, \tag{2.26}$$

that allows an easy formula for the bond price at any time s as

$$P(s,T) = \Psi^V(s,T,r_s,\theta,k,\sigma),$$

a formula that can be found, for example, in Brigo and Mercurio (2006). How can we price at time 0 any derivative paying some interest rates at some future time s? It is sufficient to generate with the model, on the different scenarios of a Monte Carlo, or at the different nodes of a binomial tree, the value $r(s)$, and from this to compute the value of all the bonds $P(s,T)$ which are required in order to know the value of the interest rates that appear in the payoff.

A totally different approach, that developed almost twenty years later, is the approach of the Libor and Swap Market Models (LMM and SMM) introduced by Brace et al. (1997) and Jamshidian (1997). There the modelling variables are directly real world rates, Libor rates in the LMM and swap rates in the SMM. There are technical reasons for this long delay, as we shall see in 6.2.2 where the LMM is explained in detail.

Here instead we give a rough intuition of the SMM, that makes it easier for us to give a sketchy view of the debate that opened in the market about the pricing of Bermudans. The idea of SMM is direct modelling of the swap rates underlying our Bermudan

$$
\begin{aligned}
dS_{a,b}(t) &= \mu_a(t)dt + \sigma_a(t)dW_i(t), \\
dS_{a+1,b}(t) &= \mu_{a+1}(t)dt + \sigma_{a+1}(t)dW_{a+1}(t), \\
&\vdots \\
dS_{b-1,b}(t) &= \mu_{b-1}(t)dt + \sigma_{b-1}(t)dW_{b-1}(t).
\end{aligned}
\tag{2.27}
$$

The drifts are determined simply by the probability measure, as explained in Chapter 6. Thus the free parameters, to be fixed in calibration or by judgement, are the volatilities functions σ_i and the *correlations* ρ_{ij} between the different *factors* dW_i. In this model it is trivial to price the Bermudan because the modelling variables coincide with the swap rates underlying the Bermudan, and from simulated rates we can also 'bootstrap' bond prices and have all to compute the Bermudan payoff. The computational methods used can for example be the Least Squares Monte Carlo for early-exercise products introduced in Longstaff and Schwartz (2001).

The analysis by Longstaff, Santa-Clara and Schwartz

LSS analyze the pricing of Bermudan swaptions. To use our terminology, they want to understand the crucial risk or element that makes a Bermudan swaption different from a standard swaption. They conclude that a crucial element are the correlations among the values of the different swaps (2.24) you can enter into by choosing the exercise date among $T_a, T_{a+1}, \ldots, T_{b-1}$:

$$Swap^{a,b}_{T_a}(K), Swap^{a+1,b}_{T_{a+1}}(K), \ldots, Swap^{b-1,b}_{T_{b-1}}(K), \tag{2.28}$$

which are the payoffs we can choose from. To understand this intuitively, imagine you are pricing the Bermudan in Monte Carlo simulation. If correlation among the payoffs was very high, say 1, then in all scenarios where the first payoff $Swap^{a,b}_{T_a}(K)$ is high, also the others tend to be high. Equally, in a scenario where the first one has little value, the others will be similar. We do not attach so much value to the fact of having the right to choose in the future: it is almost the same to us to be given the most valuable of all European swaptions written on the above swaps, an option that can be selected even at time zero.

But now consider that the correlation is much lower, maybe even negative between the first and the last swaps. When you see that in a scenario the first swap has little value, the last ones will probably be very valuable and you will exercise towards the end. If in that scenario, on the other hand, the first swap is very valuable, you will probably exercise soon because the last ones are likely to have little value. Now having a Bermudan rather than a European swaption is a great difference, and you will give the Bermudan a value higher than the European because it allows you to make money in many more scenarios, maybe even in all of them.

The analysis of LSS is much more elaborate, with a different string model and a large number of numerical results, but we simplify that drastically and go to the final consequences. We will return to this topic in Chapter 9. In a multifactor model like (2.27) you can choose the correlation matrix ρ_{ij} to control the correlation between the stochastic drivers of the underlying rates. This correlation will certainly be lower than 1 if you want to be consistent with market reality. *Can you do the same in a model like Vasicek?* The answer is: certainly not. In Vasicek *we have one single factor*, so the equivalent of ρ_{ij} for Vasicek is certainly a matrix full of 1s, and only 1s. All rates have perfect instantaneous correlation. This is certainly a dramatic element of unrealism of the model, since the real world is definitely driven by more than one factor. This has an effect not only on pricing, but also on the dynamic exercise choices that the investor will make in the future, driven by a one-factor model inconsistent with reality. In particular, and this is an interesting point to make in a chapter that deals with model comparison, LSS point out that the correct way to compare different models in terms of exercise strategy is to apply the different models, for example Vasicek and LMM, to a 'common set of paths of the term structure'. For LSS these common paths are all generated according to their view that reality has more than one factor, a view with which it is difficult to disagree.

Unfortunately, at that time most market players used one-factor models somehow similar to Vasicek. This is the billion dollar thrown away mentioned in the title: to use their words *'single factor models imply myopic exercise strategies since they assume perfectly correlated interest rates'*.

The analysis by Andersen and Andreasen

It is not surprising that such an analysis had a profound influence on the market, representing, according to Rebonato (2003), one of the main drivers of the shift from models similar to (2.26) towards models similar to (2.27). So you may be surprised to learn that there was a convincing counterargument to LSS put forward by Andersen and Andreasen (2001). Since I have simplified dramatically the arguments of LSS, I will also simplify dramatically the analysis by AA, to allow the reader to grasp a few fundamental points of the debate even at this early stage. The topic will be dealt with in more detail in Chapter 9.

One crucial remark in relation to the analysis by LSS is that the value of a Bermudan actually depends on correlations, but not so much on the correlation ρ_{ij} seen after (2.27). Those are *instantaneous correlations*, namely correlations between instantaneous changes of interest rates, roughly

$$\rho_{ij} \approx correlation\left(dS_{i,b}(t), dS_{j,b}(t)\right).$$

These *instantaneous correlations* are actually 1 in one-factor models, but what matters for pricing the Bermudans is the correlation between the swaps we can enter into when we exercise, each one evaluated at its own exercise time, as in 2.28. Therefore we should care less about the instantaneous correlations of swap rates, than about their *serial correlations*, namely

$$correlation\left(S_{i,b}(T_i), S_{j,b}(T_j)\right), \quad T_i < T_j.$$

Extrapolating from Rebonato (1998), these correlations can be very roughly approximated by

$$R_{i,j} = \frac{\int_0^{T_i} \sigma_i(t)\sigma_j(t)\rho_{i,j}\, dt}{\sqrt{\int_0^{T_i} \sigma_i^2(t)\, dt}\sqrt{\int_0^{T_j} \sigma_j^2(t)\, dt}},$$

which also depends on the dynamics of the volatilities of rates and on when the different rates expire.

These correlations need not be 1 in a one-factor model, particularly if we consider one-factor models more advanced than Vasicek. A more general one factor model may be just a collapse of (2.27), like

$$\begin{aligned}
dS_{a,b}(t) &= \mu_a(t)dt + \sigma_a dW(t),\\
dS_{a+1,b}(t) &= \mu_{a+1}(t)dt + \sigma_{a+1} dW(t),\\
&\vdots\\
dS_{b-1,b}(t) &= \mu_{b-1}(t)dt + \sigma_{b-1} dW(t),
\end{aligned}$$

where, if we avoid by model choice, or neglect the dynamics of the usually little drifts, we are still in a one-factor model thanks to choosing one single $W(t)$ and flat volatilities $\sigma_i(t) = \sigma_i$: the entire term structure can still be seen as a function of the one factor $W(t)$. In this model we have

$$\begin{aligned}
R_{i,j} &= \frac{\int_0^{T_i} \sigma_i \sigma_j 1\, dt}{\sqrt{\int_0^{T_i} \sigma_i^2\, dt}\sqrt{\int_0^{T_j} \sigma_j^2\, dt}}\\
&= \frac{T_i \sigma_i \sigma_j}{\sigma_i \sqrt{T_i}\sigma_j\sqrt{T_j}} = \frac{\sqrt{T_i}}{\sqrt{T_j}},
\end{aligned}$$

which is lower than perfect correlation 1. This $R_{i,j}$ is a rigid quantity over which we have no control, but there is a further element of realism that we can introduce, gaining control of $R_{i,j}$ while remaining in a one factor model: it is the introduction of time-dependent volatility in the following way

$$\begin{aligned}
dS_{a,b}(t) &= \mu_a dt(t) + \sigma_a v(t) dW(t),\\
dS_{a+1,b}(t) &= \mu_{a+1} dt + \sigma_{a+1} v(t) dW(t),\\
&\vdots\\
dS_{b-1,b}(t) &= \mu_{b-1} dt + \sigma_{b-1} v(t) dW(t),
\end{aligned} \tag{2.29}$$

where $v(t)$ is a time-dependent deterministic function *common to all rates*. Thus the term structure remains essentially driven by a factor $\hat{W}(t) = \int_0^t v(t)dW(t)$, but now the serial correlation is

$$\begin{aligned}
R_{i,j} &= \frac{\int_0^{T_i} \sigma_i \sigma_j v^2(t)\, dt}{\sqrt{\int_0^{T_i} v^2(t)\sigma_i^2\, dt}\sqrt{\int_0^{T_j} v^2(t)\sigma_j^2\, dt}}\\
&= \frac{\sqrt{\int_0^{T_i} v^2(t)\, dt}}{\sqrt{\int_0^{T_j} v^2(t)\, dt}}
\end{aligned}$$

which can actually be controlled by $v(t)$, and if $v(t)$ is chosen increasing it can be made more strongly lower than 1. By the way, and this is something we will see in Chapter 9, for example in (9.7), if one observes the historical behaviour of interest rates or simply performs a reasoned calibration to interest rate derivatives, one will see that the time-dependent part of interest rate volatility is dominated by an increasing behaviour: the more rates get close to their fixing, the more they are influenced by fast-changing short term expectations, becoming more volatile (with the partial exception of the 'hump' that we will describe later).

This shows that even in one-factor models there is more flexibility in pricing Bermudans than appears from the LSS analysis. This increasing flexibility is driven by the possibility of time-dependency of volatility that has a twofold effect on Bermudans: one indirect effect through the serial correlations we saw here, and one more direct through changing the volatilities of the underlying swaptions, as we will see in Chapter 9.

Thus, this example is somewhat different from the previous ones: here we have seen two modelling approaches that seem very different in the pricing of Bermudan products, and yet the simpler approach can obtain results very similar to those of the superior one by means of an adjustment that often makes the model better calibrated to the reference liquid markets as well.

This does not apply to one-factor models as simple as Vasicek (2.26), which in fact have very limited calibration power, but it can apply to models more similar to (2.29). While (2.29) is only a sketchy example, the Hull and White (1990) and (1994) models may be considered models of this kind and, even more so, those that derive from the Heath, Jarrow and Morton (1992) framework, such as Cheyette (1996).

The link between time-dependency of volatilities, calibration and the prices of early exercise derivatives will be examined in more detail in Chapter 9, where we offer some additional considerations about the other effects of time-dependent/time homogeneous parameters and the similar effects that can be created by sufficient mean-reversion of stochastic volatility. However, even the simple example given here is crucial for understanding one important feature of interest rate modelling: the fact that different rates have *different maturities*. This will be important in the detailed treatment of interest rate modelling in the second part of the book. Additionally, we have introduced the topic of interest rate correlations, that will be taken up again also in Chapter 8.

3

Stress Testing and the Mistakes of the Crisis

3.1 LEARNING STRESS TEST FROM THE CRISIS

This chapter can be read in two ways. First, it is a detailed account of three relevant problems in the practical use of the Gaussian copula, the market model for CDOs and credit derivatives that many have blamed as one of the reasons for the financial crisis. Do not be misled by the title of this chapter: as pointed out in the Preface, I do not believe that models were the main culprit behind the crisis. The main culprits can be found in some risky investment decisions that were favoured by politicians, permitted by regulators and, finally, taken by top managers of banks and other financial institutions. These decisions were based not on models, but on some noble political purposes like the desire to allow everyone to buy a house, and on less noble desires to exploit shortsighted regulations (see 1.2.1) and to adopt strategies that were dangerous for the financial system but could turn out highly lucrative for some institutions and individuals (see Remark 4).

Models had their role, however. They helped in taking the above investment decisions, as we saw in Section 1.1.3. In fact, they gave a very reassuring picture of the risks involved, helping to get on board many investors who otherwise would have not found such investments convenient. Also, models were crucial in industrializing the credit derivatives market, allowing that expansion of the exposure that was one element that led to the crisis.

Models were very efficient tools for expanding and sustaining the situation that in the end turned into the crisis. Thus now it is useful to understand which were the weaknesses, at times in the models themselves, at times in the way they were used, that made these models more useful to hide real risks than to reveal them.

This chapter gives an account of the weaknesses that I consider most crucial with respect to the Gaussian copula for default correlation. This model is here dissected and revised. We explain the model and its extension, we show where it could still be used, although with a different approach to correlations (ironically, this is CDO), and where it must be avoided at all costs (unfortunately, this is where the model is still used even by its critics). To highlight its weaknesses, I use practical examples. Then I indicate solutions for these weaknesses, which means that for all examples of a model that does not work in a given stress test, I also present a modelling solution that does work. This is crucial because without an example of what the desired model behaviour should be, it is difficult to detect model weaknesses, and also because comparison with a working solution allows for a precise assessment of the model risk associated with a model weakness.

One might wonder: if the errors pinpointed above had been avoided, would we have avoided the crisis? No. The real issue is: if the market sentiment had been such to analyze and stress the model thoroughly, we would probably not have met with the crisis. Maybe other weaknesses would have been pointed out and other solutions would have been found. But certainly there would have been an awareness of our modelling tools that was lacking dramatically before the crisis. In Section 1.5.3 we said that the Gaussian copula contributed to the crisis not so much because of its weaknesses, but because there was so little understanding of them. We can rephrase the same concept by saying that the worrying fact is not how bad the model was, but how little it was stress-tested considering the importance it had in the market.

Research was not lacking, as pointed out correctly by some books such as Brigo et al. (2010) written after the crisis. But if you look at the original versions of the papers that were written before the crisis on alternatives to Gaussian copula, you will see that most of the alternative modelling solutions proposed were presented just as more precise and complex interpolators, to use the limited liquid reference information for more elaborate payoffs. This was hardly what was needed. We needed tools for stressing the underlying market and our understanding of it, but this focus was replaced by a lot of attention to mathematical or numerical details. One consequence of this is that mathematical research never had a real impact on the modelling tools used by market operators. Probably, an analysis of the fundamental weaknesses of the modelling tools used, coupled with some simple solutions to address them, would have been more useful. We try to do this in this chapter, clearly too late for the past crisis. But we hope to be of some help for quants, analysts or traders who in the future, when similar problems surface again, would like to deal with them differently.

On the other hand, and more importantly, this chapter is devoted to stress testing. In fact in what follows we expose the weaknesses of the Gaussian copula simply by submitting the model to stress tests. The market cases are used as a playground to explain and exemplify stress testing, and to help reasoning on stress test design and the pitfalls to avoid.

We are going to look at different types of stress tests, with different purposes. But one feature is always present: we apply the model to some conditions that are extreme or in any case are different from our standard application, and we see if any problems arise. There are three problems that can actually arise, each one revealing a specific form of model risk:

1. We can discover that, with the model under analysis, it is not even possible to represent in a consistent way the stressed conditions we would like to test.
2. We can represent these conditions, but under them the model changes its behaviour and gives results that appear unreasonable or meaningless.
3. We can represent these conditions, but under them we cannot even judge the reasonableness of the results because they are not correct from a mathematical point of view.

The different kinds of stress test we consider depend on which of the above three problems we are interested in.

3.1.1 The Meaning of Stress Testing

Stress testing has recently become a buzz-word in the financial world, at times presented as a solution to every problem in the financial system. Like all words that appear to have so general a meaning, there is the risk that it means nothing. It becomes crucially important to understand which meaning of this word is relevant to model risk management and validation. There are at least three different meanings that are relevant for us.

PST *Portfolio stress testing*. Stress testing has been much used with reference to the assessments of the solidity of large banks performed by the FED in the US in 2009 and by the ECB and other European institutions in 2010 on European banks. From this perspective stress testing means assessing how a business would perform in an adverse financial scenario, in terms of predicted losses compared with capital and liquidity resources. This meaning can be applied also to a derivative or a portfolio: what would their value be if an unlikely but not impossible pessimistic scenario had to come true? It is considered a tool that complements VAR for Market Risk computations, and may appear to have nothing to do with the validation of valuation models.

MST *Model stress testing*. Under this second meaning, stress testing means subjecting the model's inputs to extreme values for understanding when a model breaks down. This is clearly relevant to model validation. However, it is not easy to say when a model has broken down. There are at least two possible scenarios:

- If the model is implemented using a non-exact computational method, for example an approximation, this approximation may become imprecise under particular conditions and clearly this may generate unexpected losses. This is the sort of model stress testing on which research focused in the past decade.
- But if the model is based on a solution that remains correct even under stress-conditions, are we sure that the model has not broken down? It may be that, in spite of mathematical integrity, under some conditions the model experiences a discontinuity and starts giving answers which contradict logic and experience. Should we say also in this case that the model has broken down?

In my opinion, both PST and MST are relevant to model risk management. PST is explicitly mentioned in the regulators' recommendation about the use of models seen in *1.4*, where they say that banks should *'assess the impact of variations in model parameters on fair value, including under stress conditions'*. MST plays an even more direct role in model risk management, and it is also mentioned by regulators when they say *'A bank is expected to test and review the performance of its valuation models under possible stress conditions, so that it understands the limitations of the models'*. I also add that both meanings of MST, one for mathematical integrity and one for financial reasonableness under different scenarios, are crucial to a quant, a trader or a validator.

3.1.2 Portfolio Stress Testing

One may well wonder how PST can be related to valuation models. Two crucial papers on PST are Berkowitz (1999) and Aragones et al. (2001). Aragones et al. define stress testing as exercises to determine the losses that might occur under unlikely but plausible circumstances, and it requires creating a scenario *'to be fed into a calculation engine'* to produce estimates of the losses (or profits) under the scenario. Berkowitz (1999) attempts a formal definition of stress testing and includes in its requirements *'a set of pricing rules $P(\cdot)$ that predict asset values as a function of the underlying factors. For example, we might price options using Black-Scholes. We will call this collection of pricing rules a valuation model'* This should make clear that any computation of the value of the portfolio under any scenario needs a valuation model. The risk manager may design a scenario using personal judgement or some statistical model. The scenario, however, provides no value for complex securities, one needs to translate the scenario into model inputs or parameters and then use the model to evaluate the portfolio.

Some works such as the aforementioned Berkowitz (1999) and Aragones et al. (2001), and more recently Rebonato (2010), have pointed out that stress testing becomes useless if the scenarios used are not associated with an estimate of their probability or likelihood. We do not enter into the debate. The aspect which is of interest to us is that, once a scenario has been devised and given a probability, we need to be able to translate it into parameters for the model.

The example we consider is stressing a credit portfolio including CDOs. The qualitative expression of the scenario may be: 'a systemic crisis that triggers an increase in default correlation'. Now we have to estimate the loss on our CDO portfolio, and the question becomes: what do you mean *precisely* by increase of *default correlation*?

Default correlation is not a single observable object in the market or in any model. For example, the Gaussian copula admits either a correlation matrix or, if this matrix is collapsed to a single number as in the market quotation system, a single number which is anyway changed for each tranche to fit each point of the correlation skew.

Fair enough, your scenario designer might think; then let's say that all points of the correlation skew will increase by 10%. Now the question becomes: are you sure this is really what you mean? Did you consider that equity tranches become less risky when you reduce correlation, while senior tranches become more risky? Did you consider that different tranches also have different sizes in their sensitivity to correlation, so that such an increase can be very great for a tranche and much less for another one? Do you know that not all possible configurations of the correlation skew are meaningful, and that some can have internal inconsistencies?

The first problem is that a model that fits a skew by changing its parameter for each different strike, like the Gaussian copula as used in the market, is very difficult to use when the goal is to translate a financial scenario into model parameters. This is unpleasant. If stress testing needs to be an important component of risk management, and be used to decide economic capital and to take business decisions, *a model must also be suitable for stress testing*. The impossibility of stress testing a portfolio to understand its value in a crisis, due to a pricing model that does not allow you to express the scenario correctly, is one important element of model risk. But there is more. We outlined previously that understanding the model is crucial to model risk management. A model that we are not able to use to represent a stress scenario is a model that is difficult to understand. Such models carry a high model risk.

A first improvement would be to eliminate the need to change the parameter set when pricing a different tranche. There are many models much more complex than the Gaussian copula that can fit consistently the tranche market. But none of these models impacted market practice. Thus in the practical example of Section 3.3 we remain in a Gaussian copula, but we give it a more reasonable correlation matrix. The surprise is that this allows an approximate but consistent fit to the correlation skew, and gives results that can be interpreted and can give insight into what happened during the credit crunch. In such an approach stress testing becomes feasible.

Fit, fat, stress

We have just introduced one more dimension for judging a model: the capability to express stressed scenarios. The literature of the first decade of the 21st century focuses much more on the capability to *calibrate or fit* a reference derivative market. This amounts to focusing on the first moment or expectation of the distribution of the underlying financial variable. This first moment is what we usually call price. This has little to do with stress testing. For stress testing we may prefer a model less precise but easy to subject to various financial scenarios.

After fitting, the second major requirement made of models by the literature of the past decade are *fat tails*. There is a branch of financial mathematics, called extreme value theory, that deals with this. Again, stress testing has little to do with fat tails, since even the tails of the distribution are computed using the model calibrated to today's data. In stress testing instead we alter this calibration, so we can force even a model which may not have very fat tails to express extreme scenarios. This seems to be the modern view in risk management: not so much the requirement to have models that are terribly precise in fitting today's market (this is crucial for the trader who has to perform hedging and mark-to-market, but not so important for model risk management), not to have models that are terribly realistic in representing the tails of the distribution of the risk factors (crucial essentially for market risk assessed with VAR), but a model with features that allow easier *stress testing*.

Incidentally, the example we show in Section 3.3 covers in a simple manner the three above aspects: if we parameterize the Gaussian copula correlation so as to fit consistently (albeit less precisely than the inconsistent copula with tranche-dependent correlations) the market skew, we get both fat tails and a framework for stress testing.

Pitfalls in stress testing

The second example of the weaknesses of the Gaussian copula, shown in Section 3.4, is the one which I find, in hindsight, the most shocking. We will see that with a Gaussian copula it is impossible to control in an easy and intuitive way the probability that at a future point there will be joint losses concentrated in a short period of time. When we increase the correlation among losses, in fact, the probability of joint losses may increase or decrease, depending on the features of the period of time we consider, and on the characteristics of the names in the portfolio. This is true even if we consider only two names, reducing correlation to a single parameter. This means that the relationship between the only parameter and the risk of concentrated losses is very unstable. At times it is not even monotonic, requiring numerical tests to see *which value of the parameter really maximizes the risk of concentrated losses*. Considering that the crisis was triggered by a sudden surge in the fear of losses concentrated in a short period of time, the market choice about the model to use for pricing and risk management of CDOs appears particularly unfortunate.

This example is also for understanding the pitfalls we may encounter in portfolio stress testing. In such a situation it will be extremely difficult to understand *which value of the parameter represents a real stress test*. Expressing a financial scenario through a quantitative model is a very delicate task, since models are difficult to understand when applied in domains which are not fully standard (in this example the non-standard application is, as you will see, the fact of considering future intervals of time). Our intuition can fail us and models can exhibit misleading behaviour, leading us to consider apparent worst-case scenarios that are actually best-case scenarios.

The above problem can render the model misleading in many practical cases. We show three of them: the computation of the probability of concentrated losses like those fear of which ignited the subprime crisis, the computation of dynamic credit VAR and the pricing of CDS counterparty risk.

Thus we see two features that a model must have to allow reasonable stress testing of our financial portfolios (PST). The model must be able to explain the market at least approximately with a single consistent set of parameters that have a financial meaning. The first example shows that the Gaussian copula applied to CDOs did not have this feature. Additionally, we have to avoid models where the relation between parameters and the risk factor is so unstable as to mislead us in stress testing. The second example shows that the Gaussian copula applied to default losses in future periods is affected also by this problem.

3.1.3 Model Stress Testing

Now let us look at the other meaning of stress testing, the one of most direct interest to us: stress testing models to find their hidden weaknesses. The first case we consider is a natural consequence of the above tests on the estimation of losses concentrated in time.

Testing different payoffs and markets

We will see in Section 3.4 that the problems of the Gaussian copula with the estimation of losses concentrated in time can be associated with the fact that the model admits some very unrealistic representations of reality. For example, for maximum correlation the model implies that the default of a company causes with certainty the default of another one, but the default of this second company is predicted to happen many years later, even decades later in some cases. This is an unrealistic feature, for whatever application of the copula. However, for a period of time starting now, or when the spreads of the different companies in a portfolio are very similar, this feature does not affect the value of the tranche so much: it does not dramatically reduce the range of possible values that the model can give.

For an evaluation in a future period of time, and for heterogeneous spreads, this unrealistic feature becomes instead dramatically relevant, leading to nonsensical results. This is a typical example of model stress testing in the second sense: detecting the situations, in terms of market configuration (the level of the spreads) or in terms of payoff features (the possibility that the period where losses are estimated is forward-start), where we have implausible and bizarre consequences from the same model assumptions that were considered reasonable in more basic situations.

Scenario design

The third weakness of the Gaussian copula that we identify does not really relate to the assumptions underlying the model. It has to do rather with one particular use of the Gaussian copula that became popular in the years immediately preceding the crisis. It is called Mapping and it is a method based on rather obscure mathematical motivations (which are exposed in a few papers by big investment banks, including Lehman) that, using the Gaussian copula as a formal tool, gives the correlations for pricing *bespoke* CDOs. These are CDOs written on portfolios which do not correspond to any quoted index. Thus mapping is a method for finding the inputs to put in the Gaussian copula when we have to price CDOs on illiquid portfolios.

The results of the tests I present, rather negative standard Mapping methods, may appear less shocking than the above results, since the Mapping methods aroused considerable perplexity even before the credit crunch. But here we do something that was not done before:

1. We test them in cases where we know what answer they should give if they were correct.
2. We show that instead there are mathematical and financial reasons for why the *standard mapping methods are bound to underestimate regularly the risk of bespoke CDOs.*
3. We show that it is possible to design equally simple methods that give approximately the right answer in the case of 1.

If we consider that, in spite of the perplexities of quants, mapping methods were used industrially, fuelling the final growth of the CDO market, and that the big losses in the crisis came when financial institutions were forced to admit that bespoke CDOs had higher risk than previously assessed, the results are not only astonishing, but really disturbing. More seriously, standard mapping methods are still used today for lack of viable alternatives.

The mapping methods move from copula parameters of liquid CDOs to copula parameters of illiquid CDOs. By definition, we do not have liquid quotes to assess their fitting capability or to perform a backtest on their validity.

Therefore, here we have to devise another, more elaborate type, of model stress test. We cannot simply move the start date forward, or move the spreads away from a common value or increase the correlation. Instead, we design different financial scenarios and apply mapping methods to them, to see if in all of these scenarios the model has a reasonable behaviour.

How do we construct these scenarios, and how could we know which behaviour was reasonable? We take the scenarios from relevant events that really happened in the past, but we use them in a way very different from backtesting. In fact, you will see that we have to carry out a 'rotation' from the time axis to the 'space axis', or the axis of different portfolios. You will also see that this cannot guarantee that methods are right, but, as a stress test should do, it can tell us if they have problems: in fact, it detects that standard mapping methods *cannot capture* a relation that we have observed historically. Having taken this from the stress test, we will be able to confirm it by mathematical analysis.

Stress testing computational methods

Finally, there is another kind of model stress test. We may be perfectly happy with the model assumptions that are considered realistic or in any case acceptable under any conditions. Still, we may make mistakes and suffer losses because we use some non-exact computational methods to translate its assumptions into numbers, and these methods can become imprecise or biased under some conditions, so that the results we get are not consistent with model assumptions.

So it makes sense to stress a model by testing, under different and extreme conditions, the behaviour of the computational methods that we use in implementation. The typical example is a model based on an approximation. For example, in the basic Libor Market Model the Libor rates are lognormal but a swap rate is not, therefore a swaption cannot be priced with a Black formula that assumes lognormality of the swap rates. However, for low volatilities and high correlations of the Libor rates the swap rate is approximately lognormal and we can price swaptions with a Black formula approximation. Here the stress test involves assessing for which levels of volatility (and correlations) the approximation remains sufficiently precise, and when instead this precision is lost. Notice that here no one is contesting the initial assumption that the Libor rates are lognormal. This is assumed to be true; and yet we have to assess whether our approximations yield results consistent with this assumption in all scenarios.

This sort of stress testing received much more attention in the past than the other kinds of stress testing we described above. I think that now we should adopt a more balanced approach where the stress testing of computational methods goes back to being only one of the passages of a validation method, and not the main or even the only one. In spite of this, it should remain an important part of stress testing because having a right model but using numbers which do not really come from that model can generate all sorts of unpredictable model risk. Due to the mathematical complexity of the issue, and to the large literature available on the topic, we devote a separate chapter to it, Chapter 6.

3.2 THE CREDIT MARKET AND THE 'FORMULA THAT KILLED WALL STREET'

3.2.1 The CDO Payoff

In Section 1.1.3 we described a CDO. Here we give more analytic details. The total loss in a portfolio of n loans or bonds, each one with notional N^i and recovery R^i is

$$L(t) = \sum_{i=1}^{n} 1_{\{\tau_i < t\}} \left(1 - R^i\right) N^i . \tag{3.1}$$

In CDO the protection seller pays the cumulated *tranched* loss of portfolio. If one buys protection on the tranche with attachment point A (the minimum level of losses to which the tranche is exposed) and detachment B (the maximum exposure), he only receives the part of the loss that exceeds A and does not exceed B, namely

$$Loss_{A,B}(t) = \begin{cases} 0 & \text{if} \quad L(t) < A \\ L(t) - A & \text{if} \quad A < L(t) \le B \, . \\ B - A & \text{if} \quad L(t) > B \end{cases}$$

Liquid markets have always existed only for tranches written on the portfolios of companies composing the main CDS indices. For Europe, the most important CDS index is the DJ-iTraxx Europe benchmark, which includes the 125 top European names in terms of CDS volumes. The tranches of the quoted CDO written on this index are:

$$\boxed{[0\% - 3\%]}\boxed{[3\% - 6\%]}\boxed{[6\% - 9\%]}\boxed{[9\% - 12\%]}\boxed{[12\% - 22\%]}. \tag{3.2}$$

If we expressed $Loss_{A,B}(t)$ relative to the size of the tranche, $B - A$, we have the percentage tranched loss

$$L_{A,B}(t) = \frac{Loss_{A,B}(t)}{B - A}, \tag{3.3}$$

which is the variable we use below to give the formulas for CDO pricing. This quantity can be written as a combination of options

$$\begin{aligned} L_{A,B}(t) &= \frac{1}{B-A}\left[(L(t) - A)1_{\{A<L(t)\le B\}} + (B - A)1_{\{L(t)>B\}}\right] \\ &= \frac{1}{B-A}\left[(L(t) - A)1_{\{A<L(t)\}} - (L(t) - B)1_{\{L(t)>B\}}\right] \\ &= \frac{1}{B-A}\left[(L(t) - A)^+ - (L(t) - B)^+\right]. \end{aligned}$$

In Section 1.1.3 we explained that a tranche $[0, X]$, that suffers all losses from the first one until a fraction X of the portfolio notional, is called an equity tranche. The equity tranched loss is defined as

$$L_X(t) = \frac{1}{X}[L(t) - (L(t) - X)^+].$$

Any tranche $[A, B]$ can actually be written as the difference of two equity tranches, since

$$L_{A,B}(t) = \frac{1}{B-A}\left[BL_B(t) - AL_A(t)\right].$$

The cashflows of a CDO starting in T_a (usually the current time) and ending in T_b (usually some years away) are

Protection buyer	$\rightarrow$ premium at $T_{a+1}, \ldots, T_b$ on outstanding notional $\rightarrow$ $\leftarrow$ tranched loss increments $dL_{A,B}(t)$ at defaults $\leftarrow$	Protection seller

The discounted protection leg can be written, for a unit notional, as

$$\int_0^{T_b} P(0,t)dL_{A,B}(t) \approx \sum_{i=1}^{b} P(0,T_i)\left[L_{A,B}(T_i) - L_{A,B}(T_{i-1})\right],$$

where we have assumed that interest rates are deterministic, as is usual in credit modelling.

In exchange, the protection buyer periodically pays a premium rate K on the CDO outstanding notional $1 - L_{A,B}(t)$. The discounted premium leg is

$$K \times \sum_{i=1}^{b} P(0,T_i)\int_{T_{i-1}}^{T_i}\left(1 - L_{A,B}(t)\right)dt \approx K \times \sum_{i=1}^{b} P(0,T_i)\alpha_i\left(1 - L_{A,B}(T_i)\right).$$

The price of a CDO tranche for the protection buyer is

$$\begin{aligned} Tranche^{A,B}(0) = & \sum_{i=1}^{b} P(0,T_i)\mathbb{E}\left[\left[L_{A,B}(T_i) - L_{A,B}(T_{i-1})\right]\right] \\ & -K \times \sum_{i=1}^{b} P(0,T_i)\alpha_i\mathbb{E}\left[\left(1 - L_{A,B}(T_i)\right)\right]. \end{aligned} \tag{3.4}$$

The tranche is quoted by the equilibrium level of K that sets the tranche to have zero value,

$$S_{A,B}(0) = \frac{\sum_{i=1}^{b} P(0,T_i)\left[\mathbb{E}\left[L_{A,B}(T_i)\right] - \mathbb{E}\left[L_{A,B}(T_{i-1})\right]\right]}{\sum_{i=1}^{b} P(0,T_i)\alpha_i\left(1 - \mathbb{E}\left[L_{A,B}(T_i)\right]\right)}.$$

Products similar to CDOs are first and last-to-default. A last-to-default with maturity T is a derivative similar to a CDS, but it references a portfolio of n companies and the protection is paid if all companies in the portfolio default before T, with the payment made at the last default time. If we adopt the simplifying assumption that all names have the same loss-given-default LGD, as is often done in the market, and we define

$$\hat{\tau} = \max(\tau_1, \tau_2, \ldots, \tau_n)$$

to be the last default time, then the protection leg of this derivative provides for the payment of LGD at $\hat{\tau}$ when $\hat{\tau} \leq T$. The risk is similar to a senior CDO tranche, while when we consider a first-to-default, paying at $\min(\tau_1, \tau_2, \ldots, \tau_n)$, we have a risk similar to an equity tranche.

3.2.2 The Copula

The payoff of a CDO depends on the default times τ_i of the names in the portfolio, $i = 1, \ldots, n$. Additionally, since the CDO pays a tranched loss which is an option on the sum of the losses on the individual names, it depends on the interdependency of their default times, as we have shown in the example in Section 1.1.3. How can one express this interdependency?

The market had already adopted the setting of intensity modelling for individual default times in the CDS market, and wanted to extend it to capture also the relations among different default times. In a standard intensity setting the default time τ_i of name i has the following distribution

$$\Pr(\tau_i \leq \tau) = F_{\tau_i}(\tau) = 1 - e^{-\int_0^\tau \lambda_i(s)ds}.$$

We set $\int_0^\tau \lambda_i(s)\, ds = \Lambda_i(\tau) = \varepsilon_i$ and we know from (2.5) that the default times on n names can be written

$$\tau_1 = \Lambda_1^{-1}(\varepsilon_1), \tau_2 = \Lambda_2^{-1}(\varepsilon_2), \ldots, \tau_n = \Lambda_n^{-1}(\varepsilon_n)$$

or, under flat intensity,

$$\tau_1 = \frac{\varepsilon_1}{\lambda_1}, \quad \tau_2 = \frac{\varepsilon_2}{\lambda_2}, \ldots, \tau_n = \frac{\varepsilon_n}{\lambda_n}. \tag{3.5}$$

How can we relate defaults in this context? The stochasticity of τ_i can come from two different sources: very likely stochasticity of ε_i, and possibly stochasticity of Λ_i when we take a stochastic intensity. Thus one sees the following fundamental ways to introduce a dependency between the different default times:

1) Put dependency in stochastic intensities of the different names and keep the ε_i of the different names independent;

2) Put dependency among the ε_i of the different names and keep the intensities (stochastic or deterministic) independent.

Let us see, from Jouanin et al. (2001), how one can apply 1). With stochastic processes for the intensities, we can relate the default times of two names by correlating the intensities

$$\begin{aligned} d\lambda_i(t) &= \mu_i(t, \lambda_i(t))\, dt + \sigma_i(t, \lambda_i(t))\, dW_i(t) \\ d\lambda_j(t) &= \mu_j\left(t, \lambda_j(t)\right) dt + \sigma_j\left(t, \lambda_j(t)\right) dW_j(t) \\ dW_i(t)\, dW_j(t) &= \rho\, dt; \qquad \varepsilon_i \perp \varepsilon_j. \end{aligned}$$

This seems an advantageous choice. The model does not require further implementation compared to single name stochastic intensity implementation. Furthermore the correlation ρ can be guessed by the historical correlations of the spreads, considering the strong link existing between intensities and spreads. Unfortunately, as shown by Jouanin et al. (2001) who use diffusive intensities, this approach fails to create sufficient dependence across $1_{\{\tau_j<t\}}$ and $1_{\{\tau_i<t\}}$, and between τ_i and τ_j. See Figure 3.1. By now we can understand the reason for this result. We have seen in Section 2.5 that in diffusive intensity models there is little link between the dynamics of the intensity and the default time. Correlating the intensities can create a strong link between the dynamics of the intensities but, due to the faint link between each intensity and the corresponding default time, the link between the default times is also weak,

$$\begin{array}{ccc} \lambda_1 & \leftrightarrow & \lambda_2 \\ \not\downarrow & & \not\downarrow \\ \tau_1 & \not\leftrightarrow & \tau_2 \end{array}.$$

Probably by now you can also guess how we could increase the dependence between default times. This can be done through reinforcing the link between intensity movements and default times. This goal was achieved in Section 2.7 by introducing jumps in the dynamics. Here we could put in the dynamics of λ_1, λ_2 the possibility of *common* jumps, such that a jump happens at the same time for λ_1, λ_2. This would create a strong link between the intensities λ_1 and λ_2 and at the same time also a stronger link between λ_i and τ_i, $i = 1, 2$, generating in the end a stronger link[1] between the default times τ_1 and τ_2.

This route was not followed by the market. Practitioners preferred to keep the intensities independent, or even better deterministic, and set dependency among the ε_i. This goal was obtained using the framework of copulas, which is recalled in the Appendix. According to Bouyè et al. (2000), copulas provide 'a way to analyze the dependence structure of multivariate distributions without studying marginal distributions'. The fundamental role of the copula function $C_{X_1,\ldots,X_n}$ for a vector of random variables $X_1, \ldots, X_n$ is to seperate marginal (individual) distributions and the joint distribution according to

$$C_{X_1,\ldots,X_n}(F_{X_1}(x_1), \ldots, F_{X_n}(x_n)) = F_{X_1,\ldots,X_n}(x_1, \ldots, x_n). \tag{3.6}$$

Given the copula, we can put the individual distributions together to find the joint distribution. We will see later on, however, that this mathematical 'seperability' does not always translate into an equivalent financial property.

The market chose, among the infinite possible copulas, the Gaussian one. It is hard to say why this was the choice. Probably the fact that the parameters of this copula were a familiar concept, correlations, played an important role. We will see later that some shortcomings of the Gaussian copula that were immediately pointed out, such as that a Gaussian copula does not feature tail dependency (see Embrechts et al. (2001) for correlation different from 1, were not as important in the crisis as one may expect, while instead the fundamental quality of this copula, the correlation as a parameter, turned out to be more confusing than intuitive. Following (12.4), from the cumulative distribution function Φ_Σ of an n-dimensional joint Gaussian distribution with correlation matrix Σ, we can compute the Gaussian copula

$$C_\Sigma^\Phi(u_1, \ldots, u_n) = \Phi_\Sigma(\Phi^{-1}(u_1), \ldots, \Phi^{-1}(u_n)).$$

This copula cannot be expressed in closed form: In the two-dimensional case we have

$$C_\Sigma^\Phi(u, v) = \int_{-\infty}^{\Phi^{-1}(u)} \int_{-\infty}^{\Phi^{-1}(v)} \frac{1}{2\pi\sqrt{1-\rho^2}} \exp\left\{\frac{s^2 - 2\rho st + t^2}{2\left(1-\rho^2\right)}\right\} ds dt. \tag{3.7}$$

The complexity of this expression did not worry practitioners so much, since this copula is in any case quite simple to simulate, following the scheme below:

Gaussian Copula: Simulation Scheme

1. Choleski/Spectral decomposition of $\Sigma = CC'$
2. Simulate n independent normal random variables $Z = z_1, \ldots, z_n$ from $\mathbb{N}(0, 1)$
3. Set $X = CZ$
4. Set $u_i = \Phi(x_i)$, $i = 1, \ldots, n$
5. $u_1, \ldots, u_n \sim C_\Sigma^\Phi$.

[1] Not an extremely strong one, however.

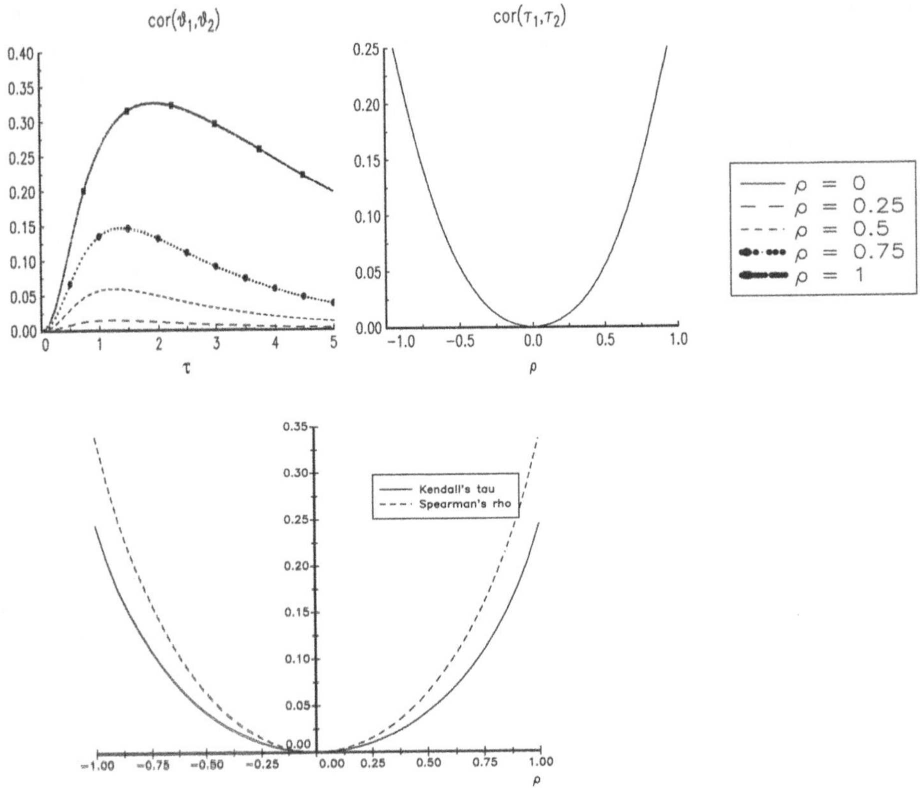

Figure 3.1 From Jouanin et al. (2001). The effect of ρ on default dependency. Notice that they use quadratic intensities and indicate $\vartheta_i = 1_{\{\tau_i < t\}}$. Kendall's tau and Spearman's rho are two indicators of dependency that reveal dependency beyond the linear one captured by correlation

3.2.3 Applying the Copula to CDOs

We look initially at the pricing of a CDO with Monte Carlo. First, calibrate individual intensities $\lambda_i(t)$ to CDS market. Then select the correlation matrix Σ. Consider scenarios $j = 1, 2, \ldots, m$. In each scenario j simulate n uniforms $u_1, \ldots, u_n$ with the above copula scheme and set

$$\tau_i = \Lambda_i^{-1}(-\ln(1-u_i)) = \frac{1}{\lambda_i}(-\ln(1-u_i)).$$

With these default times $\tau_1, \ldots, \tau_n$, we can compute at any time t the Loss, following (3.1), and the Tranched Loss following (3.3). Often for a CDO the focus is on a discrete set of payment dates $T_k = T_1, \ldots, T_M$, so one stores for each scenario

$$L_{A,B}(T_1), \ldots, L_{A,B}(T_M).$$

Averaging across all scenarios, one finds the expected Tranched Loss $\mathbb{E}\left[L_{A,B}(T_k)\right]$, and can price a CDO tranche following (3.4).

The pricing of a CDO with Monte Carlo is easy but can be time-consuming, considering that most CDOs had n equal to some hundreds. Therefore the market looked for methods to express some of the quantities needed to price a CDO in an analytic fashion. Clearly one had to avoid using the definition (3.7) of the Gaussian copula directly, since if $n = 100$ then (3.7) requires a 100-dimensional numerical integration, much heavier than any Monte Carlo.

One trick that allows to make the copula much more tractable is to assume a *one-factor correlation structure*. Define an n-dimensional distribution as follows

$$X_i = \rho_i M + \sqrt{1-\rho_i^2}Y_i \quad i = 1, \ldots, n \tag{3.8}$$

where Y_i, M are standard independent Gaussian. It is trivial to see that the distribution of X_i is Gaussian with $\mathbb{E}[X_i] = 0$ and $VAR[X_i] = P_i^2 + 1 - P_i^2 = 1$. Each X_i is a standardized Gaussian and the vector $X = [X_1, X_2, \ldots, X_n]$ is a multivariate Gaussian from which we can derive a copula. Notice that it has a peculiar correlation structure

$$Corr\left(X_i X_j\right) = \rho_i \rho_j. \tag{3.9}$$

We indicate the distribution of X as

$$\Pr(X_1 \leq x_1, \ldots, X_n \leq x_n) =: \Phi_{X_1,\ldots,X_n}(x_1, \ldots, x_n).$$

The copula is

$$C_{X_1,\ldots,X_n}(u_1, \ldots, u_n) = \Phi_{X_1,\ldots,X_n}(\Phi^{-1}(u_1), \ldots, \Phi^{-1}(u_n)).$$

How can we write this probability in the closest possible form? We can use the law of iterated expectations. Recalling that Pr(A), where A is an event, can be written as $\mathbb{E}[1_A]$, we have

$$\begin{aligned} C_{X_1,\ldots,X_n} &= \Pr\left(X_1 \leq \Phi^{-1}(u_1), \ldots, X_n \leq \Phi^{-1}(u_n)\right) \\ &= \mathbb{E}\left[\Pr\left(X_1 \leq \Phi^{-1}(u_1), \ldots, X_n \leq \Phi^{-1}(u_n)|M\right)\right]. \end{aligned}$$

One can check in (3.8) that *conditionally on M* (equivalent to saying: *for a given M*) the X_i are independent, thus

$$C_{X_1,\ldots,X_n} = \mathbb{E}\left[\prod_{i=1}^{n}\Pr\left(X_i \leq \Phi^{-1}(u_i)|M\right)\right]$$

where

$$\begin{aligned} \Pr\left(X_i \leq \Phi^{-1}(u_i)|M\right) &= \Pr\left(\rho_i M + \sqrt{1-\rho_i^2}Y_i \leq \Phi^{-1}(u_i)\right) \\ &= \Pr\left(Y_i \leq \frac{\Phi^{-1}(u_i) - \rho_i M}{\sqrt{1-\rho_i^2}}\right) = \Phi\left(\frac{\Phi^{-1}(u_i) - \rho_i M}{\sqrt{1-\rho_i^2}}\right) \end{aligned}$$

where the last passage comes from Y_i being Gaussian.

Putting together

$$\begin{aligned} C_{X_1,\ldots,X_n} &= \mathbb{E}\left[\prod_{i=1}^{n}\Phi\left(\frac{\Phi^{-1}(u_i) - \sqrt{\rho_i}M}{\sqrt{1-\rho_i}}\right)\right] \\ &= \int_{-\infty}^{+\infty}\prod_{i=1}^{n}\Phi\left(\frac{\Phi^{-1}(u_i) - \sqrt{\rho_i}M}{\sqrt{1-\rho_i}}\right) \times f^{\Phi}(M)\,dM \end{aligned} \tag{3.10}$$

where f^{Φ} is the (standard Gaussian) density of M (the first derivative of Φ). If from the copula we want to move to the joint default probability, it will be enough to apply (12.3) to find

$$\Pr(\tau_1 \leq T_1, \ldots, \tau_n \leq T_n) = \int_{-\infty}^{+\infty} \prod_{i=1}^{n} \Phi\left(\frac{\Phi^{-1}\left(1-e^{-\lambda_i T_i}\right) - \sqrt{\rho_i} M}{\sqrt{1-\rho_i}}\right) \times f^{\Phi}(M)\, dM.$$

The copula expression (3.10) may appear complex but it is much less complex than the general Gaussian copula, expressed by (3.7) in the two-dimensional case. In fact (3.10) involves, for any number n of names, only a one-dimensional integration that is numerically feasible. Instead, the general expression (3.7) would require an n-dimensional integration.

This simplification has come at the cost of simplifying the parameterization of correlation, now limited to the one-factor parameterization (3.9), but this was not seen as a problem. In fact, for a general n-dimensional portfolio we have $\frac{n(n-1)}{2}$ free correlation parameters. It can be a huge number of parameters that are very difficult to estimate, so (3.9) was considered more than enough by the market, particularly because they decided to use, for the quotation of CDOs, a simplified representation of the Gaussian copula where all the parameters ρ_{ij} of a correlation matrix, excluding the ones on the diagonal, are equal to one single number ρ. For expressing such a matrix in the one-factor parameterization (3.9) it is sufficient to take $\rho_i = \sqrt{\rho}, i = 1, \ldots, n$. The result (3.10) together with some other computational techniques introduced in pre-crisis years allowed a particularly efficient pricing of tranches.

3.2.4 The Market Quotation Standard

We have said that the market adopted, as a quotation model for tranches, a Gaussian copula with all non-diagonal correlation parameters equal to ρ. Now we describe in detail this quotation method. We have seen that the price of a tranche is (3.4), so that, from a modelling point of view, evaluating a tranche A, B means being able to compute

$$\mathbb{E}\left[L_{A,B}(t)\right] = \frac{1}{B-A}\left[B\mathbb{E}\left[L_B(t)\right] - A\mathbb{E}\left[L_A(t)\right]\right] \tag{3.11}$$

where expectation depends on the model and model parameters. When the model is the Gaussian copula with flat correlation ρ we can write $\mathbb{E}[L_X(t)] = GL_{0,X}(\rho)$.

This relation was used first of all to provide a quote for the liquid tranches written on the main index, that for example for i-Traxx were (3.2), thus a set of the kind $[0, A][A, B][B, C]\ldots$ There have been, in the brief history of the tranche market, two ways of specifying the implied correlations. The first, called *compound correlation*, uses a single correlation parameter for each single $[X, Y]$ tranche,

$$\begin{aligned}
\boxed{\rho_{0,A}} &: \mathbb{E}\left[L_{0,A}(t)\right] = \frac{1}{A-0} A\, GL_{0,A}\left(\boxed{\rho_{0,A}}\right) - 0\, GL_{0,0}(-) \\
\underline{\rho_{A,B}} &: \mathbb{E}\left[L_{A,B}(t)\right] = \frac{1}{B-A}\left[B\, GL_{0,B}\left(\underline{\rho_{A,B}}\right) - A\, GL_{0,A}\left(\underline{\rho_{A,B}}\right)\right] \\
\overline{\rho_{B,C}} &: \mathbb{E}\left[L_{B,C}(t)\right] = \frac{1}{C-B}\left[C\, GL_{0,C}\left(\overline{\rho_{B,C}}\right) - B\, GL_{0,B}\left(\overline{\rho_{B,C}}\right)\right].
\end{aligned} \tag{3.12}$$

The parameter $\rho_{0,A}$ gives the value of the first tranche $[0, A]$, then the single parameter $\rho_{A,B}$ gives the value of the tranche $[A, B]$, and so on. This way of using correlation parameters for quotations leads to a correlation skew as in Figure 3.2.

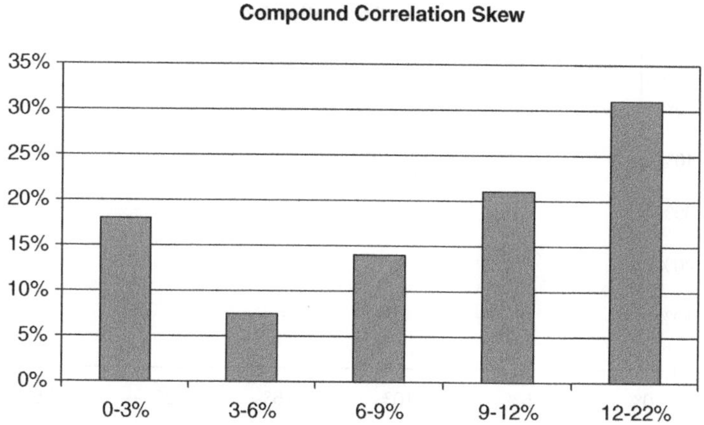

Figure 3.2 Compound correlation skew

We notice immediately that such a skew would not be easy to interpolate or extrapolate, which are the typical operations performed by traders to price non-standard products depending on a skew. Here in fact each correlation value is linked not to one number but to a pair of numbers $[X, Y]$, so interpolation and extrapolation would be non trivial. Notice also that here the model is used consistently for each quoted $[X, Y]$ tranche, since each correlation parameter is associated with one single $[X, Y]$ tranche. On the other hand, if we look at the equity tranches $[0, X]$, $[0, Y]$ into which any tranche can be decomposed, we notice that, for example, the equity $[0, B]$ is priced with two different correlations in the second and in the third line of (3.12).

The second way of specifying implied correlations, called *base correlation*, reverses this situation and makes interpolation and extrapolation easier. In this case a set of tranches $[0, A]$ $[A, B][B, C]$ ... is quoted using a correlation parameter for each one of the equity tranches $[0, Y]$ that in a representation like (3.11) can be used to express any generic $[X, Y]$ tranche:

$$\boxed{\rho_A} : \mathbb{E}\left[L_{0,A}(t)\right] = \frac{1}{A-0} A\ GL_{0,A}\left(\boxed{\rho_A}\right) - 0\ GL_{0,0}(-)$$

$$\underline{\rho_B} : \mathbb{E}\left[L_{A,B}(t)\right] = \frac{1}{B-A}\left[B\ GL_{0,B}\left(\underline{\rho_B}\right) - A\ GL_{0,A}\left(\boxed{\rho_A}\right)\right]$$

$$\overline{\rho_C} : \mathbb{E}\left[L_{B,C}(t)\right] = \frac{1}{C-B}\left[C\ GL_{0,C}\left(\overline{\rho_C}\right) - B\ GL_{0,B}\left(\underline{\rho_B}\right)\right].$$

In this the correlation skew each correlation is associated with a single point, as we can see in Figure 3.3. This second approach has become the market standard.

3.3 PORTFOLIO STRESS TESTING AND THE CORRELATION MISTAKE

In the previous chapter we have pointed out that the precision of a model in fitting a reference market does not necessarily reduce the amount of model risk when pricing a complex derivative. In fact, the same precision can be obtained by very different models. In the introduction to

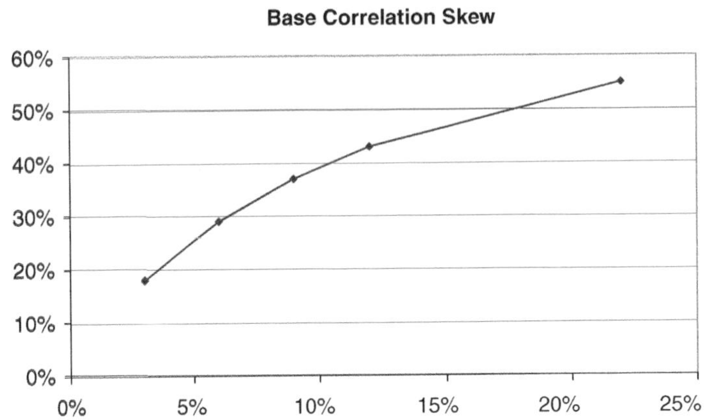

Figure 3.3 Base correlation skew

this chapter we mentioned that fitting a reference market is not a form of stress testing, since stress testing is applied to alternative scenarios to those we now see in the market.

However, in this section we show how having a model that is able to fit at least decently the reference market with one single set of parameters can be a prerequisite for fruitful stress testing. In fact it can give important insight into the risk factors that most worry the markets. Showing these risk factors gives an indication on stress testing that is missed by models that can achieve good or even perfect calibration only by making the parameters dependent on product features like strike or detachment. On the other hand, we do not care about *exact* fit: in stress testing we are in any case going to change the parameters after we have fitted them to the market.

In the following we introduce an approach that can approximately fit the market default correlation skew. This is probably the simplest model with this feature available in the literature, since it requires no more machinery than the popular one-factor Gaussian copula.

3.3.1 From Flat Correlation Towards a Realistic Approach

Figure 3.3 illustrates the typical way of representing the correlation skew in the Base Correlation standard. You know that in this setting:

1. the correlation is kept as one flat parameter;
2. this parameter needs to be changed for every different tranche if we want to calibrate to all of them.

What are the consequences of using a flat correlation? In applications to the only liquid CDOs, those written on i-Traxx or CDX indices that contain 125 names and therefore have

$$\frac{n(n-1)}{2} = \frac{125 \times 124}{2} = 7750$$

correlation parameters, this means that all the correlation parameters are set to the same number ρ.

When this feature of the model was criticized during the crisis, the usual answer of credit traders was: it is mainly a quotation model. This answer is not sufficient to justify the use of a bad model. A quotation model has a strong influence on how traders think. In the equity market the concept of implied volatility, which follows from the Black and Scholes model, remains crucial even now that the smile makes Black and Scholes only a quotation model. Analogously the implied correlation of the Gaussian copula shaped the way market operators thought about CDOs. But implied correlation is a much more complex and less intuitive concept than implied volatility.

First, a call or put option has a price that always grows with implied volatility, while relation between tranche risk and implied correlation can even change sign if we move from equity to senior tranches. Second, implied correlation summarizes in a single number a much more elaborate reality. There are names belonging to the same sector, region and with strong business links for which we can expect a high default correlation, and then there are many other name couples for which we see no obvious dependency and therefore we expect them to be little correlated. Moving from this situation to one where the correlation is average between high and low is not a simplification of this reality, it is a radically different scenario.

This makes it difficult to use this modelling framework to stress the value of our portfolios under different financial scenarios. The link between the reality and the implied correlation is not intuitive. It is also hard to say if a stress imposed to a CDO by stressing implied correlations corresponds to a reasonable – and arbitrage-free – scenario. Suppose that we decide to shock the correlation on the most senior tranche by 10% up. Is it meaningful to assume such a stress, keeping the other correlations fixed? It may not even be arbitrage-free, and in any case it is very difficult to figure out what such a stress means. Then we may decide to stress test by shifting all tranche correlations by 10%, as in the example in Section 3.1.2. Again, we are no better off. The new curve, 10% higher, may not be a feasible market scenario, and additionally the effects of such a correlation increase on different tranches are profoundly different. What is the real-world situation to which this stress corresponds? Very hard to say.

The final reason that made this quotation model extremely relevant to the market understanding of CDOs is that it was never really supported by one or more popular models that could instead explain, at least approximately, the presence and the shape of the skew. The Gaussian copula with implied flat correlation remained the only model that established itself as a market standard.

There exist, however, models that can fit all tranches consistently. The first one with this feature is probably the Hull and White (2005), (2006) and (2010) Perfect copula. This model allows us to give a general distribution to the real underlying of a CDO, which is the number of defaults in the reference portfolio at a given time. Thus in this model we can compute the probability density of the so-called default ratio

$$\frac{\sum_{i=1}^{n} 1_{\{\tau_i < T\}}}{n}$$

and also the density of the loss (3.1), which is essentially the default ratio times the individual expected loss given default.

Once this model is calibrated to all tranches, with a unique set of parameters, we can observe the market implied density of the default ratio. This would be hard in the market implied correlation approach, where we actually have five different models inconsistent with one another. We see in Figure 3.4 the implied density from a calibrated Perfect copula. The density has a peculiar shape. It is a multimodal density, or a density with bumps in the tail. There are masses of probability concentrated on particular levels in the default rate, we see them around 10–15%, around 40%, and even a slight increase of the curve around 80%. They

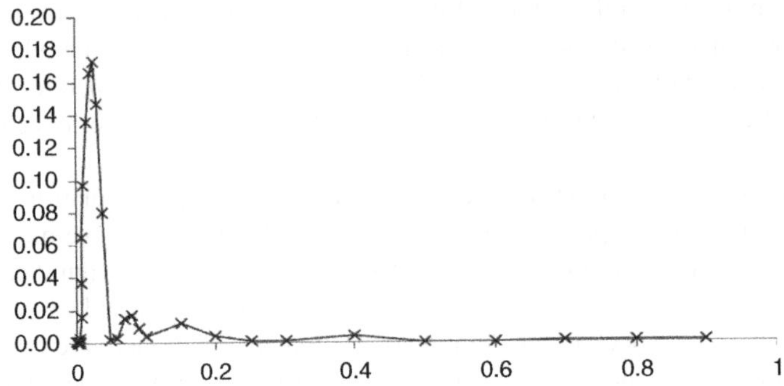

Figure 3.4 From Hull and White (2005): Plot of the Index Loss density

are likely to be associated with the fear of systemic default events at sector, regional or global level. This seems a historical regularity associated with the correlation skew.

The general market wisdom is that this kind of distribution cannot be obtained using the Gaussian copula. In Figure 3.5 we see two examples of the distribution of the loss that arise from the Gaussian copula in homogeneous portfolios where all names have the same λ (flat

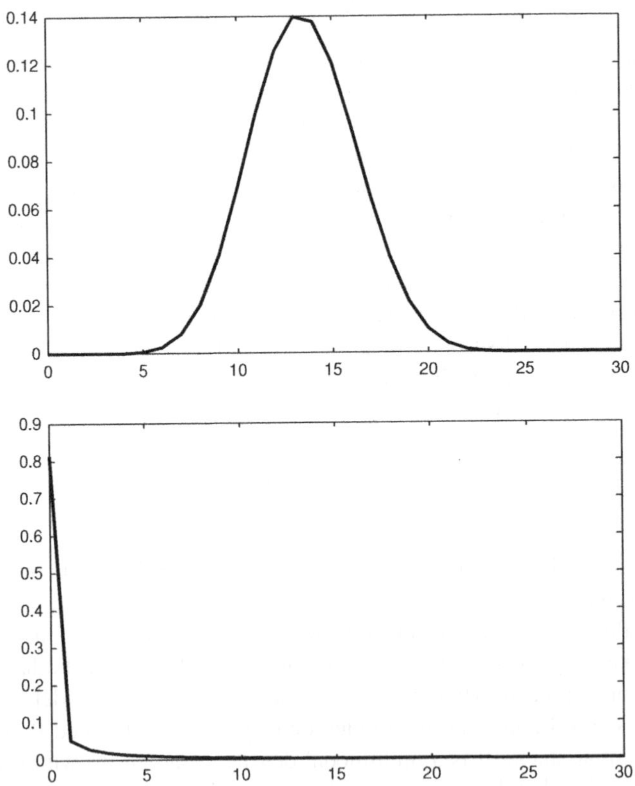

Figure 3.5 Loss densities under the Gaussian copula with flat correlation

default intensity) and the same ρ (flat correlation). In the first case, above in Figure 3.5, we have low correlation and high default risk,

$$\rho = 5\%, \lambda = 0.15$$

and the distribution appears a standard 'bell'. In the second case, below in Figure 3.5, we have higher correlation and lower default risk,

$$\rho = 70\%, \lambda = 0.01$$

the distribution is peaked on zero but we still do not see any bumps.

This is often associated with the fact that the Gaussian copula is 'Gaussian', a bad choice for obtaining fat-tail distributions since the Gaussian distribution has no excess kurtosis (the technical definition of a fat-tail distribution) and the derived Gaussian copula has no extreme tail dependency.

However, the market approach to CDO is not only a Gaussian copula, it also has a strong constraint: the correlation parameters are all kept equal. This is the most striking element of unrealism of this modelling approach. Can the existence of a correlation skew, and the associated bumps in the distribution, be somehow related to the difference between such a flat correlation and a more realistic correlation matrix? This would appear the first thing to check, but neither the scientific community nor the market pursued this line. They developed instead, particularly before the 2007–2009 crises, a battery of models based on radically different approaches, some interesting from a theoretical point of view. However, these models that were different from and more complex than the Gaussian copula were considered unusable for practical purposes.

The approach using a heterogeneous correlation matrix seems a step in the right direction. What are the effects on the distribution of the loss of the shift from a flat $\rho_{ij} = \rho$ correlation matrix to a realistic correlation matrix? A model with a flat correlation around an average level ρ tends to miss that in reality:

A) some pairs of names are characterized by a very high correlation ($\rho_{ij} = 1$ in the most extreme case);
B) some pairs of names are characterized by a very low correlation ($\rho_{ij} = 0$ in the most extreme case).

Clusters of names with high correlations make *big losses and small losses (far from expected loss) more likely*, while clusters of low correlation names make *losses around the expected loss more likely*. We are moving exactly to a fat-tail distribution. A fat-tail distribution is sometimes described sloppily with a distribution with 'more probability of extreme events', and thus fatter tails in the drawing of its density, compared to a Gaussian distribution. But if we want to make the tails fatter in the density, we can even keep a Gaussian distribution and just increase the volatility. The resulting distribution has fatter tails, but it is not a fat-tail distribution. A fat-tail distribution is a *leptokurtic distribution*. Pearson in 1905 introduced kurtosis as a measure of how flat the top of a symmetric distribution is when compared to a normal distribution of the same variance. A leptokurtic distribution, in general, has both fatter tails and a higher peak of probability around the expectation than a Gaussian distribution. Thus introducing a realistic correlation matrix is moving somewhat towards a fat-tail distribution. Can a realistic correlation allow one to have a distribution with some of the features shown by the Perfect copula of Hull and White (2005), even if we remain in the Gaussian copula?

Let us see the simplest possible example of credit portfolio with a heterogeneous correlation. We take the shortest step possible, moving from one single correlation and intensity value for all names to two correlation and intensity values. We consider a portfolio with only two types of company in it: a bigger group (60%) of *investment-grade (or senior) companies*, namely companies with low default risk ($\lambda = 0.005$), and a smaller group (40%) of *high-yield (or junior) companies*, that are quite risky companies ($\lambda = 0.015$). The companies in the latter group all have their own problems that make them risky, therefore we assume that correlation among them is quite low, say $\rho_J = 20\%$. The senior companies are instead *very* senior, therefore we think that their default risk can depend only on the possibility of some big systemic crisis that would shake even the most senior names. Consistently with this hypothesis, we give them $\rho_S = 100\%$. They have extremely low probability of default, but if they default they default all together.

With these simplified hypotheses, the resulting loss density is shown in Figure 3.6.

The Gaussian copula with heterogeneous correlations, where a subset of senior names is assumed to be perfectly correlated, gives rise to a clear multimodal loss density, featuring a bump in the far tail. This is not really surprising. Consider that when $\rho = 1$ is the only case when the Gaussian copula features a tail dependency. When we have only two random variables to correlate, choosing $\rho = 1$ is certainly not an efficient method to introduce tail dependency, because it forces us to take a very extreme view about their interdependency. But when we are considering *a portfolio of 125 names*, assuming that a subset of them has a unit correlation is not such an extreme view. We do not claim that we are able to detect exactly which names have correlation equal to 1, we only want to find a schematic representation of the portfolio where the possibility of systemic default events is not neglected. The subset of perfectly correlated names is a simple way to get this, and we see that it yields a density with

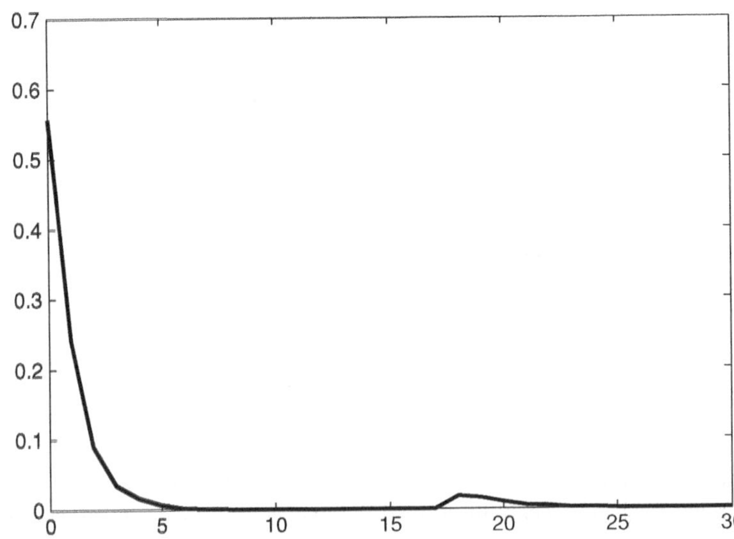

Figure 3.6 Loss density under the Gaussian copula with simple heterogeneous correlation

bumps as in the most advanced models, but here we are still in the market Gaussian copula model. This effect of a cluster of higher correlated names is not limited to the most extreme choice $\rho = 1$. A small bump in the tail can be obtained also for lower values of correlation given to the senior names as long as this value clearly remains higher than the value given to the junior names, keeping the matrix heterogeneous in a relevant way (Morini (2007).

Now let us try to go beyond this simple trick and use heterogeneous correlation even to fit the market of the quoted Index CDO. How can we attempt this? Let us reason on the above simple example, to extend it to a realistic portfolio. In the simple example, not only did we use a heterogeneous correlation, but we made correlation a function of default risk. This corresponds with the idea that names with different *levels* of credit risk are often associated to different *types* of credit risk: the risk of subinvestment grade borrowers usually comes from idiosyncratic, or firm-specific, risk factors, while the risk of senior borrowers usually comes from the risk of more systemic crisis. There are obviously many exceptions to this: senior names can become fallen angels, namely companies that jump from being considered very reliable to default in a short period of time, even without a systemic crisis. The Enron and Parmalat defaults were such cases. On the other hand, some risky names can have strong business links with each other and so actually have a high default correlation. But in spite of these exceptions, the link between low probability of default and higher correlation to systemic risk factors is a fundamental pillar for experienced loan professionals[2]:

> *The loans with the highest predictable losses have the lowest sensitivity to macroeconomic conditions. Conversely the lowest risk loans have the highest sensitivity to macroeconomic conditions (Breeden 2008).*[3]

The crisis of 2007–2009 confirms this wisdom. The most senior names in previous years had been the international financial institutions; when the crisis struck we found their health was inextricably linked to some macroeconomic factors, such as the availability of cheap liquidity and a booming house market. When these factors came to an end, the majority of these very senior names plunged all together into a near-default situation, and the near-default situation did not transform into default mainly because of enormous state intervention on a scale never seen before. Thus it seems we have a first ingredient to put in the correlation matrix: correlation must be a decreasing function of the names' default risk.

3.3.2 A Correlation Parameterization to Stress the Market Skew

Do we have to analyze the 7750 elements of the Index correlation matrix to apply this principle to a realistic portfolio? No. We can implement this principle using the simplest possible Gaussian correlation framework: One Factor Gaussian copula. We define the n-variate Gaussian distribution as in (3.8)

$$X_i = \rho_i M + \sqrt{1 - \rho_i^2} Y_i \quad i = 1, \ldots, n$$

[2] The idea is not so different from the principle that in the 20th century led the rating agencies to give low correlation to subprime borrowers, as mentioned in Section 1.1.3. Then, the new structure of the mortgage markets that linked the losses on subprime mortgages to house prices overrode this principle by creating a dramatic link with a very systemic factor, irrespective of the seniority of borrower, a distortion specific to that market.

[3] This is the application to the financial reality of a concept that we find expressed, in general terms, by Lev Tolstoy at the start of *Anna Karenina*: *'Happy families are all alike, every unhappy family is unhappy in its own way'* (thanks to Marcos Costa Santos Carreira for pointing out this analogy during a conference on derivatives).

so that

$$\rho_{ij} = Corr\left(X_i X_j\right) = \rho_i \rho_j.$$

However, now we do not assume that the individual correlation parameters ρ_i are all the same as in the market practice, but instead we make them a function of the individual intensities or spreads:

$$\rho_i = f\left(Spread_i\right).$$

Building the parameterization on the ρ_i gives a first reduction of the complexity of the problem, moving from 7750 parameters to 125. What is the effect on ρ_{ij} of the parameterization of ρ_i? Notice that if ρ_i, ρ_j are high, then ρ_{ij} will also be high, with the limit case

$$\rho_i = \rho_j = 1 \Longrightarrow \rho_{ij} = 1,$$

while if either ρ_i or ρ_j is low the resulting correlation of the two names will be lower, and will be very low when both $\rho_i \approx 0$, $\rho_j \approx 0$, for example

$$\rho_i = \rho_j = 0.03 \Longrightarrow \rho_{ij} = 0.0009.$$

If we build a decreasing parameterization

$$Spread_i < Spread_j \Longrightarrow \rho_i = f\left(Spread_i\right) > \rho_j = f\left(Spread_j\right)$$

we obtain the financial effect we want: when a senior name 'meets' another senior name in computing $\rho_i \rho_j$, their resulting correlation ρ_{ij} will be high, when a junior name meets another junior name the correlation will be low, with a slightly higher correlation for mixed meetings.

Notice that this approach is underpinned by some quantitative analysis. Glasserman et al. (2007) show analytically that it is not true that in a Gaussian copula the tails of the loss decay exponentially, as one would expect due to lack of tail-dependence. This is true for low default probabilities, but when default probabilities grow the Gaussian copula produces a heavier tail, suggesting a difference in the dependence induced by the Gaussian copula for sets of high quality credits (exponential decay of the tail) and low quality credits (power law decay of the tail). Therefore in a Gaussian copula model with flat correlations, senior names are in practice less correlated than junior names, even if the correlation parameters is the same. In our approach we contrast effectively this model behaviour by increasing correlations for more senior names. Glasserman et al. (2007) conclude that higher implied correlations for names with lower default risk may, in part, offset the diminished dependence in the Gaussian copula at low default probabilities, keeping an acceptable amount of dependency.

A second clear link is with the approach called *local correlation*, pursued for example in Turc et al. (2005). In such models, that actually fit the market correlation skew, one assumes a flat correlation ρ but

$$\rho = g(M),$$

where M is the systemic risk factor of the one-factor Gaussian copula and g is a decreasing function.

In one-factor copulas the portfolio loss is a decreasing function of M. The lower M, the higher the number of defaulted companies. This together with $g'(M) < 0$ makes correlation increase the more the loss grows and approaches the detachments of more and more senior tranches.

Why is this similar to our parameterization of correlation? Because in the parameterization the names with higher default risk have lower correlations. These names are expected to default first, and when they default – which means the loss is growing – the surviving names will have a higher average correlation. Default has taken out one of the names with correlation lower than average. The expected behaviour is an increase of correlation when the loss increases, as in the local correlation model. This tendency is stronger in the local correlation model, but somewhat more natural in the parametric correlation since it is obtained as a consequence of the correlation choice.

There is another reference in the literature that has recently been pointed out to me, one that is very interesting from the point of view of model risk analysis. An approach similar to the one above was mentioned in Andersen and Sidenius (2005), long before the crisis. However the approach is not tested on market data but is rejected a priori on the basis of some of its features, which are considered unrealistic, in particular: in such an approach correlations can reach 1, and the approach implies that the most senior names should be the most correlated to the general market trend, and therefore should be most exposed to systemic risk. Both things were considered unrealistic. These are similar to the critical comments voiced when I first presented this method in 2006. The subsequent credit crunch showed that exactly these aspects were at the core of the CDO risk: in the crisis correlation equal to 1 was observed even as implied correlation of the standard Gaussian copula, and the names which had the lowest default probability before the crisis – the banks and other financial institution – were precisely the first ones to move all together very close to default when the global economy entered the crisis.

We now have to choose a functional form for the parameterization

$$\rho_i = f\left(Spread_i\right).$$

We want the function to depend on few parameters, but to also be sufficiently general to allow for correlation factors as high as $\rho_i = 1$ and as low as $\rho_i = 0$. A simple parameterization of this kind is a 3-parameter constrained polynomial chosen in Duminuco and Morini (2008).

Let us take the 125 market spreads of the components of the i-Traxx index on 15 February 2008, and calibrate the default intensities of our portfolio to their market spreads. Then we can run an optimization on the three parameters in order to replicate as far as possible the quotation of the 5-year i-Traxx tranches on the same day. The resulting shape of f as a function of spreads is shown in Figure 3.7.

There are a few parameters ρ_i set to zero, and some set to 1. The effect of this parameterization on the elements ρ_{ij} is summarized by the three dimensional picture of the resulting correlation matrix given in Figure 3.8. On the x and y axes there are i and j for the 125 names, in the z axis there are correlations ρ_{ij}.

You see that there is a small area of names with unit correlation, representing the risk of systemic events, and an area of zero correlation names, capturing purely idiosyncratic risk.

What is the agreement of this correlation matrix with the quoted tranche prices, namely the market correlation skew? This correlation implies the rather realistic correlation skew seen in Figure 3.9 together with the market correlation skew of the same day.

Considering that we only have three parameters, and that we are still in the one-factor Gaussian copula, the fit appears surprisingly good. It is not very precise, but it captures the

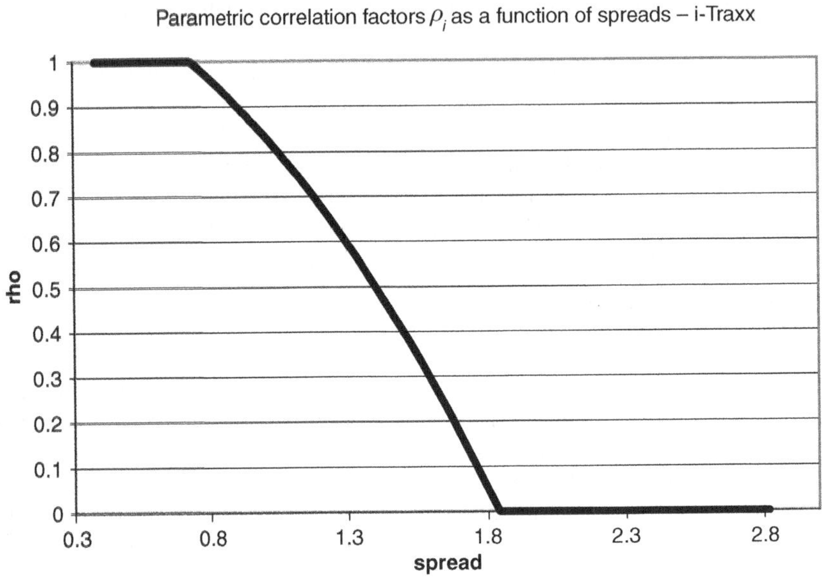

Figure 3.7 The correlation parameterization

shape of the skew very well, and this is a good result for a model that was supposed to admit a no skews or skews with no relation to market reality.[4]

The precision could probably be increased taking an even more general structure for the correlation – in the end our correlation is no longer flat but is still driven by one single stochastic factor. One can take more factors (eg the financial sector factor), to increases the flexibility in fitting correlation skews, as was done for instance by rating agencies as discussed in Section 1.1.3. However the capability of this simplified parameterization to fit the market suggests that the traditional approach of rating agencies to set correlations historically based on only two dimensions – geographical proximity and industry sector – was omitting an important aspect of correlation risk. The link between seniority and exposure to systemic introduced here captures market features much better.

The implied loss distribution can easily be computed, and it has the desired multimodal structure visible in Figure 3.10, revealing that it is possible to have it in the market implied loss density even using a Gaussian copula framework.

The representation of reality given by this approach is highly simplified. In the next section we will discuss the dynamic implication of a Gaussian copula, and in the last section of this chapter we will show that the risk of a tranche depends on more than just the level of its spreads. In spite of these limits, this approach remains the simplest explanation of the correlation skew, and is of simple application since it does not require a move away from the Gaussian copula machinery. It is less simplified than the flat correlation approach and also allows us to perform meaningful stress tests. Increasing the size of the subset of names with unit correlation, for example, has a direct positive effect on senior tranches while increasing the size of the subset

[4] This specific calibration day has been chosen as an example of the model behaviour because in the days of the crisis calibration was particularly difficult since recovery expectations had fallen while the market still used – as we did – the approach of keeping recovery at 40%.

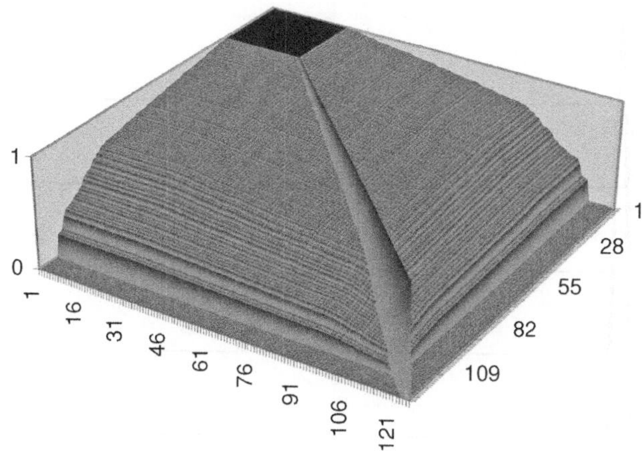

Figure 3.8 The correlation matrix resulting from the parameterization

with zero correlation has a direct positive effect on the riskiness of equity tranches. Even more interestingly, increasing the slope can increase the riskiness of both senior and equity tranches. And all stress to which one can subject the parameterization in any case results in an arbitrage-free model with a viable correlation matrix, since the correlation matrix is built from the one-factor model in a way that retains its fundamental properties. Notice also that in this framework a joint stress to spreads and correlations arises naturally from the relations we introduced among these two sets of parameters.

But before the crisis simple extensions of the market approach such as this one, which would have given more insight than the standard Gaussian copula and allowed more effective

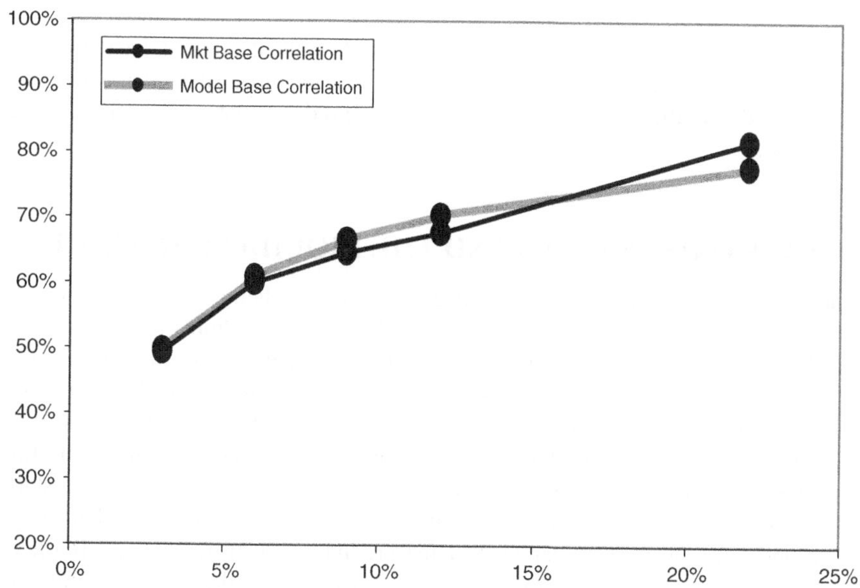

Figure 3.9 The correlation skew resulting from the parameterization

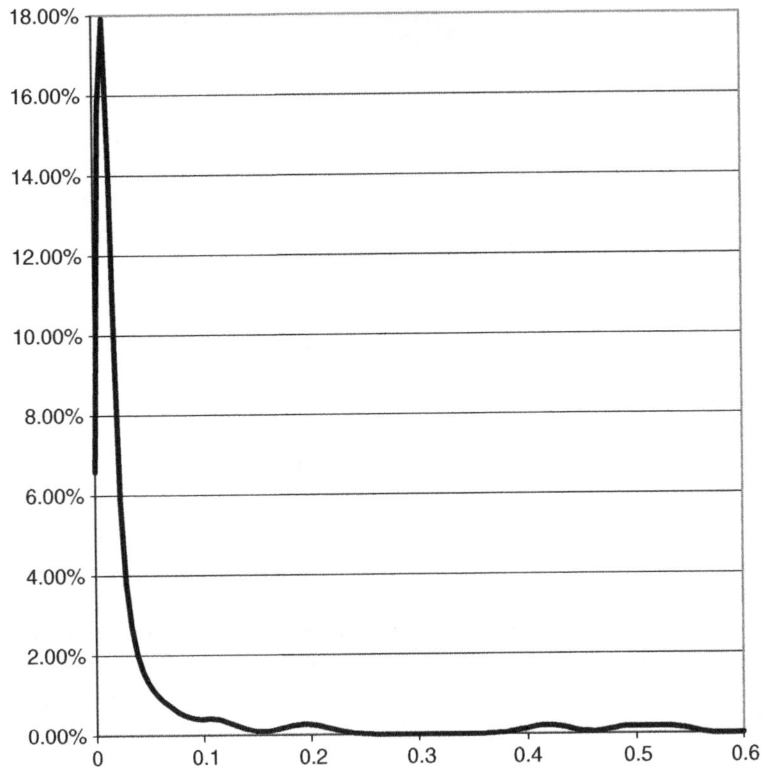

Figure 3.10 The Loss density resulting from the parameterization

stress tests, were forgotten; the far more complex models, radically alternative to the Gaussian copula, proposed by many researchers were never able to impact market practice; and the market remained with the flat-correlation or regional-based-correlation Gaussian copula until the crisis burst.

3.4 PAYOFF STRESS AND THE LIQUIDITY MISTAKE

After the crisis, the Gaussian copula was attacked mainly for being 'Gaussian'. Thus it does not create enough tail-dependency among the default events of a number of companies so that the loss of a portfolio composed of investments in those companies has a distribution that does not feature fat tails, underestimating the risk of big losses around the size of the entire portfolio.

These criticisms appear misguided. First, we have seen in the previous section that this problem can be tackled without abandoning the Gaussian distribution, but just by taking a different approach to the parameterization of correlation. Second, the crisis was not started by credit losses that wiped out entire portfolios, but by a few situations of panic that triggered a liquidity crunch. The panic was generated by a few credit losses in different portfolios that were however concentrated in a short period of time. And when the market is in a liquidity crunch, then a few additional losses concentrated in a short period can certainly lead a bank to default.

Thus, it seems that 'losses concentrated in time' were more relevant to understanding the crisis than 'losses concentrated in a portfolio'. In spite of this the modelling of the first kind of events did not receive much attention. Here we close this gap. Unfortunately, we find that the Gaussian copula can easily lead to a wrong estimation of the probability of joint credit losses from different investments in a short period of time, since the relation between this risk we want to capture and the correlation parameter of the Gaussian copula is:

1. unstable, in the sense that it changes dramatically for small changes in the features of the events we analyze;
2. irregular, since this relation is not even monotonic, making it difficult to control the risk and understand, for example, which level of correlation maximizes risk.

This makes portfolio stress testing difficult or even impossible. Additionally, our examples will show that the representation of the risk of losses near in time in the Gaussian copula can be wrong or counterintuitive also for non-stressed values of the parameters.

These unpleasant features do not appear crucially related to the model being 'Gaussian' but, unlike most other critics, point the finger at the fact of the model being 'a copula'. Our results suggest that one central fact about copulas is not true. Enthusiasts of the application of copulas in finance claim that copulas allow one to separate modelling of the interdependence between financial variables from modelling of individual variables,[5] so that we can *first* set the individual marginal distributions – for example in credit we fix them in the single name CDS market – and *then* give them the dependency structure we like through the copula function and its parameters. Unfortunately, this may be true when we use a purely mathematical definition of dependence – functional dependence – but it is no longer true anymore when we consider the meaning of dependency which is more relevant in credit modelling: losses happening in the same period of time. Copulas do not allow us to control this dependency independently from the individual distributions. The level of dependency in copulas can be limited by the individual distributions, while in different models, as will be shown, we do not have such limits and we can give a more realistic representation of dependency.

These are problems that can be overlooked in the initial model validation, because they do not surface in all applications. Efficient model stress testing should be able to detect the conditions when these problems appear. In the following we detect them by stress testing both the product dimension, moving from spot-starting to forward-starting, and the input dimension, moving correlation parameters and default intensity parameters.

3.4.1 Detecting the Problem: Losses Concentrated in Time

Let us start our analysis of the problems of Gaussian copulas by recalling a feature of this model which is well known to experienced credit traders (who often use it to show off and surprise inexperienced junior quants). In the Gaussian copula we can immediately tell the value of popular portfolio derivatives such as first-to-default and last-to-default, provided that we set the correlation parameters of the Gaussian copula equal to their maximum value 1.

[5] We recalled in 3.2.2 that Bouyé et al. (2000), one of the first popular papers that introduced copulas in finance, claim that copulas provide a way to analyze the dependence structure of multivariate distributions without studying marginal distributions.

Let us take for example a standard last-to-default, with a protection leg paying at the time of the last default,

$$\hat{\tau} = \max(\tau_1, \tau_2, \ldots, \tau_n),$$

if all defaults happen before the maturity T. What is the value of this protection leg if we work in a Gaussian copula and we take a matrix of ones

$$\begin{bmatrix} 1 & 1 & \ldots \\ 1 & 1 & \ldots \\ \vdots & \vdots & \ddots \end{bmatrix}$$

to be the correlation matrix? Any good credit trader will tell you that in this case the protection leg of the last-to-default has the same value as the protection leg of a CDS written on the least risky name in the portfolio (roughly, the one with lowest spread on the relevant maturity). Since a CDS is a much easier and liquid derivative, whose equilibrium upfront or spread is available in the market, this equivalence simplifies strongly the valuation of the last-to-default.

How come we get such a simple result? Consider the flat intensity case (3.5),

$$\tau_1 = \frac{\varepsilon_1}{\lambda_1}, \quad \tau_2 = \frac{\varepsilon_2}{\lambda_2}, \ldots, \tau_n = \frac{\varepsilon_n}{\lambda_n}.$$

We have already seen that the ε_i's are the stochastic component of the default times and have the same distribution for all names. Setting all correlations equal to 1 implies that the ε_i's not only have the same distribution, but that they are even the same random variable, namely

$$\varepsilon_1 = \varepsilon_2 = \cdots = \varepsilon_n = \varepsilon.$$

Instead, the deterministic components of the default times, which are the intensities λ_i's, are set by the CDS market and can be very different from each other. Thus we have

$$\tau_1 = \frac{\varepsilon}{\lambda_1}, \quad \tau_2 = \frac{\varepsilon}{\lambda_2}, \ldots, \tau_n = \frac{\varepsilon}{\lambda_n}, \tag{3.13}$$

which implies that the last default time $\hat{\tau}$ is the default time of the company with the lowest intensity

$$\hat{\lambda} = \min(\lambda_1, \lambda_2, \ldots, \lambda_n),$$

that corresponds to the lowest CDS spread. This explains how one can easily guess the value of the last-to-default for unit correlation, and also shows that unit correlation is the case that makes the protection of this derivative have the highest value. In fact, the protection of the last-to-default is paid only when all the CDS on the n names have paid their protection. Thus in general the payment is made less often than the payment on any of the CDS on the names in the portfolio, including the CDS on the least risky name. Only under the assumption of unit correlation do we reach this maximum value. This confirms the general wisdom that last-to-default derivatives, like senior tranches of CDOs, become more risky the more correlation increases.

So far everything seems simple and fine. However, the relation (3.13) has a few implications that sound, if not worrisome, at least bizarre.

First of all it implies that *names with extremely different default risk are allowed to have unit default correlation*. What does that mean, from a financial point of view? The usual financial intuition of high default correlations corresponds to companies that have high likelihood of defaulting at the same time, or at least at a short time from each other. Oyama (2010) speaks of '*the default correlation, that is the probability that the default of a certain loan occurs simultaneously with the default of another*'.

This is not the meaning of high default correlation in the Gaussian copula. In fact, again from (3.13), one can notice that *names with maximum default correlation can have defaults which are largely far apart in time*. In fact when two names 1 and 2 have default correlation 1 we have

$$\tau_2 = \tau_1 \frac{\lambda_1}{\lambda_2}. \tag{3.14}$$

Where for example λ_2 is 10 basis points and λ_1 is 100 basis points, the model is telling us that when the default of name 1 happens in 1 year from now, this will cause the default of name 2 in 10 years from now. This hardly corresponds to a realistic market situation. There are some cases when two companies can have such strong links that the default of one of them causes the default of the other. This includes companies where one is the main or only client of the second one, or the biggest creditor. After the birth of credit derivatives, we have to include the case in which one company has sold protection on a reference entity beyond its financial capabilities. However, in all these cases the default will be caused after a short period of time, not after 9 years.

Such a feature of the model is not, in itself, a problem. By definition models cannot be perfectly realistic and we can accept that a model has to have some unrealistic features if this lack of realism does not affect strongly the decisions we take using the model. Thus in the following we investigate whether the above fact can lead to nonsensical results in some practical cases.

3.4.2 The Problem in Practice

Unfortunately, it is not difficult to come up with practically relevant cases where the above problem is dramatically exposed. We came across one such case when trying to understand what a bank should have done to protect itself from the events that caused the credit crunch and the financial crisis of 2007–2009.

Before the crisis, market players chose the Gaussian copula as a model for assessing the risk of having a high concentration of losses in a single portfolio, over the horizon of some years from now, such as 5 or 10 years. In fact, these were the usual maturities of collateralized debt obligation (CDO), and this aspect of default correlation risk was considered the core risk involved in CDO investments. However, the problems in the credit derivatives market and structured finance that led to the credit crunch did not come from this kind of loss concentration. They came from actual or feared losses that were not high in a single portfolio, particularly being split among more equity tranches of a number of CDOs in the books of a bank and its related vehicles, but were concentrated in a short period of time, creating panic and liquidity difficulties. The recent crisis has shown that a bank, from the liquidity risk point of view, looks like a senior 'temporal' tranche. A standard senior tranche in a CDO is a product that suffers losses when *the losses concentrated in one portfolio, over a relatively long time horizon, are higher than a given threshold*. Analogously and yet differently, a bank exposed to the structured credit market runs into liquidity problems, either directly due to the losses or indirectly through the withdrawal of investors, when *the losses concentrated in a relatively short period of time, across all of its portfolios, are higher than a given threshold*.

Let us consider a bank that, after the credit crunch, wants to protect itself against this liquidity risk. We present a simplified, but realistic, example, where we can quantify this risk with precision. We take a bank which is exposed towards the default of two different investments. Of the two investments one is more senior and one is more risky, with default intensities

$$\lambda_1 = 0.03,\ \lambda_2 = 0.2.$$

The bank is not very worried that one of the two names may default, because it knows it has sufficient liquidity to face such an event. Even if they both default, but the two defaults are not very close, for example are 5 years apart, the bank believes it can cope with this without running out of liquidity. The real worry is that the two investments both default in the same, short period of time. In particular, we suppose now that the bank knows that the worst period from a liquidity point of view will be between 3 and 5 years from now, because of some planned future expenses (later we will generalize this case). How may the bank protect itself against this event, which can be the difference between survival and bankruptcy of the bank itself?

The natural choice is to buy protection on a last-to-default, but not a standard one with a start date equal to today, like the one described in the previous section, where the product protects you over a period that starts now. The bank needs a forward start last-to-default, paying protection only if both names default in the specific period of time that worries it, namely a product with payoff

$$\text{LGD at } \hat{\tau} = \max(\tau_1, \tau_2) \text{ if } 3 \le \tau_1 \le 5, 3 \le \tau_2 \le 5. \tag{3.15}$$

The value of the protection on the last default in (3.15) depends on the probability that the two names default together exactly in that short period of time,

$$\Pr(3 \le \tau_1 \le 5, 3 \le \tau_2 \le 5).$$

We may expect this probability to be higher when correlation is higher, as always happens with last to default. The higher the default correlation, the higher the probability risk that both names default in the same period of time.

However, in Figure 3.11 we see the relation and the behaviour are opposite from what was expected.

The probability of joint default *decreases* with correlation, differently from what one expects, and from what happens with a standard, spot-starting last-to-default. This fact is surprising, but it can be easily explained mathematically. When correlation is 0, the probability that the two investments default together is

$$\begin{aligned}
&\Pr(3 \le \tau_1 \le 5, 3 \le \tau_2 \le 5) \\
&= \Pr(3 \le \tau_1 \le 5) \times \Pr(3 \le \tau_2 \le 5) \\
&= 0.053 * 0.181 = 0.0096.
\end{aligned}$$

When correlation is 1, instead, $\tau_1 = \frac{\varepsilon}{\lambda_1} = \frac{\varepsilon}{0.03}$ and $\tau_2 = \frac{\varepsilon}{\lambda_2} = \frac{\varepsilon}{0.2}$, so $3 \le \tau_1 \le 5$ means $0.09 \le \varepsilon \le 0.15$ while $3 \le \tau_2 \le 5$ means $0.6 \le \varepsilon \le 1$. The two ε intervals do not overlap, so the probability

$$\Pr(3 \le \tau_1 \le 5, 3 \le \tau_2 \le 5).$$

that the two default events happen jointly is zero. For intermediate levels of correlation, the probability of joint default goes down between these two extremes.

The result is surprising because, as we have said more than once above, the market wisdom is that the risk of last-to-defaults, like senior tranches, goes up with correlation. Unfortunately,

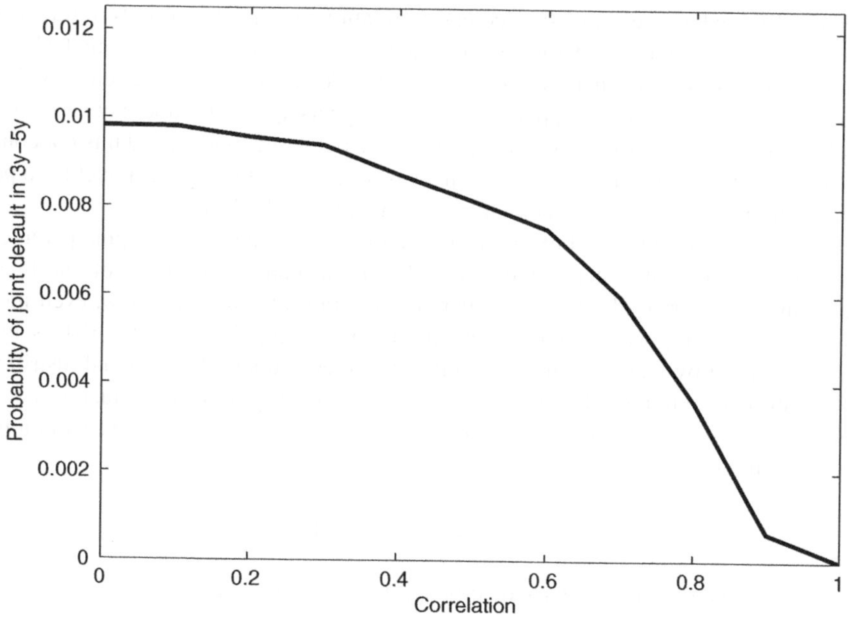

Figure 3.11 Probability of concentrated losses for different correlations

in the Gaussian copula this is guaranteed only for a last-to-default which is spot-starting, for example one that pays when both names default between today and 2 years from now. In fact, in this case we have, under independence,

$$\begin{aligned}&\Pr(0 \leq (\tau_1, \tau_2) \leq 2)\\&= \Pr(0 \leq \tau_1 \leq 2) \times \Pr(0 \leq \tau_2 \leq 2)\\&= 0.058{*}0.330 = 0.019.\end{aligned}$$

When correlation is 1, we now have $0 \leq \tau_1 \leq 2$ means $0 \leq \varepsilon \leq 0.06$ while $0 \leq \tau_2 \leq 2$ means $0 \leq \varepsilon \leq 0.4$. The two ε intervals now overlap and both inequalities hold true when the first one holds true, thus

$$\begin{aligned}&\Pr(0 \leq (\tau_1, \tau_2) \leq 2)\\&= \Pr(0 \leq \tau_1 \leq 2) = 0.058 > 0.019,\end{aligned}$$

and the probability of joint defaults goes up between these two extremes.

Thus we have shown numerically and explained mathematically that the relationship between the only parameter of the model and the financial risk in which we are really interested, namely the risk of having defaults in the same period of time, tends to invert in moving from a period of time that starts now to a period of time located in the future. The relation is clearly increasing for the 0–2 years period and clearly decreasing for the 3–5 interval. In between we can have intervals where there is almost no relation between correlation and risk, and cases where the relation is not monotonic. This makes the behaviour of the relation between model parameter and financial risk unstable and irregular.

Additionally, we have seen that the decreasing relation we have for periods of time located in the future is due to the fact that, the more correlation increases, the more the model becomes unrealistic, since it assumes that the second default is deterministically triggered by the first default but that the two defaults happen more than two years apart. This does not correspond to any real case of default dependence that we can figure out in the market, and it is not confined to the extreme level of correlation $\rho = 1$. This was revealed by testing the model for a payoff different from the standard last-to-default but of high practical relevance.

In contrast to what one would expect from the theory of copulas, the copula parameter ρ does not allow us to control neatly the risk of default dependence which is of real financial interest, which is the risk of defaults happening near in time. Now we show, even more in contrast with what one would expect from the theory of copulas, that this risk is instead strongly influenced by a change in the default intensities, namely the marginal distributions of the default times. Suppose that we keep the total probability of default equal to the above example, where $\lambda_1 + \lambda_2 = 0.03 + 0.2 = 0.23$, but we redistribute this risk evenly among the two names, setting

$$\lambda_1 = \lambda_2 = \frac{0.23}{2} = 0.115.$$

In this case, when correlation is zero the probability of joint default is

$$\begin{aligned} &\Pr(3 \le \tau_1 \le 5) \times \Pr(3 \le \tau_2 \le 5) \\ &= 0.146 * 0.146 = 0.021 \end{aligned}$$

while the probability that the two events happen together when $\rho = 1$ is simply $\Pr(3 \le \tau_1 \le 5) = 0.146$. The pattern for intermediate values is given in Figure 3.12.

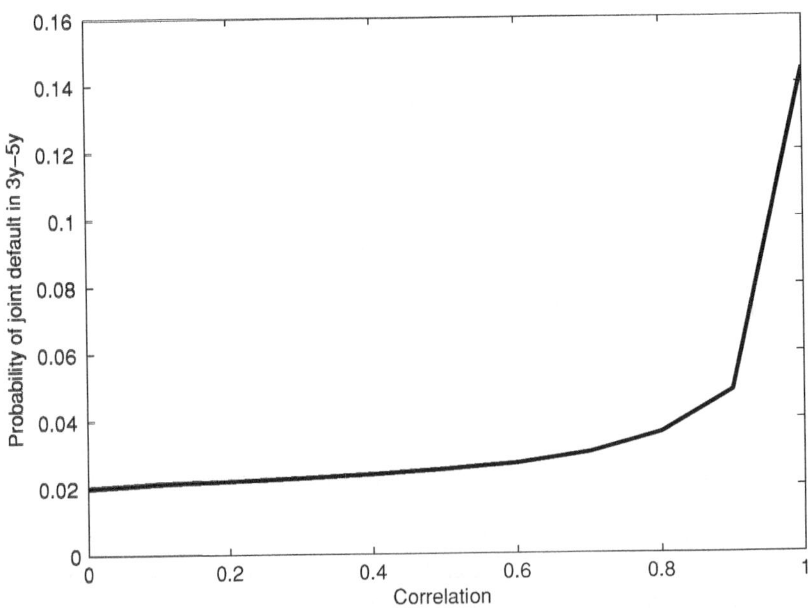

Figure 3.12 Probability of concentrated losses for different correlations. The case of names with the same default risk

This redistribution of risk between the investments has two effects. First, it allows for higher probability of joint defaults in the same period of time. Second, it alters again the relation between correlation and financial risk, which goes back to being increasing and therefore consistent with our intuition. It seems that capturing the temporal aspect of correlation risk is related more to credit spreads than to the Gaussian copula correlation ρ. The copula has not allowed us to analyze the dependence structure of multivariate distributions without studying marginal distributions, and does not give us a parameter that has a clear relation to the most relevant financial risk associated with default correlation. This does not happen in the case of homogeneous risk that was often used as a rough simplification in the market before the crisis, but it is revealed in testing the realistic case of differentiated risks in a portfolio.

Dynamic VAR

The above example can be made even more realistic. We have assumed that a bank is able to predict precisely what is the worst period for having the joint default of the two names, assuming a period of 2 years starting 3 years from now. More likely, a bank will not be able to make such a prediction, but will know that it would enter a liquidity crisis whenever the two investments default near in time. For example, it may be that the distance between the two defaults are less than three months and so is sufficient to mean the bank cannot cover its losses and so enters default. Thus in the following we compute

$$\Pr\left(|\tau_1 - \tau_2| < 3m\right) \tag{3.16}$$

and analyze how this probability behaves with correlation, limiting the analysis to a 10 year horizon, that is $\tau_1 < 10y$, $\tau_2 < 10y$. This is a much more general case than the above, and also includes the spot three-month period that starts now. It is also similar to a standard risk management computation. The main job of a risk manager is computing the notorious VAR. Given some loss $Loss\,([a,b])$ over the period of time $[a,b]$, the VAR is the maximum threshold x such that

$$\Pr(Loss\,([a,b]) > x) \le y$$

where y is the confidence level of the VAR. There exists also credit VAR's, where the loss considered comes from default events. If we assume that our bank has a capital of EUR 1bn equally divided between our investments 1 and 2, each one with a zero recovery in case of default, the probability in (3.16) can be rewritten in a VAR-like way as

$$\Pr\left(Loss\,([t, t+3m]) > 500\text{ mn}\right).$$

The behaviour of the probability as a function of correlation is shown in Figure 3.13.

Now the relation starts increasing, but suddenly it reverts to decreasing. This is particularly dangerous in stress testing. Suppose a risk manager wants to see what the price would be in the worst possible financial scenario. For the risk of two names happening together, it is likely that the poor risk manager chooses $\rho = 1$ as the worst case scenario. Unfortunately, here $\rho = 1$ is not the *most pessimistic* case, but the *most optimistic* one. Even worse, the most pessimistic case corresponds to $\rho \approx 0.7$. How could one have guessed a priori? Impossible, one must always compute (numerically or analytically when possible) the probability of losses for all levels of correlation, to find out which correlation really maximizes the risk and can be used for a stress test.

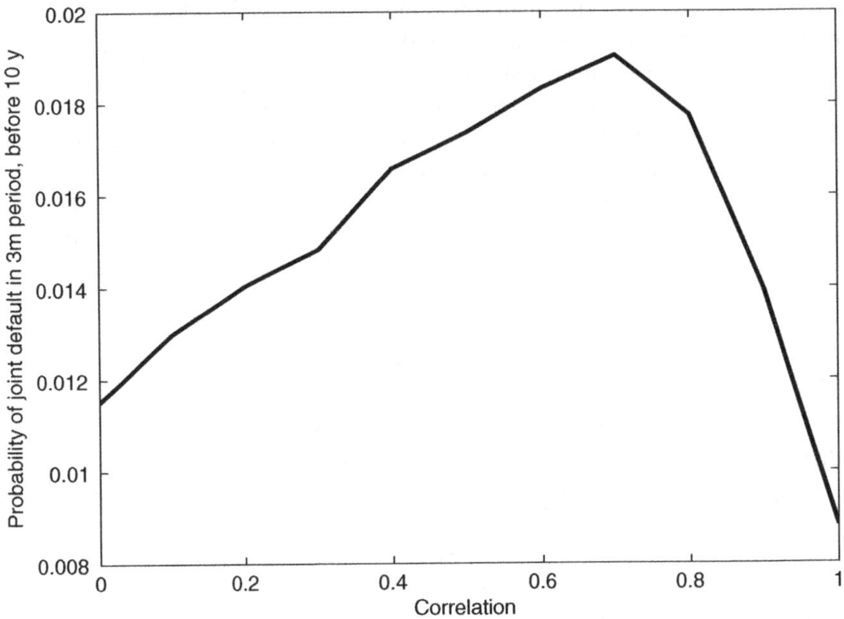

Figure 3.13 Dynamic VAR for different correlations

CDS counterparty risk

One more example is the assessment of counterparty risk in a CDS. The problem is tackled in Brigo and Chourdakis (2008), who concentrate on the possibility of default of a CDS counterparty before the default of the reference entity, thus focusing on the loss of the CDS mark-to-market at $\tau^{Counterparty} < \tau^{Reference}$. They find it natural to assume the protection seller (counterparty) to be less risky than the reference entity, $\lambda^{Counterparty} < \lambda^{Reference}$. They obtain an amazing behavior where, at some correlation levels, the credit risk adjustment for this event inverts its pattern and starts decreasing when correlation increases, contrary to the standard market expectation about the effect of high counterparty/reference correlation (wrong way risk) on CDS counterparty risk. Now we have the elements to understand this behaviour: when ρ is approaching unity, in the standard Gaussian copula credit model it becomes increasingly unlikely for the least risky name, the counterparty, to default before the most risky name, the reference entity. This paradox is simply a consequence of the Gaussian copula approach. The example is particularly relevant, since Brigo and Chourdakis (2008) use Gaussian copula for default correlation but use a stochastic default intensity. However, unless one sets a particularly high volatility for the intensity, the Gaussian copula paradox still emerges.

Here we add to the analysis in Brigo and Chourdakis (2008) by considering that there is another aspect of CDS counterparty risk that is not addressed there. It is the loss incurred when

$$\tau^{Reference} < \tau^{Counterparty},$$
$$\tau^{Counterparty} - \tau^{Reference} < \Delta T^{Settlement},$$

namely the case when the default of the reference entity precedes the default of the counterparty protection seller, or even triggers it, and the default of the counterparty happens before the

CDS has been settled.[6] In this case the loss for the protection buyer is the most severe: all the Loss Given Default.

But there is more. This case is the most relevant in CDS counterparty risk because, in difference to the case considered in Brigo and Chourdakis (2008), the loss cannot be avoided by the standard provision of collateral. In fact, standard collateral is given by the protection seller as a guarantee in an amount equal to its exposure towards the protection buyer, namely the CDS mark-to-market. But the CDS mark-to-market, even the day before default, is always much lower than the loss-given-default to which the exposure suddenly jumps at the moment of default. Consider the Lehman case: in the few days before default Lehman CDS spreads reached some hundreds of basis points. For a 1 year CDS, this can lead the exposure to be little higher than 10% of the notional. The standard collateral is posted daily only up to this amount. Suddenly there is default, and in the case of Lehman the exposure jumps to more than 80% of the notional, given the low expectations that emerged about recovery. If now the CDS protection seller reveals that he has sold heavy protection on Lehman and it is forced to default (not an unlikely possibility, excluding bailout), all the gap between today's exposure and yesterday's collateral is potentially lost. The features of a CDS, such as stochastic payment time (default time) and strong discontinuity in value just before payment time make the product risky, from a counterparty risk point of view, even when standard collateral is provided.

Let us see how the Gaussian copula deals with this risk. The time lag between default and settlement is usually at least 60 days, often 72 days. If we consider the two names of the above example, it is natural to take name 1, with lower default risk, as the protection seller, and name 2, much more risky, as the reference entity. In this example, considering a CDS with maturity 10y, the probability of suffering the heaviest CDS counterparty loss is

$$\Pr\left(|\tau_1 - \tau_2| < 3m, \tau_2 < \tau_1, \tau_1 < 10y, \tau_2 < 10y\right).$$

Also here, as shown in Figure 3.14, the probability of joint default leading to the maximum loss starts decreasing when correlation approaches one, so, differently from what one may assume, $\rho = 1$ does not correspond to the worst case scenario.

3.4.3 A Solution. From Copulas to Real Models

Can we find alternative approaches to default correlation that do not suffer from the problems of Gaussian copula? The Gaussian copula looks like a black box in these credit applications. You put in intensities and correlations, and you get a model from which it is difficult to understand and anticipate how the timing of the defaults is regulated. As an alternative, we try first to remain in the field of copulas, but we move to a copula that is constructed from a model that has a clear interpretation in terms of default events. This is the Marshall-Olkin copula, which is derived from the Marshall and Olkin (1967) model[7] which gives a physical representation of the multivariate distribution of rare events, which we can easily consider as default events.

[6] Rumour has it that similar risks related to AIG in the aftermath of Lehman's default in 2008.

[7] The paper by Marshall and Olkin (1967) that introduced this model does not mention copulas and is titled 'A Multivariate Exponential Distribution'.

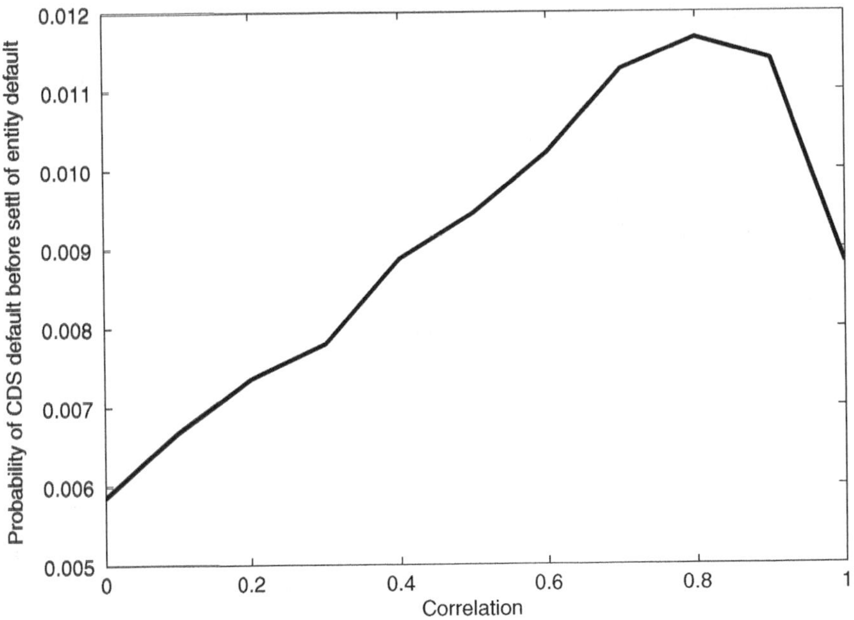

Figure 3.14 CDS counterparty risk

A model for systemic risk

Consider two names X_1, X_2. For modelling the joint distribution of default times of X_1, X_2 we take three independent Poisson processes with first jumps at $Z_1, Z_2, Z_{1,2}$ with parameters $\gamma_1, \gamma_2, \gamma_{1,2}$. The first jump of each of these processes represents a financial event. The jump Z_i leads name X_i, $i = 1, 2$, to default, while a jump $Z_{1,2}$ represents an event that makes both names default. It is not difficult to write down the joint and marginal survival probabilities in this model:

$$\begin{aligned}
&\Pr(\tau_1 > T_1, \tau_2 > T_2) \\
&\quad = \Pr(Z_1 > T_1)\Pr(Z_2 > T_2)\Pr\left(Z_{1,2} > \max(T_1, T_2)\right) \\
&\quad = e^{-\gamma_1 T_1} e^{-\gamma_2 T_2} e^{-\gamma_{12}\max(T_1, T_2)}, \\
&\Pr(\tau_i > T_i) \\
&\quad = \Pr(Z_i > T_i)\Pr\left(Z_{1,2} > T_i\right) = e^{-\gamma_i T_i} e^{-\gamma_{12} T_i}.
\end{aligned} \tag{3.17}$$

Here it is very clear how the timing of the defaults is regulated. It is not possible to have, unlike with the Gaussian copula, completely unrealistic events such as defaults that are perfectly dependent but the larger the first default time, the further away the second. There are scenarios when either of the two names, independently of the other, can default for idiosyncratic reasons, and scenarios in which instead the defaults happen for a shock that affects both. In this case the two defaults happen at the same time. This also is an approximation compared to reality, where default contagion has an effect over some time rather than instantaneously. But this is much more realistic than the 'perfectly-dependent, many-years-apart default events' of the Gaussian copula. From this model we can derive a copula, the Marshall-Olkin copula, that we hope will work better than the Gaussian copula since it is based on the above model which is natural for default risk applications. We hope this copula will work better than the Gaussian copula also because the above model leads to a multivariate exponential distribution for the default times, so the copula is derived from a multivariate distribution consistent with the marginal distribution we use in our intensity model for individual default times.

The Marshall-Olkin copula

From the joint and marginal probabilities of (3.17) we can find a family of copulas. Here it is more convenient to derive the copula from the joint survival distribution

$$S_{X_1,\dots,X_n}(x_1,\dots,x_n) = \Pr(X_1 > x_1,\dots,X_n > x_n)$$

than from the joint cumulative probability distribution. In this case we speak of *survival copulas* $\hat{C}_{x_1,\dots,x_n}$, defined by

$$\hat{C}_{X_1,\dots,X_n}(u_1,\dots,u_n) = S_{X_1,\dots,X_n}(S_{X_1}^{-1}(u_1),\dots,S_{X_n}^{-1}(u_n)),$$
$$\hat{C}_{X_1,\dots,X_n}(S_{X_i}(x_1),\dots,S_{X_i}(x_n)) = S_{X_1,\dots,X_n}(x_1,\dots,x_n).$$

From the Marshall-Olkin model we obtain the following Marshall-Olkin copula (see Muliere and Scarsini (1987)):

$$S_{\tau_i}^{-1}(u_i) = -\frac{\ln(u_i)}{\gamma_i + \gamma_{12}} \quad i = 1, 2,$$
$$\hat{C}_{\tau_1,\tau_2}(u_1,u_2) = e^{-\gamma_1 S_{\tau_1}^{-1}(u1)} e^{-\gamma_2 S_{\tau_2}^{-1}(u_2)} e^{-\gamma_{12}\max\left(S_{\tau_1}^{-1}(u1),S_{\tau_2}^{-1}(u_2)\right)}$$
$$= e^{-(\gamma_1+\gamma_{12})S_{\tau_1}^{-1}(u1)} e^{-(\gamma_2+\gamma_{12})S_{\tau_2}^{-1}(u_2)} e^{+\gamma_{12}\min\left(S_{\tau_1}^{-1}(u1),S_{\tau_2}^{-1}(u_2)\right)}$$
$$= u_1 u_2 \min\left(u_1^{-\frac{\gamma_{12}}{\gamma_1+\gamma_{12}}}, u_2^{-\frac{\gamma_{12}}{\gamma_2+\gamma_{12}}}\right).$$

Setting $\alpha_1 = \frac{\gamma_{1,2}}{\gamma_1+\gamma_{1,2}}$, $\alpha_2 = \frac{\gamma_{1,2}}{\gamma_2+\gamma_{1,2}}$, one finds

$$\hat{C}_{\tau_1,\tau_2}(u_1,u_2) = u_1 u_2 \min\left(u_1^{-\alpha_1}, u_2^{-\alpha_2}\right). \tag{3.18}$$

We are ready to apply this copula, rather than a Gaussian one, to the above case studies with

$$\lambda_1 = 0.03,\ \lambda_2 = 0.2,$$

corresponding to marginals

$$\Pr(\tau_1 > T_1) = e^{-\lambda_1 T_1}, \Pr(\tau_2 > T_2) = e^{-\lambda_2 T_2}. \tag{3.19}$$

When these marginals are introduced into the copula (3.18) we obtain a joint survival probability

$$\Pr(\tau_1 > T_1, \tau_2 > T_2) = e^{-\lambda_1 T_1} e^{-\lambda_2 T_2} \min\left(e^{\lambda_1 T_1 \alpha_1}, e^{\lambda_2 T_2 \alpha_2}\right),$$

and with this we can see how the forward probabilities of joint default change when we move the parameters of the Marshall-Olkin copula.

Let us consider again the case of joint default of two heterogeneous names in $3y$–$5y$ from now. To make sure that we are covering the entire spectrum allowed by this copula, as we did in the Gaussian copula by moving correlations from 0 to 1, we follow Embrechts

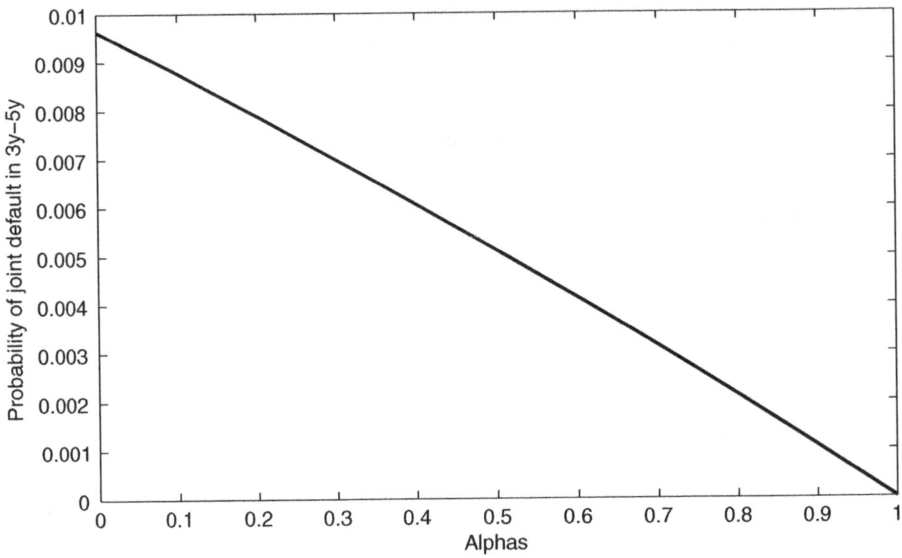

Figure 3.15 Probability of concentrated losses for different alphas in Marshall-Olkin copula

et al. (2001) who explain that in this copula independence corresponds to $\alpha_1 = \alpha_2 = 0$, while perfect dependence corresponds to $\alpha_1 = \alpha_2 = 1$. Thus we will move $\alpha_1 = \alpha_2$ from 0 to 1. We always keep $\alpha_1 = \alpha_2$ also for an easier comparison with the Gaussian copula that has a unique parameter (later on we will break this symmetry). The results are given in Figure 3.15.

In contrast to the initial expectations stated above, the Marshall-Olkin copula has a behaviour analogous to the behaviour of the Gaussian copula, seen in Figure 3.11, where maximum dependence corresponds to minimum (nil) probability of joint losses. Even in this alternative copula, defaults can be, unrealistically, perfectly dependent but largely spaced apart, although this appeared impossible in the Marshall Olkin model from which we derived the copula. We may decide to move the copula parameters differently, but we do not have a precise indication about how to do that. See Minucci (2010) for more details on these tests and those that follow.

The Marshall-Olkin model

Therefore we decide to use the Marshall-Olkin model of (3.17) without moving it to a copula. Let us see what this model implies when the marginals are (3.19), with $\lambda_1 < \lambda_2$. We start from the independence case, corresponding to assuming no probability of a common shock, $\gamma_{12} = 0$. Since we have a constraint on the marginals which must be

$$\gamma_1 + \gamma_{1,2} = \lambda_1, \quad \gamma_2 + \gamma_{1,2} = \lambda_2, \tag{3.20}$$

the independence case corresponds to

$$\gamma_1 = \lambda_1, \gamma_2 = \lambda_2, \gamma_{12} = 0.$$

Then we can start increasing $\gamma_{12} > 0$, always keeping (3.20) which corresponds to

$$\gamma_1 = \lambda_1 - \gamma_{1,2}, \quad \gamma_2 = \lambda_2 - \gamma_{1,2}.$$

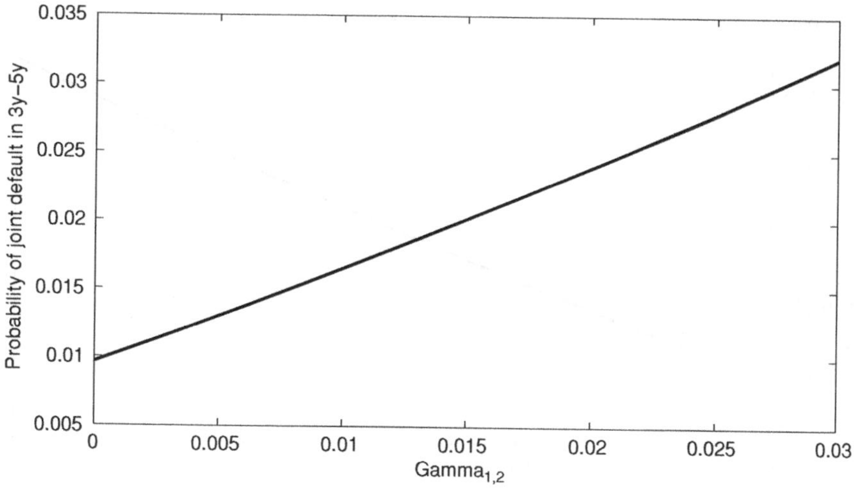

Figure 3.16 Probability of concentrated losses for different gamma in the Marshall-Olkin Model

Since $\lambda_1 < \lambda_2$, the maximum we can reach for γ_{12} is

$$\gamma_{12} = \lambda_1, \quad \gamma_1 = 0, \quad \gamma_2 = \lambda_2 - \lambda_1.$$

This is clearly the maximum codependence we can have in this model: the less risky name 1 can never default separately from 2, so that $\gamma_1 = 0$ and $\gamma_{12} = \lambda_1$, and the higher default probability $\lambda_2 > \lambda_1$ of name 2 implies that there is also a residual possibility of 2 defaulting for idiosyncratic reasons with intensity $\gamma_2 = \lambda_2 - \lambda_1$.

In this model where we have

$$\begin{aligned}\Pr(\tau_1 > T_1, \tau_2 > T_2) &= e^{-(\lambda_1 - \gamma_{1,2})T_1} e^{-(\lambda_2 - \gamma_{1,2})T_2} e^{-\gamma_{12}\max(T_1, T_2)} \\ \Pr(\tau_i > T_i) &= e^{-(\lambda_i - \gamma_{1,2})T_i} e^{-\gamma_{12}T_i} = e^{-\lambda_i T_i}\end{aligned}$$

we can compute the behaviour of joint default probabilities as γ_{12} goes from 0 to λ_1, while the other parameters move consequently. The results are shown in Figure 3.16.

Eventually, even if the marginal intensities are different from each other and the intervals have a forward start date, we have a model where the parameter that controls interdependency has a clear relationship with the financial risk of interest. Now increasing dependence increases the probability of joint losses, and this was confirmed by additional tests of ours where instead the Marshall-Olkin copula has problems similar to the Gaussian one.

Thus, even when copulas are derived from models that are easy to interpret and control, these features can be lost in passing from the model to the copula. What was wrong in the Marshall-Olkin copula above?

We can understand this based on the analysis we made in the model. In fact, the procedure that we followed in the model to increase $\gamma_{1,2}$ can be translated into the copula parameters α_1 and α_2, and leads one to move them from zero to

$$\begin{aligned}\alpha_1 &= \frac{\gamma_{1,2}}{\gamma_1 + \gamma_{1,2}} = \frac{\lambda_1}{\lambda_1} = 1, \\ \alpha_2 &= \frac{\gamma_{1,2}}{\gamma_2 + \gamma_{1,2}} = \frac{\lambda_1}{\lambda_2}\end{aligned}$$

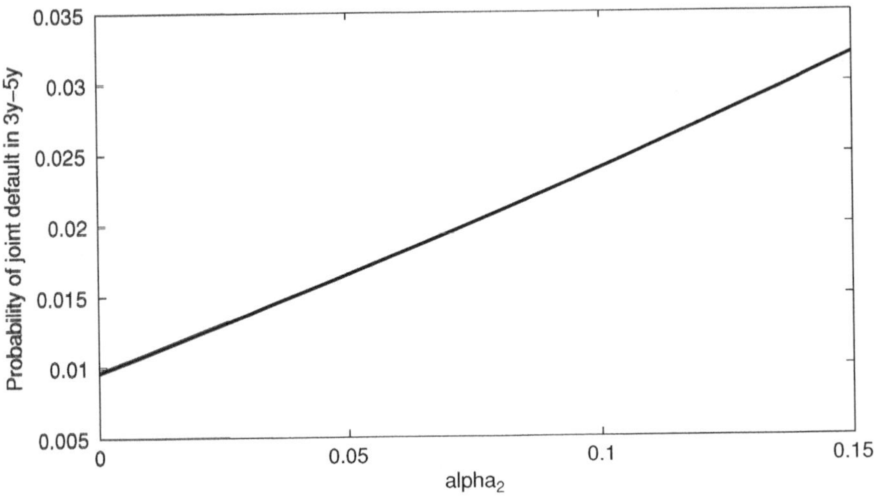

Figure 3.17 Probability of concentrated losses in a Marshall-Olkin copula when moving parameters just as in the Marshall-Olkin model

consistently with movements of $\gamma_{1,2}$. This is different from moving α_1 and α_2 keeping them equal as we did above, and it also shows that the maximum value that α_2 should reach is $\frac{\lambda_1}{\lambda_2}$, lower than the maximum value of 1 allowed by the copula. Only in this way can we get the desired behaviour, shown in Figure 3.17.

This shows that the Marshall-Olkin Copula is actually better than the Gaussian copula because with the former we have found a way to associate parameters to the financial risk we want to control. However we were to find this association only looking at the original model, thus it is not clear why one should decide to lose the clarity of a model that works very well in these applications, to get entangled in the copula black box. Additionally, we have seen that the Marshall-Olkin copula allows for scenarios such as $\alpha_1 = \alpha_2 = 1$ that have no correspondence in the original Marshall-Olkin model and that lead us to the same problems we saw in the Gaussian copula. The model (3.17) remains the safest choice.

3.4.4 Conclusions

In this section we tested the Gaussian copula for some applications that had been earlier overlooked but appear very relevant for understanding the crisis and the real risks of credit derivatives. In fact, we have considered the management of the risk of losses concentrated in time, namely the financial losses that we really saw at the beginning of the subprime crisis. We have also tested the case of homogeneous credit risk in the pool vs the more realistic case of heterogeneous credit risk. Through this simple testing of the model we have found that in the latter case the Gaussian copula does not allow one to cover the entire range of default dependencies that have a financial meaning, but instead allows it for forms of dependency that do not correspond to any possible financial scenario. While I do not think that this feature of this model 'killed Wall Street', it is definitely a worrying feature, since copulas are still widely used for pricing, hedging and risk-management computations where the probability of losses concentrated in time is a crucial risk factor.

One additional worrying feature of the Gaussian copula is that the relation between the correlation parameter and the relevant financial risk appears unstable and irregular. This problem is not limited to the Gaussian copula but extends also to the other copula examined, the Marshall-Olkin copula. Our results belie the market myth that copulas allow one to control the dependency between losses separately from the individual loss distributions. In fact, in the financial applications we consider we cannot really impose as much dependency as we like regardless of the choices we have made on the marginals. In our examples on credit modelling we have seen that the choices on the default intensities of the single names are much more important than copula correlations in determining the dependency risk we care about, namely the risk of defaults happening close together. In this case the relative size of the intensities completely alter the link between the financial risk we want to compute and the correlation copula parameter.

This makes it very difficult to understand and manage the real risk of a portfolio. For example, from standard market experience one would expect that the correlation level that corresponds to the most pessimistic financial scenario in terms of concentrated losses is correlation 1. But this is true only when we consider an interval of time that starts today or companies with equal default risk. If, instead, we consider general intervals that can start in the future and different companies, correlation 1 can even become the most optimistic scenario, with correlation 0 becoming the most pessimistic. In many cases, there is simply no monotonic relation between this parameter and financial risk, so that one has to find out numerically, for each new example, which level of the parameter represents the worst financial scenario. Doing stress testing with such models can become a nightmare, and it is dangerous. The intuition on the relation between the real risk and the model we use gets lost, which is the perfect way to run straight into another crisis.

The lack of a clear relation between copula parameters and financial risk appears to be a consequence of the use of copulas as a framework where individual default risks are modelled separately and are then joined together with an exogenous, orthogonal interdependency assumption, with shallow investigation on the consequences of this marriage. In fact, we show that a solution to this problem is to move away from the framework of copulas, which in a credit application behave like a mathematical black box, and instead to use a model with structural foundations and an easy interpretation as a physical model for default times. The example we consider is the Marshall-Olkin model, where we have a clear relation between parameters and risk, we avoid unrealistic behaviour of the default times, and the model is simple and intuitive to use. It can be used to quantify the model risk when we are using copulas in this application.

3.5 TESTING WITH HISTORICAL SCENARIOS AND THE CONCENTRATION MISTAKE

Here we test the mapping methods traditionally used for attributing a correlation to tranches of bespoke portfolios. Such methods start by using the quoted Index Tranches as a comparable, and adjust the correlations to the bespoke by assuming mathematical relations between the spreads of a portfolio and the correlation that do not have any obvious financial meaning. We notice that there exists no liquid market for backtesting the goodness of these methods, so we devise a way to use historical information to understand if these methods capture at least the historical relation between spreads and correlation. This cannot guarantee that the methods are right, but like a stress test it can tell us if they are wrong in some relevant cases. In fact, the test allows us to understand that standard methods see the relations between spreads and correlations only along one possible dimension (level of risk) while historically there has been another one (dispersion) that alternative methods can capture. We propose one such method to improve our benchmarks for evaluation and quantification of model risk.

This example is also interesting for model risk management because it gives suggestions on how to use quotations for comparables which are similar to the product of interest but are not the same, and because it shows a way to construct scenarios for stress testing.

3.5.1 The Mapping Methods for Bespoke Portfolios

In Section 3.3 we considered the problem of calibrating the market quotes for the tranches written on an index portfolio, a relatively liquid market, particularly before the crisis. But banks and funds were faced with an even more difficult problem. Most CDOs and other portfolio credit derivatives have tranches based on *bespoke* portfolios, namely portfolios constructed specifically for one structured credit derivative, for which there is no liquid information on implied correlations. In 2006–2007 this problem led to a characteristic market practice, which was called mapping. Below we describe this market technique.

In the market model based on Gaussian copula with flat correlation, to price a CDO on a portfolio an investor requires the level of the spreads of the components of the portfolio and a correlation skew (a relation between detachments of equity options and implied correlations) specific for the portfolio. When the portfolio is bespoke, we clearly have no liquid market information on correlations. In the best case, we only know the single name spreads.

The idea behind mapping is as follows. For one of the quoted indices (i-Traxx or CDX) we can observe the spreads of the components of the index and the associated correlation skew coming from the quoted tranches. For the bespoke we can observe the spreads of the components of the bespoke portfolio, and we need to find the associated correlation skew. According to mapping, the index information about index single name spreads and index correlation, together with the information about bespoke spreads, allows us to find a reasonable bespoke correlation skew.

Thus the idea is that there is some stable relation between the portfolio composition (the spreads) and the portfolio correlation skew. We can capture this relation on the index portfolio and then apply it to the bespoke portfolio. The mapping literature assumes that the level of correlation ρ_K associated with a tranche $[0, K]$ is a function of one fundamental characteristic of the tranche. This 'fundamental characteristic' is called *invariant*. Once we have decided what the invariant is, we can look at the information available on the index in order to understand what this map $f(\cdot)$ is, giving the tranche correlation as a function of the tranche invariant,

$$\rho_K^{Index} = f\left(Invariant_K^{Index}\right).$$

In other words, we are using the information available on the index portfolio to calibrate the relation between the invariant and the correlations. This calibration gives the function $f(\cdot)$. According to a believer in mapping, this function $f(\cdot)$ must also be the same for all bespokes. Hence we can apply $f(\cdot)$ to the level of the invariant computed for the tranches of the bespoke, obtaining as an output the right bespoke correlations

$$\rho_{\bar{K}}^{Bespoke} = f\left(Invariant_{\bar{K}}^{Bespoke}\right).$$

The first choice to make is to decide what the invariant is. This choice is essential, because the results are crucially influenced by this exogenous, personal judgement. Many proposals have been made in the market. Surprisingly enough, none of these proposals is underpinned by a structured financial reasoning, but only by some sketchy justification, which we try to summarize below. For more details, see for example, Baheti and Morgan (2007) and Turc et al. (2006).

1) Tranche Detachment or No Mapping

The first example of invariant we can think of is a trivial one. If the correlation skew that is correct for CDOs on the index portfolio was deemed to be correct also for CDOs written on any bespoke portfolio, then the invariant would just be the detachment K of the tranche, leading to

$$\rho_K^{Index} = f^{TD}(K), \quad \rho_{\bar{K}}^{Bespoke} = f^{TD}\left(\bar{K}\right).$$

In this case, if the index quotes were for example

$$\rho_{3\%}^{Index} = 30\%, \rho_{6\%}^{Index} = 40\%, \rho_{9\%}^{Index} = 50\%, \ldots$$

mapping would yield the following result

$$\rho_{3\%}^{Bespoke} = 30\%, \rho_{6\%}^{Bespoke} = 40\%, \rho_{9\%}^{Bespoke} = 50\%, \ldots$$

Now the correlation for, say, a tranche with detachment 7% on the bespoke would be obtained just by interpolation. This mapping approach was also called 'no mapping', because it corresponds to doing nothing to adapt correlations to the bespoke portfolio but treating the bespoke as if it was a copy of the index. This approach was used by unsophisticated market players.

Once we devise a way to test the mapping methods, 'no mapping' will be used as a benchmark to assess if the other non-trivial mapping methods described below are really useful: if they perform as well as 'no mapping', or even worse, clearly the non-trivial mapping methods are useless or even harmful, and the whole idea behind mapping should be questioned.

2) Expected Loss (EL)

This second method was widely used in the market. It was implemented by the vast majority of financial softwares and even now it is probably the most widespread approach to 'marking-to-market' CDOs on bespoke portfolios. It is just slightly more elaborate than 'no mapping', but it is intuitively appealing. The market operator believing in Expected Loss will say to the believer in Tranche Detachment:

> *'Using No Mapping for bespokes is silly. Consider a tranche with 3% detachment written on an index where the expectation of the loss (3.1), for the maturity of interest, is 0.5%. This tranche is an object completely different from a tranche with the same 3% detachment but written on a much more risky bespoke where the expected loss is, say, 10%. In the first case the expected loss is a fraction of the tranche size, in the second one the tranche is completely eaten into the expected loss. The tranche size should be rescaled by the level of the expected loss in the portfolio! A much better invariant is* $\frac{K}{\mathbb{E}[L]}$*, where L is the portfolio loss.'*

Now one must detect from the index the map

$$\rho_K^{Index} = f^{EL}\left(\frac{K}{\mathbb{E}\left[L^{Index}\right]}\right)$$

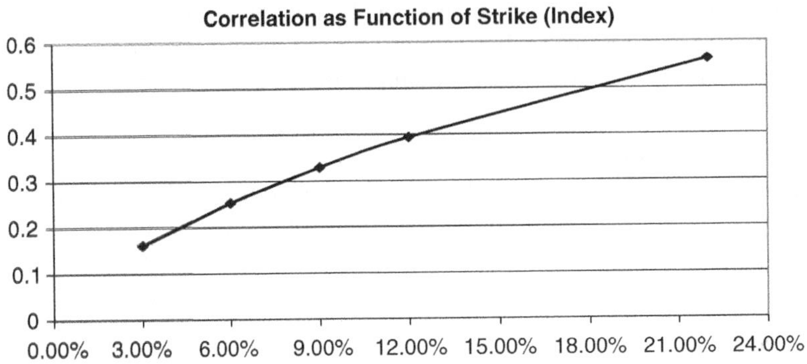

Figure 3.18 EL Mapping A): the market correlation skew

and then one can apply it to the bespoke, so that

$$\rho_{\bar{K}}^{Bespoke} = f^{EL}\left(\frac{\bar{K}}{\mathbb{E}\left[L^{Bespoke}\right]}\right).$$

From a computational point of view, the effort involved in implementing this mapping method is minimal. We can easily visualize it on a chart. We start from the index correlation skew for some maturity given in Figure 3.18.

Then we compute the expected loss for the index at the same maturity and we find $E\left[L^{Index}\right] = 3\%$ (this is a convenient number since the first i-Traxx detachments are multiples of 3%). We rewrite the correlation skew as a function of $\frac{K}{\mathbb{E}[L]}$ rather than K, as in Figure 3.19.

According to mapping, this relation must be the same for all portfolios in the market. Thus we assume it also holds true for the bespoke of interest. We compute the expected loss of the bespoke using the bespoke spreads, and find $E\left[L^{Bespoke}\right] = 6\%$. With this we can rewrite the above relation between correlation and invariant as a normal correlation skew, which means multiplying the x-axis by $E\left[L^{Bespoke}\right]$. It gives the renormalized correlation skew for the bespoke shown in Figure 3.20.

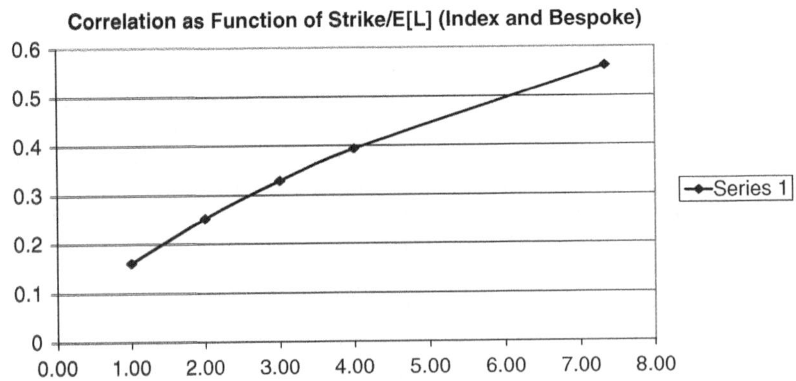

Figure 3.19 EL Mapping B): the skew in terms of detachments over Expected Loss

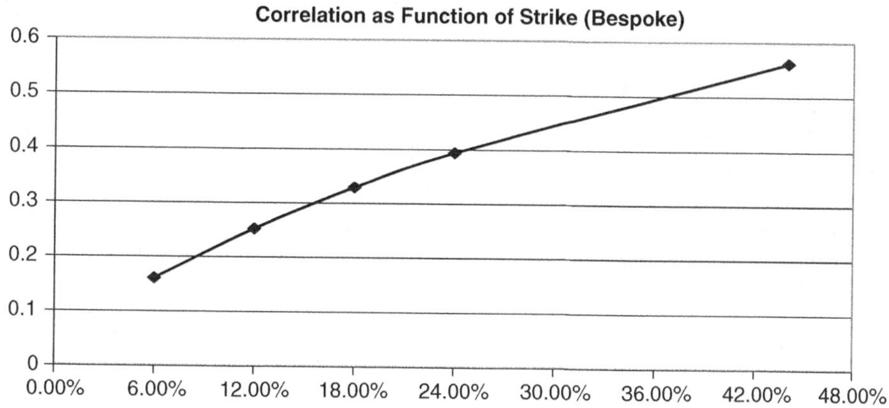

Figure 3.20 EL Mapping C): the correlation skew of the bespoke

3) Expected Tranched Loss (ETL)

This third method was considered an improvement on the Expected Loss method, although it was similar in spirit. The believer in Expected Tranched Loss would have said to the believer in EL:

'EL is too simplified an invariant. It depends on one single moment of the Loss distribution, the first moment. But the loss has many more moments that shape its distribution, and you need the invariant to account also for them. In fact an equity tranche has a payoff which is an option on the Loss,

$$L_K = L - (L - K)^+$$

and as such it depends on moments of order higher than one. An invariant better than EL will be

$$\frac{\mathbb{E}[L_K]}{\mathbb{E}[L]}.$$

Unlike EL, with the ETL method we no longer write down explicitly the relation between the correlation and the invariant, because the invariant itself now depends on correlation. The relation has now to be intended as an implicit function. The practical methodology to ensure that this implicit function is detected on the index and then applied to the bespoke, consistently with the mapping logic, works as follows: one starts from a correlation ρ_K^{Index} in the index, and with a numerical procedure finds the detachment $\bar{K}$ in the bespoke such that, using the same correlation ρ_K^{Index} for the index K tranche and for the bespoke $\bar{K}$ tranche, we have

$$\frac{\mathbb{E}\left[L_{0,\bar{K}}^{Bespoke}\right]}{\mathbb{E}\left[L^{Bespoke}\right]} = \frac{\mathbb{E}\left[L_{0,K}^{Index}\right]}{\mathbb{E}\left[L^{Index}\right]}.$$

The tranche with detachment $\bar{K}$ in the bespoke is called *equivalent* to tranche K in the Index. For the set of quoted index tranches $K_1, K_2, \ldots$ associated with correlations $\rho_{K_1}^{Index}, \rho_{K_2}^{Index} \ldots$

one finds a set of equivalent bespoke tranches $\bar{K}_1, \bar{K}_2 \ldots$ associated with the correlations

$$\rho_{\bar{K}_1}^{Bespoke} = \rho_{K_1}^{Index}, \rho_{\bar{K}_2}^{Bespoke} = \rho_{K_2}^{Index}, \ldots$$

This set is the backbone of the correlation skew for the bespoke, from which through interpolation and extrapolation we can find a correlation for any bespoke tranche.

There is another method which is similar to ETL but considers a different invariant. It is called Probability Matching. We do not cover it in the tests below, but it is covered in Sardo (2010), and the results obtained are analogous to those obtained here for ETL.

3.5.2 The Lehman Test

The mapping methods have been tested in a Lehman research paper by Baheti and Morgan (2007). The test is based on a simple reasoning. Mapping methods claim that correlation is just a function of the invariant, and the function is the same for all portfolios in the market. If this is true, one can detect this function from any index with quoted tranches, for example the CDX Investment Grade which is the index of the American 'senior' names, the names with lower spreads and higher rating. The function can then be applied to the spreads of another index with quoted tranches, such as i-Traxx Main, which is the index of the European senior names, or CDX High Yield, which is the index of the American 'junior' names, with higher spreads and lower rating. This will return a correlation skew for either index. If mapping works, these correlation skew will be – at least approximately – equal to the corresponding correlation skew quoted in the market.

Clearly, a mapping sceptic would find this attempt entirely hopeless, and would consider any success an unlikely miracle. In my opinion the two tests mentioned above have two different probabilities of success. The first test, where one tries to guess the European senior skew from the American senior skew,

$$\textit{CDX Investment Grade} \longrightarrow i - \textit{Traxx Investment Grade},$$

seems very difficult. In fact, the mapping methods only know the spreads about the European market, and must use these spreads to adapt the American skew to the European reality. But how can one guess from the spreads the crucial features that make Europe different from America? Features such as the fact that the US is one country while Europe is divided into different countries or the different legal system treatment of bankruptcy are not trivially revealed by the sheer comparison of the two vectors of spreads. Indeed, even for an experienced trader it would be difficult, given two 125-element vectors of spreads without labels, to distinguish the vector corresponding to i-Traxx from the vector corresponding to CDX.

Things should be easier when one tries to guess the American junior skew from the American senior skew,

$$\textit{CDX Investment Grade} \longrightarrow \textit{CDX High.Yield}.$$

Here the crucial difference between the senior (investment grade) and the junior (high yield) market is indeed revealed trivially by the sheer comparison of the two vectors of spreads. Even a child would be able to tell the two markets apart by the sheer comparison of the two vectors of spreads: the investment grade vector has lower spreads than the high yield vector. If there is a stable relationship between the seniority of the names in a portfolio and their correlation, that allows one to modify a senior skew to elicit a more junior skew, this modification can be performed by the mapping method that only sees information about spreads.

Baheti and Morgan (2007) perform exactly these tests, for 5y tranches, based on the market data for one trading day in the past. Below we show their results, in terms of tranche net present value.

CDX.NA.IG↦iTraxx Main : Tranches 5y NPV

	Market	NM	EL	ETL
0–3%	10.53	10.83	9.58	10.35
3–6%	42.2	38.5	36	42.9
6–9%	12.3	7.2	6.4	10.3
9–12%	5.6	2.5	1	4.7
12–22%	2.2	0.8	0	1.9

CDX.NA.IG↦CDX.NA.HY : Tranches 5y NPV

	Market	NM	EL	ETL
0–10%	68.75	61.73	74.92	74.79
10–15%	26.07	19.31	28.85	22.78
15–25%	225.7	230.2	155.2	136.7
25–35%	56.1	134.2	21.3	28.1

The results are the opposite of what I would expect. In the US↦Europe exercise one mapping method, ETL, works pretty well, with a clear advantage over no-mapping. Which feature of the US–Europe relationship is captured by this exercise? That is hard to tell.

In the Senior↦Junior exercise, on the other hand, mapping methods all perform badly. Either there is no relationship between seniority and correlation, or the relationship is not the one implicit in these mapping methods.

3.5.3 Historical Scenarios to Test Mapping Methods

It is hard to make a judgement on mapping methods based on the above two tests. They apply mapping to portfolios which are very different from one another (this is particularly true for the first test, but it applies to some extent also to the second). It would be better, for a validation, to apply mapping to portfolios that are similar, but have some specific differences which must be easy to detect and interpret, so that we can check if the effect of such a difference on the correlation skew is captured by mapping. In particular, we need such a difference to be detectable just by the spreads of the two portfolios, otherwise mapping has no way of capturing its effect on correlation, and the success or failure of mapping appears a matter of pure chance. This is what one may suspect about the above tests, particularly the successful US↦Europe one. Unfortunately, the only portfolios available worldwide having liquid markets for tranches are the three portfolios considered by Baheti and Morgan (2007).

In what follows we suggest an alternative use of our information about the indices that provides us with portfolios which are similar, but differ for some specific features which are easy to detect even by looking at the spreads alone. We advise against using *different portfolios at the same time*, as in the Lehman test, but recommend using *the same portfolio at different times*. We can consider two different days, let us say yesterday and today. We treat the spreads and the skew of yesterday as the spreads and the skew of the index. Then the spreads of today are treated as the spreads of the bespoke. By applying a mapping method to these three inputs we obtain a guess for the correlation skew of today (our bespoke) that can be compared with the actual correlation skew quoted in the market for today. The test will be even more relevant if we take two dates which are a few days apart, and such that in the meantime some relevant market facts have happened, changing the index portfolio in a limited and clear way.

This is the first baseline test that a mapping method must pass. In fact every mapping method is based on assuming a relation between the spreads of a portfolio and its correlation skew. The above test allows us to see if the spread-correlation relationship implied by the mapping method is at least consistent with the historical spread-correlation relationship. Failing this test would set alarm bells ringing. Moreover, this test is a relatively easy task for the mapping methods, because we consider two portfolios which are still very similar, since they are composed of the same names and separated only by the changes that occurred to the spreads in a few trading days. If a mapping method works well in this simple test, it may also work in a real bespoke mapping. If it does not work here, it is even more dubious to apply it to more complex situations like bespoke mapping.

Remark 9. ***Mapping for hedging (or the real story of these tests).*** *When I set out to perform these tests of mapping methods, I was not really interested in the mapping methods for pricing bespoke CDOs. My purpose was not to be unfair towards credit derivatives traders compared to interest rate derivatives traders. As a quant on interest-rate derivatives I had worked on the issue of the 'shadow delta' faced by interest rate traders. This issue is explained in detail in Section 5.3 on hedging. Here we summarize it briefly. When traders use a quotation model that requires a smile on some parameter to fit the market, in equity or interest-rates for example, even delta-hedging becomes a non-trivial issue. Suppose a simple context with European options with one maturity written on some underlying, and a volatility smile as in Figure 3.21.*

Computing the delta of a derivative means repricing the derivative after a small shift of the underlying F *from its current value* F_0 *to* $F_0 + \varepsilon$. *Is it reasonable to assume that, if tomorrow there is such a shift of the underlying, the smile will remain unchanged? This is a strong assumption, called* sticky-strike *assumption and represented by a null movement of the smile*

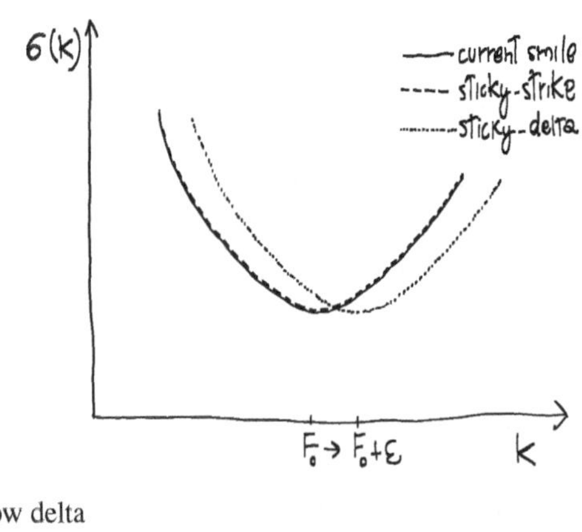

Figure 3.21 The shadow delta

curve when moving from F_0 *to* $F_0 + \varepsilon$, *so that the continuous line in the figure (today smile) coincides with the dashed line (smile after a movement of the underlying under the sticky strike assumption). Market operators, for example in the world of interest rate options, do not believe this assumption to be reasonable. Many find the* sticky-delta *assumption more realistic, where the smile moves to the right following the movement of* F, *as in the situation represented by the dotted line. Capturing the relation correctly is paramount for efficient hedging. A sticky-strike strategy in a sticky-delta market, for example, condemns the hedges computed to be belied by the realized market behaviour with a regular outflow of money.*

When considering the Gaussian copula applied to the tranche market, we confront a similar issue. Traders compute the delta of a tranche by repricing the tranche after shifting the spreads of the underlying portfolio. There are different kind of reasonable deltas. One is the portfolio delta *where the spreads of all* n *names in the portfolio are increased, say, by 1 basis point. Another is the* single name delta *where only the spread of one name in the portfolio is increased by* n *basis points. Is it reasonable to assume that, where such movements really happen in the market, the correlation skew does not move? The answer should be* no. *For example, an increase in the risk of one single name is likely to be associated with some reduction in the default correlation, since this name is experiencing an individual crisis. Mapping methods change the correlation skew in reaction to a change in the spreads, thus they can also be used to adjust the correlation skew when spreads are changed to compute spread sensitivities. Clearly, to trust the movement of correlation they impose one needs to ascertain that this movement is consistent with usual market moves, which can be done only by means of testing against historical behaviour. If this test fails, it is an alarm bell about the mapping methods that can eventually give us some insight into their structural behaviour. This is by way of explanation about how the tests below on mapping, from Morini (2007), occurred to me.*

In this section we perform the historical testing of the mapping methods explained above. Each one of these tests is based on two dates, the 'index date' used for a form of calibrating the mapping method, and the 'bespoke date' whose correlation skew needs to be guessed. The two dates used come just before and just after an important event or relevant crisis that happened in the past. In this case the interpretation of the difference between the pre-crisis portfolio and the post-crisis portfolio is easier because the market operators have already analyzed and interpreted the crisis with hindsight. It is easier to say, for example, if the change in the risk of the portfolio is idiosyncratic or systemic.

In the usual market standard, historical analysis or backtesting are data mining exercises which include at least hundreds of observation times. In model validation, on the other hand, the quality of the data is much more important than its quantity. Rating agency analyses have often been invalidated by the fact that a large dataset was analyzed, but did not include any period of distress or any shift in the economic data. Additionally, the data mining with hundreds of days gives results that are very difficult to interpret. Thus we concentrate on only two pairs of days, but we have selected periods during which we are sure that the market went through relevant changes.

The first event-study looks at what happened in the so-called 'May 2005 correlation crisis'. After the credit crunch of 2007–2009, it may seem ironic that such relatively minor market turmoil merited being called a crisis. In fact, it was an important event, but it did not have the dramatic consequences of the credit crunch because it was the typical example of an idiosyncratic crisis, namely a crisis that only affected a few names, all belonging to a single sector, the car-makers. On 5 May Standard&Poor's downgraded General Motors and Ford

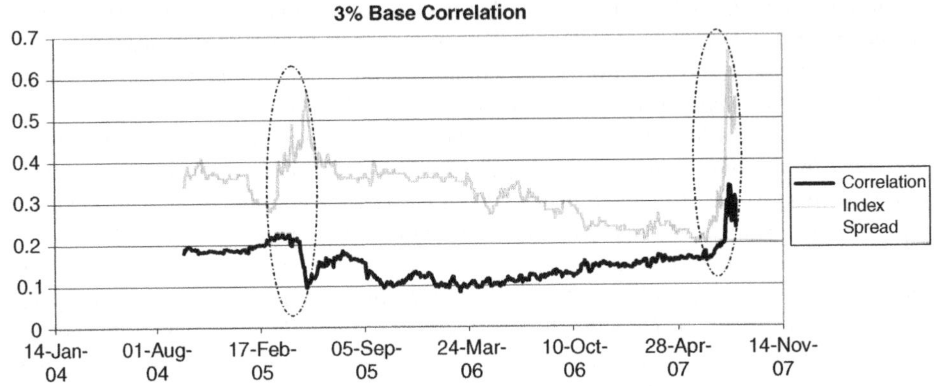

Figure 3.22 Correlations and spreads in the 2005 carmakers correlation crisis

to junk status, provoking a sharp increase in the credit spreads of all companies related to the automobile sector, both in Europe and in the US. In the same days the correlation skew plunged, as illustrated in the historical chart in Figure 3.22, with a decrease particularly strong in the equity 3% tranche (when equity correlation gets lower, the equity tranche becomes more risky). This makes sense, since a crisis focused on few names with no fear of generalized contagion should lower the average default correlation in the portfolio.

The second event-study is firmly impressed on the minds of everyone who was working in the market at the time. It is the week in July 2007 when CDS spreads, after years of impressive calm and low volatility broken only by occasional turmoils such as the May 2005 event, suddenly rocketed with an increase never seen before. We saw in Section 1.1.3 that this market move was fuelled by the situation of subprime mortgages, to which banks were strongly exposed. When the financial system is in trouble, banks will have to reduce their lending and this will in turn trigger an increased risk of default for all economic players worldwide. Many operators suspected that it was the beginning of a typical systemic crisis, doomed sooner or later to affect the whole economy. This explains why, together with the growth of the CDS spreads of almost all names, implied default correlation increased sharply, as can be seen in the chart in Figure 3.23.

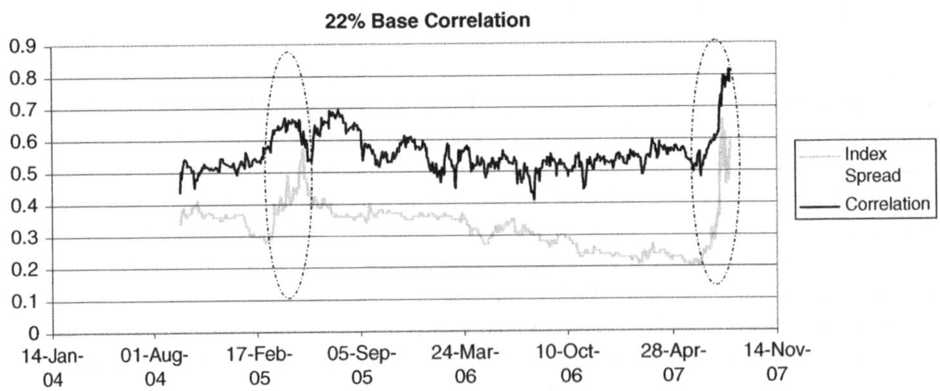

Figure 3.23 Correlations and spreads in the 2007 Subprime correlation crisis

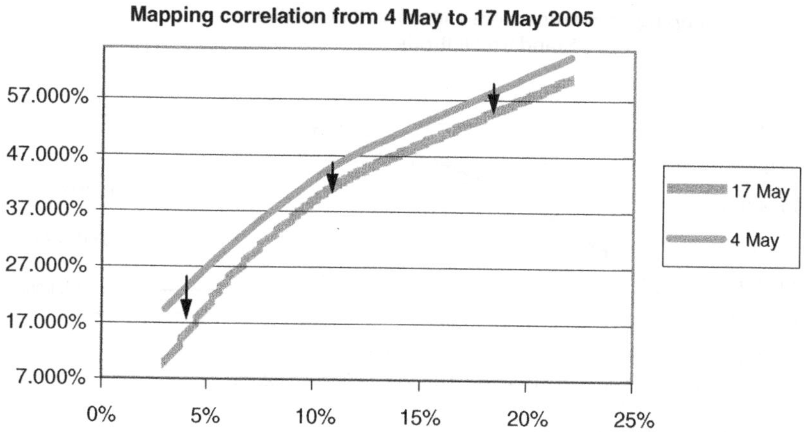

Figure 3.24 May 2005 market correlation shift

In what follows we analyze if and how these two different joint behaviours of spreads and correlations (May 2005 first, and then July 2007) can be explained by the spread-correlation relations implied by the mapping methods.

The idiosyncratic crisis: May 2005

Let us consider the period between 4 May 2005 and 17 May 2005. In-between these two days the iTraxx Main index spread increased strongly, while the correlation skew decrease is much as shown in Figure 3.24 and in the table below, where all quoted tranches are reported for maturity 5y.

Correlations	0%–3%	0%–6%	0%–9%	0%–12%	0%–22%
Market Initial ρ	**19.38%**	**30.43%**	**39.75%**	**47.45%**	**64.72%**
Market Final ρ	**9.66%**	**24.73%**	**35.74%**	**43.78%**	**60.88%**
Difference	**−9.72%**	**−5.71%**	**−4.00%**	**−3.68%**	**−3.85%**

Now let us apply the two mapping methods explained (EL and ETL) to the skew of 5 May (the index day) and the 5y spreads of 5 May and 17 May (the bespoke day), to see how mapping would have guessed the correlation skew of 17 May. In the table below we report the correlation one would obtain with no mapping, which obviously equals the correlation of 5 May (Market Initial ρ), and the correlations guessed by EL and ETL for 17 May (EL/ETL Mapping Final ρ), to be compared with the true market correlation on 17 May (Market Final ρ).

Correlations	0%–3%	0%–6%	0%–9%	0%–12%	0%–22%
Market Initial ρ	**19.38%**	**30.43%**	**39.75%**	**47.45%**	**64.72%**
EL Mapping Final ρ	**17.22%**	**26.22%**	**34.55%**	**41.72%**	**57.66%**
ETL Mapping Final ρ	**17.17%**	**26.62%**	**35.58%**	**43.47%**	**61.65%**
Market Final ρ	**9.66%**	**24.73%**	**35.74%**	**43.78%**	**60.88%**

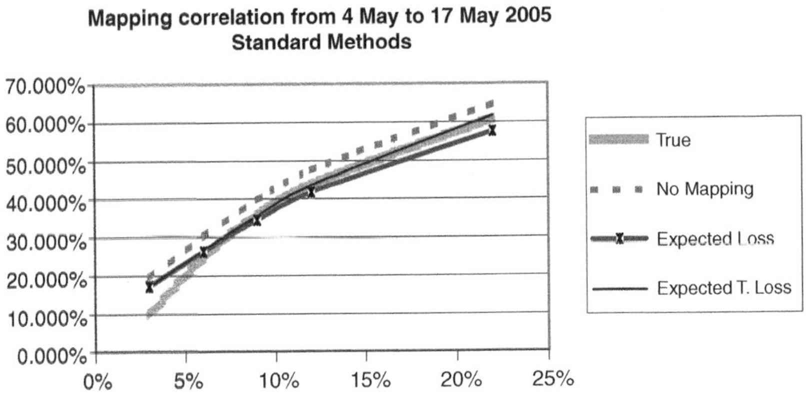

Figure 3.25 Mapping results

Figure 3.25 shows graphically the four correlation skews: the one by no mapping, the two skews guessed by the mapping methods, and the true, realized skew. The errors associated with the three guessed skews are in the following table.

Correlation Errors	0%–3%	0%–6%	0%–9%	0%–12%	0%–22%
No Mapping	**−9.7%**	**−5.7%**	**−4.0%**	**−3.7%**	**−3.8%**
EL Mapping	**−7.6%**	**−1.5%**	**+1.2%**	**+2.1%**	**+3.2%**
ETL Mapping	**−7.5%**	**−1.9%**	**+0.2%**	**+0.3%**	**−0.8%**

The mapping methods definitely work well. The reader may have noticed my perplexities about the mapping methods, mainly due to their lack of structural foundations. Looking at the results of this test, I had to admit that in this case they prove capable of moving the correlation in a way surprisingly similar to the real behaviour of the i-Traxx index, representing a real improvement compared to no-mapping. The error is low particularly for ETL, confirming that this more complex method is better than simple EL. Let us now look at how the mapping methods perform in an opposite situation, the systemic crisis.

The systemic crisis: July 2007

From 20 July 2007 and 27 July 2007, we have a large increase in spreads – one that affects almost all names – associated with a movement in the correlation skew. We have selected this period since both the increase in the index spread and the movement of the correlation skew are comparable in size to those seen in the May 2005 test. In both cases spreads have increased, but for the correlation skew the two moves followed opposite directions. This time we have an increase of correlation, as shown in Figure 3.26 and in the table below.

Correlations	0%–3%	0%–6%	0%–9%	0%–12%	0%–22%
Market Initial ρ	**19.61%**	**28.93%**	**36.76%**	**43.38%**	**60.70%**
Market Final ρ	**24.92%**	**36.37%**	**44.93%**	**52.09%**	**69.34%**
Difference	**+5.31%**	**+7.44%**	**+8.17%**	**+8.71%**	**+8.64%**

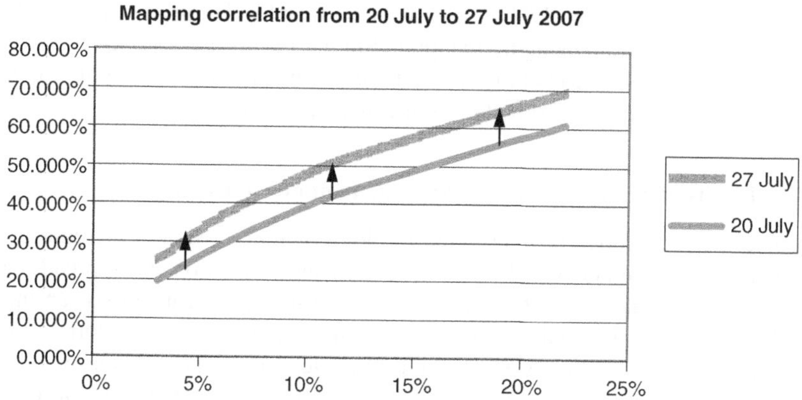

Figure 3.26 July 2007 market correlation shift

The mapping results are shown in the following table and in Figure 3.27.

Correlations	0%–3%	0%–6%	0%–9%	0%–12%	0%–22%
No Mapping Final ρ	**19.61%**	**28.93%**	**36.76%**	**43.38%**	**60.70%**
EL Mapping Final ρ	**16.81%**	**23.33%**	**29.71%**	**35.18%**	**49.26%**
ETL Mapping Final ρ	**17.61%**	**25.26%**	**32.57%**	**39.11%**	**56.61%**
Market Final ρ	**24.92%**	**36.37%**	**44.93%**	**52.09%**	**69.34%**

This time the behaviour of the mapping methods is wrong. The true final correlation is much higher than the initial correlations, but the mapping methods predict instead a decrease in correlation, leading to a bigger error than would result using no mapping. The table below shows the size of the correlation errors.

Correlation Errors	0%–3%	0%–6%	0%–9%	0%–12%	0%–22%
No Mapping	+**5.31%**	+**7.44%**	+**8.17%**	+**8.71%**	+**8.64%**
EL Mapping	+**8.11%**	+**13.04%**	+**15.22%**	+**16.91%**	+**20.08%**
ETL Mapping	+**7.31%**	+**11.11%**	+**12.36%**	+**12.98%**	+**12.73%**

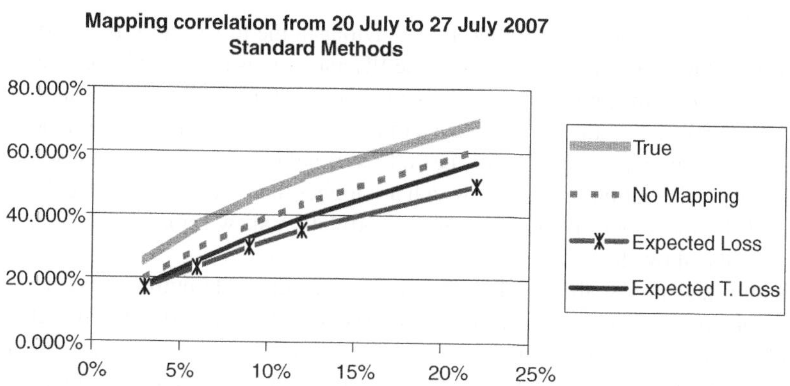

Figure 3.27 Mapping results

Among the mapping methods ETL is slightly better than EL, but in any case both lead to an error larger than results from using no mapping. Similar results are obtained in Sardo (2010) for the so-called Probability Matching method which, in spite of turning out slightly better than ETL, gives the same wrong direction to the mapping movement.

3.5.4 The Limits of Mapping and the Management of Model Risk

The mapping methods correctly interpreted the idiosyncratic crisis (an increase of spreads concentrated on a small minority of the names), decreasing correlation when spreads increased, but unfortunately they also exhibit the same behaviour in the systemic crisis (an increase of spreads which affects a large majority of the names in the portfolio), when correlation should instead be increased. Notice that 'systemic' must be intended at a portfolio level: what makes an increase of risk systemic, from the point of view of mapping, is the fact that it affects the majority of the names *in the portfolio*.

The evidence from these tests leads us to make a relevant observation. Let us go back to the initial pictures about the behaviour of EL, the most widespread mapping method. Look at passage from EL Mapping Figure A (Figure 3.18) to EL Mapping Figure B (Figure 3.19), and then at the passage from EL Mapping Figure B (Figure 3.19) to EL Mapping Figure C (Figure 3.20). It is clear that every time the bespoke is more risky than the index the entire correlation skew is shifted to the right. Due to the fact that in the market we have always seen an increasing correlation skew, this always translates into a reduction of correlation.

Let us examine this analytically. According to the mapping principle, the correlation $\rho_K^{Bespoke}$ given to the bespoke tranche with detachment K must be the correlation $\rho_{K'}^{Index}$ given to the index tranche with detachment K' such that

$$\frac{K}{\mathbb{E}\left[L^{Bespoke}\right]} = \frac{K'}{\mathbb{E}\left[L^{Index}\right]}.$$

If $\mathbb{E}\left[L^{Bespoke}\right] > \mathbb{E}\left[L^{Index}\right]$, we must have $K' < K$. Since the correlation skew is increasing,

$$K' < K \Longrightarrow \rho_{K'}^{Index} < \rho_K^{Index}.$$

Given that $\rho_{K'}^{Index} = \rho_K^{Bespoke}$, we have that

$$\rho_K^{Bespoke} < \rho_K^{Index}.$$

Thus, as far as EL is concerned, the wrong behaviour in the test is not due to a one-off error associated with the fine details of this test. The EL mapping is bound to lower the correlation every time we move to a bespoke which is more risky, thus making a mistake every time this increase of risk is, on the contrary, systemic. The ETL method, which replaces K at the numerator of the invariant with $\mathbb{E}[L_K]$, has a less trivial behaviour, since it also depends on moments of the distribution of the loss which are higher than the first moment $\mathbb{E}[L]$, but the backbone of the movement it imposes on the correlation skew remains the same as EL, as confirmed by the above tests.

The rigidity and predictability of standard mapping methods outlined by these tests are surprising for two reasons. First, such a finding has never been noted in the literature in spite of the widespread use of this method, confirming that in the years before the crisis there was little analysis of the practical implications of such methods. Second, it is obvious that this method leads in some common practical cases to painful errors with mathematical certainty.

Suppose we are given a bespoke which is more risky than the index because all names in the bespoke belong to the same sector which is now in crisis. Intuitively, a CDO on this portfolio should be priced with rather high correlation skew. The mapping, instead, will always lower the correlation skew.

If we want to get an increase in the correlation skew we have to *invert* the invariant of EL: from $\frac{K}{\mathbb{E}[L]}$ to $K\mathbb{E}[L]$. We call this method 'Inverted EL'. Below are the results for the July 2007 test.

Correlations	0%–3%	0%–6%	0%–9%	0%–12%	0%–22%
No Mapping Final ρ	19.61%	28.93%	36.76%	43.38%	60.70%
EL Mapping Final ρ	16.81%	23.33%	29.71%	35.18%	49.26%
ETL Mapping Final ρ	17.61%	25.26%	32.57%	39.11%	56.61%
Inverted EL Mapping Final ρ	**23.61%**	**35.65%**	**44.87%**	**52.30%**	**65.46%**
Market Final ρ	**24.92%**	**36.37%**	**44.93%**	**52.09%**	**69.34%**

If one considers $K\mathbb{E}[L]$ as an invariant the skew is moved in the right direction, with surprisingly high precision. However, such a mapping has a problem which is opposite to EL: it only works when there is a systemic increase of risk, failing every time the increase of risk is due to idiosyncratic issues.

Introducing dispersion as a benchmark for model risk

Is this the end of the mapping illusion? Probably. A simple algorithm like mapping is too rigid to express sensible relations between the composition of a portfolio and its correlation skew. However, it is interesting to point out that it is not difficult to improve on the standard methods proposed before the crisis. In the following we propose a method that captures the behaviour of the correlation skew both when the increase in risk is systemic and when it is idiosyncratic, recognizing the two different situations and adapting itself to give a realistic outcome. The idea behind this method was suggested to me not by complex mathematical considerations, but by the market experience picked up from expert tranche traders. Such traders usually looked at the movements of a market indicator called the *spread dispersion index*. It is a simple quantity. Consider the vector

$$[s_1, s_2, \ldots, s_n]$$

containing the spreads of the names in the portfolio for some maturity (here we consider 5y, consistently with the correlation data). Define the average spread

$$\bar{s} = \frac{1}{n}\sum_{i=1}^{n} s_i$$

and the spread standard deviation

$$\hat{s} = \sqrt{\frac{1}{n}\sum_{i=1}^{n}(s_i - \bar{s})^2}.$$

What is the minimum standard deviation we can get keeping the average $\bar{s}$ fixed? It is a case of minimum dispersion, when all names have the average risk, $s_i = \bar{s}\ \forall i$, leading to

$$\min \hat{s} = 0.$$

Conversely, what is the maximum standard deviation we can get keeping the average $\bar{s}$ fixed? It is when the dispersion in the portfolio is maximum, corresponding to the case where all risk stays on one single name k, $s_k = n\bar{s}$ with $s_i = 0$ for $i \neq k$, leading to

$$\begin{aligned}\max \hat{s} &= \sqrt{\frac{1}{n}\left[(n\bar{s}-\bar{s})^2 + (n-1)(0-\bar{s})^2\right]}\\ &= \times\sqrt{\frac{1}{n}\left[(n-1)^2\,\bar{s}^2 + (n-1)\,\bar{s}^2\right]}\\ &= \bar{s}\sqrt{\frac{1}{n}(n-1)(n-1+1)} = \bar{s}\sqrt{(n-1)}\end{aligned}$$

The dispersion index is the ratio between the spread standard deviation and its maximum value,

$$s^* = \frac{\hat{s}}{\max \hat{s}} = \frac{\hat{s}}{\bar{s}\sqrt{(n-1)}}.$$

It captures how dispersed is the risk in a portfolio, rescaling standard deviation by the average risk of the portfolio. When $s^* = 1$ we have the maximum dispersion we can get given the average portfolio risk expressed by $\bar{s}$.

The two indicators usually looked at by traders are $\bar{s}$ and s^*. The information conveyed by $\bar{s}$ is very close to the information conveyed by $\mathbb{E}[L]$, which is the invariant of EL. On the other hand, the information conveyed by s^* is not considered by EL. It could be included to some extent in ETL, but the tests above have shown that the behaviour of ETL is rather similar to EL. Thus we create a new invariant based on s^*, whose information appears to be omitted by standard methods. The functional form we choose for this invariant is simply

$$K^{s^*}.$$

From 20 to 27 July 2007 the dispersion index has moved from $s^*_{20/7} = 11.28\%$ to $s^*_{27/7} = 8.40\%$, namely the dispersion has reduced. This is what one expects in a systemic crisis because increasing the risk of all names by similar amounts redistributes the risk among all names. The results of the mapping test in the systemic crisis using K^{s^*} as a mapping invariant (dispersion mapping) are reported in the following table and the chart in Figure 3.28.

Correlations	0%–3%	0%–6%	0%–9%	0%–12%	0%–22%
No Mapping Final ρ	19.61%	28.93%	36.76%	43.38%	60.70%
EL Mapping Final ρ	16.81%	23.33%	29.71%	35.18%	49.26%
ETL Mapping Final ρ	17.61%	25.26%	32.57%	39.11%	56.61%
Dispersion Mapping Final ρ	**26.76%**	**37.88%**	**45.61%**	**51.78%**	**63.36%**
Market Final ρ	**24.92%**	**36.37%**	**44.93%**	**52.09%**	**69.34%**

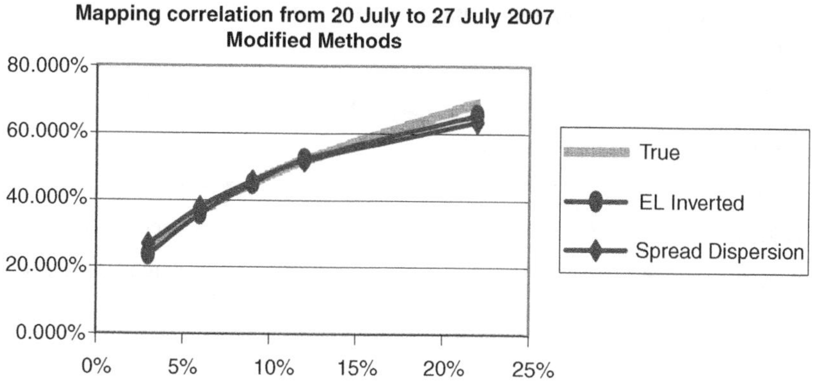

Figure 3.28 Mapping results

Dispersion mapping works well for explaining this systemic crisis, which one can readily appreciate by looking at the correlation errors in the table below.

Correlation Errors	0%–3%	0%–6%	0%–9%	0%–12%	0%–22%
No Mapping	**+5.31%**	**+7.44%**	**+8.17%**	**+8.71%**	**+8.64%**
EL Mapping	**+8.11%**	**+13.04%**	**+15.22%**	**+16.91%**	**+20.08%**
ETL Mapping	**+7.31%**	**+11.11%**	**+12.36%**	**+12.98%**	**+12.73%**
Dispersion	**−1.84%**	**−1.51%**	**−0.68%**	**+0.31%**	**+5.98%**

What makes this method more interesting than the methods seen previously is that not only does it work well in explaining the systemic crisis of July 2007, but it also explains well our other case study, the idiosyncratic crisis of May 2005. In the idiosyncratic crisis the dispersion index moved in a direction opposite to that for the systemic crisis: it increased from $s^*_{4/5} = 5.70\%$ to $s^*_{17/5} = 6.15\%$. This is consistent with intuition: a crisis concentrated on a few names raises the dispersion by increasing one or a few spreads while the others are almost unaffected. The results of dispersion mapping in the May 2005 test are given in the table below and in Figure 3.29.

Correlation Errors	0%–3%	0%–6%	0%–9%	0%–12%	0%–22%
No Mapping	**−9.7%**	**−5.7%**	**−4.0%**	**−3.7%**	**−3.8%**
EL Mapping	**−7.6%**	**−1.5%**	**+1.2%**	**+2.1%**	**+3.2%**
ETL Mapping	**−7.5%**	**−1.9%**	**+0.2%**	**+0.3%**	**−0.8%**
Dispersion	**−7.2%**	**−1.3%**	**+0.8%**	**+1.1%**	**+0.4%**

Dispersion mapping also works well for explaining the idiosyncratic crisis (which was explained also by standard methods) and for explaining the systemic crisis (which was instead missed by standard methods).

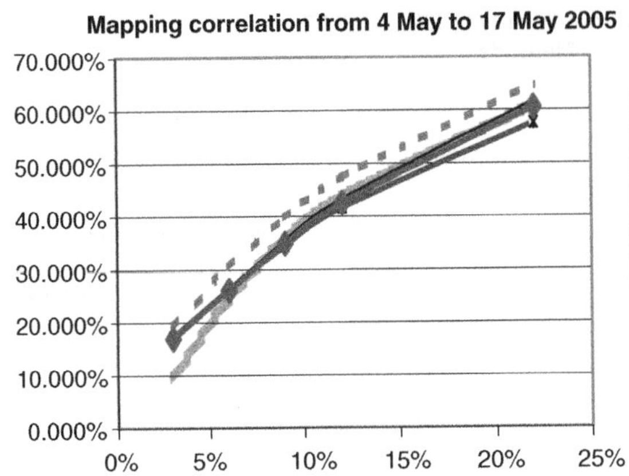

Figure 3.29 Mapping results

3.5.5 Conclusions

We have tested the standard mapping methods against the historical joint behaviour of spreads and correlations during two relevant market dislocations in the past. The two events were selected in order to allow us to assess mapping both in the case of idiosyncratic changes of risk and of systemic changes. The analysis has been used as a stress test of the mapping methods, and in fact it has allowed us to detect that standard mapping methods treat any increase in risk as an idiosyncratic increase.

This is also a problem in the standard application of mapping to the pricing of bespoke CDOs. In fact when we consider senior tranches, which represent the majority of the tranches bought by institutional investors before the crisis, mapping has the effect of watering down increases of risk due to higher spreads in the bespoke compared to the index by diminishing the correlation at the same time. This causes an underestimation of risk every time we have to price a CDO with a sector or regional concentration higher than the index, since in this case one would expect some increase in correlation.

The underestimation may also have affected the pricing of CDOs on mortgage-related securities that, as the crisis clearly revealed, were strongly subject to systemic risk. When mapping was used to price very risky CDOs, the senior tranches had their risk reduced by the lower correlation imposed by mapping methods. This matched the underestimation of risk typical of rating agency methods based on historical correlations.

Was it impossible to devise mapping methods capable of recognizing a systemic increase of risk? No, as we have shown by displaying the performance of a simple method based not on complex mathematical considerations but on an indicator, the dispersion index, that was well known to practitioners in the field. The method we introduced is not proposed as a solution to the problems of mapping methods, because all mapping methods, including dispersion mapping, appear too simple for the task they are supposed to perform. More information about the bespoke portfolio should be used in attributing a correlation skew to the portfolios, and a more structural analysis of the behaviour of the different credit markets should be the foundation for the design of algorithms used to price bespoke. Simple mathematical recipes with no structural foundation should certainly not be relied upon as much as was the case before the crisis.

The interesting aspect of the dispersion mapping is the fact that it shows an alternative dimension for performing mapping: standard mapping was driven mainly by the level of the spread or expected loss; dispersion is driven by the standard deviation of the spreads and, in some cases, such as the systemic crisis situation of 2007, it can yield better results. This is a first step in the direction of reasoning on the factors that should affect mapping methods, going beyond the oversimplified methods relied upon in the past. And, more importantly, the dispersion mapping gives us a way to quantify the model risk involved in the use of standard mapping methods by comparing them with an alternative but reasonable assumption.

4
Preparing for Model Change. Rates and Funding in the New Era

In Chapter 3 we saw that one crucial '*task of the risk manager is to surmise how today's accepted pricing methodology might change in the future*'. This point, suggested by Rebonato (2003), seems particularly hard to satisfy. Two things can help in this task: an in-depth knowledge of the history of financial models, to understand how pricing methodologies have changed in the past, and an in-depth understanding of the assumptions underlying a model, to be ready to anticipate which assumptions may suddenly be dismissed and replaced by different assumptions more in line with a new market sentiment.

We have already mentioned different examples of models that were suddenly replaced by a different set of assumptions, usually during a time of crisis. We have spoken of the sudden revision of the default correlation assumptions at the beginning of the credit crunch, and of the passage to stochastic volatility in interest rate modelling after the LTCM crisis at the end of the 1990s. Based on these examples, in Section 1.1.4 we concluded that the one crucial fact that can trigger a model change are events in the economic reality of financial markets, such as a decrease in house prices or a period of supply and demand shocks for caps and swaptions.

In this chapter, which is devoted to the analysis of model changes, I have decided to focus on different examples, which are recent since they were triggered by the credit crunch but do not relate to credit derivatives.

The first example is the transformations that happened in the interest rate derivatives market as a consequence of the credit crunch, a story that we have already anticipated in Section 1.3.4 as an example of the hidden model assumptions underlying the relations we observe among market prices of different products. Now we shall analyze this case study in much more detail, focusing on how these assumptions suddenly changed and were replaced by more realistic ones.

One of the outcomes of the first example is that we understand how to deal, after the credit crunch, with collateralized derivatives, namely derivatives which are traded jointly with a provision of liquidity eliminating both the risk of default and the need to look for liquidity to fund the derivative. However, in the market there are also derivatives which are not collateralized, but affected by risk of default and liquidity costs. The approach to these derivatives is now changing, disrupting some long-standing assumptions in the approach of banks to pricing. This is the topic of the second example we will see below.

4.1 EXPLAINING THE PUZZLE IN THE INTEREST RATES MARKET AND MODELS

This section is relevant first of all because it gives a detailed analysis of how the interest rate market has changed after the credit crunch, with the explosion of basis spreads between rates of different tenors, the loss of the possibility of replicating swaps with spot rates, and the separation between the curve used for discounting and the interest rate curve that appears in the payoffs of interest rate derivatives. It is an analysis that explains the new patterns quantitatively and gives insight into how to model interest rates in the new era.

Secondly it is an example of analysis of a global change in the modelling consensus. We analyze here how the data can be used to understand whether a model representation of the market is correctly specified by observing which new factors must be introduced, which are the important independent variables, what can be simplified as deterministic and what, crucially, must be kept stochastic.

This example, aside from confirming the conclusions reached in Section 1.1.4 about what can trigger a model change, is more interesting and intriguing than the other examples of model change we have seen so far. As we anticipated in Section 1.3.4, here the change in market consensus about modelling, which is an issue that naturally affects mainly illiquid and complex products, was revealed by the change in the prices of liquid products. One may wonder how the prices of liquid products, which are not directly computed with models, can have anything to say about the market consensus on modelling. It is *the relations* among observable prices that change, revealing that some modelling assumptions are no longer a good representation of reality.

Here we commit to finding new replications, at least approximate, that can replace the old broken one and really explain the new market patterns. Detecting with precision how the implicit model consensus changed is not trivial. We know the exact timing of the model change, we even know the exact day: 9 August 2007. However, the simplest hypotheses that quants could make at that time on the possible new consensus model did not explain the new patterns. A deeper analysis was required, which we review in the following. This analysis reveals that there are assumptions underlying a model practice whose consequences are not superficially obvious and that is difficult to anticipate the consequences of a new model standard. Knowing what happened to the pre-crisis interest rate market model can help us to detect similar assumptions underlying other consensus models and to anticipate what can happen if the consensus breaks down.

Even if you think that trying to anticipate how a model can change is a task too difficult to be fulfilled, you will find this example useful. In fact in this case market patterns had already changed and yet modellers were not able to come up with a model that explained, at least approximately, the new patterns. You will agree that, once the model has already changed, understanding precisely how it has changed is something that must be done if you do not want to accumulate losses. The example will be useful at least for this a-posteriori analysis of a big breakdown in market consensus.

Additionally, this example shows that, even if you cannot anticipate a market change, understanding the hidden assumptions of a market standard allows you to set up a procedure to monitor the relations that depend on these assumptions. This way, as soon as these relations break down you understand that the model consensus is changing. And this helps in detecting the relevant stress test that should be performed to the value of a portfolio in order to know what its value could be in a situation of 'crisis' when the foundations of the modelling consensus are shaken.

Here we will consider three different models before finding one that can explain the change that happened to liquid interest rate products like swaps and FRAs. We start from the modelling consensus that could be found in all pre-crisis textbooks: the risk-free interest rate model, where there are no default or liquidity risks affecting the level of lending rates. We see that this model implies very precise no-arbitrage relations between interest rate products, relations that were approximately confirmed by market behaviour for very many years before the crisis, in spite of the fact that the reference market of interest rate derivatives, which is the interbank lending market, was not completely free of default or liquidity risks.

Secondly, we consider a model where such risks are introduced in a basic way: we suppose that there is default risk in the interbank market, but that this risk is homogeneously distributed among the banks (an assumption that was common before the crisis) and is hardly volatile (exactly the same is assumed in the deterministic default intensity models which are the market standard in the credit default swap market, as we saw in Section 2.2.3). This was the initial model change that many quants thought was sufficient to explain the changes in interest rate derivatives patterns. We show analytically that this model does not in fact explain the new relations observed after July 2007. Although all rates products have a different meaning under this new model compared to the risk-free one, *the relations* among the observable variables remain the old ones. However, this attempt is not useless, since it shows how a risk-free model can appear a good representation even for a market which is not fully risk-free, as long as the new risks are homogeneous and not volatile.

Then we also try to see if the new patterns can be explained by the fact that, even when there is non-negligible credit risk in the market, the liquid derivatives are collateralized so they have no credit risk. This discrepancy generates a 'convexity adjustment' that some people thought to be the real reason for the market discrepancy (ironically, at the beginning I was among those people). We hint at the fact that convexity adjustments can explain only a minimal part of the discrepancies we observe in the market.

The third model we introduce is based on an analysis of what really happened to interest rate quotes after the beginning of the credit crunch. We do not anticipate the analysis, but simply mention that under this third model interest rate derivatives appear in a completely new light: we recognize that they are similar to basket derivatives, and that there is optionality even in linear interest rate derivatives. It is only this third model that gets us at least close to the new post credit-crunch market patterns.

One last remark is in order before starting our journey. You may notice that in the following we tend to obtain the fundamental results based not only on the standard tools of mathematical finance (risk-adjusted expectations) but also through replication arguments. The reason for this is simple. In this work we are trying to explain the changes that happened in the market with the credit crunch, well before any quantitative analysis was performed. Thus we are essentially trying to explain the model of the market implicitly applied by traders when market conditions changed and so we focus on relations that can be derived based on replication arguments, which traders usually understand long before mathematical results are obtained.

4.1.1 The Death of a Market Model: 9 August 2007

In Section 1.3.4 we saw that the first relation that broke down when the crisis burst related to Forward Rate Agreements (FRA). An FRA with fixing T, payment time T' and fixed rate K has a payoff at T' given by

$$[L(T,T') - K](T' - T),$$

where we recall that $L(t,T)$ is the spot Libor rate set at t for maturity T. We indicate by $F(t;T,T')$ the equilibrium level of K quoted in the market at time t.

Another crucial relation regards Basis Swaps (BS). A Basis Swap is a contract where two parties exchange two floating legs, both with last payment at T, based on two different payment tenors, α and α', $\alpha < \alpha'$. The α leg has a higher frequency of payment, and pays Libor rates with a shorter tenor. A spread Z is added to the payments of the α leg to make the two legs have the same value. We indicate by $B(t;\alpha/\alpha';T)$ this equilibrium level of Z as quoted in the market at time t.

We can now introduce the long-standing relationships. Define the following functions of the market Libor rate:

$$P_L(t,T) = \frac{1}{1+L(t,T)(T-t)},$$
$$F_L(t;T,T') = \frac{1}{T'-T}\left(\frac{P_L(t,T)}{P_L(t,T')} - 1\right)$$
$$= \frac{1}{T'-T}\left(\frac{1+L(t,T')(T'-t)}{1+L(t,T)(T-t)} - 1\right).$$

Notice that $P_L(t,T)$ is what we might call a 'Libor bond', namely a deterministic discount factor based on the Libor rate. Having defined $P_L(t,T)$, it is easy to understand $F_L(t;T,T')$, which is what standard textbooks call a 'Libor Forward rate'.

Before the crisis, the market evidence was

$$F(t;T,T') \approx F_L(t;T,T'), \qquad (4.1)$$
$$B(t;\alpha/\alpha';T) \approx 0.$$

The first relation says that the market quoted equilibrium rate for a forward rate agreement was very close to the result of a simple formula based on Libor spot quotations, the formula of the so-called forward rate. The second relation regards Basis Swaps and says that the spread required to make two floating legs with different tenor have the same value was almost zero, suggesting that tenor is not a crucial variable for the value of a floating leg. Both sets of evidence were easily explained by using replication arguments that can be found in every textbook on fixed income finance.

After the crisis (and particularly after 9 August 2007), the market evidence became

$$F(t;T,T') \ll F_L(t;T,T'), \qquad (4.2)$$
$$B(t;\alpha/\alpha';T) \gg 0.$$

In Figure 4.1 we see the difference between $F_L(t;t+6m,t+12m)$ and $F(t;t+6m,t+12m)$ with t covering a period of more than 6 years, so we can verify whether the above relations really held before the crisis.

The market FRA rate F and the textbooks' forward rate F_L almost coincide in the three years preceding July 2007, as predicted by the textbooks, with a difference averaging 0.88bp (0.000088). In summer 2007, when the subprime crisis bursts, a gap $F_L - F$ opens up. The gap is very large, is clearly positive, and reaches a peak around the time of Lehman's default in September 2008. It averages 50bp from August 2007 to May 2009.

4.1.2 Finding the New Market Model

How can we understand which changes in the fundamental risk factors led to the new patterns (4.2)? One first point is to observe what else happened in the market at the same time. In those days, as we see in Figure 4.2, another major discrepancy arose in the market: the discrepancy between Libor and Eonia OIS (Overnight Indexed Swaps) rates.

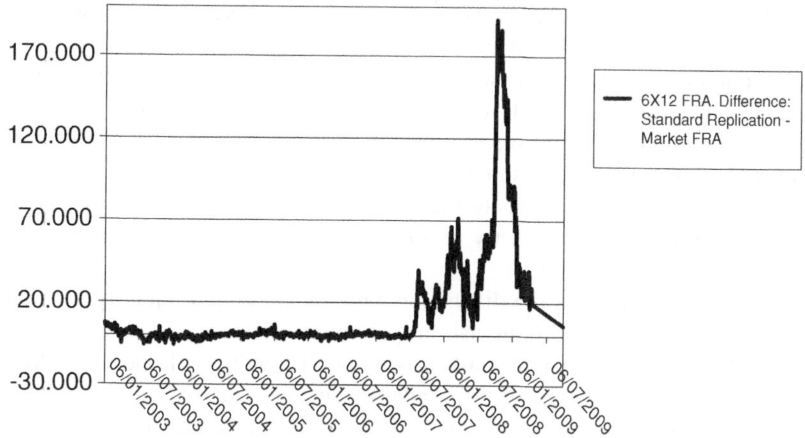

Figure 4.1 Standard Replication – Market FRA (6*m* fixing, 12*m* payment)

An OIS is a fixed/floating interest rate swap with the floating leg tied to a published index of a daily overnight reference rate, for example the Eonia rate in the Euro market. According to experienced market operators, an overnight rate incorporates negligible credit or liquidity risk. An OIS rate with maturity T can be seen as an average of the market expectations about future overnight rates until T, so it somewhat 'extends' overnight rates to longer terms remaining free of credit or liquidity risk. Since, on the other hand, Libor is considered a rate that incorporates some credit/liquidity risk in the interbank market, the market interpreted the explosion of the Libor-OIS gap as a sign of the explosion of these two risks in the rates market. Thus they are the two risks on which we will focus in the following.

The reader may find the above statements rather generic. Why should an overnight rate be free of default or liquidity risk? Why, exactly, can the OIS rate be treated as a risk free rate to apply to a generic term T? And about Libor, what is meant by the statement that it incorporates some credit/liquidity risk? Libor does not refer to any specific counterparty; does it depend on some average liquidity/credit risk? To which companies does this average refer?

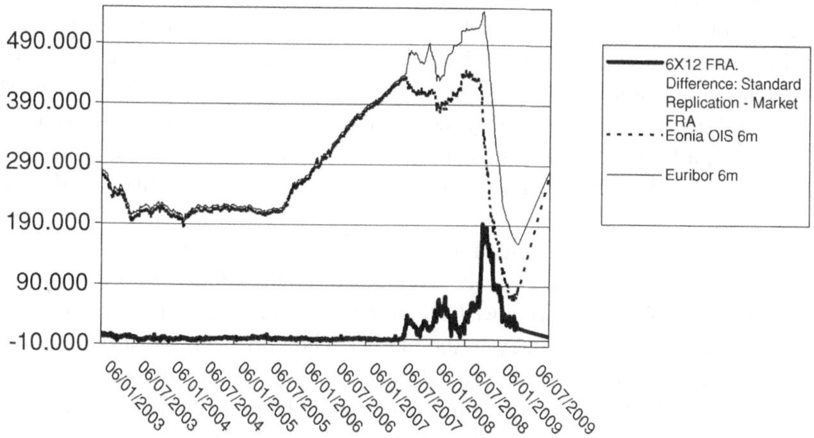

Figure 4.2 OIS (6m), Libor (6m), and FRA anomalies

The reader is right. Many claims we make about the interest rate market are actually imprecise, especially when we start talking of credit and liquidity. In fact we have a very nice interest rate theory for a perfect market with no such risks as default. In such a market, as we will see, there exists naturally one single interest rate even if there are thousands of counterparties. On the other hand we also have a very nice theory for the risk of default of single counterparties and the credit spread that applies to such counterparties, but this does not allow us to understand what happens to the interest rate market as a whole when its players are subject to such risks. Below we try to go beyond this situation by introducing different models of the interest rate market.

The one thing we simplify is the distinction between credit and liquidity. It is difficult to disentangle liquidity risk from credit risk, in particular when one is analyzing not a single derivative deal but the interest rate market as whole. Liquidity risk can be either funding liquidity risk (the risk of running short of available funds) or market liquidity risk (the risk of having large exposures to markets where it is difficult to sell a security).

Funding liquidity risk for a bank is normally strongly correlated to its own risk of default, since an increase of the cost of funding of a bank is usually both a cause and a consequence of an increase in risk of default.

As to market liquidity risk, we will soon see that the market which is of interest to us is the market for cash loans from one bank to another bank. In fact the Libor rates, which are the underlying of FRAs and swaps, are based on these contracts, called deposits. Therefore, in this context market illiquidity is the difficulty of transferring a cash loan with a specific counterparty, and as such it is always strongly correlated to the risk of default by the counterparty.

The crisis of 2007 has taught us that deciding which came first, credit or liquidity crunch in the interbank market, is akin to asking which came first, the chicken or the egg. For this reason we do not attempt to separate precisely liquidity from credit in the spreads over risk-free rates. We summarize both terms in a single expression: 'credit spread'. This simplification does not prevent us from finding very interesting results. A similar view is taken in Duffie and Singleton (1997) and in Collin-Dufresne and Solnik (2001), who claim that the two effects cannot be disentangled, in the absence of a theory for liquidity. Later on, however, we contradict this view – we are now in desperate need of a theory of liquidity, which is another major model change that is unfolding now – and we outline how the two components could be separated. Finally we tackle liquidity directly.

Yet there is one first thing we have to introduce to make our representation minimally realistic. Interest rate derivatives never have one single underlying, unlike the scenario we usually pretend in our models. Even if we consider the above FRA, where the underlying is the rate $L(T, T')$, the product is in reality more similar to a basket or index derivative. In fact, the rate $L(T, T')$, a Libor rate in this example (other derivatives may have as an underlying other rates such as Euribor which are all pretty similar to Libor), comes out of a rather elaborate process.

Let us recall the discussion in Section 1.1.4, and add some more details. The level of Libor is provided by the fixings, *trimmed* averages of contributions from a panel including the most relevant banks in the market *with the highest credit quality*. The banks contribute the rate at which they can borrow money in the market. The borrowing must be *unsecured* (not collateralized), therefore it corresponds to a *deposit* contract. Usually the quotes in the deposit market closely track the Libor fixings, since banks should simply contribute the funding rate they see in the deposit market, and the players in the deposit market are normally a set larger than Libor contributors but similar in composition. Indeed, since deposits are unsecured only borrowers with high credit quality can access this market. This is why the deposit market is also called the Libor market. In what follows, when we speak of Libor banks we mean both those banks belonging to the panel and those belonging only to the Libor market. When the distinction becomes relevant, in Section 4.1.5, we will be more precise.

The way we interpret the Libor rates in our models is crucial to the pricing of even the simplest interest rate derivative, the swap. This issue has never been investigated in depth since it is trivially solved when the market is risk-free, or even when there is a homogeneous and stable amount of credit risk in interbank transactions, as we will see. The issue becomes non-trivial when neither of these conditions holds.

Below we will consider different models of the interest rate market. You will see that some quantities, that in a risk free model appear to be one single thing, turn out to be a multiplicity in more realistic models. To make things clearer, we try to use a notation that recalls, as often as possible, which model we are using and what are the assumptions that underlie a given relation. First we have a notation for rates $L^?(t,T)$ and discount bonds $P^?(t,T)$. These quantities can be subject to risk of default by the counterparty, or not (because the counterparty cannot default or because the deal is collateralized). In the latter case we will use a superscript as in

$$L^{rf}(t,T),\, P^{rf}(t,T)$$

where rf stands for 'risk-free'. In the former case we will use the symbols

$$L^{dA}(t,T),\, P^{dA}(t,T)$$

where d stands for 'defaultable' and A indicates the counterparty. In fact, when there is default risk one needs to specify the counterparty.

Then we consider derivative quantities, such as the equilibrium rate $F_?^?(t;T,T')$ of a forward rate agreement, and the equilibrium basis spread $B_?^?(t;\alpha/\alpha';T)$ of a Basis Swap. These quantities will be defined differently depending on:

A) whether or not the product is subject to counterparty risk, recalled as in the above by the superscript

$$F_?^{rf}(t;T,T'),\, B_?^{rf}(t;\alpha/\alpha';T) \text{ or } F_?^{dA}(t;T,T'),\, B_?^{dA}(t;\alpha/\alpha';T)$$

B) the model chosen for the underlying interest rate, recalled by the subscript. We consider three models.
   1. interest rate market free of default risk: $F_{rf}^?(t;T,T'),\, B_{rf}^?(t;\alpha/\alpha';T)$
   2. interest rate market with stable default risk: $F_{dX_0}^?(t;T,T'),\, B_{dX_0}^?(t;\alpha/\alpha';T)$, where the subscript indicates that Libor is linked to the default risk of a counterparty X_0 chosen at 0
   3. interest rate market with volatile default risk:

$$F_{dX_0,X_\alpha,\ldots}^?(t;T,T'),\, B_{dX_0,X_\alpha,\ldots}^?(t;\alpha/\alpha';T)$$

   where the subscript indicates that Libor is linked to the default risk of a sequence of counterparties.

The same holds for the prices of the above products,

$$FRA_?^?(t;T,T';K), \quad BS_?^?(t;\alpha/\alpha';T;Z)$$

where K and Z are the fixed rate of the FRA and the contractual spread of the Basis Swap.

4.1.3 The Classic Risk-free Market Model

Let us start from the classic assumption of absence of default risk. We call $L^{rf}(t,T)$ the fair simply-compounded interest rate applying to a loan from a bank to another bank from t to T when the loan is free of default (or liquidity) risk. In this case the rate $L^{rf}(t,T)$ gives an indication of the time-value of money, namely what, according to the market consensus, is the compensation that a lender must request for giving up his money for the period from t to T. If the market is arbitrage-free, the same rate $L^{rf}(t,T)$ applies whichever bank we choose as a borrower, because there are no bank-specific issues, such as default risk, that can justify different quotes for the same payoff.

If we assume that the entire interbank lending market is free of default risk, the meaning of the Libor rate $L(t,T)$ is clear. All banks borrow at the same rate $L^{rf}(t,T)$ that embeds the time-value of money, therefore

$$L(t,T) = L^{rf}(t,T). \tag{4.3}$$

The risk-free bond has a price

$$P^{rf}(0,T) = \mathbb{E}[D(0,T)].$$

In an arbitrage-free market the rate $L^{rf}(0,T)$ that applies to a loan for a notional equal to 1, needs to satisfy

$$1 = \mathbb{E}\left[D(0,T)(1 + L^{rf}(0,T)T)\right]$$

leading to

$$1 = P^{rf}(0,T)(1 + L^{rf}(0,T)T),$$

$$P^{rf}(t,T) = \frac{1}{1 + L^{rf}(t,T)(T-t)}$$

and, considering (4.3),

$$P_L(t,T) = \frac{1}{1 + L(t,T)(T-t)} = P^{rf}(t,T).$$

Also the link between Libor fixings and the Deposit market is clear: fixings and Deposit quotes simply coincide, being two ways of giving information on $L^{rf}(t,T)$. This leads to the possibility of very simple replication procedures to price fundamental interest rate derivatives such as swaps.

The Swap

A standard spot-starting swap with notional equal to 1, first fixing today at $t = 0$, tenor α and M payments involves payments at the set of dates

$$\alpha, 2\alpha, \ldots, M\alpha.$$

You can think of α as 6 months, as it will be in all the following practical examples. The fixed leg, if the fixed rate is K, is trivially evaluated as

$$\sum_{i=1}^{M} P^{rf}(0,\alpha i)K\alpha$$

since it is made up of purely deterministic payments. But even a floating leg is very simply replicated by basic instruments. An investor can:

1) borrow today an amount $P^{rf}(0, M\alpha)$. It is fair that he gives back 1 at maturity $M\alpha$;
2) lend 1 to an interbank counterparty until α. At α the investor receives $1 + L^{rf}(0, \alpha) = 1 + L(0, \alpha)$, and lends 1 again to the counterparty until 2α. At 2α the investor receives $1 + L^{rf}(\alpha, 2\alpha) = 1 + L(\alpha, 2\alpha)$, and lends 1 again to the counterparty until 3α, repeating this until $M\alpha$. We call this part of the strategy a 'rolled lending'.

At $M\alpha$ the investor receives $1 + L((M-1)\alpha, M\alpha)$ from the rolled lending in 2) and pays 1 to the counterparty of the borrowing in 1). Since the notional payments of amount 1 cancel each other out, the payoff of this strategy is the same as the one for a swap floating leg: only the regular interest rate payments are left.

The value of the strategy is the value of the rolled lending of point 2), which has a unit value since implementing it costs exactly 1, minus the value $P^{rf}(0, M\alpha)$ of the borrowed money of point 1), namely

$$1 - P^{rf}(0, M\alpha),$$

and in a market with no arbitrage this must be the fair value of the equivalent floating leg,

$$Float^{rf}_{rf}(0; 0, M\alpha) = 1 - P^{rf}(0, M\alpha).$$

This is an extremely powerful result, and makes the life of an interest rate modeller much easier. We are so accustomed to it that we forget how surprising it is: we have concluded that a relatively complex product like the floating leg of a swap with last payment at $M\alpha$, which involves a number of future stochastic rate payments, can be priced based only on the current quote for one Libor rate,

$$Float^{rf}_{rf}(0; 0, M\alpha) = 1 - \frac{1}{1 + L(0, M\alpha)M\alpha} = \frac{L(0, M\alpha)M\alpha}{1 + L(0, M\alpha)M\alpha}. \tag{4.4}$$

We call this the *fundamental result of the risk-free market*. Similar relations would hold at a generic $t > 0$ for a swap with payoffs at

$$t + \alpha, t + 2\alpha, \ldots, t + M\alpha,$$

but keeping $t = 0$ makes simpler notation.

The FRA

Let us now consider a Forward Rate Agreement with fixing at α and maturity 2α. This is a one-period forward-starting swap. Actually, we have already priced it by replication in Section 1.3.4, but now we apply the general swap replication just seen. Since the FRA can be viewed as the difference between two spot starting swaps, the value of the floating leg is

$$\begin{aligned} Float^{rf}_{rf}(0; \alpha, 2\alpha) &= Float^{rf}_{rf}(0; 0, 2\alpha) - Float^{rf}_{rf}(0; 0, \alpha) \\ &= 1 - P^{rf}(0, 2\alpha) - 1 + P^{rf}(0, \alpha) \\ &= P^{rf}(0, \alpha) - P^{rf}(0, 2\alpha). \end{aligned}$$

The value of the fixed leg is $P^{rf}(0, 2\alpha)K\alpha$, leading to

$$FRA^{rf}_{rf}(0; \alpha, 2\alpha; K) = P^{rf}(0, \alpha) - P^{rf}(0, 2\alpha) - P^{rf}(0, 2\alpha)K\alpha, \tag{4.5}$$

so that the equilibrium FRA rate is

$$\begin{aligned} F^{rf}_{rf}(0; \alpha, 2\alpha) &= \frac{1}{\alpha}\left(\frac{P^{rf}(0, \alpha)}{P^{rf}(0, 2\alpha)} - 1\right) \\ &= \frac{1}{\alpha}\left(\frac{P_L(0, \alpha)}{P_L(0, 2\alpha)} - 1\right) = F_L(0; \alpha, 2\alpha). \end{aligned} \tag{4.6}$$

Thus in this model of the market we expect the first equation of (4.1) to hold,

$$F(t; T, T') \approx F_L(t; T, T').$$

The basis swap

Now let us consider a basis swap where two parties exchange two floating legs, both with last payment at T, based on two different payment tenors, α and α', $\alpha < \alpha'$, plus a spread Z added to the α leg. In this setting both floating legs have value

$$Float^{rf}_{rf}(0; 0, T; \alpha) = Float^{rf}_{rf}(0; 0, T; \alpha') = 1 - P^{rf}(0, T)$$

since the fundamental result (4.4) shows clearly that the value of a floating leg does not depend on its frequency. Thus we need no spread Z to equal the value of two legs with different frequencies. We just have

$$B^{rf}_{rf}(0; \alpha/\alpha'; T) = 0.$$

In fact, recalling the above swap replication, we notice that we could indeed replicate a basis swap with notional X by borrowing at one frequency and lending at the other the same amount X. By definition, this strategy costs nothing thus the fair value of the basis swap, without any additional spread, is already zero. Thus in a risk-free market we would also expect the second equation of (4.1) to hold.

Comparing the model results with reality

Thus, based on the above replication arguments, standard financial theory expects this forward rate $F_L(t; T, T')$ to be equal to $F(t; T, T')$, and B to be zero. This was almost true in the past but it is not so anymore. We have already seen in the Figure 4.1 the difference between $F_L(t; t + 6m, t + 12m)$ and $F(t; t + 6m, t + 12m)$ on a 6 year period. In Figure 4.3 we can see in more detail both F_L and F in the second half of 2008 and first half of 2009.

Analogously, the Basis Swap spreads widened from very few basis points to much larger values after the crisis. From August 2008 to April 2009, the Basis Swap spread to exchange 6 Month Libor with 12 Month Libor over 1 year was strongly positive and averaged 40bps, as we see in Figure 4.4.

Clearly, the risk-free model was no longer valid after the beginning of the credit crunch.

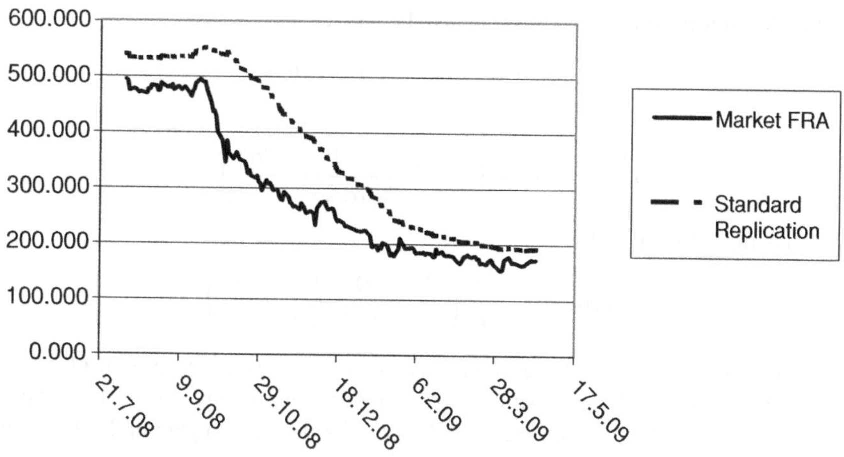

Figure 4.3 Market FRA and standard replication (6m fixing, 12m payment)

FRA as an expectation in the risk-free market

Above we have priced an FRA through replication. The same result could also have been obtained with the standard tools of mathematical finance. The price of the FRA is

$$FRA_{rf}^{rf}(0;\alpha,2\alpha;K) = \mathbb{E}[D(0,2\alpha)((L(\alpha,2\alpha)-K)\alpha)]. \tag{4.7}$$

We can use change of numeraire (see Appendix) to get rid of the stochastic discount factor that appears inside the expectation (notice that interest rates are necessarily stochastic here). We move from expectation under the risk-neutral measure to expectation under the forward measure $Q^{rf2\alpha}$ associated with numeraire $P^{rf}(t,2\alpha)$,

$$FRA_{rf}^{rf}(0;\alpha,2\alpha;K) = P^{rf}(0,2\alpha)\mathbb{E}^{rf2\alpha}[((L(\alpha,2\alpha)-K)\alpha)].$$

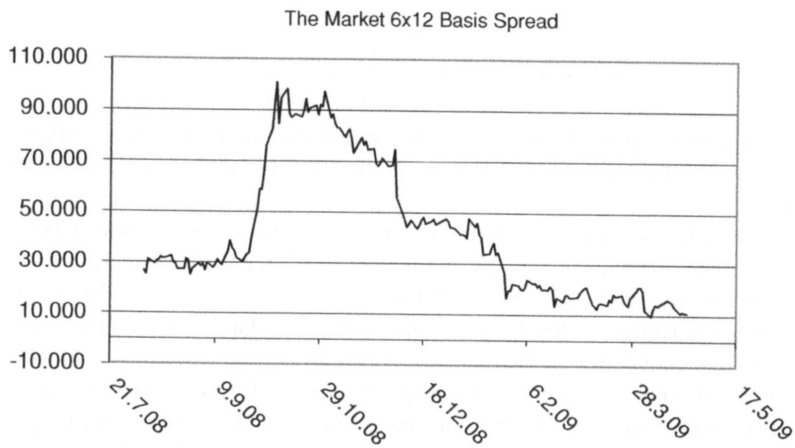

Figure 4.4 Basis swap spread 6 × 12, maturity 1y

We see that the equilibrium value of K can also be written as

$$F_{rf}^{rf}(0;\alpha,2\alpha)=\mathbb{E}^{rf2\alpha}[L(\alpha,2\alpha)].$$

We know

$$L(\alpha,2\alpha)=\frac{1}{\alpha}\left(\frac{P_{rf}(\alpha,\alpha)-P_{rf}(\alpha,2\alpha)}{P_{rf}(\alpha,2\alpha)}\right) \tag{4.8}$$

so $L(\alpha,2\alpha)$ is the value at α of

$$F_L(t;\alpha,2\alpha)=\frac{1}{\alpha}\left(\frac{P_{rf}(t,\alpha)-P_{rf}(t,2\alpha)}{P_{rf}(t,2\alpha)}\right)$$

which can be seen as *the price of a tradable asset divided by the numeraire* of $Q^{rf2\alpha}$. Thanks to the definition of probability measure associated with a numeraire given in the Appendix, we know that if the market is arbitrage-free, $F_L(t;\alpha,2\alpha)$ is a martingale under $Q^{rf2\alpha}$ and we get

$$\begin{aligned}F_{rf}^{rf}(0;\alpha,2\alpha)&=\mathbb{E}^{rf2\alpha}[L(\alpha,2\alpha)]=\mathbb{E}^{rf2\alpha}[F_L(\alpha;\alpha,2\alpha)]\\&=\frac{1}{\alpha}\left(\frac{P_{rf}(0,\alpha)}{P_{rf}(0,2\alpha)}-1\right).\end{aligned} \tag{4.9}$$

4.1.4 A Market Model with Stable Default Risk

When we allow for default, each bank has its own default risk, and its own default time. The defaultable bond with maturity T issued by a counterparty A has a price

$$P^{dA}(0,T)=\mathbb{E}\left[1_{\{\tau^A>T\}}D(0,T)\right]$$

where τ^A is the default time of A. In an arbitrage-free market the rate $L^{dA}(0,T)$ that applies to a loan to counterparty A, for a notional equal to 1, needs to satisfy

$$1=\mathbb{E}\left[1_{\{\tau^A>T\}}D(0,T)(1+L^{dA}(0,T)T)\right]$$

leading to

$$\begin{aligned}1&=P^{dA}(0,T)(1+L^{dA}(0,T)T),\\P^{dA}(t,T)&=\frac{1}{1+L^{dA}(t,T)(T-t)}.\end{aligned}$$

Thus the relation between bonds and rates is the same as we had in a risk-free market, although both rates and bonds have a different meaning. Notice that we have assumed zero recovery for simplicity.

In this context, the meaning of the Libor rate $L(t,T)$ fixed at t for maturity T is not as easy as in a risk-free market, where there was a unique rate applying to all counterparties. Let $\mathbb{L}_t$ be the set of Libor banks. Each bank $A\in\mathbb{L}_t$ will borrow at a different rate $L^{dA}(t,T)$. The Libor rate is the trimmed average of the $L^{dA}(t,T)$ across all Libor banks, a quantity more complex to model or to replicate than a single rate.

Are we forced to model each rate separately? If this was the only way to study the market when there is risk of default, interest rate modelling would become extremely complex. Before the credit crunch, risk of default was not completely null, and yet the rules of a risk-free market were safely used. Can we understand how this was possible? Are there some assumptions – maybe unrealistic now but common before the crisis – that allow us to simplify the representation of the interest rate market even if there is risk of default? The two assumptions we make are *homogeneity* and *stability*, explained in the following.

Homogeneity, or **All Libors were created equal.** We say that the set $\mathbb{L}_t$ of Libor banks is *homogeneous* when

$$L^{dA}(t,T) = L^{dX_t}(t,T) \quad \forall A \in \mathbb{L}_t,$$

which means that all Libor banks have *the same* borrowing rate $L^{dX_t}(t,T)$, where by X_t we indicate under this assumption the generic Libor bank at t. Notice that an obvious consequence of X_t being a Libor bank at t is that $\tau^{X_t} > t$. The homogeneity assumption is the mathematical extremization of the idea, which was very commonly expressed in the market before the crisis, that all banks that participate in the interbank market have a similar risk of default. Usual descriptions such as 'Libor contains a few basis points of bank vs bank counterparty risk' imply the idea that, for all practical purposes, Libor banks can be treated as all having the same (low) credit risk, expressed simply by the Libor fixing itself.[1]

When credit risk is homogeneous we do no longer need to differentiate between counterparties and we can write

$$P^{dX_t}(t,T) = \frac{1}{1 + L^{dX_t}(t,T)(T-t)},$$

and the Libor quotes have a simple meaning

$$\begin{aligned} L(t,T) &= L^{dX_t}(t,T), \\ P_L(t,T) &= P^{dX_t}(t,T). \end{aligned} \tag{4.10}$$

Stability, or **Libor today will be Libor forever**

$$A \in \mathbb{L}_0 \Longrightarrow A \in \mathbb{L}_t \quad \mathit{if} \quad \tau^A > t$$

which means that if today a bank is part of the Libor market, so that it can borrow money unsecured at levels near to Libor fixings, we expect it to remain in the Libor market (unless it defaults). This is the mathematical extremization of the idea that the Libor market has a stable composition, which corresponds to expecting the group of the most relevant and reliable banks in the market to be stable, an hypothesis not that far removed from the pre-crisis mood when it was unlikely for market operators to display any worries that banks such as Citigroup or Lehman could be thrown out of the Libor market.

Homogeneity with stability is equivalent to assuming that the future Libor rate $L(t,T)$ at any date $t > 0$ will coincide with the future borrowing rate $L^{dX_0}(t,T)$ of the Libor counterparty chosen at 0, if the latter has not defaulted. Namely

$$L(t,T) \overset{\mathit{by\ Hom}}{=} L^{dX_t}(t,T) \overset{\mathit{by\ Stab}}{=} L^{dX_0}(t,T), \quad \tau^{X_0} > t. \tag{4.11}$$

[1] Grinblatt (2001), for example, says: 'A 6-month LIBOR loan is a loan to an AA or AAA-rated borrower. Occasionally, LIBOR is the rate charged to an A-rated borrower. We refer to LIBOR as if it is a single rate, when in fact, different banks can in theory quote different LIBOR lending rates. In practice, the variation in quoted rates is small with the vast majority of banks having identical LIBOR rates. The rates at which simultaneous transactions take place exhibit even less variation. Hence, it is appropriate to treat LIBOR as if it were a single rate.'

This identification between the index rate, Libor in our example, and the rate of the counterparty chosen at 0 in the deal, is the same feature that we have in a risk-free market. This gives us the possibility of performing efficient evaluations through replication, as we show in the following.

The defaultable swap

Thanks to (4.11), if we consider the same swap as in Section 4.1.3, paying at

$$\alpha, 2\alpha, \ldots, M\alpha,$$

it is still possible even to evaluate its floating leg by replication, at least from the perspective of an investor that is another bank in the Libor market. The main difference is that now both counterparties are defaultable, and we assume the swap to be not collateralized, and thus subject to risk of default.

Let us suppose that the investor that receives the floating leg adopts the following strategy

1) he borrows $P^{dX_0}(0, M\alpha)$ until $M\alpha$. Since the investor is a Libor bank, his credit risk is expressed by $L^{dX_0}(0, M\alpha)$ and it is fair for him to borrow $P^{dX_0}(0, M\alpha)$ and agree to give back 1 at $M\alpha$ in case of no default.
2) he lends 1 to another Libor counterparty until α. At α, thanks to homogeneity and stability, the investor receives $1 + L^{dX_0}(0, \alpha) = 1 + L(0, \alpha)$ in case of no default, and lends 1 again to the same counterparty until 2α. At 2α the investor receives (again in case of no default) $1 + L^{dX_0}(\alpha, 2\alpha) = 1 + L(\alpha, 2\alpha)$, and lends 1 again to the same counterparty until 3α, repeating this until $M\alpha$.

This is similar to the replication strategy of a swap floating leg in the risk-free market. The cost of the strategy is given by the value of the rolled lending of 2), which is 1 because it costs 1 to implement it, minus the value $P^{dX_0}(0, M\alpha)$ of the money borrowed in 1), namely

$$1 - P^{dX_0}(0, M\alpha).$$

However, in difference to the risk-free case, this strategy does not have exactly the same cashflows as the floating leg of a defaultable swap. Rather, this strategy involves receiving a stream of floating payments equal to those of the floating leg, and subject to the same risk of default as a floating leg. But it involves also two capital payments that do not appear in the floating leg of a swap: the capital to be paid back at $M\alpha$ in 1), and the capital to be received at $M\alpha$ at the end of the rolled lending of 2). In difference to the risk-free case, these two payments do not necessarily cancel out each other, because the first payment is contingent upon the survival of the investor, while the second payment is contingent upon the survival of the counterparty. Thus we have to take them into account explicitly. If we define $Float_{dX_0}^{dX_0}(0; 0, M\alpha; \alpha)$ to be the value of the floating leg of the swap, we have the value of the combined strategy of 1) and 2) as equal to the value of the floating leg plus the value of the two capital payments:

$$1 - P^{dX_0}(0, M\alpha) = Float_{dX_0}^{dX_0}(0; 0, M\alpha; \alpha)$$
$$+ \mathbb{E}\left[D(0, M\alpha) 1_{\{\tau^{Count} > M\alpha\}}\right] - \mathbb{E}\left[D(0, M\alpha) 1_{\{\tau^{Inv} > M\alpha\}}\right].$$

However, since both the investor and the counterparties are Libor banks at 0, and thanks to homogeneity they have the same risk of default, we have

$$\begin{aligned}1 - P^{dX_0}(0, M\alpha) &= Float_{dX_0}^{dX_0}(0; 0, M\alpha; \alpha) + P^{dX_0}(0, M\alpha) - P^{dX_0}(0, M\alpha) \\ &= Float_{dX_0}^{dX_0}(0; 0, M\alpha; \alpha).\end{aligned}$$

Thus we are still able to evaluate the floating leg of the swap

$$Float_{dX_0}^{dX_0}(0; 0, M\alpha; \alpha) = 1 - P^{dX_0}(0, M\alpha).$$

Although we now have risk of default and rates and derivatives have different definitions and payoffs compared to the risk-free case, we have retained the fundamental result of the risk-free market: the floating leg of a swap with last payment at $M\alpha$ can be priced based only on a Libor rate as

$$\begin{aligned}&Float_{dX_0}^{dX_0}(0; 0, T; \alpha) = 1 - P^{dX_0}(0, M\alpha) \\ &= 1 - \frac{1}{1 + L(0, M\alpha)M\alpha} = \frac{L(0, M\alpha)M\alpha}{1 + L(0, M\alpha)M\alpha}.\end{aligned}$$

From the defaultable swap to the market FRA

Now let us consider a defaultable swap floating leg lasting one single period, for example fixing first at α and ending at 2α. It has a discounted payoff

$$D(0, 2\alpha)1_{\{\tau^{X_0} > 2\alpha\}} L(\alpha, 2\alpha)\alpha. \tag{4.12}$$

We price it first by replication. We can interpret it as the difference between two swaps fixing first today, like the swap replicated above, with one swap ending in 2α and the other ending in α. From the above we deduce that this floating leg has value

$$\begin{aligned}Float_{dX_0}^{dX_0}(0; \alpha, 2\alpha; \alpha) &= P^{dX_0}(0, \alpha) - P^{dX_0}(0, 2\alpha) \\ &= P_L(0, \alpha) - P_L(0, 2\alpha)\end{aligned} \tag{4.13}$$

The fixed leg of this swap is composed of one single K payment at 2α, therefore it has value

$$P^{dX_0}(0, 2\alpha)K\alpha = P_L(0, 2\alpha)K\alpha.$$

If we put together the value of the fixed leg and the value of the floating leg we have

$$P_L(0, \alpha) - P_L(0, 2\alpha) - P_L(0, 2\alpha)K\alpha. \tag{4.14}$$

In the risk-free market a one-period swap like the one just described was considered equivalent to a forward rate agreement. If this was the case also in the defaultable market we are analyzing, we could compute the level of K that makes (4.14) zero and this would be

$$F_{dX_0}^{dX_0}(0; \alpha, 2\alpha) = \frac{1}{\alpha}\left(\frac{P_L(0, \alpha)}{P_L(0, 2\alpha)} - 1\right). \tag{4.15}$$

We could conclude that again

$$F(t; T, T') = F_L(t; T, T').$$

However, in a defaultable market the product evaluated in (4.14) cannot correspond to the real market FRA. Let us see two facts that do not correspond with FRA market reality.

Collateralized derivatives

The first unrealistic feature is that, for *uncollateralized* derivatives, when a default happens the two legs of a swap are not treated separately, as we did above, but there is a *netting* between them. The second unrealistic feature is more important and actually cancels out the first one: the forward rate agreements are a particular kind of swap which is regularly *collateralized*. As we explained earlier, collateral is the amount of guarantees exchanged between banks in order to protect the reciprocal exposures from counterparty risk. The amount of collateral must be kept equal to the expected discounted exposure, which corresponds approximately to the price of all deals existing between two counterparties. For interbank products like FRA collateral is usually cash, and it is updated daily. It makes the product become essentially default-free.

Additionally, collateral provides funding for a deal. A trader who buys a non-collateralized $5y$ option, for example, will need $5y$ funding for an amount equal to the price he has to pay. If the deal is collateralized, funding is needed only for one day: the day after inception, in fact, an amount of liquidity equal to the current price will be received through the collateral. Then the interest on the collateral until maturity is paid daily and indexed to overnight rates. As we saw in Chapter 1, the cost of our funding (our account $B(t)$) gives the time-value of money for us and the curve we have to use for discounting. Thus collateralized derivatives should be discounted with a curve indexed to overnight rates (OIS) for two reasons: because for these deals the funding account is indexed to overnight, and because the overnight, as the best approximation of a risk-free rate, is the right one to apply to default-free contracts.

This reasoning shows that an FRA cannot be priced with the above replication for a *defaultable swap in a defaultable market*, since in reality the market is defaultable today, so that Libor is really linked to default risk, but the market FRA is not a defaultable swap since it is collateralized. Neither can we price a market FRA with the replication for a *risk-free swap in a risk-free market*. If we follow the risk-free replication the fair rate that the risk-free counterparty pays is $L^{rf}(\alpha, 2\alpha)$, which in a defaultable market does not coincide with the Libor rate paid by the FRA. We need to price a *risk-free swap in a defaultable market*. We have a risk-free (collateralized) derivative with a defaultable (uncollateralized) underlying. This mismatch leads to the impossibility of a simple exact replication. One initial approach to deal with this issue is to keep homogeneity and stability and perform the computations shown below.

Collateralized FRA with convexity adjustments

We can still price the FRA as the expectation of its payoff, using formula

$$FRA^{rf}_{dX_0}(0; \alpha, 2\alpha; K) = \mathbb{E}[D(0, 2\alpha)((L(\alpha, 2\alpha) - K)\alpha)],$$

that looks analogous to the one used for the risk-free market, but now we have a different model representation of the market quantity $L(\alpha, 2\alpha)$. What has not changed is the discounting by the risk-free $D(0, 2\alpha)$, due to collateralization. Therefore in today's market $L(\alpha, 2\alpha)$ comes from the Libor curve which is affected by default risk, while $D(0, 2\alpha)$ is linked to a risk-free OIS curve. Again we can use change of numeraire to move to expectation under the same forward measure $Q^{rf2\alpha}$ associated with $P^{rf}(t,2\alpha)$ and used for the risk free market, getting again

$$FRA^{rf}_{dX_0}(0;\alpha,2\alpha;K) = P^{rf}(0,2\alpha)\mathbb{E}^{rf2\alpha}[((L(\alpha,2\alpha)-K)\alpha)],$$
$$F^{rf}_{dX_0}(0;\alpha,2\alpha) = \mathbb{E}^{rf2\alpha}[L(\alpha,2\alpha)]. \tag{4.16}$$

However, in the risk-free market we have $L(\alpha,2\alpha) = \frac{1}{\alpha}(\frac{P^{rf}(\alpha,\alpha)}{P^{rf}(\alpha,2\alpha)} - 1)$ which is a martingale since it is a tradable asset divided by the numeraire $P^{rf}(t,2\alpha)$, leading to an FRA rate equal to the replication forward rate as in (4.9). In the risky market we have instead

$$F^{rf}_{dX_0}(0;\alpha,2\alpha) = \mathbb{E}^{rf2\alpha}[L(\alpha,2\alpha)] = \mathbb{E}^{rf2\alpha}\left[\frac{1}{\alpha}\left(\frac{1}{P^{dX_\alpha}(\alpha,2\alpha)} - 1\right)\right]$$
$$= \mathbb{E}^{rf2\alpha}\left[\frac{1}{\alpha}\left(\frac{P^{dX_\alpha}(\alpha,\alpha)}{P^{dX_\alpha}(\alpha,2\alpha)} - 1\right)\right] \neq \frac{1}{\alpha}\left(\frac{P^{dX_\alpha}(0,\alpha)}{P^{dX_\alpha}(0,2\alpha)} - 1\right)$$

where $P^{dX_\alpha}(\alpha,\alpha) = 1$ comes from the fact that a Libor party X_α at α is necessarily alive at α. Now $L(t,2\alpha) = \frac{1}{\alpha}(\frac{P^{dX_\alpha}(t,\alpha)}{P^{dX_\alpha}(t,2\alpha)} - 1)$ is not a martingale since it is not a tradable asset divided by the numeraire $P^{rf}(t,2\alpha)$. We have a *measure mismatch* exactly as in the case of Constant Maturity Swaps, which will be analyzed in Section 6.3. How can we compute its expectation without the martingale property? An approach is to detect a measure Q^N, associated with some numeraire N_t, such that $\frac{1}{\alpha}(\frac{P^{dX_\alpha}(t,\alpha)}{P^{dX_\alpha}(t,2\alpha)} - 1)$ is a martingale under this measure:

$$\mathbb{E}^N\left[\frac{1}{\alpha}\left(\frac{P^{dX_\alpha}(\alpha,\alpha)}{P^{dX_\alpha}(\alpha,2\alpha)} - 1\right)\right] = \frac{1}{\alpha}\left(\frac{P^{dX_\alpha}(0,2\alpha)}{P^{dX_\alpha}(0,2\alpha)} - 1\right) = F_L(0;\alpha,2\alpha)$$

and then use the mathematical relations between the expectation of $\frac{P^{dX_\alpha}(\alpha,\alpha)}{P^{dX_\alpha}(\alpha,2\alpha)}$ under Q^N and the one under $Q^{rf2\alpha}$ provided by the change of numeraire techniques, see for example Brigo and Mercurio (2006). Exactly as in the case of Constant Maturity Swaps in Section 6.3, we will find that the expectation we are interested in depends on a convexity adjustment $\mathbf{CA}^{N/rf}$:

$$F^{rf}_{dX_0}(0;\alpha,2\alpha) = \mathbb{E}^{rf2\alpha}\left[\frac{1}{\alpha}\left(\frac{P^{dX_\alpha}(\alpha,\alpha)}{P^{dX_\alpha}(\alpha,2\alpha)} - 1\right)\right] = F_L(0;\alpha,2\alpha) + \mathbf{CA}^{N/rf}. \tag{4.17}$$

These computations, assuming a market with stable and homogeneous credit risk, are feasible and are performed in Morini (2010). The formula obtained is applied to an FRA with $\alpha = 6m$, namely the most liquid market FRA in the market with expiry in 6 months and payment in 1 year, using historically estimated parameters. The result is that $\mathbf{CA}^{N/rf}$ *for this product is a number lower in absolute value than one basis point*. Thus, in spite of convexity adjustment brought about by collateralization, in a market with stable and homogeneous credit risk we still obtain approximately the old relation

$$F(0;\alpha,2\alpha) = F^{rf}_{dX_0}(0;\alpha,2\alpha) \approx F_L(0;\alpha,2\alpha). \tag{4.18}$$

The small size of the convexity adjustment, computed for this $6m$ maturity, should not surprise experienced interest rate traders or quants: convexity adjustments are usually very small for short maturities. Look at Figure 6.5 for a confirmation from the CMS world. However, even for such a short maturity, the difference between the market FRA rate F and F_L has been as large as 200bps during the crisis, confirming that there is something more to these anomalies than the above convexity adjustments. The representation of the market with the homogeneity and stability hypothesis is probably a good model to explain why before the crisis we had the relations of a risk-free market in spite of some bank credit risk, but to explain the post-crisis patterns we need some different assumptions.[2]

Before looking for an effective explanation, we make a few useful digressions.

In spite of the fact that the computation of convexity adjustments in Morini (2010) does not solve the problem we have here, the rather complex mathematics used there turns out to be not entirely useless. In fact, it shows how to deal consistently with two different bonds, the Libor bond $P_L(t,T)$ and the risk-free bond $P^{rf}(t,T)$, which embed different risk in spite of the fact that they give the same non-defaultable payoff of 1 at T. This apparent *arbitrage* is explained by the fact that only the risk-free bond is a tradable asset, and therefore can be chosen as a numeraire, while $P_L(t,T)$ is not a tradable asset. This explains how it can embed default risk without defaulting, but cannot be used as a numeraire. Furthermore, the analysis of Morini (2010) shows precisely how the relations between risk-free interest rates and risky rates are analogous to the relations between term structures under two different currencies, with a survival probability playing the role of a rate of exchange. This extends and specifies the original intuition in Bianchetti (2009).

Remark 10. ***The agnostic market model.*** *We have seen above that after the crisis what changed in the FRA pricing problem*

$$\mathbb{E}[D(0,2\alpha)((L(\alpha,2\alpha)-K)\alpha)]$$

is not the risk of default of the FRA, thanks to collateralization, but the nature of $L(\alpha,2\alpha)$ that may have changed with the explosion of credit/liquidity risk. Thus $L(\alpha,2\alpha)$ is no longer a risk-free rate and we can no longer write it in terms of risk-free bonds and use the martingale property to prove the equivalence between the FRA rate and a standard forward rate. The approach to modelling interest rates after the credit crunch which is proposed by Mercurio (2008) stops here in the attempt to understand the new market. It exploits instead the fact that even when $L(\alpha,2\alpha)$ is undetermined we can still express the equilibrium rate of a FRA as the expectation of $L(\alpha,2\alpha)$ under the risk-free forward measure, as shown in (4.16). Thanks to this, the FRA rate may not coincide anymore with the standard forward rate but it is still a martingale under the pricing measure and still coincides with $L(\alpha,2\alpha)$ at expiry α. These properties allow us to define a framework where the market patterns are not explained but we can still perform some interest rate modelling, although with a higher number of variables. I believe this approach is clever and that the market is likely to go on following it to perform operations on interest rate quotations like bootstrapping curves and volatilities. However, as long as the market patterns are not explained with some more structural model, the very many variables of the new agnostic approach to interest rate modelling remain largely undetermined in their dynamics and their relations, leaving room for large model risk. Some of this is mentioned in Section 8.2. Therefore in what follows we will take a different route and explain, at least approximately, the interest rate market patterns. This may also have the side-effect of giving indications for a more aware specification of the properties of rates in the agnostic approach.

[2] To give a numerical value to the convexity adjustment, Morini (2010) performs historical estimation of some volatilities and correlations of Libor and OIS rates. You may distrust historically estimated parameters. However, the resulting difference between $F^{rf}_{dX_0}$ and F_L is so low that no reasonable changes in the estimated parameters could explain a market difference that was as large as 200bps.

Remark 11. ***The relation between the FRA and the Basis.*** *The result I present in this section is usually well known to traders specializing in the interbank market, but it usually comes as a surprise for other, even experienced, market operators, particularly quants. I thank my colleague trader Silvia Schiavo for clarifying the issue, actually with arguments different from those I use below. The issue is: if we now want to see the consequence of a modelling assumption on basis swaps, should we redo all the work done for FRAs? Not really. In fact Basis Swaps are also collateralized derivatives, so they can also be treated as default-free contracts. Thanks to this property we can write a precise relationship between FRA rates and Basis spreads that holds irrespective of what we assume about the interbank market. Thus we use for this section the notation*

$$FRA_?^{rf}(t;T,T';K), \quad BS_?^{rf}(t;\alpha/\alpha';T;Z),$$

to underline that the following equalities hold irrespective of the model assumed. To make our analysis simpler, we select the simplest Basis Swap: the exchange of a leg with frequency α that lasts until 2α (two payments), and of a leg with frequency 2α that lasts until 2α (one payment). In the empirical application we will see later, we consider the one year vs six month Basis Swap, so α corresponds to six months. As explained in Ametrano and Bianchetti (2009), the current Euro quotation system for basis swaps is slightly different from the classic description we gave in Section 4.1.3, so that for this basis it is more realistic to assume that the basis spread Z, rather than added to the 6 month leg, is subtracted to the one year leg. In this case the value of the Basis swap is

$$\begin{aligned}BS_?^{rf}(0;\alpha/2\alpha;2\alpha;Z) = &\mathbb{E}\left[D(0,\alpha)\alpha L(0,\alpha) + D(0,2\alpha)\alpha L(\alpha,2\alpha) + \right.\\ &\left. - D(0,2\alpha)2\alpha(L(0,2\alpha) - Z)\right].\end{aligned}$$

Notice that only the component

$$\mathbb{E}[D(0,\alpha)\alpha L(0,\alpha)]$$

really involves the expectation of an unknown, model dependent quantity, the rest are deterministic payments that are evaluated by pure discounting,

$$\begin{aligned}BS_?^{rf}(0;\alpha/2\alpha;2\alpha;Z) &= P^{rf}(0,\alpha)\alpha L(0,\alpha) + \mathbb{E}[D(0,2\alpha)\alpha L(\alpha,2\alpha)]\\ &- P^{rf}(0,2\alpha)2\alpha(L(0,2\alpha) - Z).\end{aligned}$$

If we define the deterministic quantity

$$\tilde{K}(Z) = \left(\frac{1}{P_L(0,2\alpha)} - 1 - 2Z\alpha - \frac{P^{rf}(0,\alpha)}{P^{rf}(0,2\alpha)}\left(\frac{1}{P_L(0,\alpha)} - 1\right)\right)/\alpha,$$

we can write

$$BS_?^{rf}(0;\alpha/2\alpha;2\alpha;Z) = \mathbb{E}\left[D(0,2\alpha)\alpha(L(\alpha,2\alpha)\right] - P^{rf}(0,2\alpha)\tilde{K}(Z)\alpha. \tag{4.19}$$

Compare this with FRA:

$$FRA_?^{rf}(0;\alpha,2\alpha;K) = \mathbb{E}\left[D(0,2\alpha)\alpha L(\alpha,2\alpha)\right] - P^{rf}(0,2\alpha)K\alpha.$$

If one sets $K = \tilde{K}(Z)$ the FRA price is equal to the price of a Basis Swap when the spread is set to Z. The first component, the only one that involves a model-dependent expectation of a future Libor rate, is the same for FRA and Basis, so that the two derivatives depend on the

Replicating an FRA

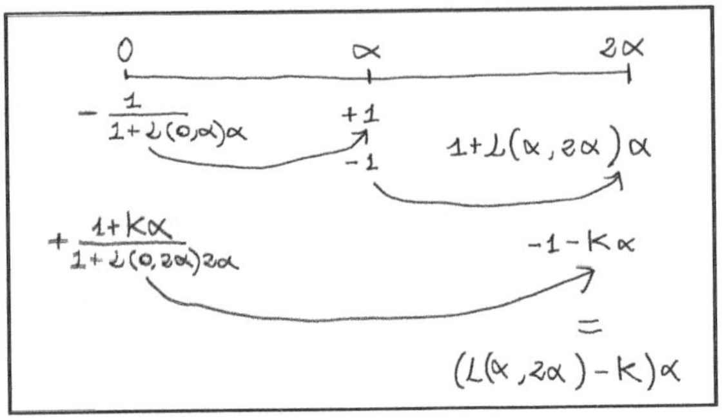

Figure 4.5 FRA Standard Replication Scheme

same information. Intuitively, consider the FRA replication strategy, summarized in Figure 4.5. The fixed leg is replicated by a bond with maturity 2α*, while the floating leg is replicated by lending* α*, followed by another lending from* α *to* 2α*. One leg has* α *tenor, the other leg has* 2α *tenor. It is clear that an FRA replication is affected by the presence of non-negligible Basis Swap spreads in the market.*

We have not yet been able to understand how

$$\mathbb{E}[D(0,2\alpha)\alpha L(\alpha,2\alpha)]$$

should be computed to match the patterns observed in the crisis, but if the above relation between FRA and Basis is correct, and the market is arbitrage-free, we should at least be able to replicate the equilibrium FRA quote observed in the market using the equilibrium Basis swap spread quote and applying (4.19). This is indeed the case, as shown in Figure 4.6, taking as usual $\alpha = 6m$*. Conversely, if one sets*

$$Z = \tilde{Z}(K) := \left(\frac{1}{P_L(0,2\alpha)} - \alpha K - \frac{P^{rf}(0,\alpha)}{P^{rf}(0,2\alpha)} \left(\frac{1}{P_L(0,\alpha)} - 1 \right) - 1 \right) / (2\alpha) \qquad (4.20)$$

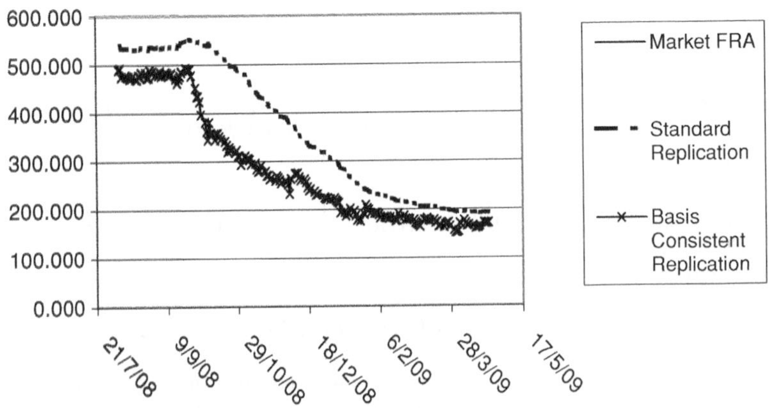

Figure 4.6 6 × 12 Market FRA, Standard Replication, and Basis-consistent Replication

the Basis Swap will have the same value as the FRA when the fixed rate is set to K. *This allows us to compute the Basis Spread implied by the FRA rate that we obtained assuming stable and homogeneous credit risk. This basis turns out almost null, as one would expect. This confirms we are still far from explaining the new market pattern, but (4.19) has reduced our two problems to only one. If we are able to explain the basis, the FRA will also be explained.*

Before moving to an effective explanation of the basis, we recall a few common misconceptions.

Remark 12. ***Common misconceptions in explanations of the basis.*** *If you asked a market operator to give you a reason for the basis that exploded during the credit crunch, for example between* 6*m-tenor rates and* 12*m-tenor rates, it is very likely that you will get an answer along the following lines:*

> 'Compare a strategy where you lend for $12m$ with a strategy where you roll over twice a $6m$ lending. In the latter case, after $6m$, if the counterparty default risk has increased, you can stop lending with no cost (at par). If instead you are a $12m$ lender, you will have to unwind at a cost that incorporates the increased risk of default. Thus, *those who roll the 6m investment have an option to exit when the credit risk grows, and move to a counterparty with lower risk*, and this explains the basis.'

Is this true? Not at all. The 6*m roller does* not *have an option to exit after* $6m$, because he will always exit at $6m$, including when the default risk of the counterparty has decreased instead of increased. *In case of a decrease of the risk of default by the counterparty, it is the* 12*m lender who has the advantage (he receives a yield higher than the actual risk). Thus the expected gain of the* 6*m lender when the counterparty worsens is compensated by its expected loss when the counterparty gets better, this fact cannot explain the basis. Also the second part of the argument, to say that after* 6*m if the risk of the counterparty has increased the roller will* 'move to a counterparty with lower risk' *is a financial nonsense. In fact, such a counterparty will pay a lower yield, and if the investor is looking for yield he may move to an even more risky counterparty. This is normal in the market and it is no explanation for the basis. Ironically, it seems that the fear of default that characterized the credit crunch has made us forget that default risk can both increase and decrease, and that a normal investor does not necessarily run away from credit risk but, as happens with any other form of risk, can accept it as long as it is fairly remunerated.*

The above explanations are not totally off the mark, but miss a crucial aspect: the basis does not regard two strategies with different frequencies of payment, but two derivatives which are indexed to Libor rates with different frequencies. The mechanism for the basis must be looked for there, in the Libor panel and market that determine the future level of Libor.

A final misconception worth mentioning relates to the claim that 'overnight rates are risk-free, they do not incorporate bank vs bank credit risk'. This is often used today, but it seldom comes with consistent explanations. Overnight lending is unsecured, so there is no protection from default. How come the overnight rates do not include credit risk? 'Because the length of the lending is very short,' says someone. But this is no answer. Think of the standard CDS intensity credit model seen earlier: if the instantaneous default probability is flat λ, *credit spreads are close to* λ *for any term of lending. The length of the lending is captured by the year fraction by which the rate is multiplied, not by the credit spread. Once during a course, exasperated by not finding a defendable justification, someone told me: 'overnight is risk-free because companies do not default overnight!' So when do they default? In the afternoon?!? The truth is that even this person was not totally off the mark, but a defensible explanation must be less trivial, as we see below.*

4.1.5 A Market with Volatile Credit Risk

In the previous sections we saw that neither a risk-free market nor a market assuming homogeneous and stable credit risk can explain the new interest rate patterns.

The market with homogeneity and stability is the mathematical representation of a market where all banks have similar risk of default, and this risk of default is not volatile. In practice, such a situation can be an approximation of reality only when the risk of default is very low. This is probably a good model to use to understand why, before the crisis, we had the relations of a risk-free market, in spite of there being some default risk. But we need different assumptions to explore the new patterns. In the old setting, we can take a bank that is today a member of the Libor market and consider its spread a good representation of the Libor rate also for the future.

Now we suppose instead that risk of default grows and becomes more volatile, as happened with the burst of the subprime crisis. In this context it is unrealistic to assume that the expected future spread of a current Libor contributor coincides with the expected future of Libor. There are in fact many reasons why a bank that is today a member of the Libor market may cease being a good representation of Libor in the future. We see four simple reasons to explain this.

Banks can exit the Libor panel

Recall the Libor panel rules:

> *'The banks represented on the panels are the most active in the cash markets and have the highest credit ratings'*
> *'The BBA is committed to reviewing the panels at least twice annually'*

When the credit standing of a bank in the Libor panel deteriorates too much, a bank may even be excluded by the Libor panel and replaced with a better one. This does not happen very often, but it has happened a few times, for example during the credit crunch. This worst case is paradigmatic: clearly, in this case the spread of the original Libor counterparty will not influence the future Libor rate, which will be *lower* than the spread of the counterparty, now ejected from the panel.

Banks can exit the deposit Libor market

But we do not need a bank to be officially thrown out of the Libor panel to see the above mechanism at work. A bank can exit the Libor market, even if is does not exit the Libor panel. This was the case for many banks during the subprime crisis. The Libor market is the market where loans are made, unsecured, at a rate which is very similar to the Libor fixings. The Libor fixings are computed by asking banks the rate at which they can borrow unsecured. If a bank has difficulties in borrowing unsecured at quotes close to previous Libor fixings or, even worse, it has difficulties in borrowing unsecured at all, how will the bank answer the Libor panel? Very likely, it will contribute a fictive rate, which rather than being their true rate for unsecured borrowing is their guess at the rate for unsecured borrowing that applies to those other banks that can still afford it.

This is the thesis exposed, precisely for the credit crunch period which is of interest to us, in Peng et al. (2008). The argument is that many banks were contributing to the Libor panel rates lower than their actual lending costs, as confirmed by a number of market observations, since 'any bank posting a high Libor level runs the risk of being perceived as needing funding'. Consistently with our above considerations, Peng et al. (2008) conclude that, particularly for distressed banks, their Libor contribution did not reflect the actual cost of their funding.[3]

What is the effect of a bank replacing its real cost of funding, which has become too high, with a fictive, lower one when making its Libor contribution? It is exactly the same effect as if the bank were thrown off the panel and replaced by a better bank.

This conclusion is confirmed by practical evidence from the credit crunch. During this crisis the Libor deposit market thinned dramatically, confirming that only a very few banks, if any, were able to borrow unsecured. Brunnermeier (2009) even speaks of the *freezing up of the interbank market on 9 August* 2007. In spite of this, contributions for unsecured lending rates went on reaching the panel with no apparent discontinuity.

Banks can exit the interquartile part of the Libor panel

The bank can remain in the Libor panel and in the Libor market and yet no longer be a good representative of Libor. In fact, Libor is a trimmed average, in the sense that the highest and lowest quartiles of the contributions are taken away before averaging; when risk of default is stable and homogeneous, this fact is negligible, but when there is more variability this may have a relevance. Our initial reference counterparty can turn out to have a borrowing rate either higher or lower than average Libor contributions. Which one of the two cases is more relevant? If there is a crisis that interests some banks, it is unlikely that a few contributions appear strongly lower than the average of the others, while it is more probable that there will be a few contributions strongly higher than the average. In a systemic crisis the situation can be different, but the evidence from the credit crunch, the prototypical systemic crisis, shows skewed Libor contributions, with a lower average and a few outliers with higher spreads. This suggests that the case with quantitatively more relevant consequences is the case when the counterparty's credit spread is higher than average Libor contributions.

Banks can exit the world of the living banks . . .

Eventually, if their credit standing deteriorates too much, unless they are bailed out by a government, banks can default. This is what happened to Lehman. Since we are considering collateralized derivatives, the possibility of default by banks does not impact our derivatives directly, but it still has an impact on the payoff of interest rate derivatives since it operates as one of the events that can bring a bank out of the Libor market when its spreads worsen too much. Default is one more selection mechanism that creates a bias in Libor towards banks with *lower* risk.

[3] Notice that Peng et al. (2008) is a research report by a large Libor contributor bank, whose CDS spread reached levels much higher than the Libor spread during the crisis, so it is indeed a knowledgeable source!

Market quotes when credit risk is volatile

Any of the above reasons show that there is some non-negligible likelihood that the spread of a current Libor counterparty will not be a good representative of future Libor, because there is a cap to how much the credit spread of a bank can grow and still influence the future level of Libor. When the situation of a counterparty deteriorates too far, its spread stops having an influence on Libor. Therefore, *the expected future spread of Libor is lower than the expected spread in the future of a bank which is now a Libor counterparty*. This means that we have lost the *stability assumption*. And without stability, *homogeneity* cannot strictly hold: one bank can deteriorate becoming necessarily different from the others before being thrown out. We can assume homogeneity to hold at time 0 for simplicity, but it cannot hold in the future.

The swap

What is the effect of this conclusion on our approach to replicate the floating leg of a swap? A disruptive effect. The standard replication strategy of a floating leg no longer makes sense. Suppose that the investor willing to replicate the floating leg starts doing it as we did in the previous section: we start lending today 1 for α years to a counterparty X_0 which is today a Libor counterparty. After α years she will receive $1 + L^{dX_0}(0, \alpha) = 1 + L(0, \alpha)$. So far so good, the old strategy works, but at α, for the first stochastic payment, the investor needs to change approach. At α the investor should check whether the counterparty is still a Libor bank, namely one of the banks with the lowest credit risk. If the answer is no, namely $X_0 \notin \mathbb{L}_\alpha$ because it is too risky, she cannot lend the money again to the same counterparty, otherwise she would receive $1 + L^{dX_0}(\alpha, 2\alpha) > 1 + L(\alpha, 2\alpha)$. Even the first fundamental part of the replication would be wrong, overestimating the level of Libor.

The investor must instead choose another counterparty X_α with a lower credit risk and thus a lower credit spread, so that $X_\alpha \in \mathbb{L}_\alpha$ and the investor will receive $1 + L^{dX_\alpha}(\alpha, 2\alpha) = 1 + L(\alpha, 2\alpha)$. This process, involving at every α an assessment of the risk of the counterparty with possible substitution with a counterparty with *lower* credit spread, must be repeated until $M\alpha$. The credit quality of the counterparty is assessed, and improved if necessary, every α years.

The FRA

Now let us suppose we are in a market FRA, a collateralized product where only one stochastic payment is involved, the one at α. Compared to the risk-free or stable-risk cases in which one did not change the counterparty, lending always at X_0, now at α we may need to move to a counterparty better than X_0 in case X_0 exits the Libor panel or market. Therefore the α-payment $L^{dX_\alpha}(\alpha, 2\alpha)$ will be lower than $L^{dX_0}(\alpha, 2\alpha)$ that we had in the previous market models, so that the fixed rate needed to set the two legs in equilibrium will also be lower, giving an intuitive understanding, that we will also verify analytically below, of why during the crisis

$$F^{rf}_{dX_0 X_\alpha}(0; \alpha, 2\alpha) \ll \frac{1}{\alpha}\left(\frac{P_L(0, \alpha)}{P_L(0, 2\alpha)} - 1\right).$$

Notice that the subscript we use for this model of the market indicates the mechanism for which the Libor counterparty gets refreshed at fixing time, and cannot be identified with the initial one.

The Basis Swap

Let us now consider Basis Swaps. In order to gain intuition on how such swaps behave in this context, it becomes important to understand what changes when, from a swap with α tenor ($\frac{1}{\alpha}$ frequency) like the one above, we move to different tenors. If the tenor of the interest rate payment in the floating leg was 2α (thus with payments at $2\alpha, 4\alpha, 6\alpha \ldots$), the process of assessment and improvement of the counterparty credit quality would be done less often. The investor will be exposed to all possible worsening of the counterparty credit that can happen along 2α years. Thus the 2α-year Libor leg involves more credit risk than the α-year Libor leg, and this higher credit risk is embedded in higher rates paid. If instead the tenor of the interest rate payment in the floating leg was $\frac{\alpha}{2}$ (thus with payments at $\frac{\alpha}{2}, \alpha, \frac{3}{2}\alpha \ldots$), this assessment and improvement of the counterparty should be done every $\frac{\alpha}{2}$ years, reducing the risk of default even further than in the α-year Libor leg.

In the α leg the Libor rates are higher since they embed higher credit spreads, a compensation for the higher counterparty risk. But with collateralization the two legs have the same null counterparty risk. To reach equilibrium a spread Z needs to be added to the $\frac{\alpha}{2}$ leg,

$$B(t; \frac{\alpha}{2}/\alpha; T) \gg 0.$$

The overnight rate

There is another important implication of this representation of the interest rate market. In the replication of a floating leg, the more frequent the payments, the lower the credit risk, until payment reaches the shortest tenor available in the market: the overnight. To replicate a leg with overnight payments, one should assess and if necessary improve the credit quality of the counterparty everyday, leading to a leg involving an extremely low level of counterparty risk. Who is admitted to the overnight lending market? Those borrowers whose risk of default is negligible over the next day. This explains why the overnight quote is usually considered to be default-free. Since only banks with a negligible default risk over the term of the lending are admitted to this market, its quote represents a very good approximation of a risk-free interest rate.

A model to replicate today's basis

We want to go beyond intuition and model Libor rates when credit risk is high and volatile, so that homogeneity holds only at time 0 and stability does not hold at all, meaning that banks can exit the Libor market. Here, however, the model is independent of how we interpret the reasons for spread movements, it can be credit, liquidity, or both. With homogeneity and stability we had,

$$L(\alpha, 2\alpha) \overset{by\ Hom}{=} L^{dX_\alpha}(\alpha, 2\alpha) \overset{by\ Stab}{=} L^{dX_0}(\alpha, 2\alpha).$$

If they are replaced by the assumption that the current Libor counterparty will exit the Libor market when its borrowing rate is too high, we have

$$L(\alpha, 2\alpha) \leq L^{dX_0}(\alpha, 2\alpha). \tag{4.21}$$

We still suppose that at time 0

$$L(0, \alpha) = L^{dX_0}(0, \alpha),$$

so that we can initially identify Libor with a current Libor counterparty that we call X_0. But then, at α, we will have to verify whether we can continue with this identification or not, by checking if $L^{dX_0}(\alpha, 2\alpha)$ satisfies the requirements for X_0 still being a Libor bank at α.

Notice that both $L(\alpha, 2\alpha)$ and $L^{dX_0}(\alpha, 2\alpha)$ are given by the risk-free rate $L^{rf}(\alpha, 2\alpha)$ plus a spread,

$$L(\alpha, 2\alpha) =: L^{rf}(\alpha, 2\alpha) + S(\alpha, 2\alpha),$$
$$L^{dX_0}(\alpha, 2\alpha) =: L^{rf}(\alpha, 2\alpha) + S^{dX_0}(\alpha, 2\alpha).$$

What do we know about the rates and spreads involved in our computations? In (4.9) we computed the expectation of $L(\alpha, 2\alpha)$ under the hypothesis that $L(\alpha, 2\alpha) = L^{rf}(\alpha, 2\alpha)$, thus (4.9) tells us that

$$\mathbb{E}^{rf2\alpha}\left[L^{rf}(\alpha, 2\alpha)\right] = \frac{1}{\alpha}\left(\frac{P^{rf}(0,\alpha)}{P^{rf}(0,2\alpha)} - 1\right).$$

Instead formula (4.17) gives a result on $L(\alpha, 2\alpha)$ under the hypothesis that $L(\alpha, 2\alpha) = L^{dX_\alpha}(\alpha, 2\alpha)$, thus (4.17) tells us that

$$\mathbb{E}^{rf2\alpha}\left[L^{dX_0}(\alpha, 2\alpha)\right] \approx \frac{1}{\alpha}\left(\frac{P^{dX_0}(0,\alpha)}{P^{dX_0}(0,2\alpha)} - 1\right) = F_L(0;\alpha, 2\alpha),$$

where X_0 is one counterparty that was Libor at X_0 and that is still alive at α. We have a '$\approx$' sign instead of a plain '=' because of the convexity adjustment we have in (4.17), that appears smaller than a basis point. In the following we neglect the very small convexity adjustment and the data on L^{rf} and P^{rf} come from OIS quotes, while those on L^{dX_0} and P^{dX_0} come from Libor.

Having neglected the small convexity adjustment, we have

$$\begin{aligned}\mathbb{E}^{rf2\alpha}\left[S^{dX_0}(\alpha, 2\alpha)\right] &= \mathbb{E}^{rf2\alpha}\left[L^{rf}(\alpha, 2\alpha)\right] - \mathbb{E}^{rf2\alpha}\left[L^{dX_0}(t, T)\right] \\ &= \frac{1}{\alpha}\left(\frac{P^{rf}(0,\alpha)}{P^{rf}(0,2\alpha)} - \frac{P^{dX_0}(0,\alpha)}{P^{dX_0}(0,2\alpha)}\right),\end{aligned}$$

so we introduce the variable

$$S^{dX_0}(t;\alpha, 2\alpha) = \frac{1}{\alpha}\left(\frac{P^{rf}(t,\alpha)}{P^{rf}(t,2\alpha)} - \frac{P^{dX_0}(t,\alpha)}{P^{dX_0}(t,2\alpha)}\right),$$

that we call the forward spread of X_0 and that has the property of being a martingale (still neglecting the small convexity adjustment) and that

$$S^{dX_0}(\alpha;\alpha, 2\alpha) = S^{dX_0}(\alpha, 2\alpha).$$

Notice that our Libor condition (4.21) corresponds to

$$S(\alpha, 2\alpha) \le S^{dX_0}(\alpha, 2\alpha) \text{ or equivalently}$$
$$S(\alpha, 2\alpha) \le S^{dX_0}(\alpha;\alpha, 2\alpha).$$

A simple scheme to represent the potential refreshment of the counterparty is:

$$\boxed{S(\alpha, 2\alpha) = \begin{cases} S^{dX_0}(\alpha, 2\alpha) & \text{if } S^{dX_0}(\alpha, 2\alpha) \le S^{Exit} \\ S^{Subst} & \text{if } S^{dX_0}(\alpha, 2\alpha) > S^{Exit} \end{cases}}, \tag{4.22}$$

where

- **S^{Exit} is the maximum level of the spread for X_0 to still be a Libor counterparty at α**
- **S^{Subst} is the spread of Libor in case $X_0 \notin \mathbb{L}_\alpha$ because $S^{dX_0}(\alpha, 2\alpha) > S^{Exit}$**

This is the same as writing

$$\begin{aligned} L(\alpha, 2\alpha) &= L^{rf}(\alpha, 2\alpha) + 1_{\{S^{dX_0}(\alpha,2\alpha) \le S^{Exit}\}} S^{dX_0}(\alpha, 2\alpha) + 1_{\{S^{dX_0}(\alpha,2\alpha) > S^{Exit}\}} S^{Subst} \\ &= L^{rf}(\alpha, 2\alpha) + S^{dX_0}(\alpha, 2\alpha) - 1_{\{S^{dX_0}(\alpha,2\alpha) > S^{Exit}\}} \left(S^{dX_0}(\alpha, 2\alpha) - S^{Subst}\right) \\ &= L^{dX_0}(\alpha, 2\alpha) - 1_{\{S^{dX_0}(\alpha,2\alpha) > S^{Exit}\}} \left(S^{dX_0}(\alpha, 2\alpha) - S^{Subst}\right). \end{aligned}$$

First we have to make a choice on S^{Exit}, then on S^{Subst}, with necessarily

$$S^{Subst} \le S^{Exit}.$$

We will not aim to make any precise representation of reality; we will propose as an example some extremely simple possible values and we will see if even such simplified assumptions can lead to relevant improvements in explaining the market compared to the old risk-free or stable-risk-of-default approaches.

The level S^{Exit} is the level over which a Libor bank is considered an underperformer. Thus S^{Exit} can be close to the current expectation of $S^{dX_0}(\alpha, 2\alpha)$, so that *a counterparty will be excluded from Libor banks if it performs worse than expected*:

$$\boxed{S^{Exit} = \mathbb{E}\left[S^{dX_0}(\alpha, 2\alpha)\right] = S^{dX_0}(0; \alpha, 2\alpha)}.$$

We also make a simple choice for S^{Subst}. The counterparty X_0 is excluded by Libor because its spread is higher than today expectation by an amount

$$S^{dX_0}(\alpha, 2\alpha) - S^{dX_0}(0; \alpha, 2\alpha) > 0;$$

in this case we assume that the prototypical counterparty that replaces the underperformer did as well as X_0 did badly, thus we move to a Libor counterparty *whose spread S^{Subst} is lower than today expectation by the same amount $S^{dX_0}(\alpha, 2\alpha) - S^{dX_0}(0; \alpha, 2\alpha)$*, so that

$$S^{Subst} = S^{dX_0}(0; \alpha, 2\alpha) - \left[S^{dX_0}(\alpha, 2\alpha) - S^{dX_0}(0; \alpha, 2\alpha)\right]$$

$$\boxed{S^{Subst} = 2S^{dX_0}(0; \alpha, 2\alpha) - S^{dX_0}(\alpha, 2\alpha)}.$$

This leads to

$$\begin{aligned} L(\alpha, 2\alpha) &= L^{dX_0}(\alpha, 2\alpha) - 1_{\{S^{dX_0}(\alpha,2\alpha) > S^{Exit}\}} \left(S^{dX_0}(\alpha, 2\alpha) - S^{Subst}\right) \\ &= L^{dX_0}(\alpha, 2\alpha) - 1_{\{S^{dX_0}(\alpha,2\alpha) > S^{dX_0}(0;\alpha,2\alpha)\}} \left(S^{dX_0}(\alpha, 2\alpha) - 2S^{dX_0}(0; \alpha, 2\alpha) + S^{dX_0}(\alpha, 2\alpha)\right) \\ &= L^{dX_0}(\alpha, 2\alpha) - 2 \times 1_{\{S^{dX_0}(\alpha,2\alpha) > S^{dX_0}(0;\alpha,2\alpha)\}} \left(S^{dX_0}(\alpha, 2\alpha) - S^{dX_0}(0; \alpha, 2\alpha)\right) \\ &= L^{dX_0}(\alpha, 2\alpha) - 2\left(S^{dX_0}(\alpha, 2\alpha) - S^{dX_0}(0; \alpha, 2\alpha)\right)^+ \\ &= L^{dX_0}(\alpha, 2\alpha) - 2\left(S^{dX_0}(\alpha; \alpha, 2\alpha) - S^{dX_0}(0; \alpha, 2\alpha)\right)^+. \end{aligned}$$

Now we are ready to solve our problem:

$$\mathbb{E}^{rf2\alpha}[L(\alpha, 2\alpha)] = F_L(0;\alpha, 2\alpha) - 2\mathbb{E}^{rf2\alpha}\left[\left(S^{dX_0}(\alpha;\alpha, 2\alpha) - S^{dX_0}(0;\alpha, 2\alpha)\right)^+\right].$$

If we assume that $S^{dX_0}(t, \alpha, 2\alpha)$ evolves as a geometric Brownian motion

$$dS^{dX_0}(t, \alpha, 2\alpha) = S^{dX_0}(t, \alpha, 2\alpha)\sigma_\alpha dW_\alpha(t),$$

we have the simple option formula

$$\begin{aligned}\mathbb{E}^{rf2\alpha}[L(\alpha, 2\alpha)] &= F_L(0;\alpha, 2\alpha) \\ &-2Black\left(S^{dX_0}(0;\alpha, 2\alpha), S^{dX_0}(0;\alpha, 2\alpha), \sigma_\alpha^2\alpha\right).\end{aligned} \tag{4.23}$$

As in the old $F_L(0;\alpha, 2\alpha)$, this formula gives expected future Libor based on current Libor. But now it includes a refreshment mechanism that can explain the market patterns of FRA. This shows very precisely why in this model the FRA equilibrium rate is lower than $F_L(0;\alpha, 2\alpha)$, since

$$F^{rf}_{dX_0,X_\alpha}(0;\alpha, 2\alpha) = \mathbb{E}[L(\alpha, 2\alpha)] \leq F_L(0;\alpha, 2\alpha),$$

with the inequality collapsing to an equality only if $S^{dX_0}(0;\alpha, 2\alpha)$ is zero, which would bring us to the risk-free market or if the credit volatility is zero, which would bring us back to the stable-default-risk market.

This formulation can also explain the non-null basis spread, as is clear from the relation (4.20) between the FRA rate and the Basis spread. But we do not only want to explain the sign of the Basis spread, but also its magnitude, so we will test our formula (4.23) on real market quotes of Basis Swaps. Consider the Basis Swap where as usual $\alpha = 6m$. We have that

$$\begin{aligned}B^{rf}(0;\alpha/2\alpha;2\alpha) = &\frac{1}{2}F_L(0;\alpha, 2\alpha) + \frac{1}{2}\left(\frac{1}{P_L(0,\alpha)} - 1\right) \\ &\times\left(F_L(0;\alpha, 2\alpha) - F^{rf}_{rf}(0;\alpha, 2\alpha)\right) - \frac{1}{2}\frac{\mathbb{E}\left[D(0, 2\alpha)\alpha(L(\alpha, 2\alpha)\right]}{P^{rf}(0, 2\alpha)\alpha}.\end{aligned}$$

Replacing expectation with its value in the model with volatile credit we have

$$\begin{aligned}B^{rf}_{dX_0,X_\alpha}(0;\alpha/2\alpha;2\alpha) = &\frac{1}{2}\left(\frac{1}{P_L(0,\alpha)} - 1\right) \\ &\times\left(F_L(0;\alpha, 2\alpha) - F^{rf}_{rf}(0;\alpha, 2\alpha)\right) \\ &+ Black\left(S^{dX_0}(0;\alpha, 2\alpha), S^{dX_0}(0;\alpha, 2\alpha), \sigma_\alpha^2\alpha\right).\end{aligned} \tag{4.24}$$

This formula for the Basis is simple. We have all the rates we need from Libor and OIS rate quotes. The only input we do not have immediately available is the volatility. It is the volatility of the credit spread of one generic counterparty. Since we are working on Euro data, as a proxy we use the volatility of the i-Traxx Index spread, the average credit spread of the 125 most liquid entities in the Euro market. We extract the volatility information from the ATM options on the $5y$ i-Traxx spread with expiry $\alpha = 6m$, that are quoted daily. Options with $6m$ expiry for a $6m$ spread would be more appropriate, but such options are not traded in the market.

The simple formula (4.24), based uniquely on Euribor and Eonia OIS data, with a credit volatility input, yields a good replication of the historical behaviour of the traded $6m/12m$ basis, as shown in Figure 4.7. Thanks to (4.20), we know that a similar result is obtained

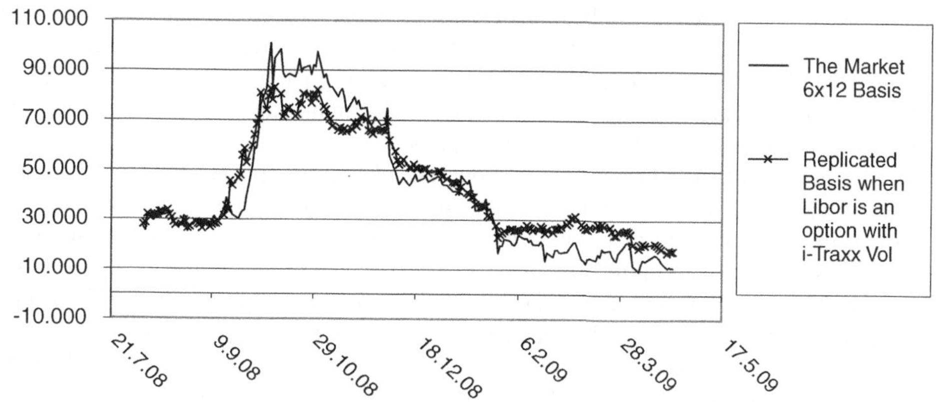

Figure 4.7 The market Basis and the model replication with realistic credit

for market FRA. We intend the formula we derived as a very schematic representation of a refreshment mechanism or pull-to-quality that we can observe in Libor quotations. We do not want to overextend the interpretation of the mechanism underlying this formula by trying to make it fit the data exactly. The improvement of the scheme, compared to the previous models of the market that only implied an almost zero basis, is already very satisfactory for our goals.

We point out that some of the discrepancies between the historical pattern and our replication can be explained also by the lack of a more appropriate volatility input. For example, in the aftermath of the Lehman default, the option replication tends to underestimate the historical pattern. This may be related to the fact that we are using as volatility proxy a value that refers to the 125 most liquid companies in Europe, an index more than half of which is composed of corporate, nonfinancial firms, while the Libor spread should refer to financials only. The volatility of financials was perceived to be higher than the average volatility after Lehman's default, so that our volatility input may underestimate the correct one. This issue may partially explain also why, in the final part of the sample, referring to a period where banks were perceived as less risky while the crisis was hitting hard non-financial companies, the replicated basis is higher than the quoted one.

In spite of the details, the relevance of this result is to show that an extremely simple explanatory model based on counterparty risk in Libor, and on the optionality implicit in Libor, allows an approximate replication of the Basis swap (and FRA) market patterns, even though in the model there are no parameters used to fit to the Basis Swap or FRA market. This representation of the Basis as an option has the advantage of giving a general explanation of why the Basis gets higher the higher the difference in tenor between the two legs of the swap. A $6m$-tenor Libor leg is lower than a $1y$-tenor Libor leg since the $6m$ leg involves a stream of counterparties whose credit risk is checked and refreshed every $6m$, down to reaching an overnight leg (OIS) whose risk of default is checked and refreshed overnight. This risk is sufficiently low to consider such a leg approximately riskless.

Some critical observations are in order. The model is obviously too simple to constitute a detailed representation of the Basis Swap or FRA dynamics. The spread behaviour could be represented by more realistic stochastic dynamics. Various elements of realism could be added even without changing the assumptions on the stochastic dynamics. For example, we modelled Libor as a kind of cap contract, but one may notice that in normal market conditions Libor is rather a collar, since there is not only a cap on the level of the forward rate of a counterparty for it to be considered Libor, but also a floor. In fact, there are counterparties that are considered less risky than Libor, and in any case Libor is a trimmed average from which both the lowest and highest quartiles are excluded. This may even justify, in market conditions different from those in the recent crisis, negative Basis Swap spreads.

We also point out that the choice made about the substitution spread $S^{Subst}(\alpha, 2\alpha)$ implies that this spread over OIS can turn negative in some cases. More generally the choice appears optimistic in respect of the Libor counterparty that substitutes for the original one when the latter underperforms. A less optimistic choice, however, would underestimate the market basis, if the remaining assumptions are unchanged. On the contrary, the choice about S^{Exit} is quite conservative. It may be that these discrepancies, with what appears realistic, are due to the fact that in market prices we observe risk-adjusted, and not objective, probabilities. But there are also few reasonable alternative assumptions that would lead to a result similar to (4.24). For example, we could be less optimistic about the substitute counterparty S^{Subst}, but we could bring into the picture some other elements not introduced explicitly in the final simple model. In particular, we could allow for the fact that the conditions of a lending contract depend not only on the borrower's credit conditions, but also on the lender's credit/liquidity conditions. And a lending contract can exit the Libor world not only because of borrower's credit problems, as assumed here, but also because of the lender's liquidity problems. If we consider for example the model representation of liquidity in Section 4.2, we will see that there are at least four variables that may be involved in a rate like Libor: the credit spread of the borrower, which is obvious, *the credit spread of the lender*, which is less obvious but that appears clearly in the representation given in Piterbarg (2010), and two liquidity bases for the two parties. The joint consideration of these terms could provide an alternative mechanism to remain in line with market quotes with a less optimistic assumption about the substitute counterparty.

4.1.6 Conclusions

The previous analysis has given us a number of clues for dealing with sudden shifts in the modelling consensus prevailing in a market. We have seen clearly in the patterns of market data just how a very strong hypothesis like the idea of a risk-free market was *confirmed* by market data for many years, and we have also seen *how suddenly* it was rejected when economic conditions changed. After being very pessimistic about the information derived from market data in the case study about the pricing of a credit-linked note (presented in Chapter 2), where many would expect all the answers to be found in the market data, we now show conversely that we can in fact extract a precise answer from the market in a specific situation, the sudden change of a modelling paradigm, about which some people I have spoken to simply thought that 'the market had gone crazy'.

Although here the focus has been on understanding a big change in model consensus, the analysis performed has been just one more example of model comparison, that adds to those shown in Chapter 2, and an example of *live* stress testing like those considered in Chapter 3, since we have shown which of the assumptions in the old model paradigm actually broke down in a time of crisis, and that those assumptions were quite hidden. The results provided here give a number of indications about how to model an interest rates market with counterparty risk, supported by analytic results, empirical testing and financial considerations. Flows of floating rates with different frequency should embed different levels of default risk and different levels of default risk volatility to represent the fact that the credit quality of the Libor counterparty is periodically updated. Otherwise credit risk as it is modelled in the reference market for credit, the CDS market, does not explain the rates' patterns.

These results illustrate many of the possible pitfalls in the analysis of the evolution of modelling paradigms. We saw how the pre-crisis reality made us forget the true complexity in the payoff of interest rate derivatives, leading to an oversimplified representation that entered many textbooks. We also forgot the relation between forward rate agreements and basis spreads, something that was well known to traders but overlooked by quants when they found a simplified mathematical scheme that allowed them to ignore the existence of Basis spreads. We can add that, for example, Basis spreads *were never really zero*, although they were very near to zero. Greater attention to this fact, plus attempts to explain it with a modelling tool, would have provided useful insights so that all the financial players would have been less taken aback by the market shift.

As pointed out in Remark 10, some clever solutions have been found that allow one to perform interest rate modelling in the new context even without a structural explanation of the new market patterns. These 'agnostic' models will certainly be very useful in practice, but they involve many variables which are modelled separately, like a curve of OIS rates and many different curves of Libor rates with different tenors, and in this modelling framework such curves can be given any dependence, from independence to perfect dependence. The model risk coming from the indetermination of the relationship between these curves can be high, as we point out again in Section 8.2. A structural framework such as the one we have seen here gives some indication of the dependencies between the different curves, which appear to be neither perfect nor null.

The structural explanation we have finally given above reaches empirical results far superior than those arrived at by alternative explanations, and this is a fact we must take into account. But in times of change of the model paradigms, we should not stop questioning and improving our explanations. In the next section we try to dig a bit deeper into the concept of liquidity risks and costs, a topic that we temporarily overlooked in this section.

4.2 RETHINKING THE VALUE OF MONEY: THE EFFECT OF LIQUIDITY IN PRICING

In the previous section we saw how a large spread opened in August 2007 between Libor rates, incorporating the default and liquidity costs of a 'refreshed' prime bank, and OIS rates, which can be considered free of risk of default and liquidity costs. This created the first major disruption in standard pricing practices: the old way of building one term structure of discount factors and using it for pricing all derivatives was no longer valid. In fact, the discount factors used to be bootstrapped by the quotes of derivatives indexed to Libor, and these discount factors were considered approximately valid to price both risk-free derivatives and derivatives subject to the default risk of a bank counterparty, confirmed by the fact that Libor quotes and OIS quotes were extremely close. Once Libor rates became much higher than OIS quotes, Libor discounts were clearly no longer correct to discount those derivatives which are risk-free due to the provision of collateral.

A new term structure, based on OIS quotes, needed to be introduced, and the resulting discounts used for collateralized derivatives. For collateralized *interest rate* derivatives this created a big discontinuity in modelling: previously these derivatives had indexing and discounting associated with the same term structure, the Libor term structure. Now they have discounting associated with OIS and indexing associated with Libor. This complication is compounded by the fact that Libor quotes with high credit risk are affected by the presence of a basis between the different tenors. All these problems, all related to collateralized interest rate derivatives, brought about one important change of modelling paradigm, which we analyzed in the Section 4.1.

But collateralized derivatives are only half of the story. The other half are derivatives with no provision of collateral, and these amount to a minority of the outstanding notional but are still very common, particularly between banks and corporates and banks and public institutions, and at times even between banks. These derivatives too used to be discounted with a Libor curve and then a credit value adjustment (CVA) was added to the price to take into account the risk that the counterparty may default before maturity.

Remark CVA and DVA. *If 'party 1' in a deal is pricing a derivative with a CVA that takes into account the risk of default of 'party 2', and then the two parties agree on the price, this means in principle that 'party 2' is making a price with some adjustment that takes into account its own risk of default. Awareness of this scenario grew in banks in the years around the credit crunch, when banks started to have a risk of default that was clearly not negligible; and people in banks started to talk of debt value adjustment (DVA) as an additional correction that a party must apply to a price to take into account its own risk of default.*

Was Libor discounting still valid at least for non-collateralized derivatives? The first answer that the market gave was 'No'. In fact, Libor today includes an important spread for default risk, and this is not actually needed since the specific and precise risk of default for the counterparties is taken into account by CVA and DVA. More importantly, each bank would like to use a discounting that includes its own specific and precise cost of *funding liquidity*.

It is an old market wisdom that the discount factor used by a bank to price its own assets and liabilities should be based on its own cost of funding, that is the interest paid when it borrows funds. If you recall Section 1.2.1, we introduced our abstract discount factor exactly as follows: $D(t, T) = B(t)/B(T)$, where $B(t)$ is the value of our abstract bank account at t, used both to invest and to withdraw funds. It is a very reasonable principle: the cost of financing ourselves for a period of time measures what is for us the *time value of money*, and the time value of money is exactly what we want to be incorporated in our discount factors.

One unrealistic element of the bank account representation is that in practice borrowing rates are different from lending rates. Henrard (2007) explains why it is justified to base discounting only on a funding or borrowing curve without also considering one lending or depositing curve. The point is that an investment bank is naturally short cash, so it never really deposits, it simply borrows less.

The importance of basing discounting on the cost of funding became very evident just after the credit crunch, as confirmed by the extreme popularity of the paper by Piterbarg (2010), where this principle is formalized. Piterbarg (2010) shows how funding determines the discount factor by obtaining the derivative price via replication, in line with the classic paper by Black and Scholes (1973) but considering different costs of funding. Piterbarg (2010) points out that collateralized deals are funded by the collateral itself. Since collateral is regulated overnight at an overnight interest rate $r_C(t)$, collateralized derivatives are discounted at such a rate. Instead, in Piterbarg (2010) a repo rate $r_R(t)$ applies to assets where the asset itself is used in repo for getting funding, and finally a rate $r_F(t)$ which is used for unsecured (non-collateralized) deals. Piterbarg (2010) says that $r_F(t) - r_C(t)$ can be thought of as the intensity of default or the credit spread of a bank, although he points out that in his formalism the possibility of counterparty default is ignored.

In 2009 and 2010 banks were facing fast-increasing funding costs. Libor was becoming more and more separate from the funding costs of the majority of banks, since, as explained in the previous section, it was now referenced only by a real or more often hypothetical minority of prime banks that, while no longer default-free, could still borrow in the interbank market. The old assumption 'that the borrowing or lending would normally be done at Libor' (as we can read in Hull's (2006) popular book) was no longer valid even as a rough approximation. Banks were struggling to find a consistent approach to charge their real funding costs when pricing non-collateralized derivatives, so as to protect them both from the risk of running short of liquidity due to undercharging of funding costs and from the risk of becoming non-competitive due to overcharging of these costs. The picture was complicated by the fact that funding costs were an issue for non-collateralized derivatives (collateralized derivatives are funded by collateral itself), and non-collateralized derivatives are also those subject to credit risk. Thus the banks had to compute for these derivatives both a credit charge and a funding charge. Could these two items be treated independently of each other?

The increased importance of the concept of funding charge, something that was not that crucial in the old days of Libor discounting, and that was going to affect all traditional unsecured derivatives, was another change of modelling paradigm that touched the very roots of pricing. Notice that, if two banks have different funding costs, which is quite likely, we are throwing away one principle that used to be considered fundamental: that two banks using the same models and the same data should reach the same price for a given derivative. If discounting becomes different for different banks because their funding costs are different, we must expect each bank to compute a different price even if they are in perfect agreement on models and market data.

In those years I was doing research on the topic with my colleague Andrea Prampolini, who worked in the Treasury, while I was working for Trading. We saw the importance of a consistent pricing of funding liquidity from the different perspectives of the Treasury, which looks after the management of liquidity resources for the banks, and the front office that saw liquidity charging as a crucial issue for remaining competitive in a market undergoing big transformations.

We noticed that many market operators with whom we were corresponding were applying the standard principle of liquidity charging, 'discount with your own cost of funding', together with the standard principle of credit charging, 'take into account the default probability of your counterparty, and yours too'. When something like that is done, putting together two relatively new approaches without studying their interactions, one is clearly exposed to a big risk of model error. Intuitively, the pricing of funding liquidity and the pricing of counterparty credit risk should be closely related. Companies, in fact, compute a funding spread that comes from the market of their bond issuances and thus includes compensation for their own risk of default, namely their own credit spread. What happens when credit spreads enter the pricing *twice*, once when discounting with funding and once when computing credit adjustments?

In Morini and Prampolini (2011) we showed that a naive application of the standard approach to include funding costs by modifying the discounting rate, when it is put in place together with the standard approach for the computation of CVA and DVA, does in fact lead to double-counting. In order to show this, and also show how this issue can be avoided, we had to build some cornerstones for a unified consistent modelling framework for liquidity and credit risk adjustments that turned out to be different from the simple summation of two separate adjustments. The first thing we had to do was to take explicitly into account, in the valuation of a derivative, the funding strategy that needs to be put in place to manage the liquidity absorbed or generated by the derivative, and study in particular the effect of a default on this strategy. We showed that without this joint consideration of funding and credit, we were bound to make modelling mistakes in this new foundation of pricing after a credit and liquidity crunch. Together with some other papers on the topic, this also was very popular, remaining for many months in the top ranking of *www.defaultrisk.com*.

The analysis touched another very hot and important issue: meaning, the necessity, risks and consequences of DVA, namely the practice of taking our own default into account in the pricing of assets and liabilities. From one point of view, DVA seems obvious and hardly new: if we as a bank compute CVA for our counterparties, we must expect that they compute CVA for us, and therefore we must compute DVA for ourselves. This is what a bank may think if it looks at itself from outside, as the counterparties do: there is a probability that the bank will not pay its own liabilities, and this fact must enter the price of a deal.

On the other hand, DVA appears to lead to a distortion of financial choices and of financial communications, even to moral hazard. Computing DVA means taking into account our own default, so reducing our expected liabilities, because we introduce scenarios – our default scenarios – where we are not paying our liabilities. DVA is an 'asset', the value of which increases the more the bank approaches default. (As Algorithmics (2009) put it, 'can you profit now from your own future default?') If the bank looks at itself subjectively, DVA is an absurdity: there will be no gains the day the bank defaults! Default should be avoided at all costs, not priced in as an asset.

Morini and Prampolini (2011) show some steps towards a solution of this DVA puzzle, because they display analytically how DVA can be evaluated as a funding term, and not as a default gain. They show that even if a company does not take its own risk of default explicitly into account, a full accounting of the funding elements generates a term equal to DVA.

However, the fact that a bank can reach the same price by taking into account explicitly its own risk of default or by taking into account funding benefits with no default considered explicitly, in this way reconciling the 'internal point of view' in looking at a bank with the external one, only relates to the evaluation of a bank's liabilities, as we shall see in what follows. For *assets*, they reach two different prices whether or not they take into account explicitly their own risk of default. What is the right choice? The authors do not give an answer, and as one of the two authors, I must admit that I don't have the answer. But I will show sufficient reasons why *both approaches, at the current state of the art, appear difficult to sustain*. This is a special adventure on our journey into model risk: a crucial pillar of pricing where all modelling solutions we have appear wrong, and we do not as yet know the right answer. Now let us go through the reasoning that led to a solution of the DVA problem, and to the advent of this new problem.

4.2.1 The Setting

Let us consider a deal in which one entity, what we call B (borrower), commits to pay a fixed amount K at time T to a party L (lender). This is a very simple payoff that allows us to focus on liquidity and credit costs without unnecessary complications. The simple payoff has several advantages. It is the derivative equivalent of a zero-coupon bond issued by B or a loan from L to B, so that we will be able to compare the results of our analysis with the well established market practice for such products. It is also a payoff where it is always clear who is a net borrower and who is a net lender, thus we always have a premium when the deal is struck, in which we can incorporate a liquidity charge, similar to real-world bank practice. The same would apply to stochastic option payoffs. Alternatively, in case of bilateral stochastic payoffs like swaps, the deal is struck at equilibrium but stochastic market movements will generate then a net lender and a net borrower, analogously to the simple payoff analyzed here, so that the extension to bilateral payoffs should be done in line with the results shown here.

We keep the modelling assumptions simple. We assume that party X, with $X \in \{B, L\}$, has a recovery rate R_X and that the risk free interest rate that applies to maturity T has a deterministic value r. As usual, r represents the time-value of money on which the market agrees, excluding effects of liquidity or credit risk (it is an approximation for the OIS rate). A party X makes funding in the *bond market*. Party X is also reference entity in the CDS market. We have therefore the following information:

1. the CDS spread π_X. We take this spread to be deterministic and paid instantaneously, and following the standard market model for credit risk in the CDS market, the reduced-form or intensity model we saw in Section 2.2.3, the spread π_X can be written

$$\pi_X = \lambda_X \, \mathrm{LGD}_X. \tag{4.25}$$

where λ_X is the deterministic default intensity and $\mathrm{LGD}_X = 1 - \mathrm{R}_X$ is the loss given default of entity X. If recovery is null, we have $\mathrm{LGD}_X = 1$ and the CDS spread coincides with λ_X, so that $\Pr(\tau_X > T) = e^{-\pi_X T}$. Therefore π_X must be intended as the best estimate of the risk-adjusted instantaneous default probability of X, taking expected recovery into account as in (4.25). Notice that when the CDS market is illiquid or strongly affected by the default risk of protection sellers, CDS spreads may not fully satisfy this requirement. Clearly $\pi_X \geq 0$.

2. the cost of funding s_X. For most issuers this is measured in the secondary bond market and represents the best estimate of the spread over a risk-free rate that a party pays on its funding. Notice that since nowadays the basis between Libor and OIS in non-negligible, the spread s_X must be intended as a spread over OIS. We take s_X to be instantaneous and deterministic too, so that we can compute by difference a liquidity basis γ_X such that

$$s_X = \pi_X + \gamma_X.$$

A proxy for the liquidity basis can be found in the bond-CDS basis, or more precisely its opposite, since in market jargon the CDS-bond basis is defined as the difference between the CDS spread and a bond spread, thus its sign is opposite to γ_X. The bond-CDS basis has generally been negative and particularly high in absolute terms during the credit crunch. Positive values for the bond-CDS basis are possible, but they are now mainly observed for certain sovereign issuers, therefore we assume for now $\gamma_X \geq 0$. The name 'liquidity basis' is justified by the fact that it is usually associated with the cost of the liquidity provision which the buyer makes to the issuer when buying the bond. This is dependent on the greater or lesser ease with which the bonds of X can be sold in the secondary market, thus γ_X is related to both funding liquidity costs and market liquidity risk. In particular, in the following we will shed more light on the role of the liquidity spread in the valuation of funding costs and benefits.

Our aim is to describe the net present value V_X (at time zero) of all cashflows generated by the transaction for the party by consistently accounting for liquidity and counterparty risk. We shall proceed as follows: we first consider the current standard approach to CVA and DVA, then we attempt to introduce liquidity costs by the standard approach adjusting the discount rate, and show that this path would lead to double accounting. Then we introduce the approach that includes risky funding and discuss some interesting implications. We start with the assumption $R_X = 0$ and Section 4.2.7 we will extend the results to the case of positive recovery.

4.2.2 Standard DVA: Is Something Missing?

Let's start from the market standard for CVA and DVA. Following for example Brigo and Capponi (2009), the above deal has a total value given by

$$V_L = e^{-rT} K - \text{CVA}_L - P, \tag{4.26}$$

where P is the premium paid by the lender L at inception, and CVA takes into account the probability that the borrower B defaults before maturity, thus

$$\begin{aligned} \text{CVA}_L &= \mathbb{E}[e^{-rT} K 1_{\{\tau_B \leq T\}}] = e^{-rT} K \Pr[\tau_B \leq T] \\ &= e^{-rT} K \left[1 - e^{-\pi_B T}\right]. \end{aligned}$$

We have that

$$V_L = 0 \quad \Rightarrow \quad P = e^{-rT} K - \text{CVA}_L.$$

At the same time party B sees a value

$$V_B = -e^{-rT} K + \text{DVA}_B + P \tag{4.27}$$

$$V_B = 0 \quad \Rightarrow \quad P = e^{-rT} K - \text{DVA}_B$$

with $\text{CVA}_L = \text{DVA}_B$.

This guarantees the symmetry $V_B = V_L = 0$ and the possibility for the parties to agree on the premium of the deal,

$$P = e^{-rT} e^{-\pi_B T} K. \tag{4.28}$$

This approach does not consider explicitly the value of liquidity. In fact, in exchange for the claim, at time 0 party B receives a cash flow from party L equal to P and therefore, while party L has to finance the amount until the maturity of the deal at its funding spread s_L, party B can reduce its funding by P. So party B should see a funding benefit and party L should see the fair value of its claim reduced by the financing costs. How come these funding components do not appear in the above valuation? Can we justify it by assuming that the two companies have negligible funding costs? Not entirely. In fact the absence of the funding term for L can indeed be justified by assuming $s_L = 0$. This implies $\pi_L = 0$. However the same assumption cannot be made for B without completely changing the nature of the deal. In fact assuming $s_B = 0$ would imply $\pi_B = 0$, which would cancel the DVA and CVA term. Thus when B is a party with non-negligible risk of default it must have a funding cost given at least by $s_B = \pi_B > 0$. The effect of this funding cost seems to be missing in the above formula. In the next sections we analyze if that is really the case.

4.2.3 Standard DVA plus Liquidity: Is Something Duplicated?

We introduce liquidity costs by adjusting the discounting term, along the lines of Piterbarg (2010), but we also introduce defaultability of the payoff along the lines of Brigo and Capponi (2009), getting for the lender

$$\begin{aligned} V_L &= \mathbb{E}\left[e^{-(r+s_L)T} K 1_{\{\tau_B > T\}}\right] - P \\ &= \mathbb{E}\left[e^{-rT} e^{-\gamma_L T} e^{-\pi_L T} K 1_{\{\tau_B > T\}}\right] - P \\ &= e^{-(r+\gamma_L+\pi_L+\pi_B)T} K - P, \end{aligned} \tag{4.29}$$

and, by analogy, for the borrower

$$\begin{aligned} V_B &= -\mathbb{E}\left[e^{-(r+s_B)T} K 1_{\{\tau_B > T\}}\right] + P \\ &= -\mathbb{E}\left[e^{-rT} e^{-\pi_B T} e^{-\gamma_B T} K 1_{\{\tau_B > T\}}\right] + P \\ &= -e^{-rT} e^{-\pi_B T} e^{-\gamma_B T} K e^{-\pi_B T} + P \\ &= -e^{-(r+\gamma_B+2\pi_B)T} K + P. \end{aligned} \tag{4.30}$$

To compare these results, including CVA, DVA and liquidity from discounting, with results on DVA obtained in the previous section 4.2.2, it is convenient to consider the simplest situation where L is default free and with no liquidity spread, while B is defaultable and has the minimum liquidity spread allowed in this case: $s_L = 0$, $s_B = \pi_B > 0$. Imposing $V_L = V_B = 0$, we have

$$\begin{aligned} P_L &= e^{-rT} e^{-\pi_B T} K \\ P_B &= e^{-rT} e^{-2\pi_B T} K = e^{-rT} e^{-\pi_B T} \boxed{e^{-\pi_B T}} K. \end{aligned}$$

There are two bizarre aspects to this representation. First, even in a situation where we have assumed no liquidity spread, two counterparties do not agree on the simplest transaction with default risk. A *day-one profit* should be accounted by borrowers in all transactions with CVA. This belies years of market reality. Secondly, the explicit inclusion of the DVA term results in the duplication of the funding benefit for the party that assumes the liability. The formula implies, against all the evidence, that the benefit is remunerated twice. If this were correct then a consistent accounting of liabilities at fair value would require pricing zero-coupon bonds by multiplying *twice* their risk-free present value by their survival probabilities. This also belies years of market reality.

4.2.4 Solving the Puzzle

In order to solve the puzzle, we do not compute liquidity by the adjusted discounting of (4.29) and (4.30), but generate liquidity costs and benefits by modelling explicitly the funding strategy. The approach we take is that companies capitalize and discount money with the risk-free rate r, and then they add or subtract the actual credit and funding costs that arise in the management of the deal. This allows us to introduce explicitly into the picture both credit and liquidity, an approach pursued neither by Brigo nor by Capponi (2009) nor by Piterbarg (2010), and to investigate more precisely where credit/liquidity gains and losses are financially generated. We now take into account that the above deal has two legs. If we consider for example the lender L, one leg is the 'deal leg', with net present value

$$\mathbb{E}\left[-P + e^{-rT}\,\Pi\right]$$

where Π is the payoff at T, including a potential default indicator; the other leg is the 'funding leg' with net present value

$$\mathbb{E}\left[+P - e^{-rT} F\right]$$

where F is the funding payback at T, including a potential default indicator. When there is no default risk or liquidity cost involved, this funding leg can be overlooked because it has a value

$$\mathbb{E}\left[+P - e^{-rT} e^{rT} P\right] = 0.$$

Instead, in general the total net present value is

$$\begin{aligned} V_L &= \mathbb{E}\left[-P + e^{-rT}\,\Pi + P - e^{-rT} F\right] \\ &= \mathbb{E}\left[e^{-rT}\,\Pi - e^{-rT} F\right]. \end{aligned}$$

Thus the premium at time 0 cancels out with its funding, and we are left with the discounting of a total payoff including the deal's payoff and the liquidity payback. An analogous relationship applies to the borrower, as detailed in the next section. In what follows we work on the assumption that all liquidity management happens in the cash market, so that funding is made by issuing bonds and excess funds are used to reduce or to avoid increasing the stock of bonds. This is the most natural assumption since it is similar to that made by banks in their internal liquidity management, namely what the treasury desk assumes in charging or rewarding trading desks.

4.2.5 Risky Funding for the Borrower

The borrower B has a liquidity advantage from receiving the premium P at time zero, as it allows it to reduce its funding requirement by an equivalent amount P. The amount P of funding would have generated a negative cashflow at T, when funding must be paid back, equal to

$$-\,P\, e^{rT} e^{s_B T}\, 1_{\{\tau_B > T\}}. \tag{4.31}$$

The outflow equals P capitalized at the cost of funding, times a default indicator $1_{\{\tau_B>T\}}$. Why do we need to include a default indicator $1_{\{\tau_B>T\}}$? Because in the case of default, under the assumption of zero recovery, the borrower does not pay back the borrowed funding and there is no outflow. Thus reducing the funding by P corresponds to receiving at T a positive amount equal to (4.31) in absolute value,

$$\begin{aligned} &P\, e^{rT} e^{s_B T}\, 1_{\{\tau_B>T\}} \\ &= P\, e^{rT} e^{\pi_B T} e^{\gamma_B T}\, 1_{\{\tau_B>T\}} \end{aligned} \tag{4.32}$$

to be added to what B has to pay in the deal: $-K\, 1_{\{\tau_B>T\}}$.

Thus the total payoff at T is

$$1_{\{\tau_B>T\}} P\, e^{rT} e^{\pi_B T} e^{\gamma_B T} - 1_{\{\tau_B>T\}} K. \tag{4.33}$$

Taking discounted expectation,

$$\begin{aligned} V_B &= e^{-\pi_B T}\, P\, e^{\pi_B T} e^{\gamma_B T} - K\, e^{-\pi_B T} e^{-rT} \\ &= P\, e^{\gamma_B T} - K\, e^{-\pi_B T} e^{-rT}. \end{aligned} \tag{4.34}$$

Compare this with (4.30). Now we have no unrealistic double accounting of default probability. Notice that

$$V_B = 0 \quad \Rightarrow \quad P_B = K\, e^{-\pi_B T} e^{-\gamma_B T}\; e^{-rT} \tag{4.35}$$

where P_B is the breakeven premium for the borrower, in the sense that the borrower will find this deal convenient as long as

$$V_B \geq 0 \quad \Rightarrow \quad P \geq P_B.$$

Assume, as in (4.27), that $\gamma_B = 0$ so that in this case

$$P_B = K\, e^{-\pi_B T}\; e^{-rT}. \tag{4.36}$$

Compare with (4.28). We can conclude that in this case the standard computation from Section 4.2.2 is correct, since taking into account the probability of default in the valuation of the funding benefit removes any liquidity advantage for the borrower. We no more have the double counting of 4.2.3. Formula 4.3.5 shows what happens when there is a 'pure liquidity basis' component in the funding cost, $\gamma_B > 0$. On the other hand, charging liquidity costs by an adjusted funding spread as in Section 4.2.3 cannot be naturally extended to the case where we want to observe explicitly the possibility of default events in our derivatives; for it to be consistent we need, as in Piterbarg (2010), to exclude the default events. We will discuss this further in Section 4.2.8. In writing the payoff for the borrower we have not explicitly considered the case in which the deal is interrupted by the default of the lender, since, following standard derivative documentation such as ISDA (2009), page 15, the closeout amount at default of the lender should allow the borrower to replace the transaction with an identical one with a new counterparty (see Section 10.2). This keeps V_B independent of the default time of the lender, as it is consistent with the reality of bond and deposit markets.

4.2.6 Risky Funding for the Lender and the Conditions for Market Agreement

If the lender pays P at time 0, he incurs a liquidity cost. In fact he needs to finance (borrow) P until T. At T, L will give back the borrowed money with interest, but only if he has not defaulted. Otherwise he gives back nothing, so the outflow is

$$\begin{aligned} &P\, e^{rT}\, e^{s_L T}\; 1_{\{\tau_L > T\}} \\ &= P\, e^{rT}\, e^{\gamma_L T}\; e^{\pi_L T}\; 1_{\{\tau_L > T\}} \end{aligned} \tag{4.37}$$

while he receives in the deal: $K\; 1_{\{\tau_B > T\}}$. The total payoff at T is therefore

$$-\,P\, e^{rT}\, e^{\gamma_L T}\, e^{\pi_L T}\; 1_{\{\tau_L > T\}} + K\; 1_{\{\tau_B > T\}}. \tag{4.38}$$

Taking discounted expectation

$$\begin{aligned} V_L &= -P\, e^{\gamma_L T}\; e^{-\pi_L T}\; e^{\pi_L T} + K\, e^{-rT}\; e^{-\pi_B T} \\ &= -P\, e^{\gamma_L T} + K\, e^{-rT}\; e^{-\pi_B T} \end{aligned} \tag{4.39}$$

The condition that makes the deal convenient for the lender is

$$\begin{aligned} &V_L \geq 0 \quad \Rightarrow \quad P \;\leq\; P_L, \\ &P_L = K\, e^{-rT}\; e^{-\gamma_L T}\; e^{-\pi_B T} \end{aligned} \tag{4.40}$$

where P_L is the breakeven premium for the lender. It is interesting to note that the lender, when he computes the value of the deal taking into account all future cashflows as they are seen from the counterparties, does not include a charge to the borrower for that component π_L of its cost of funding which is associated with its own risk of default. This is cancelled out by the fact that funding is not given back in case of default. In terms of relative valuation of a deal this fact about the lender mirrors exactly the fact that for the borrower the inclusion of the DVA eliminates the liquidity advantage associated with π_B. In terms of managing cashflows, on the other hand, there is an important difference between borrower and lender, which is discussed in Section 4.2.8. To reach an agreement in the market we need

$$V_L \geq 0, \; V_B \geq 0$$

which, recalling (4.35) and (4.40), implies

$$\begin{aligned} P_L &\geq P \geq P_B \\ K\, e^{-rT}\, e^{-\gamma_L T}\, e^{-\pi_B T} &\geq P \geq K e^{-rT} e^{-\gamma_B T} e^{-\pi_B T} \end{aligned} \tag{4.41}$$

Thus an agreement can be found whenever

$$\gamma_B \geq \gamma_L.$$

This solves the puzzle, and shows that, if we only want to guarantee a positive *expected* return from the deal, the liquidity cost that needs to be charged to the counterparty of an uncollateralized derivative transaction is just the liquidity basis, rather than the bond spread or the CDS spread. The results of the last two sections go beyond Piterbarg (2010) in showing that only the bond-CDS basis is a proper liquidity spread, while the CDS spread associated with the default intensity is a component of the funding cost offset by the probability of defaulting in the funding strategy. In Section 4.2.8 we will show how the picture changes when we look at possible *realized* cashflows (as opposed to the expected cashflow), and explore further the connections between these results and Piterbarg (2010).

4.2.7 Positive Recovery Extension

In this section we look at what happens if we relax the assumption of zero recovery. The discounted payoff for the borrower is now

$$\begin{aligned} &1_{\{\tau_B > T\}} e^{-rT}\; P\, e^{\pi_B T}\; e^{\gamma_B T}\; e^{rT} \\ &+1_{\{\tau_B \leq T\}} e^{-r\,\tau_B}\; \mathrm{R}_B\, e^{-r\,(T-\tau_B)}\; P\, e^{\pi_B T}\; e^{\gamma_B T}\, e^{rT} \\ &-1_{\{\tau_B > T\}} e^{-rT}\; K \\ &-1_{\{\tau_B \leq T\}} e^{-r\,\tau_B}\; \mathrm{R}_B\, e^{-r\,(T-\tau_B)}\; K \end{aligned}$$

where the recovery is a fraction R_X of the present value of the claims at the time of default of the borrower, consistent with standard derivative documentation. Notice that B acts as a borrower both in the deal and in the funding leg, since we represented the latter as a reduction of the existing funding of B. Simplifying the terms and taking the expectation at 0 we obtain

$$\begin{aligned} V_B &= \Pr\{\tau_B > T\}\, P\, e^{\pi_B T}\; e^{\gamma_B T} + \Pr\{\tau_B \leq T\}\, e^{-rT}\, \mathrm{R}_B\; P\, e^{\pi_B T}\; e^{\gamma_B T}\, e^{rT} \\ &\quad - \Pr\{\tau_B > T\}\, e^{-rT}\, K - \Pr\{\tau_B \leq T\}\mathrm{R}_B\, e^{-rT}\, K \\ &= [1 - \mathrm{L{\small GD}}_B\, \Pr\{\tau_B \leq T\}]\, \left(P\, e^{\pi_B T}\; e^{\gamma_B T} - e^{-rT}\, K\right). \end{aligned} \tag{4.42}$$

Using (4.25), we can write the first order approximation

$$1 - e^{-\pi_B T} \approx \text{LGD}_B \left(1 - e^{-\lambda_B T}\right)$$

which allows us to approximate (4.42) as

$$\begin{aligned} V_B &\approx e^{-\pi_B T} \left(P\, e^{\pi_B T}\, e^{\gamma_B T} - e^{-rT}\, K\right) \\ &= P\, e^{\gamma_B T} - e^{-\pi_B T}\, e^{-rT}\, K. \end{aligned}$$

We have thus shown that (4.34) is recovered as a first order approximation in the general case of positive recovery rate. Similar arguments apply to the value of the claim for L, which acts as a lender in the deal and as a borrower in the funding leg. For L, (4.39) is recovered as a first order approximation of

$$\begin{aligned} V_L = &- [1 - \text{LGD}_L\ \Pr\{\tau_L \leq T\}]\ P\, e^{\pi_L T}\, e^{\gamma_L T} \\ &+ [1 - \text{LGD}_B\ \Pr\{\tau_B \leq T\}]\ e^{-rT}\, K. \end{aligned}$$

In the following we show for simplicity a few more results on the assumption that $\text{R}_X = 0$. The extension to the general case can be performed along the lines of this section.

4.2.8 Two Ways of Looking at the Problem: Default Risk or Funding Benefit? The Accountant vs the Salesman

One of the most controversial aspects of DVA relates to its consequences in the accounting of liabilities in the balance sheet of a company. In fact the DVA allows a borrower to condition future liabilities on survival, and this may create a distorted perspective in which our default is our lucky day. However, liabilities are already reduced by risk of default in the case of bonds when banks use the *fair value option* according to international accounting standards, and even when banks mark the bond liabilities at historical cost. What is the meaning of DVA? Are we really taking into account a benefit that will be concretely observed only in case of our default? In this section we show what happens if the borrower does not condition its liabilities upon survival, namely pretends to be default-free thereby ignoring DVA and avoiding a possibly distorted view where default is a positive event.

Let a party B pretend, for accounting purposes, to be default-free. The premium P paid by the lender gives B a reduction of the funding payback at T corresponding to a cashflow at T

$$P e^{rT} e^{s_B T},$$

where there is no default indicator because B is treating itself as default-free. This cashflow must be compared with the payout of the deal at T, which is

$$-K$$

again without indicator, ie without DVA. Thus the total payoff at T is

$$P e^{rT} e^{s_B T} - K. \tag{4.43}$$

By discounting to zero we obtain an accounting value V_B such that

$$V_B = P\, e^{s_B T} - K\, e^{-rT}$$

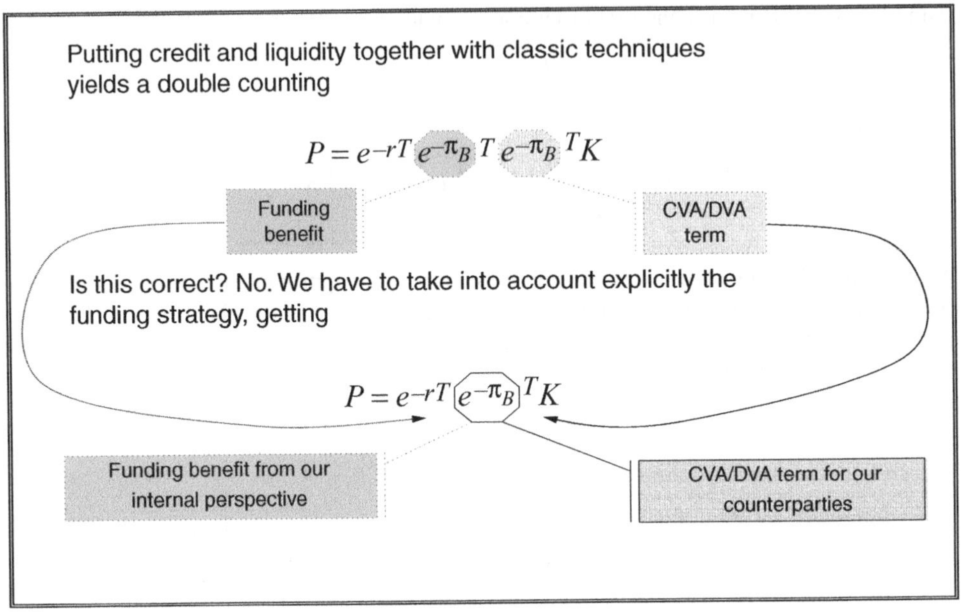

Figure 4.8 Liquidity and funding for a borrower: no double-counting and convergence of internal and external valuation

which yields an accounting breakeven premium P_B for the borrower equal to the breakeven of (4.35),

$$P_B = K\, e^{-rT} e^{-\pi_B T} e^{-\gamma_B T}. \tag{4.44}$$

So in this case the borrower B recognizes on its liability a funding benefit that actually takes into account its own market risk of default π_B, plus additional liquidity basis γ_B, thereby matching the premium computed by the lender that includes the CVA/ DVA term. But now this term is accounted for as a funding benefit and not as a benefit coming from the reduction of future expected liabilities thanks to default. Thus, putting together the results of Section 4.2.5 with what we have just seen, we get the result summarized in Figure 4.8.

The results of these sections give an indication of how the DVA term can be realized. When a bank enters a deal in a borrower position, it is making funding for an amount as large as the premium. If this premium is used to reduce existing funding which is equally or more expensive, which in our context means buying bonds or avoiding some issuance that would otherwise be necessary, this provides a tangible financial benefit that is enjoyed in survival by a reduction of the payments at maturity.[4] The reduction is given by the difference in (4.43). The implementation of such a strategy involves difficulties that vary from bank to bank. In any case we have shown how the DVA term can be seen not as a 'default benefit', but rather as a natural consequence of taking into account funding costs.

[4] We point out that a bank can buy back its own bonds. In fact, this is actually 'selling protection on yourself', but it is fully *funded*. When a sale of protection is funded, there is no counterparty risk and therefore no limit to who can sell protection, in difference to the case of an unfunded CDS. In fact buying their own bonds is a common activity by banks.

The above results show that the borrower's valuation does not change if he considers himself default-free, and it does not depend on how the funding spread in the market is divided into credit spread and liquidity basis. Do we have a similar property also for the lender? Not at all. Since, following Section 4.2.6, we have

$$P_L = K\,e^{-rT}\,e^{-\gamma_L T}\,e^{-\pi_B T},$$

the breakeven premium and the agreement that will be reached in the market depend crucially on γ_L. This is not the only difference between the situations of borrower and lender. Notice that the borrower's net payout at maturity T is given in (4.33) and is non-negative in all states of the world if we keep $P \geq P_B$, although the latter condition was designed only to guarantee that the *expected* payout is non-negative. For the lender, on the other hand, the payout at maturity is given by (4.38). The condition (4.40) for the non-negativity of the expected payout of the lender does not imply the non-negativity of (4.38), particularly since we can have a negative carry even if we assume that both counterparties will survive until maturity. If we want to guarantee a non-negative carry at least when nobody defaults, in addition to (4.40) we need the following condition to be satisfied

$$\pi_L \leq \pi_B. \tag{4.45}$$

Otherwise the lender, in difference to the borrower, is exposed to liquidity shortage and negative carry even if the deal is, in an expectation considering all scenarios, convenient for him. Liquidity shortages when no one defaults can be excluded by imposing for each deal (4.45), or, with a solution working for whatever deal with whatever counterparty, by working as if the lender was default-free. Only if the lender pretends for accounting purposes to be default-free does the condition for the convenience of the deal based on expected cashflows become

$$P \leq K\,e^{-rT}\,e^{-s_L T}\,e^{-\pi_B T} = K\,e^{-rT}\,e^{-\gamma_L T}\,e^{-\pi_L T}e^{-\pi_B T}$$

which clearly implies the non-negativity of (4.38).

Assuming that to be default-free leads to results equivalent to Piterbarg (2010). In fact, under this assumption, uncollateralized payoffs should also be discounted at the full funding in our simple setting. Let's consider a bank X that pretends to be default-free. When the bank is in the borrower position we have

$$P_B = P_X = e^{-s_X T}e^{-rT}K$$

while when it is in a lender position with respect to a *risk-free* counterparty (as in the example of Piterbarg (2010)) the breakeven premium will be given by

$$P_L = e^{-s_X T}e^{-rT}K = P_B = P_X,$$

and the discounting at the funding rate $r + s_X$ is recovered for both positive and negative exposures.

On the other hand, for general counterparties with non-null credit risk and liquidity costs, the lender's assumption of being default-free makes a market agreement very difficult, since in this case the agreement

$$K\,e^{-rT}\,e^{-\gamma_B T}\,e^{-\pi_B T} \leq P \leq K\,e^{-rT}\,e^{-\gamma_L T}\,e^{-\pi_L T}e^{-\pi_B T}$$

implies

$$\boxed{\gamma_B \geq \gamma_L + \pi_L}$$

rather than

$$\boxed{\gamma_B \geq \gamma_L}.$$

In a market where everyone treats himself as default-free and counterparties as defaultable, a party wants to fund itself at a spread that includes only its own CDS

$$(\gamma_B + \pi_B)$$

but when it finances other parties it charges them a spread including *two* CDS spreads

$$(\gamma_L + \pi_L + \pi_B).$$

4.2.9 Which Direction for Future Pricing?

Which one is the right solution? Both have their own pros and cons. In the first case a bank looks at itself as counterparties do it taking into account its own default and thus reduces the discounting rate for assets sufficiently to avoid charging two credit spreads to counterparties that borrow money from the bank. This is good because one of the two credit spreads is just what the bank must pay due to its own risk of not paying its obligations, and there is no financial rationale to charge it to borrowers. This way the bank charges to borrowers a total cost which is consistent with the way the bank computes its own funding costs, the bank will remain competitive and an agreement in the market will not be impossible.

On the other hand, in this way the bank bases its decisions on treating its own default as a financial advantage: a strategy may look convenient only because the bank is pricing in the fact that, if it defaults, it will not pay back its own funding. But if the bank does not default, this will appear an absurdity! Where is it going to find the money to finance deals that could lead to negative carry when both parties survive?

In the second case the bank avoids this problem; it assumes it cannot default and in this way it risks no moral hazard and no funding losses if it does not default: all its funding costs are fully charged to counterparties. However, this is a viewpoint that is in contrast with how counterparties look at the bank: they know the bank can default, they know that part of the funding costs of the bank are only due to this, and may not accept being charged this cost when they are borrowing money from the bank. Consider this: if you asked a bank for a mortgage, would you find it fair if the bank told you: you have a credit spread of 3% because this is your default probability, but we have a spread of 4% because this is our probability of default, so we will charge you 7%. Would you accept?

So, note the following. The above analysis provides a possible solution to the DVA problem. In fact, it shows that DVA does not create a double counting with funding costs if we remember the possibility of default in our funding. It also shows that an asset similar to DVA appears, whether a bank considers explicitly its own risk of default consistently both in a deal and in the funding of the deal, or if it neglects this risk of default in both deal and funding. This reconciles the way a bank looks at itself from inside with the way the market looks at it from outside. However, the same analysis opens up another issue: the DVA is associated with the discounting spread that a bank must use when it is the borrower in a deal, but there is also the other side of the coin, the discounting spread that must be charged when a bank is a lender. In this second case, assuming the bank is defaultable or not makes a difference and as we saw the choice is not easy.

How can we find a way out between what appear to be two opposing model errors? Certainly everyone recognizes that the business of borrowing and lending money gets more difficult when, as today, banks have high credit spreads. At the moment various proposals are being made to find a practical solution to this issue for the business of derivatives.

Maybe a bank should neglect its own risk of default, and charge the total funding costs to counterparties, in the hope that this will be accepted as part of the margin compensation for the service the bank provides. This may work for some banks and some counterparties, but not for banks with too high credit spreads or for counterparties that can easily get the same services from other banks.

Maybe a bank should take into account its own risk of default, but at the same time lend only to companies which are more risky than the bank itself, following (4.45), so avoiding negative cashflows when no one defaults. Isn't this, in the end, one of the most basic principles of the lending and borrowing business? It sounds rather unsatisfactory.

Perhaps the solution to the problem is to recognize that the funding spread we consider above, read in the secondary bond market and incorporating fully the credit risk of the bank on the maturity of the funding, is just a marginal funding cost while the true average funding cost is much lower. The funding cost should include all those forms of funding, such as bank deposits or overnight funding, that, as we saw in the previous section, do not incorporate fully the credit spread of the bank, moving the resulting funding spread much closer to the one that the bank would compute if it took the credit spread away from its funding as suggested in (4.40).

Some, however, might argue that forms of funding such as deposits or overnight borrowing can disappear at any time, exposing a bank to a risk, and that the protection from this risk would bring the cost of funding back to the one read in the bond market for the maturity of the funding. Others might counter that the bond market makes an external evaluation of this funding risk that can be more conservative than the internal evaluation by a bank, due to asymmetric information, and in any case when speaking of non-collateralized deals we are back to the traditional bank business of borrowing money on a short term, transforming the maturity and lending a higher rate for longer terms. In traditional banking a bank does not buy protection on all its liquidity risk, nor does it do so on all its credit risks because this would eliminate the rationale of the business.

We do not yet know the answer. We are seeing in real time the birth of a new foundation for pricing. But notice the irony: these are open problems from the very birth of modern markets. But in the years before the crisis, the smallness of banks' credit spreads made them practically irrelevant. The crisis, just by increasing the size of these spreads, has forced a total rethink of the foundations of pricing.

Part II

Snakes in the Grass: Where Model Risk Hides

5
Hedging

5.1 MODEL RISK AND HEDGING

This book is devoted to the management of model risk in the use of valuation models. However, valuation models are not used only for valuation. They are used also for another purpose which is at least equally important for a financial institution, and very difficult: hedging. In spite of this, the predominant part of the literature on financial models only regards pricing, and the limited existing literature on hedging is mainly theoretical, attempting to give a rigorous foundation to hedging but bearing little relation to what hedging is in practice. Thus hedging remains a very heuristic discipline, more art than science, and it is very difficult to find examples of model risk in hedging in the literature.

Notwithstanding hedging is a crucial topic when talking of model risk and model validation. Hedging enters model risk management in two ways:

1. Since the birth of the modern option market observation of the performances of a model in replicating a derivative has been a traditional technique used in the validation of models for valuation. Hedging enters the picture since replicating a derivative means building a hedging strategy that yields the same profits and losses (P&L) as holding the derivative itself.
2. The real hedging strategy put in place by a trader always makes some use of valuation models, and is an activity that can generate important losses for a bank. Therefore many institutions also include in model validation the validation of the hedging strategies implemented by traders.

While in point 1) hedging enters model validation as a tool for assessing the quality of a valuation, in 2) the hedging strategy actually implemented by traders with the help of some models is the focus of a validation that can potentially be separate from the validation of the same models when used only for pricing. In the following we consider both ways in which hedging can affect model validation.

The first point, tackled in Section 5.2, relates to what most risk management units call the **P&L Explain Test**, where the pricing model is applied to a set of historical data to build a hedging portfolio and perform the exercise of replicating a derivative on this dataset. From a less ambitious perspective, this test is performed just to have an example of how the model would have worked in the past, making clearer which market movements have generated the trader's P&L and double-checking that all technicalities for the management of a derivative have been taken into account. In a more ambitious application, this is a backtest that can confirm or belie the correspondence between the pricing model and the market reality.

Here we try to reason on the real meaning of this kind of test, taking into account both the theory and the practice. First we describe how a prototypical P&L exercise works, and see how under ideal market conditions this P&L test, which only requires the observation of the hedging behaviour of a model in the past, could really reveal whether the model is effective for pricing and consistent with reality. This is based on the principle that the true price of a derivative is the cost of its self-financing hedging strategy, as done by Black and Scholes (1973) in their seminal paper. If one believes that results obtained in the P&L backtesting also apply to the relevant future, model validation may be considered successfully computed when a P&L Explain test is satisfactorily passed.

Then we dash the extremely optimistic expectations just created by showing that the market conditions required for a P&L Explain test to be really successful are so idealized that they do not apply to any real model in any real market, and that the lack of these conditions is sufficient to annul much of this test's theoretical meaning. In spite of this, we show that the test remains interesting and potentially useful, particularly to compare models and to rank them. In fact, a worse performance by a model in a P&L Explain test, compared to an alternative model, may mean that the underperforming model requires more frequent recalibration, is less robust when used in the real world, and is rather unstable, overreacting to small market changes, all features that make a model less desirable for both pricing and hedging.

The analysis of Section 5.2 has an important implication, among others that even when a P&L analysis can be performed and is of some use in assessing a model, the hedging test typical of a P&L analysis bears little relation to a real hedging strategy. The crucial difference is that in a P&L analysis the model must never be recalibrated during the life of a derivative, while in the real world hedging is performed with a model which is regularly recalibrated. Real hedging strategies take this fact into account, and therefore do not appear consistent with the theoretical hedging strategy suggested by the valuation model, which clearly does not consider any recalibration. Thus the assessment of a real hedging strategy, called **Hedge-Analysis**, is related to the validation of the pricing model but different from it.

In Section 5.3 we analyze how a real hedging strategy works, how it relates to the underlying valuation model, and how it can be assessed, by means of a practical case study regarding the behaviour of local vs stochastic volatility models in hedging plain-vanilla options. This may appear a simple issue, but it has been the subject of fierce debate for a long time, and is by no means resolved. Chapter 2 reported one piece of research that shows that there are actual and important differences between local and stochastic volatility models; the results we see here in hedging demystify a little, at least in regard to hedging performances, the debate about which of the two modelling frameworks 'is better'. In fact, we show that, in contrast to what one may have found in the literature until quite recently, both local and stochastic volatility models have an undesirable hedging behaviour, even when they are assumed to give an acceptable valuation. We also show that, for both models, this undesirable behaviour can be simply corrected with heuristic adjustments which are trivially implemented by most traders.

Confirming what we guessed in the theoretical analysis at 5.2, the practical case study shows that the analysis of a real hedging strategy is not trivial, and is not redundant even after the model used in hedging has been validated for pricing. In fact, first of all it is difficult to understand the implications of model assumptions on hedging, a topic on which quants expend much less effort than on the analysis of pricing. Secondly, real hedging strategies put in place by traders have a high likelihood of differing from the model-implied hedging suggested by the theory. Even if traders are happy with the price coming out of a model, they may be unhappy with its dynamic behaviour and apply a hedging strategy based on ad hoc adjustments and tricks that can be in absolute contradiction with the assumptions underlying the model. In this case the hedging strategy must be validated and analyzed as something different from the validation of the pricing model, and we may find that the real hedging strategy implemented uses the model in a way, not implicit in the theory, that makes hedging much more effective.

There is one final lesson to be learned from this story: even the inventors of a model can be misled about its hedging behaviour, even if they are among the best quants that ever trod the boards of a trading floor... a useful warning for all of us, model developers and model users alike.

5.2 HEDGING AND MODEL VALIDATION: WHAT IS EXPLAINED BY P&L EXPLAIN?

In this section I do not provide any new results. I would just like to spark some reasoning on quite old issues based on some informal considerations of my own and on many discussions with practitioners and researchers.

The question to be tackled is: can we use the hedging performances of a model applied to a derivative to assess the goodness of the model itself? We assume that some complex, illiquid derivative is hedged according to some pricing model, and that all risk factors that are considered relevant are hedged. At time t_0 the derivative has a price

$$V_{t_0} = f\left(A_{t_0}, \theta\right)$$

where the vector

$$A = A^1, \ldots, A^{NA}$$

indicates the prices of the underlying instruments depending on the risk factors which affect pricing. These instruments are also the ingredients of the hedging portfolio, while the vector

$$\theta = \theta^1, \ldots, \theta^{Np}$$

indicates the parameters. The function $f(\ldots)$ is the pricing function for the derivative in the valuation model.

We want to perform a P&L Explain analysis of this model applied to this derivative. We set A at the current market value A_{t_0}, we calibrate the parameters and then we compute all the sensitivities of the derivative

$$w^1_{t_0} = \frac{\partial f}{\partial A^1_t}|_{t=t_0}, \ldots, w^{NA}_{t_0} = \frac{\partial f}{\partial A^{NA}_t}|_{t=t_0}.$$

We construct a replicating portfolio based on these sensitivities, with value

$$\Pi_{t_0} = \sum_i w^i_{t_0} A^i_{t_0} + B_{t_0}$$

where B is an amount kept in cash that guarantees equality of the portfolio value Π_{t_0} with the *model value* of the derivative V_{t_0}

$$B_{t_0} = V_{t_0} - \sum_i w^i_{t_0} A^i_{t_0}.$$

At t_1 we compute the price of the derivative V_{t_1}, and we compare this change in price

$$\Delta V_{t_1} = V_{t_1} - V_{t_0}$$

with the change in value of the hedging portfolio

$$\Delta\Pi_{t_1} = \sum_i w^i_{t_0} \Delta A^i_{t_1} + r B_{t_0} \Delta t_1,$$

where

$$\Delta x_{t_i} = x_{t_i} - x_{t_i - 1}$$

We repeat this for all dates $t_i \in \bar{T} = t_1, \ldots, t_m$. We have negative evidence for the validity of the model when

$$Err = \sum_{t_i \in \bar{T}} \left(\Delta \Pi_{t_i} - \Delta V_{t_i}\right)^2$$

is large, and positive evidence when it is small. What 'small' and 'large' mean depends on your view about the meaning of this test. You will see that a 'fundamentalist view' may consider $Err \approx 0$ a feasible target and be very satisfied with the model only when this target is at least approached, while a 'sceptical view' would not expect $Err \approx 0$ to be a feasible target and, if it is reached, will conclude that it was a matter of chance or that it was obtained by construction. A moderate view will probably consider this test good enough for a comparison, so that a model will be considered better than another, limited to this test, when it gets a lower level for Err, with no view on an absolute level of Err to be taken as a target.

5.2.1 The Sceptical View

A sceptic will tell you that, even if the test works, *the results mean nothing*. I have heard this view expressed in the market many times, among both traders and quants. One common argument is: this test never compares the price V_t from the model with a market price, since it is usually applied to complex derivatives for which there is no liquid market. Everything is computed *within* the model: the derivative price and the sensitivities. If we have a function $V_t = f(A_t)$ (assuming $NA = 1$ for simplicity), what is the surprise in finding that

$$dV_t \approx \frac{\partial f(A_t)}{\partial A_t} dA_t \tag{5.1}$$

over a short time interval? According to the sceptic, this is just a 'first-order Taylor expansion' and there is no surprise if (5.1) holds approximately. A real validation based on market data can only be obtained by comparing $f(A_t)$ with some real market price for the derivative.

Another argument is: a model has the purpose of defining a probability distribution for the possible states of the world $\omega_1, \omega_2, \ldots$ in order to set the pricing probability measure P and be able to compute

$$P(\omega_1), P(\omega_2), \ldots$$

The backtesting of the hedging strategy seen above is instead based only on the observation of *one* ω_i. What can it tell us about the measure P? According to the sceptic, nothing.

In these sceptical positions one element is usually forgotten: that to be valid a P&L Explain analysis, should take care to ensure that the hedging strategy considered *is self-financing*.

5.2.2 The Fundamentalist View and Black and Scholes

Now let us look at the test from what we shall call a fundamentalist point of view, where the fundamentalist here is a hypothetical market operator who strongly believes in the typical assumptions of the theory of mathematical finance, basically those that underlie the Black and Scholes (1973) seminal result. I have never met a pure fundamentalist but I have met some mathematicians so little used to challenge the foundations of our job, and some traders so much in awe of mathematical assumptions, that they ended up having a fundamentalist position.

To understand this position, go back to the replication argument on which the Black and Scholes formula is based. Consider a European derivative with an initial cost and a payoff at maturity. If one is able to construct a replication strategy that is *self-financing*, in the sense that I will add no money to it and I will withdraw no money until maturity, and the strategy replicates the payoff of the derivative at maturity in all states of the world, the initial cost of the strategy must be the same as the price of the derivative, if we want the market to remain arbitrage-free. Otherwise one could short the strategy and buy the derivative, or the other way around, and get a free lunch.

Saying that the above strategy must be constructed as self-financing does not mean that there are no gains and no losses. There will be gains and losses in the process of readjusting the vector of weights (sensitivities) w_t as time goes on, but these gains and losses will simply not be taken away but will increase or decrease the cash amount B, which may become negative (we borrow cash).

In this framework we build the replicating portfolio as a hedging portfolio based on model sensitivities in order to replicate each instantaneous variation of the value of a derivative (recall that the Black and Scholes framework is considered for continuous processes in continuous time). We never withdraw/add any money from/to the hedging and portfolio, if the model we use corresponds to the true process of the underlying risk factors, we expect that, in any state of the world, the T (maturity) cost/benefit of closing the positions in all A_i and in B equals the payoff. In an arbitrage-free market this also implies that the value of the replication strategy equals the value of the derivatives at any time $0 \leq t \leq T$, otherwise, again, one could go long/short in the derivative and short/long in the strategy and create an arbitrage opportunity. This implies

$$\Delta \Pi_t - \Delta V_t = 0, \quad \forall t$$

and therefore $Err = 0$. When we are performing the P&L Explain test on some historical data, we are testing if this happens for one specific state of the world. Getting $Err = 0$ is a necessary condition – although not sufficient, since we are assessing only one specific state of the world – for the model to be right, namely to correspond to the true process of the underlying risk factors.

This is what happens when the replicating strategy is based on the sensitivities of the Black and Scholes formula and the underlying is supposed to move as in Black and Scholes,

$$\begin{aligned}
A^1 &= S, \ B = B \\
dS &= \mu S dt + \sigma S dW_t, \\
V_t &= B\&S\left(S_t, K, 0, \sigma^2 (T - t)\right),
\end{aligned}$$

where we took zero rates for simplicity. In this case a delta-hedging strategy is enough to replicate the option, since the only stochastic factor is the unique underlying. According to Ito's Lemma

$$\begin{aligned}
dV_t &= \frac{\partial V_t}{\partial t} dt + \frac{\partial V_t}{\partial S} dS + \frac{1}{2} \frac{\partial^2 V_t}{\partial S^2} \sigma^2 S^2 dt \\
&= Theta \times dt + Delta \times dS + \frac{1}{2} Gamma \times \sigma^2 S^2 dt.
\end{aligned}$$

To match the sensitivity to the underlying at the first step, the replicating portfolio must contain *Delta* stocks, and to match the sensitivity to 'time' it must contain $\left(Theta + \frac{1}{2}Gamma \times \sigma^2 S^2\right)\frac{1}{r}$ in cash. Is it true that this strategy has the same value as the option? For this to be true we need the amount of cash at time zero to be

$$B\&S\left(S_t, K, 0, \sigma^2(T-t)\right) - Delta \times S$$

thus we need

$$B\&S\left(S_t, K, 0, \sigma^2(T-t)\right) - Delta \times S = \frac{\left(Theta + \frac{1}{2}Gamma \times \sigma^2 S^2\right)}{r}.$$

Since

$$\frac{\left(Theta + \frac{1}{2}Gamma \times \sigma^2 S^2\right)}{r} = e^{-(T-t)} K N(d_2),$$

the condition is satisfied. Rebonato (1998) shows in practice that if one simulates the Black and Scholes model *with a very small simulation step* and then performs a hedging strategy (or equivalently a P&L Explain test) of a call using the Black and Scholes sensitivities *with a very small rebalancing period*, the strategy really replicates the payoff in all scenarios and always has the same value as the option priced with the Black and Scholes formula.

This reveals the meaning of the test a bit better. The test is not trivial, since we are not only verifying the first order derivatives, as in the sceptic critique, but we also require the self-financing condition. The brilliant element of the P&L Explain test lies in noticing that in the Black and Scholes framework we can actually use one single state of the world, which is given by our historical data, to 'falsify' the model, namely to show that the model cannot be the correct one. We have only to perform a P&L Explain test: if even in a single state of the world the model-based self-financing replication strategy does not replicate the derivative price, the model cannot be the right one. If, instead, the test is successful, we can't claim we have 'verified' the model because we should test all possible states of the world, but we have certainly obtained strong confirmation of its validity. The question now is: do we really live in a Black and Scholes framework?

5.2.3 Back to Reality

We already know that we do not live in the 'wonderful world of Black and Scholes'. But if in pricing the discrepancies between such a world and the reality are usually neglected, they seem sufficient to denude the P&L Explain test of a lot of its power:

1. In reality we work in *discrete time* with *transaction costs*. Thus we never really observe 'dS' or 'dV', and in any case we cannot replicate them with no cost.
2. The concept of perfect replication so crucial to Black and Scholes requires the market to be *complete*. All risk factors need to be hedgeable, which almost by definition is not the case when we are speaking of a complex derivative, as we saw in Section 1.2.2. Some risk factors cannot be really accessible, meaning that there are no liquid derivatives depending on them.
3. Some other risk factors, if not all risk factors, may not be pure diffusions. With jumps we cannot even attempt perfect hedging through standard sensitivities. The perfect replication idea is the privilege of diffusion models in continuous time, like Black and Scholes. Only when we observe *continuous changes* of the underlying in *continuous time* can we hope

for a real replication. As Cont and Tankov (2004) put it, 'when moving from diffusion-based complete market models to more realistic models, the concept of replication does not provide the right framework for hedging and risk management'.

These three points show that the interpretation of a P&L Explain test given by a fundamentalist view clashes dramatically with reality. The relevance of a P&L test in the real world is much lower than it would be if we lived in a Black and Scholes world. This is the answer to one of the questions we raised at the beginning.

Now let us look at the other question: is the hedging test required by a P&L Explain test similar to the hedging strategy put in place by real-world traders? This cannot be the case because of the three points above and, even more importantly, because of the next one:

4. In a rigorous P&L Explain test inspired by the Black and Scholes framework the model *should never be recalibrated during the life of an option*. One updates the A_t but the set of parameters θ must remain the same as established at the beginning. Today no model is calibrated to a single point in time; all models are regularly recalibrated, particularly when they are used for dynamic hedging. See Buraschi and Corielli (2005) for interesting results on the justifications for this standard practice. What matters to us now it that the issue of recalibration is the crucial element that shows how the rigorous P&L Explain test is not a test of the model as it is really used in hedging, and that we need a different test called 'Hedge Analysis'.

The above points suggest that a fundamentalist view of a P&L test is not justified. However, in difference to the sceptical view, we have seen that in an ideal world P&L Explain would be a good way to assess model validity. We can add that the measurement and the analysis of the test quantity

$$Err = \sum_{t \in T} \|\Delta \Pi_t - \Delta V_t\|^2 \tag{5.2}$$

may retain a practical interest, and, abandoning the dogmatic requirements of a rigorous P&L test, can still be a useful part of model validation.

Consider the above point 1. There we showed that for an effective replication the theory prescribes hedging to be continuous, while in practice hedging and rebalancing are done in discrete time. Even in a numerical simulation of the test like the one performed by Rebonato (1998), where the 'market data' are in reality generated by a Black and Scholes Monte Carlo, there is the same issue, since Monte Carlo is performed at discrete time. Rebonato tackles the issue as follows: the tests are considered successful if the hedging error reduces as we increase the hedging frequency. Then he applies the idea to the numerically generated data and finds that really, *along all Monte Carlo paths*, namely all possible scenarios of his artificial world, as the hedging frequency increases the derivative and the replication strategy actually converge.

A similar test may be also useful with real market data, even with no illusion about perfect convergence. In real hedging we try at t_0 to hedge the future price movement

$$V_{t_1}\left(A_{t_1}^{mkt}\right) - V_{t_0}\left(A_{t_0}^{mkt}\right)$$

by the movement of the hedge:

$$\frac{dV}{dA}|_{A=A_{t_0}^{mkt}}\left(A_{t_1}^{mkt} - A_{t_0}^{mkt}\right).$$

We know that real

$$V_{t_1}\left(A_{t_1}^{mkt}\right)-V_{t_0}\left(A_{t_0}^{mkt}\right) \quad \text{and} \quad A_{t_1}^{mkt}-A_{t_0}^{mkt}$$

will surely be different from

$$dV \quad \text{and} \quad dA$$

that we use in computing our greeks and hedges, but we do not know how different they are. The analysis of *Err* in (5.2) allows us to measure how much our sensitivities, theoretically constructed for infinitesimal changes of the underlying, are robust to real-world daily changes. If *Err* is too big, it may be an indication that the time-step in our hedging strategy is not adequate, we should reduce the time-step or use higher order sensitivities in hedging (gamma hedging).

Consider the above point 4. Since traders actually recalibrate the model when they hedge, they are trying to hedge the future price movement

$$V_{t_1}^{\text{mod}(t_1)}\left(A_{t_1}^{mkt}\right)-V_{t_0}^{\text{mod}(t_0)}\left(A_{t_0}^{mkt}\right) \tag{5.3}$$

with

$$\frac{dV^{\text{mod}(t_0)}}{dA}|_{A_{t_0}=A_{t_0}^{mkt}}\left(A_{t_1}^{mkt}-A_{t_0}^{mkt}\right), \tag{5.4}$$

where in the notation I have pointed out that *the model actually changes between* t_0 *and* t_1 since the recalibration of parameters at t_1 moves us from the model mod (t_0) to the model mod (t_1). Instead, the sensitivity computed at t_0 is fully based on mod (t_0).

If we observe *Err* in the hedging strategy based on (5.4), obtaining a quantity *Err* which is small (or smaller than the quantity obtained with an alternative model) usually indicates that we had on average a small difference between mod (t_0) and mod (t_1), since only in such a case is it likely that the sensitivity based on mod (t_0) matches the realized price change. To an extent the model is making 'good short-term predictions about future prices'. As an experienced trader once told me, we commonly say that valuation models are not used to make *predictions*. This is not true when they are applied to hedging: here the capability to predict short-term movement is crucial. In other words, the test can show that on average recalibration does not change the model dramatically. This can be seen as an assessment of model correct specification and model stability.

5.2.4 Remarks: Recalibration, Hedges and Model Instability

Some observations are now in order. First, saying that the model requires recalibration implies that in

$$V_t = f(A,\theta),$$

there are also some parameters that we do not hedge against but that we need to recalibrate, thus we have parameters θ that change in time even if the model assumes they do not change. We should write

$$V_{t_0}^{\text{mod}(t_0)} = f\left(A_{t_0},\theta_{t_0}\right) \quad \text{and} \quad V_{t_1}^{\text{mod}(t_1)} = f\left(A_{t_1},\theta_{t_1}\right),$$

where θ_t is not a parameter that the model assumes to be a predictable function of time, like $\sigma(t)$ in Black and Scholes with time-dependent volatility, but a model parameter which is changed, in an unpredictable way, every time the model is recalibrated. In a situation of this kind, traders often decide also to hedge against movements of θ. This is the case of the real-world use of the Black and Scholes model, where the volatility σ can be deterministic in the model but actually changes due to recalibration, so that *vega-hedging* is performed for immunization from such changes. We need to add one asset Z such that its price is a function of the parameter, $Z_t = g(\theta_t)$, so that

$$\theta_t = g^{-1}(Z_t).$$

In the Black and Scholes example, we would have $\theta_t = \sigma_t$ and the additional asset would be an option, priced with its own Black and Scholes formula, corresponding to $g(\cdot)$. Now we can write the price of the derivative we are hedging as

$$f(A_t, \theta_t) = f\left(A_t, g^{-1}(Z_t)\right) =: \hat{f}(A_t, Z_t).$$

In this case, should one even try to find a cost of the hedging strategy equal to the price of the option in the model, namely $Err = 0$? Not at all. In fact, according to the model, the parameter θ is not stochastic and there is no hedge to perform on it. Since the model price is always the price of the self-financing hedging strategy, it cannot embed the cost of this 'out-of-the model' hedging. This has, firstly, practical consequences for risk managers who need to compute reserves and, secondly, can imply *instability* problems, as we shall see.

Hedges vs Model Reserves

The strategy that also hedges against movements of θ will have a cost Π different from the one predicted by the model, and this cost appears a better estimation of the true price of the derivative because it takes into account a material risk neglected by the model, the risk associated with changes of θ. Should this be considered a *model reserve*? According to experienced risk managers it should not, because the hedging of θ is an *expected cost* while model reserves relate to losses which are *feared* but not expected. Thus it makes sense to charge our estimate of the amount

$$\Pi - V_{t_0}^{\text{mod}(t_0)} \tag{5.5}$$

to the buyer of the derivative, as we do with expected costs, rather than setting up a model reserve.

Now pay attention to the following consequence of this observation. One natural outcome of the above situation, where there is regular hedging against stochastic movements of a parameter that the model treats as deterministic, is that an alternative model with stochastic θ, which we call mod θ, will be considered. For example, if Black and Scholes is our base model we may move to the Heston model where volatility is stochastic. Do we expect to find again discrepancy

$$\Pi - V_{t_0}^{\text{mod}\theta(t_0)}$$

between the cost of hedging and the model price as large as (5.5)? No, because a model with stochastic θ gives a price $V_{t_0}^{\text{mod}\theta(t_0)}$ that already incorporates θ hedging, thus the above hedge charge may disappear completely. But it is also possible that new hedge charges may be needed, even if they will probably be smaller. Consider, for example, the above case of the passage from Black and Scholes to Heston. Now there will be other parameters, such as the volatility of volatility, that are recalibrated even if the model assumes them to be constant ... the 'true' model does not exist; we have only the possibility to move to 'better' models.

Model instability

Additionally, when we use the model mod where θ should be flat or deterministic, but in practice we hedge against movements of θ_t by buying and selling Z_t, we have to recalibrate θ_t to Z_t day-by-day. This may not be as simple an exercise as was indicated above,

$$\theta_t = g^{-1}(Z_t).$$

In general recalibration is performed via optimization, so we have

$$\theta_t = \arg\min_{\theta}\left(\left(Z_t - Z_t^{\text{mod}}\right)^2\right),$$

with the further complication that θ_t and Z_t may actually be vectors. Thus we can have an *ill-posed calibration problem*, such that even small changes from Z_{t_i} to $Z_{t_{i+1}}$ can lead to large changes between θ_{t_i} and $\theta_{t_{i+1}}$.

In this case it is particularly difficult for the model to explain its own hedges, ie getting (5.3) close to (5.4). In fact the hedges are computed by mod_{t_i} but the realized change of value is also computed using $\text{mod}_{t_{i+1}}$ which can be very different from mod_{t_i} due to the calibration problem. A large *Err* can be an indication of this problem, which is often also detected through the following tests:

1) test of the variability of parameters when the model is calibrated through time. The higher the variability, the more unstable the model.

2) test of the evolution of the derivative prices in the future according to the model. The more these predicted prices differ from those that will be revealed in the market in the future, the more unstable the model. The issue of model stability is touched on and exemplified in Chapter 9.

5.2.5 Conclusions: from Black and Scholes to Real Hedging

In this section we saw how the P&L Explain test inspired by the Black and Scholes replication would be a solid and general assessment of the correspondence of the model with reality only if the reality conformed to the fundamental assumptions of Black Scholes, such as continuous time trading, no transaction costs, a complete market and purely diffusive stochastic processes. Since these do not hold in practice, P&L Explain loses a lot of its power.

Additionally, we have seen that a rigorous P&L explain test must be performed with a model whose deterministic parameters are never recalibrated. This opens a relevant gap between P&L Explain and the reality of hedging, which is performed with regular recalibration.

Yet, as we showed, it can be useful in model validation to compute the P&L of a hedging exercise, even if this hedging exercise considers recalibration and discrete-time hedging. A lower P&L volatility indicates that the model does not require too much recalibration, which is a sign of good dynamic behaviour, and that the model sensitivities, constructed for instantaneous changes of the underlying, are robust to real-world discrete-time changes. Obtaining a good performance in these tests is a positive feature of a model, both for hedging and for pricing.

However, we are still not speaking of the validation of a real hedging strategy. In fact, for all the above tests we are still assuming that the traders compute the sensitivities consistently with the model, without modifying the sensitivity ad hoc. The sensitivity used to construct the hedging portfolio is still the first derivative (analytic or numeric) of the price computed within the model. In reality, traders know that the model will be recalibrated tomorrow and that this is not taken into account by the first derivative computed today. Therefore they can decide to adjust the sensitivity. This is what we explore and explain in the next section.

5.3 FROM THEORY TO PRACTICE: REAL HEDGING

This analysis takes as its starting point one of the most popular pieces of research in mathematical finance. I refer to the first sections of the Hagan et al. (2002) paper that introduces the SABR model. This paper does more than introduce a model: in the first sections it performs an analysis of the requirements that an option model should satisfy in its hedging behaviour, and of how the most common option models actually behave with respect to these requirements. In particular, it shows analytically the behaviour of local volatility models. This part of the paper had a profound influence on the trading world.

In option markets characterized by smile and skew there is the issue, recognized for many years, of the *shadow-delta*. I anticipated it in Remark 9 and I now revisit it briefly. When dealing with a classic Black and Scholes market with flat smile, delta hedging is a simple exercise. Delta is computed as the sensitivity of the option price to a small change of the underlying price F, with no change of the implied volatility of options, that remains at the level σ predicted by Black and Scholes. When, however, traders are using Black and Scholes as a quotation model in a market with a smile, things are not so simple. Consider a volatility smile as in Figure 5.1.

Computing the delta of a derivative means repricing the derivative after a small shift of the underlying F from its current value F_0 to $F_0 + \varepsilon$. Is it reasonable to assume that, if tomorrow there occurs such a shift of the underlying, the smile will remain unchanged? This is a strong assumption, called a *sticky-strike* assumption and represented by a null movement of the smile curve when moving from F_0 to $F_0 + \varepsilon$, such that the continuous line in the figure (today smile) coincides with the smile after a movement of the underlying.

Hagan et al. (2002) claim that this assumption is wrong. In real markets the smile would move to the right following the movement of F, as in the situation represented by the dotted

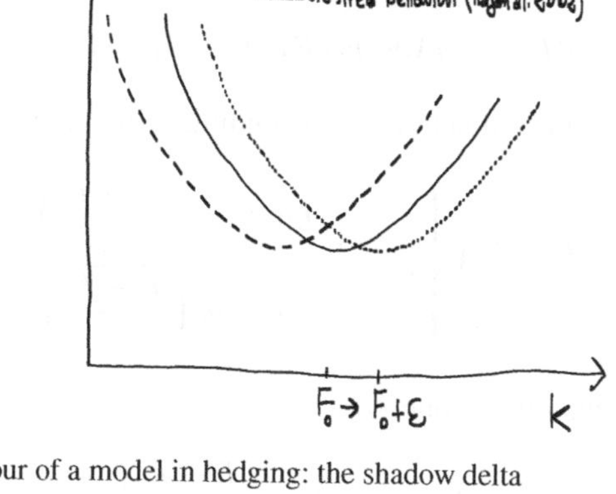

Figure 5.1 The behaviour of a model in hedging: the shadow delta

line. Here I do not discuss this initial assumption. In my experience the majority of traders agree with it; some of them disagree or claim that it depends on many other factors. In any case, from my limited trading experience I point out that the assumption sounds reasonable. In fact for many markets there are regularities in the shape of the smile. For example, I have often heard traders say that in the interest rate market, for short maturities, 'the minimum of the smile is around the ATM strike'. The Hagan et al. (2002) assumption is the one that guarantees that in the model, when the underlying moves, these kinds of properties persist, as they actually persist in the market.

Consequently, Hagan et al. (2002) claim that, when using a model that is not Black and Scholes but implies a non-flat option smile, if we assess the effect of a change in the level of the underlying, for example from F to $F+\varepsilon$, it is desirable to observe that the model implied smile curve moves in the same direction. We call this a *comonotonic* behaviour. Since this appears to be the usual pattern observed in the market, if the model is able to predict it the hedging of derivatives will be less expensive, with reduced rebalancing costs.

For performing this analysis, Hagan et al. (2002) consider the volatility curve $\sigma_F(K)$, implied by a model when the underlying forward is F. Namely $\sigma_F(K)$ is the function such that model call and put option prices coincide with Black prices when Black volatility is given by $\sigma_F(K)$,

$$\Pi^{MOD}(K, F, \theta) = Black\left(K, F, \sigma_F^2(K)\,T\right).$$

For assessing the dynamic behaviour of the model in delta-hedging, we must consider the movement of $\sigma_F(K)$ caused by variations of F. We would like to observe that

$$F \to F+\varepsilon \Rightarrow \sigma_{F+\varepsilon}(K) \approx \sigma_F(K-\varepsilon). \tag{5.6}$$

This means, as we said, that if we move the underlying to the right, namely increase it, the implied volatility curve will also move to the right. In this way, for example, the property such as 'the minimum of the smile is at the ATM strike' is preserved by changes in the underlying itself, since (5.6) implies

$$F \to F+\varepsilon \Rightarrow \sigma_{F+\varepsilon}(F+\varepsilon) \approx \sigma_F(F).$$

Hagan et al. (2002), using singular perturbation techniques, show that in a local volatility model with dynamics

$$dF_t = LocVol(F_t)\,F_t\,dW, \qquad F_0 = F, \tag{5.7}$$

ie a model with a local volatility function not depending on time, the implied volatility is

$$\sigma_F(K) = LocVol\left(\frac{F+K}{2}\right)\left\{1 + \frac{1}{24}\frac{LocVol''\left(\frac{F+K}{2}\right)}{LocVol\left(\frac{F+K}{2}\right)}(F-K)^2 + \cdots\right\}.$$

The first term dominates the second one, so

$$\sigma_F(K) \approx LocVol\left(\frac{F+K}{2}\right).$$

After the model has been calibrated, we can assess its predictions for an increase in the underlying,

$$\begin{aligned} F &\to F+\varepsilon \Rightarrow \\ \sigma_{F+\varepsilon}(K) &\approx LocVol\left(\frac{(F+\varepsilon)+K}{2}\right) \\ &= LocVol\left(\frac{F+(\varepsilon+K)}{2}\right) \approx \sigma_F(K+\varepsilon). \end{aligned}$$

Comparing with (5.6), we see this is the opposite of the desired behaviour. In particular, if the forward price F increases to $F+\varepsilon$, $\varepsilon>0$, the implied volatility curve moves to the left; if F decreases to $F-\varepsilon$, the implied volatility curve moves to the right. Local volatility models predict that the market smile/skew moves in the opposite direction to the price of the underlying asset. This is opposite to typical market behaviour.

This can have consequences on hedging performance. Under any model, the delta is

$$\Delta = \frac{Black\left(K, F, \sigma_F^2(K)T\right)}{\partial F} = \frac{\partial Black}{\partial F} + \frac{\partial Black}{\partial \sigma}\boxed{\frac{\partial \sigma_F(K)}{\partial F}}.$$

The first term is the Black delta. The second term is the model correction to the Black delta, which consists of the Black vega risk multiplied by the predicted change in volatility due to changes in the underlying forward price. If the sign of this latter term is opposite to what it should be according to market evidence, the entire correction has the wrong sign. It would be better, in practice, to hedge with the Black model. According to the above analysis, this is exactly the situation with local volatility models.

To resolve this problem, Hagan et al. (2002) introduce a stochastic volatility model which has become the most popular stochastic volatility model in the market, the SABR model.

5.3.1 Stochastic Volatility Models: SABR

In the SABR model, the forward price F is assumed to evolve under the associated natural forward measure Q^T according to

$$\begin{aligned} dF(t) &= V(t)F(t)^{\beta}\, dW_F(t), \\ dV(t) &= \epsilon V(t)\, dW_V(t), \\ V(0) &= \alpha, \end{aligned} \tag{5.8}$$

where W_F and W_V are Q^{T} standard Brownian motions with

$$\mathbb{E}\left[dW_V\, dW_F\right] = \rho\, dt.$$

The β exponent makes the dynamics of the underlying analogous to the CEV (constant elasticity of variance) local volatility model, perturbed by the lognormal stochastic volatility term V. Setting the local volatility exponent $\beta<1$ allows us to explain typical market skews (monotonically decreasing, asymmetric smiles). When associated with stochastic volatility it allows us to fit more general hockey-stick smiles. The skew component of the smile can also be explained by assuming $\rho<0$ (alternatively to $\beta<1$ or jointly with it, as we will see in Section 7.1). The parameter ϵ is the volatility of volatility, what we often call the *volvol*.

Using singular perturbation techniques, Hagan et al. (2002) obtain a closed-form approximation for the model implied volatility $\sigma_F(K)$,

$$\sigma_F^{SABR}(K) := \frac{\alpha}{(FK)^{\frac{1-\beta}{2}}\left[1+\frac{(1-\beta)^2}{24}\ln^2\left(\frac{F}{K}\right)+\frac{(1-\beta)^4}{1920}\ln^4\left(\frac{F}{K}\right)+\cdots\right]}\frac{z}{x(z)}.$$

$$\left\{1+\left[\frac{(1-\beta)^2\alpha^2}{24(FK)^{1-\beta}}+\frac{\rho\beta\epsilon\alpha}{4(FK)^{\frac{1-\beta}{2}}}+\epsilon^2\frac{2-3\rho^2}{24}\right]T_{j-1}+\cdots\right\},$$

$$z := \frac{\epsilon}{\alpha}(FK)^{\frac{1-\beta}{2}}\ln\left(\frac{F}{K}\right),$$

$$x(z) := \ln\left\{\frac{\sqrt{1-2\rho z+z^2}+z-\rho}{1-\rho}\right\} \tag{5.9}$$

so that

$$E^T\left[(F(T)-K)^+\right] = Black\left(K, F(0), \left(\sigma_F^{SABR}(K)\right)^2 T\right). \tag{5.10}$$

Hagan et al. (2002) remark that, using this formula and moving from F to $F+\varepsilon$, leaving all else unchanged, we can assess that the underlying and the implied volatility curve move in the same direction, consistently with desired dynamic behaviour.

5.3.2 Test Hedging Behaviour Leaving Nothing Out

We start by reviewing a few simple tests, where we use the SABR closed-form formula to assess model hedging behaviour with a test consistent with the approach detailed above: observing the calibrated implied volatility curve, changing in the implied volatility curve the input F for the new input $F+\varepsilon$, and then by observing how the implied volatility curve has moved. In particular, we consider sample tests where we start from $F = 0.08$ and then move to $(F+\varepsilon) = 0.1$.

Simple hedging tests

The first observation we make is trivial. The SABR model, by definition, cannot always have a dynamic behaviour different from local volatility models. In fact, when $\epsilon = 0$ and $\beta < 1$, the SABR model is reduced to a local volatility model. This is the case for the model in Figure 5.2.

In Figure 5.2 we see that, as for local volatility models, the smile moves backwards when increasing $F = 0.08$ (continuous curve) to $(F+\varepsilon) = 0.1$ (dotted curve).

However, what is more relevant is that even moving to a real stochastic volatility model the local volatility part may still dominate, as in the example at Figure 5.3 (parameters are given below the chart).

Here we have again the undesirable behaviour. If we further increase the volatility of volatility, as in Figure 5.4, we have a mixed behaviour that is still not consistent with the desired pattern.

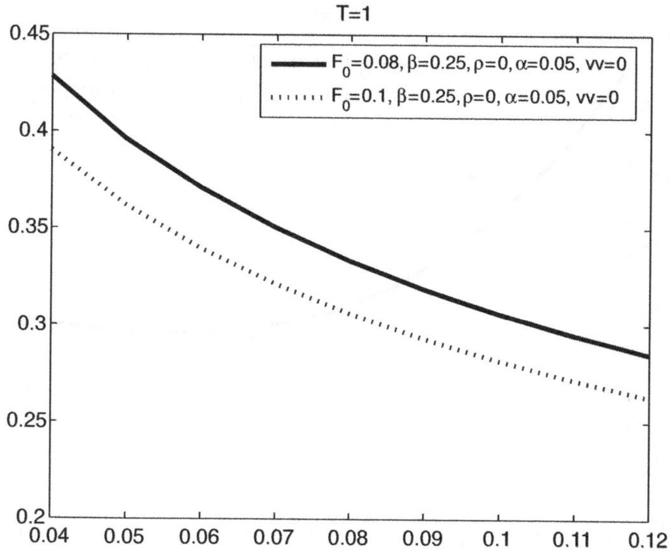

Figure 5.2 $\epsilon = 0$, $\alpha = 5\%$, $\beta = 0.25$, $\rho = 0$, $F = 0.08$

A choice of parameters that gives a behaviour consistent with market patterns is given in Figure 5.5.

However, this parameter configuration is good for representing an almost symmetric smile, not the hockey-stick shape with a dominant skew that we often observe in market quotations. Is there a way to represent a situation where the skew is important in the smile shape, but, in the above hedging test, we keep the desired behaviour of (5.6)? This is obtained by fitting the

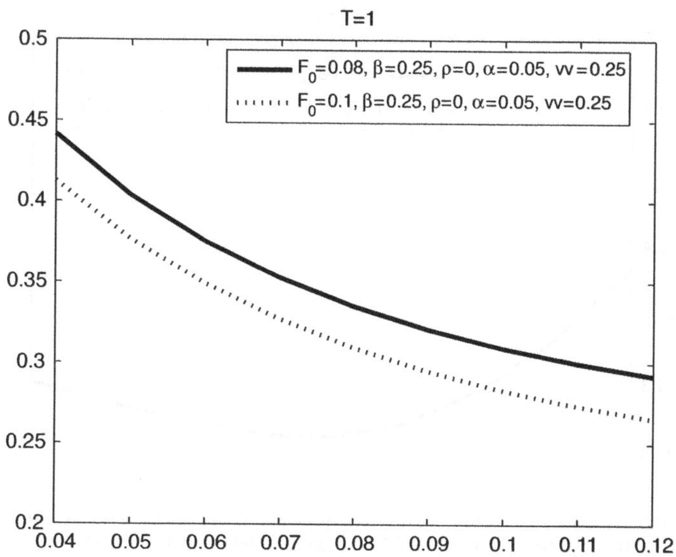

Figure 5.3 $\epsilon = 0.25$, $\alpha = 5\%$, $\beta = 0.25$, $\rho = 0$

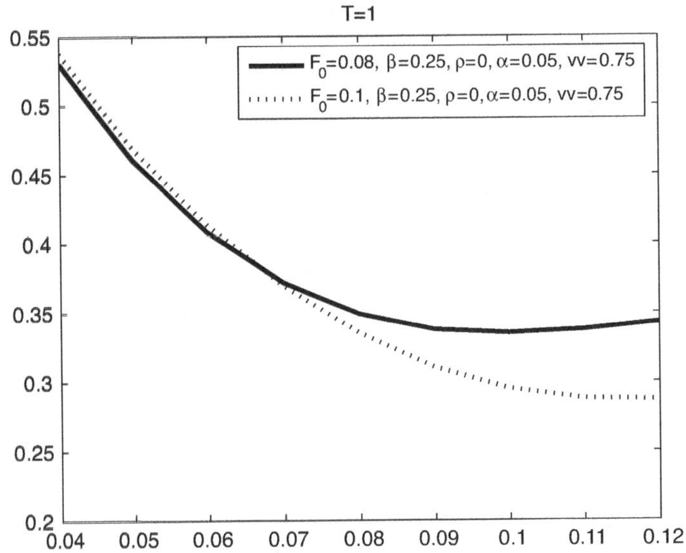

Figure 5.4 $\epsilon = 0.50$, $\alpha = 5\%$, $\beta = 0.25$, $\rho = 0$

skew through $\rho < 0$ rather than by $\beta < 1$, as most market practitioners know. This is shown in the example at Figure 5.6, where the continuous curve represents a smile very similar to the continuous curve of Figure 5.3, but with a totally different set of parameters, and in particular $\rho < 0$ and $\beta = 1$ rather than $\rho = 0$ and $\beta < 1$. In spite of the strong analogy of the curves before shifting the underlying, the behaviour after the shift is radically different.

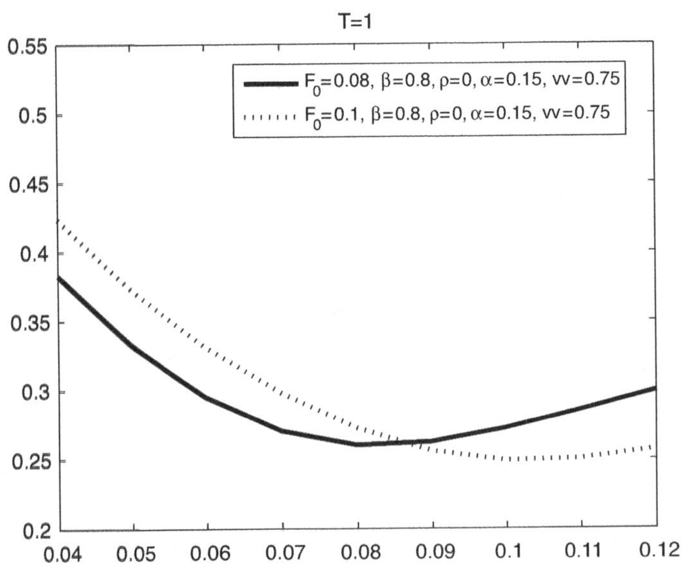

Figure 5.5 $\epsilon = 1$, $\alpha = 5\%$, $\beta = 0.8$, $\rho = 0$

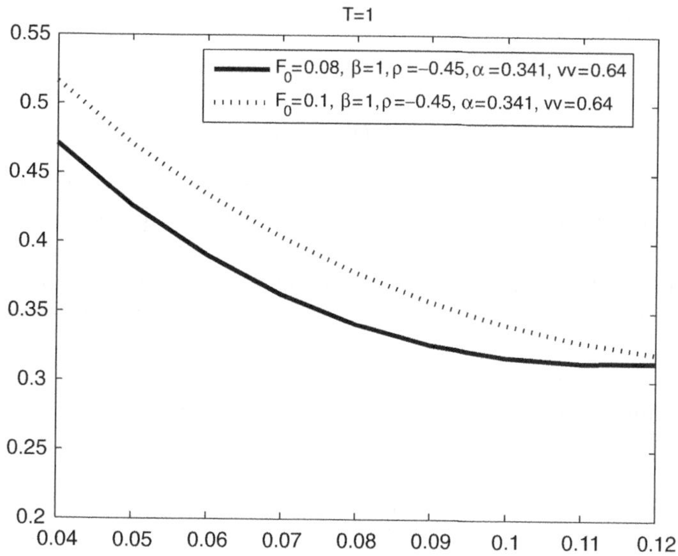

Figure 5.6 $\epsilon = 0.6$, $\alpha = 33.24\%$, $\beta = 1$, $\rho = -0.41$

The local volatility part of SABR behaves as in local volatility models, such that in case of a smile with a relevant skew the SABR model behaves as desired in terms of hedging behaviour only when the skew is determined by the correlation between underlying and stochastic volatility, possibly with the local exponent β set to 1 as in a standard lognormal model. So the desired behaviour in the above test is a property of the model only with specific parameterization, negative correlation, otherwise the implied model skew continues to move opposite to the underlying, as in the simplest local volatility models. But now an important observation is in order.

Hedging when $\rho \neq 0$

All the tests seen above, used for assessing the hedging behaviour of both local volatility and SABR models, require assessing smile dynamics for a shift in the underlying *with the other parameters left unchanged.* The question we now raise is the following: is it consistent with model assumptions to test smile dynamics in this way when using a stochastic volatility model where the underlying and the stochastic volatility are correlated, with $\rho \neq 0$?

The answer is a resounding *no*. In the above tests one is neglecting an important implication of $\rho \neq 0$. The model predicts that a shift in the underlying is accompanied by a corresponding expected movement of the stochastic volatility. Let us examine this in more detail. If we want to perform a hedging test consistent with model assumptions (termed model-consistent or in-the-model hedging), we need to assume that a shift ΔF is due to a stochastic shock ΔW_F (there are no other sources of randomness directly affecting the underlying). Recall that assuming correlation between underlying and stochastic volatility amounts to set

$$dW_V = \sqrt{1-\rho^2}dZ + \rho dW_F,$$

where $Z \perp W_F$. This way

$$\mathbb{E}[dW_V \, dW_F] = \rho \, dt$$

$$\mathbb{E}[dW_V \mid dW_F] = \rho dW_F. \tag{5.11}$$

Therefore assuming a shift dW_F in the underlying corresponds to expecting a contemporary shift ρdW_F in the volatility, if we are performing model-consistent hedging. Assuming we have a shock to the underlying forward price with unchanged volatility is not necessarily wrong, but corresponds to one of an infinity of possible scenarios, and is not the average or expected scenario. On average we will have a non-null corresponding volatility shift ρdW_F.

How does this affect the results of our hedging test? Let us look at a numerical example where, as in a Monte Carlo simulation, we discretize the dynamics moving from the instantaneous dW_F, dW_V to discrete increments ΔW_F, ΔW_V over a short but not instantaneous interval of time.

In delta-hedging we want to assess the effect of a shift of the underlying, say a swap rate, from 0.05 to 0.051. Suppose values for parameters such as $\alpha = 0.1$, $volvol = 0.3$, $\beta = 1, \rho = -0.7$.

This corresponds to a stochastic shock

$$\Delta W_F = \frac{\Delta F}{\alpha F} = 0.2. \tag{5.12}$$

Following (5.11), this corresponds to an expected stochastic volatility shock

$$\mathbb{E}[\Delta W_V \mid \Delta W_F = 0.2] = \rho \Delta W_F = -0.14, \tag{5.13}$$

leading to a shock of the initial value of volatility α from $\alpha = 0.1$ to 0.096.

If we neglect this expected change in volatility, as was done in the typical hedging test mentioned above, we have the model behaviour of Figure 5.7 for a shift in F from 0.05 to 0.051.

This is the desired behaviour: for an increase in the forward, the smile moves right. Figure 5.8 tests what happens if we take into account the expected change in volatility implied by the model.

In this case, the behaviour is not what we desire: the smile has moved back. Dupire (2006) and Bartlett (2006), in contexts different from ours, reach similar conclusions about the actual behaviour of the SABR model.

These results are quite surprising. We started by observing that a comonotonic behaviour of underlying and volatility curve in hedging is the most realistic and desirable behaviour for a model. We observed that even SABR does not have this behaviour when the skew is reproduced through $\beta \neq 1$ with $\rho = 0$; in order to have the comonotonic behaviour we need to reproduce market skew through correlation between underlying and volatility, namely $\rho \neq 0$.

However, we have assessed this fact through the simplest possible delta-hedging test: assessing smile dynamics in case of a shift in the underlying with all other parameters left unchanged. Such a test, although it is meaningful and fully consistent with model assumptions in the case of local volatility models or stochastic volatility models with $\rho = 0$, turns out to be model-inconsistent precisely when $\rho \neq 0$, the only case in which the test was giving the desired result. If, instead, we perform a model-consistent test taking into account the expected

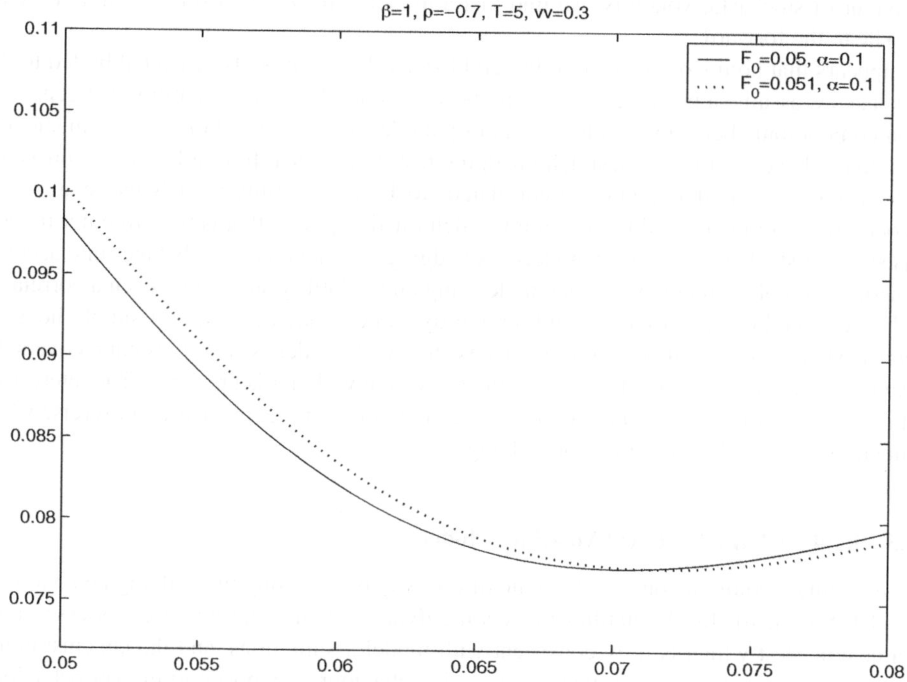

Figure 5.7 SABR: model-inconsistent hedging

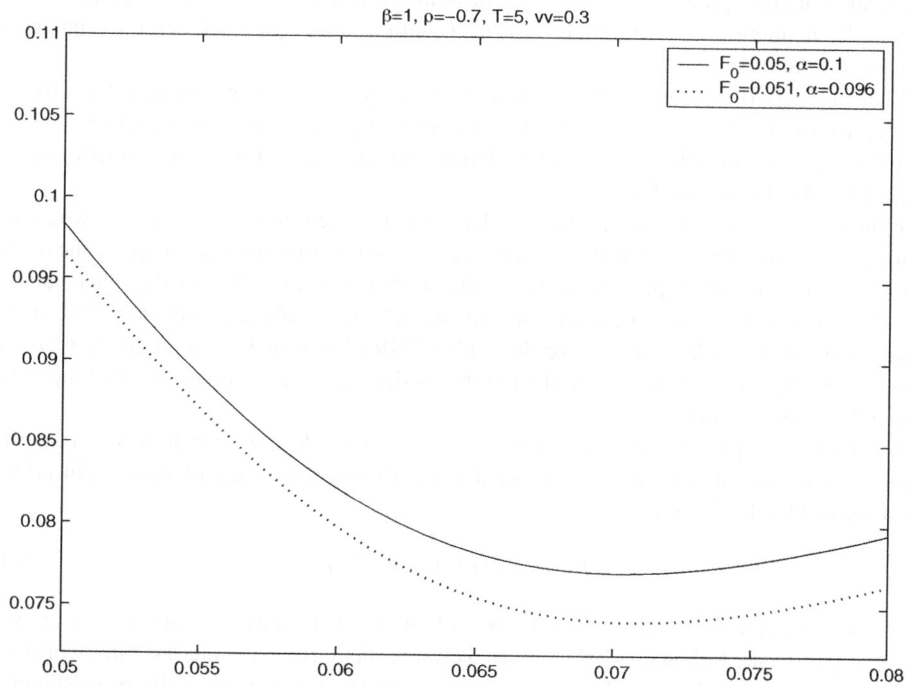

Figure 5.8 SABR: model-consistent hedging

behaviour of stochastic volatility, we find that a model with $\rho \neq 0$ also has a smile moving opposite to the forward.

It appears that both stochastic volatility and local volatility models, when calibrated to the market skew, assume a negative relationship between underlying and volatility that generates a non-comonotonic behaviour. In local volatility models this relationship is deterministic and thus captured even in the simplest delta-hedging test (that is therefore fully model-consistent for local volatility models), while in correlated stochastic volatility models the relationship is stochastic and thus missed by the simplest delta-hedging test (that is therefore not model-consistent for stochastic volatility models). A hedging test that consistently takes into account the assumption of correlation between underlying and volatility shows that even a correlated stochastic volatility model has an undesirable dynamic behaviour, while a simple hedging exercise where only F is altered appears inconsistent with model assumptions but recovers the behaviour that a trader would desire for being consistent with market patterns. The interesting fact is that most traders in the market perform exactly this simple, inconsistent exercise when computing the model sensitivities for hedging.

5.3.3 Real Hedging for Local Volatility Models

These findings require a consistent update of our way of assessing the hedging behaviour of a model. So far, for local volatility models the dynamic behaviour has been assessed only by a hedging test which is fully consistent with model assumptions, and the conclusion has been, as in Hagan et al. (2002), that its dynamic behaviour is opposite to market behaviour. However, we have seen that stochastic volatility models can also have a similar, undesirable behaviour when the dynamic behaviour is assessed by a fully model-consistent procedure. Stochastic volatility models only work in a desirable way when used in a model-inconsistent but simpler hedging practice (namely shifting F with all other parameters left unchanged in spite of correlation).

What happens if we reverse the perspective and try a similar inconsistent but effective hedging for local volatility models? Is anything like that possible and reasonable? We show in the following that not only is this possible, but it is the most common market practice among users of local volatility models.

In the previous section we saw that model-consistent hedging is a procedure where one treats a shift in the underlying as the consequence of a stochastic shock admitted by the model, taking into account all implications, as we did in (5.12) and (5.13). On the other hand, in model-inconsistent hedging one just restarts the model with a different level of the underlying. In model-inconsistent hedging, as we did with SABR changing F without changing α, the change in F is not an endogenous product of the model, but an exogenous restart of the model from a different position.

In order to exemplify this approach for local volatility models, we will look at it as applied to the simplest possible local volatility model, the shifted lognormal of Rubinstein (1983), characterized by the dynamics

$$dF(t) = \sigma\,[F(t) + \lambda]\,dZ(t). \tag{5.14}$$

This model is consistent with (5.7) and can calibrate market skews. It is also consistent with the assumption (see Rebonato (2002b)) that skews, particularly in the interest rates world, can relate to the fact that the underlying does not react to shocks in a way fully proportional to its level (a typical implication of the lognormal assumption) but is in-between a proportional reaction and an absolute reaction (a typical implication of the normal/Gaussian assumption).

In fact, notice that 5.14 can be derived as a dynamics intermediate between the following two dynamics: a lognormal model

$$dF(t) = \sigma^{rel} F(t)\, dZ(t) \qquad \text{(Lognormal)}$$

and a normal model

$$dF(t) = \sigma^{abs}\, dZ(t). \qquad \text{(Normal)}$$

The simplest way of obtaining an intermediate behaviour is to combine the above two dynamics by assuming

$$dF(t) = A \cdot \sigma^{rel} F(t) dZ(t) + (1 - A) \cdot \sigma^{abs} dZ(t). \qquad (5.15)$$

How to choose the parameters σ^{rel} and σ^{abs}? If the lognormal model is calibrated to ATM options, as is typical for lognormal models, we simply have $\sigma^{rel} = \sigma^{ATM}$, where σ^{ATM} is the market implied volatility for ATM options. Then, how to choose σ^{abs} in such a way that ATM options are also calibrated as well as possible in the normal model? Intuitively, the idea is to make the dynamics (normal) as similar as possible to the calibrated dynamics (lognormal) at least near time 0, setting

$$\sigma^{abs} = \sigma^{rel} F(0) = \sigma^{ATM} F(0). \qquad (5.16)$$

See Marris (1999) for more details on why this trick allows us to get a combined model (5.15) which is well calibrated to ATM options. We now have

$$dF(t) = A \cdot \sigma^{ATM} F(t) dZ(t) + (1 - A) \cdot \sigma^{ATM} F(0) dZ(t)$$

that setting

$$\sigma = \sigma^{ATM} A \quad \text{and} \quad \lambda = \frac{(1 - A)}{A} F(0),$$

can be rewritten as in (5.14),

$$dF(t) = \sigma\, [F(t) + \lambda]\, dZ(t).$$

Notice that

$$\lambda = \frac{(1 - A)}{A} F(0) \Longrightarrow A = \frac{F(0)}{F(0) + \lambda}.$$

From this comes the recipe that Marris (1999) gives to calibrate approximately the model to ATM options for any λ: just set

$$\sigma = \sigma^{ATM} A = \sigma^{ATM} \frac{F(0)}{F(0) + \lambda}.$$

It is clear that both σ and λ in the model definition (5.14) are fixed when the model is first calibrated. Then, when assessing the effect of a change $F(0) = F \to F(0) = F + \varepsilon$, for being theoretically consistent these parameters should be left unchanged and only the initial value of the underlying in the dynamics should be altered. Results of this model-consistent hedging test are shown in Figure 5.8 on the left, and are, as expected, opposite to the desired behaviour.

Often, traders in the market do not use local volatility models in this way. In the case of this simple local volatility model, one would take into account that the value of λ comes from $\lambda = \frac{(1-A)}{A}F(0)$, and that only the latter representation guarantees calibration to ATM implied volatility. Thus, when assessing a change from $F(0) = F$ to $F(0) = F + \varepsilon$ one would also change λ to $\lambda = \frac{(1-A)}{A}(F(0) + \varepsilon)$, while this is a model parameter that should not be altered. This is an example of model-inconsistent hedging, where a shift in the underlying is not treated as an endogenous product of a model shock but rather the model is restarted with this different level of the underlying, with consequent implicit recalibration to ATM options. Results are given in Figures 5.9 and 5.10.

The behaviour of the model is not comonotonic in the first, model-consistent hedging test, as we expected. However, we see that if we move to a model-inconsistent (but common and not unreasonable) delta hedging test, local volatility models also exhibit the desired comonotonic smile movement.

Thus we have confirmation of the conclusions in the above section. Traders know that a model will be recalibrated tomorrow, therefore they do not care over much about being consistent with model assumptions in computing sensitivities. On the contrary, traders build sensitivities that try to anticipate the effect of tomorrow's recalibration. In the example of local and stochastic volatility models, they see that the model assumes that the smile tomorrow will move opposite to the underlying. But they know, if they agree with Pat Hagan, that the opposite will happen in most cases in the market. Therefore tomorrow the model will need recalibration to adjust this inconsistency. Traders try to anticipate recalibration, building a sensitivity that, as we saw in this local volatility hedging test, also incorporates a recalibration to ATM volatilities

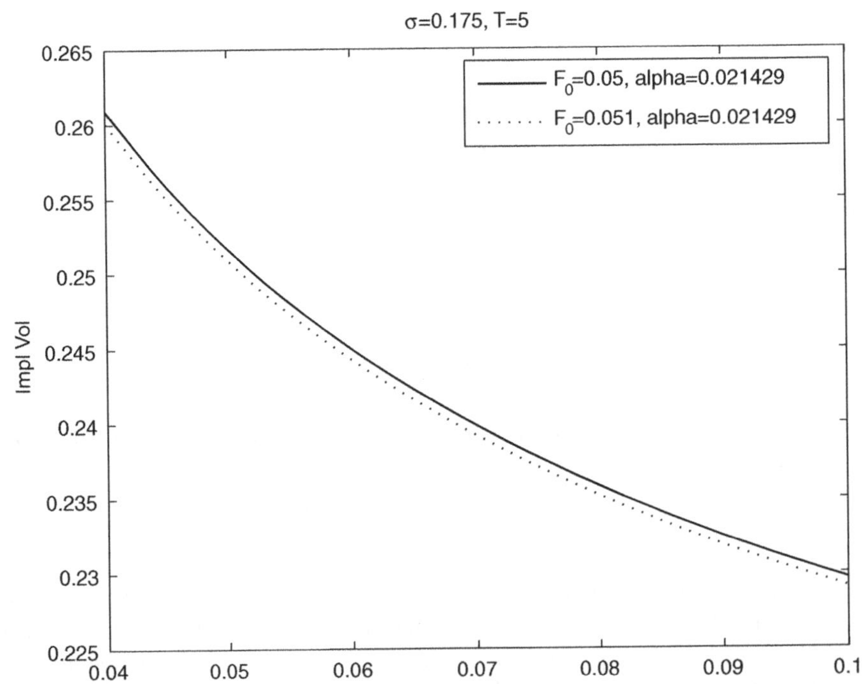

Figure 5.9 The shifted lognormal: model consistent hedging

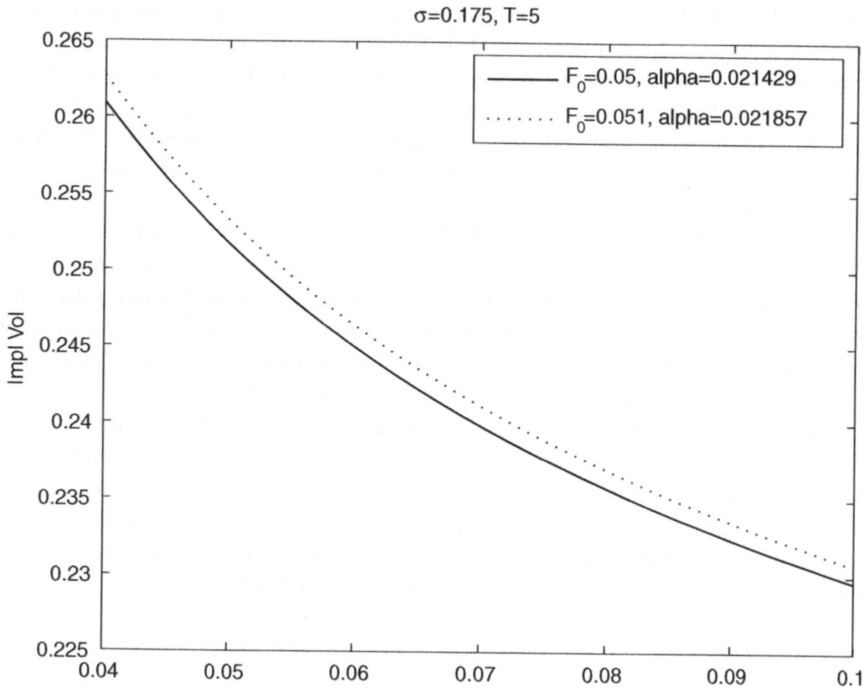

Figure 5.10 The shifted lognormal: model-inconsistent hedging

that has the effect of moving the smile in the same direction as the underlying. The sensitivity is not consistent with model assumptions, but it takes into account the reality of market movements and the practice of recalibration.

5.3.4 Conclusions: the Reality of Hedging Strategies

It is common market wisdom that local volatility models do not possess a desirable dynamic behaviour. Hagan et al. (2002) show in particular that, in case of an increase of the underlying, local volatility models predict the implied volatility curve will move in the opposite direction, contrary to the market empirical behaviour. This is undesirable since it implies wrong hedges. Stochastic volatility models are instead deemed not to suffer from this shortcoming, in particular when they fit the market skew through a negative correlation between volatility and asset price. Here we have provided results suggesting that, however, if one assesses the dynamic behaviour taking into account all model assumptions (in particular the correlation between stochastic volatility and the underlying) stochastic volatility models also have a dynamic behaviour that is not qualitatively different from the wrong behaviour of local volatility models.

This may appear discomforting, and lead to the conclusion that almost all common financial models are inapt for hedging. However, this conclusion is belied by further tests showing that both local volatility and stochastic volatility models can imply correct hedges when hedging is performed by techniques that are of simple implementation and widespread in the marketplace. These techniques are not consistent with the initial model assumptions, but they are consistent with the reality of markets where models are regularly recalibrated.

In my experience, model-inconsistent hedging is considered a natural choice by many traders, since they deem common pricing models to be reliable for representing the relative values of different financial assets but not realistic enough as a representation of the dynamics of actual market variables. Since hedging also depends on the latter dynamics, it must be adjusted ad hoc to be effective in practice.

As Li (2006) recalls, 'most derivatives dealers tend to believe there are too few factors in a model to sufficiently capture the evolution of the underlying', so that the model is used for valuation purposes but the hedging strategy implied by the model is discarded. In such an approach a variation of the underlying from F to $F + \varepsilon$ is not treated as an endogenous product of the model, but simply as an exogenous new starting point for re-evaluation, all else being equal, or with ad hoc adjustments to the other variables that may recover a more realistic joint dynamics of fundamental market variables. Of course, it is a relevant goal for research in our field to commit to develop models that reconcile model implications and market practice in terms of hedging behaviour. In the meanwhile, for the purposes of validation, we must be able to understand how hedging is done in practice and what are the differences between the implications of a model and the way they are modified for hedging, assessing the hedging practice as something related to but different from the pricing model.

6
Approximations

In Chapter 3 we focused on stress testing the assumptions of a model. We saw that model assumptions have many implications that are difficult to predict. The model may appear a reasonable simplified representation of reality in a given market condition or for a given range of payoffs. However, if something changes in the market or if the model is applied to a new problem, we may discover that some implications of model assumptions that are unreasonable and not realistic now have a relevant impact and make the model unreliable.

In this chapter we consider a further step. If a model passes tests like those in Chapter 3, we can be happy with the model: its assumptions are considered sufficiently realistic and we have tools to deal with those cases where these assumptions may be inapt. However, model assumptions do not automatically generate the numbers we need in order to evaluate or risk manage. The model must be implemented, and often this implementation requires the use of computational methods which are not exact formulas: they may be numerical methods like Monte Carlo, or analytical methods that are obtained through introducing some approximation to the model assumptions.

When, for example, an approximation used for computation becomes imprecise, introducing a large bias between the output of the approximation and the correct computation, we have a new form of model risk: even if the assumptions are reasonable, the results we have are not consistent with our assumptions and losses can arise.

These problems can arise suddenly, because an approximation is often precise only for a range of model parameters. When market changes lead to a change in the parameters, the bias between the approximation and the correct result can explode. Therefore we must be able not only to validate an approximation under current market conditions but also to understand under which market conditions the formula breaks down, so as to introduce quantitative indicators to monitor the approximation in the future. This is the issue we tackle next.

6.1 VALIDATE AND MONITOR THE RISK OF APPROXIMATIONS

Here we do not test the consistency of the model with our views on reality, something already addressed, but the internal consistency between the model and the results we obtain from the computational methods. As stated in Section 3.1.3, this is logically the last step to consider in stress testing: only when we feel confident about the validity of model assumption can we act to remain consistent with them in any practical application. But this last step is crucial, because having found a satisfactory model but then using numbers which, *due to approximation error, do not really come from that model* spoils all the analysis performed for model choice. In practice, this test is often performed first, to make sure that subsequent tests are performed with reliable implementations.

The analysis in the previous chapters provides additional reasons for being careful in performing this step. We have seen that the core of model risk, when we use complex models, is model misunderstanding. When the results from our computational methods become inconsistent with the original assumptions, we can easily lose track of the model behaviour and implications, creating dramatic misunderstanding. We have also seen that a crucial step in model risk management is being ready for changes in the model paradigm adopted by the market. When an approximation or a numerical method loses its precision, the market is likely to abandon it, and also often to abandon the model itself. We must understand this risk in advance if we do not want to be taken by surprise.

The risks that we run when an approximation loses precision are exemplified clearly in the examples below. Here the playground we choose is interest rate modelling. Credit modelling was the perfect playground for Chapter 3 where we stress-tested model assumptions, since in credit the main mistakes that led to the crisis were in the bias between model assumptions and economic reality. Now that we focus on implementation bias, interest rate modelling is a natural choice, because it is here that market practitioners use the mathematically most complex models that require the most massive use of approximations or numerical methods for implementation. We describe the main approximations used in the market practice for interest rate derivatives, looking in particular at the Libor Market Models, the most modern framework for representing the dynamic of the term structure, and at the SABR model, which is the most popular dynamics to price interest rate derivatives consistently with the smile. We describe in detail the models and the derivation of the approximations, because without understanding both it becomes impossible to detect what are the potential weaknesses of the approximations.

We consider some popular approximations: the formula for swaption pricing with the Libor Market Model in Section 6.2.4 and the formulas for the computation of convexity adjustments in Section 6.3. These approximations must first be validated against alternative computational methods less subject to deviations from the correct results. One such method is often Monte Carlo simulation, which is often disliked for everyday use since it can be very time-consuming and also noisy in the computation of sensitivities (the Monte Carlo price comes with a range of uncertainty; if the sensitivity is of a size comparable to the uncertainty, we may even get the sign of the sensitivity wrong). Yet Monte Carlo can be used, allowing it plenty of time to get results as precise as possible, as a useful benchmark to test an analytical approximation.

We look at the steps to follow for performing such tests. We will then point out that the sneakiest model risk arises from most approximations being based on features of the market that are considered permanent. Thus, even if the initial tests confirm that the formula is valid under initial market conditions, there can be a residual risk that we need to monitor. This is the case for these approximations that started to break down with the credit crunch. Observing what happened in the crisis is a good way to understand how to manage these residual risks.

In the third example, presented in Section 6.4, we focus on the SABR approximation for pricing options. Here we show an alternative way to test an approximation: not against Monte Carlo (which for SABR can be as biased as the approximation), but against the exact formula that we are able to compute for a few special cases. Here we will show how to choose special cases that are sufficiently general to reveal the real weaknesses of the formula.

Finally, in Section 6.5 the reader is given three exercises, taken from three practical market cases. In the first exercise the lesson learned from the above examples on approximations can help him/her detect easily the problem involved with a recently developed approximation. This approximation has not yet been challenged by market shifts, but we need to understand which market moves could invalidate it, and how we can control and monitor this risk. In the second and third exercises we go beyond approximations and lead the reader to an understanding of the problems that can arise in the use of two more numerical methods that are usually considered less risky than approximations but can at times give serious problems: Monte Carlo simulation and numerical integration. In the end, of course, we sketch the solution to the exercises.

6.2 THE SWAPTION APPROXIMATION IN THE LIBOR MARKET MODEL

Let us first review the technicalities and financial motivations which are fundamental to an understanding of how the pricing of interest rate derivatives works. We follow the pre-crisis framework of interest rate modelling, called the *risk-free model* in Chapter 4, since this is still the one used by most practitioners for complex derivatives. In any case, even those who recognize that the old risk-free model is no longer valid do not discard the framework but try to make minimal changes to deal with the new features of the market see Mercurio (2008). Thus we keep the notation introduced in Chapter 4 but drop the superscripts and subscripts indicating the underlying model, since the modelling framework is always the risk-free one.

6.2.1 The Three Technical Problems in Interest Rate Modelling

One fundamental technicality has already been used: the change of numeraire. Its results can appear at first sight of mainly theoretical interest. But on the contrary, the introduction of change of numeraire around 1995 dramatically altered the practice of interest rate modelling. The first application was providing a rigorous justification to the main formula that had been in use in the interest rate derivatives market since the markets inception. This is the Black formula, an heuristic application to interest rate derivatives such as caps and swaptions of an approach for the pricing of commodity derivatives introduced in Black (1976).

The formula is similar to the Black and Scholes formula used for pricing equity derivatives. In its application to caps and swaptions it is based on assuming a standard lognormal dynamics for the market rates directly involved in the payoffs, and it was liked by traders since immediate to calibrate and intuitive, for the expression of views in terms of comfortable concepts such as implied volatility and, when skew and smile became more relevant for interest rate derivatives, it also allowed for expression and control in a way similar to that for other markets which had earlier experienced the same phenomenon.

Unfortunately, the heuristic motivations justifying the application of this formula to the interest rate market – an application that was born on the trading floors – appeared inconsistent or arbitrary. This did not discourage traders from using it, but it still created a serious practical problem: in the absence of a sound theoretical background it is difficult to extend an approach to more advanced issues, such as exotic payoffs or smile-consistent trading. Therefore traders used Black whenever possible, and then used completely different models such as short rate models like Vasicek or Hull and White to price complex derivatives or to study the stochastic behaviour of the term structure. This situation was disturbing and many traders, particularly those working on advanced derivatives, would have been happy to have a modelling framework consistent with the Black formula and yet applicable to more complex issues.

The first step in this direction was to use change of numeraire to justify formally the Black formula. We explain this with reference to caps. A cap can be represented as a portfolio of options on individual Libor forward rates, each called a *caplet*. We have seen in (4.6) that the equilibrium rate of a Forward Rate Agreement with expiry (fixing time) T and maturity (payment time) T' is the *Forward Libor Rate* $F(t; T, T')$ that can be written as

$$F(t; T, T') = \frac{1}{(T' - T)} \left[\frac{P(t, T)}{P(t, T')} - 1 \right], \tag{6.1}$$

A caplet fixing at T_{k-1} and paying at T_k has a payoff

$$\alpha_k(F(T_{k-1};T_{k-1},T_k)-K)^+, \tag{6.2}$$

so it is an option on a FRA. As usual it is priced as a risk-neutral expectation of the payoff

$$Caplet^{T_k}=\mathbb{E}\left[D\left(0,T_k\right)\alpha_k(F(T_{k-1};T_{k-1},T_k)-K)^+\right]. \tag{6.3}$$

There is an initial complication in pricing this payoff that we call *the first problem of interest rate modelling*. In interest rate modelling interest rates are obviously stochastic, and this implies that *the discount factor* $D\left(t,T_k\right)$ *is stochastic*, because discount factors are derived from interest rates. For this reason $D\left(t,T_k\right)$ is also correlated to the underlying F, since both depend on the same source of risk, interest rates risk. In difference to what Black and Scholes (1973) or Black (1976) can do in their equity or commodity models, here we cannot take $D\left(t,T_k\right)$ out of the expectation based on considering it deterministic or independent from the rest of the payoff.

Change of numeraire shows a way to solve this complication. We can get rid of the problem of this stochastic discount factor, as we did in the Appendix result (12.6), by changing to the T_k forward measure Q^k

$$\begin{aligned}Caplet^{T_k}&=\mathbb{E}\left[D\left(0,T_k\right)\alpha_k(F(T_{k-1};T_{k-1},T_k)-K)^+\right]\\&P(0,T_k)\mathbb{E}^{T_k}\left[\alpha_k(F(T_{k-1};T_{k-1},T_k)-K)^+\right].\end{aligned}$$

Now we have a pricing problem similar to the pricing of a call option, but we find ourselves faced with *the second problem of interest rate modelling*. We have seen in 1.2.1 how intuition justifies that in an arbitrage-free market the prices of tradable assets should be martingales under the risk-neutral measure. But here, in contrast to the case of equity or commodity derivatives, the underlying $F_k(t)$ *is not a tradable asset* (you cannot buy or sell, say, 'one billion of interest rates'). How to give it an arbitrage-free dynamics?

Change of numeraire also solves this problem, because we show in the Appendix that in an arbitrage-free market the underlying $F(t;T_{k-1},T_k)$ must be a martingale not under the risk-neutral measure, but under the forward measure Q^k, that here is our most convenient pricing measure. Now we are free to assume, as in Black and Scholes (1973) or Black (1976), that the underlying is lognormal with dynamics

$$dF(t;T_{k-1},T_k)=\sigma^{T_k}F(t;T_{k-1},T_k)dW^k(t) \tag{6.4}$$

under our pricing measure, and this leads consistently to the following pricing formula

$$Caplet^{T_k}=P(0,T_k)\alpha_k Black\left(F(0;T_{k-1},T_k),K,T_{k-1}\left(\sigma^{T_k}\right)^2\right).$$

This formula has always been used for quoting caplets, but before the introduction of change of numeraire it was presented as an 'approximation' where discount factors were inconsistently treated as deterministic and the martingale assumption was arbitrary.[1]

[1] It is interesting to note that market practitioners had developed this approach well before any quant could prove its consistency. When the possibility of verifying the approach was subsequently developed, the approach was proved consistent, arbitrage-free and involving no approximation. We will see similar convergence between practice and theory again when speaking of convexity adjustments. They are surprising confirmations of the rationality and lack of arbitrage of very big and liquid markets like the interest rate market. In such markets a formula that sruvives for decades without big losses associated to it is likely to be consistent.

There is one issue that we have not solved yet and that we can call *the third problem of interest rate modelling*. The Black formula cited is about the pricing of a derivative *depending on one single rate*. The above results give no indication about how to treat a payoff depending on more than one rate and that cannot be decomposed into more elementary payoffs, each one dependent on one single rate. It is very unlikely that this can be done just by treating each rate separately as done in the above derivation. The above derivations tells us nothing about the relations that can exist among different forward rates, and yet such relations should exist since different forward rates are only *different bits* of *the same term structure*. We expect no-arbitrage relations to link them, avoiding that what today appears as a consistent term structure simply moves randomly in the future becoming a scatter of points. This issue was solved easily in simple models like Vasicek (1977), which derive the entire term structure on the unique simple variable $r(t)$, but in multidimensional models of real-world rates it was not solved until the introduction of the Libor Market Model, a model whose foundation is in the above change of numeraire principles but that generalizes them to a full model of the term structure.

The explanation of the Black formula, the introduction of the Libor Market Model, and the precise formula for pricing the constant maturity swaps were all important consequences of the discovery of the change of numeraire toolkit, and probably also the most important technical advances in interest rate modelling in the decade preceding the crisis. We see all of them in the following.

6.2.2 The Libor Market Model and the Swaption Market

The Libor Market Model of Brace, Gatarek and Musiela (1997) is based on the above fundamental results about the no-arbitrage behaviour of real-world forward rates. First, we have to fix a set of dates $\{T_0, \ldots, T_M\}$, that represents the expiry and maturity dates for the forward rates. This set is called the *tenor structure*. Since in this modelling framework we want to model real rates, which are characterized by precise fixing and payment times, the tenor structure must be chosen such that it is as consistent as possible with the liquid maturities of the underlying market which we want to consider. Following the notation of Brigo and Mercurio (2001), we shall denote by $\{\alpha_0, \ldots, \alpha_M\}$ the corresponding year fractions, so that, calling $T_{-1} = 0$ the current time, α_k is the year fraction associated with the pair of dates T_{k-1}, T_k.

To simplify notation further, we denote by $F_k(t)$ the simply compounded forward rate $F(t; T_{k-1}, T_k)$, the forward rate fixing at T_{k-1} and with maturity T_k. We consider all $F_k(t)$ with maturities going from $T_1, \ldots, T_M$, so we have M forward rates in the model. These are the state variables in this model. Each forward rate expires at T_{k-1}, when it becomes a spot rate. Before T_{k-1} it is a stochastic process, and it is this stochastic process which we must model. The scheme of the model is summarized in Figure 6.1

First, now that we know there are different possible pricing measures associated with different numeraires, we have to choose one of them. We have already noted from (4.9) that, if for each forward rate $F_k(t)$ we change to the T_k-forward measure associated with the numeraire bond $P(t, T_k)$, we have that $F_k(t)$ is a martingale. So, we choose to model directly under this measure, which for simplicity we indicate here as Q^k.

No arbitrage forces us to take $F_k(t)$ as a martingale, but we are free to choose any martingale dynamics for $F_k(t)$. We could select a stochastic or local volatility dynamics, as for example in Mercurio and Morini (2009a) where a SABR dynamics is chosen. But when Brace, Gatarek and Musiela (1997) introduced this approach for the first time, there was no clear smile in

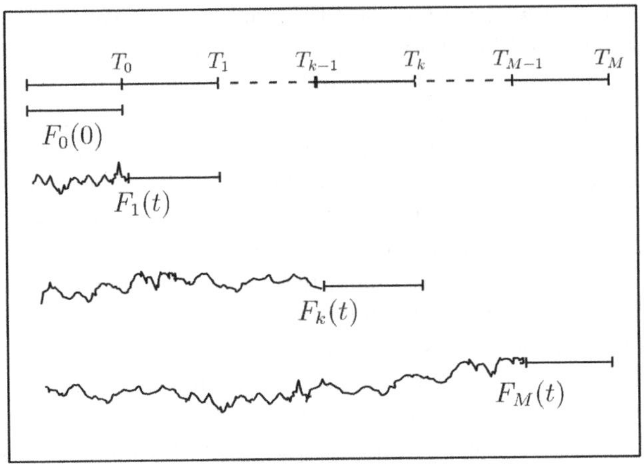

Figure 6.1 The Libor Market Model. Tenor structure and forward rates

the interest rate market and the lognormal dynamics appeared the best choice. The lognormal Libor Market Model they introduced is still considered the reference LMM, and is still crucial because although the interest rate market now has a clear smile, usually captured with SABR, the quotation system is still based on a lognormal dynamics. In the first part of this chapter, where we speak of two very fundamental market approximations (for swaptions and for CMS), we describe them and show how to validate and monitor them in the context of the lognormal LMM, because the approximations look very similar under all dynamics but are easier to understand in the lognormal context. Later in this chapter we will also consider approximations specific to smile LMM dynamics.

If we assume that $F_k(t)$ under Q^k is a diffusion with a percentage volatility which is a deterministic function, we have the original LMM, that assumes for every $k = 1, \ldots, M$,

$$dF_k(t) = \sigma_k(t) F_k(t)\, dZ_k^k(t), \quad t \le T_{k-1}, \tag{6.5}$$

where $Z_k^k(t)$ is the k-th component of an M-dimensional Brownian motion $Z^k(t)$ under Q^k (notice that the superscripts indicate the modelling measure, the subscript indicates the component of the vector). This vector $Z(t)$ collects the different Brownian shocks driving the different rates, and is characterized by a $M \times M$ matrix of instantaneous correlations, called ρ. This is called the *instantaneous correlation* of the LMM, and is the second set of parameters characterizing the model. The first set are the time functions $\sigma_k(t)$, called the *instantaneous volatilities* of the LMM.

Interest rate models usually need first a calibration to the term structure, which can be expressed as a vector of rates or a vector of bonds. Then the user desires also a calibration to the two main liquid interest rate derivatives, caps and swaptions.

In the Libor market model the calibration to the term structure is automatic, as long as we set $F_k(0) = F_k^{Market}$, namely we set the initial value of each rate to be equal to the forward rates observed today on the market. This is one of the advantages of this modelling framework where one models directly market rates rather than instantaneous theoretical quantities such as the short rate modelled by Vasicek (1977) or Hull and White (1990).

Further, the pricing of caps, and consequently cap calibration, is very easy, because in the LMM we model directly the underlyings of caps, and in a way consistent with the pricing-quoting system of the cap market, as we will see in detail in Chapter 9. This ease of caplet pricing in the LMM depends strictly on the fact that each caplet is an option *on one single rate*, the rate $F_i(t)$, and since it pays *at the maturity* T_i *of the rate*, it is naturally priced under the measure Q^i which is exactly the one under which we have given the dynamics of $F_i(t)$ in the LMM.

But this is a very special case. What can we do if we have to price a payoff depending on more than one rate, for example a payoff paid at T_5 and given by

$$(w_1 F_3(T_2) + w_2 F_4(T_3) + w_3 F_5(T_4))^+ \ ? \tag{6.6}$$

This cannot be decomposed into the sum of payoffs each one depending on a single rate. I have a pricing problem

$$\mathbb{E}\left[D(0, T_5)(w_1 F_3(T_2) + w_2 F_4(T_3) + w_3 F_5(T_4))^+\right]$$

and the first thing that one can do to simplify it is to get rid of the stochastic discount factor $D(0, T_5)$, which as we know can be done by a change to the measure Q^5 associated with the bond numeraire $P(t, T_5)$, moving to the new problem

$$P(0, T_5)\mathbb{E}^5\left[(w_1 F_3(T_2) + w_2 F_4(T_3) + w_3 F_5(T_4))^+\right]$$

Now we are pricing under measure Q^5. We know that $F_5(t)$ is a lognormal martingale under this measure, but what about the other rates F_3 and F_4? For pricing a generic product, (6.5) is no longer sufficient. We need to know the dynamics of a rate $F_k(t)$ under a measure Q^i, with $k \neq i$.

This dynamics can be computed using the Girsanov theorem see, for example, Brigo and Mercurio (2006). Unfortunately, when we have to consider $F_k(t)$ under Q^i, $k \neq i$, we will not find a simple martingale dynamics. We have a very complex no arbitrage drift, given in general by the following:

Proposition 13. *The dynamics of forward rate* $F_k(t)$ *under the forward measure* Q^i

- $i < k, \quad t \leq T_i :$

$$dF_k(t) = \sigma_k(t)F_k(t)\sum_{j=i+1}^{k}\frac{\rho_{k,j}\alpha_j\sigma_j(t)F_j(t)}{1+\alpha_j F_j(t)}dt + \sigma_k(t)F_k(t)dZ_k^i(t)$$

- $i = k, \quad t \leq T_{k-1} :$ $\qquad dF_k(t) = \sigma_k(t)F_k(t)dZ_k^i(t)$
- $i > k, \quad t \leq T_{k-1} :$

$$dF_k(t) = -\sigma_k(t)F_k(t)\sum_{j=k+1}^{i}\frac{\rho_{k,j}\alpha_j\sigma_j(t)F_j(t)}{1+\alpha_j F_j(t)}dt + \sigma_k(t)F_k(t)dZ_k^i(t).$$

Somehow, this result should not be surprising. We have found that, when a rate is modelled jointly with other rates, and therefore we have to choose a common measure, one rate has a dynamics *that also depends on the other rates in the term structure and their parameters*, that appear in its drift. These drifts do exactly what we expected our model to do: they capture the no-arbitrage relationships that link together the different bits of the term structure, represented by our different forward rates. Notice what happens to our toy derivative (6.6). We find it convenient to price under Q^5 and under this measure F_5 is a martingale and as such does not depend on any other rate. But then the rate F_4 has a dynamics that depends on F_5 and its parameters, as you can see above for the case $i > k$, and F_3 has a dynamics that depends on F_4 and F_5 and their parameters, keeping consistency among different bits of the term structure.

These dynamics are a solution to the 'third problem of interest rate modelling', but they create a computational problem. In fact, apart from $i = k$, they do not feature known transition densities. For most products involving the joint dynamics of forward rates we have to resort to discretization and Monte Carlo simulation – or we can look for approximations. This is exactly what happens for swaptions, which form the core of our case study.

6.2.3 Pricing Swaptions

Swaptions are the other important reference market for interest rate derivatives. Swaptions are options on forward starting swaps. Consider a swap with payments scheduled at $T_{\alpha+1}, \ldots, T_\beta$. We have already seen in 2.8.2 that it can be priced by replication getting

$$Swap_t^{\alpha,\beta}(K) = P(t, T_\alpha) - P(t, T_\beta) - \sum_{i=\alpha+1}^{\beta} P(t, T_i)\alpha_i K.$$

This price can be equivalently expressed by making use of the definition of forward rates given in (6.1),

$$Swap_t^{\alpha,\beta}(K) = \sum_{i=\alpha+1}^{\beta} P(t, T_i)\alpha_i(F(t, T_{i-1}, T_i) - K)$$

or using the definition (2.23) of the equilibrium swap rate to write

$$Swap_t^{\alpha,\beta}(K) = \sum_{i=\alpha+1}^{\beta} P(t, T_i)\alpha_i(S_{\alpha,\beta}(t) - K).$$

The payoff of a swaption, which is an option to enter at time T_α into a swap with a fixed rate equal to K, can be written as

$$\begin{aligned} & D(t, T_\alpha)\left(Swap_{T\alpha}^{\alpha,\beta}(K)\right)^+ \qquad (6.7) \\ &= D(t, T_\alpha) \sum_{i=\alpha+1}^{\beta} P(T_\alpha, T_i)\alpha_i(S_{\alpha,\beta}(T_\alpha) - K)^+. \end{aligned}$$

In the market swaptions are quoted with the following Black formula:

$$Swaption_t = \sum_{i=\alpha+1}^{\beta} P(t, T_i)\alpha_i Black\left(S_{\alpha,\beta}(t), K, \int_t^{T_\alpha} \sigma_{\alpha,\beta}(t)^2\, dt\right). \qquad (6.8)$$

Can we also find in this case a change of measure that allows us to justify this Black formula? Yes, but we need to change to a new measure, the $Q^{\alpha,\beta}$ swap measure, associated with the annuity or bond portfolio numeraire $\sum_{i=\alpha+1}^{\beta} P(t, T_i)\alpha_i$. Then

$$\begin{aligned}
Swaption_t &= \mathbb{E}_t\left[D(t, T_\alpha) \sum_{i=\alpha+1}^{\beta} P(T_\alpha, T_i)\alpha_i (S_{\alpha,\beta}(T_\alpha) - K)^+\right] \\
&= \sum_{i=\alpha+1}^{\beta} P(t, T_i)\alpha_i \mathbb{E}_t^{\alpha,\beta}\left[\frac{\sum_{i=\alpha+1}^{\beta} P(T_\alpha, T_i)\alpha_i}{\sum_{i=\alpha+1}^{\beta} P(T_\alpha, T_i)\alpha_i}(S_{\alpha,\beta}(T_\alpha) - K)^+\right] \\
&= \sum_{i=\alpha+1}^{\beta} P(t, T_i)\alpha_i \mathbb{E}_t^{\alpha,\beta}\left[(S_{\alpha,\beta}(T_\alpha) - K)^+\right]. \qquad (6.9)
\end{aligned}$$

We have now simplified the pricing expression as we did by moving to the forward measure in the case of caplets. Next we have to find out what the no-arbitrage dynamics of the underlying swap rate $S_{\alpha,\beta}(t)$ is under the pricing measure $Q^{\alpha,\beta}$. Again, change of numeraire can help us: the swap rate is defined as (2.23), which is a tradable asset (a portfolio of bonds) divided by the numeraire of the swap measure $Q^{\alpha,\beta}$, such that the swap rate is a martingale under the swap measure. Now we can assume that this martingale is lognormal

$$dS_{\alpha,\beta}(t) = \sigma_{\alpha,\beta}(t) S_{\alpha,\beta}(t)\, dW_t^{\alpha,\beta} \qquad (6.10)$$

and under this assumption we get that a swaption is priced with (6.8).

We have seen that the Libor Market Model was consistent with the market quotation practices for caplets, since it was based on the assumption of lognormality of forward rates. Is the LMM also consistent with the Black formula for swaptions or, equivalently, are swap rates lognormal in the LMM as they are in the derivation of the Black formula for swaptions? Here the answer is more difficult, because swap rates are not the variables modelled in the LMM, which is based on forward rates.

However it is possible to give an answer to this question, although answering is not trivial. In fact a swap rate can be written as a function of forward rates:

$$S_{\alpha,\beta}(t) = \sum_{i=\alpha+1}^{\beta} w_i(t)\, F_i(t), \quad w_i(t) = \frac{\alpha_i \prod_{j=\alpha+1}^{i} \frac{1}{1+\alpha_j F_j(t)}}{\sum_{k=\alpha+1}^{\beta} \alpha_k \prod_{j=\alpha+1}^{k} \frac{1}{1+\alpha_j F_j(t)}} \qquad (6.11)$$

where in computing $w_i(t)$ we have used the fact that

$$\begin{aligned}
\frac{P(t, T_i)}{P(t, T_\alpha)} &= \frac{P(t, T_i)}{P(t, T_{i-1})} \frac{P(t, T_{i-1})}{P(t, T_{i-2})} \cdots \frac{P(t, T_{\alpha+2})}{P(t, T_{\alpha+1})} \frac{P(t, T_{\alpha+1})}{P(t, T_\alpha)} \\
by\ (6.1) &= \prod_{j=\alpha+1}^{i} \frac{1}{1+\alpha_j F_j(t)}.
\end{aligned}$$

We know which stochastic processes are followed by forward rates in the LMM. The swap is just a function of these stochastic processes. Using Ito's Lemma we can compute which stochastic process is followed by the swap rate itself, and by change of numeraire we can see this process under the swap measure. This test has been done, see, for example, Brigo and Mercurio (2006), and the answer is *no*, the swap rate is *not* lognormal according to the assumptions of the LMM. It has a complex dynamics that does not feature any analytic solution, let alone a lognormal solution. We can simplify this result by saying: lognormal forward rates, as in the LMM, imply a swap rate which is not lognormal. And this result extends to more complex versions of the LMM: forward rates modelled following the SABR model of Hagan et al. (2002) do not imply a SABR swap rate; forward rates modelled following the Heston model do not imply a Heston swap rate, and so on.

This is a serious drawback of the LMM. We have seen that one of the features motivating the introduction of the BGM was the desire to have a model consistent with the quotation practice for caplets that could be calibrated to caplets instantaneously and analytically. Now we know that we do not have the same very desirable property when we look at the other, at least equally important, liquid interest rate derivative market.

But there is something worse. Since in this model the dynamics of the swap rate features no analytic solution, it seems that we cannot price swaptions with any analytical formula, but just via numerical methods such as Monte Carlo simulation. How does this work?

Monte Carlo pricing in the LMM

We should recall the payoff of a swaption given in (6.7) and compute its price as

$$
\begin{aligned}
Swaption_t &= \mathbb{E}_t\left(D(0,T_\alpha)\sum_{i=\alpha+1}^{\beta}\alpha_i P(T_\alpha,T_i)\,(S_{\alpha,\beta}(T_\alpha)-K)^+\right)\\
&= P(0,T_\alpha)E^\alpha\left[\sum_{i=\alpha+1}^{\beta}\alpha_i P(T_\alpha,T_i)(S_{\alpha,\beta}(T_\alpha)-K)^+\right]\\
&= P(0,T_\alpha)E^\alpha\underbrace{\left[\sum_{i=\alpha+1}^{\beta}\alpha_i P(T_\alpha,T_i)\left(\sum_{i=\alpha+1}^{\beta}w_i(T_\alpha)\,F_i(T_\alpha)-K\right)^+\right]}_{\Psi(F_{\alpha+1}(T_\alpha),F_{\alpha+2}(T_\alpha),\ldots,F_\beta(T_\alpha))}.
\end{aligned}
$$

In the above passages we had two goals:

1. revealing that the payoff of a swaption can be written just as a function of the forward rates that we model in the LMM;
2. pricing under one of the natural measures of the LMM, the forward measure Q^α.

Thanks to Proposition 13 we know that the dynamics of F_k under Q^α, $\alpha < k$ is

$$
dF_k(t) = \sigma_k(t)F_k(t)\sum_{j=\alpha+1}^{k}\frac{\rho_{j,k}\alpha_j\sigma_j(t)F_j(t)}{1+\alpha_j F_j(t)}\,dt + \sigma_k(t)F_k(t)\,dZ_k^\alpha(t),
$$

which we have to discretize, getting in the simplest Euler discretization:

$$
\begin{aligned}
&\bar{F}_k(t+\Delta t)\\
&= \bar{F}_k(t)+\sigma_k(t)\bar{F}_k(t)\sum_{j=\alpha+1}^{k}\frac{\rho_{j,k}\alpha_j\sigma_j(t)\bar{F}_j(t)}{1+\alpha_j\bar{F}_j(t)}\,\Delta t+\sigma_k(t)\bar{F}_k(t)\left[Z_k^\alpha(t+\Delta t)-Z_k^\alpha(t)\right].
\end{aligned}
$$

For each scenario z, $z = 1, \ldots, N$, we store $\bar{F}^z(T_\alpha) = \left[\bar{F}^z_{\alpha+1}(T_\alpha), \ldots, \bar{F}^z_\beta(T_\alpha)\right]$ and we price as usual in simulation

$$Swaption_t^{MC} = P(0, T_\alpha)\frac{1}{N}\sum_{z=1}^{N} \Psi\left(\bar{F}^z(T_\alpha)\right).$$

We have recalled these simple passages to point out that Monte Carlo simulation applied to a problem such as pricing swaptions with a LMM is computationally very burdensome. In fact a swaption, for example a swaption 10×10 which is a swaption with $T_\alpha = 10y$ and $T_\beta = 20y$, depends on 10 annual forward rates. Each one of these rates has a dynamics that needs to be discretized, usually by a discretization step of at least 4 steps a year (often many more if we were in a smile LMM with different dynamics), and simulated for 10 years until the maturity T_α. A reasonable number of scenarios used for the Monte Carlo is between 100,000 and 1,000,000, or even more. If you multiply these numbers by each other, you see that pricing swaptions with Monte Carlo involves a large number of operations and, however powerful your greed computers or even your GPUs, it cannot be performed instantaneously like pricing with a Black formula. This would not be a problem for just pricing or hedging: any trader is used to non-negligible computational times for this. The real issue is that traders would like to *calibrate* the model to swaptions, of which there are hundreds in the market, and calibration means putting the swaption pricing procedure inside an optimization algorithm, which usually requires dozens if not hundreds of iterations, and that needs to be repeated every time we want to use the model for pricing or hedging other derivatives with a freshly calibrated model. This is not really feasible, as was discovered by those who, in the early days of the LMM, tried this approach. So market practitioners started to look for alternative ways to price swaptions in the LMM.

6.2.4 Understanding and Deriving the Approximation

The first idea that suggested itself for how an alternative method could be derived came from the earliest attempts to Monte Carlo pricing of swaptions. A LMM Monte Carlo simulation to price a swaption with maturity T_α and length of the underlying swap equal to $T_\beta - T_\alpha$ generates N realizations of the value of the swap rate $S_{\alpha,\beta}$ at T_α according to LMM assumptions. With these realizations one can build a sort of 'empirical density', that might more correctly be called numerical density. One divides the space of the possible swap values in many small intervals, and then counts how many realizations fall into each of the buckets, so as to obtain a histogram representing the distribution of $S_{\alpha,\beta}(T_\alpha)$ according to the LMM simulation. This was done, for example by Brigo and Mercurio (2001), and their results are presented in Figure 6.2.

The distribution of the swap rate in the LMM according to the simulation is the saw-toothed line. But that is not the only line shown in the picture, there is actually another one, showing a lognormal distribution with the same volatility and mean as the LMM distribution. However, this lognormal density is not very visible because *the two distributions overlap almost perfectly*.

What is this chart telling us? That, although in principle, from a mathematical point of view, the assumptions of the LMM do not lead to a swap rate which is exactly lognormal, in practice the distribution of the swap rate in the LMM and a lognormal distribution are hardly distinguishable. This suggests that we could make a small error if we priced swaptions in the

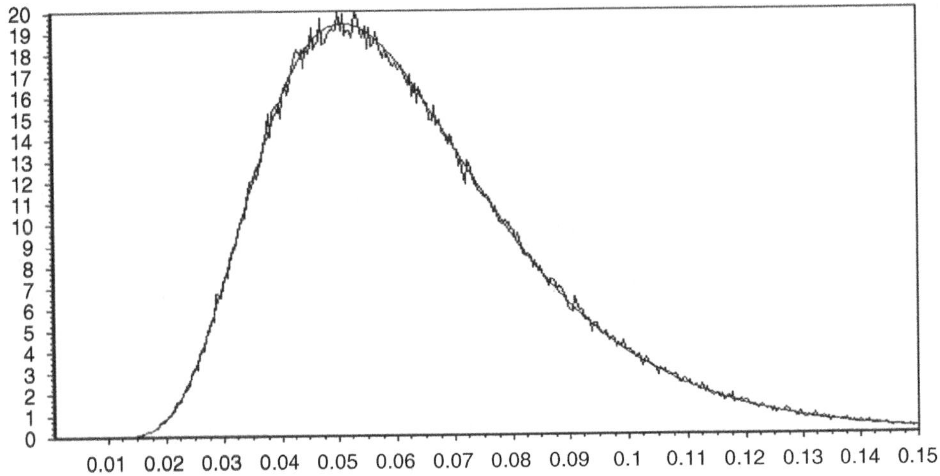

Figure 6.2 LMM swap rate density from simulation vs a lognormal density, from Brigo and Mercurio (2001)

LMM with the simplest possible formula: a Black formula, which we saw to be desirable for a number of reasons and which is based on assuming that the underlying swap rate is lognormal:

$$Swaption_t^{LMM} \approx \sum_{i=\alpha+1}^{\beta} P(t, T_i)\alpha_i\, Black\left(S_{\alpha,\beta}(t), K, \hat{V}_{\alpha,\beta}\right).$$

This would necessarily be an approximation, since we know that in the LMM the swap rate is not lognormal. But the chart of the numerical distribution gives us hope that the distribution is not so far off. To reach this approximation, we have to estimate the parameters of the lognormal distribution which is nearest to the LMM swap rate distribution. Equivalently, to use the terminology of Piterbarg (2007), we have to project the LMM distribution of the swap rate onto the space of the lognormal distributions, and use the parameters of this distribution in a Black formula. We already know from the no-arbitrage argument in (2.23) that when we price using a Black formula the underlying swap rate is a martingale, therefore the mean of the distribution is zero. We are left with the task of estimating the variance of this nearest lognormal distribution, which I have indicated by $\hat{V}$ in the above formula. Having a Black approximation for swaptions in the LMM amounts to estimating $\hat{V}$.

If we were modelling the swap rate as an exactly lognormal process, as in (6.10), this variance would just be the integral of the square of the volatility from now to T_α,

$$\int_t^{T_\alpha} \sigma_{\alpha,\beta}(t)^2\, dt.$$

But this property is typical of lognormal dynamics only. In fact lognormal dynamics is characterized by the fact that its *relative volatility*, which is the diffusion coefficient (namely the term that multiplies dW in a diffusion) divided by the underlying, is a deterministic parameter, and the integral of its square gives the variance of the underlying. For the other dynamics this does not work, and in fact there is no such parameter as the volatility $\sigma_{\alpha,\beta}(t)$ of the underlying.

For example, in the LMM we model the swap rate indirectly as a function of forward rates, and the only parameters are volatilities and correlations of forward rates.

Even if we do not have $\int_t^{T_\alpha} \sigma_{\alpha,\beta}(t)^2\, dt$, we can try and find the *nearest suitable quantity*. How to find this quantity was not established by some famous quants in a formal paper, but by market practitioners. Although the passages of this derivation were subsequently detailed by Jäckel and Rebonato (2000), they explain that the origin of the formula lies in a routine market procedure. As such, the derivation appears quite heuristic, as we see below.

The idea is to mimic the passages that in (6.10) would allow us to compute $\int_t^{T_\alpha} \sigma_{\alpha,\beta}(t)^2\, dt$ without using explicitly $\sigma_{\alpha,\beta}(t)$.

Approximation scheme

When we have a driftless lognormal dynamics

$$dX(t) = \nu(t) X(t)\, dW,$$

we can price an option on $X(T)$ by means of a Black formula with input

$$V^2 = \int_0^T \nu(t)^2\, dt.$$

This input can be obtained without using explicitly $\nu(t)$ by these three passages:

1. Divide the dynamics by the underlying
$$\frac{dX(t)}{X(t)} = \nu(t)\, dW.$$
2. Multiply the dynamics by itself
$$\frac{dX(t)\, dX(t)}{X(t)^2} = \nu(t)\nu(t)\, dW\, dW = \nu(t)^2\, dt,$$
where we have used the thumb rule of stochastic calculus saying that $dWdW = dt$, based on the fact that $dWdW$ is a random variable with expectation dt and negligible variance.
3. Now integrate
$$V^2 = \int_0^T \frac{dX(t)dX(t)}{X(t)^2} = \int_0^T \nu(t)^2\, dt.$$

These passages can be performed in any model. But are we sure that with these passages we find a quantity which is suitable for our purposes, namely one that can be used as an input in a Black formula? Not yet, because after performing 1) and 2) one can expect to find a deterministic number only when one really starts from a lognormal dynamics. Only in a lognormal model is the relative volatility deterministic. When the dynamics is different, we may find at 2) a stochastic relative volatility

$$\tilde{\nu}(t, X(t,\omega))^2\, dt.$$

This would not be suitable for our purposes, because it does not correspond to lognormal dynamics. Only if we now manage to approximate, with no big errors, this quantity with a deterministic quantity have we reached the approximation we were looking for.

Applying the scheme to swaptions

Let us see how this has been applied to the LMM and swaption case. It is clear that starting from the lognormal swap rate (6.10) the passages to perform are

$$\begin{aligned}&\int_0^{T_\alpha} \frac{dS_{\alpha,\beta}(t)\, dS_{\alpha,\beta}(t)}{S_{\alpha,\beta}(t)^2}\\ &= \int_0^{T_\alpha} \frac{S_{\alpha,\beta}(t)^2 \sigma_{\alpha,\beta}(t)^2 dt}{S_{\alpha,\beta}(t)^2}\\ &= \int_0^{T_\alpha} \sigma_{\alpha,\beta}(t)^2 dt. \end{aligned} \tag{6.12}$$

What, instead, is the dynamics of the swap rate in the LMM? In the LMM we just have

$$\begin{aligned} S_{\alpha,\beta}(t) &= \sum_{i=\alpha+1}^{\beta} w_i(t) F_i(t), \\ dF_i(t) &= drift + \sigma_i(t) F_i(t) dZ_i(t), \end{aligned} \tag{6.13}$$

thus the swap dynamics must be computed via Ito's Lemma. Then we have to mimic the passages in (6.12) and finally approximate the result with a deterministic number.

The market actually reversed this order, first making an approximation that strongly simplifies the following computations. You will recall from (6.11) that the weights $w_i(t)$ are stochastic and depend on the rates $F(t)$. These weights, however, are often deemed to be less volatile than $F(t)$'s themselves, for the heuristic observation that in the weights 'the rates $F(t)$ appear both at numerator and denominator, so part of the movements of the $F(t)$'s at the numerator cancels out with the movements of the $F(t)$'s at the denominator'. This is likely to reduce the volatility of the ratios. At the time the approximation was developed, at the end of the 1990s, this seemed confirmed by market observations. This inspired the idea of treating the weights as if they were deterministic, which means keeping them at the level observed at time 0 when the formula is computed, so that

$$\text{(First Freezing)} \quad S_{\alpha,\beta}(t) \cong \sum_{i=\alpha+1}^{\beta} w_i(0) F_i(t).$$

This is called a *freezing* in market jargon, and simplifies dramatically the computation of the dynamics of $S_{\alpha,\beta}(t)$ via Ito's Lemma, which becomes

$$dS_{\alpha,\beta}(t) \cong \sum_{i=\alpha+1}^{\beta} w_i(0)\, dF_i(t) = \sum_{i=\alpha+1}^{\beta} w_i(0)\, F_i(t) \sigma_i(t) dZ_i(t)$$

leading to (see Section 12.2.2 in the Appendix)

$$dS_{\alpha,\beta}(t)\, dS_{\alpha,\beta}(t) \cong \sum_{i=\alpha+1}^{\beta} \sum_{j=\alpha+1}^{\beta} w_i(0) w_j(0) F_i(t) F_j(t) \rho_{i,j} \sigma_i(t) \sigma_j(t)\, dt,$$

and then to

$$\frac{dS_{\alpha,\beta}(t)dS_{\alpha,\beta}(t)}{S_{\alpha,\beta}(t)^2} \cong \sum_{i=\alpha+1}^{\beta}\sum_{j=\alpha+1}^{\beta} \frac{w_i(0)w_j(0)F_i(t)F_j(t)\rho_{i,j}\sigma_i(t)\sigma_j(t)}{\left(\sum_{i=\alpha+1}^{\beta} w_i(0)\, F_i(t)\right)^2} dt.$$

We have performed step 1 and step 2 of the above approximation scheme, and we can now look at the result. In spite of (First Freezing), we still have a stochastic quantity. In fact, it depends on the rates $F(t)$ which are stochastic, and when we then integrate to apply step 3 we would be integrating over the future unknown behaviour of these rates. Thus at this point the heuristic principle we have seen above is applied again: in the terms of the above double summation, 'the rates $F(t)$ appear both at numerator and denominator, so part of the movements of the $F(t)$'s at the numerator cancels out with the movements of the $F(t)$'s at the denominator', and this consideration justified the conclusion that these rates had a reduced impact on the total volatility. This leads to the following

$$\text{(Second Freezing)} \frac{dS_{\alpha,\beta}(t)dS_{\alpha,\beta}(t)}{S_{\alpha,\beta}(t)^2} \cong \sum_{i=\alpha+1}^{\beta}\sum_{j=\alpha+1}^{\beta} \frac{w_i(0)w_j(0)F_i(0)F_j(0)\rho_{i,j}\sigma_i(t)\sigma_j(t)}{\left(\sum_{i=\alpha+1}^{\beta} w_i(0)\, F_i(0)\right)^2} dt.$$

In the end the LMM variance for swaptions is

$$\boxed{\sum_{i=\alpha+1}^{\beta}\sum_{j=\alpha+1}^{\beta} \frac{w_i(0)w_j(0)F_i(0)F_j(0)\rho_{i,j}}{S_{\alpha,\beta}(0)^2} \int_0^{T_\alpha} \sigma_i(t)\sigma_j(t)\,dt =: \hat{V}_{\alpha,\beta}.} \tag{6.14}$$

Thus in the market practice swaptions are quoted as

$$Swaption_t = \sum_{i=\alpha+1}^{\beta} P(t,T_i)\alpha_i Black\left(S_{\alpha,\beta}(t), K, \sigma_{\alpha,\beta}^2 T_\alpha\right)$$

while in a Libor Market Model, where Libor rates are the modelling variables, we have the following approximation

$$Swaption_t \approx \sum_{i=\alpha+1}^{\beta} P(t,T_i)\alpha_i Black\left(S_{\alpha,\beta}(t), K,\ \hat{V}_{\alpha,\beta}\right). \tag{6.15}$$

Can we accept an approximation based on such intuitive motivations with no further testing or monitoring? Of course not. This is the topic of the next section.

6.2.5 Testing the Approximation

How can we check if the above approximation is sufficiently precise? Let us consider the problem of testing a valuation method in general, using the above case as a specific example.

The goal

The first point is that when a decision has been taken on the modelling assumptions we want to make, we would like these assumptions to be used consistently in all valuations we perform. It is not difficult to understand why we need this consistency. For example, in the LMM above we have assumed that forward rates are lognormal. This is not necessarily a good assumption. What matters now is that if we use the lognormal assumption in one part of our valuation, we also need to use it elsewhere. For example, if we have consistently used the lognormality assumption to calibrate exactly to the market prices of ATM caps, then we must price derivatives with consistent computational methods, otherwise we will be pricing with a model different from the one which is really calibrated to the market.

The problems

Second, we have to understand why we can experience difficulties in guaranteeing the above consistency. The reason is that models do not have exact analytic methods to evaluate all payoffs. Therefore for pricing we have to resort to methods which are not exact or not analytic.

The non-exact analytic methods are what we call analytic approximations, and clearly they give rise to problems in getting consistency with the initial assumptions because they are obtained by introducing simplifications, and therefore errors, to the exact consequences of the initial assumptions.

The non-analytic, or numerical, methods are either Monte Carlo simulation or finite-difference methods (trees) or numerical integration. These methods are also by definition not exact. At the end of this chapter we will give two examples of conditions in which such methods can go seriously wrong, but these are special cases. Usually there are standard techniques to obtain very precise results from these methods.[2] Approximations, on the other hand, all differ from each other, therefore our practical examples focus on them.

When we have to price a product, we look first for an exact analytic method. Where this is not available, the first choice is usually a numerical method. Numerical methods, however are computationally lengthy and somehow noisy. This rules them out for many pricing problems. In the example on swaptions they are excluded because swaptions need to be included in calibration and this requires particular speed.

Testing approximations and testing numerical methods

In general, any non-exact method for valuation is tested by comparison with some alternative method which we expect to be more precise. Numerical methods are usually tested on some simplified problem, in terms of model parameters or in terms of payoff, where exact analytic methods are also available. The numerical method optimized through this comparison can then be used with general model parameters and payoffs for which exact analytic methods are not available.

When instead we use an approximation, analytic but non-exact, the approach to testing may be different. Analytic approximations are usually applied to simple products, so it is more difficult to test them against exact methods on even simpler payoffs. The above swaption approximation, for example, could not be tested on a caplet (which is sort of elementary swaption), because on a caplet the approximation would collapse to the exact method, without this meaning that the approximation is good for general swaptions. At times it is possible to perform a test by simplifying the model, setting some parameters to special values. We will test the SABR analytic approximation in this way in Section 6.4, but this will work as a method

[2] Some valuation methods that, strictly, should be considered not analytic and not exact are in fact so fast and precise that everyone treats them as analytic and exact. Most notably, the Black and Scholes formula involves a numerical integration for the computation of the Gaussian probability distribution. In spite of this it is considered the analytic formula *par excellence*.

to point out where the formula is not working, and not to validate the formula in general. In fact, the quality of approximations changes considerably with the value of parameters, and a test on special values gives little guarantee for different values. Therefore numerical methods are most often used to test an analytic approximation.

In the example of the above approximation (6.15), we can make comparison with Monte Carlo simulation. Monte Carlo is not an exact method, but if we make it sufficiently precise it can be very useful for testing.

There are two main errors in the way Monte Carlo is used for LMM: the *discretization error* and the *simulation error* in the strict sense of the word, associated with the fact that Monte Carlo pricing is just an estimate based on a finite number of realizations. The latter can be evaluated and controlled precisely by making use of the Monte Carlo confidence interval or error windows, as we will see. The discretization error is more tricky, and must be considered separately. Do we expect the discretization error in the LMM Monte Carlo to be lower or higher than the error we make in the analytic approximation (6.17)? The error in the analytic approximation is associated with freezing: the underlying stochastic variables that appear in the dynamics (6.13) are kept at their 0 value until maturity T_α. The discretization in the Monte Carlo is a freezing error too, in some sense: the underlying stochastic variables are kept at their t value from $t + \Delta t$, although they would have a continuous stochastic dynamics in the exact model. However, in Monte Carlo they are updated every Δt, so the simulation step is shorter than the maturity and we expect the Monte Carlo error to be smaller than the error in the approximation.

Thus, Monte Carlo appears a good test for our approximation. The test requires a computational time that would be unacceptable if it had to be repeated every time the approximation is used; in fact, the low speed of Monte Carlo is the reason why we found an alternative method. But we don't need to perform it every time. We have to perform it when we first introduce the approximation, and then we have to repeat it periodically or when quantitative indicators show that certain relevant market conditions have changed and the formula needs retesting. We see this in practice for the above approximation.

The setting of tests against Monte Carlo simulation

The tests of an analytic approximation against a Monte Carlo price make clever use of the fact that, due to the simulation error, Monte Carlo price is never a single price but a range of prices. The Monte Carlo price $\hat{\Pi}^{MC}$ of a payoff Π is computed, based on the N simulated paths, as an average

$$\hat{\Pi}^{MC} = \sum_{j=1}^{N} \Pi^j / N,$$

where Π^j is the realization of the payoff Π in scenario j. We can consider the Π^j as independent and identically distributed random variables, since they are independent draws from the model distribution of Π. Thus the Monte Carlo price is a *sample mean* with a distribution with average equal to the exact model price of the payoff, $\mathbb{E}[\Pi]$, and a standard deviation which is

$$\frac{Std(\Pi)}{\sqrt{N}},$$

the standard deviation of the payoff divided by the number of draws, which in this case are scenarios. By the Central Limit Theorem, when N is very large, we have

$$\frac{\sum_{j=1}^{N} \Pi^j/N - \mathbb{E}[\Pi]}{Std(\Pi)/\sqrt{N}} \sim \mathbb{N}(0, 1).$$

Notice that N can really be very large in Monte Carlo simulations, larger than it is for historical estimations, for example. From the above formula, it follows that

$$\Pr\left\{\left|\frac{\sum_{j=1}^{N} \Pi^j}{N} - \mathbb{E}[\Pi]\right| < \epsilon\right\} = \Pr\left\{|\mathbb{N}(0, 1)| < \epsilon \frac{\sqrt{N}}{Std(\Pi)}\right\}.$$

This gives us the probability that our Monte Carlo estimate $\sum_{j=1}^{N} \Pi^j/N$ is not farther than ϵ from the true expectation $\mathbb{E}[\Pi(T)]$ we wish to estimate. One sets a desired value for this probability, say 0.98, and by solving

$$2\Phi\left(\epsilon \frac{\sqrt{N}}{Std(\Pi)}\right) - 1 = 0.98,$$

one gets

$$\epsilon = 2.33 \frac{Std(\Pi)}{\sqrt{N}}.$$

This means that the exact price $\mathbb{E}[\Pi(T)]$ is inside the 'window'

$$\left[\hat{\Pi}^{MC} - 2.33 \frac{Std(\Pi)}{\sqrt{N}}, \quad \hat{\Pi}^{MC} + 2.33 \frac{Std(\Pi)}{\sqrt{N}}\right]$$

with a 98% probability. This window is sometimes called a 98% confidence interval. We can see that, all things being equal, as N increases, the window shrinks as $1/\sqrt{N}$.

The true standard deviation $Std(\Pi)$ of the payoff is usually unknown. This is replaced by the known sample standard deviation obtained by the simulated paths

$$(\widehat{Std}(\Pi; N))^2 := \sum_{j=1}^{N} (\Pi^j)^2/N - \left(\sum_{j=1}^{N} \Pi^j/N\right)^2$$

and the actual 98% Monte Carlo window we compute is

$$\left[\hat{\Pi}^{MC} - 2.33 \frac{\widehat{Std}(\Pi; N)}{\sqrt{N}}, \quad \hat{\Pi}^{MC} + 2.33 \frac{\widehat{Std}(\Pi; N)}{\sqrt{N}}\right].$$

To obtain a 95% (narrower) window it is sufficient to replace 2.33 by 1.96, and to obtain a (still narrower) 90% window it is sufficient to replace 2.33 by 1.65. All other sizes may be derived by the Φ tables.

When we have to test an analytic approximation against Monte Carlo, we want to keep the confidence probability high, usually 98%. Then we also want to keep the window narrow, in particular we want the window to be smaller than the bid-ask spread that we observe in the market (or that we estimate if we are pricing a non-quoted product). This means increasing N

until $\hat{N}$ for which

$$\frac{\widehat{Std}(\Pi;\hat{N})}{\sqrt{\hat{N}}}2.33 < \frac{Ask - Bid}{2}.$$

Then we price the same payoff Π with the analytic approximation, which yields a price $\hat{\Pi}^{AA}$. If

$$\underbrace{\hat{\Pi}^{MC} - 2.33\frac{\widehat{Std}(\Pi;N)}{\sqrt{N}}}_{\text{MC inf}} \leq \hat{\Pi}^{AA} \leq \underbrace{\hat{\Pi}^{MC} + 2.33\frac{\widehat{Std}(\Pi;N)}{\sqrt{N}}}_{\text{MC sup}},$$

then *the approximation price is indistinguishable from the Monte Carlo price* both from a statistical point of view, since it is inside the Monte Carlo window computed with a high confidence probability, and from a financial point of view, since their difference is smaller than the price range that we see in the market. The difference between the two prices is smaller than both the statistical uncertainty we have on the Monte Carlo price and the financial uncertainty that we have on market prices. Thus, if the Monte Carlo price is considered a viable valuation method, the approximation must also be considered valid, and will be the method of choice when required by computational constraints.

The results

As an example, we can look at the tests of this kind that were made on (6.14) in Brigo and Morini (2003). Similar tests are also to be found in Brigo and Mercurio (2001) and Jäckel and Rebonato (2000). In particular, since the output of (6.14) is an implied volatility to be put in the Black formula, the procedure first involved the inversion of the Black formula (6.8) to find the implied volatilities corresponding to $\hat{\Pi}^{MC}$ and $\hat{\Pi}^{MC} \pm 2.33\,\frac{\widehat{Std}(\Pi;N)}{\sqrt{N}}$, transforming our price window into a volatility window. The volatility window is smaller than the usual bid-ask spread on the liquid swaptions (close-to-the-money, with maturities and tenors of few years), often estimated around 30bps (see Mercurio and Morini (2009a) and Fan, Gupta and Ritchken (2007)).

The tests were performed for different swaptions and under different market conditions, and are indicated by swaption maturity (T_α) $\times$ length ($T_\beta - T_\alpha$) in years. The rank of the correlation matrix ρ used is also indicated. The role of the rank in the LMM is well explained in Brigo and Morini (2006), and is mentioned again in Chapter 8. For the time being, keep in mind the following facts. When rank is 1, the correlations all collapse to their maximum value 1. When correlation is 0 for all rates, rank has its maximum value M. This gives a rough intuition: low-rank correlations are 'higher' than high-rank correlations.

We can divide these results into four groups, which are shown separately in the tables below.

A) In the first tests Libor volatilities come from calibrations to market conditions which were ordinary in 2002–2003.

One could halt the test of the approximation here, if the approximation had only to be used for a very short period of time. This is almost never the case – use of the approximation continues even in times when market conditions may be significantly different. Therefore these tests also have to be performed under stressed market conditions in order to anticipate when this approximation will need to be revised. This is done in tests B, C and D.

B) Here a single swaption is considered, 6×7, and rank is 10. The approximation is also tested in case of stressed values for the input σ volatilities. 'Cal. vol's' stands for calibrated volatilities. Then the calibrated volatilities σ_k, which range from around 10% to around 15%, are increased by $20\% = 0.2$ and the test is repeated.

C) The same as for B), but with a 10×10 swaption, with historically estimated correlation at full rank 19.

D) Here the stress test relates to the input forward rates, which are all increased by $2\% = 0.02$.

I have highlighted the failures with a rectangle around those approximated volatilities that do not fall inside the Monte Carlo window.

A) Tests under normal market conditions			
	MC inf	MC sup	Approx.
5 × 6 rank 2	0.10811	0.10911	0.10900
5 × 6 rank 5	0.10832	0.10933	0.10900
10 × 10 rank 2	0.09753	0.09841	0.09800
10 × 10 rank 7	0.09558	0.09643	0.09600
B) Tests under stressed volatility (6x7, rank 10)			
	MC inf	MC sup	Approx.
Cal. vol's	0.104131	0.105085	0.105000
Cal. vol's +0.2	0.285133	0.288272	[0.289777]
C) Tests under stressed volatility (10x10, rank 19)			
	MC inf	MC sup	Approx.
Cal. vol's	0.094512	0.095363	0.095000
Cal. vol's +0.2	0.272064	0.274788	[0.277094]
D) Tests under stressed initial forward rates			
	MC inf	MC sup	Approx.
5 × 6 rank 2	0.10844	0.10941	0.10914
10 × 10 rank 19	0.09730	0.09813	0.09805

Analysis of the results

Results of tests conducted under ordinary market conditions show that the formula is accurate when compared to Monte Carlo pricing. Obviously, those shown here are just a few of the available tests. The more tests performed, the better. But notice that if you perform, for example, 100 tests you should not expect 100 successes, not even if the formula was exact: *in fact, for the Monte Carlo we are considering a 98% confidence interval.*

In test B), on the other hand, with a swaption with average maturity and length and intermediate rank of ρ, the approximated formula still works well with calibrated volatility. However, when we consider a stressed volatility the formula result falls outside the Monte Carlo window, showing a loss of accuracy, which is even more evident in test C) where we have full rank coupled with a 'far' and 'long' swaption.

We have detected a crucial market condition in relation to the working of the formula: it loses accuracy when the variance of the underlying swap rate increases. We get an increase of the variance whenever the volatilities of forward rates σ_k get higher, and also when the maturity T gets longer, increasing the integrated volatility $\int_0^T \sigma_k^2(t)dt$. This result confirms the intuition about the above approximation, computed by *freezing*, namely treating some objects that have non null variance, as if they had no variance. When the volatility is actually relatively

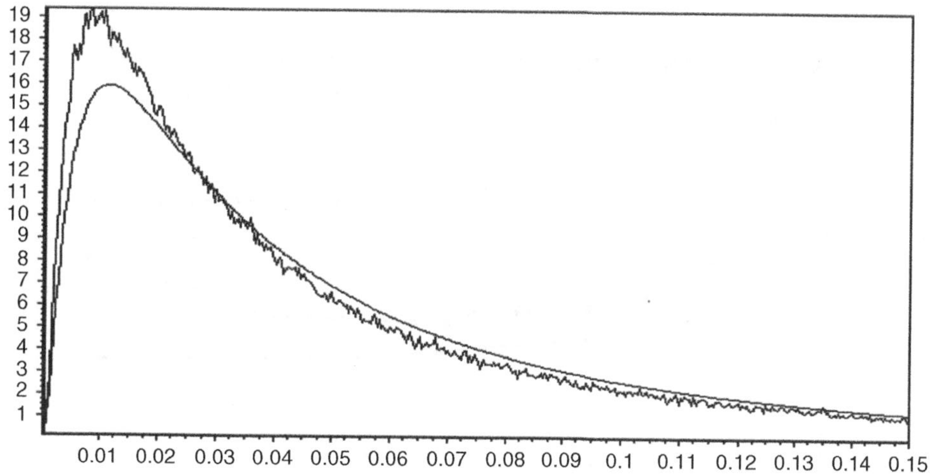

Figure 6.3 LMM swap rate from simulation vs a lognormal density (stress case), from Brigo and Mercurio (2001)

low, this approximation is reasonable when it gets higher; it starts losing accuracy. This gives us a quantitative indicator to monitor in order to understand when the formula needs revision.

These results can be visually confirmed comparing the LMM numerical distribution of a swap rate with a lognormal distribution where the volatility has been stressed as above, as carried out by Brigo and Mercurio (2001) in a test illustrated in Figure 6.3.

Note that the two distributions are no longer as similar as we observed them to be when using non-stressed parameters.

The market evidence

When these results, and similar results obtained by other researchers, were made public in the first years after 2000, they were interpreted by concluding that the formula (6.14) was fully reliable, since it seemed highly unlikely that volatility could increase by as much as 20%. Brigo and Mercurio (2001) call these volatilities 'pathological'. Yet with the credit crunch the market entered a truly pathological state and stayed there for years. In Figure 6.4 you can compare a plot of non-stressed volatilities σ_k of forward rates as calibrated to the market for the period of the Brigo and Morini (2003) tests; these volatilities stressed by increasing them by 20% as in above 2003 test; and, finally, volatilities from a calibration performed in 2009. You can see that in the short term market volatilities reached the levels we considered exhibited pathological stress in 2003. And in the long end the old stressed data and the more recent market data are worryingly close.

This shows that it was certainly not a waste of time to test the formula under stressed conditions, and that the levels considered in 2003 for the stresses were not excessive. Comparison of the 2003 tests with the 2009 data acts as a warning against continuing to use this formula, under 2009 conditions, with as much confidence as in the past. The old tests show that we have now reached a market condition critical for the performances of this formula. More robust approximations must be looked for, and if they cannot be found the precision of the old formula must now be monitored closely and its use minimized, with greater reliance

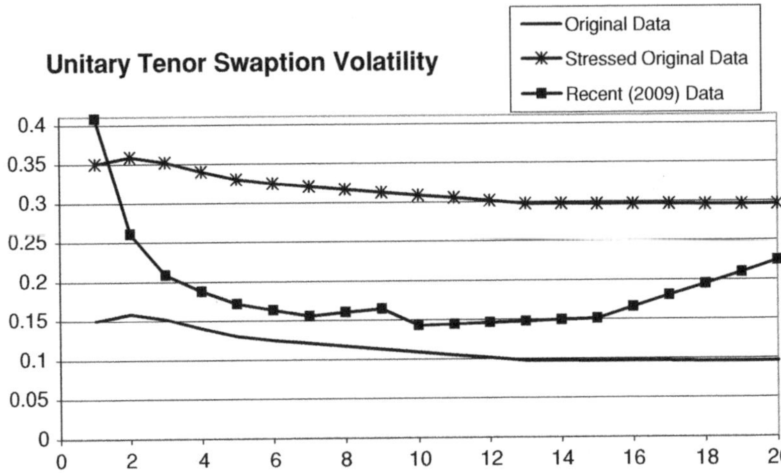

Figure 6.4 Volatilities of annual forward rates. The lowest line is obtained by calibration in the period of the 2003 test. The line with stars indicates the latter volatilities stressed by 20%, as in the 2003 test. The line with squares is obtained by calibration in January 2009

being placed instead on Monte Carlo simulation. If none of the above works, and we must go on using the same formula, we should consider setting up a model reserve based on the difference between the formula and the Monte Carlo results.

The favoured solution is to find an alternative formula. In this case a good candidate is the formula in Hull and White (1999), which is derived as (6.14), but it avoids the approximation that we have called (First Freezing); in fact, in computing the swap rate dynamics it takes precisely into account that the weights $w_i(t)$ are functions of the rates, and is essentially based only on the last approximation that we called (Second Freezing).

Exercise

I leave the reader with two problems to think about:

1. Considering the results of the tests above, and looking with precision at the parameters used in the tests, can you spot another element, different from maturity or volatility, that may have affected the results, and in particular the failures of the approximation? The answer is at the end of Section 6.3.
2. Considering the revolution in the patterns of interest rate products that we have seen in Chapter 4, do you think there are additional post credit crunch elements that could affect the efficiency of the swaption approximation? Think in particular about the validity of (6.11), which is the foundation of the swaption approximation. The answer is (quite hidden!) in Sections 11.3 and 11.4.

6.3 APPROXIMATIONS FOR CMS AND THE SHAPE OF THE TERM STRUCTURE

In this section we derive and then test the approximation commonly used in the market for an interest rate product that has been very liquid in the past years, with a peak around 2006. We speak of constant maturity swaps (CMS). They are often included in the calibration of interest rate models, since there are various more complex derivatives which are based on them, such as CMS spread options, and because they give invaluable information on the market-implied distribution of swap rates, as we will see in Section 7.1.

The complication in the pricing of CMS is the computation of *convexity adjustment*, defined below. These convexity adjustments are usually computed in the market with a formula that was developed by market practitioners, and then explained rigorously and improved by Hagan (2003). To the best of our knowledge, however, the formula has never been tested. Thus in the following we explain how CMS work, we derive the market formula, and then we test it against Monte Carlo following the approach explained in 6.2.5, trying to understand which conditions can impair its precision. To make the testing even more relevant, we compare it with an alternative approximation for convexity adjustments that can be derived from the Libor market model. Since the two approximations are very different from each other, we will see that the conditions that can impair their precision are also different.

6.3.1 The CMS Payoff

Constant maturity swaps are contracts in which two flows of payments, or legs, are exchanged. One of the two legs, which we call the CMS leg, pays at regular dates T_i

$$T_1, \ldots, T_n \text{ with } T_i - T_{i-1} = \delta$$

the swap rates $S_{i,i+c}(T_i)$, where $S_{i,i+c}$ is the equilibrium rate of a swap with length c having the following reset and payment dates

$$\underbrace{\bar{T}_i = T_i}_{\text{First Reset}}, \bar{T}_{i+1}, \bar{T}_{i+2}, \ldots, \underbrace{\bar{T}_{i+c}}_{\text{Last Payment}} \quad \text{with } \bar{T}_j - \bar{T}_{j-1} = \alpha,$$

so that the swap resets first at the moment T_i when it is paid in the CMS. This CMS is called *set in arrears*.

A typical CMS leg may pay every 3 months (δ equal to three months) the swap rates with length 5 years (c equal to 5 years) and annual frequency (α equal to 1 year). What complicates the representation of this derivative is that two sets of payment times are involved: the dates of payment of the CMS (T_i) and the dates of payment defining the swap rates ($\bar{T}_i$), two sets that can be very different from each other.

The other leg is a standard floating leg that pays Libor rates $F_i(t)$ plus a spread X. In the price of this contract the standard floating leg can be evaluated through replication as we did for plain-vanilla swaps, while the CMS leg is evaluated making use of the concept of *convexity adjustment* $\mathbf{CA}^{i,i+c}$:

$$\mathbb{E}\left[\sum_{i=0}^{n-1} D(0,T_i)(S_{i,i+c}(T_i) - F_i(T_{i-1}) - X)\delta\right] \tag{6.16}$$

$$= \sum_{i=0}^{n-1} P(0,T_i)\underbrace{\left[S_{i,i+c}(0) + \mathbf{CA}^{i,i+c}\right]}_{\textit{Current forward + adjustment}}\delta - (1 - P(0,T_{n-1})) - X\sum_{i=0}^{n-1} P(0,T_i)\delta.$$

How can we compute **CA**? First of all we need to understand what CA actually replaces. What we have learned about change of numeraire in the Appendix turns out very useful here.

6.3.2 Understanding Convexity Adjustments

Notice that the payment at T_i is multiplied by a stochastic discount factor $D(0, T_i)$, which we can eliminate by changing to the T_i-forward measure, so that we can write the price as

$$\begin{aligned}
&\mathbb{E}\left[\sum_{i=0}^{n-1} D(0,T_i)(S_{i,i+c}(T_i) - F_i(T_{i-1}) - X_{n,c})\delta\right] \\
&= \sum_{i=0}^{n-1} P(0,T_i)\left(\mathbb{E}^{T_i}\left[S_{i,i+c}(T_i)\right] - \mathbb{E}^{T_i}\left[F_i(T_{i-1})\right] - \mathbb{E}^{T_i}\left[X_{n,c}\right]\right)\delta \\
&= \sum_{i=0}^{n-1} P(0,T_i)\left(\mathbb{E}^{T_i}\left[S_{i,i+c}(T_i)\right] - F_i(0) - X_{n,c}\right)\delta.
\end{aligned}$$

The difficulty is to compute $\mathbb{E}^{T_i}\left[S_{i,i+c}(T_i)\right]$. It is not a problem to compute $\mathbb{E}^{T_i}\left[F_i(T_{i-1})\right]$ since we know that $F_i(t)$ is a martingale under Q^i: Q^i is the *natural pricing measure* for $F_i(t)$, in the sense that the expectation is just the current value of the forward. This does not happen for the swap rate, the forward measure is not its natural measure, the swap rate is a martingale only when we price under the swap measure. This is what makes the CMS non trivial to price: the rates which are paid are paid in a way that is not natural.

Swap rates naturally arise as equilibrium rates of standard swaps and not as payments at T_i. We can understand this by noticing that there is no replication for the payment of $S_{i,i+c}(T_i)$ at T_i (this is actually what the market noticed), or by change of numeraire, noticing that the expectation of a swap rate under a forward measure is *not* the current value of the swap rate. However in this case the market also decided to start from the current value of the rate, but understood that this was not exact and an adjustment was needed, the convexity adjustment. So the convexity adjustment is a way to express a change of measure, and the market approximation is necessarily rough since it has been around for quite a while before the concept of change of numeraire had been fully understood even by academics. With our knowledge of this formalism we can write

$$\begin{aligned}
\mathbb{E}^{T_i}\left[S_{i,i+c}(T_i)\right] &= S_{i,i+c}(0) + \mathbf{CA}^{i,i+c}, \\
\mathbf{CA}^{i,i+c} &= \mathbb{E}^{T_i}\left[S_{i,i+c}(T_i)\right] - S_{i,i+c}(0), \\
\mathbf{CA}^{i,i+c} &= \mathbb{E}^{T_i}\left[S_{i,i+c}(T_i)\right] - \mathbb{E}^{i,i+c}\left[S_{i,i+c}(T_i)\right]
\end{aligned}$$

where $\mathbb{E}^{i,i+c}$ is, as we know, the expectation under the swap measure $Q^{i,i+c}$, associated with the annuity numeraire $A(t) = \sum_{j=i+1}^{i+c} P(t,\bar{T}_j)\alpha$. Under this measure the swap rate is a martingale.

How to compute $\mathbf{CA}^{i,i+c}$? To obtain the market approximation in a rigorous way, following Hagan (2003), we move also the Q^{T_i} expectation to the second measure using 12.18,

$$\mathbb{E}^{T_i}\left[S_{i,i+c}(T_i)\right] = \mathbb{E}^{i,i+c}\left[S_{i,i+c}(T_i)\frac{P(T_i,T_i)/A(T_i)}{P(0,T_i)/A(0)}\right].$$

The quantity $A(T_i)$ depends on the entire evolution of the yield curve, which does not make it easy to compute its expectation. First, let us call

$$G_t = P(t,T_i)/A(t).$$

Remark 14. ***Convexity Adjustments as Covariances***. *Just a short digression to understand better the financial meaning of convexity adjustments. Notice that G_t is a martingale under $Q^{i,i+c}$, so that*

$$\begin{aligned}\mathbf{CA}^{i,i+c} &= \mathbb{E}^{T_i}\left[S_{i,i+c}(T_i)\right] - \mathbb{E}^{i,i+c}\left[S_{i,i+c}(T_i)\right] \\ &= \mathbb{E}^{i,i+c}\left[S_{i,i+c}(T_i)\frac{G_{T_i}}{G_0} - S_{i,i+c}(T_i)\right] \\ &= \mathbb{E}^{i,i+c}\left[S_{i,i+c}(T_i)\left(\frac{G_{T_i}}{G_0} - 1\right)\right],\end{aligned}$$

where $\left(\frac{G_{T_i}}{G_0} - 1\right)$ has zero mean. So we can write

$$\begin{aligned}\mathbf{CA} &= \frac{1}{G_0}\left\{\mathbb{E}^{i,i+c}\left[S_{i,i+c}(T_i)G_{T_i}\right] - G_0 S_{i,i+c}(0)\right\} \\ &= \frac{1}{G_0} Cov\left(S_{i,i+c}(T_i), G_{T_i}\right),\end{aligned}$$

where Cov *stands for* covariance. *What we want to compute is simply a covariance/correlation between a numeraire/discount-bond ratio and the underlying rate. This is not relevant for the next computation, but it can help your intuition (it helped mine). In fact, we can roughly say that what creates all these issues about change of measure in interest rate derivatives is simply the correlation between the underlying and the discount factors. Again roughly, we can say that without correlation we could just separate expectation of the swap and expectation of the discount ratio, with no change of measure involved. Since in the above approach (6.16) we do something similar even when there is correlation, it is intuitive that the correction we have to add depends on correlation/covariance.*

6.3.3 The Market Approximation for Convexity Adjustments

Let us return to our main problem: how do we compute

$$CA^{i,i+c} = \mathbb{E}^{i,i+c}\left[S_{i,i+c}(T_i)\left(\frac{G_{T_i}}{G_0} - 1\right)\right]$$

in closed form? The market looked for a simple approximation, and set out to compute it with two desiderata

1. we would like to express approximately G_{T_i} as a function of $S_{i,i+c}(T_i)$, such that then we have to compute the expectation of a function of a martingale. Basically we are looking for approximation of $P(t, T_i)/\sum_{j=i+1}^{i+c} P(t, \bar{T}_j)\alpha$ as a function of one single swap rate.
2. we would like this function to be easy, so that it's easy to compute its expectation.

Let us start from problem 1), namely finding an expression for G_{T_i} in terms of the swap rate,

$$G_t \approx g\left(S_{i,i+c}(t)\right).$$

How can we express bond prices/discount factors of different maturities with one single swap rate? One idea is to use at t the forward swap rate $S_{i,i+c}(t)$ as a constant, flat rate for discounting all payments in the period spanned by the underlying swap. This makes some sense, because a swap rate $S_{i,i+c}(t)$ is really a sort of average of the forward rates from $T_i = \bar{T}_i$ to $\bar{T}_{i+c}$. So for the period from $\bar{T}_i$ to $\bar{T}_{i+c}$ we set $S_{i,i+c}(T_i) = S$ and perform discounting with the factor $\frac{1}{(1+S\alpha)}$, to be applied to all periods of length α. This way, using standard bond mathematics,

$$\begin{aligned} A(t) &= \sum_{j=i+1}^{i+c} P(t, \bar{T}_j)\alpha \qquad [1^{st} \text{ Approx.}] \\ &\approx P(t, T_i) \sum_{j=1}^{c} \frac{\alpha}{(1+S\alpha)^j} \\ &= P(t, T_i) \frac{\alpha}{(1+S\alpha)} \left(\frac{1 - \frac{1}{(1+S\alpha)^c}}{1 - \frac{1}{(1+S\alpha)}} \right) \\ &= P(t, T_i) \frac{1}{S} \left(1 - \frac{1}{(1+S\alpha)^c} \right). \end{aligned}$$

where we have used the elementary school formula for the sum of the first terms of a series in geometric progression. Now we have the approximation $g\left(S_{i,i+c}(t)\right)$ we were looking for

$$G_{T_i} \approx g\left(S_{i,i+c}(T_i)\right) = \frac{P(t, T_i)}{P(t, T_i)\frac{1}{S}\left(1 - \frac{1}{(1+S\alpha)^c}\right)} = \frac{S_{i,i+c}(0)}{\left(1 - \frac{1}{(1+S_{i,i+c}(0)\alpha)^c}\right)}.$$

Notice something that will be useful later on for understanding the strong and the weak points of the market formula for convexity adjustments: apart from the use of continuous compounding, this first approximation involves two main simplifications:

- the curve is always assumed to be flat;
- as a consequence, we have perfect correlation between rates (forward rates) of different maturities (only parallel movements of the term structure).

We have solved point 1, namely we have found a function $g\left(S_{i,i+c}(t)\right)$. In what follows we continue the computation of an analytic formula for convexity adjustments making different approximations, in particular we perform a first order expansion of g and use the lognormality assumption. The approximations that follow and the lognormality assumption can be avoided, as they are in the most advanced formulas for convexity adjustments used in the market (see, for example, Berrahoui (2005) and the computations in Section 7.1). But the above approximation, where the term structure is assumed to be flat, is used in all market formulas. That is what we want to test.

Now we can tackle the second goal, simplifying g. The simplest way is a first order expansion, which turns any function in to a linear one,

$$\begin{aligned} g(S_t) &\approx g(S_0) + g'(S_0)(S_t - S_0), \qquad [2^{nd} \text{ Approx.}] \\ \frac{g(S_t)}{g(S_0)} - 1 &\approx \frac{g'(S_0)}{g(S_0)}(S_t - S_0), \end{aligned}$$

so that

$$\begin{aligned}\mathbf{CA}^{i,i+c} &= \mathbb{E}^{i,i+c}\left[S_{i,i+c}(T_i)\left(\frac{G_{T_i}}{G_0}-1\right)\right]\\ &\approx \mathbb{E}^{i,i+c}\left[S_{i,i+c}(T_i)\frac{g'\left(S_{i,i+c}(0)\right)}{g\left(S_{i,i+c}(0)\right)}\left(S_{i,i+c}(T_i)-S_{i,i+c}(0)\right)\right]\\ &= \frac{g'\left(S_{i,i+c}(0)\right)}{g\left(S_{i,i+c}(0)\right)}\mathbb{E}^{i,i+c}\left[\left(S_{i,i+c}(T_i)^2-S_{i,i+c}(T_i)S_{i,i+c}(0)\right)\right]\\ &= \frac{g'\left(S_{i,i+c}(0)\right)}{g\left(S_{i,i+c}(0)\right)}\mathbb{E}^{i,i+c}\left[\left(S_{i,i+c}(T_i)^2-S_{i,i+c}(0)^2\right)\right]\\ &= S_{i,i+c}(0)^2\frac{g'\left(S_{i,i+c}(0)\right)}{g\left(S_{i,i+c}(0)\right)}\mathbb{E}^{i,i+c}\left[\frac{S_{i,i+c}(T_i)^2}{S_{i,i+c}(0)^2}-1\right].\end{aligned}$$

Since

$$\begin{aligned}\frac{g'\left(S_{i,i+c}(0)\right)}{g\left(S_{i,i+c}(0)\right)} &= \frac{1}{S_{i,i+c}(0)}\left(1-\frac{S_{i,i+c}(0)\,\alpha}{1+S_{i,i+c}(0)\,\alpha}\right)\frac{c}{\left(1+S_{i,i+c}(0)\,\alpha\right)^c-1}\\ &=: \frac{1}{S_{i,i+c}(0)}\Psi\left(S_{i,i+c}(0),\alpha,c\right)\end{aligned}$$

the adjustment is

$$\mathbf{CA}^{i,i+c} \approx S_{i,i+c}(0)\Psi\left(S_{i,i+c}(0),\alpha,c\right)\mathbb{E}^{i,i+c}\left[\frac{S_{i,i+c}(T_i)^2}{S_{i,i+c}(0)^2}-1\right] \tag{6.17}$$

Notice that the only quantity which is model dependent is $\mathbb{E}^{i,i+c}\left[S_{i,i+c}(T_i)^2\right]$, the second moment of the distribution of the swap measure under the natural measure where the swap rate is a martingale. If we are in a world without smile, where

$$dS_{i,i+c}(t) = \sigma_{i,i+c}S_{i,i+c}(t)\,dW^{i,i+c}(t), \tag{6.18}$$

as in (6.10), we know by the moment generating function of a Gaussian random variable that

$$\mathbb{E}^{i,i+c}\left[S_{i,i+c}(T_i)^2\right] = S_{i,i+c}(T_i)^2\,e^{\sigma^2_{i,i+c}T_i},$$

which leads to the classical convexity adjustment

$$\mathbf{CA}^{i,i+c} \approx \mathbf{CA}^{i,i+c}_{MKT} := S_{i,i+c}(0)\Psi\left(S_{i,i+c}(0),\alpha,c\right)\left(e^{\sigma^2_{i,i+c}T_i}-1\right). \tag{6.19}$$

Before testing this formula against Monte Carlo following the procedure outlined in Section 6.2.5, we present an alternative approximation for convexity adjustments, based on Brigo and Mercurio (2006) and derived in the LMM framework via approximations very similar to those presented in Section 6.2.4. Then all three approaches (market approximation, LMM approximation and Monte Carlo) will be compared.

6.3.4 A General LMM Approximation

In the first part of this chapter the LMM was explained and we saw how many computational complications arise from the fact that the forward rates modelled in the LMM have complicated no-arbitrage drifts, which one needs to use every time $F_k(t)$ is modelled under a measure Q^i, $i \neq k$:

$$dF_k(t) = \mu_k^i(t, F(t))F_k(t)\,dt + \sigma_k(t)F_k(t)\,dZ_k(t),$$

$$\mu_k^i(t, F(t)) = \begin{cases} -\sigma_k(t)\sum_{j=k+1}^{i} \frac{\rho_{k,j}\alpha_j\sigma_j(t)F_j(t)}{1+\alpha_j F_j(t)} & k < i \\ \sigma_k(t)\sum_{j=i+1}^{k} \frac{\rho_{k,j}\alpha_j\sigma_j(t)F_j(t)}{1+\alpha_j F_j(t)} & k > i \end{cases}.$$

These diffusions admit no analytic expression for the distribution of the rate. If μ_k^i was deterministic, we would have again a geometric Brownian motion as in the case $i = k$, although not driftless. But notice that μ_k^i depends on the values at t of forward rates with maturities in-between the maturity of the rate and that of the numeraire, so it is stochastic. The consequence is that when many rates are involved jointly in a payoff we do not have transition densities and we need to discretize the dynamics of each forward rate and simulate all of them, with a considerable computational burden.

How can we approximate this drift with a deterministic function? Simple. The drift is a known, deterministic quantity only at current time $t = 0$, when the values of interest rates are known. This is a typical freezing approximation, which we have already used in Section 6.2.4, but here applied in general to the dynamics of forward rates:

$$\text{(Drift Freezing Approximation)}\ dF_k(t) \approx \mu_k^i(t, F(0))\,F_k(t)\,dt + \sigma_k(t)F_k(t)\,dZ_k(t).$$

This approximation can be justified in the usual way, which may well sound boring at this point: also in the drifts μ_k^i rates are both at numerator and at denominator, so their movements may partially cancel each other out, reducing the volatility. With this approximation forward rates go back to having an explicit transition distribution under any forward measure, and this distribution is the easy lognormal one,

$$F_k(t) = F_k(0)\exp\underbrace{\left[\int_0^t \mu_k^i(t)\,ds - \int_0^t \frac{1}{2}\sigma_k^2(s)\,ds + \int_0^t \sigma_k(s)\,dZ_k(s).\right]}_{\sim \mathbb{N}\left(\int_0^t \mu_k^i(t)\,ds - \int_0^t \frac{1}{2}\sigma_k^2(s)ds,\ \int_0^t \sigma_k^2(s)\,ds\right)}.$$

Recalling the moment generating function of $\mathbb{N}(\mu, \sigma^2)$ we see that

$$\mathbb{E}^i[F_k(t)] = F_k(0)\,e^{\int_0^t \mu_k^i(t)\,dt}.$$

In case we have to deal with swap rates we can, by analogy to the above approximation, also simplify the computation of swap rates. A swap rate, you may recall (6.11), is almost a linear combination of forward rates, but weights are stochastic. These weights, however, have low volatility, and thus we can find an approximation by keeping the weights w_i at their initial value

$$\text{(Weight Freezing Approximation)}\quad S_{\alpha,\beta}(t) \approx \sum_{i=\alpha+1}^{\beta} w_i^{\alpha,\beta}(0)\,F_i(t).$$

It is exactly the same approximation made in (First Freezing), but here it is used in general.

These two approximations can make the LMM a rather easy model for any payoff, but the market understood that these approximations are acceptable only if they are tested for each new payoff of application.

Among the payoffs whose pricing would be dramatically simplified by this approximation are CMS. To price a CMS we only need to be able to compute

$$S_{i,i+c}(0) + \mathbf{CA}^{i,i+c} = \mathbb{E}^{T_i}\left[S_{i,i+c}(T_i)\right].$$

We can resort to (Weight Freezing Approximation) so that

$$\begin{aligned}\mathbb{E}^{T_i}\left[S_{i,i+c}(T_i)\right] &\approx \mathbb{E}^{T_i}\left[\sum_{j=i+1}^{i+c} w_j^{i,i+c}(0)F_j(T_i)\right]\\ &= \sum_{j=i+1}^{i+c} w_j^{i,i+c}(0)\mathbb{E}^{T_i}\left[F_j(T_i)\right]\end{aligned}$$

and compute the expectation using (Drift Freezing Approximation) so that

$$\mathbb{E}^{T_i}\left[S_{i,i+c}(T_i)\right] \approx \sum_{j=i+1}^{i+c} w_j^{i,i+c}(0)F_j(0)e^{\int_0^{T_i}\mu_j^i(t)dt}. \tag{6.20}$$

6.3.5 Comparing and Testing the Approximations

The chart presented at Figure 6.5 shows the results of the comparison between the different methods for computing convexity adjustments $\mathbf{CA}^{i,i+c}$. We consider swap rates $S_{i,i+c}$ with annual payments. The different T_i's considered are given in the first row ('Maturity', in years) and the different c's are given in the second row ('Tenor', in years). The third row presents the volatility of the underlying swap rate, $\sigma_{i,i+c}$. They are taken from market ATM swaption on

PRICING CMS SWAPS: MONTE CARLO, APPROXIMATIONS AND CONVEXITY ADJUSTMENTS

Maturity	2	2	2	6	6	6	10	10	10
Tenor	2	6	10	2	6	10	2	6	10
Swap Volatility	0.142000	0.122000	0.113000	0.116019	0.107059	0.101703	0.106000	0.098693	0.098000
MC Low	0.051377	0.054669	0.055913	0.057628	0.058373	0.058798	0.058889	0.059235	0.059406
MC Expect	**0.051343**	**0.054696**	**0.055937**	**0.057708**	**0.058441**	**0.058861**	**0.059000**	**0.059331**	**0.059502**
MC High	0.051308	0.054724	0.055961	0.057788	0.058509	0.058924	0.059110	0.059426	0.059599
MC Correction	**0.000174**	**0.000285**	**0.000376**	**0.000363**	**0.000783**	**0.001025**	**0.000571**	**0.001052**	**0.001605**
LMM Approx.	**0.051324**	**0.054708**	**0.055959**	**0.057745**	**0.058407**	**0.058903**	**0.059016**	**0.059402**	**0.059557**
%Err on Corr	**0.109195**	**-0.042105**	**-0.058511**	**-0.101928**	**0.043423**	**-0.040976**	**-0.028021**	**-0.067490**	**-0.034268**
Error	**0.000019**	**-0.000012**	**-0.000022**	**-0.000037**	**0.000034**	**-0.000042**	**-0.000016**	**-0.000071**	**-0.000055**
SMM Adjusted	**0.051321**	**0.054695**	**0.055943**	**0.057734**	**0.058405**	**0.058856**	**0.058999**	**0.059374**	**0.059506**
%Err Corr	**0.123705**	**0.004045**	**-0.017249**	**-0.070952**	**0.046412**	**0.004759**	**0.001931**	**-0.040912**	**-0.002620**
Error	**0.000022**	**0.000001**	**-0.000006**	**-0.000026**	**0.000036**	**0.000005**	**0.000001**	**-0.000043**	**-0.000004**

Figure 6.5 Results of the comparison between different methods to compute convexity adjustments

1 February 2002. All data, including forward rates, come from the same day, at the beginning of the growing interest in CMS and the industrial use of the market approximation.

The row labelled as 'MC Expect' is nothing other than

$$\mathbb{E}^{T_i}\left[S_{i,i+c}(T_i)\right]$$

computed with an LMM calibrated exactly to swaptions data with exogenous historical correlations (see Brigo and Morini (2006) for details of the method used). Immediately above and below the lower and upper bounds of the 98% confidence window are given. In the row 'MC correction' we have

$$\mathbf{CA}_{MC}^{i,i+c} = \mathbb{E}^{T_i}\left[S_{i,i+c}(T_i)\right] - S_{i,i+c}(0)$$

when the expectation is taken via Monte Carlo. The results from the Monte Carlo simulation can be considered our best estimate for the convexity adjustments, since they do not involve the relevant simplifications of the market approximation (6.19) and the LMM formula (6.20). However, bear in mind that these Monte Carlo results are the best estimation of convexity adjustments *in the Libor Market Model*; the model is calibrated exactly to the market (ATM quotes since we are assuming absence of smile in the Monte Carlo and in the approximations), but the results remain absolutely model dependent, as we will see in Section 7.1 where we change the model and convexity adjustments also change. The approximation of 6.3.4 which is closest to the Monte Carlo assumptions is the LMM one, since it is derived from the same model.

The results

Looking at the results obtained with the Monte Carlo, one of the most obvious considerations is that the convexity adjustment starts becoming relevant when maturity and tenor increases. It grows by a factor of 10 in moving from the shortest and closest swap to the maximum maturity and tenor considered, equal to 10 years. This is well known to all interest rate derivatives traders (as has already been mentioned in Section 4.1.4); the really relevant convexity adjustments are for maturities and tenors even longer than those considered in this test, such as 20×20 years. This is something we must take into account. The error we commit in pricing is more meaningful when expressed in relative terms (the difference between the Monte Carlo convexity and the approximated convexity, relative to the Monte Carlo convexity), so that we understand if an approximation maintains the same degree of precision across the different maturities. However, even a very large relative error can be acceptable for short maturity, because here the small size of the adjustment would lead to a small absolute 'dollar' error. This is not the case when we move to longer maturities. Here the dollar error would be much larger, and the dollar error is what traders actually look at.

Below we show both relative errors ('% Err') and absolute errors ('Error'), first for the 'LMM approximation' which is (6.20), and then for the 'SMM Adjusted' which is Hagan's market formula (6.19).[3]

From this selection of results, the LMM approximation appears acceptable. It falls within the Monte Carlo window for all maturities. This is somewhat surprising. This approximation, based on freezing, is better the lower the variance of the underlying at maturity. The variance is the integral of the squared volatility from now to maturity, so we would expect the formula to

[3] The name comes from the fact that it assumes the underlying swap rate to be lognormal, like the swap market model of Jamshidian (1997).

lose its accuracy for longer maturity, when we need to be most precise. This problem does not arise. The relative error even tends to decrease with maturity and tenor, keeping the absolute dollar error stable. Can you give one possible reason to explain an increase in accuracy for longer maturities contrasting the above effect? One reason is shown in the third row: market volatility decreases with maturity and tenor, thus the increase of the integral of the squared volatility, due to the growth of the integration interval, is contrasted with the decrease in the volatility integrand.

The results are quite similar for the market approximation (6.19). If we want to look at the fine details, it is interesting to notice that the market formula appears even more precise, compared to the LMM Monte Carlo, than the LMM approximation. The relative error decreases (therefore accuracy increases) even faster with maturity, and often also with tenor. So accuracy increases when the relevance of the correction increases, leading to an absolute error extremely small on large maturities and tenors, which may well explain its popularity with market traders. This is even more surprising, since this approximation is based on an alternative description of the problem and is not even related to the LMM used in simulation.

Understanding the results

Can you give one possible reason for this increase in accuracy for longer maturities and tenors? Should we look again at the term structure of volatility? Well, there is no freezing involved in this approximation. Probably we need to look for another fundamental explanation. Have a look at Figure 6.6, which sets out the term structure of forward rates in the market for the day of this test, 1 February 2002, and recall the simplifying assumptions we made in computing this approximation.

The crucial approximation was assuming that *the curve is considered flat*. But you see that with increasing maturity and tenor the curve really gets much flatter, so that this simplifying assumption becomes so close to reality that we are making almost no approximation at all!

This is a paradigmatic case of an approximation that in theory seems quite bad, since it completely neglects crucial market information such as the slope of the term structure. But for the computation of convexity adjustments it turns out to be very practical, since the curve

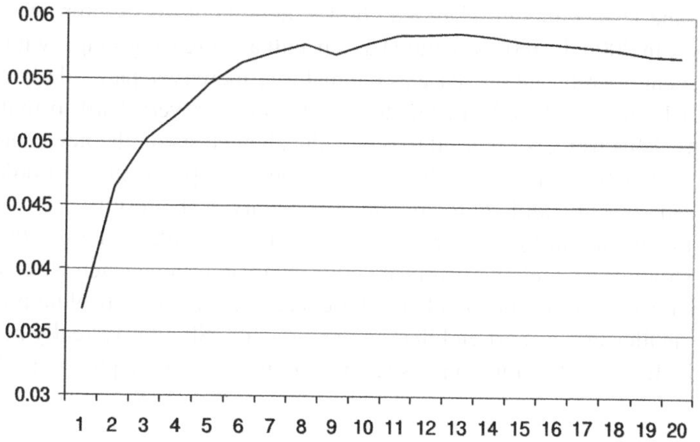

Figure 6.6 Term structure of forward rates used in the CMS tests

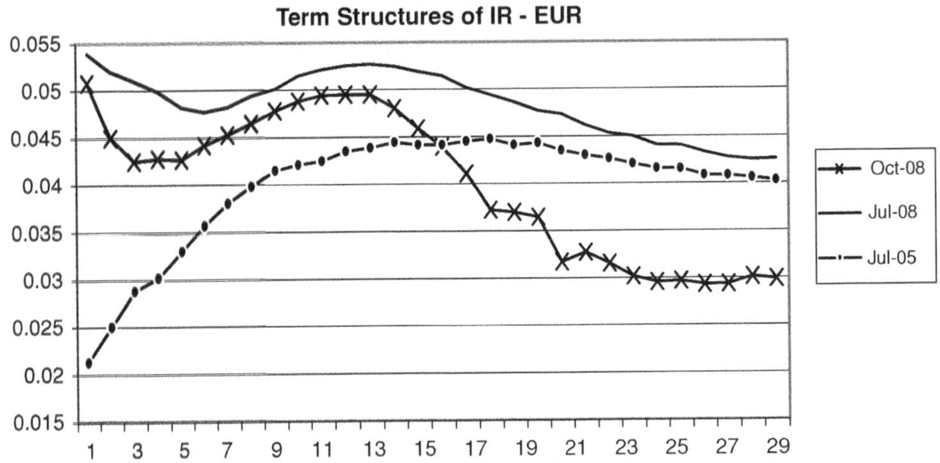

Figure 6.7 How the shape of the term structured changed in different years

is typically very different from flat in the short term, when however convexity adjustment is so small that even a large relative error is irrelevant. On the other hand, where convexity adjustments become important in size and we need a precise method, the term structure is typically almost flat.

In the previous section we learned that detecting which market feature crucially explains the efficiency of an approximation allows us to detect when the formula needs revision and retesting. The time has already arrived for this formula. The claims I have made above about the 'typical' shape of a term structure have also been belied by market reality, not in this case in the early days of the credit crunch but later on, starting with the troubles in the interest rate derivatives market triggered by the speech by ECB President Jean Claude Trichet on 5 June 2008,[4] and with a climax continuing at least until 2009.

Figure 6.7 shows that before the crisis (see the 2005 curve) the term structure remained similar to that of 2002. This gives us some confidence that during the years of maximum market interest in CMS products the fundamental market tool remained reliable.

But we become less confident when we observe how the term structure was transformed during the crisis. In 2008 the term structure has a peculiar decreasing shape, with a little hump in the short term and a relevant decrease as the maturity increases, particularly marked in the data from after Lehman's default. In this term structure it is very hard to find the features described above. This triggers the need to repeat the above tests on the new market situation, changing however only the term structure and not the other parameters, in order to identify whether this really is a crucial feature affecting the quality of the results.

The first set of results in Figure 6.8 seems to confirm our interpretation. In 2005, with a 'typical' term structure, the relative errors are quite small and stable when we change maturity and tenor. When we move to the October 2008 curve, we have the absolute novelty that the error is much smaller in the short end than in the long end. Should we really be surprised by this? Not really. In 2008 the situation has reversed compared to the pre-crisis situation: now

[4] The episode is recalled Chapter 9, where I focus on the effect on the term structure of rate volatilities. Here instead the focus is on the fact that the speech triggered first an inversion of the terms structure of rates.

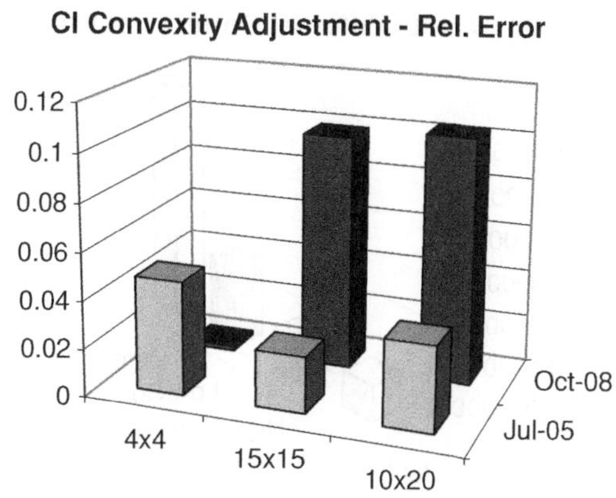

Figure 6.8 Classic CA approximations under different term structures

in the short end the term structure makes a hump but it varies by less than 1%, while in the longer end it goes down from more than 5% to less than 3%, being not flat at all. Consistently, the relative error for the long maturity and long end convexities is much bigger than it was in 2005.

Clearly, this situation also changes the comparison of this formula with the LMM one, as we see in Figure 6.9. The market formula is clearly superior on July 2005 term structure, but the comparison is less clear-cut with an October 2008 term structure. Each of the two formulas could be considered a good alternative to the other when market conditions make one of them imprecise, but unfortunately the market conditions that invalidate them tend to occur together.

Additionally, there is an event typical of interest rate crises that affects both approximations. It is the decrease in interest rate correlations (measured by estimating historically a matrix ρ like the one seen for the LMM). When the term structure of interest rates experienced the changes in shape that we see in Figures 6.8 and 6.9, with the short end of the term structure increasing and the long end decreasing, this obviously turned into plunging estimated forward rate correlations. Long and short end of the term structure were moving oppositely.

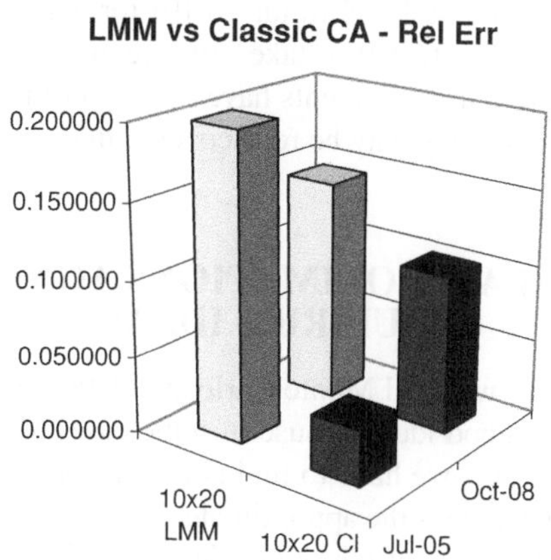

Figure 6.9 LMM vs classic CA approximations under different term structures

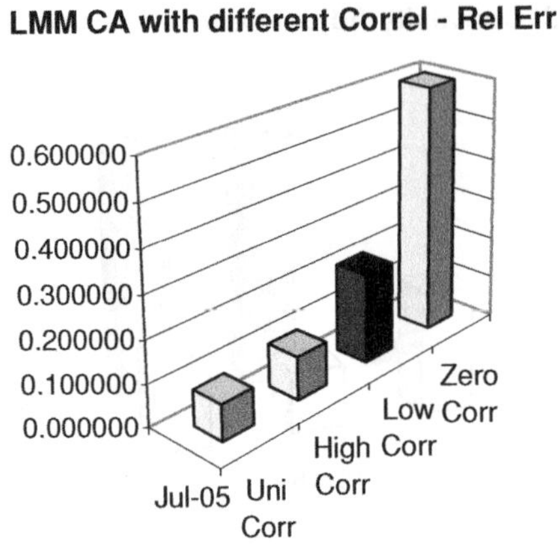

Figure 6.10 LMM CA approximation under different correlations

The market formula (6.19) is negatively affected by this since it is based on assuming a flat curve, which means only parallel movements and perfect correlations among rates. The LMM formula (6.20) is negatively affected for a more subtle reason: the freezing approximations are based on the usual consideration that 'the rates $F(t)$ appear both at numerator and denominator, so part of the movements of the $F(t)$'s at the numerator cancels out with the movements of the $F(t)$'s at the denominator'. But if we consider for example the weights $w_i^{\alpha,\beta}(0)$ which are frozen in (Weight Freezing Approximation), we see that the rates do not appear exactly in the same way in numerator and denominator. As long as the curve moves in parallel and all rates therefore move by almost the same amount, this can be irrelevant. But when correlations are low and different rates can move in very different ways, the above consideration loses a lot of its sense, as confirmed by the numerical results in Figure 6.10.

This gives an answer to the question I posed at the end of Section 6.2.4: the other element that can affect the results of the testing of the swaption formula (6.14), also based on freezing, are correlations. The different tests are made at different correlations, and the failures are when the rank of the correlation matrix is highest, which roughly means lowest correlations.

Interesting alternatives to the market formula (6.19) for convexity adjustments are given in Hagan (2003), which modifies (6.19) to take into account a non-flat term structure with non-parallel movements. These improvements have usually been disregarded and considered irrelevant by market operators. They may be rediscovered in the new market evidence.

6.4 TESTING APPROXIMATIONS AGAINST EXACT. DUPIRE'S IDEA

In the two previous examples we used Monte Carlo simulation to test an analytical approximation. This is not always a good idea because in some cases Monte Carlo can be as biased as approximations. In such cases we have to find alternative ways to assess the quality of an approximation. One such example is the approximated formula (5.9) for the implied volatility of a call option in the SABR model, introduced in Chapter 5. We saw in (5.8) that in the SABR model the forward price F of an asset for maturity T is assumed to evolve under the T forward measure according to

$$dF(t) = V(t)F(t)^{\beta}\,dW(t),$$
$$dV(t) = \epsilon V(t)\,dW_V(t), \qquad V(0) = \alpha,$$

where W and W_V are standard Brownian motions with

$$\mathbb{E}\,[dW_V\,dW] = \rho\,dt.$$

The Hagan et al. (2002) closed-form approximation (5.9) is derived under the assumption that the volatility of volatility ϵ is small. Under this assumption Hagan et al. (2002) obtain an approximation for the probability density of $F(T)$, and from this density they derive an analytic implied volatility $\sigma_F^{\text{SABR}}(K)$. This passage from the density to the implied volatility introduces further approximation.

The precision of this formula has been questioned, both by practitioners and in the literature, particularly for long maturities, high volatility of volatility, and low strikes. For example, Mercurio and Morini (2009a) compare the approximation price with the price of an option computed through direct Monte Carlo simulation of the SABR dynamics (5.8). They show an error of the approximation that for long maturity and low strike can be more than 30bps in terms of implied volatility. However, the latter comparison proved difficult to verify by the majority of market players, since the SABR model was not usually implemented through Monte Carlo simulation but only through the above approximated formula. Additionally, the SABR model does not lend itself easily to simulation, since F in the above dynamics should in theory always remain non-negative, while in a Monte Carlo simulation where the dynamics is discretized negative values are unavoidable and must be eliminated with ad hoc techniques that may be suspected of introducing a bias in the Monte Carlo simulation (see also Section 6.5.3).

Therefore, in 2009 I was looking for confirmation of the imprecision of the SABR formula alternative to the Monte Carlo results I had presented with Fabio Mercurio (Mercurio and Morini (2009a)). And I wanted this confirmation to be non debatable, therefore I wanted it to be based on comparison with a clearly unbiased method, possibly an exact method. In general, there are no exact methods to price an option in the SABR model. However, for some special values of the parameters exact formulas are available. For example, all market practitioners know that the SABR model embeds, for special parameters, the Constant Elasticity of Variance model, and therefore in these special cases the formula (5.9) can be compared with the exact closed-form formulas available for these models. However, reducing SABR to a Constant Elasticity of Variance model means setting the volatility of volatility $\epsilon = 0$, which is not a very interesting case because the model is no longer a stochastic volatility model, and because the suspicion is that formula (5.9), coming from an expansion for small ϵ, loses precision when ϵ is high, not when $\epsilon = 0$. How to find a case where the price of a call option in (5.8) can be computed exactly without restricting oneself to the uninteresting case $\epsilon = 0$?

The solution was given to me by Bruno Dupire one evening, during a dinner in Rome in spring 2009. This is what you get for going to dinner with one of the best quants in the world!

Bruno's idea is based on a special choice of the SABR parameters that yields a very easy and exact closed-form for option pricing allowing for any value for ϵ. We will compare this exact formula with (5.9) for different strikes, maturities, and levels of ϵ. This allows us to understand better the behaviour of the formula (5.9), understanding when it is a reliable solution for the model (5.8), and when it is not.

6.4.1 Perfect Positive Correlation

The first special case allowing a closed-form, exact (in the Black and Scholes sense) solution for the above model requires considering a Gaussian backbone and perfect positive correlation. Thus we assume

$$\rho = 1, \beta = 0$$

so that

$$\begin{aligned} dF(t) &= V(t)\,dW(t), \\ dV(t) &= \epsilon V(t)\,dW(t), \qquad V(0) = \alpha. \end{aligned} \tag{6.21}$$

This implies

$$\frac{dV(t)}{\epsilon} = V(t)dW(t) = dF(t),$$

so that, by integration,

$$\frac{V(T)}{\epsilon} - \frac{\alpha}{\epsilon} = F(T) - F(0),$$
$$F(T) = F(0) + \frac{V(T)}{\epsilon} - \frac{\alpha}{\epsilon}$$

where $V(t)$ is lognormal with instantaneous volatility ϵ. The price of a call with maturity T and strike K can be computed exactly as follows,

$$\begin{aligned} Call(F, K, T) &= P(0, T)\mathbb{E}\left[(F(T) - K)^+\right] \\ &= \frac{1}{\epsilon}P(0, T)\mathbb{E}\left[(V(T) - \alpha - K\epsilon + F(0)\epsilon)^+\right] \\ &= \frac{1}{\epsilon}P(0, T)\,Black\left(\alpha, \alpha + K\epsilon - F(0)\epsilon, \epsilon^2 T\right). \end{aligned} \tag{6.22}$$

This can be compared with the approximated pricing formula (5.9) proposed by Hagan et al. (2002). Notice that this special case can involve a singularity in the formula (5.9). If $z < 1$, we have an indetermination $\ln \frac{0}{0}$. We apply De L'Hôpital rule,

$$\lim_{\rho\to 1} \frac{\sqrt{1 - 2\rho z + z^2} + z - \rho}{1 - \rho} = \lim_{\rho\to 1} z\left(1 - 2\rho z + z^2\right)^{-\frac{1}{2}} + 1$$
$$= \lim_{\rho\to 1} \frac{z}{\sqrt{1 - 2\rho z + z^2}} + 1 = \frac{z}{1 - z} + 1 = \frac{1}{1 - z}.$$

If $z > 1$, we have $\ln \frac{-1+z+z-1}{0} = +\infty$ and $\sigma_F^{\mathrm{SABR}}(K) = 0$. Notice that $z > 1$ implies

$$\sqrt{FK}\ln\left(\frac{F}{K}\right) > \frac{\alpha}{\epsilon}.$$

When $F \leq K$, this is impossible, thus it is a case that applies only to ITM options, $F > K$. But when $F > K$, we have $\sqrt{FK}\ln\left(\frac{F}{K}\right) < (F - K)$, so that

$$\sqrt{FK}\ln\left(\frac{F}{K}\right) > \frac{\alpha}{\epsilon} \Longrightarrow F - K > \frac{\alpha}{\epsilon}.$$

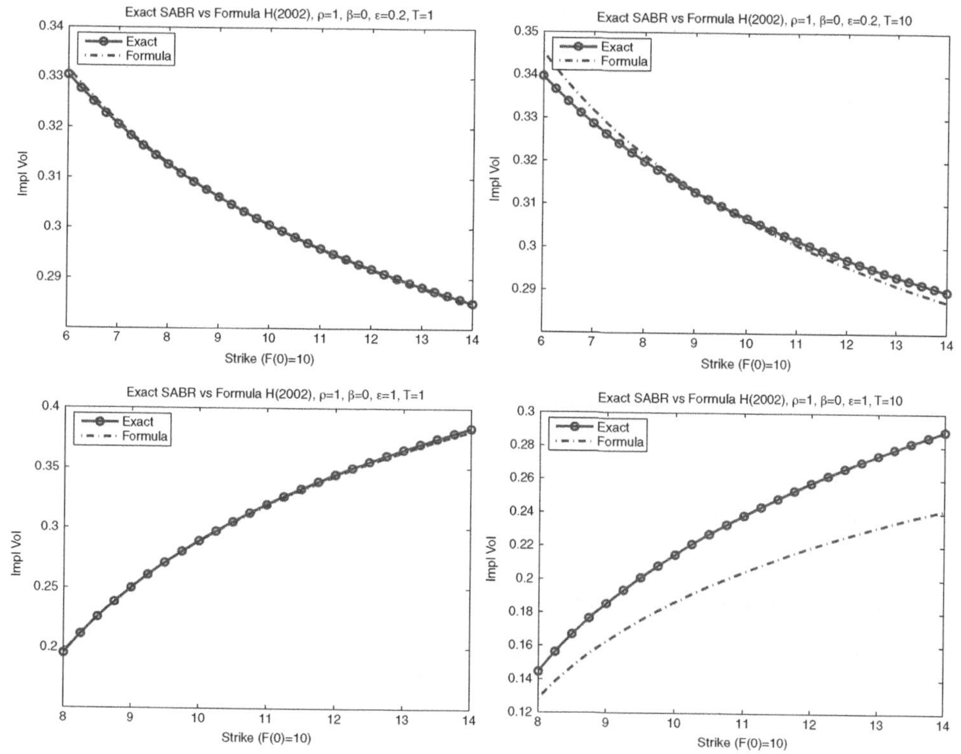

Figure 6.11 Exact SABR vs approximation when $\beta = 0$, $\rho = 1$

In turn,

$$F - K > \frac{\alpha}{\epsilon} \Longrightarrow \alpha + K\epsilon - F(0)\epsilon < 0$$

thus the strike in the call option (5.9), when seen as an option on a lognormal random variable, is negative, so its price is the option intrinsic value and it is correctly evaluated with underlying volatility set to 0.

We now consider the pricing of a stream of call options, with different strikes, when the underlying is $F(0) = 10$ and the (absolute) volatility is 30% of $F(0)$, namely $\alpha = 3$. We use $P(0, T) = 1$. We consider different scenarios for the option maturity T and the volatility of volatility ϵ. The results are shown in the charts at Figure 6.11.

The Hagan et al. (2002) formula appears very precise when the volatility of volatility is very low ($\epsilon = 0.1$) and the maturity is short (1 year). The precision worsens when we increase the maturity (10y). It gets definitely imprecise when, along with the maturity, we also increase the volatility of volatility ($\epsilon = 1$).

Notice that in the two cases where $\epsilon = 1$, if we extend the range of strikes we also cover an area where, confirming the analytical results, the volatility goes to zero since the option has a value equal to its intrinsic value. This is what we see in Figure 6.12.

Another interesting case is $\epsilon = 0.3$, since in this case one can prove that the model reduces to lognormal. This case is illustrated in Figure 6.13. Although in the latter case the level of the volatility is not high, the formula is not very precise, particularly if we extend the range of

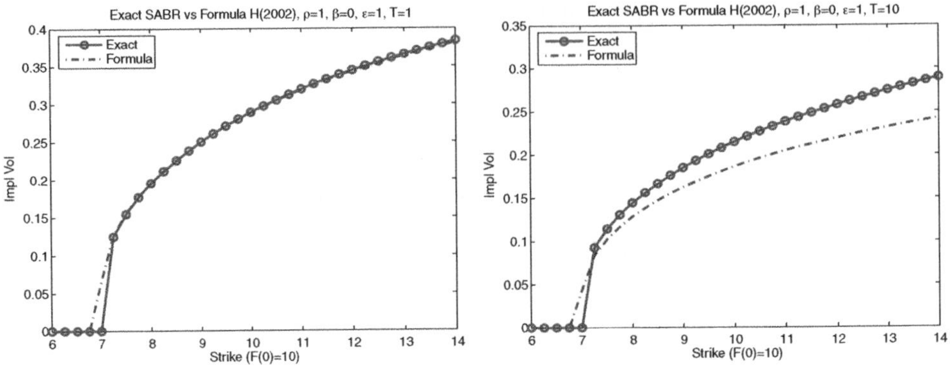

Figure 6.12 Exact SABR vs approximation when $\beta = 0$, $\rho = 1$. More strikes.

strikes (right pane in the above figure). The case of strikes close to zero is particularly relevant for some applications of the formula such as interest rate derivatives.

6.4.2 Perfect Negative Correlation

The second special case allowing for an exact closed-form formula considers instead perfect anticorrelation between volatility and the underlying. If we assume

$$\rho = -1, \ \beta = 0$$

so that

$$dF(t) = V(t)\,dW(t),$$
$$dV(t) = -\epsilon V(t)\,dW(t), \quad V(0) = \alpha,$$

this implies

$$\frac{dV(t)}{\epsilon} = -\,V(t)dW(t) = -dF(t),$$

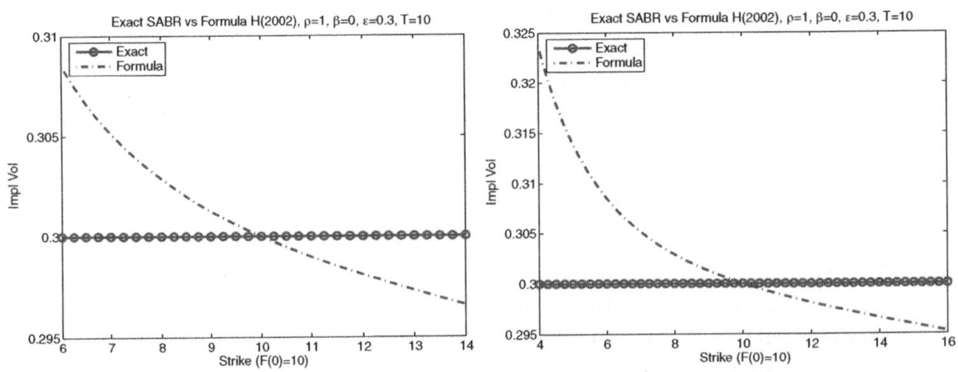

Figure 6.13 Exact SABR vs approximation. Log normal case.

so that, by integration,

$$\frac{V(T)}{\epsilon} - \frac{\alpha}{\epsilon} = -F(T) + F(0),$$
$$F(T) = F(0) - \frac{V(T)}{\epsilon} + \frac{\alpha}{\epsilon}$$

where $V(t)$ is lognormal with instantaneous volatility ϵ. The price of a call with maturity T and K can be computed exactly

$$\begin{aligned} Call(F, K, T) &= P(0, T)\mathbb{E}\left[(F(T) - K)^+\right] \\ &= \frac{1}{\epsilon} P(0, T)\mathbb{E}\left[(-V(T) + \alpha - K\epsilon + F(0)\epsilon)^+\right] \\ &= \frac{1}{\epsilon} P(0, T) Black^{Put}\left(\alpha, \alpha - K\epsilon + F(0)\epsilon, \epsilon^2 T\right), \end{aligned}$$

where

$$Black^{Put}(F, K, v) = K\ \Phi(-d_2) - F\ \Phi(-d_1).$$

When using the Hagan et al. (2002) approach, the formula corresponds to (5.9), with the difference on the $x(z)$ term, which is now

$$x(z) := \ln \lim_{\rho \to -1} \left\{ \frac{\sqrt{1 - 2\rho z + z^2} + z - \rho}{1 - \rho} \right\} = \ln \left\{ \frac{|z + 1| + z + 1}{2} \right\}$$

When $z > -1$, $x(z) = z + 1$. When $z < -1$, the volatility goes to 0. Notice, however, that in this case $F < K$, and this implies $\sqrt{FK} \ln\left(\frac{F}{K}\right) > (F - K)$, so that

$$\sqrt{FK} \ln\left(\frac{F}{K}\right) < -\frac{\alpha}{\epsilon} \Longrightarrow F - K < -\frac{\alpha}{\epsilon}.$$

In turn,

$$F - K < -\frac{\alpha}{\epsilon} \Longrightarrow \alpha - K\epsilon + F\epsilon < 0,$$

thus the put has zero value, and this is correctly evaluated with 0 volatility. Results for the comparison with the Hagan et al. (2002) formula are given in the charts at Figure 6.14.

The results obtained for the $\rho = 1$ case also appear to be confirmed by the opposite $\rho = -1$ case. Again, in the two cases where $\epsilon = 1$, if we extend the range of strike we also cover an area where, confirming the analytical results, the volatility goes to zero since the option has a value equal to its intrinsic value, as we see in Figure 6.15. We also show, in Figure 6.16, the case when $\epsilon = 0.3$. Now this does not correspond to lognormal, but shows that discrepancies between the Hagan et al. (2002) approximated volatility and the exact value also start to appear for moderate value for the volatility of volatility ϵ, for long maturities and low strikes.

Again the results for the larger range of strikes, on the right in Figure 6.15, appear particularly relevant for interest rate modelling applications. Finally, we should mention that for $\rho = -1$ all configurations obtained correspond to decreasing skews similar to those that appear in the market, and the same applies to the $\rho = 1$ case for low or moderate volatility of volatility.[5] In all these cases the results using the exact formulas we introduced confirm that the standard

[5] The case $\rho = 1$ with very high ϵ is an exception since it leads to increasing skews.

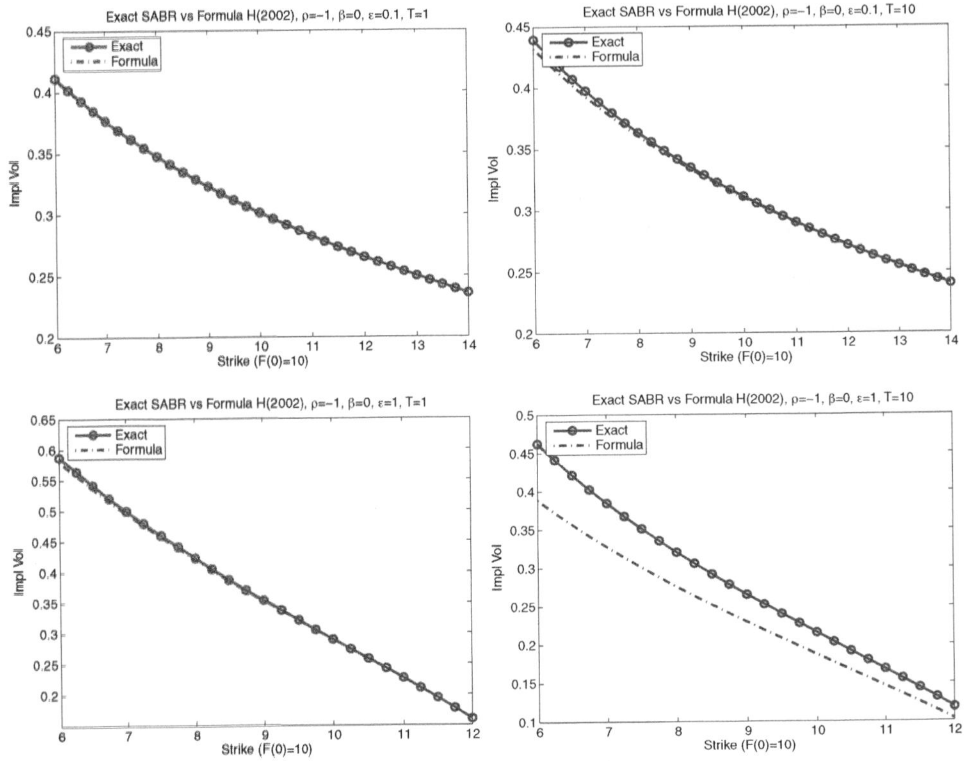

Figure 6.14 Exact SABR vs approximation when $\beta = 0$, $\rho = -1$

market SABR formula becomes less precise, as a representation of the SABR model, when ϵ increases, the maturity increases, and the strike gets lower. This can be put in relation to the way the approximation is derived in Hagan et al. (2002). First, an expansion valid only for small ϵ is performed. No wonder the approximation may become less precise for large ϵ. The test above, however, adds crucial information: it shows that ϵ can be considered too 'large' also when it has values that are not unlikely in a calibrated SABR model. Secondly,

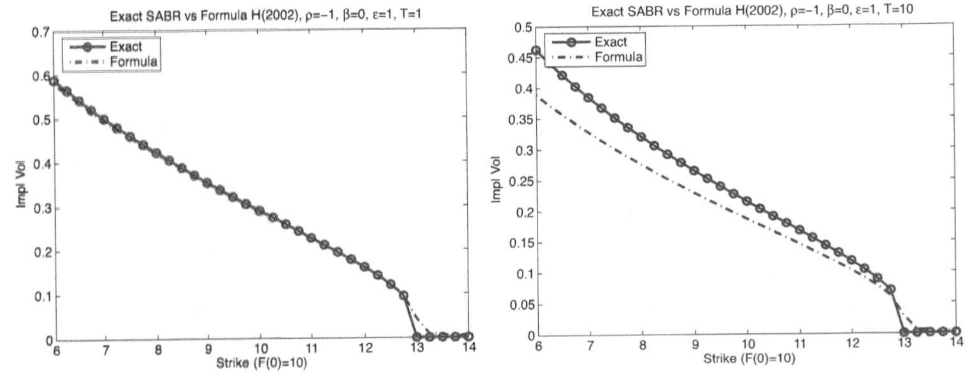

Figure 6.15 Exact SABR vs approximation when $\beta = 0$, $\rho = -1$. More strikes

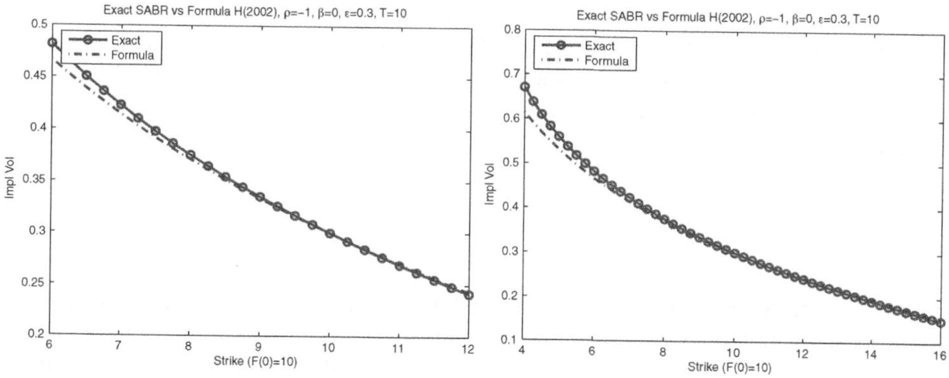

Figure 6.16 The case $\epsilon = 0.3$

in the derivation of the formula the density of the underlying obtained after the expansion is further approximated so as to express the formula as an implied volatility, and this yields, as all practitioners using SABR know, that the density of the underlying implicit in the SABR formula can turn negative for values of the underlying close to zero. A negative density is an absurdity that certainly leads to a bias compared to the correct density implied by the SABR dynamics. Since this happens for low values of the underlying, options with low strikes are naturally more affected.

The above example has shown how we can find interesting special cases where a model can be implemented to an exact formula, and how to use this to understand the behaviour of an approximation. Unfortunately, we do not always have the opportunity to ask a legendary quant in front of a plate of *abbacchio scottadito*. Mostly, we have to think hard to find special cases that are not so special as to rule out the very situations where an approximation can become imprecise.

6.5 EXERCISES ON RISK IN COMPUTATIONAL METHODS

In this final section we present a few more cases relating to the precision, or lack of it, of computational methods used in the market. The first one is still focused on approximations, and you should use the above examples, as well as some results on SABR seen in Chapter 5, to anticipate both problem and solution. The second relates to numerical integration, which is clearly a non-exact method but today can be approached in such an efficient way that at times it is treated as if it is an exact method. And yet it can still present some critical issues, as we will see. Finally, we consider briefly one problem that can arise in what has often been our benchmark in terms of precision: Monte Carlo simulation.

6.5.1 Approximation

In Section 6.3.4 we saw how in a standard lognormal LMM, the no-arbitrage drifts of rates are at times approximated through the following freezing:

$$\sum_{j=i+1}^{k} \frac{\alpha_j \sigma_j \rho_{k,j} F_j(t)}{1+\alpha_j F_j(t)} \approx \sum_{j=i+1}^{k} \frac{\alpha_j \sigma_j \rho_{k,j} F_j(0)}{1+\alpha_j F_j(0)}. \tag{6.23}$$

We saw why it can work, and when instead, it can have problems: when volatilities get high and correlations get low. When in 2005 I was developing with Fabio Mercurio an LMM based, rather than on a lognormal dynamics, on SABR dynamics (5.8) applied to each forward rate, we had to deal with the no-arbitrage drift of the stochastic volatility (one volatility for all rates) that contained the following term

$$\sum_{j=z+1}^{k} \frac{\alpha_j \sigma_j \rho_{j,V} F_j^{\beta}(t)}{1+\alpha_j F_j(t)}, \tag{6.24}$$

where $\rho_{j,V}$ is the correlation between a rate and the stochastic volatility term, while β is the SABR local volatility exponent that appears in the dynamics of forward rates (one for each rate). As we saw in Section 5.3.2, $\rho_{j,V} < 0$, concurrently with $\beta < 1$, are the two parametric configurations used to capture the market skew. In order still to be able to use the SABR closed-form formula, the drift 6.26 needed to be turned into a deterministic quantity. We decided to apply the usual freezing which works relatively well with lognormal LMM,

$$\sum_{j=\gamma(t)+1}^{k} \frac{\alpha_j \sigma_j \rho_{j,V} F_j^{\beta}(t)}{1+\alpha_j F_j(t)} \approx \sum_{j=z+1}^{k} \frac{\alpha_j \sigma_j \rho_{j,V} F_j^{\beta}(0)}{1+\alpha_j F_j(0)}. \tag{6.25}$$

And here come the questions.

1. The approximation made at (6.25) appears more dubious, and less reliable, than the standard freezing (6.23). Why?
   Because the freezing approximations are based on the idea that 'the rates $F(t)$ appear both at numerator and denominator, so part of the movements of the $F(t)$'s at the numerator cancels out with the movements of the $F(t)$'s at the denominator'. But in (6.25) rates at numerator have an exponent β that can be $\beta < 1$. Since interest rates are – usually – lower than unit, we can expect this exponent to magnify the movements of rates at numerator, or to shrink their movements when the exponent gets close to zero. In any case, the movements of these numerator rates are not likely to cancel out with movements of rates at denominator even if correlations are relatively high and volatilities are relatively low.
2. In spite of this, in Mercurio and Morini (2009a) the SABR LMM model is calibrated to the correlation skew, and then the above approximation is compared with Monte Carlo simulation, and the error on swaption implied volatilities turns out very low, usually less than one basis point. Can we think of a good justification for this result?
   When Fabio Mercurio and I looked at the results of our test, we realized that after the model is calibrated to the swaption market smile, which includes a decreasing correlation skew, parameters tend to have very typical patterns. In fact, as we saw in Chapter 5, $\rho_{j,V} < 0$ is concurrent with $\beta < 1$ in fitting the skewness of market quotations. Thus the calibrated model often captures the skew via correlation, so it has $\rho_{j,V} \ll 0$ and $\beta \approx 1$, and in this case there is no relevant exponent in the rates at numerator, making the precision of (6.25) comparable with the standard freezing (6.23). Otherwise, the skew is fit by $\beta \ll 1$ with $\rho_{j,V} \approx 0$. In this case rates at numerator have a behaviour strongly different from those at denominator, impairing the precision of the freezing of the drift. But when $\rho_{j,V} \approx 0$ the drift will in any case be almost null, so precision in its approximation becomes practically irrelevant! When both correlation and local skew are intermediate, the approximation error remains very low for a mixed contribution of the two effects just explained.

3. Can you now guess under which market conditions the approximation may break down? *The approximation would certainly break down if for some reason the smile inverts its slope, leading to different configurations of β and $\rho_{j,V}$ that eliminate the above mechanism. It is hard to imagine an interest rate market with an increasing skew, but in some cases this may be possible. Another dangerous configuration for this approximation is when the skew becomes so steeply decreasing that* both $\rho_{j,V} \ll 0$ *and* $\beta \ll 1$ *are required for skew fitting.*

6.5.2 Integration

Now let us consider very briefly a case of possible problems not in an approximation, but in a numerical procedure which is quite common in finance: numerical integration. In the past few years very efficient methods have been devised for numerical integration, yet the precision of the results still depends on the features of the financial problems to solve and from issues, like the value of parameters, similar to those that affect the precision of approximations. In fact, also in this case the issue arose after the credit crunch burst.

Consider, for example, the integral we saw in (3.10), which gives the one-factor Gaussian copula

$$C_{X_1,\ldots,X_n} = \mathbb{E}\left[\prod_{i=1}^{n} \Phi\left(\frac{\Phi^{-1}(u_i) - \sqrt{\rho}M}{\sqrt{1-\rho}}\right)\right]$$
$$= \int_{-\infty}^{+\infty} \prod_{i=1}^{n} \Phi\left(\frac{\Phi^{-1}(u_i) - \sqrt{\rho}M}{\sqrt{1-\rho}}\right) \times f^{\Phi}(M)\,dM,$$

where the variable over which we integrate is a standardized Gaussian variable M.

The issue in this kind of integration is that M can take values from $-\infty$ to $+\infty$. When we perform a numerical integration, we obviously have to decide a domain smaller than infinity, say between $-\gamma$ and $+\gamma$, with γ a finite number. Often γ as low as 30 or even 10 can be a good approximation of infinity! Can you guess why? It is because of the standardized Gaussian density $f^{\Phi}(M)$, that becomes negligible for high values of $|M|$, and usually makes the entire integrand negligible, giving a negligible contribution to the value of the integral. However, a level $\bar{\gamma}$ that was sufficient for precise computation for normal values of the parameters, can become insufficient *when correlation ρ gets higher or even close to 1*, because this makes the other part of the integrand bigger, and can send $\frac{\Phi^{-1}(u_i)-\sqrt{\rho}M}{\sqrt{1-\rho}}$ to very high values. This problem becomes particularly noticeable when we are pricing CDOs and we integrate not only over joint default probability, which is in any case capped by 1, but also over the loss seen as a function of M. It was only after the credit crunch that correlation values as high as 1 became typical in portfolio credit modelling.

6.5.3 Monte Carlo

Very briefly, we conclude the chapter by recalling that Monte Carlo simulation must also be carefully designed to avoid problems. Think of the Cox, Ingersoll and Ross process (2.16) that we used in credit modelling:

$$d\lambda(t) = k[\theta - \lambda(t)]dt + \sigma\sqrt{\lambda(t)}dW(t).$$

This process has been widely used also for interest rate derivatives to give a dynamics to the short rate, and you can see this process implemented too in equity desks because the stochastic volatility of the popular Heston model, seen in (2.21), follows a CIR process. Thus the need to simulate this dynamics is ubiquitous in quantitative finance, and yet it is not at all a trivial task. The process has been chosen for so many applications not only because it often allows one to find a close-form or semi-closed-form solution for important quantities like survival probabilities, bonds and option prices, but also, and even more importantly, because setting the Feller condition

$$2k\theta > \sigma^2$$

we can guarantee that the process remains positive. And notice something else. Even if you do not set the Feller conditions, under normal conditions this model can reach zero but does not reach negative values. As soon as λ, which is a continuous process, reaches zero, the diffusion coefficient disappears

$$\sigma\sqrt{\lambda(t)}dW(t) = 0$$

and we are left with only the following drift

$$d\lambda(t) = k\theta dt.$$

The long-term mean θ and the speed of mean reversion k are usually positive, so this drift corresponds to an increase that takes λ back to positive.

But this only holds in continuous time. Thus it holds for all analytic solutions that do not require any approximation of the continuous time dynamics above. But when we need to perform Monte Carlo simulation, we need to discretize the dynamics,

$$\bar{\lambda}(t_i) = \bar{\lambda}(t_{i-1}) + k[\theta - \bar{\lambda}(t_{i-1})]\Delta t + \sigma\sqrt{\bar{\lambda}(t_{i-1})}\Delta W(t_i).$$

Now $\bar{\lambda}(t_i)$ is a discrete-time process and is certainly not continuous. $\Delta W(t)$ is no longer an instantaneous change of a stochastic process, and, from t_{i-1} to t_i, $\bar{\lambda}$ can become negative. This means a serious deviation from the theoretical positive dynamics that we would like to simulate, and leads us into trouble because at the next step we will have to compute $\sqrt{\bar{\lambda}(t_i)}$. If $\bar{\lambda}(t_i)$ is negative we will get an imaginary number, which is no good for rate, intensity or volatility simulation! Therefore schemes must be implemented that avoid $\bar{\lambda}$ becoming negative, or, more frequently, schemes must be used such that when $\bar{\lambda}$ turns negative it is replaced by a different non-negative quantity. I will not give you the technicalities because what I want here is simply to show you a typical example of the issues that can impair Monte Carlo precision and thus need to be addressed and monitored. For more information on the subject, see the paper by Lord et al. (2006) that surveys different possible methodologies and puts forward its own proposal, motivated by the attempt to make corrections to the $\bar{\lambda}(t_i)$ discrete dynamics that at the same time avoid negative $\bar{\lambda}(t_i)$ and keep the behaviour of the process as similar as possible to the continuous time dynamics. For more complex and advanced methods see also Andersen (2006) and Glasserman and Kim (2008).

7
Extrapolations

Interpolation is defined as the joining of two or more known points using some functional form that often comes from a modelling assumption. Extrapolation is instead the use of a functional form or a modelling assumption to move from a few known points to areas not surrounded by available information. Modelling in the financial markets has a lot to do with interpolating and extrapolating. We calibrate a model to few quotes for liquid products (our known points) and then we use the calibrated model to price very similar products (in this case we are doing interpolation) or products which are related but that have relevant differences from the calibration products (in this case we are often doing extrapolation[1]).

In terms of model risk, interpolation is less dangerous. It is the case when we have market information for risks very similar to those we want to assess with our models. We know that the market information can fit with different models that can have very different behaviours, leaving room for model uncertainty. But as long as we consider products in the area where all models are fit to the same market points, the different behaviours cannot be very different. It is when we extrapolate to really different products that the differences can become crucially important. Extrapolation must be singled out because most model risk hides here.

In this sense, many other parts of the book have already dealt with the risk of extrapolation with models: the model comparison exercise in Chapter 2, and the mapping in Section 3.5 are two of the most relevant examples. There we saw that assessing the quality of models beyond their fitting capabilities is necessary to reduce model risk.

Here we highlight something more. In the first example we show that the risks of extrapolation remain even if we fully trust the model we are using. We see an extrapolation exercise that we may consider safe because, once the model has been calibrated, the extrapolation seems fully determined by the market quotes and by our trusted model. In the example the SABR model appears to determine exotic prices based on market information about the liquid vanilla swaptions just calibrated; actually, it leads to prices based on an extrapolation that has little foundation in market prices since it is influenced by an indetermination in model parameters. We explain how this extrapolation can be turned into an interpolation, reducing model risk, by adding market information.

The first example covers extrapolation performed with a model. The second example covers an even more dangerous issue. Often in the market we interpolate and extrapolate only with some simple functional form, based on no model. This can happen when dealing with the strike-dependent parameters of some quotation model inconsistent with market patterns, such as the implied volatility of Black and Scholes in a market with smile or the implied correlation of the Gaussian copula for the credit correlation skew. When we simply interpolate using some functional form, the risks are limited, but they increase rapidly when we extrapolate in the absence of any modelling clue on how to do this. Here we illustrated with an example on the correlation skew how in some cases one can move from interpolation on the

[1] At the Global Derivatives Conference in 2011 I heard Jim Gatheral define financial modelling as glorified extrapolation.

parameters of the quotation model to interpolation on quantities that have clearer meaning and for which interpolation bounds are more easily derived. More importantly, this change of variable can also turn extrapolation into safer interpolation, even with no addition of market information.

7.1 USING THE MARKET TO COMPLETE INFORMATION: ASYMPTOTIC SMILE

Here we show, with a case based on the SABR model, the indetermination that can affect extrapolations. We show first how this problem can arise even in the pricing of common and relatively simple derivatives, and eventually how to use the prices of such derivatives to fix the indetermination and turn extrapolation into interpolation.

7.1.1 The Indetermination in the Asymptotic Smile

Section 5.3.1 introduced the SABR model and in 5.3.2 we showed the behaviour of the model implied smile for different configurations of the parameters. Now please go back and look at the continuous line in Figure 5.4, where the volatility skew is obtained by the parameter β being lower than 1. Now look at the continuous line in Figure 5.6 where the value of the underlying is the same but here we have a skew given by the correlation parameter ρ being negative with $\beta = 1$.

What do you notice about these two skews? They almost overlap, as we can appreciate by putting them on the same chart in Figure 7.1.

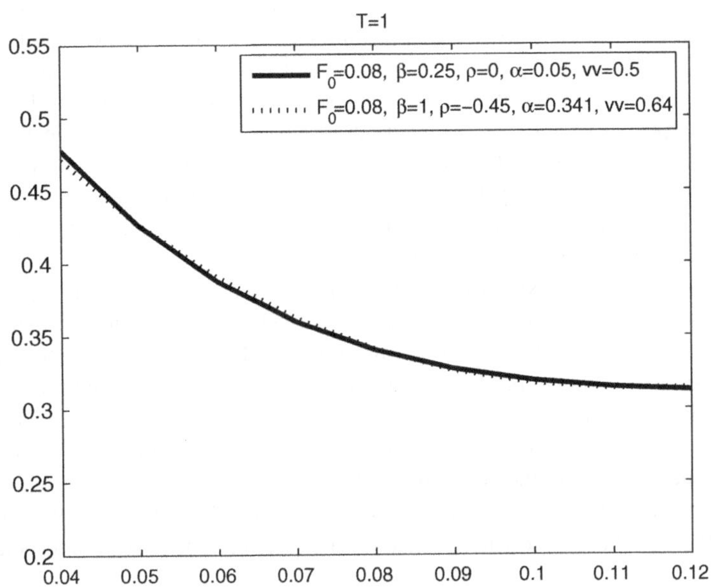

Figure 7.1 The skews for two different configurations of SABR parameters

The models suffer from parameter indetermination: one can fit a given market skew using either a model with a lognormal behaviour asymmetrically disturbed by a correlated stochastic volatility ($\beta = 1, \rho < 0$) or using a model where the skew is fit by local volatility without correlation between rates and stochastic volatility ($\beta < 1, \rho = 0$).

The main application of SABR is in interest rate modelling, in particular it is the market model for the swaption smile. Therefore in all the above examples it is natural to think that the underlying F is a swap rate, and the skew is a swaption skew. Hagan et al. (2002) suggest solving the β indetermination by choosing β according to personal preference, depending on one leaning more towards normal rather than lognormal behaviour of interest rates, or to determine β by historical estimation. In fact, from the SABR option formula (5.9) one can derive an approximated relation between the implied volatility σ^{ATM} of ATM options and the forward price F of the underlying,

$$\ln\left(\sigma^{ATM}\right) \approx \ln(\alpha) - (1-\beta)\ln(F),$$

from which β can be obtained with a linear regression applied to the historical behaviour of swap rates and corresponding swaption ATM implied volatilities.

Is the indetermination problem now solved? We may think it is. In fact, although the idea of estimating β historically, or even choosing it by personal preference, may be disturbing, the choice seems irrelevant since whatever β we choose *we get from calibration exactly the same skew*, by playing with the parameter ρ. One might think that in spite of this a different β may lead to a different dynamic behaviour of the model. But in Chapter 5 we saw that in the end the fact of having a skew by local volatility or by correlation does not lead to very different hedging behaviour; and in any case even different dynamic behaviours would have no effect on the majority of derivatives, which are 'European' in the sense that they depend only on the distribution of the underlying at a given maturity.

The problem with this conclusion is that it is not true that *we get from calibration exactly the same skew* irrespective of the choice we make on β. This conclusion is a consequence of the limited observable information we have about the smile. For any underlying, we only observe options quoted for a limited range of strikes. For example, in the swaption market we only see strikes down to 200*bps* below the ATM strike and up to 200*bps* above the ATM strike. This is a range even more limited than that shown in Figure 7.1.

If we base our judgement only on this limited information, the two smiles appear equal. But they are not, as we can see by looking at them on a less limited domain, as in Figure. 7.2.

If we consider strikes more extreme than those typically quoted in the market, we find that implied volatilities for these 'asymptotic' strikes are very different if we use β rather than ρ to fit the skew. In particular, Figure 7.3 shows that β is the parameter really relevant for determining the asymptotic smile. In fact when using very different values of correlation ρ, while keeping the same values for all other parameters, the asymptotic smile behaviour is only slightly altered. Instead, different values of β clearly lead to different configurations. In the specific case a tendency to a flat behaviour is very clear in case $\beta = 0$, while a much faster growth is evident in case $\beta = 1$. The case $\beta = 0.5$ is intermediate, although it appears to lean more towards the flat tendency. These empirical results are confirmed by the mathematical analysis of Andersen and Piterbarg (2006).

So, the indetermination of β leads to unpredictable extrapolations of the SABR smile for asymptotic strikes. Now our practical trader may say:

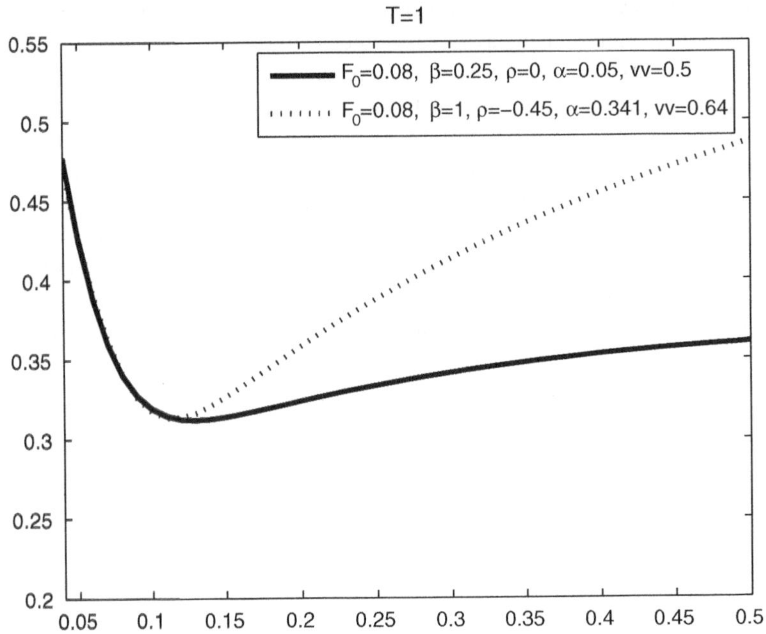

Figure 7.2 Skews for two different configurations of SABR parameters when the range of strikes is larger

Practical Trader: *And so what? Why should we care about the behaviour of the model for asymptotic strikes? There are no swaptions in the market with such high strikes so I just don't care about it.*

Wise Quant: *There is a caveat also in this conclusion. It is true that derivatives with strikes very far away from those quoted in the market are quite unlikely for examples in the interest rate world. However, there are derivatives very common in the interest rate market like Bermudan swaptions that are strongly affected by what the model implies for strikes outside the range of moneyness quoted in the market. In fact, from now to an exercise date t of a Bermudan the underlying can move to values S_t far away from its current value S_0; and when, for example in a Monte Carlo simulation, we have to assess if at t it is more convenient to exercise or to hold until maturity $T > t$, we will be using the different values of S_t in the different scenarios. Suppose the Bermudan has strike K: in many scenarios $S_t - K$, namely the moneyness of the Bermudan seen from t will be much higher than $S_0 - K$, and also of that maximum moneyness $S_0 - K_{\min}$ that we can observe today.*

Practical Trader: *Fair enough. Strikes outside the observable range can be relevant for products like Bermudans even if the strike K of the Bermudan is today within the observable range. But this relates to a larger but still limited range of strikes, there is in any case no influence of asymptotic strikes! And since I have never seen a termsheet quoting an asymptotic strike, I don't care about them.*

Wise Quant: *I am sorry but you are wrong again. There are interest rate derivatives that depend on asymptotic strikes in a relevant way, and they are among the most liquid after caps and swaptions. They are CMS derivatives, starting from the simplest constant maturity swap. Have a look at the next section.*

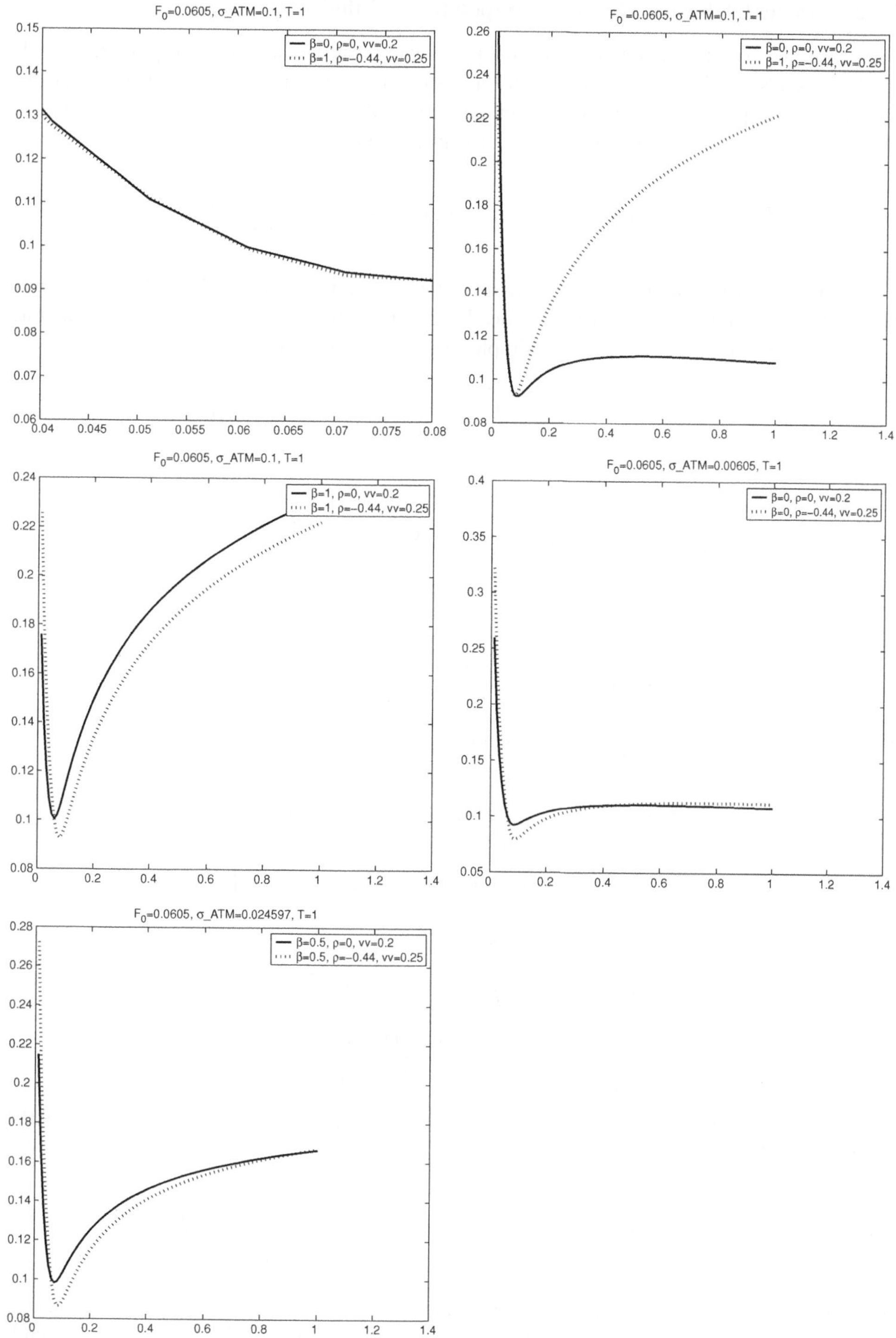

Figure 7.3 Different model choices and asymptotic smile

7.1.2 Pricing CMS with a Smile: Extrapolating to Infinity

In Section 6.3 we introduced constant maturity swaps, and we saw that the pricing formula (6.16) depends crucially on the convexity adjustments to be added to the current values of the forward swap rates that will be paid in the future. After a number of computations, (6.17) showed that the general formula for convexity adjustment is

$$\mathbf{CA}^{i,i+c} \approx S_{i,i+c}(0)\Psi\left(S_{i,i+c}(0), \alpha, c\right)\left(\frac{\mathbb{E}^{i,i+c}\left[S_{i,i+c}(T_i)^2\right]}{S_{i,i+c}(0)^2} - 1\right).$$

This formula depends on the second moment of the swap rate $\mathbb{E}^{a,b}\left[S_{a,b}(T_i)^2\right]$. This is the only part that depends on the model. Here we need to compute the second moment of the swap rate in the SABR model. We can exploit a simple result that shows that

$$\mathbb{E}^{a,b}\left[S_{a,b}(T_a)^2\right] = 2\int_0^\infty \mathbb{E}^{a,b}\left[(S_{a,b}(T_a) - K)^+\right] dK. \tag{7.1}$$

In fact,

$$\begin{aligned}
&\int_0^\infty \mathbb{E}^{a,b}\left[(S_{a,b}(T_a) - K)^+\right] dK \\
&= \mathbb{E}^{a,b}\left[\int_0^{S_{a,b}(T_a)} \left(S_{a,b}(T_a) - K\right) dK\right] \\
&= \mathbb{E}^{a,b}\left[S_{a,b}(T_a)^2 - \frac{S_{a,b}(T_a)^2}{2}\right] = \mathbb{E}^{a,b}\left[\frac{S_{a,b}(T_a)^2}{2}\right].
\end{aligned}$$

If we apply the result to swaptions, whose price is, as we saw in (6.9),

$$\begin{aligned}
\text{SWAPTION}_0(K) &= \sum_{i=a+1}^{b} P(0, T_i)\alpha_i \mathbb{E}^{a,b}\left[(S_{a,b}(T_a) - K)^+\right] \\
&=: Annuity_0 \mathbb{E}^{a,b}\left[(S_{a,b}(T_a) - K)^+\right]
\end{aligned}$$

we have that

$$\begin{aligned}
\mathbb{E}^{a,b}\left[S_{a,b}^2(T_a)\right] &= 2\int_0^\infty \mathbb{E}^{a,b}\left[(S_{a,b}(T_a) - K)^+\right] dK \\
&= 2\int_0^\infty \frac{\text{SWAPTION}_0(K)}{Annuity_0} dK.
\end{aligned}$$

This quantity is easily priced when the swap rate $S_{a,b}(t)$ is supposed to follow the SABR dynamics. Following (5.10), we get

$$\mathbb{E}^{a,b}\left[S_{a,b}^2(T_a)\right] = 2\int_0^\infty Black(S_{a,b}(0), K, \left(\sigma_S^{SABR}(K)\right)^2 T_a)dK. \tag{7.2}$$

What should the practical trader note from these passages? That in a model which implies a smile, the value of convexity adjustments, and therefore the price of CMS derivatives, depends on the model implied volatility for all possible strikes, including the asymptotic strikes. If we break our integral into

$$\int_0^{\infty} Black(S_{a,b}(0), K, \left(\sigma_S^{SABR}(K)\right)^2 T_a)dK$$
$$= \int_0^{K_{\max}} Black(S_{a,b}(0), K, \left(\sigma_S^{SABR}(K)\right)^2 T_a)dK$$
$$+ \int_{K_{\max}}^{\infty} Black(S_{a,b}(0), K, \left(\sigma_S^{SABR}(K)\right)^2 T_a)dK$$

the second integral turns out fundamental for the final price. The second integral is not determined by calibration, but depends on the model extrapolation towards infinity and we know that this extrapolation depends on β, a parameter which remains largely undetermined in spite of swaption calibration. Thus the way you fix β amounts to the way you price your CMS; if you fix β based on your personal taste, this is not irrelevant to pricing. It will decide the price of CMS.

7.1.3 Using CMS Information to Transform Extrapolation into Interpolation and Fix the Indetermination

From the above section it seems we are in the worst situation possible. The price of CMS depends on how SABR extrapolates above the maximum observable strike. This extrapolation depends on β, and we do not have enough observable liquid swaption quotes to fix β in an unambiguous way. Is there any solution to this?

Yes, and it is a simple one. Reverse the approach. We have shown that there is a strong link between CMS prices and the value of β. For some maturities and tenors liquid CMS quotes are available. If we include them in our calibration, adding them to swaptions, we may solve our indetermination on β and transform our extrapolation into interpolation. CMS quotes contain market information about the implied volatility for asymptotic strikes, so they could replace the lack of those swaptions with asymptotic strikes which, if available, would eliminate our uncertainty about β.

This route is suggested and tested in Mercurio and Pallavicini (2006). They include liquid CMS in the SABR calibration by computing numerically the integral in (7.2). They show first of all that, as we suspected based on the above reasoning, convexity adjustments do depend on β. This can be seen in Table 7.1.

They try to calibrate the entire swaption cube (available maturities, tenors and strikes) and the available CMS quotes, keeping a unique β . They succeed in this, and discover that with this approach there is actually no more indetermination about β. We refer to Mercurio and Pallavicini (2006) for more details on the data used and the methodologies applied.

A value of β that was obtained in the market in 2006 applying this approach, together with the value for the other parameters, is shown in Tables 7.2, 7.3 and 7.4. We notice that the other SABR parameters are changed when considering different expiries and tenors, but β is unique.

What is of interest to us here is the idea behind these results. If we have understood well the relations between our model parameters and the available derivatives, we can add market information that reduces the need to perform extrapolations outside the information we can get from market quotes. This is not an irrelevant increase of the calibration set such as the one mentioned in Section 2.6.1, which may create a sense of false confidence. Here we are adding relevant information, which helps reduce our model uncertainty.

Table 7.1 CMS convexity adjustments (in bp) for different expiries, obtained after calibration of the SABR functional form to the swaption smile for different choices of β

	β					
Expiry	0.2	0.3	0.4	0.5	0.6	0.7
5y	9.6	10.5	10.6	10.7	10.7	10.8
10y	19.7	19.9	20.1	20.4	20.8	21.5
20y	25.4	32.5	33.8	35.7	39.3	49.4
30y	32.5	43.9	46.7	51.7	62.9	107.6

Table 7.2 SABR calibrated parameters. Tenor = 10

expiry:	0	1	5	10	20	30
alpha	0.054093	0.0537	0.052345	0.048698	0.04285	0.04129
beta	0.679529	0.679529	0.679529	0.679529	0.679529	0.679529
rho	0.105087	−0.04913	−0.20976	−0.26018	−0.29182	−0.30872
vv	0.403646	0.392924	0.319015	0.259055	0.228857	0.204484

Table 7.3 SABR calibrated parameters. Tenor = 20

expiry:	0	1	5	10	20	30
alpha	0.047448	0.047285	0.049107	0.045248	0.039197	0.038541
beta	0.679529	0.679529	0.679529	0.679529	0.679529	0.679529
rho	−0.11305	−0.12924	−0.22288	−0.26415	−0.30342	−0.31083
vv	0.402065	0.390207	0.31951	0.258021	0.22615	0.208255

Table 7.4 SABR calibrated parameters. Tenor = 30

expiry:	0	1	5	10	20	30
alpha	0.045105	0.045226	0.047169	0.043614	0.038355	0.038558
beta	0.679529	0.679529	0.679529	0.679529	0.679529	0.679529
rho	−0.21316	−0.1507	−0.22162	−0.26858	−0.31036	−0.31843
vv	0.400915	0.390826	0.319456	0.25761	0.224685	0.213075

7.2 USING MATHEMATICS TO COMPLETE INFORMATION: CORRELATION SKEW

This example relates to the Gaussian copula used in the market of portfolio credit derivatives, covered in Chapter 3. We did not refer to this example there, among the errors that led to the crisis, because we consider it a minor issue, but nevertheless it carries a good amount of model risk that is better avoided. It also provides a very good example of how we can use our mathematical information about the behaviour of the different quantities in the model in order to make interpolation as controlled as possible and transform extrapolation into interpolation. Unlike in the previous section, here we do not use any additional market information, which is any way not available, but we change the variable we use to express market quotes. With this new variable, we can compute the values it assumes at the boundaries of its domain, eliminating the need for extrapolation. Additionally, it makes it much easier to understand the properties an interpolator must have.

7.2.1 The Expected Tranched Loss

Section 3.2.1 showed that the equilibrium spread of the tranche $[A, B]$ of a CDO is given by

$$S_{A,B} = \frac{\sum_{i=1}^{b} P(0, T_i)\left[\mathbb{E}\left[L_{A,B}(T_i)\right] - \mathbb{E}\left[L_{A,B}(T_{i-1})\right]\right]}{\sum_{i=1}^{b} P(0, T_i)\alpha_i\left(1 - \mathbb{E}\left[L_{A,B}(T_i)\right]\right)},$$

where $\mathbb{E}\left[L_{A,B}(t)\right]$ can be decomposed into a combination of expected tranched losses of simple equity tranches $[0, A]$, $[0, B]$ according to

$$\mathbb{E}\left[L_{A,B}(t)\right] = \frac{1}{B-A}\left[B\mathbb{E}\left[L_B(t)\right] - A\mathbb{E}\left[L_A(t)\right]\right].$$

When the expected tranched loss of equity tranche $[0, K]$ is expressed using the Gaussian copula with a flat correlation ρ_K, we can write

$$\mathbb{E}\left[L_K(t)\right] = Etl_{0,K}(\rho_K).$$

Clearly, from market quotations for the sequence of tranches of a CDO, such as the i-Traxx tranches:

0% − 3%	3% − 6%	6% − 9%	9% − 12%	12% − 22%

one can bootstrap a curve of correlations, that is the correlation skew:

3%	6%	9%	12%	22%	→	$\rho_{3\%}$	$\rho_{6\%}$	$\rho_{9\%}$	$\rho_{12\%}$	$\rho_{22\%}$

What is to be done with tranches that have attachments and detachments different from those? A natural approach (see Parcell and Wood (2007) for the results that follow) may be to interpolate among these points, and extrapolate for points below 3% and above 22%, as in Figure 7.4.

Here the interpolation is piecewise linear, and the extrapolation continues the gradient of the last linear segment. Other popular choices in the market suggest setting the correlation at $\rho_{0\%} = 0$ for 0-detachment, and at $\rho_{100\%} = 1$ for 100%-detachment, or to extrapolate flat: $\rho_{0\%} = \rho_{3\%}$, $\rho_{100\%} = \rho_{22\%}$.

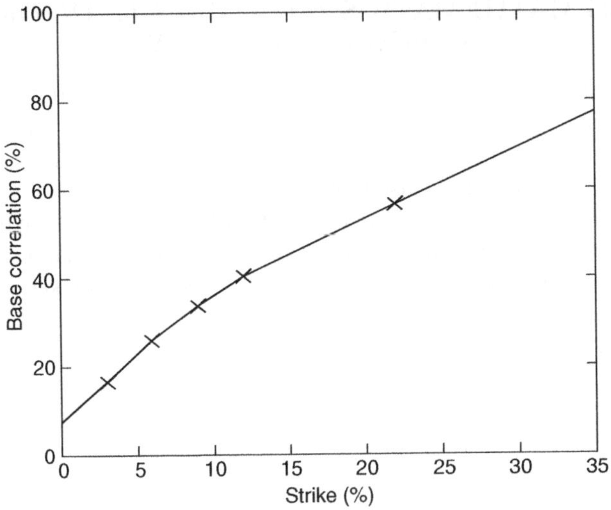

Figure 7.4 Bootstrapped correlation from Parcell and Wood (2007), interpolated and extrapolated with piecewise linear parameterization

The first choice may even lead to correlations below 0 (not possible for large portfolios since the correlation matrix must remain positive semidefinite, see Chapter 8) or above 1. The latter two choices are strongly arbitrary.

Even when it does not lead to correlation lower than 0 or higher than 1, linear interpolation can give meaningless results, as shown in Figure 7.5, where we show the equilibrium spreads for all 'tranchelets'

$$[X\% - (X + 0.5)\%]\,,$$

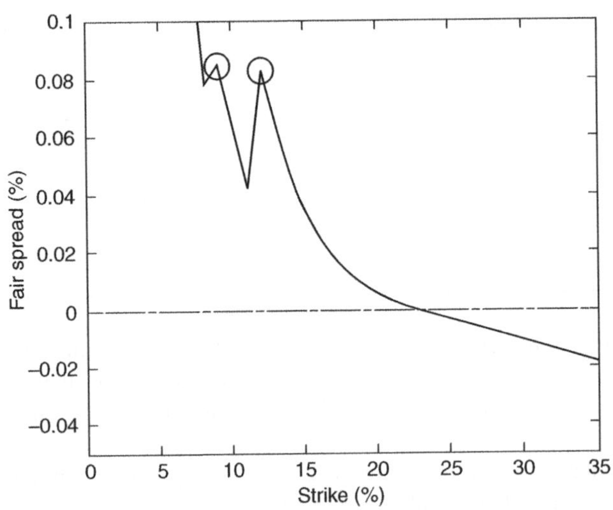

Figure 7.5 Tranchelet spreads from Parcell and Wood (2007) when inter/extrapolating Gaussian correlation

computed using correlations $\rho_{X\%}$, $\rho_{(X+0.5)\%}$ computed according to the above linear interpolations.

Spreads increase at 9% and 12%, which is impossible since increase in subordination must decrease risk, and they even get negative above 23%. The problem is that:

1. we are forced to extrapolate outside the area where the market provides information;
2. we have no indication on which interpolation methods we should use.

The proposal of Parcell and Wood (2007) is to change the variable we use to express tranche value, moving to the expected tranche loss $Etl_{0,K}(\rho_K)$ rather than the base correlation ρ_K. First of all, with little loss of generality but with noticeable simplification of notation, we redefine the expected tranched loss as follows. We take a notional of the tranche equal to a fraction K of the portfolio size, so that for this notional

$$Etl_K(\rho_K) := \mathbb{E}[L(T) - (L(T) - K)^+] \tag{7.3}$$

Then Parcell and Wood (2007) redefine the loss as a *discounted loss*

$$L(T) := P(0, T) L(T).$$

Here, again for simplicity of notation, we simply consider interest rates equal to zero. The relations we get are the same as are obtained by Parcell and Wood (2007), but intuition is simpler. Now the equilibrium spread of the tranche can be written as

$$S_{A,B} = \frac{\sum_{i=1}^{b} \mathbb{E}\left[L_{A,B}(T_i)\right] - \mathbb{E}\left[L_{A,B}(T_{i-1})\right]}{\sum_{i=1}^{b} \alpha_i \left(1 - \mathbb{E}\left[L_{A,B}(T_i)\right]\right)}. \tag{7.4}$$

Notice first the telescopic property of the numerator of this ratio,

$$\begin{aligned}\sum_{i=1}^{b} \mathbb{E}\left[L_{A,B}(T_i)\right] - \mathbb{E}\left[L_{A,B}(T_{i-1})\right] &= \mathbb{E}\left[L_{A,B}(T_b)\right] - \mathbb{E}\left[L_{A,B}(T_0)\right] \\ &= \mathbb{E}\left[L_{A,B}(T_b)\right].\end{aligned} \tag{7.5}$$

In the market, where there are certainly less quoted tranche maturities that dates in our discretization $T_1, \ldots, T_b$, it is common to simplify the denominator by assuming a parametric growth of the loss between $\mathbb{E}\left[L_{A,B}(0)\right] = 0$ and $\mathbb{E}\left[L_{A,B}(T_b)\right]$. We speak of parametric 'growth' since the expected tranched loss is a non-decreasing quantity thanks to the fact that default probabilities are non-decreasing in time. The simplest assumption is to take, for t with $0 < t < T_b$,

$$\mathbb{E}\left[L_{A,B}(t)\right] = \mathbb{E}\left[L_{A,B}(T_b)\right] \frac{t}{T_b} \tag{7.6}$$

so that, putting (7.5) and (7.6) into (7.4), we have

$$S_{A,B} = \frac{\mathbb{E}\left[L_{A,B}(T_b)\right]}{\sum_{i=1}^{b} \alpha_i \left(1 - \frac{T_i}{T_b} \mathbb{E}\left[L_{A,B}(T_b)\right]\right)}.$$

This formula clearly shows that the expected tranched loss $\mathbb{E}\left[L_{A,B}(T_b)\right]$ is the fundamental driver of the value of a tranche, thus it can be used as an alternative quotation system. Recall, however, that in the base correlation quotation system described in Section 3.2.4, we decompose $L_{A,B}(T)$ as

$$L_{A,B}(T) = \frac{1}{B-A}\left[BL_B(T) - AL_A(T)\right]$$

where

$$L_K(T) = \frac{1}{K}\left[L(T) - (L(T)-X)^+\right] = \frac{1}{K}Etl_K(\rho k).$$

The quotation object we will use for interpolation and extrapolation is the expected tranched loss (ETL) defined in (7.3).

7.2.2 Properties for Interpolation

The first advantage of this object it that we can compute, calling $F_{L(T)}$ the cumulative distribution of $L(T)$, the following derivative

$$\begin{aligned}\frac{\partial}{\partial K}Etl_K &= \frac{\partial}{\partial K}\mathbb{E}\left[L(T) - (L(T)-K)^+\right]\\ &= -\frac{\partial}{\partial K}\int_0^\infty (L(T)-K)^+\, dF_{L(T)}\\ &= \frac{\partial}{\partial K}\int_K^\infty (K - L(T))\, dF_{L(T)} = \Pr(L(T) > K).\end{aligned}$$

A probability must be non-negative, so we have *a condition on the first derivative* that the interpolation needs to satisfy. If we derive again we have, recalling also (2.22),

$$\frac{\partial^2}{\partial K^2}Etl_K = -f_{L(T)},$$

where $f_{L(T)}$ is the probability density of $L(T)$. Since a density must be non-negative, we know that the *second derivative must be non-positive*. We have much more information than we had when interpolating correlation.

7.2.3 Properties for Turning Extrapolation into Interpolation

But there is more. For the expected tranched loss we do not have the same indetermination about the boundary levels Etl_0 and $Etl_{100\%}$ that we had with ρ_0 and $\rho_{100\%}$. We can also use the mathematical properties of Etl_K to turn extrapolation into interpolation. In fact Etl_0 and $Etl_{100\%}$ do not really depend on ρ_0 and $\rho_{100\%}$, and they are known:

$$\begin{aligned}Etl_0 &= \mathbb{E}\left[L(T) - (L(T)-0)^+\right] = 0,\\ Etl_{100\%} &= \mathbb{E}\left[L(T) - (L(T)-100\%)^+\right] = \mathbb{E}\left[L(T)\right].\end{aligned}$$

The non-tranched expected loss $\mathbb{E}[L(T)]$ involves no optionality on the loss and thus it depends only on the default probability of the portfolio components, available and easy to compute. Thus when we work on expected tranched loss *there is no extrapolation*, it is all interpolation, and we have conditions on the first two derivatives of the interpolator. We have reduced strongly our indetermination. First of all, we can compute the boundaries that an *Etl* curve must respect. This is computed in Parcell and Wood (2007) and shown here in Figure 7.6.

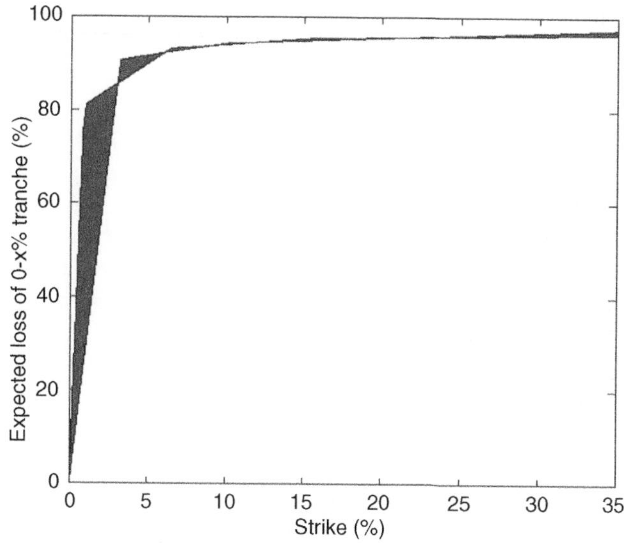

Figure 7.6 From Parcell and Wood (2007): boundaries on expected tranched loss

From the boundaries on expected tranched loss we can also deduce the boundaries that must be respected by a correlation interpolator/extrapolator, shown in Figure 7.7.

In some areas the bounds are tight, too much to be respected by a piecewise linear interpolation/extrapolation for correlation like the one typically used in the market.

Parcell and Wood (2007) also compute an interpolated ETL using a piecewise quadratic interpolator on which they constrain the sign of the derivatives and fix the extreme points to

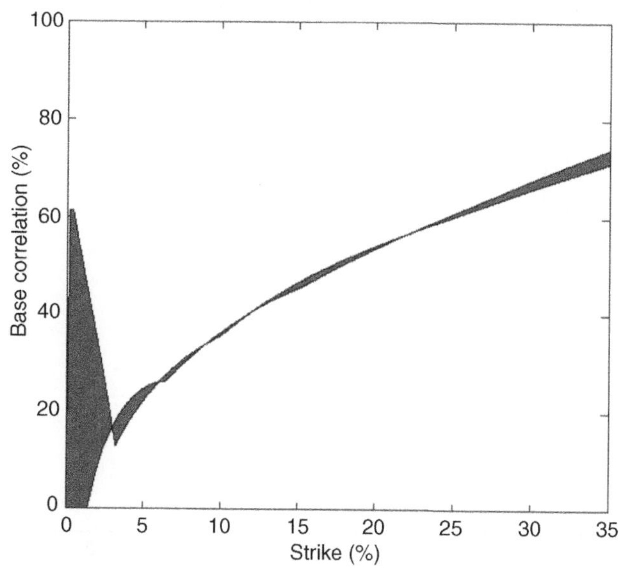

Figure 7.7 From Parcell and Wood (2007): boundaries on Gaussian correlation coming from boundaries on ETL

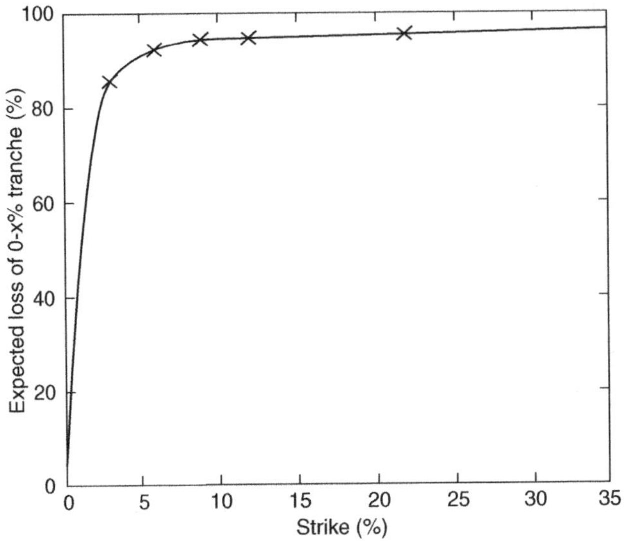

Figure 7.8 Bootstrapped ETL from Parcell and Wood (2007)

zero and to the non-tranched expected portfolio loss. The resulting spreads can be seen in Figure 7.8.

As done for inter/extrapolated correlations, one can now compute the equilibrium spreads for all tranchelets

$$[X\% - (X + 0.5)\,\%]\,.$$

In difference to the correlation case, with interpolated ETL there are neither negative spreads nor spreads increasing with subordination, as shown in Figure 7.9.

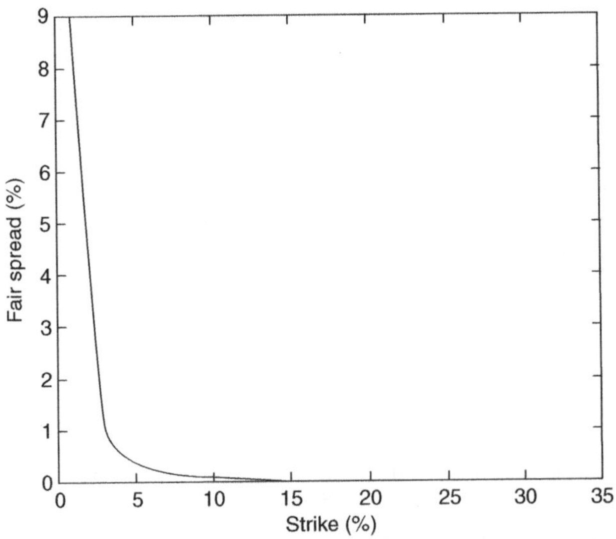

Figure 7.9 Tranchelet spreads from Parcell and Wood (2007) when inter/extrapolating ETL

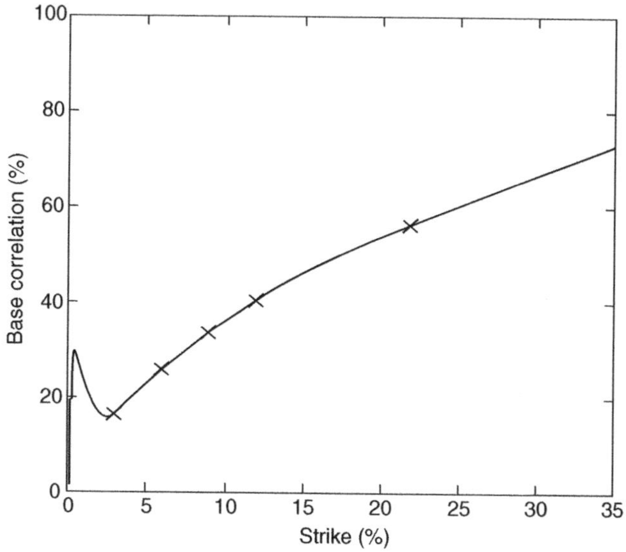

Figure 7.10 Gaussian correlation from Parcell and Wood (2007) when inter/extrapolating ETL

Interestingly, we can see which base correlation curve is implied by the *Etl* curve. The resulting curve is shown in Figure 7.10 and it is very different from the one obtained via direct interpolation of correlation that we saw in Figure 7.4. This is confirmed by different types of interpolator.

For more details the reader is again referred to Parcell and Wood (2007). Here the interest has been to show how a simple change of the variable we use to express, for example, a market skew can eliminate the need to extrapolate and can give us useful constraints to guarantee that our interpolation is consistent.

8
Correlations

During the credit crunch, all trading desks in banks suffered big losses. For credit desks, the most unexpected and painful losses were associated with CDO tranches, in particular senior tranches, which lost almost all their value due to default correlation breaking new high ground until it reached the maximum value possible, 1. The worst moment for interest rate derivatives desks was in June 2008 when, particularly in the Euro market, the term structure inverted with the short end, usually the lowest, jumping up and the long end, usually the highest, falling down. The losses were particularly high on spread options, where the difference between a long end rate and a short end rate is the underlying. The implied correlations jumped down from a historically high level, and even negative correlations were feared, consistent with the observation that the two opposite ends of the term structure were moving in opposite directions. Equity derivatives suffered losses particularly in the segment of basket derivatives: they had been priced using historical correlations, but during the crisis, when all stock prices decreased together, correlations went up. What do all these losses have in common? They were all correlation losses.

Here we tackle the risk in correlation modelling from two different perspectives. First we cover the technical difficulties in controlling the correlations among the different risk factors in a model. This requires parameterizing correlations consistently with market patterns, guaranteeing the resulting matrix is well defined and controlling model dimensionality. We provide examples of the correlation of stochastic volatility and the underlying, interest rate correlations and cross-currency correlations.

Second, we focus on those more fundamental errors that we can make in designing correlations (or, more precisely, dependencies) in our models: assuming rigid relations for factors that have a higher degree of independence, and conversely taking as unrelated things that have stronger structural links. The history of financial losses and crises is paved with similar errors. Some of them have already been analyzed in other parts of the book. Here we recall some of them and analyze two further examples, a 'zero-correlation error' (underestimation of high correlation) and a 'one-correlation error'(introduction of strong links that may not exist). While one of the two errors has recently been exposed, we still run the risk of the second one. Finally, we explain that dynamics models of term structures involve three kinds of correlations: instantaneous, final and serial, that are then extensively used in the next chapter.

8.1 THE TECHNICAL DIFFICULTIES IN COMPUTING CORRELATIONS

Here we focus not on dependency but on correlations in the strict sense. See Embrechts et al. (1999) for the difference between the two. In fact, in finance dependencies are usually represented in three main possible ways.

1. One first possibility is through the use of common factors in structural models for the dynamics of variables. Two examples of this kind have been given in Chapter 3. One

example is the Marshall-Olkin model, where there exists a factor that can trigger the simultaneous default of two names. Another example is the possibility we hint at of creating default dependency through putting a common jump in the intensity of two names.
2. The second relatively common possibility for introducing dependency is using copulas, which have also been dealt with in Chapter 3.
3. The third, and by far most common, possibility to create dependence is the use of correlation matrices in models where the drivers are Brownian motions, and therefore their instantaneous movements have a multivariate Gaussian distribution. Here dependencies are controlled by matrices of correlations between instantaneous variations of random shocks and are at times called *instantaneous correlations* (see Section 8.2 for other types of correlation). This is the focus of this section.

Clearly this distinction is largely conventional, since correlations can also be seen as dependencies created by the presence of common Gaussian factors. However the distinction is practically relevant because solution 3) is ubiquitous in finance and presents a number of technical difficulties that can arise in all asset classes and all derivatives, while solutions 1) and 2) are all problem-specific.

First of all, correlation matrices must respect a number of properties that appear formal but are instead crucial for avoiding embarrassing modelling mistakes. An $M \times M$ correlation matrix ρ must have

1. **every element not higher than one**: $\left|\rho_{i,j}\right| \leq 1 \quad \forall\, i, j$
2. **unitary diagonal**: $\rho_{i,i} = 1,\ \forall\, i$
3. **symmetric**: $\rho_{i,j} = \rho_{j,i},\ \forall\, i, j$
4. **positive semidefinite**: $x'\rho x \geq 0,\ \forall x$.

Properties 1-2-3 are obvious, recalling that correlation is an index of inter-dependence normalized, symmetric, and maximum when measuring correlation of a variable with itself. Notice that property 1 is anyway implied by the three other properties. In fact, through the Cauchy-Schwartz inequality, for any symmetric positive semidefinite matrix ρ we have $\left|\rho_{ij}\right| \leq \sqrt{\rho_{ii}\rho_{jj}}$.

The least intuitive property is 4, but it is crucial. Consider the following example. If x is a column vector whose components are the quantities z_i of M assets in a portfolio, each one multiplied by the standard deviation σ_i of the value of the corresponding asset ($x_i = z_i\sigma_i$), and ρ is the $M \times M$ correlation among the values, then $x'\rho x$ is the variance of the portfolio value. A variance must be non-negative, therefore for any model to be meaningful it must imply positive semidefinite correlation matrices.

Properties above hold for all correlation matrices. When, then, we consider specific asset classes and specific models, the correlations involved may require additional properties, and technical solutions have been proposed in the literature to deal with them, particularly in the form of parametric functions for correlations. Some examples are given below, skipping credit for which correlation solutions and in particular parameterizations have already been analyzed in Chapter 3, but focusing on interest rate and cross-currency where there are always correlations due to the intrinsic multifactor nature of these markets. Many of the solutions shown here can also be applied to asset classes, such as equity or commodities, that while being mainly single asset can involve both basket or spread derivatives and even correlations between the different single name model factors. This relates in particular to the third example, which deals with correlations between assets and a common stochastic volatility factor.

8.1.1 Correlations in Interest Rate Modelling

In the Libor market model introduced in Section 6.2 the instantaneous correlations between forward rates are modelled through a matrix ρ. There are specific properties that we would like a matrix of rate correlations to enjoy, based both on intuition and on empirical observation. The first desired characteristic, at times called *decorrelation*, is the reduction in correlation as the distance between maturities increases, namely

$$\rho_{i,j} \geq \rho_{i,j+h}, h > 1.$$

For example, this implies that in an $M \times M$ correlation matrix of annual forward rates we have $\rho_{1,2} \geq \rho_{1,M}$, the correlation between the rate that expires in 1 year and the rate that expires in 2 years is larger than the correlation between the rate that expires in 1 year and the rate that expires in M years. Graphically this means that column entries decrease when moving away from the main diagonal.

A second feature that is considered desirable in the market does not regard the distance between the maturity of rates, but the role of the maturity for couples of rates which are equally spaced. To make things simpler, think of $\rho_{1,2}$ and $\rho_{M-1,M}$. What do you expect,

$$\rho_{1,2} \lesseqgtr \rho_{M-1,M}?$$

The right answer is

$$\rho_{1,2} \leq \rho_{M-1,M}, \quad M > 1.$$

In fact we expect an increase in interdependency between equally spaced forward rates as their maturities increase. Graphically it means that sub-diagonals of the correlation matrix are increasing when moving south-eastwards. This *sub-diagonal trend* can be intuitively justified since adjacent, or equally spaced, forward rates appear less distinguishable when their maturities are higher. An investor asked to choose between an investment with 1 year horizon or one with 2 year horizon will probably make a precise choice, while he will probably be indifferent between an horizon of 19 years and one of 20 years. This indifference turns into higher correlation. Both properties are approximately visible in the historically estimated correlations among the daily changes of forward rates presented in Figure 8.1.

In the LMM there are many correlation parameters. If the rates are $M + 1$ including the first deterministic spot rate, the free correlation parameters (different from 1 and from each other)

$\mathrm{Corr}(dF_i^d, dF_j^d)$	1	2	3	4	5	6	7	8	9	10
1	1.00	0.79	0.46	0.50	0.48	0.39	0.37	0.42	0.38	0.38
2	0.79	1.00	0.63	0.67	0.68	0.57	0.54	0.64	0.62	0.60
3	0.46	0.63	1.00	0.85	0.71	0.65	0.57	0.67	0.64	0.62
4	0.50	0.67	0.85	1.00	0.77	0.66	0.62	0.74	0.72	0.69
5	0.48	0.68	0.71	0.77	1.00	0.93	0.91	0.89	0.77	0.76
6	0.39	0.57	0.65	0.66	0.93	1.00	0.96	0.86	0.71	0.70
7	0.37	0.54	0.57	0.62	0.91	0.96	1.00	0.84	0.69	0.68
8	0.42	0.64	0.67	0.74	0.89	0.86	0.84	1.00	0.93	0.92
9	0.38	0.62	0.64	0.72	0.77	0.71	0.69	0.93	1.00	0.99
10	0.38	0.60	0.62	0.69	0.76	0.70	0.68	0.92	0.99	1.00

Figure 8.1 Historical estimation of correlations for annual forward rates – 1 year of data (2008)

will be $M(M-1)/2$. When the correlations in the model are determined implicitly as free parameters through calibration, for instance to swaptions, it is very hard to recover the above properties. Often implied correlations extracted by market derivatives quotations are not very meaningful, and are highly irregular. Examples of this type were given in Brigo and Mercurio (2001). Probably this is mainly due to the fact that products vitally dependent on correlation, such as spread options, are not sufficiently liquid for use in calibration, while the liquid ones such as swaptions have only a faint dependence on correlations.

One solution is to take correlations exogenously, for instance fixing correlations according to historical market estimates. In this case we can usually find meaningful correlations, and still have enough freedom to calibrate to reference products by means of the volatility function, as we will see in the Brigo and Morini (2006) calibration approach analyzed in Chapter 9. Otherwise, if one wants to use correlations as calibration parameters, it is better to reduce the number of correlation parameters and impose some structure. This can be obtained by parameterizations, such as

- classic two-parameter exponential form. It guarantees properties 1-2-3-4 and decorrelation, but sub-diagonals are flat

$$\rho_{i,j} = \rho_\infty + (1 - \rho_\infty)\exp[-\beta|i - j|], \quad \beta \geq 0. \tag{8.1}$$

Instead, to also gain control of the sub-diagonal trend, the form above must be modified, for example as in

- Rebonato (1998) three-parameter exponential form (guarantees properties 1-2-3, decorrelation, and increasing sub-diagonals, but 4 (positive-semidefiniteness) is not guaranteed)

$$\rho_{i,j} = \rho_\infty + (1 - \rho_\infty)\exp[-|i - j|(\beta - \alpha(\max(i, j) - 1))]. \tag{8.2}$$

  Since this form is not automatically positive semidefinite, one has to check a posteriori that the resulting matrix enjoys such a property.

Additionally, in interest rate modelling one also wants to control the *rank* of a correlation matrix. The rank of a matrix is the number of its non-null eigenvalues. Why should we care about a property that sounds so theoretical? Because the correlation rank, in a multidimensional model with a Gaussian structure of the shocks, equals the real number of independent stochastic factors affecting the variables dynamics, namely the number of actual random numbers that one has to generate in Monte Carlo simulation of a model. If a Libor market model with M rates is driven by M-dimensional vector of shocks dZ with $M \times M$ correlation ρ, we do not necessarily have an 'M factor' model. In fact, if $rank(\rho) = r < M$, there exists a matrix B which $M \times r$ such that $\rho = BB'$ so that

$$dZ \sim BdY,$$

where dY is r-dimensional, made up of just r independent stochastic shocks. The actual number of independent stochastic factors in the model is just r. If r was for example 2, we have a 'two-factor' model. When the number of factors is high, numerical methods often used to price exotic derivatives become computationally burdensome, while correct prices could often be efficiently expressed even with a model representing variables as combinations of a lower number of independent stochastic factors. This is particularly true when speaking of interest rate modelling, as confirmed by the numerous pieces of research performing *principal component analysis* and finding that only a few factors are really relevant in describing the movements of the term structure.

To meet this different need, parameterizations have been developed that not only allow one to guarantee the properties 1-2-3-4, but also to control the rank. They can be used on all asset classes. The most popular was proposed by Rebonato and Jäckel (1999). The space of $M \times M$ correlation matrices with rank $r < M$ can be represented as

$$BB'$$

where B is $M \times r$ with rows as follows

$$\begin{aligned} b_{i,1} &= \cos\theta_{i,1} \\ b_{i,k} &= \cos\theta_{i,k}\sin\theta_{i,1}\cdots\sin\theta_{i,k-1}, \quad 1 < k < r, \\ b_{i,r} &= \sin\theta_{i,1}\cdots\sin\theta_{i,r-1}, \quad i = 1,\ldots,M. \end{aligned}$$

The matrix of angles θ are the parameters of this functional form, which can be used in all asset classes since it does not focus on the properties of forward rate correlation matrices or on the reduction of the number of parameters but only on the representation of all correlations with reduced rank. Alternatively, the rank of a correlation matrix can be modified by algorithms that allow one to find low rank approximations of full rank matrices, such as the method presented in Morini and Webber (2006).

8.1.2 Cross-currency Correlations

The parameterizations (8.1) and (8.2) in the above section are based on exponential functions, and they fit very well the behaviour of forward interest rate correlations, which in fact is characterized by an exponential decline in the columns of a correlation matrix starting from the unit entry on the main diagonal, $i \geq j$ (we look at the lower triangle of the matrix). We can observe this in the correlation matrix of Figure 8.1, whose columns are plotted in Figure 8.2.

Correlations decrease rapidly as $|i - j|$ increases at the beginning of the column, allowing the exponential forms to fit this behaviour very well.

In dealing with cross currency swaps, contracts where a flow of payments in domestic currency is exchanged with a flow of payments in foreign currency, both flows paying at dates T_i, $i = 0, 1, \ldots, M$, the variables that enter pricing are the forward rates of exchange, defined as

$$\Phi_i(t) = \frac{\varphi_t P^f(t, T_i)}{P(t, T_i)},$$

where φ_t is the rate of exchange (number of domestic currency units for a unit of foreign currency), $P^f(t, T_i)$ is the price of a foreign bond with maturity T_i expressed in foreign currency, and as usual $P(0, T_i)$ is the price of a domestic bond with the same maturity. When pricing options on cross-currency swaps, an issue that arises for example in evaluating the counterparty risk of a cross currency swap, the correlations among the $\Phi_i(t)$, $i = 0, 1, \ldots, M$, are also involved. We do not give more details on this pricing problem because they are of no interest here. What is of interest is that the correlations among forward exchange rates, when

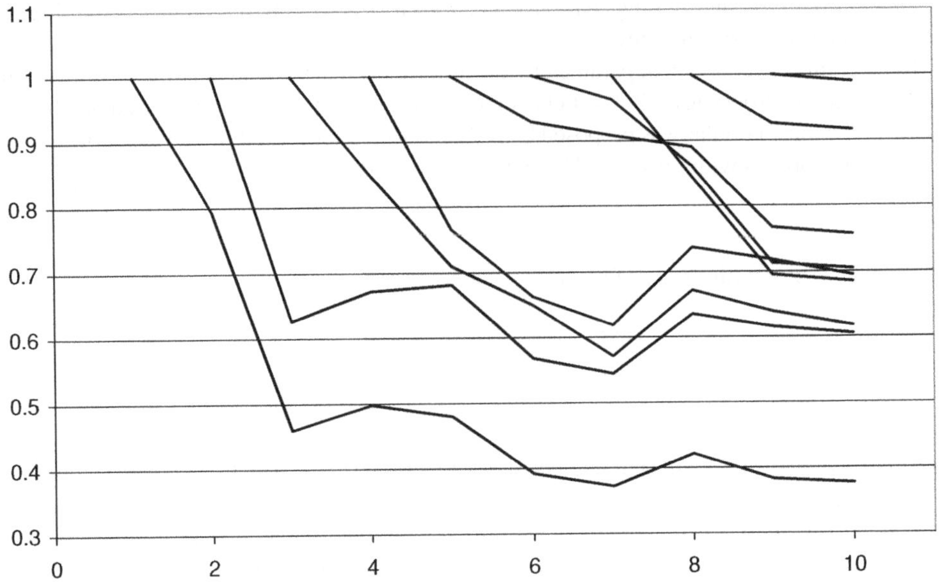

Figure 8.2 Interest rate correlation matrix (columns). Historical estimation, 2008

estimated historically, reveal features different from those of forward rate correlations, as can be seen looking at a forward exchange correlation matrix in Table 8.1 and Figure 8.3.

We see that forward exchange rate correlations do not decrease rapidly at the beginning of the columns. On the contrary, the decrease in correlation is slower at the beginning, and then gets steeper. Towards the end of the column, the steepness reduces again. Alternatively, we could say that correlation, seen as a function of the distance between the maturities of the forward exchange rates, is a concave function at the short end and a convex function at the long end of the range under consideration.

How can we get a parameterization that allows for such a behaviour? One possibility is to modify the general framework of Schoenmakers and Coffey (2003), which was devised for

Table 8.1 FX (forward exchange rates) correlation. EUR/USD. Historical estimation, 2008

$\mathrm{Corr}(d\Phi_i, d\Phi_j)$	1	2	3	4	5	6	7	8	9	10
1	1.00	0.99	0.93	0.91	0.86	0.74	0.71	0.64	0.61	0.59
2	0.99	1.00	0.97	0.92	0.88	0.75	0.73	0.66	0.63	0.61
3	0.93	0.97	1.00	0.89	0.86	0.75	0.72	0.66	0.62	0.60
4	0.91	0.92	0.89	1.00	0.99	0.80	0.79	0.73	0.70	0.68
5	0.86	0.88	0.86	0.99	1.00	0.81	0.79	0.74	0.71	0.69
6	0.74	0.75	0.75	0.80	0.81	1.00	0.98	0.96	0.93	0.92
7	0.71	0.73	0.72	0.79	0.79	0.98	1.00	0.97	0.94	0.95
8	0.64	0.66	0.66	0.73	0.74	0.96	0.97	1.00	0.96	0.96
9	0.61	0.63	0.62	0.70	0.71	0.93	0.94	0.96	1.00	0.96
10	0.59	0.61	0.60	0.68	0.69	0.92	0.95	0.96	0.96	1.00

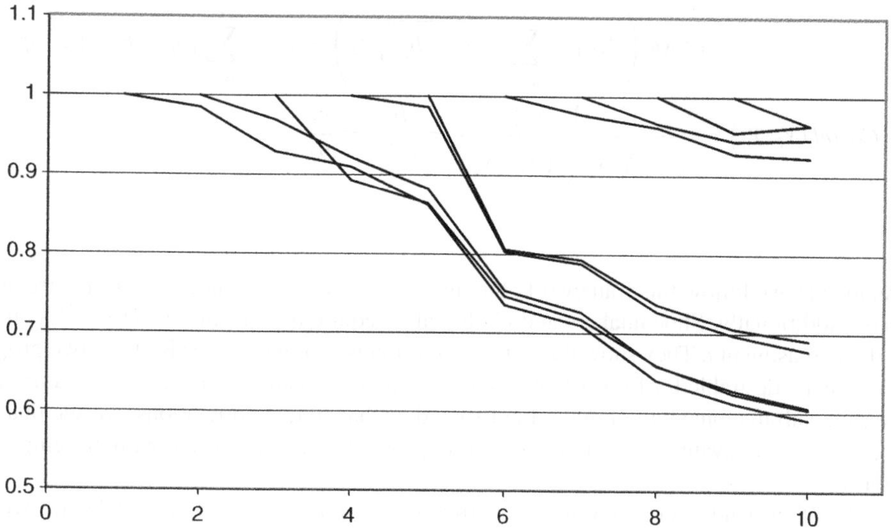

Figure 8.3 FX correlation matrix (columns). EUR/USD. Historical estimation, 2008

interest rate correlations but can be adapted to much more general situations, as we show in the following. We first recall the general result by Schoenmakers and Coffey (2003).

Proposition 15. *Schoenmakers and Coffey (2003) show that setting*

$$\rho i, J = \frac{b(i)}{b(j)}, \quad j \geq i$$

where $b(j) > 0$ and $b(j)$ strictly increasing in j *on $[1, n]$, then properties 1-2-3-4 of a correlation matrix are guaranteed.*

Proof. Let $b_i, i = 1, \ldots, n$ be positive increasing numbers. Then set

$$c_i \triangleq \begin{cases} \sqrt{b_i^2 - b_{i-1}^2} \text{when } i = 2, \ldots, n \\ b_1 \text{when } i = 1 \end{cases}.$$

Let $Z_i, i = 1, \ldots, n$ be independent standard Gaussian and set $Y_i = \sum_{k=1}^{i} c_k Z_k$. Then, for $i \leq j$,

$$Cov\left(Y_i, Y_j\right) = \mathbb{E}\left[\sum_{k=1}^{i} c_k Z_k \times \sum_{h=1}^{j} c_h Z_h\right]$$

$$\begin{aligned} Cov\left(Y_i, Y_j\right) &= \mathbb{E}\left[\sum_{k=1}^{i} c_k Z_k \times \left(\sum_{k=1}^{i} c_k Z_k + \sum_{h=i+1}^{j} c_h Z_h\right)\right] \\ &= \mathbb{E}\left[\left(\sum_{k=1}^{i} c_k Z_k\right)^2\right] = VAR\left(\sum_{k=1}^{i} c_k Z_k\right) \end{aligned}$$

$$= VAR\left(Z_1 b_1 + \sum_{k=2}^{i} \sqrt{b_k^2 - b_{k-1}^2} Z_k\right) = b_1^2 + \sum_{k=2}^{i} (b_k^2 - b_{k-1}^2) = b_i^2$$

$$Correl\left(Y_i, Y_j\right) = \frac{Cov\left(Y_i, Y_j\right)}{\sqrt{VAR(Y_i)}\sqrt{VAR\left(Y_j\right)}} = \frac{b_i^2}{b_i b_j} = \frac{b_i}{b_j}$$

■

As long as we follow this framework, the matrix we build is guaranteed to be a correlation matrix. Additionally, Shoenmakers and Coffey also require the function $h(j) = \frac{b(j)}{b(j+1)}$ to be strictly increasing in j. They show that if this condition is guaranteed we also have two properties which are desirable for forward interest rate correlation matrices: decreasing columns and increasing sub-diagonals. Looking at the forward exchange rate correlations, we see that the first property is relevant to us, while the second property is not consistent with our empirical evidence.

On the other hand, there are other properties we are interested in, in particular we would like to be able to control the convexity of the columns. In this framework, we can control the behaviour of the columns of the correlation matrix by controlling the behaviour of the function $b(j)$. To understand this point it is convenient to rewrite Schoenmakers' and Coffey's condition as

$$\rho i, J = \frac{b(j)}{b(i)}, \ i \geq j$$

and define $a(j) = \frac{1}{b(j)}$ so that

$$\rho(i, j) = \frac{b(j)}{b(i)} = \frac{a(i)}{a(j)}, \ i \geq j,$$

so that now controlling the behaviour of the matrix columns corresponds to controlling the behaviour of $\rho i, J$ as a function of i for J and fixed in particular, since for each column J is a positive constant, the behaviour of each column replicates that of $a(i)$.

In order to remain in the framework that guarantees that the matrix is well defined we have to choose a decreasing function $a(i)$ (corresponding to increasing $b(i)$). This translates into decreasing columns (Property 1 by Schoenmakers and Coffey), and this is desirable since it corresponds to our empirical evidence. Additionally, we would like the function to be concave on the short end, turning convex for longer maturities. A decreasing function with such behaviour of the second derivative is, for example, the cosine in the range $[0, \pi]$.

Obviously, we will need to turn it into an always positive function and be flexible about the inflection point where the convexity reverts. Such a goal can be obtained by

$$a(i) = \cos\left(\pi\alpha + \pi(\beta - \alpha)\frac{i}{n}\right) - \cos(\beta\pi) + \gamma, \quad 0 \leq \alpha \leq \beta \leq 1, \gamma > 0, \qquad (8.3)$$

where the addition of $-\cos(\beta\pi)$ moves the minimum of the function to zero, and γ gives some more flexibility in recovering market patterns by shifting the function in the positive semiplan (the condition $\gamma > 0$ guarantees that $a(i) > 0$, required for $\rho i, J$ is well defined). The coefficients α and β allow us to choose the 'convexity area' of the cosine

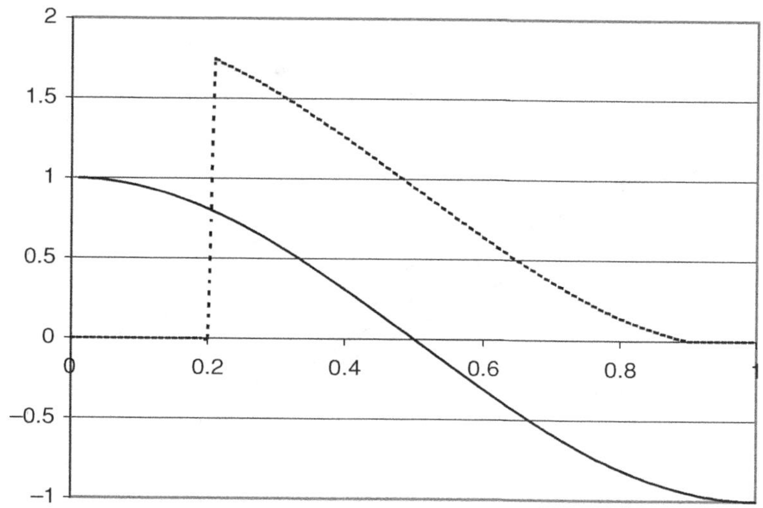

Figure 8.4 A cosine parameterization for FX correlations

which best corresponds to market patterns. In Figure 8.4 we plot $\cos(x\pi)$ for $x \in (0, 1]$ and $\cos(\pi\alpha + \pi(\beta - \alpha)x) - \cos(\beta\pi)$ for $x \in (0, 1]$, having set $\alpha = 0.2$ and $\beta = 0.9$.

Notice that if we write $x = \frac{i}{n}$, we have

$$a(i) = y(x) = \cos(\pi\alpha + \pi(\beta - \alpha)x) - \cos(\beta\pi) + \gamma, \quad x \in (0, 1]. \tag{8.4}$$

The argument $\pi\alpha + \pi(\beta - \alpha)x$ of the cosine function can take values in the set $[0, \pi]$ since $0 \leq \alpha \leq \beta \leq 1$. We have

$$y'(x) = -\sin(\pi\alpha + \pi(\beta - \alpha)x)\pi(\beta - \alpha)$$
$$y''(x) = -\cos(\pi\alpha + \pi(\beta - \alpha)x)\pi^2(\beta - \alpha)^2$$

thus

$$y'(x) > 0 \Longrightarrow x > \frac{1-\alpha}{\beta-\alpha},$$
$$y''(x) \geq 0 \Longrightarrow \frac{1/2-\alpha}{\beta-\alpha} \leq x \leq \frac{3/2-\alpha}{\beta-\alpha}.$$

Since $\frac{1-\alpha}{\beta-\alpha} \geq 1$, the condition on the first derivative is never satisfied, thus correlation cannot be increasing, approximately consistently with the typical market patterns. Since $\frac{3/2-\alpha}{\beta-\alpha} > 1$, the condition on the second derivative reduces to the fact that for $\alpha \geq 1/2$ the convexity is always non-negative, otherwise we can have a change of convexity from negative to positive at $x = \frac{1/2-\alpha}{\beta-\alpha}$.

We fit this form onto the historical estimation of Figure 8.1, and we do the same with the exponential parameterization (8.2). The fit of our form is slightly better than (8.2), but what really matters is visible from the plot of the first column in Figure 8.5: while the best the exponential form can do to fit the market patterns is to become a straight line, our parameterization can reproduce the actual behaviour of correlations. See Facchinetti and Morini (2008) for more details.

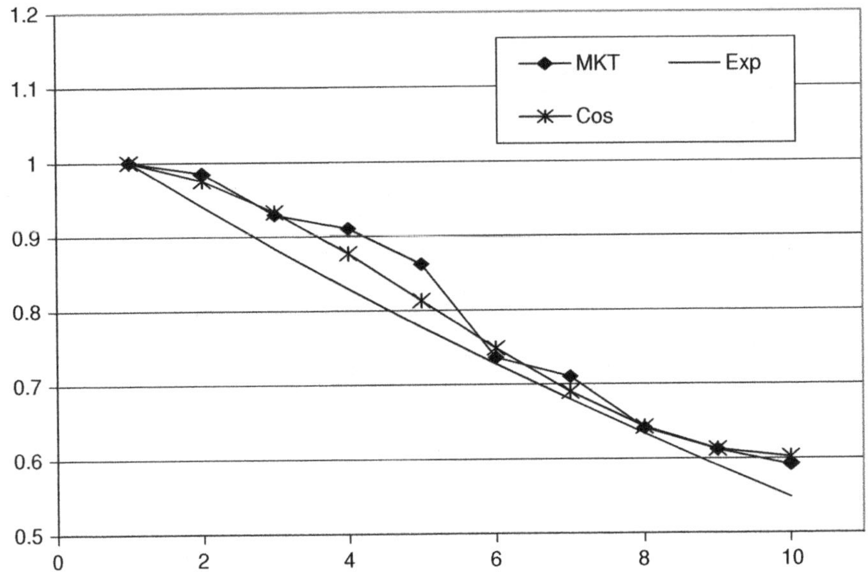

Figure 8.5 Fit to historical FX correlations by different parameterizations

8.1.3 Stochastic Volatility Correlations

This approach can be used in stochastic volatility models for basket equity or commodity derivatives, or for multifactor rare models. We follow the rare case in Mercurio and Morini (2007) that introduced this approach. In a stochastic volatility Libor model involving M forward rates $F_k(t)$ and one stochastic volatility factor $V(t)$,

$$dF_k(t) = \sigma_k(t)V(t)F_k(t)dW_k(t)$$
$$dV(t) = D(t, V)dt + \upsilon(t)\psi(V(t))\, dW^{\upsilon}(t),$$

like the model mentioned in Section 6.5.1, there are two different kinds of (measure-independent) instantaneous correlations involved: the rate-rate correlations, an $M \times M$ matrix ρ^r given by

$$\mathbb{E}\left[dW_i(t)dW_j(t)\right] = \rho_{ij}^r dt$$

and the rate-vol correlations, an M-dimension column vector ρ^{υ} given by

$$\mathbb{E}\left[dW^{\upsilon}(t)dW_i(t)\right] = \rho_i^{\upsilon} dt.$$

They are often modelled independently, assuming some synthetic parameterization for ρ^r, depending on few parameters and consistent with the typical properties of forward rate correlations, while there are no standard parameterizations for ρ^{υ}. However, when the model is implemented for pricing, the model involves an $M + 1$ stochastic vector

$$X = [F_1, \ldots, F_M, V]$$

characterized by a vector of Wiener shocks

$$dW = \left[dW_1, \ldots, dW_M, dW^{\upsilon}\right]$$

with a matrix ρ of instantaneous correlations given by

$$\rho = \left[\begin{array}{c|c} \rho^r & \rho^v \\ \hline (\rho^v)' & 1 \end{array}\right].$$

This matrix is required to be a valid correlation matrix for the model to be consistent and arbitrage-free, in particular it has to be positive semidefinite. Moreover, only if the last property is satisfied is it possible to use Monte Carlo simulation, since simulation requires us to find a matrix C such that $\rho = CC'$, so as to simulate dW as CdZ, $dZ \sim \mathbb{N}(0, Idt)$. We have that $\rho = CC'$ if and only if it is positive semidefinite.

Even when the parameterization chosen for ρ^r is guaranteed to be positive semidefinite, when it is 'fringed' by ρ^v it is very easy for this property to get lost in the final matrix ρ. Thus we need a global parameterization for the matrix ρ.

This global parameterization is characterized by two desiderata:

- the submatrix ρ^r must be modelled through few parameters and must respect the typical features of a forward rate correlation matrix;
- for ρ^v one can accept M parameter and would desire as much freedom as possible, in order to fit the market skew.

In our approach, described in the following, building the global parameterization of correlations requires building first a preliminary covariance matrix, which has to be positive semidefinite. We can build such a matrix and assess its properties both starting from a simple stochastic model or from matrix analysis. Both approaches are illustrated below.

We consider a preliminary vector of stochastic processes

$$dY = \left[dY_1, \ldots, dY_M, dY^v\right]$$

based on the dynamics

$$dY_i = \bar{\rho}_i^v dY^v + dZ_i;$$

where dY^v, dZ_i are Wiener processes and

$$dZ_i \perp dY^v, \ \mathbb{E}\left[dZ_i dZ_j\right] = \theta_{ij} dt.$$

Obviously the $M \times M$ matrix θ must be taken positive-semidefinite. This leads to the following covariance structure.

$$\begin{aligned} Cov\left(dY_i, dY_j\right) &= \bar{\rho}_i^v \bar{\rho}_j^v \, dt + \theta_{ij} \, dt \\ Cov\left(dY_i, dY^v\right) &= \bar{\rho}_i^v \, dt \\ Cov\left(dY^v, dY^v\right) &= dt. \end{aligned} \tag{8.5}$$

The covariance structure in (8.5) can also be studied by matrix analysis. It corresponds to taking two different matrices A and B, both of dimension $(M+1) \times (M+1)$, and characterized as follows

$$A\,dt = \left[\begin{array}{c|c} \left[\bar{\rho}_i^v \bar{\rho}_j^v\right] & \bar{\rho}^v \\ \hline (\bar{\rho}^v)' & 1 \end{array}\right] dt$$

$$B\,dt = \left[\begin{array}{c|c} [\theta_{ij}] & [0] \\ \hline [0] & 0 \end{array}\right] dt.$$

Notice that A is a viable covariance matrix (typical, for example, of a one factor model $dY_i = \bar{\rho}_i^v dY^v$), positive semidefinite since $A = \begin{bmatrix} \bar{\rho}^v \\ 1 \end{bmatrix} \begin{bmatrix} \bar{\rho}^v \\ 1 \end{bmatrix}'$. B also is positive semidefinite when θ_{ij} has been chosen to be so (apart from the addition of a zero eigenvalue, the spectral properties are not altered by the 'fringing' with null vectors that leads to B starting from θ).

When these two matrices have been defined, one takes for the preliminary vector

$$dY = \left[dY_1, \ldots, dY_M, dY^v\right],$$

a covariance matrix given by $Cov = A + B$, which coincides with the covariance structure in (8.5) and is a positive semidefinite matrix, since the sum of two positive semidefinite matrices is always positive semidefinite.

Notice that in this parameterization through $\bar{\rho}_i^v$ we have full freedom to choose the covariance $Cov\,(dY_i, dY^v)$ between the factors dY_i and the unique factor dY^v, while the covariance $Cov\left(dY_i, dY_j\right)$ between the factors dY_i is dominated by the features we have chosen for θ_{ij}. In particular, θ can be modelled through some classic parameterization for forward rates correlation, such as (8.1) which is guaranteed to be positive semidefinite and to exhibit the *decorrelation* feature typical of forward rates correlations.

The parameterization θ_{ij} is then modified by the $\bar{\rho}_i^v \bar{\rho}_j^v$ term; however, we usually have $\bar{\rho}_i^v \bar{\rho}_j^v \ll 1$ when $\bar{\rho}_i^v$ are chosen in line with low correlation terms. This is shown in Figure 8.6.

It is clear the matrix $Cov = A + B$ is not a correlation matrix since, while being symmetric and positive semidefinite, it does not have a unitary diagonal. So in order to move to a valid

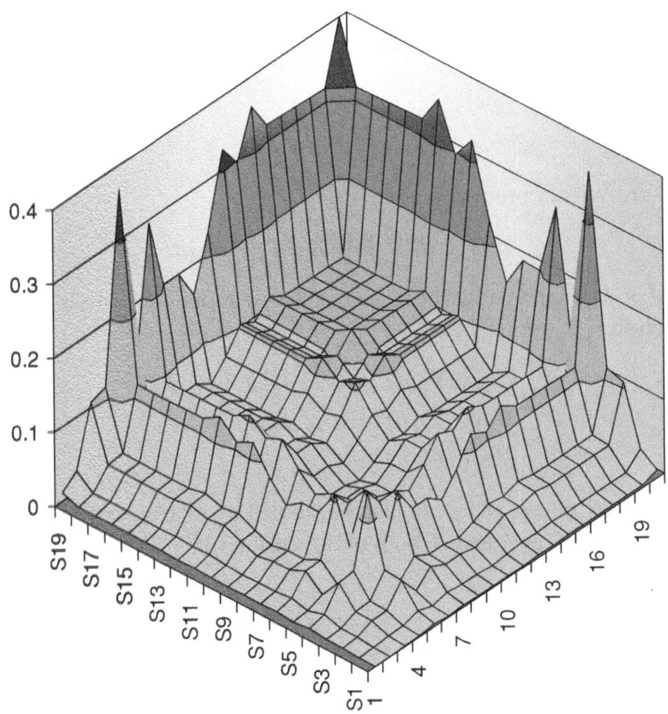

Figure 8.6 The parameterization A

correlation matrix we have to apply some normalization method preserving the fundamental properties. A simple choice is a rescaling, leading to the following definition of the final parameterization:

$$\rho_{ij} = \frac{Cov_{ij}}{\sqrt{Cov_{ii}Cov_{jj}}}, \tag{8.6}$$

$$Cov = \left[\begin{array}{c|c} \left[\theta_{ij} + \bar{\rho}_i^v \bar{\rho}_j^v\right] & \bar{\rho}^v \\ \hline (\bar{\rho}^v)' & 1 \end{array}\right],$$

$$\theta_{i,j} = k + (1-k)e^{-\beta|i-j|}.$$

Notice ρ is positive semidefinite when Cov is, since when a matrix X is positive semidefinite, PXP' is always positive semidefinite.

A real-world application of the above parameterization to a Libor market model with stochastic volatility is performed in Mercurio and Morini (2007), where the global parameterization (8.6) is first introduced. The analysis reported there shows that using the global parameterization above does not reduce the fitting capability of the model compared to a less constrained model where ρ^r is parameterized via (8.1) while ρ^v is a free skew-fitting parameter. Additionally, the global parameterization makes correlation parameters more regular. But the most relevant issue in favour of the use of the above parameterization comes from spectral analysis of the two correlation matrices

Rates Only Param.	19.024	1.924	0.046	0.013	0.006	0.003	0.002	...	0.000	−1.026
Global Param.	18.628	1.301	0.041	0.012	0.005	0.003	0.002	...	0.000	0.000

8.2 FUNDAMENTAL ERRORS IN MODELLING CORRELATIONS

Whenever we devise a model, we are probably making a correlation mistake. A model is always a simplification. In performing a simplification, we certainly represent the market with a number of variables lower than those actually existing in reality. Therefore, some objects which are distinct and, even if correlated, have a correlation lower than 1, are collapsed to a single object, implicitly making their correlation 1. Another unavoidable simplification is that some quantities which are actually stochastic, because they move in an unpredictable way, are represented in the model with deterministic quantities or even flat quantities. This is not only a volatility mistake. Most of the time it is a correlation mistake. The original stochastic quantity had some correlation with the other stochastic variables that almost certainly was not zero. When this stochastic quantity is reduced to a deterministic one, usually a flat parameter, all these correlations are implicitly set to zero.

Even in this simple consideration we have seen the two most typical, and most dangerous, mistakes we can make in specifying correlations, which are:

$\rho = 0$ **mistake** Taking as unrelated things that have structural links.
$\rho = 1$ **mistake** Assuming a rigid relation for things that have a degree of independence.

Clearly, also assuming a correlation $\rho = 30\%$ when the most reasonable value is $\rho = 70\%$ is a correlation mistake. However, such errors are usually less dramatic and, more importantly, they are less common. Most often dramatic correlation errors are perpetrated with the purpose of simplifying a model, and the simplest cases of correlations are ± 1 and 0. The two cases 1 and -1 do not need separate treatment since a correlation -1 with X can always be written as a correlation 1 with $-X$.

There are also cases in which the two errors can be performed jointly! The correlation error we saw in Section (3.3) is of this type: an average correlation was used while market reality, and also market quotes, would have been much more effectively explained by a parameterization that involved more extreme values in the correlation matrix, including 0 and 1 .

8.2.1 The Zero-correlation Error

In his paper 'A Free Lunch and the Credit Crunch', Jon Gregory talks of monoline insurers. These are companies that provide insurance for high-rating transactions in structured finance. The most typical transactions of this kind in the years before the crisis were senior tranches of CDOs. In offering guarantees in case of losses of senior tranches, monolines are essentially financial companies taking most of their risk in selling protection on very senior credit derivatives.

Monolines were usually given very high ratings – AAA – by rating agencies. This was motivated mainly by the fact that monolines are only subject to losses when AAA derivatives make losses, and this may at first sight appear a logical and obvious justification for the rating. Secondly, a monoline had to follow strict guidelines that forced it to unwind some of its trades when its capital started to be reduced by losses. Thanks to their AAA rating, monolines did not have to post collateral when selling protection on senior tranches. Therefore buyers of insurance from monolines were fully subject to the default risk of the monoline counterparty, but again this was considered negligible thanks to the AAA rating.

Inspired by the arguments of Gregory (2008) but following a different route, below we show that such a state of things was motivated essentially by a zero-correlation error. Even if the AAA rating were a correct assessment of the *unconditional* probability of default of monolines, the conclusion that this made their sale of protection on senior tranches a reliable commitment can only have been motivated by a wrong assessment of the correlations involved in this issue.

Detailed treatment of counterparty risk is undertaken in Chapter 10, and we will not anticipate it here. However, we will anticipate a concept which is quite intuitive. The counterparty credit risk grows with:

1. the risk of default of the counterparty, obviously;
2. the value of the obligation that the counterparty has towards us. If the counterparty defaults, but at that moment its obligations towards us have very little value, our loss will be small.

Thus the worst case is where there is a strong correlation between the risk of default of the counterparty and the value of the obligation that the counterparty has towards us. For example, buying a put option on the stock of company X from company X itself is rarely a good deal: when the value of the stock is low, and therefore the put has maximum value, is also when we have the highest probability of default of the counterparty. In the counterparty risk literature, this is called *wrong way risk*.

Let us translate this into our case of interest. We will be very exposed to the counterparty when there is a high risk of default for a high number of CDO components, so that the risk of losses in the senior tranche is high. The exposure is highest when the defaults have already generated losses in the senior tranche and we are waiting for the protection payment. Thus the worst element here is a high correlation between the default time of the counterparty monoline and the occurrence of losses in senior tranches.

Let us analyze the situation with the tools we have developed in the rest of the book. We have seen that a very simple framework for dealing with default correlation are factor models, and in Section 3.2 we saw that the most common framework is the one-factor Gaussian copula, where we link the defaults τ_i through a Gaussian copula generated from the Gaussian random variables seen in (3.8):

$$X_i = \rho_i M + \sqrt{1-\rho_i^2} Y_i \quad i = 1, \ldots, n.$$

This is the simplest way to represent a reality where we believe that there is some systemic factor determining default – represented by M – together with idiosyncratic factors Y_i. In Chapter 3 we criticized many aspects of the Gaussian copula framework used in the credit market, but this fundamental assumption is one of its most solid aspects.

Section 3.2 showed how, within this framework, conditional to M the default times are independent, so that

$$\Pr(\tau_1 \le T_1, \ldots, \tau_n \le T_n | M) = \prod_{i=1}^{n} \Pr(\tau_i \le T | M) \tag{8.7}$$

$$= \prod_{i=1}^{n} \Pr\left(Y_i \le \frac{\Phi^{-1}\left(1 - e^{-\lambda_i T}\right) - \rho_i M}{\sqrt{1-\rho_i^2}} | M \right).$$

Since the representation (3.8) is assumed for all names in the market, the above formula $\Pr(\tau_1 \le T_1, \ldots, \tau_n \le T_n | M)$ applies to any set of n names we choose. We can take the above n names as the names that have to default in order for us to see losses in a senior tranche. Each name has default driven either by its own idiosyncratic factor Y_i or by the common systemic factor M. The expression $\Pr(\tau_1 \le T_1, \ldots, \tau_n \le T_n | M)$ shows that, whatever values of Y_i we get, we can always find an M that makes the probability of joint default as close to 1 as desired, since

$$\lim_{M \to -\infty} \Pr(\tau_1 \le T_1, \ldots, \tau_n \le T_n | M) = 1.$$

It would not be possible to obtain such a result playing with any of the Y_i. Each Y_i can influence only the default of name i, not the others, so even when it goes to $-\infty$ we have the default of the name i but possibly no effect on a senior tranche. Only M can influence n names together. Therefore losses in senior tranches (on *any* senior tranche) will be strongly associated with very low values of M.

If we now look at that special name which is our monoline, what will the level of the correlation parameter ρ_{Mono} be in the one-factor representation

$$X_{Mono} = \rho_{Mono} M + \sqrt{1-\rho_{Mono}^2} Y_{Mono} \quad ?$$

This name suffers losses only when senior tranches make losses. Normally this happens due to very low values of M. We expect the default time of the monoline to be crucially associated with the level of M, so that

$$\rho_{Mono} \approx 1,$$
$$X_{Mono} \approx M.$$

In this case, recalling that when we apply copulas we first generate the Gaussian X_i, then we transform it into a uniform and finally we apply (2.4), we get for the monoline

$$\tau_{Mono} \approx -\frac{1}{\lambda_{Mono}} \ln(1 - \Phi(M)).$$

The lower M, the closer τ_{Mono} will be to today, and that's the only important factor deciding the default time of a monoline. The lower the risk of default of the monoline λ_{Mono}, the higher the sensitivity of its default time to M. What have we found out? That both the monoline defaults and the losses on *any* senior tranches are associated with the same scenarios, those where M is very low.

The above analytical derivation is probably oversimplified, and one may argue about many of its simplifications. But it is actually still too complex to prove a very simple and intuitive concept: that an insurance on a systemic risk – like the risk which mainly affects senior CDO tranches – is a very unreliable insurance, because all the claims towards the insurer are likely to be made at the same time, making the insurer default exactly when its help would be most needed. When Jon Gregory explained this reasoning to me in Budapest in 2008, my comment was that buying monoline insurance on senior tranches looked like buying house fire insurance in London in the 17th century, when all houses were of wood and built very close to each other, so that a fire in one house was likely to set the entire city on fire. It is highly unlikely that, in the moment of need, the insurer would have had enough money to pay all the insurance claims. This is another example of insurance against systemic risk.

In spite of this, the market acted as if the insurance from monolines was valuable, treating the risk of default of monolines as if it were not correlated with the risk of default of senior tranches and giving monolines AAA rating as insurers. This appears a zero correlation error. In practice, when during the credit crunch CDO problems started to mount, the two biggest American monoline insurers of structured finance actually defaulted, and their counterparties suffered limited losses only thanks to government help.

See Gregory (2008) for an analysis that shows how the situation of monoline insurance buyers is similar to that of bank customers in a run on a bank, and for results showing how, again due to default correlation between monolines and senior tranches, even the strict guidelines imposed on monolines before the credit crunch were doomed to be ineffective in reducing counterparty risk for insurance buyers.

Mistakes where correlations are set to 0 in spite of strong dependencies can arise even more naturally. Consider the problem we analyzed in Section 4.1. This problem originated in the burst of a gap between Libor and OIS rates. These two curves, which used to be almost equal and almost perfectly correlated as shown in Figure 4.2, separated out in summer 2007. Where we had one $L(t, T)$, now we have $L(t, T)$ which just represents Libor and another rate $OIS(t, T)$ which represents an OIS rate. They are both important because Libor rates $L(t, T)$ are the underlying of most interest rate derivatives, while the rates $OIS(t, T)$ are those used to bootstrap term structure of default-free interest rates, to be used for discounting of all collateralized derivatives.

How can we price a standard interest rate derivative, which is indexed to L but must be discounted with OIS? Mercurio (2008) makes a model where the two rates are modelled separately, and we can set a correlation ρ among them, which can take all possible values from -1 to 1. The easiest value for this correlation is 0, which leads to a rather simple implementation of the model. But are we sure that such a choice makes sense? We have seen that the gap between L and OIS is due to the fact that, differently from OIS, L is not default-free but is affected by a special risk of default associated with banks in the Libor panel. Therefore we can write

$$L(t, T) = OIS(t, T) + S(t, T),$$

where $S(t, T)$ captures this Libor risk of default. This implies that the instantaneous correlation ρ can be written as

$$\begin{aligned} \rho &= InstCorrel(L(t, T), OIS(t, T)) \\ &= InstCorrel(OIS(t, T) + S(t, T), OIS(t, T)). \end{aligned}$$

And here the problem arises. How can these two objects, that have the rate $L(t, T)$ in common, have a correlation that can be 0 or even negative? It makes no sense. Therefore, in spite of the comfort that users may find in the zero correlation hypothesis, research has moved on and the market has followed. Funnily enough, the market seems to have moved from a 0-correlation error to a 1-correlation error.

8.2.2 The 1-Correlation Error

Mercurio (2009) correctly adresses the above issue by proposing to model $OIS(t, T)$ and $S(t, T)$, taking $L(t, T)$ simply as their sum. Again, what is the easiest choice for modelling $S(t, T)$, a choice taken by many banks? It is to take $S(t, T)$ as a deterministic quantity. But now we have a different problem, which is

$$\begin{aligned} & InstCorrel(L(t, T), OIS(t, T)) \\ &= InstCorrel(OIS(t, T) + S(t, T), OIS(t, T)) \\ &= InstCorrel(OIS(t, T), OIS(t, T)) = 1. \end{aligned} \tag{8.8}$$

We are taking the two variables L and OIS perfectly correlated, a hypothesis easily falsified just by looking at the historical behaviour of the two variables seen at 4.2. Faced with this new problem, the market is oscillating between the two classic mistakes.

Notice, in addition, that not only can this issue be important for the pricing of derivatives, but also for hedging. Let us consider the simplest interest rate derivative analyzed at length in 4.1. Before the credit crunch its price could be written as

$$\begin{aligned} & P(t, T)\mathbb{E}^T\left[\left(L\left(T', T\right) - K\right)\right] \\ &= P(t, T)\left[L\left(t; T', T\right) - K\right] \end{aligned}$$

where P came from the same Libor curve as L. A trader could compute a sensitivity to a part of the Libor term structure,

$$\frac{\partial P(t, T)\left[L\left(t; T', T\right) - K\right]}{\partial L(t; T', T)},$$

and this took into account both the effect of a movement of the curve on $P(t, T)$ and the more direct effect on $\left[L\left(t; T', T\right) - K\right]$. Notice that the sensitivity to the discounting has a sign opposite to the sensitivity to the expectation of the payoff. When rates go up, the expectation of the payoff goes up, but the discount goes down, reducing the total sensitivity.

After the credit crunch we have that the price is

$$\begin{aligned} & P^{OIS}(t,T)\mathbb{E}^{T\_OIS}\left[\left(L\left(T',T\right)-K\right)\right] \\ &= P^{OIS}(t,T)\left[\bar{L}\left(t;T',T\right)-K\right] \end{aligned}$$

where $\bar{L}\left(t;T',T\right)$ is a sort of forward rate (see Mercurio 2008) belonging to a curve linked to Libor and different from the curve of $P^{OIS}(t,T)$. If the trader assumes that the two curves are perfectly correlated as in (8.8), he or she could be tempted to see again one single sensitivity to the term structure, and will take as a hedge either an interest rate product linked to the OIS curve or one linked to the Libor curve, because they assume that in any case these will move in unison. If, instead, they move discordantly, the trader will not be hedged. Conversely, if the trader assumes independence of OIS and Libor curves, he or she will see two fully separate sensitivities, one to expected payoff and one to discounting, and will build an hedging portfolio with some investment in OIS and some in Libor. In this case the trader will always be hedged, but if OIS and Libor turn out to be perfectly correlated the trader may be wasting time and money. Knowing whether correlation is zero or 1 or some intermediate value is very important, with a particularly high risk associated with the 1-correlation error.

Instantaneous, terminal and serial correlations

Another 1-correlation mistake was analyzed in Section 2.8.2, where we showed that the simplest version of one-factor models for the term structure imposed an extremely high correlation among rates, which can reduce the value of early-exercise derivatives like Bermudan swaptions. There we also showed, however, that more elaborate models can put a patch on this problem because, although instantaneous correlation is constrained in one-factor models, other types of correlation are not because they are also influenced by the time-dependency of volatility. In fact, there are three important types of correlation that have been analyzed in the literature, particularly with reference to the LMM presented in Chapter 6 where modelling variables are Libor forward rates $F_i(t)$. They are:

1. Instantaneous correlations

$$\rho_{ij} \approx correl\left(dF_i(t), F_j(t)\right), \tag{8.9}$$

   that are the controllable model parameters.

2. Terminal correlations

$$TC_{i,j}(T) = correl\left(F_i(T), F_j(T)\right), \quad T \le T_i < T_j,$$

   that influence in particular the pricing of a swaption with expiry T. In fact, such a derivative is an option on a combination of Libor rates and thus depends on their correlations. But since these options are European with expiry T, they depend only on the joint distribution of Libor rates at T and are influenced by ρ_{ij} through the effect that ρ_{ij} has on $TC_{i,j}(T)$. What is this effect? Rebonato (1998) shows that, although $TC_{i,j}(T)$ cannot be computed in closed-form, they can be well approximated by

$$TC_{i,j}(T) \approx \frac{\int_0^T \sigma_i(t)\sigma_j(t)\rho_{i,j}\,dt}{\sqrt{\int_0^T \sigma_i^2(t)\,dt}\sqrt{\int_0^T \sigma_j^2(t)\,dt}}. \tag{8.10}$$

This shows that terminal correlations depend on instantaneous correlations $\rho_{i,j}$ but also on the volatilities. If volatilities were flat, we would have $TC_{i,j}(T) \approx \rho_{i,j}$, while in general we know that $TC_{i,j}(T) \leq \rho_{i,j}$ thanks to Cauchy-Schwartz inequality. In particular, even starting from $\rho_{i,j} = 1$ we can always make $TC_{i,j}(T) = 0$. Think of this stupid example:

	$\sigma_i(t)$	$\sigma_j(t)$
$0 \leq t < T/2$	$\sigma_i > 0$	0
$T/2 \leq t < T$	0	$\sigma_i > 0$

Low factor short rate models rely heavily on time-dependency of volatility to try to represent the terminal correlations lower than 1 that are implied in market prices. This is one of the reasons why they often use very irregular volatilities to calibrate swaption data.

3. Serial correlations

$$R_{i,j} = correl\left(F_i(T_i), F_j(T_j)\right), \quad T \leq T_i < T_j, \tag{8.11}$$

which influence in particular the prices of Bermudan swaptions, as we saw in 2.8.2, where we also provided an approximation for them based on (8.10). We will talk of this again in the next chapter.

9
Calibration

The topic of calibration is covered throughout the book. In Chapters 1 and 2 we analyzed calibration capability as the first element that must be assessed in model selection. In the chapter on stress tests and copulas Section 3.3 was devoted to showing how to transform an inconsistent quotation system, like the Gaussian copula for i-Traxx CDOs, into a model consistently able to calibrate the market, at least approximately. In this case reaching a good calibration turns out to be important as a way to understand a market better. Then Section 4.1 gives the analysis of an attempt to devise a model able to calibrate a new market. In Chapter 5 we saw the link between frequency of calibration and hedging, introducing the topic of model stability which we develop further here. In the following we will touch on the topic of calibration again, for example in Chapter 11, where we see that the difficulty of a model to calibrate jointly different quotes can be interpreted by many market operators as a sign of arbitrage opportunities.

This chapter completes the analysis of calibration in practice. What do we want from a calibration procedure? Formally, calibrating a model M to a product for which the model has a pricing function $\Pi^M(\Theta)$, depending on some parameters Θ, means solving the following problem

$$\Theta^* = \arg\min_{\Theta} \left\| \Pi^M(\Theta) - \Pi^{Mkt} \right\|, \tag{9.1}$$

namely finding the set of optimal model parameters Θ^* that *minimize the pricing error*, that is, the distance between model prices and market prices Π^{Mkt}. However, this is only the mathematical side of the problem. This is not sufficient in finance.

First of all, the market will crucially require that the above problem is performed with *computational efficiency*. This is understandable, since in current market practice the model is recalibrated before performing any operation: giving a quote for a product, evaluating a position, computing a sensitivity. With such frequent recalibration, this step must be performed as quickly as possible. Yet, even reaching a solution to (9.1) in a very efficient way is not sufficient to feel confident about a calibration procedure.

We need to be concerned in particular about three aspects:

1. minimization of the pricing error;
2. efficiency of the numerical procedure;
3. correct implications of the calibrated parameters.

The third point usually appears disturbing to many, but nowadays it is considered an unavoidable step in any reasonable calibration procedure. And in any case at this point of the book I expect you to appreciate its importance. Why should one *verify the implications of the calibrated parameter*, instead of just feeling glad that market prices are replicated as well as possible with an efficient procedure?

Well, if the model were calibrated to some reference derivatives, and then used only to price very similar derivatives, we could probably do without the third step. The example could be of a model calibrated to European options and then used to price other European options with maturities and strikes intermediate between the calibrated ones. Unfortunately, this is almost never the case. Models are usually applied to products that are relevantly different from those used in calibration. Just think of the example in Section 7.1: in that example it is enough that the strike is not intermediate between the calibrated ones, but higher, to have a situation where the option price does not depend so much on your calibration as on the value of a parameter that was arbitrarily fixed. Other examples were given in Chapter 2 : the note with trigger is given completely different assessments of gap risk by moving a parameter, the jump size, that is essentially unaffected by model calibration; the trigger option of the equity example is given different prices by two models, local and stochastic volatility models, that are equally calibrated to European options. In particular, in Section 2.6.1 we saw how, at times, enlarging the calibration set has no effect on our description of the relevant risks and only generates misunderstandings. Definitely, calibration is not the end of model specification. One must still consider the usual issues: are these parameters consistent with the market consensus on the modelling of this risk factor? Do they imply a behaviour which is reasonable and consistent with real market patterns?

A satisfactory calibration can leave room for extensive indetermination and model risk when pricing derivatives more complex than those in the calibration set. On the other hand, some extensions of the calibration set, performed taking into account the features of the complex derivative we are pricing, can be a crucial element to reduce model risk and avoid embarrassing mistakes. This has been shown for example in Section 7.1, where enlarging the calibration set transforms an arbitrary extrapolation into a safer interpolation pinned by liquid market information.

The literature has focused on one fundamental issue relating to the indetermination of a calibration procedure: the fact that calibrating a model to European options, which are products that depend on the density of the underlying at one single maturity, should not determine unambiguously the prices of derivatives which have dynamic features, like path-dependent or early exercise derivatives. We have already hinted at this issue, and the debate it triggered, in Chapter 2. Here we analyze it in much more detail, going in-depth into the model risk that can remain after calibration, and how to reduce model risk by improving calibration. In the process we present two important tools for model assessment: the evolution of the term structure of volatility, and the evolution of the term structure of smile.

We do not focus here on calibration as an optimization problem, first because such a topic would take up an entire book, and second because the most subtle model risk is the one that remains after an efficient optimization has been performed. When, however, the constraints of an optimization are the crucial point generating model risk, we consider this, as is done in Chapter 5. Very good references on calibration are Wilmott (2006), Cont and Tankov (2007).

9.1 CALIBRATING TO CAPS/SWAPTIONS AND PRICING BERMUDANS

We analyze this issue starting from the simplest interest rate derivative: caps. A cap is a stream of options on single rates, namely the caplets seen in 6.2. Calibrating caps reduces to calibrate the embedded caplets. The model we consider is the Libor Market Model introduced in Section 6.2.2.

9.1.1 Calibrating Caplets

The market quotes of caplets are expressed by giving, for the caplet fixing in T_{k-1} and paying in T_k with strike X, the flat implied volatility σ_k^{Caplet} that must be plugged into the Black formula, based on the assumption of lognormal Libor rates, in order to find the market price:

$$Caplet_k^{MKT} = P(0, T_k)\alpha_k Black\left(F_k(0), X, \left(\sigma_k^{Caplet}\right)^2 T_{k-1}\right). \tag{9.2}$$

What is the LMM formula for pricing a caplet? The standard lognormal LMM assumes lognormal forward rates with possibly time-dependent volatility, so

$$Caplet_k^{LMM} = P(0, T_k)\alpha_k Black\left(F_k(0), X, \int_0^{T_{k-1}} \sigma_k^2(t)dt\right).$$

This is equal to the market Black formula (9.2), apart from the fact that the market quotation system uses a flat volatility σ_k^{Caplet} rather than the time-dependent volatility $\sigma_k(t)$. When pricing European options in a lognormal model, their value is completely determined by the integral of the square of the volatility of the underlying from now to expiry. Thus calibrating the LMM to caplets amounts to fixing the instantaneous volatility $\sigma_k(t)$ so that the integrated square volatility in the model matches the one implied by the market formula (9.2), namely

$$\boxed{\int_0^{T_{k-1}} \sigma_k^2(t)dt = T_{k-1}\left[\sigma_k^{Caplet}\right]^2 := V_k^{Caplet}(0).}$$

This allows us to understand, first, that caplet calibration in the LMM is simple, and, second, that the market quote σ_k^{Caplet}, is a sort of average volatility of rate F_k from now to its expiry.

Traders often look at these quotes organized in the *term structure of volatility* (TSV), given by volatilities σ_k^{Caplet} plotted against the expiries T_{k-1} of the associated rates F_k, as in the example at Figure 9.1. We start by explaining the TSV assuming that we are working with a lognormal model. We then extend the treatment to the smile case in Section 9.2.

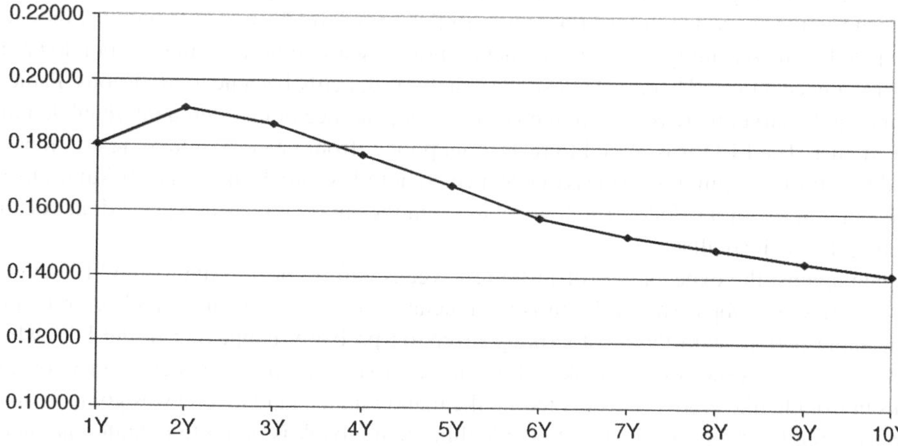

Figure 9.1 Term structure of volatility on 16 May 2000. Data used in Brigo and Mercurio (2006)

9.1.2 Understanding the Term Structure of Volatility

The TSV shown in Figure 9.1 has not been chosen only because it has been shown in a classic book on interest rate modelling. The TSV had a very similar shape in the market from the end of the LTCM crisis to the beginning of the subprime crisis. In spite of market variations, one could always observe a humped shape, with relatively low volatility on the short end, a peak between few months and two year maturity, and then a decreasing volatility towards the long end of the maturity spectrum.

The usual (Rebonato (1998)) explanation for this shape is based on the fact that, the more we move towards short-term rates, the more they are driven by policies of monetary authorities and rumours and expectations about them. Rates in the long end of the term structure, on the other hand, depend more on expectations regarding the macroeconomic prospects of growth and inflation in the long run. Since expectations on monetary policy can change with any comment from central bank officers, they have a high variability. Instead, expectation on the long-term perspective of an economy changes less easily, and this reduces the volatility of rates in the long end. This explains the backbone of the TSV, but one might wonder: why the hump? Why in the very short term does volatility go down again? Because monetary authorities tend to make their moves in the next few months as predictable and as expected as possible, reducing short-term volatility.

If this traditional interpretation for the standard shape of the TSV is valid, then there must have been moments in the past, particularly during crises, when the TSV must have changed shape dramatically. In fact, the above description of the volatility of expectations and the behaviour of monetary authorities does not fit times of crisis well. Let us take a couple of market cases from the credit crunch.

In the charts in Figure 9.2 we see the term structure of volatility in the US dollar market. Just before the start of the subprime crisis, in July 2007, we see, as the chart also quotes expiries of few months or weeks, that caplet volatilities decreased sharply in the very short run. According to classic interpretations, this should be due to the high predictability of the US monetary policies of the next few months. This interpretation makes sense, since US authorities, led mostly by Alan Greespan, were famous from 1987 to 2007 for the care they took not to surprise the market unnecessarily.

Then, in mid-July 2007, the first serious problems in the subprime market arose. Central banks did not seem to pay a lot of attention to this event. In the previous months, they had anticipated an increasingly restrictive monetary policy, with liquidity drains to cool down the fast-growing economy. Then, in August, the situation suddenly became more serious. Panic in the interbank market increased, until the virtual disappearance of unsecured interbank lending on 9 August. The FED was forced to reverse its policy: from promising more restrictions on liquidity, it turned to pumping a mass of unexpected liquidity into the market on 9 August itself. What can you see in the TSV? The low volatility in the short end has increased dramatically, the hump is much smaller.

Again against the expectations of just a few weeks before, on 17 August the FED cut the reference rate by 50bps. Similar U-turns in monetary policy affected almost all central banks in the same period, with the most striking inversion probably happening in the UK, where Mervyn King, governor of the Bank of England, at first adopted a very stern stance towards banks in trouble like Northern Rock, letting the market understand that he was going to allow them to default. Unfortunately, to let people think that a bank is going to default amounts to making this default certain: on 13 September people with money in Northern Rock started a

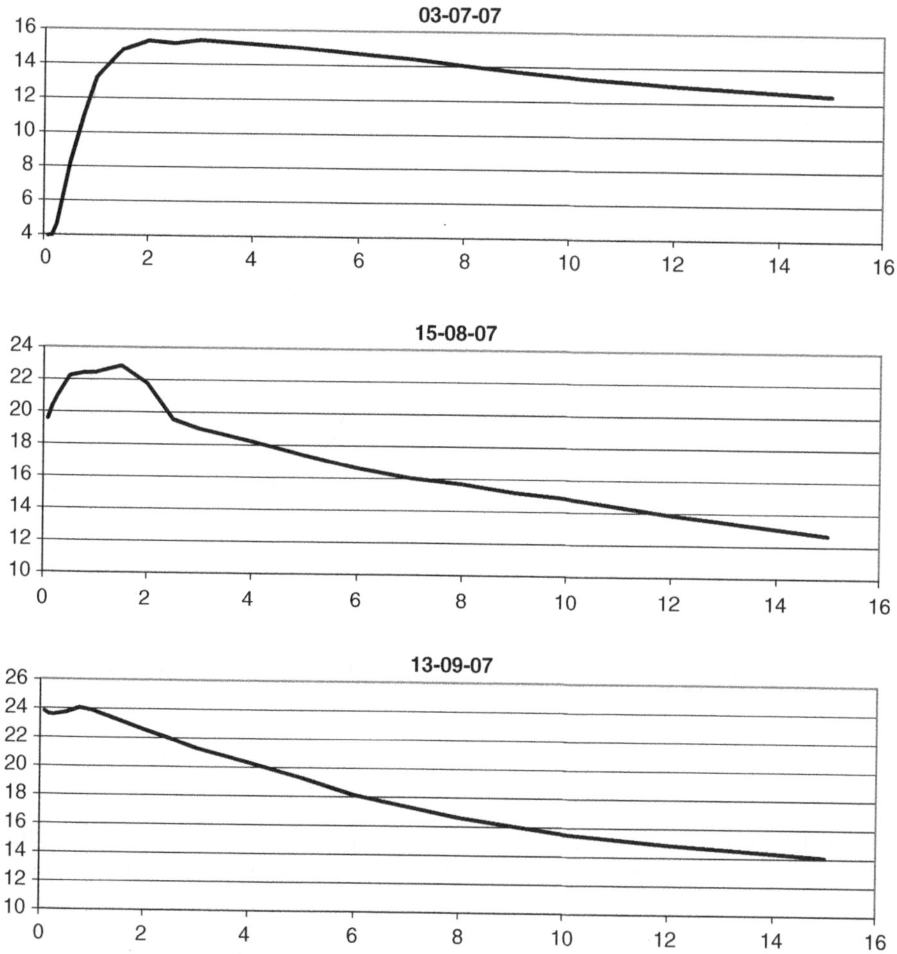

Figure 9.2 US term structure of caplet volatility. Percentage volatility on y-axis, years on x-axis

run on the bank to withdraw all of their deposits. No bank, even one in perfect health, has enough liquidity to pay back all of its deposits in one day. To avoid a default much faster and more dramatic than anticipated, Mervyn King had to go totally back on his words about banks in trouble: he declared he was going to provide as much liquidity as needed to help banks in trouble, starting with Northern Rock. No surprise that, when we look at the TSV in September, the hump has essentially disappeared. Central banks were no longer considered predictable.

This happened in the US and in the UK. The situation in the Euro area was slightly different. The crisis struck later and less dramatically, and ECB showed more stability than most Central banks. We see in Figure 9.3 that on 2 June 2008 the hump in the volatility, usually associated with confidence in the predictability of central bank action, is still there. In those days, as we now know all too well, we were still in the middle of the crisis. The feeling of people in the banking market was not very optimistic, and they were quite right, as confirmed by

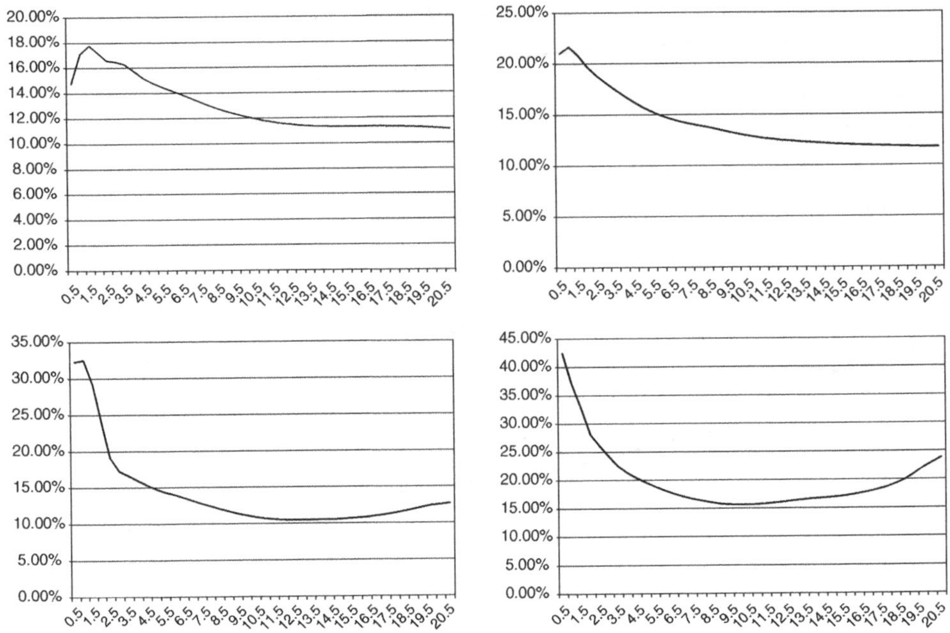

Figure 9.3 TS of Caplets vols in the Euro market. From left to right, top down: A) 2 June 2008. B) 13 June. C) 22 October. D) 5 January 2009

Lehman's default a few months later. These people expected that at the next meeting of the ECB rates would have to be kept stable, if not decreased, to help the economy out of its problems.

Instead, on 5 June, the president of the ECB, Jean Claude Trichet, said *'we could decide to move our rates by a small amount at our next meeting in order to secure the solid anchoring of inflation expectations'*. No one in the market anticipated increases in rates for worries about inflation; people in banks were actually speaking more of the risk of deflation. The comment by the ECB head led to considerable turmoil in the market and, as you can see in Figure 9.3, on 12 June the hump has also almost disappeared from the Euro market TSV.

For a complete disappearance, we have to wait until after Lehman's default, as becomes visible in the TSV of January 2009. Notice one more thing from these charts: all the previous examples we have recalled about the behaviour of central banks have only moved the short end of the TSV. But then, in the last snapshot, the one after the Lehman default, the long end volatility has moved by more than 10%. It seems that the long end of the rates curve really is touched by far fewer events than the short end. It takes a dramatic unexpected event like Lehman's default and the turmoil that followed to move it fast and a lot, also increasing its volatility.

This fresher analysis seems to confirm the older literature: the near end of the TSV is more volatile because driven by expectations about monetary policy, the hump is a sign of predictability over the very short term, the long end is less volatile because influenced by long-term expectations.

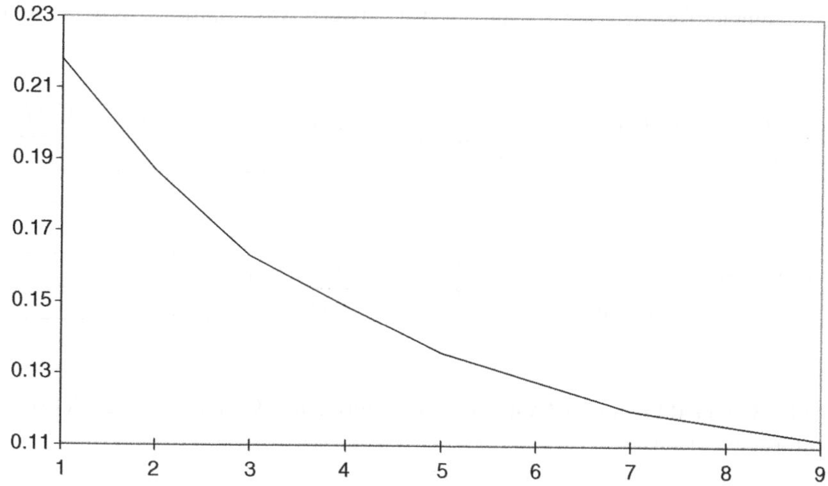

Figure 9.4 Term structure of volatility for 10 December 2002. Volatility on y-axis, years on x-axis

9.1.3 Different parameterizations

This analysis can help us choose a functional shape for volatility, which hitherto we have indicated just as a generic function $\sigma_k(t)$. In the following numerical examples we use the data from 10 December 2002. Here we assume yearly caplet; in the Euro market reality caplets are three-month or six-month spaced. The information on the volatility of yearly forward rates, and therefore on synthetic yearly caplets, can however be captured by unitary tenor swaptions, as we do here.[1] The annual volatility for that period shows no hump, as we see in Figure 9.4, because the hump in the market actually occurred before one year.

The data represented in this TSV are, for the first 5 points:

Caplet	Expiry	Underlying		Vol
$Caplet_1^{MKT}$	1Y (T_0)	$F_1(t) = F(t; 1Y, 2Y)$	$\sigma_1^{Caplet} =$	0.218
$Caplet_2^{MKT}$	2Y (T_1)	$F_2(t) = F(t; 2Y, 3Y)$	$\sigma_2^{Caplet} =$	0.187
$Caplet_3^{MKT}$	3Y (T_2)	$F_3(t) = F(t; 3Y, 4Y)$	$\sigma_3^{Caplet} =$	0.163
$Caplet_4^{MKT}$	4Y (T_3)	$F_4(t) = F(t; 4Y, 5Y)$	$\sigma_4^{Caplet} =$	0.149
$Caplet_5^{MKT}$	5Y (T_4)	$F_5(t) = F(t; 5Y, 6Y)$	$\sigma_5^{Caplet} =$	0.136

The market often chooses piecewise constant parameterizations (step functions), since the main interest in calibration is having the freedom to change volatility in order to calibrate different quotes, which are available only for maturities spaced by months or years (one year in our example). A very general choice for a piecewise constant structure may allow a different

[1] Thus here we are assuming by construction consistency between caps and swaptions, because this allows us better to understand the mathematical implications of calibrating to caps or swaptions. The issue of the actual differences to be found in the caplets market compared to the one for swaptions is treated in Section 11.3.

volatility parameter for each rate in each interval between two maturities, as in the following table:

	$t \in (0, 1Y]$	$(1Y, 2Y]$	$(2Y, 3Y]$	...	$((M-2)Y, (M-1)Y]$	$((M-1)Y, MY]$
$F_1(t)$	$\sigma_{1,1}$	—	—	...	—	
$F_2(t)$	$\sigma_{2,1}$	$\sigma_{2,2}$	—	...	—	
$\vdots$	...	...	...	...	...	
$F_{M-1}(t)$	$\sigma_{M-1,1}$	$\sigma_{M-1,2}$	$\sigma_{M-1,3}$	...	$\sigma_{M-1,M-1}$	—
$F_M(t)$	$\sigma_{M,1}$	$\sigma_{M,2}$	$\sigma_{M,3}$	...	$\sigma_{M,M-1}$	$\sigma_{M,M}$

(9.3)

This is called **General Piecewise Constant** parameterization. Calibrating to caplet volatilities means in this case ensuring

$$\sqrt{\int_0^{T_{k-1}} \sigma_k^2(t)\,dt} = \sqrt{\sum_{j=0}^{k-1} (T_j - T_{j-1})\,\sigma_{k,j+1}^2} = \sqrt{T_{k-1}}\sigma_k^{Caplet}.$$

Notice that we can fit caplets perfectly with multiple configurations. Such a structure has many parameters, which are redundant compared to the M caplets, and it will turn out useful only if we add more derivatives to calibration. How to subparameterize this structure when dealing with caps only? One possibility is simply to make volatility **maturity-dependent**,

$$\sigma_k(t) = s_k$$

getting a table as follows

	$t \in (0, 1Y]$	$(1Y, 2Y]$	$(2Y, 3Y]$	...	$((M-2)Y, (M-1)Y]$	$((M-1)Y, MY]$
$F_1(t)$	s_1	—	—	...	—	
$F_2(t)$	s_2	s_2	—	...	—	
$\vdots$	...	...	...	...	...	
$F_{M-1}(t)$	s_{M-1}	s_{M-1}	s_{M-1}	...	s_{M-1}	—
$F_M(t)$	s_M	s_M	s_M	...	s_M	s_M

(9.4)

In this case calibration is trivial, since we are using the same assumption of flat volatility that is used by the market to provide caplet quotes. Calibration reduces to setting

$$s_k = \sigma_k^{Caplet},$$

so that, with reference to the above data, we have

$$\begin{array}{|l|}\hline \sigma_1^{Caplet} = 0.218 \\ \hline \sigma_2^{Caplet} = 0.187 \\ \hline \sigma_3^{Caplet} = 0.163 \\ \hline \sigma_4^{Caplet} = 0.149 \\ \hline \sigma_5^{Caplet} = 0.136 \\ \hline \end{array} \Rightarrow \begin{array}{|l|}\hline s_1 = 0.218 \\ \hline s_2 = 0.187 \\ \hline s_3 = 0.163 \\ \hline s_4 = 0.149 \\ \hline s_5 = 0.136 \\ \hline \end{array} \qquad (9.5)$$

If this parameterization is chosen, one believes that what drives the volatility of a rate is the calendar date of its expiry and maturity. The rate expiring in May 2015 has a volatility associated with the fact of fixing on 2015, no matter whether we are looking at it 5 years earlier, in May 2010, or just six months earlier, in November 2014. Someone might say: if you believe in this parameterization, you have understood nothing of the above interpretation. What matters for volatility is not the specific calendar date of the fixing, but how far you are from that date! So volatility for the rate expiring in 2015 should be different in 2014 from what it was in 2010. In 2010 the rate had a volatility associated with being 5 years from the expiry. In 2015 it will have a (probably higher) volatility associated with being six month from expiry. If one believes in this second concept, the parameterization should be **time-to-maturity-dependent**,

$$\sigma_k(t) = \psi_{k-z} \quad \text{when } t \in [T_{z-1}, T_z]$$

leading to the following table

	$t \in (0, 1Y]$	$(1Y, 2Y]$	$(2Y, 3Y]$	...	$((M-2)Y, (M-1)Y]$	$((M-1)Y, MY]$
$F_1(t)$	ψ_1	–	–	...	–	
$F_2(t)$	ψ_2	ψ_1	–	...	–	
$\vdots$	...	...	...	...	...	
$F_{M-1}(t)$	ψ_{M-1}	ψ_{M-2}	ψ_{M-3}	...	ψ_1	–
$F_M(t)$	ψ_M	ψ_{M-1}	ψ_{M-2}	...	ψ_2	ψ_1

(9.6)

This is a **time-homogeneous** parameterization, where volatility depends only on $T-t$, the time-to-maturity, and not on calendar time. This is a typical goal for many market operators (see the discussion in Nawalkha and Rebonato (2011)). Calibrating now means enforcing

$$\sqrt{1year}\,\psi_1 = \sqrt{1year}\,\sigma_1^{Caplet} \Rightarrow \psi_1 = \sigma_1^{Caplet}$$

$$\sqrt{\psi_2^2 + \psi_1^2} = \sqrt{2}\sigma_2^{Caplet} \Rightarrow \psi_2 = \sqrt{2\left[\sigma_2^{Caplet}\right]^2 - \psi_1^2}$$

$$\sqrt{\psi_3^2 + \psi_2^2 + \psi_1^2} = \sqrt{3}\sigma_3^{Caplet} \Rightarrow \psi_3 = \sqrt{3\left[\sigma_3^{Caplet}\right]^2 - \psi_1^2 - \psi_2^2}.$$

and so on. With the above numbers we get

$$\begin{array}{|l|}\hline \sigma_1^{Caplet} = 0.218 \\ \hline \sigma_2^{Caplet} = 0.187 \\ \hline \sigma_3^{Caplet} = 0.163 \\ \hline \sigma_4^{Caplet} = 0.149 \\ \hline \sigma_5^{Caplet} = 0.136 \\ \hline \end{array} \Rightarrow \begin{array}{|l|}\hline \psi_1 = 0.218 \\ \hline \psi_2 = 0.150 \\ \hline \psi_3 = 0.099 \\ \hline \psi_4 = 0.095 \\ \hline \psi_5 = 0.061 \\ \hline \end{array}. \qquad (9.7)$$

Who is right? Possibly the truth lies in the middle, and changes with time: before the crisis time-to-maturity seemed the driver of volatility, but during the crisis market operators were often associating different volatilities with rates expiring in 2010 rather than in 2009, for example, *not because they had different time-to-maturity* but because they believed that in 2010 it was more likely that the market would be out of the crisis. If a trader has this view, he or she should consider making at least part of the volatility function maturity-dependent. In fact, the time-to-maturity dependent parameterization had some difficulty calibrating the market during the crisis without implying unacceptable negative variances. This shows that time-homogeneity is very important in a stable market, but that this requirement also needs to be put into perspective: particularly in times of turmoil, dependence on calendar time has a relevant meaning. In the literature this has led to the proposal of more general parameterizations. The issue has also been extended to the parameters of smile models, with implications not dissimilar from those that we cover in this chapter.

But this is not our focus here. The question we want to answer is: leaving aside some special cases when one of the above parameterizations could not calibrate the market, in all cases where both can fit perfectly the cap market, is it irrelevant which parameterization is chosen? The answer is no, and the reason is that the two parameterizations can give the same prices to caps and yet disagree on the prices of more complex derivatives. In terms of model risk management, this can be analyzed precisely by looking at the so-called evolution of the TSV implied by the model.

9.1.4 The Evolution of the Term Structure of Volatility

The term structure of volatility today is given by market data in Figure 9.4, and a calibrated model will incorporate it irrespective of the volatility parameterizations. But looking at the above tables, we notice that the model is also telling us what it implies about *the future term structure of volatility*, for example in one year from now. Take the table in (9.3). To see the TSV in 1y you can erase the first column, labelled '$t \in (0, 1Y]$', because the first period has elapsed, and the first row, because rate $F_1(t)$ has fixed and it will have no more volatility

	$(1Y, 2Y]$	$(2Y, 3Y]$	$\dots$	$((M-2)Y, (M-1)Y]$	$((M-1)Y, MY]$
$F_2(t)$	$\sigma_{2,2}$	$-$	$\dots$	$-$	
$\vdots$	$\dots$	$\dots$	$\dots$	$\dots$	
$F_{M-1}(t)$	$\sigma_{M-1,2}$	$\sigma_{M-1,3}$	$\dots$	$\sigma_{M-1,M} - 1$	$-$
$F_M(t)$	$\sigma_{M,2}$	$\sigma_{M,3}$	$\dots$	$\sigma_{M,M-1}$	$\sigma_{M,M}$

This is the model representation of the situation in one year from now. From this, you can compute the implied volatilities of caplets in one year from now, according to the model: it is just a matter of integrating, on each row, the square of the volatilities until fixing. In general, at a future time $t = T_j$ the Term Structure of Volatility is given plotting the average volatilities of the forward rates with fixing times $T_{j+1} = t + 1y$, $T_{j+2} = t + 2y \dots$:

Fixing times of rates		Average vol's of rates
$T_{j+1} = t + 1y$	$\longmapsto$	$V_1^{Caplet}(T_j) = \sqrt{\frac{1}{T_{j+1}-T_j}\int_{T_j}^{T_{j+1}} \sigma_{j+2}^2(t)dt}$
$T_{j+2} = t + 2y$	$\longmapsto$	$V_2^{Caplet}(T_j) = \sqrt{\frac{1}{T_{j+2}-T_j}\int_{T_j}^{T_{j+2}} \sigma_{j+3}^2(t)dt}$
$\vdots$		$\vdots$
$T_{M-1} = t + (M-1)y$	$\longmapsto$	$V_{M-1}^{Caplet}(T_j) = \sqrt{\frac{1}{T_{M-1}-T_j}\int_{T_j}^{T_{M-1}} \sigma_M^2(t)dt}$

(9.8)

This will not be the same under different parameterizations. Take the table at (9.4), associated with maturity-dependent volatility, and do the same job of erasing the first row and first column. You get

	$(1Y, 2Y]$	$(2Y, 3Y]$	...	$((M-2)Y, (M-1)Y]$	$((M-1)Y, MY]$
$F_2(t)$	s_2	—	...	—	
$\vdots$	...	...	...	...	
$F_{M-1}(t)$	s_{M-1}	s_{M-1}	...	s_{M-1}	—
$F_M(t)$	s_M	s_M	...	s_M	s_M

If you do the same with the table at (9.6), associated with time-to-maturity-dependent volatility, you get

	$(1Y, 2Y]$	$(2Y, 3Y]$	...	$((M-2)Y, (M-1)Y]$	$((M-1)Y, MY]$
$F_2(t)$	ψ_1	—	...	—	
$\vdots$	...	...	...	...	
$F_{M-1}(t)$	ψ_{M-2}	ψ_{M-3}	...	ψ_1	—
$F_M(t)$	ψ_{M-1}	ψ_{M-2}	...	ψ_2	ψ_1

The first difference you should notice is that under maturity-dependent volatility in one year from now you lose the 'head' of the TSV, the parameter s_1 has disappeared. The TSV will look like the one at time 0 seen in Figure 9.4, only you will have to *cut the beginning*, as many years at the beginning as the years forward you are considering. The evolution of the TSV appears as in Figure 9.5.

On the other hand, under the time-to-maturity-dependent parameterization you lose the 'tail' of the parameterization (I am using the terminology of Brigo and Mercurio (2006) where they present this evidence). The TSV will look like the one at time 0 seen in 9.4, only you will have to *cut the end*, as many years at the *end* as the years forward you are considering, such as in Figure 9.6.

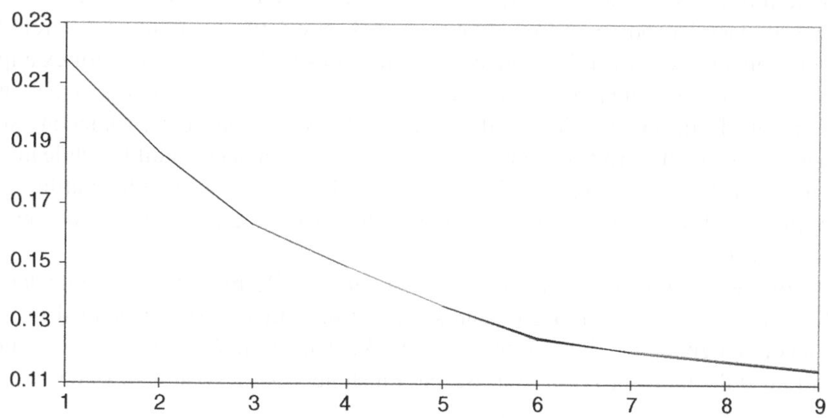

Figure 9.5 Evolution of the term structure of volatilities when volatility depends on the **maturity** of a forward rate. The structures overlap, but they start at different times

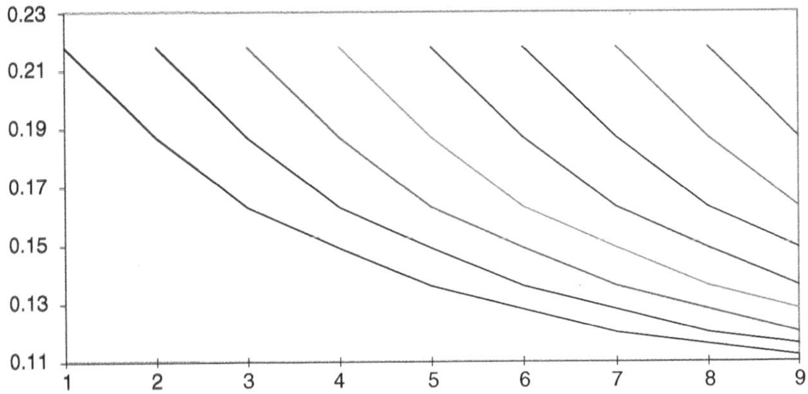

Figure 9.6 Evolution of the term structure of volatilities when volatility depends on the **time-to-maturity** of a forward rate

9.1.5 The Effect on Early-Exercise Derivatives

We anticipated that the choice of the parameterizations does not affect caplets (that are European options with expiry at fixing of rates), but it does imply different dynamic behaviours of forward rates, so it implies different prices for less simple products: options with intermediate maturities (swaptions), path dependent derivatives, and early exercise derivatives. In equity early exercise derivatives are mainly American options, where the investor can decide when to exercise, choosing any day from inception to maturity. In interest rates we have instead *callable* or *Bermudan* derivatives, where the investor can decide when to exercise but is limited to a discrete set of dates between now and maturity, for example every year.

Why do different parameterizations influence this type of derivative? Exactly because different parameterizations lead to different evolutions of the term structure of volatility.

In such products, for pricing we have to evaluate, given today information embedded in the model, if, at the future exercise dates, it will be more convenient for us to exercise or to hold (exercise value vs expected continuation value conditional to market information at that point in the future). We could have a right to decide if we want to early exercise to enter into a financial product depending on forward rates and their volatilities at one of different future times. For evaluating what will be more convenient for us at that future time, for example 4y, according to today-calibrated model, we have to set ourselves in 4y using the model, and we have to evaluate the different options as if we were at 4y. Notice that at 4y a caplet on $F_5(t)$ has to be priced with volatility 13.6% if one is using maturity-dependent volatility, while in case of time-to-maturity dependent volatility the same option has to be priced with volatility 21.8%. A non-negligible difference, in terms of value of the underlying products and potentially in terms of the decision to exercise or not.

Let us consider a numerical example. The most common Bermudan interest rate derivative is the Bermudan swaption. The Bermudan swaption has already been explained in Section 2.8.2 as an option giving the right to enter at strike K, at any time T_{ex} in $T_a, \ldots, T_{b-1}$, into the swap starting at the moment T_{ex} of exercise and finishing at T_b, a swap with value

$$Swap_{T_{ex}}^{ex,b}(K) = \sum_{i=ex+1}^{b} P(T_{ex}, T_i)\alpha_i(S_{ex,b}(T_{ex}) - K).$$

We consider here a Bermudan with first exercise date $1y$, exercise right every year, maturity $10y$, and written on underlying yearly swaps, so that the T_i's are yearly spaced, $T_a = 1y$, $T_{b-1} = 9y$, $T_b = 10y$. This is called a 10-noncall-1 bermudan swaption. The data we use for pricing are those from 10 December 2002, when interest rates were

F_0	F_1	F_2	F_3	F_4	F_5	F_6	F_7	F_8	F_9
2.86%	3.35%	4.05%	4.44%	4.77%	5.03%	5.26%	5.39%	5.47%	5.53%

The strike selected is 6.3%, so that the underlying swaptions are out-of-the-money, but not very out-of-the-money, at the moment of valuation. The method used is the least squares Monte Carlo for early exercise products of Longstaff and Schwartz (2001). Monte Carlo standard error (mc-low and mc-up) is at 98% confidence. We consider first that rates have volatilities from a maturity-dependent parameterization calibrated to caplets, as in (9.5), and then rates with time-to-maturity-dependent parameterization as in (9.7). In both cases we assume the same unit correlation among rates. The two prices for the Bermudan are, for 100mn notional,

maturity-dependent vol, unit ρ		
$mc - low$	$mc - mid$	$mc - up$
1,300,000.00	1,340,000.00	1,380,000.00
time-to-mat-dependent vol, unit ρ		
$mc - low$	$mc - mid$	$mc - up$
1,000,000.00	1,030,000.00	1,060,000.00

. (9.9)

It is a sizeable difference of about 30% of NPV. Such a price difference would point to a high model risk when pricing Bermudans with a Libor market model, since it means that a feature of the model which is not determined by our calibration, the evolution of the TSV, can lead to very different prices. However, we have mentioned that there are other derivatives that depend on this evolution: among them we have swaptions. Swaptions are the other liquid derivative in the interest rates market. Let us see what happens when we add it to our calibration set.

9.1.6 Reducing Our Indetermination in Pricing Bermudans: Liquid European Swaptions

A calibration to swaptions, which were described in 6.2.3, can fix a lot of the above indetermination about the shape of the volatility functions $\sigma_k(t)$. This can be understood most precisely if we consider an exact calibration to swaptions, such as the one in Brigo and Morini (2006). In this case the parameterization of volatility is the General Piecewise Constant of (9.3). We do not need to choose a subparameterization like (9.4) or (9.6) because in calibrating to swaptions we have more data than with caps and the parameters of (9.3) will be fixed by swaption data. The computational method used is the analytic formula (6.15) derived and tested previously, which when specified for the GPC parameterization gives a volatility

$$V_{\alpha,\beta}^2 = \sum_{i,j=\alpha+1}^{\beta} \frac{w_i(0)w_j(0)F_i(0)F_j(0)\rho_{i,j}}{T_\alpha\ S_{\alpha,\beta}(0)^2} \sum_{h=0}^{\alpha}(T_h - T_{h-1})\sigma_{i,h+1}\sigma_{j,h+1} \tag{9.10}$$

that must be plugged into a Black formula like (6.8) to price the swaption on the swap with first fixing T_α and last payment T_β. In the market jargon, if T_α corresponds approximately to k

years, and $T_\beta - T_\alpha$ is n years, we say that this swaption has *maturity* k and *tenor* n, or that it is the $k \times n$ (called 'k *into* n') swaption. The correlations $\rho_{i,j}$ among rates, which, as we see in (9.10), enter the pricing, are selected exogenously through historical estimation in Brigo and Morini (2006).

Since we are using a lognormal model, we will focus on ATM swaptions. The ATM swaption data are usually organized in the market by a matrix of implied volatilities to be plugged into (6.8) to get the market price, with the different maturities on the rows and the tenors on the columns. The volatility matrix for 10 December 2002, the same day considered in the above test, is given in (9.11). The maturities which are not shown were not liquidly quoted in the Euro market.

		n									
		1	2	3	4	5	6	7	8	9	10
	1	21.8%	19.7%	17.7%	16.5%	15.5%	14.8%	14.2%	13.7%	13.3%	12.9%
	2	18.7%	16.7%	15.5%	14.5%	13.9%	13.4%	13.0%	12.6%	12.3%	12.1%
	3	16.3%	15.0%	14.0%	13.4%	12.9%	12.5%	12.2%	12.0%	11.8%	11.6%
k	4	14.9%	13.8%	13.1%	12.6%	12.2%	11.9%	11.7%	11.5%	11.3%	11.1%
	5	13.6%	12.8%	12.4%	11.9%	11.6%	11.4%	11.2%	11.0%	10.9%	10.7%
	7	12.0%	11.5%	11.3%	11.0%	10.6%	10.5%	10.4%	10.3%	10.2%	10.1%
	10	10.8%	10.4%	10.2%	10.0%	9.9%	9.8%	9.7%	9.7%	9.6%	9.5%

(9.11)

The possibility of calibrating precisely the GPC parameterization given these data is exemplified in Figure 9.7. Consider the first swaption we have in the swaption matrix. It is the 1×1 swaption. This is essentially a yearly caplet, an option of F_1 with expiry in 1 year. It depends only on the volatility of this rate in the first year, $\sigma_{1,1}$ so we can fix this parameter by calibrating this swaption. Then move to consider swaptions of increasing tenor for the same maturity. One moves to the 1×2 swaption. Now not only the volatility of F_1 matters for pricing, but also the volatility of F_2. However, what matters is only volatility in the first year, since the swaption still has expiry in 1 year. Thus the price depends on $\sigma_{1,1}$, obtained previously, and on $\sigma_{2,1}$ which can now be fixed to calibrate exactly this 1×2 swaption. Of course, the correlation $\rho_{1,2}$ between F_1 and F_2 also enters the picture, but this is obtained by historical estimation. If one now moves to a swaption of increasing maturity, the first one is 2×1. It is again an option on a single rate, this time F_2, and it has expiry in 2 years, therefore it depends on $\sigma_{2,1}$ and $\sigma_{2,2}$. But $\sigma_{2,1}$ has been found previously, so we can use the constraint to calibrate the 2×1 swaption to back out the value of $\sigma_{2,2}$ implied b swaption data. As you will note, we have found values for $\sigma_{2,1}$ and $\sigma_{2,2}$, and therefore defined the time-dependency of F_2 through swaption calibration.

We refer to Brigo and Morini (2003) and (2006) for an explanation of how this approach can be extended to the entire swaption matrix, to which problems this can give rise and how they can be solved.[2] Similar reasoning on the relation between market swaption volatilities and model parameters has also been applied to smile models, as in Piterbarg (2005). What matters is that with this approach we can get a behaviour of volatility of rates in time, and therefore *an implied evolution of the term structure of volatility*, that comes not from our assumptions but from swaption market data. Of course, it does not only come from swaption market data: it depends also on the choice of the exogenous correlation. Which sort of evolution do we obtain?

[2] In any attempt to achieve a perfect, analytic fit there is a risk of fitting noise and getting irregular and unstable parameters. These issues are covered in Brigo and Morini (2006).

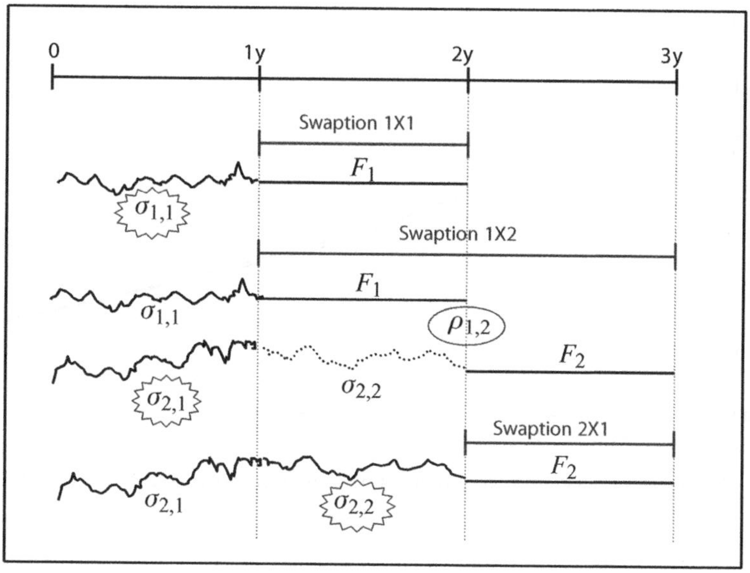

Figure 9.7 Calibrating LMM to the swaption matrix

One more similar to the time homogeneous evolution in Figure 9.6, associated with time-to-maturity dependence of volatility, or one more similar to the constant volatility evolution in Figure 9.5? Interestingly, it depends exactly on the exogenous correlation assumption.

We show here two different correlation assumptions. The first correlation used is simply historical estimation of ρ, unaltered. The first portion is shown in (9.12).

	1	2	3	4	5
1	1.00	0.89	0.77	0.77	0.70
2	0.89	1.00	0.86	0.84	0.79
3	0.77	0.86	1.00	0.87	0.82
4	0.77	0.84	0.87	1.00	0.92
5	0.70	0.79	0.82	0.92	1.00

(9.12)

The second correlation used also comes from historical estimation, but we apply to (9.12) the rank reduction of Morini and Webber (2006) to get the best rank 2 approximation. The first portion is shown in (9.13).

	1	2	3	4	5
1	1.00	0.99	0.98	0.94	0.91
2	0.99	1.00	1.00	0.98	0.96
3	0.98	1.00	1.00	0.99	0.98
4	0.94	0.98	0.99	1.00	1.00
5	0.91	0.96	0.98	1.00	1.00

(9.13)

The most superficial difference from (9.12) is that correlations look higher in (9.13), but we saw in Section 8.1.1 that it has the very important effect of reducing the model to a two factor model.

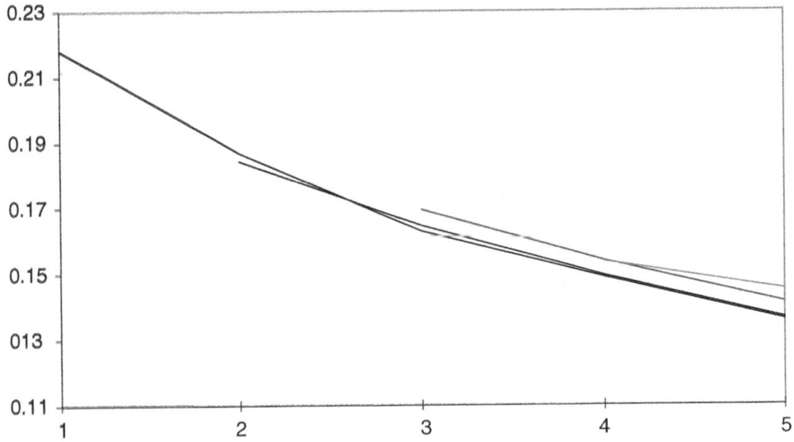

Figure 9.8 Evolution of TSV from swaption calibration when exogenous correlation has maximum rank

When the correlation comes from (9.12), the evolution of the term structure of volatility we obtain from calibration is shown in Figure 9.8, where we have zoomed in on the first part of it which is more regular and not affected by the missing quotes in the Euro market. We can hazard that it seems a maturity-dependent evolution, in spite of the fact that we did not impose anything of this kind but just calibrated swaptions.

When the correlation comes instead from (9.13), the evolution we get is shown in Figure 9.9. It is certainly different from the one above, and we can hazard that it is closer to a time-homogeneous, time-to-maturity dependent evolution, although in this case also we have imposed nothing of the kind.

Mathematically speaking, these results are not terribly difficult to explain. We have seen in Section 8.2.2 that swaptions are strongly affected by terminal correlation *TC* rather than instantaneous correlations ρ, so what you can hope to fix by calibrating to swaptions are just

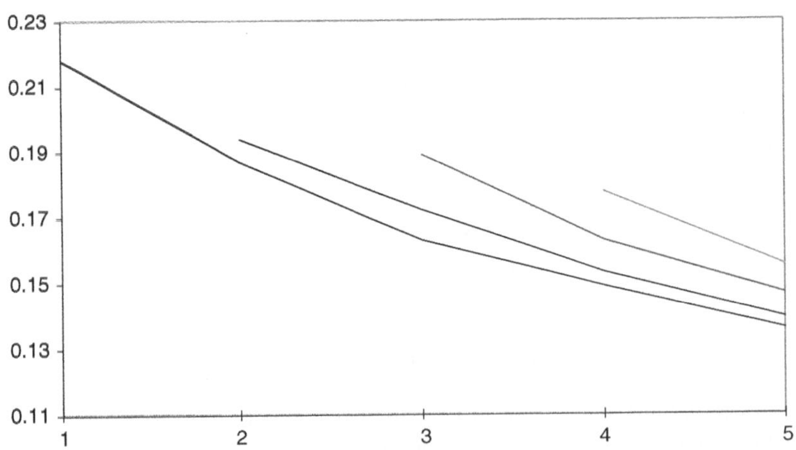

Figure 9.9 Evolution of TSV from swaption calibration when exogenous correlation has rank 2

terminal correlations TC. The results seem to imply that historical unaltered ρ should be pretty similar to the implied swaption TC, so that we do not need strongly time-dependent volatilities to move from the exogenous ρ to implied TC. When, instead, exogenous instantaneous correlations are higher, as we have seen them to be in (9.13), to fit the same implied terminal correlation we have to introduce stronger time-dependency of volatilities. In the context of financial interpretation, some might prefer the results from calibration with (9.13), because here the correlation is that of a low factor model, which is likely to be the one most commonly used in the market, and TSV evolves in a way that is more similar to the regularity typical of the pre-crisis years, when TSV looked quite stable in time. Someone else, however, may prefer the results form calibration with (9.12), because here correlation is an objective unaltered historical estimation while the volatilities are almost flat as in the market quotation system of caplets.

But this sort of interpretation is of no great interest to us now. The real question we have in mind is: has this calibration to swaptions reduced our model uncertainty and model risk in the pricing of Bermudan swaptions? Certainly, calibration to swaptions does not fix our parameters, since it can be performed with different correlations leading to different volatilities. But if the two equally fitting alternatives give similar prices to Bermudan, we have strongly reduced our model risk. We are now in a position to look at the dispute between Longstaff, Santa-Clara and Schwartz (LSS) and Andersen and Andreasen (AA) sketched in Section 2.8.2, but without oversimplifying the setting.

The real question is: a different correlation assumption among rates has an effect on the pricing of Bermudans, as LSS point out, and in particular lower correlations, associated with models with many factors, should make Bermudans more valuable. However, AA assert that once a different correlation, and therefore a different number of factors in the model, has been chosen, the model must then be calibrated to available market data, in particular European swaptions. After this calibration, the two models will also have different time-dependencies of volatility. Moreover, the time-dependency of volatility has an effect on Bermudans, as we saw in (9.9), directly through changing the value of the embedded European swaptions and indirectly through the effect on serial correlations. Thus the final effect on a Bermudan is not determined. In particular, one effect AA mention is that since swaption calibration, to use our terminology, fixes a large number of terminal correlations (8.10), making them similar in the two models, a large amount of serial correlation (8.11) will also be fixed by that, making the Bermudan value similar in the two models. Then, empirically, they register that the prices are indeed similar, but the ones given by the low-factor model are slightly *higher*.

We performed the test, repricing the 10-non-call-1 swaption seen above under the two different calibrations: the one that assumes the two-factor model (9.13), arriving at the approximately time-homogeneous evolution in Figure 9.9, and the other calibration that assumes a very-high-factor model (9.12), arriving at the approximately flat volatility evolution in Figure 9.8. The differences in the Bermuolan swaption price are as follows.

high-rank ρ, calibrated vol		
mc-low	mc-mid	mc-up
1,180,000.00	1,220,000.00	1,260,000.00

low-rank ρ, calibrated vol		
mc-low	mc-mid	mc-up
1,210,000.00	1,250,000.00	1,280,000.00

We would need to conduct systematic tests in order to express a solid opinion. But the result of our single test strikingly confirms the view of AA: the difference in pricing is very low, almost the same size as the Monte Carlo uncertainty, and in any case the low-factor model gives a slightly higher price.

It seems that we do not necessarily throw away a billion dollars when we use a low-factor model. We can avoid this model error if we perform a precise calibration to market swaptions. Notice that this conclusion could be made stronger in our setting than in the original one of AA. In fact, here the low-factor model is really exactly calibrated to swaptions, due to the fact of deriving the two-factor model from the LMM and applying the precise calibration approach of Brigo and Morini (2006), while traditional low-factor models used in the market for Bermudans usually have serious difficulties in getting such precise calibration. On the other hand, our model is a 'two-factor model' in the sense that it is driven by only two independent random shocks, but traditional two-factor models also have the feature, which is very important from a computational point of view, of allowing us to write the entire term structure at any time as a function of only two variables. We do not have this property, due to the fact that here we allowed each rate to have its own time-dependency of volatility rather than a common one. This issue has already been mentioned in Section 2.8.2 while describing the model (2.29).

This exercise has shown that calibration to swaptions reduces model uncertainty in the pricing of a Bermudan like the one considered, although the different volatility/correlation configurations can leave room for model risk for some other early exercise derivatives. We have seen one more interplay between precision and scope of calibration, model indetermination, and the pricing of exotics, adding some elements to the debate in the literature. Interestingly, after many examples where we have shown cases of model uncertainty apparently missed by practitioners and researchers, here we have had to scale down an issue of model uncertainty that created considerable concern in the market.

9.2 THE EVOLUTION OF THE FORWARD SMILES

Additionally, this example has allowed us to cover the issue of *stability*, namely *what a model predicts about future prices*. When we assess the behaviour of a model, including model risk assessment, we focus mainly on the *today* prices that the model generates. Checking which *future* prices it implies, as we did above with the analysis of the implied evolution of the TSV, is an additional aspect that has important consequences for applications that are affected by the dynamic behaviour of the model. An example is hedging, and we mentioned this issue in Chapter 5. Another relevant example is the pricing of early exercise derivatives that crucially depend on model-implied future prices, such as the Bermudans considered above.

In the following we see some additional facts on how stability can be controlled and assessed in model risk management. The formula (9.8) for the Evolution of the Term Structure of Volatility is applicable only to a lognormal Libor market model, since it is based on the volatility parameter $\sigma_i(t)$. However, the TSV is a concept which is also relevant in a market with a smile. Even today traders derive a TSV from the *quotes of ATM caplets*, and use this pattern to understand how the market allocates volatility to the different maturities of rates. How can we understand what a non-lognormal model, fit to the caplet smile, implies for the future Evolution of the Term Structure of Volatility?

Let us analyze in more detail the procedure for computing the evolution of the TSV seen in Section 9.1.4. The price of an ATM caplet in the market is given by $Caplet_i^{mkt}$. The mathematical representation of this price is

$$Caplet_i = P(0, T_i)\mathbb{E}^i\left[\alpha_i(F(T_{i-1}; T_{i-1}, T_i) - F(0; T_{i-1}, T_i))^+\right],$$

and market quotes are provided by using a Black formula with an input σ_k^{Caplet} that makes the price equal to $Caplet_i^{mkt}$. Rewriting the Black formula (9.2) as a function of the implied integrated volatility, with the other inputs treated as fixed parameters, we have

$$Caplet^{mkt} = P(0, T_i)\alpha_i Black_\sigma\left(\sqrt{T_{k-1}}\sigma_k^{Caplet}|0, T_i, F(0; T_{i-1}, T_i), F(0; T_{i-1}, T_i)\right).$$

Operators who use a lognormal model have an analogous pricing formula based, however, on a time-dependent volatility $\sigma_i(t)$, so that after calibration they get

$$V_i^{Caplet}(0) = \sqrt{\int_0^{T_{i-1}} \sigma_i^2(t)dt}/\sqrt{T_{i-1}} = Black_\sigma^{-1}\left(Caplet^{mkt}/P(0, T_i)\alpha_i\right)/\sqrt{T_{i-1}}.$$

Then in order to know what the model implies as a future term-structure of volatility at a time T_j they simply have to move the lower bound of the integration domain forward, getting

$$T_j: \qquad V_i^{Caplet}(T_j) = \sqrt{\int_{T_j}^{T_{i-1}} \sigma_i^2(t)dt}/\sqrt{T_{i-1} - T_j} \text{ for } i = j+2, \ldots, M.$$

There exists, however, another more general way, to justify this result. When in a future time T_j traders look at the term structure of volatility, they will look at caplets with maturity T_i and fixing at T_{i-1}, $i \geq j+2$, *that are ATM at* T_j. Such a derivative, seen from time 0, is a forward starting caplet: a caplet with the strike fixing at T_j to the level $F(T_j; T_{i-1}, T_i)$. Its price is given by

$$Caplet_i = P(0, T_i)\mathbb{E}^i\left[\alpha_i(F(T_{i-1}; T_{i-1}, T_i) - F(T_j; T_{i-1}, T_i))^+\right]. \tag{9.14}$$

It is a special kind of an option to exchange an asset with a different one: the two assets are the same rate but observed at two different times. In the lognormal model this kind of option can be priced via the Margrabe formula. For two generic assets $F^A(t)$, $F^B(t)$, with dynamics under a T-forward measure given by

$$dF^A(t) = \mu^A(t)F^A(t)dt + \sigma_A(t)F^A(t)dW^A(t),$$
$$dF^B(t) = \mu^B(t)F^B(t)dt + \sigma_B(t)F^B(t)dW^B(t),$$
$$corr\left(dW^A(t), dW^B(t)\right) = \rho$$

the Margrabe formula gives the price of the option to exchange the assets at T as

$$P(0,T)\mathbb{E}^T\left[(F^A(T)-F^B(T))^+\right]=P(0,T)\,F^A(0)\exp\left[e^{\int_0^T \mu^A(s)ds}\right]$$

$$\cdot\Phi\left(\frac{\ln\frac{F^A(0)}{F^B(0)}+\int_0^T \mu^A(s)-\mu^B(s)\,ds+\hat{\sigma}^2(s)/2ds}{\sqrt{\Sigma}}\right)$$

$$-F^B(0)\exp\left[e^{\int_0^T \mu^B(s)ds}\right]\Phi\left(\frac{\ln\frac{F^A(0)}{F^B(0)}+\int_0^T \mu^A(s)-\mu^B(s)\,ds-\Sigma(0,T)/2}{\sqrt{\Sigma}}\right).$$

$$\Sigma=\int_0^T \sigma_A^2(s)+\sigma_B^2(s)-2\rho\sigma_A(s)\sigma_B(s)\,ds.$$

In the simple case of (9.14) we have

$$P(0,T_i)\mathbb{E}^i\left[\alpha_i(F_i(T_{i-1})-F_i(T_j))^+\right]=P(0,T_i)F_i(0)\left[2\Phi\left(\frac{1}{2}\sqrt{\Sigma(T_{i-1})}\right)-1\right]$$

$$\Sigma=\int_0^{T_{i-1}}\sigma_i^2(s)\,ds+\int_0^{T_j}\sigma_i^2(s)\,ds-2\int_0^{T_j}\sigma_i^2(s)\,ds=\int_{T_j}^{T_{i-1}}\sigma_i^2(s)\,ds$$

where the correlation is 1 because the two assets we exchange are two copies of the same rate until T_j, when the second one is frozen and its volatility jumps to zero, making correlation irrelevant. The freezing of the second asset also explains why some integrals are stopped at T_j. The final formula for the forward-starting caplet is simply

$$P(0,T_i)\alpha Black_\sigma\left(\int_{T_j}^{T_{i-1}}\sigma_i^2(s)\,ds|0,T_i,F_i(0),F_i(0)\right)$$

$$=P(0,T_i)\alpha_i F_i(0)\left[2\Phi\left(\frac{1}{2}\sqrt{\int_{T_j}^{T_{i-1}}\sigma_i^2(s)\,ds}\right)-1\right].$$

We see that the volatility input of the pricing function of a forward-starting caplet with maturity T_i and the strike setting at T_j is exactly the element $V_i^{Caplet}(T_j)$ in the evolution of the TSV. Thus, for getting the model implied evolution of the TSV, one could compute the prices of a complete strip of forward starting caplets that will be ATM at T_j, with prices $FSCaplet_i^j(F_i(0), ATM)$, and then invert these prices and get the required $V_i^{Caplet}(T_j)$ as

$$V_i^{Caplet}(T_j)=Black_\sigma^{-1}\left(\frac{FSCaplet_i^j(F_i(0),ATM)}{P(0,T_i)\alpha}|0,T_i,F_i(0),F_i(0)\right)/\sqrt{T_{i-1}-T_j}. \tag{9.15}$$

We can test this new general method (9.15) by computing with it the evolution of the TSV of a *lognormal* model, so that we also have the analytic method (9.8) and we can compare the outputs. In Figure 9.10 you see the evolution for the above calibrated lognormal model, computed with (9.8), while in Figure 9.11 we have the same evolution computed through (9.15) after the forward starting caplets (9.14) have been priced via Monte Carlo, and so making no use of the analytic formula that we have in a lognormal model but treating it like a general model.

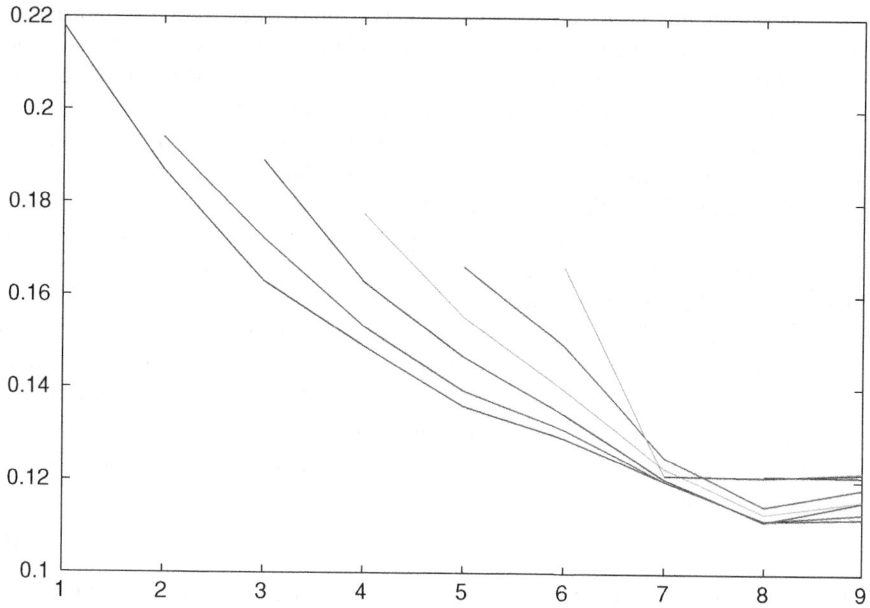

Figure 9.10 Evolution of TSV analytic

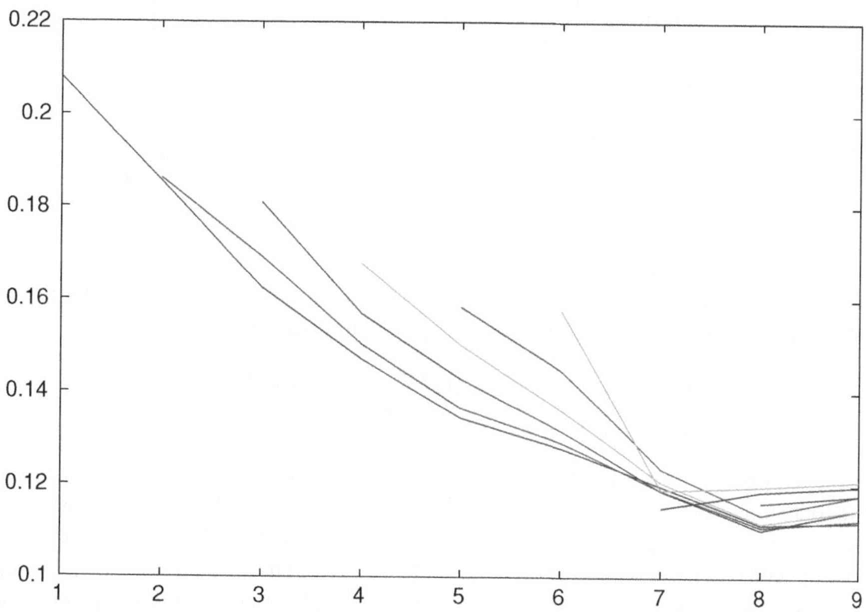

Figure 9.11 Evolution of TSV by Monte Carlo

As you can see the qualitative answers from the two approaches are indistinguishable, but the first method (9.8) is available only for lognormal while (9.15) is available for all models.

There are differences in the details of the two evolutions, since the Monte Carlo expression is affected by the simulation error. But this approach works for whatever model we have, for which we only need to be able to compute prices $FSCaplet_i^j(F_i(0), ATM)$. These can be computed even in very complex models, for example via Monte Carlo simulation, and then we can apply (9.15) to derive the evolution of the term structure of volatility. Thus with this approach we can express the model prices of caplets that will be ATM at the future date T_j (exactly the products that will be used by traders for the future TSV) in terms of implied volatilities, through the usual lognormal metric.

And what if now using this advanced model, we want to extract the implied evolution of the smile? Again, smiles are prices of options far-from-the-money expressed as implied volatilities using the lognormal metric. Computing the model implied T_i smile for future time T_j requires first computing the model prices today $FSCaplet_i^j(F_i(0), \chi_k)$ of the caplets with expiry T_i that will set a not-necessarily-ATM strike $\chi_k F_i(T_j)$ at T_j, where χ_k is an element of a vector χ that could be for example

$$\chi = [0.7,\ 0.85,\ 1,\ 1.15,\ 1.3]\,. \tag{9.16}$$

Then these prices, which can be computed in any model for example by Monte Carlo simulation, need to be expressed with an implied Black volatility following the usual lognormal metrics. This is not difficult because a caplet with expiry T_i that will set a strike $\chi_k F_i(T_j)$ at T_j can be priced in the Black model with formula

$$P(0,T_i)\alpha Black_\sigma\left(\int_{T_j}^{T_{i-1}} \left(\sigma_i^k(s)\right)^2 ds | 0, T_i, F_i(0), \chi_k F_i(0)\right),$$

so that the implied smile will be given by the

$$V_i^{k-Caplet}(T_j) = Black_\sigma^{-1}\left(\frac{FSCaplet_i^j(F_i(0), \chi_k F_i(0))}{P(0,T_i)\alpha} | 0, T_i, F_i(0), \chi_k F_i(0)\right) / \sqrt{T_{i-1} - T_j} \tag{9.17}$$

for k running all the elements of (9.16).

Consider a stochastic volatility Libor market model with a single stochastic volatility factor with the same Heston dynamics as (2.21), but applied to forward rates:

$$\begin{aligned} dF_k(t) &= \sigma_k(t)\sqrt{V(t)}F_k(t)dZ_k^k(t), \quad k = 1, 2, \ldots, M \\ dV(t) &= \kappa(\theta - V(t))\,dt + \epsilon\sqrt{V(t)}\,dW(t), \end{aligned}$$

where the volatility is mean-reverting, and we assume no correlation between $Z_k(t)$ and $W(t)$, leading to a smile symmetric around the ATM strike. We can use (9.17) to see how the smile evolves in time according to the model. For example, we can consider dates $T_0, T_1, \ldots, T_9$, each one spaced by one year, so that $T_0 = 1y$ and $T_9 = 10y$. Then we can look at the so-called forward smile: how, according to the model, the smile at T_i looks for all subsequent maturities T_{i+1} (one year when seen at T_i), T_{i+2} (two years), and so on until T_9. We have an evolution of the term structure of smiles. We see in Figure 9.12 the term structure of smile for dates T_1, T_4 and T_7, so that we would observe the evolution of the term structure. The picture is what we would expect from model properties: since the stochastic volatility is mean reverting, the

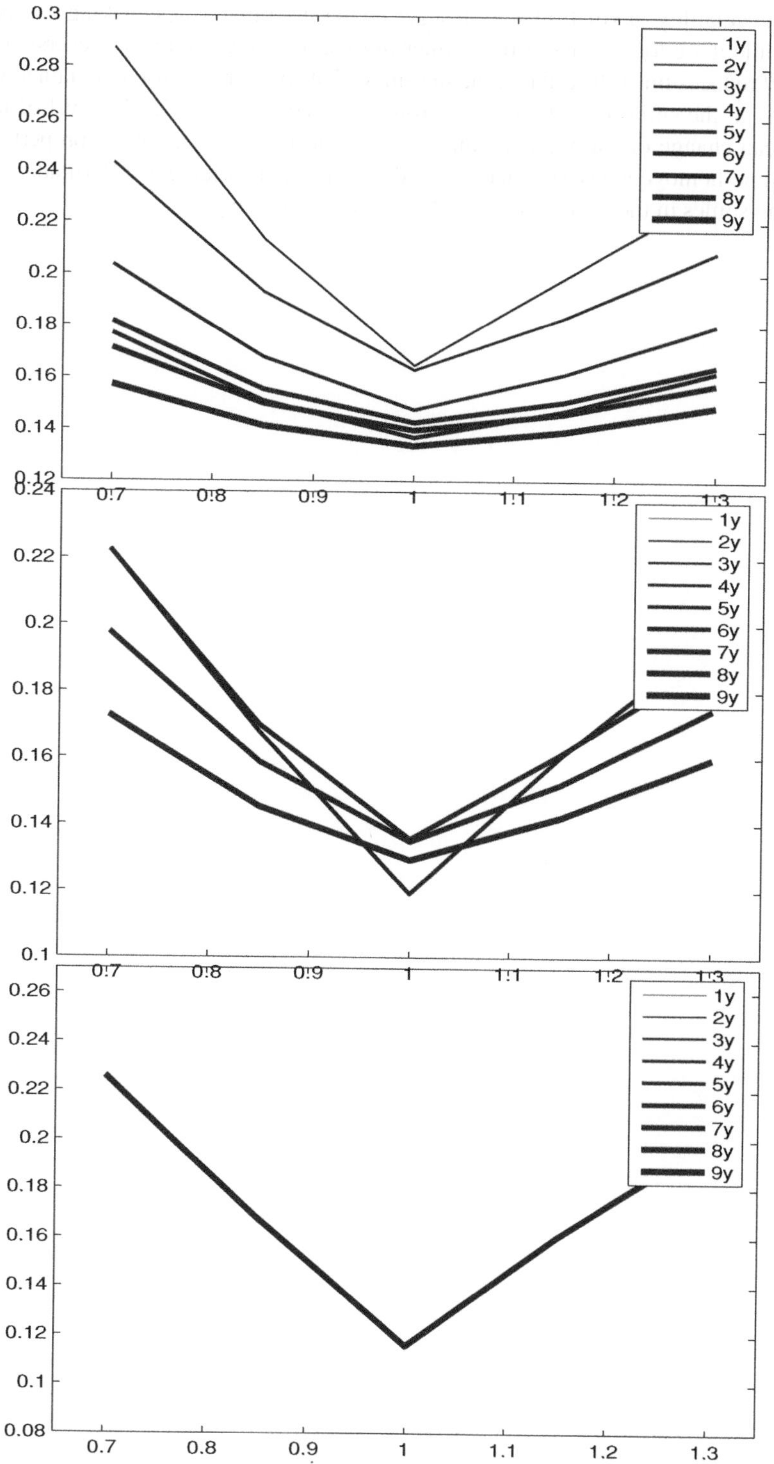

Figure 9.12 Evolution of smile for a Heston Libor Market Model. In the legend '3y' indicates, for example, the rate that expires in 3*y* from inception. From top to bottom: the term structure in 2, 3 and 8 years

effect of the volatility of volatility ϵ is stronger on the short maturities, making the smile very convex, while if we look at maturities further in time the effect of a mean reversion towards flat value θ reduces this effect, flattening the smile. This property is also maintained when we do not look at the smile from time 0 but from a subsequent date T_i. The level of the ATM volatility can change due to the combined effect of all parameters, but the properties of the smile are time-homogeneous, so that exercise decisions in the pricing of a Bermudan are taken considering smiles in the future similar to the ones we see today.

10

When the Payoff is Wrong

10.1 THE LINK BETWEEN MODEL ERRORS AND PAYOFF ERRORS

In this chapter we consider a risk of mistakes that does not relate to models, but can be even more dangerous than model risk. We are speaking of the mistakes that we can make when we give a mathematical representation of a payoff. There are various reason why I have included this topic.

Often the first precise analysis of a payoff is performed by a quantitative modeller, or even, as in the cases we consider in this chapter, it is performed by the quantitative researchers who are writing papers on how to price the payoff with a model. The other categories of people who work with a new payoff, such as salespeople, traders, legal consultants and even accountants, can deal with the new payoff having only a verbal description and an intuitive understanding of it. The quant, on the other hand, when making the model to price the payoff, is forced to give the payoff a precise analytic representation. If he or she makes a mistake at this step, they risk being held responsible, even if the source of the error came from misunderstandings or lack of clarity on the part of those who introduced the payoff. For this reason, this is a topic all quants should pay attention to.

There is another reason why I have included this topic in the book. Considering the complexity of many payoffs, in their representation the modeller uses mathematical tools not so different from those he or she uses to represent the behaviour of market variables – 'the model' in the strict sense of the word – and he is subject to similar mistakes. At times a formalism that proved useful to describe a class of payoffs may not be suitable for describing an extension of this class of payoffs, or the same payoffs but considered in a new context. We can miss some elements in the reality of the market that make the representation of the payoff unrealistic or at least partial, exactly as can happen when we are designing a new model. An example is the representation of CDS counterparty risk given in the literature mentioned in 3.4.2: the fact of excluding that the protection seller can default between default of the reference entity and settlement, which are simplistically represented as coinciding, is an example of how an approximation typical of mathematical modelling can lead to a very important mistake about a payoff.

This is also the case in the first example we report below. It relates to the *default closeout*, namely the payoff of a derivative in case of default of one counterparty. In particular we focus on what this default payment is likely to be when both the counterparty and the institution which is pricing the payoff have a non-negligible default risk. This case is often called 'bilateral counterparty risk'. We will see that the representation of this default payment given in the quantitative literature about 'unilateral counterparty risk', where the possible default of the party that is pricing the derivative is not considered, may not be trivially extendable to the case of bilateral counterparty risk. Instead, all published papers assumed exactly the same form of default payment used in the analysis of unilateral default risk. Morini (2010) and Brigo and Morini (2010) show that this assumption contradicts both the standard market practice of popular financial products like bonds and some prescriptions given in the legal documentation about derivatives, and suggest an alternative description based on the analysis of what can happen in practice when there is bilateral risk of default.

The interesting point, for a book about model risk, is not whether the previous literature was right or wrong. It is possible that the debate recently opened will lead to the creation of a clear standard on this issue. Otherwise, we will only have a practical answer when the next important default happens.

What is relevant is to note that there were different possibilities for the analytic description of the future default payoff, which can have a dramatic effect on the value of the counterparty risk adjustments, and that the quantitative research side-stepped the issue by choosing the simplest possibility. The description of the payoff has probably been considered much less relevant than the study of the models for default events. The results we show below, however, confirm that payoff imprecision may have created large and unexpected losses had the real default payoff turned out different from the one assumed in pricing. Therefore, attention to the payoff description should be given high importance even by modellers, particularly because, as we will see, the risk of a payoff misinterpretation can be understood even without any knowledge of legal issues but only from experience of standard practice on simple financial products, and with a clever analysis of the effects of the payoff description in specific future scenarios. An analysis, by the way, that is made remarkably easier by the use of quantitative models.

Additionally, for pricing a payoff one often finds it natural to introduce some minor simplifications to the payoff itself, which may go unnoticed or appear negligible in most market situations, but become relevant in special market situations. This is the case with the second example we consider, where we describe the evolution in the representation of the payoff of a credit index or portfolio option that has been observable in published research ever since this product was introduced. The product has not changed; but the increasing understanding of it on the part of the quants led to an evolution in its representation. A first flaw in the market practice was pointed out by Pedersen (2003), who showed that the market formula corresponded to a payoff different from the real one. This observation led to an improvement in the market formula. A second issue was noted by Morini and Brigo (2009) and (2010), that point out that even the improved market standard fails in a specific scenario of systemic default. Here the risk of mistakes is more related to mathematical issues, such that the analysis of Morini and Brigo (2009) and (2010) was actually motivated not by perplexities about the payoff but by the search for a mathematically more precise definition of the martingale pricing measure used implicitly in the market formula. Their finding that the representation of the payoff in the market formula was not yet fully consistent with the true payoff was merely a by-product of this more theoretical analysis. What is interesting to us is that, similarly to some considerations we made when speaking of approximations in Chapter 6, the inconsistency was initially judged practically irrelevant since it referred to a very extreme scenario. But then empirical testing revealed that the probability of this scenario, evaluated on market inputs registered during the credit crunch, was no more negligible since default correlation had reached a peak.

10.2 THE RIGHT PAYOFF AT DEFAULT: THE IMPACT OF THE CLOSEOUT CONVENTION

In this section we focus on the description of the default payoff in a context where both counterparties to a deal can default, showing the ambiguities that a quant faces in describing this future payment, and the financial and mathematical considerations one can make in order to understand which one of the possible payoffs is more likely. I follow mainly Brigo and Morini (2010), although, for the reasons explained in Section 3.4, I will not make use of the hypothesis of comonotonic defaults to represent the case of high default dependency. Although this hypothesis is used in Brigo and Morini (2010) just as a toy model to represent an extreme scenario, some of its features are so unrealistic – in particular the implication that once a default happens, the second default time is known with certainty – that I fear it may confuse the reader. I will explain the effects of default dependency with market examples without making use of that model assumption.

When a default event happens to one of the counterparties in a deal, the deal is stopped and marked-to-market: the net present value of the residual part of the deal is computed. This net present value, called closeout amount, is then used to determine the default payments. Before the credit crunch, and actually up to the Lehman default, there appeared to be no ambiguity in the above computation: the net present value of the residual deal was usually computed as the expectation of the future payments discounted back to the default day by a Libor-based curve of discount factors.

Today, however, we are aware (see Chapter 4) that discounting a deal which is default-free and backed by a liquid collateral should be performed using a default-free curve of discount factors, based on overnight quotations, whereas a deal which is not collateralized and is thus subject to default risk should be discounted taking liquidity costs into account and should include a Credit Valuation Adjustment. Therefore, when we speak of net present value, we are now aware that this must be computed in different ways even for equal payoffs, depending on the liquidity and credit conditions of the deal. In case of a default, which net present value should we compute?

Before the credit crunch, the answer was obvious. Default risk related mainly to deals between a bank and a corporation. The bank usually had a credit quality so much higher than the corporate that the bank could safely be assumed to be default-free, and only the risk of default of the corporate was considered. This setting is called ‘unilateral counterparty risk’. In such a case the net present value after a default will be computed as if the residual deal was default-free: in fact, the only party that can default has just defaulted, while the surviving party has been assumed to be risk-free from the start. We call this assumption a *risk-free closeout.*

Nowadays almost no counterparty can be considered to be default-free, and some corporates have much higher credit quality than most banks. Thus the literature has moved to the so-called ‘bilateral counterparty risk’, where both counterparties are risky.[1] In this case when a default happens the surviving party is not default-free, since it can still default before the maturity of the deal. In spite of that, current literature still assumes that the net present value of the deal at default will be computed as if the surviving party was default-free. Now, this is not an obvious choice as it was in the unilateral setting, and seems driven more by a simplistic extension of the unilateral formulas rather than by a reasoning on the financial reality in case of default. In fact, if the survived counterparty wants to replace the defaulted deal with a new deal equal to the residual part of the defaulted deal, this new deal will have a price which is certainly not risk-free: it will take into account the default probability of the survived entity. We call this a *replacement closeout*, and in Section 10.2.2 we show that such a description of the default payment is supported by legal documentation produced by ISDA. If the reader is interested in the topic but does not want to dwell on technical issues, he/she can move to Section 10.2.4 which

[1] We have already hinted at this framework, and at a number of its implications, in Section 4.2. Here we look at it in greater detail, focusing on a different aspect.

gives an intuitive summary of the findings of this section, perhaps reading first the next two sections but certainly skipping the computation in Section 10.2.3. The latter section, however, can be useful for seeing how quantitative tools can be applied to the analysis of payouts.

10.2.1 How Much Will be Paid at Closeout, Really?

We consider two parties in a derivative transaction: I (investor) and C (counterparty). We call τ^X, R^X and $L^X = 1 - R^X$, respectively, the default time, the recovery and the loss given default of party X, with $X \in \{I, C\}$. We define $\Pi_I(t, T)$ to be the discounted cashflows of the derivative from t to T seen from the point of view of I, assuming both parties are risk-free. The risk-free net present value of the derivative at t is

$$V_I^0(t) := \mathbb{E}_t[\Pi_I(t, T)].$$

The subscript I indicates that this value is seen from the point of view of I; the superscript 0 indicates that we are considering both parties as default-free.

In the early literature on counterparty risk adjustment, see for example Brigo and Masetti (2005), only the default of counterparty C is considered, while the investor I is treated as default free. Under this assumption, the value of the transaction is

$$\begin{aligned} V_I^C(t) = \mathbb{E}_t\left\{1_{\{\tau^C > T\}}\Pi_I(t, T)\right\} \\ +\mathbb{E}_t\left\{1_{\{\tau^C \le T\}}\left[\Pi_I\left(t, \tau^C\right) + D\left(t, \tau^C\right)\left(R^C\left(V_I^0\left(\tau^C\right)\right)^+ - \left(-V_I^0\left(\tau^C\right)\right)^+\right)\right]\right\}. \end{aligned} \tag{10.1}$$

You see that the cashflows considered are split between those received before default, $\Pi_I(t, \tau)$, and the present value of the payout at default time τ. What happens at τ? At τ the residual deal is marked-to-market. The mark-to-market of the residual deal at an early termination time is called *closeout amount* in the jargon of ISDA documentation. Here it is given by

$$V_I^0\left(\tau^C\right).$$

If this is negative to the survived party, namely the investor I, I will pay this amount entirely to the liquidators of the counterparty. If it is positive to I, the liquidators will pay to I only a recovery fraction of the closeout amount, leading to a payout at default given by

$$\left(R^1\left(V_I^0\left(\tau^C\right)\right)^+ - \left(-V_I^0\left(\tau^C\right)\right)^+\right). \tag{10.2}$$

Here the closeout amount $V_I^0(\tau)$ is computed treating the residual deal as a *default-free* deal. The reason for this is obvious. There are two parties I and C, and party I is supposed default-free so it will never default, while party C has already defaulted and this is taken into account by the fact that, in case $V_C^0(\tau) > 0$, C will pay only a recovery fraction of the default-free closeout amount. This default-free closeout could also be called a *replacement closeout*, in the sense that, if I wanted to substitute the defaulted deal with another one where the counterparty is default-free, the counterparty would ask I to pay $V_I^0(\tau)$, a risk-free closeout since both parties are risk-free.

Nowadays almost no counterparty can be considered to be default-free. The extension to the case when both I and C can default is called 'bilateral risk of default' and is introduced for interest rate swaps in Bielecki and Rutkowski (2001) and Picoult (2005), but became a real issue only after the credit crunch, when a number of papers were written on the topic, for example Gregory (2009), Brigo and Capponi (2009), and Brigo, Pallavicini and Papatheodorou (2009). In these previous works the net present value adjusted by the default probabilities of both parties is given by

$$\begin{aligned} V_I(t) &= \mathbb{E}_t\left\{1_0 \Pi_I(t,T)\right\} \\ &+ \mathbb{E}_t\left\{1_I\left[\Pi_I\left(t,\tau^I\right) + D\left(t,\tau^I\right)\left(\left(V_I^0\left(\tau^I\right)\right)^+ - R^I\left(-V_I^0\left(\tau^I\right)\right)^+\right)\right]\right\} \\ &+ \mathbb{E}_t\left\{1_C\left[\Pi_I\left(t,\tau^C\right) + D\left(t,\tau^C\right)\left(R^C\left(V_I^0\left(\tau^C\right)\right)^+ - \left(-V_I^0\left(\tau^C\right)\right)^+\right)\right]\right\}, \end{aligned} \quad (10.3)$$

where we use the following event indicators

$$\begin{aligned} 1_0 &= 1_{\{T<\min(\tau^I,\tau^C)\}}, \quad 1_I = 1_{\{\tau^I \le \min(T,\tau^C)\}} \\ 1_C &= 1 - 1_I - 1_0 = 1_{\{\tau^C<\tau^I\}} 1_{\{\tau^C \le T\}}. \end{aligned}$$

Here both parties can default, and it will be the *first* default that interrupts the deal. *We indicate by* 1 *the party that defaults first, and by* 2 *the party that defaults last*, so that

$$\tau^1 = \min\left(\tau^I, \tau^C\right).$$

Then the pricing formula (10.3) simplifies to

$$\begin{aligned} V_I(t) &= \mathbb{E}_t\left\{1_0 \Pi_I(t,T)\right\} \\ &+ \mathbb{E}_t\left\{(1_C - 1_I)\left[\Pi_2\left(t,\tau^1\right) + D\left(t,\tau^1\right)\left(R^1\left(V_2^0\left(\tau^1\right)\right)^+ - \left(-V_2^0\left(\tau^1\right)\right)^+\right)\right]\right\}. \end{aligned} \quad (10.4)$$

Let us see how this treats the default payout. It is

$$(1_C - 1_I)\left[R^1\left(V_2^0\left(\tau^1\right)\right)^+ - \left(-V_2^0\left(\tau^1\right)\right)^+\right].$$

If the counterparty C defaults first, then $1_C = 1, 1_I = 0, \tau^1 = \tau^C$ and we have the same payout as in the unilateral case of (10.2). If the investor I defaults first, the payout is reversed: when the closeout amount is positive to the defaulted investor, this amount is received fully, while if it is negative only a recovery fraction will be paid to the counterparty. Notice that, as in the unilateral case, with bilateral risk of default the closeout amount *is computed treating the residual deal as default-free*

$$V_2^0\left(\tau^1\right). \quad (10.5)$$

We are again excluding the possibility of default of either party in pricing the residual payoff. Is this assumption as obviously justified here as it was in the unilateral case? Not quite. Only the assumption of ignoring the risk of default of 1 is justified, obviously. In fact 1 has defaulted and this is accounted for correctly by computing a closeout amount where there is no possibility of another default of 1, and then, in case this amount is negative to 1, by assuming that 1 will pay only a recovery fraction of it. But the other party 2 has not defaulted, and now it is not true that it will never default in the future. There is a non-negligible probability that it defaults before the maturity T of the residual deal. Thus it is unclear why the mark-to-market of a residual deal where one of the two parties has not yet defaulted and may default in the future should be treated as default-free. Here the *risk-free closeout is not a replacement closeout*. In fact, if the survived party 2 wanted to substitute the defaulted deal with another one where the market counterparty is default-free, the counterparty would ask 2 to pay not

$$V_2^{\boxed{0}}(\tau^1)$$

but

$$V_2^{\boxed{2}}(\tau^1), \tag{10.6}$$

because the market counterparty cannot ignore the default risk of party 2 from τ^1 to the maturity T of the residual deal. Thus the amount (10.6) will be called in the following *replacement closeout amount*. It is given by (10.1) when $1 = I$, while when $1 = C$ (now only the default of I is still possible) it is given by

$$\begin{aligned} V_I^I(t) &= \mathbb{E}_t\left\{1_{\{\tau^I > T\}}\Pi_I(t,T)\right\} \\ &\quad + \mathbb{E}_t\left\{1_{\{\tau^I \leq T\}}\left[\Pi_I\left(t,\tau^I\right) + D\left(t,\tau^I\right)\left(\left(V_I^0\left(\tau^I\right)\right)^+ - R^I\left(-V_I^0\left(\tau^I\right)\right)^+\right)\right]\right\}. \end{aligned} \tag{10.7}$$

If we consider the replacement closeout, the pricing formula in case of bilateral counterparty risk becomes

$$\begin{aligned} \hat{V}_I(t) &= \mathbb{E}_t\left\{1_0\Pi_I(t,T)\right\} \\ &\quad + \mathbb{E}_t\left\{1_I\left[\Pi_I\left(t,\tau^I\right) + D\left(t,\tau^I\right)\left(\left(V_I^C\left(\tau^I\right)\right)^+ - R^I\left(-V_I^C\left(\tau^I\right)\right)^+\right)\right]\right\} \\ &\quad + \mathbb{E}_t\left\{1_C\left[\Pi_I\left(t,\tau^C\right) + D\left(t,\tau^C\right)\left(R^C\left(V_I^I\left(\tau^C\right)\right)^+ - \left(-V_I^I\left(\tau^C\right)\right)^+\right)\right]\right\}, \end{aligned} \tag{10.8}$$

as given in Brigo and Morini (2010) and in Morini (2010).

10.2.2 What the Market Says and What the ISDA Says

The reader may think that the first step to take is to ask experienced practitioners which approach is applied in practice for the computation of closeout. We have done this (and we thank for that in particular the participants to Global Derivatives Conference 2010 in Paris) and surprisingly enough we found that opinions differed. This variety of opinions can be related to the fact that the ISDA documentation had given a (relatively) open definition of closeout amount and, more importantly, to the fact that full awareness of the importance of CVA and DVA has happened only *after* Lehman's default, the last important default that may work as a benchmark. At that time 'Libor discounting' was mainly used for closeout, and this is somewhat in-between a risk-free discounting and a discounting taking full consideration of the risk of default of the remaining party.

Which one of the two closeout assumptions is backed by legal documentation? Let us have a look. The Market Review of OTC Derivative Bilateral Collateralization Practices, published by ISDA on 1 March 2010, says: 'Upon default close-out, valuations will in many circumstances reflect the replacement cost of transactions calculated at the terminating party's bid or offer side of the market, and will often take into account the credit-worthiness of the terminating party'.

Analogously the ISDA Close-out Amount Protocol, published in 2009, says that in determining a closeout amount the information used includes 'quotations (either firm or indicative) for replacement transactions supplied by one or more third parties that may take into account the creditworthiness of the Determining Party at the time the quotation is provided'.

It is clear that a replacement closeout, rather than a risk-free closeout, is mentioned by the ISDA documentation. On the other hand, the wording is careful, and documentation speaks of credit-worthiness which is taken into account 'often', not always, and that 'may', not must, be included in the quotations from third parties. This leaves room for a risk-free closeout, which is probably easier to compute because it is the same independently of the features of the survived counterparty.

There are still grey areas in how the closeout will actually be computed in a real default, and therefore in what we have to assume about closeout when we compute the credit valuation adjustment of a non-collateralized derivative. Is this issue practically relevant, or would it have a negligible impact in the computation of the credit valuation adjustment?

In the following we show, with a quantitative analysis, that the impact can be dramatic. If you want to skip the technical details and get a summary of the findings, you can go to Section 10.2.4.

10.2.3 A Quantitative Analysis of the Closeout

Since we are dealing with a matter that would affect even the simplest derivative in case of default, we find an analysis with very simple – albeit not unrealistic – models and transactions to be much more instructive than the application of some elaborate model to a complex derivative that would just risk increasing the confusion. We consider a contract where party C enters at time 0 into the commitment to pay a unit of money at time T to party I. Similarly to the claim already put forward in Section 4.2, it has exactly the same payoff as the prototypical zero-coupon bond or loan of the textbooks on finance.[2] Party C is the borrower or bond issuer, and I is the lender or bond holder. Again, this payoff is convenient for our purposes because there is a consolidated standard on how to price it. We will see which one between risk-free and replacement liquidation is consistent with the practice developed in the loan and bond markets. In the following we take deterministic interest rates.

The unilateral case

First we evaluate this 'derivative bond' deal using unilateral formulas, namely considering only the default of the borrower counterparty C (here the default of I is omitted from the payout irrespective of the fact that it may or may not default). We apply (10.1) to this payoff, getting

$$\begin{aligned}
&\mathbb{E}_t\left\{1_{\{\tau^C>T\}}e^{-\int_t^T r(s)ds}\right\}+\mathbb{E}_t\left\{1_{\{\tau^C\le T\}}\left[e^{-\int_t^{\tau^C} r(s)ds}R^C\left(e^{-\int_{\tau^C}^T r(s)ds}\right)^+\right]\right\}\\
&=e^{-\int_t^T r(s)ds}\mathbb{E}_t\left[1_{\{\tau^C>T\}}\right]+R^C e^{-\int_t^T r(s)ds}\mathbb{E}_t\left[1_{\{\tau^C\le T\}}\right]. \qquad (10.9)
\end{aligned}$$

---

[2] It is really astonishing how many things are still to be understood about such a simple payoff!

This is the standard formula for the pricing of a defaultable bond or loan,

$$V_I^C(0) = e^{-\int_0^T r(s)ds} \Pr\left(\tau^C > T\right) + R^C e^{-\int_0^T r(s)ds} \Pr\left(\tau^C \leq T\right),$$

which says that the price of a defaultable bond equals the price of a default-free bond multiplied by the survival probability of the issuer, plus a recovery part received when the issuer defaults.

By applying (10.7) to this payoff we can compute easily also $V_I^I(t)$, the value when only the default of the lender I is taken into account. We have

$$V_I^I(t) = \mathbb{E}_t\left\{1_{\{\tau^I > T\}} e^{-\int_t^T r(s)ds}\right\} + \mathbb{E}_t\left\{1_{\{\tau^I \leq T\}} e^{-\int_t^{\tau^I} r(s)ds} \left(e^{-\int_{\tau^I}^T r(s)ds}\right)^+\right\} = e^{-\int_t^T r(s)ds}. \tag{10.10}$$

We have obtained the price of a risk-free bond, thus the formula says that in a loan or bond what matters is the risk of default of the borrower. We have no influence on the risk of default of a party, the lender, that in this contract has no future obligations. Both formula (10.9) and (10.10) are in line with market practice.

The bilateral case with replacement closeout

Now we price the deal considering the default risk of both parties, *and assuming first a replacement closeout*. We apply formula (10.8) introduced above, putting (10.9) and (10.10) into this formula. We get

$$\begin{aligned}
\hat{V}_I(t) &= \mathbb{E}_t\left\{1_0 e^{-\int_t^T r(s)ds}\right\} \\
&+ \mathbb{E}_t\left\{1_I\left[e^{-\int_t^T r(s)ds}\mathbb{E}_{\tau^I}\left[1_{\{\tau^C > T\}}\right] + R^C e^{-\int_t^T r(s)ds}\mathbb{E}_{\tau^I}\left[1_{\{\tau^C \leq T\}}\right]\right]\right\} \\
&+ \mathbb{E}_t\left\{1_C\left[R^C e^{-\int_t^T r(s)ds}\right]\right\}.
\end{aligned}$$

Notice that

$$1_I = 1_{\{\tau^I \leq \min(T, \tau^C)\}}$$

is τ^I-measurable, namely it is known at τ^I, so that the second one of the three terms of $\hat{V}_I(t)$ above can be rewritten as

$$\begin{aligned}
&\mathbb{E}_t\left\{1_I\left[e^{-\int_t^T r(s)ds}\mathbb{E}_{\tau^I}\left[1_{\{\tau^C > T\}}\right] + R^C e^{-\int_t^T r(s)ds}\mathbb{E}_{\tau^I}\left[1_{\{\tau^C \leq T\}}\right]\right]\right\} \\
&= e^{-\int_t^T r(s)ds}\mathbb{E}_t\left[\mathbb{E}_{\tau^I}\left[1_I 1_{\{\tau^C > T\}}\right]\right] + R^C e^{-\int_t^T r(s)ds}\mathbb{E}_t\left[\mathbb{E}_{\tau^I}\left[1_I 1_{\{\tau^C \leq T\}}\right]\right] \\
&= e^{-\int_t^T r(s)ds}\mathbb{E}_t\left[1_I 1_{\{\tau^C > T\}}\right] + R^C e^{-\int_t^T r(s)ds}\mathbb{E}_t\left[1_I 1_{\{\tau^C \leq T\}}\right]
\end{aligned}$$

where in the last passage we have used the law of iterated expectations. Now in $\hat{V}_I(t)$ we can factor together the terms that are multiplied by R^C and those that are not, getting

$$\hat{V}_I(t) = e^{-\int_t^T r(s)ds}\left(\mathbb{E}_t\left[1_0 + 1_I 1_{\{\tau^C > T\}}\right] + R^C \mathbb{E}_t\left[1_I 1_{\{\tau^C \leq T\}} + 1_C\right]\right).$$

Playing with indicators we get

$$\begin{aligned}\hat{V}_I(t) &= e^{-\int_t^T r(s)ds}\mathbb{E}_t\left[1_{\{T<\tau^I\}}1_{\{T<\tau^C\}} + 1_{\{\tau^I \leq T\}}1_{\{\tau^C > T\}}\right]\\ &\quad + R^C e^{-\int_t^T r(s)ds}\mathbb{E}_t\left[1_{\{\tau^I \leq \tau^C\}}1_{\{\tau^C \leq T\}} + 1_{\{\tau^C<\tau^I\}}1_{\{\tau^C \leq T\}}\right].\end{aligned}$$

Since $1_{\{T<\tau^I\}} + 1_{\{\tau^I \leq T\}} = 1_{\{\tau^I \leq \tau^C\}} + 1_{\{\tau^C<\tau^I\}} = 1$, we have

$$\begin{aligned}\hat{V}_I(t) &= e^{-\int_t^T r(s)ds}\mathbb{E}_t\left[1_{\{\tau^C > T\}}\right] + R^C e^{-\int_t^T r(s)ds}\mathbb{E}_t\left[1_{\{\tau^C \leq T\}}\right]\\ &= e^{-\int_t^T r(s)ds}\left[\Pr_t\left(\tau^C > T\right) + R^C \Pr_t\left(\tau^C \leq T\right)\right]. \qquad (10.11)\end{aligned}$$

In spite of the somewhat lengthy computations, we have reached a very simple and reasonable result. We have $\hat{V}_I(t) = V_I^C(t)$, so the risk of default of the bond-holder in a bond, or the lender in a loan, does not influence the value of the contract. When the contract has no future obligations for a party I the risk of default of I does not influence the price. Only the risk of default of the bond-issuer or borrower matters for valuation. This result is also in line with market practice.[3]

The bilateral case with risk-free closeout

Now we apply instead *the formula (10.3) that assumes a risk-free closeout*. Since $V_I^0(\tau) = e^{-\int_\tau^T r(s)ds}$, we have

$$\begin{aligned}V_I(t) &= \mathbb{E}_t\left\{1_0 e^{-\int_t^T r(s)ds}\right\} + \mathbb{E}_t\left\{1_I\left[e^{-\int_t^{\tau^I} r(s)ds}\left(e^{-\int_{\tau^I}^T r(s)ds}\right)^+\right]\right\}\\ &\quad + \mathbb{E}_t\left\{1_C\left[e^{-\int_t^{\tau^C} r(s)ds} R^C\left(e^{-\int_{\tau^C}^T r(s)ds}\right)^+\right]\right\}\\ &= e^{-\int_t^T r(s)ds}\mathbb{E}_t\left[1_0 + 1_I\right] + e^{-\int_t^T r(s)ds} R^C \mathbb{E}_t\left[1_C\right].\\ &= e^{-\int_t^T r(s)ds}\left(\Pr_t\left[T < \min\left(\tau^I, \tau^C\right) \cup \tau^I \leq \min\left(T, \tau^C\right)\right]\right.\\ &\quad \left. + R^C \Pr_t\left[\tau^C < \tau^I \cap \tau^C \leq T\right]\right). \qquad (10.12)\end{aligned}$$

Playing with indicators one can obtain

$$\begin{aligned}V_I(t) &= e^{-\int_t^T r(s)ds}\left(\Pr_t[\tau^C > T] + \Pr_t[\tau^I < \tau^C < T] + R^C \Pr_t[\tau^C < \min(\tau^I, T)]\right)\\ &= e^{-\int_t^T r(s)ds}\left(\Pr_t[\tau^C > T] + R^C \Pr_t[\tau^C < T] + \left(1 - R^C\right)\Pr_t[\tau^I < \tau^C < T]\right). \quad (10.13)\end{aligned}$$

---

[3] The reader may think that the risk of default of the lender could in practice influence the price of a bond or loan through its effect on the cost of funding for the lender. See Section 4.2 for a discussion on this. However, when liquidity costs are not considered, as is the case here, this effect does not exist and, as in classic bond pricing, one expects the risk of default of the holder not to influence the price of a bond.

Comparing the two closeout formulations

Reaching this result for V_I applied to a 'derivative bond' has been far easier than reaching the analogous one for $\hat{V}_I$, but the result looks more complex. In fact it introduces a dependence on the risk of default of the lender even at time 0, and on the exact individuation of the first default that was not there in $\hat{V}_I$. As we can easily see by comparing (10.13) with (10.11), a risk-free liquidation increases the value of a 'derivative bond' to the bond holder compared to the value that a bond has in the market practice. Symmetrically, the value is reduced to the bond issuer, and this reduction is an increasing function of the default risk of the bond holder.

A numerical example

To quantify the size of the above difference, and to analyze numerically the practical effect of either assumption on closeout, we need to have a model for the default times of our two names. Consistently with the purpose of keeping complexity as low as possible since we are dealing with very fundamental issues, we will use the simplest bivariate extension of the standard single name credit model. As in the single name market credit model, we assume that the default time of the name X, $X \in \{I, C\}$, is exponentially distributed. We take a flat default intensity λ_X, so that the survival probability is

$$\Pr(\tau_X > T) = e^{-\lambda_X T},$$

and for consistency also $r(s)$ is taken flat so that the default-free bond is

$$P_T = e^{-rT}.$$

As baseline hypotheses, we consider the case when the default times of the two names are independent. Later we consider what happens when there is a link between the credit risk of I and C. It is well known that in case of independence $\min\left(\tau^I, \tau^C\right)$ is also exponentially distributed of parameter $\lambda_I + \lambda_C$, since

$$\begin{aligned}\Pr\left(\min\left(\tau^I, \tau^C\right) > T\right) &= \Pr\left(\tau^I > T\right)\Pr\left(\tau^C > T\right)\\ &= e^{-(\lambda_I+\lambda_C)T}\end{aligned}$$

It is easy to compute the terms needed to apply Formula (10.12) assuming risk-free closeout. First, one has

$$\Pr\left(\tau^I < \min(\tau^C, T)\right) = \frac{\lambda_I}{\lambda_I + \lambda_C}\left(1 - e^{-(\lambda_I+\lambda_C)T}\right),$$

We also have the special case

$$\Pr\left(\tau^I < \tau^C\right) = \frac{\lambda_I}{\lambda_I + \lambda_C}$$

which is obtained as a limit case of the earlier expression when $T \uparrow \infty$. We have all we need for computing (10.13), which corresponds to

$$e^{-rT}\left\{e^{-(\lambda_I+\lambda_C)T} + \frac{\lambda_I}{\lambda_I + \lambda_C}\left(1 - e^{-(\lambda_I+\lambda_C)T}\right) + R^C\frac{\lambda_C}{\lambda_I + \lambda_C}\left(1 - e^{-(\lambda_I+\lambda_C)T}\right)\right\}. \tag{10.14}$$

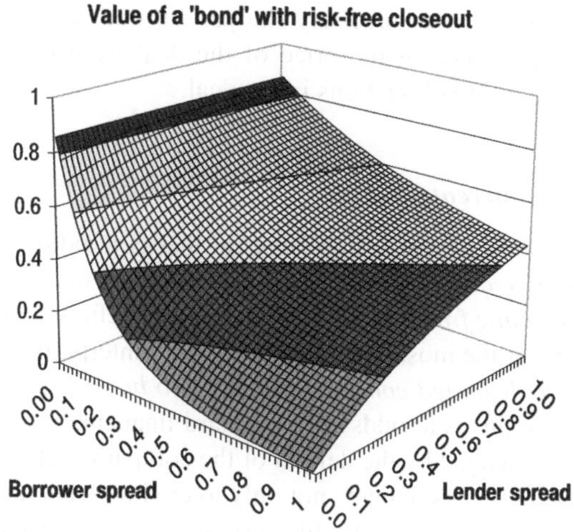

Figure 10.1 Pricing under risk-free closeout

With this simple model we can test numerically the behaviour of the formula (10.3) or (10.14) with risk-free closeout. Set the risk-free rate at $r = 3\%$, and consider a bond with maturity 5 years. The price of the bond varies with the default risk of the borrower, as usual, and here also with the default risk of the lender, due to the risk-free closeout. In Figure 10.1 we show the price of the bond for intensities λ_{Lender}, $\lambda_{Borrower}$ going from zero to 100%. We consider $R^{Borrower} = 0$ so that the level of the intensity approximately coincides with the market CDS spread on the 5 year maturity.

We see that the effect of the lender's risk of default is not negligible, and is particularly decisive when the borrower's risk is high. Market operators should be aware of this consequence of a risk-free closeout.

The results in Figure 10.1 can be compared with those in Figure 10.2, where we apply formula (10.8) or (10.11) that assumes a replacement closeout.

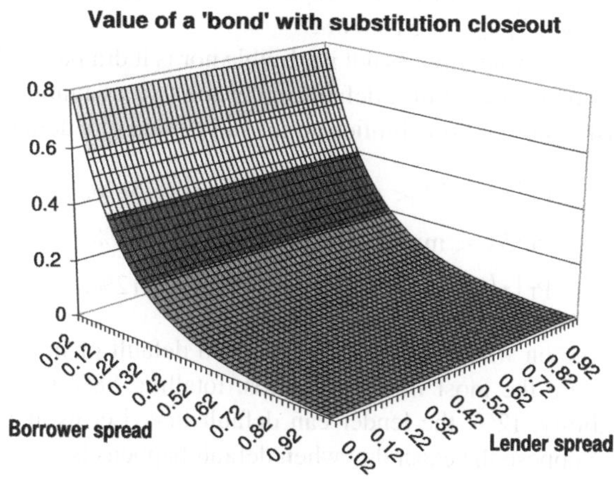

Figure 10.2 Pricing under substitution closeout

The pattern in Figure 10.2 traces precisely the pattern one would expect from standard financial principles: independence of the price of the deal from the risk of default of the counterparty which has no future obligations in the deal.

Default contagion under different closeouts

There is a further implication of a risk-free closeout that is at odds with market standards: *a company that has a net creditor position in a derivative and suddenly defaults can have a strong financial gain stemming from default itself*, whose benefit will go to its liquidators.

Symmetrically, and this is the most worrying part, the counterparty that *did not default and that is a net debtor of the defaulted company will have to book a sudden loss due to default of the creditor*. Notice that this is at odds with standard financial wisdom. It is natural that a *creditor* of a company is damaged by the default of the company, but here we have something more: when (10.3) is used, there is damage not only to creditors, but also to *debtors*.

Let us observe a numerical example. In this case it becomes relevant if we have assumed independence between the default risks of the two names, or if we assume a dependence exists. We start with a numerical example under the assumption of independence, then we explain with a market example what would be the difference in case a form of dependence was assumed. We consider the above $r = 3\%$ and a bond with maturity 5 years, for a 1bn notional. Now we take $R^{Borrower} = 20\%$ and two risky parties. We suppose the borrower has a very low credit quality, as expressed by $\lambda_{Borrower} = 0.2$, which means

$$\Pr\left(\tau^{Borrower} \leq 5y\right) = 63.2\%.$$

The lender has a much higher credit quality, as expressed by $\lambda_{Lender} = 0.04$. This means a lower probability of default that is, however, not negligible, being

$$\Pr\left(\tau^{Lender} \leq 5y\right) = 18.1\%.$$

A risk-free bond issuance with the same maturity and notional would cost $P_T = 860.7\ mn$. Using the formula with risk-free closeout, we get that a risky bond, within the two parties above, has price $V_{Lender} = 359.5\ mn$ to be compared with the price coming from the formula with replacement closeout, $\hat{V}_{Lender} = 316.6\ mn$.

The difference in the two valuations is not negligible nor is it dramatic. More relevant is the difference in what happens in case of a default under the two assumptions on closeout. We have the following risk-adjusted probabilities on the happening of a default event

$$\Pr\left[\tau^{Borrower} < \min\left(5y, \tau^{Lender}\right)\right] = 58\%,$$
$$\Pr\left[5y < \min\left(\tau^{Lender}, \tau^{Borrower}\right)\right] = 30\%,$$
$$\Pr\left[\tau^{Lender} < \min\left(5y, \tau^{Borrower}\right)\right] = 12\%.$$

The two formulas agree on what happens in case of no default or in case of default of the borrower first. These are the most likely scenarios, totalling 88% probability. But with a non-negligible probability, 12%, the lender can default first. Let us analyze in detail what happens in this case. Suppose the exact day when default happens is

$$\tau^{Lender} = 2.5\ years.$$

Just before default, at 2.5 years less one day, we have for the borrower the following book value of the liability produced by the above deal:

$$V_{Borrower}\left(\tau^{Lender} - 1d\right) = -578.9 \text{ mln}$$

if he assumes a risk-free closeout, or

$$\hat{V}_{Borrower}\left(\tau^{Lender} - 1d\right) = -562.7 \text{ mln}$$

if he assumes a replacement closeout.

Now default of the lender happens. In the case of a risk-free closeout, one can easily check in (10.3) or (10.14), calling the lender I and the borrower C, that when $\tau^I \leq \min\left(T, \tau^C\right)$ and

$$V_C^0\left(\tau^I\right) \leq 0,$$

as here, we have

$$V_C\left(\tau^I\right) = V_C^0\left(\tau^I\right).$$

Thus the book value of the bond becomes simply the value of a risk-free bond,

$$V_C\left(\tau^I + 1d\right) = -927.7 \text{ mln}.$$

The borrower, who has not defaulted, must pay this amount entirely to the defaulted lender. He has a sudden loss of

$$927.7 \text{ mln} - 578.9 \text{ mln} = 348.8 \text{ mln}$$

due to default of the lender. This way of regulating bilateral counterparty risk leads to a default contagion that extends not only to the creditors, but also, and in a more sudden way, to the debtors of the defaulted company, as we show in the simple scheme in Figure 10.3.

Additionally, formulas (10.3) and (10.14) show clearly that the loss is higher the higher the credit spreads, and this is what makes this kind of contagion particularly dangerous. Finally, notice that this book loss of 365 mln will soon become a material, realized loss because the borrower has to pay it to the liquidators of the defaulted lender well before the original maturity of the deal.

Furthermore, this behaviour is not consistent with financial practice in the bond and loan market, where there are no big losses to the borrower or bond issuer due to the default of a lender or a bond-holder. This makes the behaviour particularly undesirable. The bond practice is instead consistent with the replacement closeout. In this case, applying (10.8) we have

$$\hat{V}_{Borrower}\left(\tau^{Lender} + 1d\right) = -578.9 \text{ mln}.$$

There is no discontinuity and no loss for the borrower in case of default of the lender.

This would not be the case if there was a dependence between the default risk of the two counterparties. Suppose, for example, that the party that defaults has a relevant systemic impact. In this case the surviving counterparty will be affected by this default, and will see its credit spreads grow, may be dramatically, as happened, for example, for many banks that were Lehman's counterparties when Lehman defaulted. In this case the risk-free closeout is unaffected by this dependency, since it does not take into account the risk of default of the surviving party. It works exactly as above. The replacement closeout, instead, will be lower than above; the lower, the higher is the correlation with the default risk of the defaulted company. In terms of default closeout, the borrower in the above example will have an advantage from

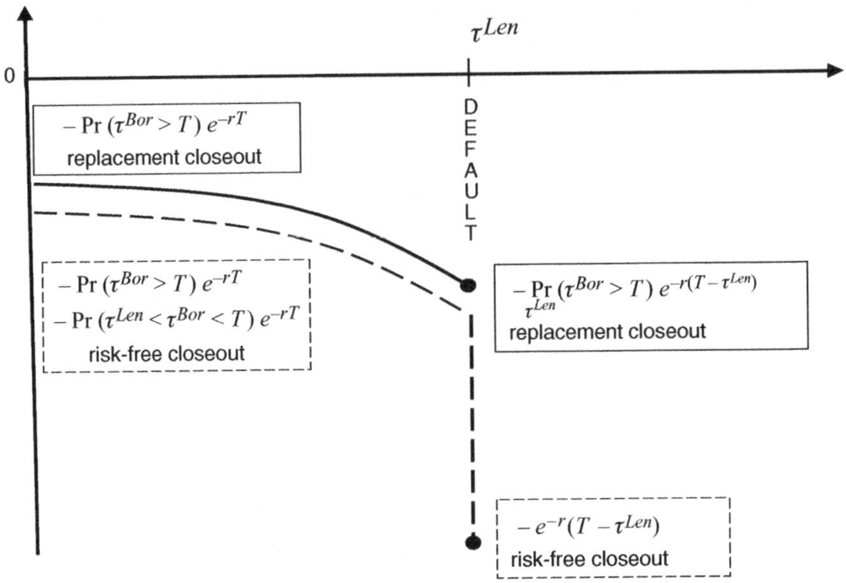

Figure 10.3 The loss for the borrower at default of the lender under risk-free closeout: the value of the risky liability jumps since it becomes a risk-free one

this, because its liabilities will be deflated by the increase of the borrower's default probability, as shown in Figure 10.4.

The replacement closeout may even lead to an almost null closeout amount in the most extreme case, when the borrower is led to the verge of default by the default of the lender. The creditors and the liquidators of the defaulted party, however, will be less happy, since they see the claims of the defaulted party towards its debtors lose their value, and this will reduce the recovery value that sooner or later will go to the creditors. This effect is greater, the stronger the default dependence between the defaulted entity and its borrowers. In Brigo and Morini (2010) also the effect of the two different closeouts on collateralized deals is also analyzed.

10.2.4 A Summary of the Findings and Some Conclusions on Payoff Uncertainty

There can be more uncertainty about the payoff of a deal than we may think. This creates a relevant risk that affects quants directly, since they are often the first people to give a mathematical description to the payoff. In the specific example analyzed, comparing the risk-free closeout assumed in the earlier literature with the replacement closeout inspired by the financial rationale contained in the recent ISDA documentation, we have seen analytically how dramatic can be the effect of slightly different assumptions about the rules to compute future payments.

We have first reckoned that the replacement closeout is consistent with market standard for bonds and loans, while the risk-free closeout introduces at time 0 a dependence on the risk of default of the party with no future obligations. We can grasp the fundamental conclusions

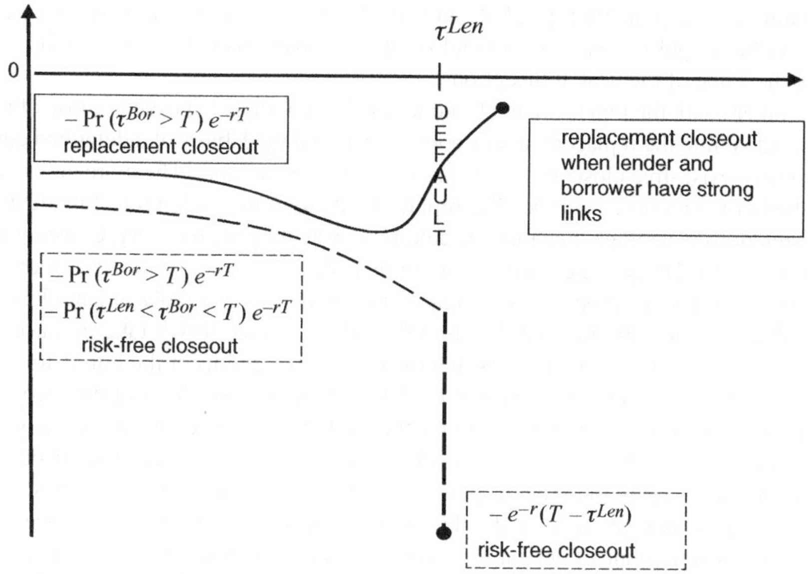

Figure 10.4 Lower recovery for creditors at systemic default under replacement closeout: the value of the risky liability jumps down since deflated by the increase of spreads

even without looking at the precise numbers. If the owner of a bond defaults, or if the lender in a loan defaults, this means no losses to the bond issuer or to the loan borrower. Instead, if the risk-free default closeout applies, when there is default of the party which is a net creditor in a derivative (thus in a position similar to a bond owner or loan lender), the value of the liability of the net debtor will suddenly jump. In fact, before the default the liability of the net debtor had a mark-to-market that took into account the risk of default of the debtor itself: if the debtor is liable for a nominal of \$100 but has a non-negligible risk of default, the market value of its liability is surely lower than the risk-free present value of \$100, even much lower if the credit spreads of the debtor are very high. After the default of the creditor, if a risk-free closeout applies, this liability transforms into a risk-free liability, with a value equal to the risk-free present value of \$100, surely larger than the pre-default liability.

We have illustrated this by sketching a practical example where a bank funded itself through a derivative. The bank finds out that default of the lender makes its liabilities grow from 579 million to 927 million just as an effect of the closeout assumption. This is a loss of 348 million on a funding deal of 1 billion notional.

The increase will be larger the larger the credit spreads of the debtor. This is a dramatic surprise for the debtor that will soon have to pay this increased amount of money to the liquidators of the defaulted party. There is a true contagion of a default event towards the debtors of a defaulted entity that does not exist in the bond or loan market. Net debtors at default will not like a risk-free closeout. They will prefer a replacement closeout, which does not imply a necessary increase of the liabilities since it continues taking into account the credit-worthiness of the debtor also after the default of the creditor, consistently with what happens in the bond or loan markets. Additionally, as we showed analytically, the replacement closeout inherits one property typical of fundamental markets: if one of the two parties in the deal has no future obligations, like a bond or option buyer, his default probability does not influence the value of the deal at inception.

On the other hand, the replacement closeout has shortcomings opposite to those of the risk-free closeout. While the replacement closeout is preferred by debtors of a defaulted company, symmetrically a risk-free closeout will be preferred by the creditors. The more money debtors pay, the higher the recovery will be. The replacement closeout, while protecting debtors, can in some situations worryingly penalize the creditors by abating the recovery. Consider the case when the defaulted entity is a company with high systemic impact, so that the credit spreads of the counterparties are expected to increase at default. Under a replacement closeout, the market value of their liabilities will be strongly reduced, since it will take into account the reduced credit-worthiness of its debtors themselves. All the claims of the liquidators towards the debtors of the defaulted company will be deflated, and the low level of the recovery may be again a dramatic surprise, but this time for the creditors of the defaulted company.

In-depth analysis of the issue has brought about much more understanding of the consequences of the two possible default payoffs. This evidence suggests that banks and other operators in the derivatives market should be aware of this issue. The prevalence of either closeout has an important effect on the credit valuation adjustment. For example, if the risk-free closeout introduced in the previous literature prevails, banks should understand the consequences of this. Banks usually perform stress tests and set aside reserves for the risk of default of their borrowers, but do not do the same for the default of lenders. Should a risk-free closeout prevail, banks had better set aside important reserves against this risk. On the other hand, under the replacement closeout banks can expect the recovery to be lowered when their net borrowers default, compared to the case when a risk free closeout applies.

The question is of some interest also to regulators, since the two closeouts have different systemic implications. The risk-free closeout increases the number of operators subject to contagion from a default, including parties that currently seem not to think they are exposed. On the other hand, it spreads the default losses over a higher number of parties and reduces the classic contagion channel affecting creditors. The analysis may even help regulators to introduce more certainty into a issue that still creates a risk at least as high as the risk created by many cases of model uncertainty, confirming strongly our decision to include the description of the payoffs among the points to be paid attention to in model risk management.

10.3 MATHEMATICAL ERRORS IN THE PAYOFF OF INDEX OPTIONS

The underlying of a Credit Index is a portfolio of credit default swaps for n different entities, each one with a weight $\frac{1}{n}$. The index Protection Leg pays the losses associated with the credit default swaps when defaults happen. If the entities have default times τ_i, and a fixed recovery R, we can indicate the loss at t by

$$L(t) = \frac{(1-R)}{n} \sum_{i=1}^{n} 1_{\{\tau_i \leq t\}}.$$

By $N(t)$ we indicate the outstanding notional, given by the initial portfolio notional minus the notional of the defaulted entities in the index. Starting from an initial notional of 1, we have

$$N(t) = 1 - \frac{L(t)}{1-R} = \sum_{i=1}^{n} \frac{1}{n} 1_{\{\tau_i > t\}}. \tag{10.15}$$

In a Credit Index starting at T_A and ending in T_M the discounted payoff of the Protection leg can be represented mathematically as

$$Prot_t = \int_{T_A}^{T_M} D(t,u)\, dL(u),$$

while the Premium leg that must be paid to receive protection is made of periodic payments of a rate K made at different times T_j and proportional to the outstanding notional. We can write the discounted Premium leg as

$$Prem_t(K) = \underbrace{\left[\sum_{j=A+1}^{M} D\left(t, T_j\right) \alpha_j N\left(T_j\right) \right]}_{DV_t} K.$$

The value of the index deal $I_t(K)$ for the protection buyer is given by

$$\mathbb{E}_t\left[I_t(K)\right] = \mathbb{E}_t\left[Prot_t\right] - \mathbb{E}_t\left[Prem_t(K)\right] = \mathbb{E}_t\left[Prot_t\right] - \mathbb{E}_t\left[DV_t\right] K.$$

The quantity

$$\mathbb{E}_t\left[DV_t\right] = \sum_{j=A+1}^{M} \alpha_j \mathbb{E}_t\left[D\left(t, T_j\right) N\left(T_j\right)\right] \tag{10.16}$$

is the index annuity or risky duration. In the simplest definition, the equilibrium spread of the Index at time t is the value of K that sets $\mathbb{E}_t\left[I_t(K)\right]$ to zero, i.e.

$$S_t = \frac{\mathbb{E}_t\left[Prot_t\right]}{\mathbb{E}_t\left[DV_t\right]},$$

so that

$$\mathbb{E}_t\left[I_t(K)\right] = \mathbb{E}_t\left[DV_t\right](S_t - K).$$

A Payer Index Option is a contract giving the right to enter at T_A into the running Index with final payment at T_M as protection buyer paying a fixed rate K, receiving additionally, upon exercise, the payment of the losses $L(T_A) - L(t)$ from the option inception t to T_A, the so-called *front end protection*. What is the reason for this contract provision? The purpose of a Credit Index Option is to allow the protection buyer to lock in a particular premium spread K, that the protection buyer has the right, not the obligation, to make effective at a future time. However, if the above simple payoff was considered without Front End Protection, the option buyer would not be protected from losses in the period between t and maturity T_A. The front end protection was introduced to avoid this downside and attract more investors.

Thus if an option is entered into at time $t = 0$ the payoff in case of exercise is

$$\mathbb{E}_{T_A}\left[I_{T_A}(K)\right] + L(T_A) = \mathbb{E}_{T_A}\left[DV_{T_A}\right]\left(S_{T_A} - K\right) + L(T_A).$$

In the first market approach, this option is evaluated by performing the decomposition

$$\mathbb{E}\left[D(0,T_A)\mathbb{E}_{T_A}\left[DV_{T_A}\right]\left(S_{T_A}-K\right)^+\right]+\mathbb{E}\left[D(0,T_A)L(T_A)\right]$$

and then by expressing the first component through a standard Black formula, leading to the following price for the option,

$$\mathbb{E}\left[DV_0\right]Black\left(S_0,K,\sigma^2 T_A\right)+\mathbb{E}\left[D(0,T_A)L(T_A)\right],$$

where σ is the volatility of the forward spread. Can you see an evident error in this pricing approach?

10.3.1 Too Much Left Out

If you did not see the error, do not worry too much. Although it may appear obvious once you have spotted it, the market took some years to correct it, and the correction came from a paper by Pedersen (2003). He noticed that, leaving the value

$$\mathbb{E}\left[D(0,T_A)L(T_A)\right]$$

of the front end protection outside the Black formula, that is outside the positive part operator, the above formula neglects the fact that the front end protection is received only upon exercise, so the correct payoff is not

$$\left(\mathbb{E}_{T_A}\left[DV_{T_A}\right]\left(S_{T_A}-K\right)\right)^+ + L(T_A),$$

as implicit in the above formula, but

$$\left(\mathbb{E}_{T_A}\left[DV_{T_A}\right]\left(S_{T_A}-K\right)+L(T_A)\right)^+.$$

It is surprising that several years were required to correct this mistake, but such is the history of finance. The observations and the results of Pedersen (2003) led to an improved Black formula approach, based on the following redefinition of the underlying index spread. We can define a loss-adjusted index

$$\tilde{I}_t(K)=Prot_t-Prem_t(K)+L(t)$$

and give a new spread definition, setting to zero $\mathbb{E}_t\left[\tilde{I}_t(K)\right]$ rather than $\mathbb{E}_t\left[I_t(K)\right]$. This leads to the following *Loss-Adjusted* index spread

$$\tilde{S}_t=\frac{\mathbb{E}_t\left[Prot_t\right]+\mathbb{E}_t\left[D(t,T_A)L(T_A)\right]}{\mathbb{E}_t\left[DV_t\right]}$$

that allows the option pricing problem to be written as

$$\mathbb{E}_t\left[D(t,T_A)\mathbb{E}_{T_A}\left[DV_{T_A}\right]\left(\tilde{S}_{T_A}-K\right)^+\right], \tag{10.17}$$

which, by assuming $\tilde{S}_t$ to be lognormal with volatility σ, justifies pricing with a Black formula as follows

$$\mathbb{E}_t\left[DV_t\right]Black\left(\tilde{S}_t,K,\sigma^2(T_A-t)\right). \tag{10.18}$$

Can you suggest a particular scenario when this formula will give a meaningless answer, one which is not in line with the true value of the option?

10.3.2 Too Much Left In

If you did not spot the scenario, again do not worry too much. That scenario only became relevant during the 2007–2009 credit crunch. The answer to the above question is as follows. Notice that, if the value $\mathbb{E}_t[DV_t]$ of the defaultable annuity is zero, the spread is not defined – it jumps to infinity – and the formula is meaningless. When can the defaultable annuity have zero value? Look at (10.16) and (10.15). This happens when all names in the portfolio default. This looks like an unlikely scenario. If the reference portfolio is composed of few names, the event can have a low but non negligible probability. When the option is instead written on one of the quoted credit indices such as i-Traxx Main, which includes 125 entities selected from among the most relevant in the European credit market, the probability of such an event seems completely negligible. And yet Morini and Brigo (2009) and (2010) find that this Armageddon scenario, on market data from 2007, after the burst of the credit crunch, has a probability which is not negligible.

The analysis of Morini and Brigo (2009) and (2010) goes as follows. They first notice that, since $\mathbb{E}_t[DV_t]$ goes to zero when all names default, it is not strictly positive and cannot be used as a numeraire. The passage from (10.17) to (10.18) would require a change of measure like the one shown in the Appendix in 12.4. But if the numeraire is not positive, standard change of numeraire does not work. This is a problem with the market approach, but it is essentially a theoretical one. However it led to recognition that the formula (10.18) is not defined when all names default while the payoff in that scenario is simply $L(T_A)$.

In fact, Morini and Brigo (2009) and (2010) find a mathematical solution to overcome both problems. Consult the paper for the technical details, which are quite heavy, since they involve the definition of an appropriate *subfiltration* and a consequent probability measure. I do not deny that the paper is of interest to mathematicians working in finance, but I do not find it relevant for this book, so I will provide only the practical consequences of those computations. The practical outcome is a formula for the pricing of credit index options that modifies the above approach also to take into account the right payoff when all names default. The final formula is

$$\mathbb{E}[DV_0]\left[Black\left(\tilde{S}_0 - \frac{\boxed{(1-R)P(0,T_A)\Pr(\hat{\tau}\le T_A)}}{\mathbb{E}_0[DV_0]}, K, \hat{\sigma}^2 T_A\right)\right.$$
$$\left.+\boxed{(1-R)P(0,T_A)\Pr(\hat{\tau}\le T_A)}\right], \qquad (10.19)$$

where $\hat{\tau}$ is the moment of the default of all names in the portfolio,

$$\hat{\tau} = \max(\tau_1, \tau_2, \ldots, \tau_n).$$

Comparing with the standard market formula $\mathbb{E}[DV_0]\,Black\left(\tilde{S}_0, K, \sigma^2 T_A\right)$, we see that while Pedersen's correction to the first market pricing standard was to show that there was something more, the front end protection, to bring *inside* the Black formula (or the positive part operator), here the observation about the current, Pedersen-based market standard is that for making pricing arbitrage-free there is something that must be brought *outside* the Black formula: the value of the payoff in case of portfolio Armageddon.

10.3.3 Empirical Results with the Armageddon Formula

Now let us check whether the improvement of the arbitrage-free option formula (10.19) over the market option formula (10.18) has a relevant impact on pricing. We test this first with inputs in line with market conditions at the beginning of 2007, before the credit crunch, and then using more recent 2008 market data.

Notice first that, unlike the formula (10.18), the newer formula (10.19) is impacted by the interdependence of default times of the names of the index, because it takes into account the probability of a portfolio Armageddon. How can we compute this probability in line with some market quotations? Recall from Chapter 3 that in a tranche the protection buyer receives the changes of the *tranched loss,*

$$L_{a,b}(t) = \left[(L(t) - a)\,1_{\{a \le L(t) < b\}} + (b-a)\,1_{\{L(t) > b\}}\right] / (b-a), \quad \{a, b\} \in [0, 1], \ b > a,$$

so that from a market quote for a tranche $[a, b)$ we can infer the expected tranched loss $\mathbb{E}\left[L_{a,b}(T)\right]$. Notice that, when the underlying index contains n names, the probability of a portfolio Armageddon,

$$\Pr(\hat{\tau} \le T_A) = \mathbb{E}\left[1_{\{\hat{\tau} \le T_A\}}\right],$$

coincides with

$$\mathbb{E}\left[L_{a,b}(T_A)\right], \ a = \frac{(n-1)(1-R)}{n}, \ b = (1-R), \tag{10.20}$$

namely the expected tranched loss for the most senior tranche possible, corresponding to a last-to-default on the index. With a quote for this tranche, we could get a probability of portfolio Armageddon from the market.

The underlying i-Traxx index has quoted tranches, however with $R = 0.4$ we need a tranche having $a = 0.5952$, $b = 0.6$, a tranche more senior than any quoted. The standard market practice would be to extrapolate correlations to get the number we need. Morini and Brigo (2009), instead, simply consider for $\rho_a = \rho_b$ a range of equally spaced correlations in-between the highest correlations of i-Traxx ($\rho^I_{0.22}$) and CDX ($\rho^C_{0.3}$). Thus, while extrapolation would suggest we should increase correlation beyond any quoted ρ_x, they limit it to the market quoted CDX $\rho_{0.3}$, limiting the tests to values which are observable in the market, and making a choice that should underestimate the probability of $\hat{\tau}$. One may question the crucial foundation of this procedure, namely the market practice of quoting tranches with the above correlations and a deterministic recovery. We have made this and several other criticisms in Chapter 3. But the results of the empirical application of this procedure remain very interesting, because we are using market quotes in the same way in which traders used them at that time.

The input data, from JP Morgan, are obtained using base correlation and homogeneous pool assumptions and are given in Table 10.1. The considered options have expiry in 9 months and

Table 10.1 Market inputs

	9 March 2007	11 March 2008
Spot Spread 5y: S_0^{5y}	**22.50 bp**	**154.50 bp**
Implied Volatility, $K = \tilde{S}_0^{9m,5y} \times 0.9$	52%	108%
Implied Volatility, $K = \tilde{S}_0^{9m,5y} \times 1.1$	54%	113%
Correlation 22% I-Traxx Main: $\rho^I_{0.22}$	**0.545**	**0.912**
Correlation 30% CDX IG: $\rho^C_{0.3}$	**0.701**	**0.999**

Table 10.2 Options on i-Traxx 5y, Maturity 9m. 9 March 2007

Strike (Call)	26	21	Strike (Put)	26	21
Market Formula	**23.289**	**11.619**	**Market Formula**	**13.840**	**21.069**
No-Arb. Form. $\rho = 0.545$	23.289	11.619	No-Arb. Form. $\rho = 0.545$	13.840	21.069
No-Arb. Form. $\rho = 0.597$	23.289	11.619	No-Arb. Form. $\rho = 0.597$	13.840	21.069
No-Arb. Form. $\rho = 0.649$	23.289	11.618	No-Arb. Form. $\rho = 0.649$	13.840	21.069
No-Arb. Form. $\rho = 0.701$	23.286	11.614	No-Arb. Form. $\rho = 0.701$	13.843	21.071

allow entry to the I-Traxx index with maturity in 5 years. We consider one *in-the-money* option and one *out-of-the-money* option. We price options first using market inputs as of 9 March 2007, and then using market inputs as of 11 March 2011.

The results for 9 March 2007 inputs are shown in Table 10.2. In the first row is the price using the market option formula, below is the price computed with the arbitrage-free option formula (10.19), with the different correlation values considered. The differences are negligible, considering that the bid-offer spread was higher than 1 bp.

The results for 11 March 2008 inputs are shown in Table 10.3. Here the difference between (10.18) and the price with the arbitrage-free option formula (10.19) is dramatically larger. For out-of-the-money call options differences range from 9.45 bp to 81.45 bp, compared to a bid-offer spread that was in the range 5–8 bp. The perceived higher systemic risk, triggered by the subprime crisis, means that the risk-neutral probability of an Armageddon is no longer negligible. This is also relevant in normal times when considering smaller portfolios or options on tranches.

10.3.4 Payoff Errors and Armageddon Probability

We have seen in the above example on index options two errors in the representation of a payoff that were introduced by modellers in designing an approach for pricing. Both were introduced in the process of developing an easier analytic formula for the pricing, therefore these errors appear similar to the model simplifications considered in Chapter 6 about approximations. In fact there are similarities between the two issues. We notice that, however, an approximation of a payoff, which is a contract that does not depend on our assumptions and

Table 10.3 Options on i-Traxx 5y, Maturity 9m. 11 March 2008

Strike (Call)	180	147	Strike (Put)	180	147
Market Formula	**286.24**	**189.08**	**Market Formula**	**222.24**	**253.08**
No-Arb. Form. $\rho = 0.912$	277.67	179.62	No-Arb. Form. $\rho = 0.912$	226.87	256.83
Difference	**8.57**	**9.45**	**Difference**	**4.63**	**3.75**
No-Arb. Form. $\rho = 0.941$	271.46	172.77	No-Arb. Form. $\rho = 0.941$	230.323	259.63
Difference	**14.78**	**16.31**	**Difference**	**8.08**	**6.56**
No-Arb. Form. $\rho = 0.970$	258.89	158.86	No-Arb. Form. $\rho = 0.970$	237.61	265.58
Difference	**27.35**	**30.22**	**Difference**	**15.37**	**12.50**
No-Arb. Form. $\rho = 0.999$	212.87	107.63	No-Arb. Form. $\rho = 0.999$	268.19	290.95
Difference	**73.37**	**81.45**	**Difference**	**45.95**	**37.87**

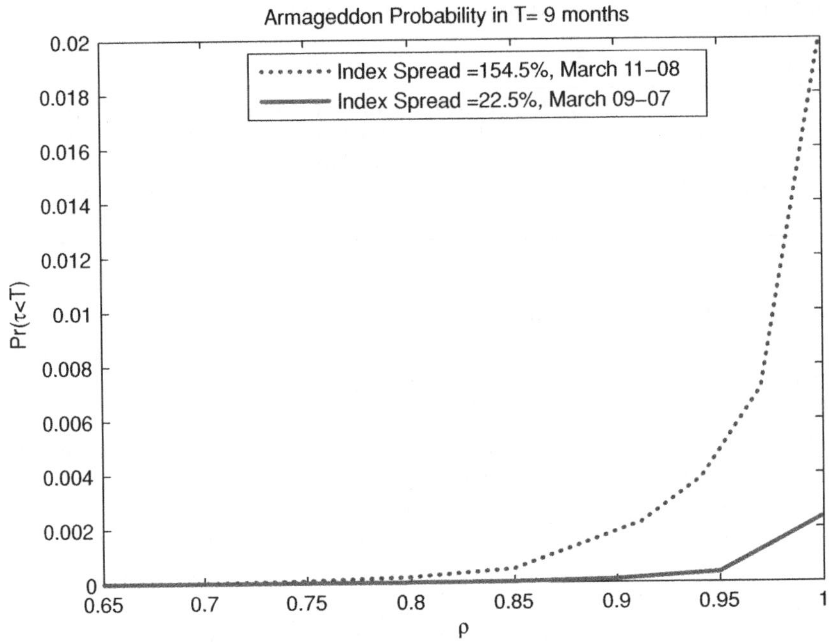

Figure 10.5 Armageddon Probability by spreads and correlations

fully verifiable at maturity, may be considered by some a more serious problem than a model approximation.

Neither of the two errors or approximations was large. However, the first one became relevant when the credit derivative market grew and options became more liquid. Before that, such an error would have probably been smaller than the bid-ask spread. The second error was much smaller. But we have seen that under peculiar market conditions, such as that generated by the credit crunch, it became relevant in pricing, as confirmed by the above empirical tests.

We show in Figure 10.5 the relation between the portfolio Armageddon risk neutral probability and the level of default correlation. The Armageddon probability is an indicator associated with both features typical of a systemic credit crisis: higher correlations and higher default probabilities.

We have seen an easy example of Armageddon risk priced in by the credit correlation market also in the empirical tests in Section 3.3, where the probability density of a credit portfolio loss computed by a model with a realistic correlation includes a probability mass concentrated on a very high level of losses, which we can rightly call an Armageddon level. There is evidence that the Armageddon risk is priced also in normal market conditions. Brigo et al. (2007) and Longstaff and Rajan (2008) show that dynamic Loss models needed to include a jump process associated with an Armageddon event so as to fit the correlation skew, even before the credit crisis.

But the probability obtained in the crisis, as shown in Morini and Brigo (2009), appears incredibly high, even for the credit crunch. However, remember that what we can extract from a market quotation is not a historical or real-world probability, but a *risk-neutral* or *risk-adjusted probability*. Even if the actual probability of this Armageddon event remained relatively small even during the crisis, it may be that the risk premium associated with such a painful event was extremely high. This is an important factor to take into consideration when we are stress testing our model approximations or our payoff simplifications: in future they may be subject to stresses higher than any real-world observation because prices are arrived at by the fears of traders incorporated into the *risk-adjusted* probabilities.

11
Model Arbitrage

11.1 INTRODUCTION

Here we analyze an application of models which is typical of hedge funds or proprietary trading desks: using models for arbitrage, exploiting temporary inconsistencies among related markets. Models often introduce relationships among securities. If they did not, they could not be used for hedging derivatives. At times they introduce a relationship between liquid securities: interest rate term structure models imply a relation between caps and swaptions, which are both liquid interest rate options; structural models for credit risk, which we have seen in Section 2.2.2, of the family of the Merton (1974) models, introduce a relation between the price of the stocks of a company, and its credit risk, which in turn influence the price of bonds and credit default swaps. We are talking here of models that can price two different securities with a single set of parameters.

When an arbitrageur finds such a model, one frequent approach to exploit it is to calibrate the model to both securities. Once the model is calibrated, there is a precise relation between the two sets of securities priced by the model. If joint calibration is possible for all dates of a given time series, the model is considered a reliable picture of the relationship between the two markets. If at some point the joint calibration stops working, or it continues working but requires a relevant change to a parameter which earlier appeared very stable, the arbitrageur interprets it as a deviation from the long term relationship. If he believes that this deviation is only temporary, he will bet that the market will go back to the previous equilibrium by building a trading strategy that makes money when the long-standing equilibrium relationship returns.

We see in the following two examples of this 'model arbitrage' or 'statistical arbitrage'. One is the cap-swaption arbitrage, which has been the focus of a lot of attention between the end of the 1990s and the beginning of the 2000s. Go back to the times before the credit crunch, when in the mind of traders there was *one single term structure of interest rates*. A portfolio of caps and a portfolio of swaptions can have payoffs depending *exactly on the same rates*: although caps and swaptions are traded in two separate markets, knowing the value of the same set of interest rates in the future will be a necessary and sufficient condition to know how much the swaptions and the caps will pay. So a model for the future evolution of interest rates can price both caps and swaptions and introduce precise relationships between their prices. The relationship can be specified by jointly calibrating the model to caps and swaptions on a given day. Towards the end on the '90s some models were available to advanced traders which, for the first time, performed this joint calibration rather easily: they are the Libor Market Models of Brace, Gatarek and Musiela (1997), which we saw in Section 6.2.2. Thanks to these models, traders learned that there was a rather stable relation between cap and swaption prices. For arbitrageurs this was potentially a source of profit: if there were temporary deviations of the parameters in the relation from their long-term equilibrium value, one could bet that the parameter was bound to go back to the equilibrium value, making money when this actually happened. This strategy worked for some time, and arbitrageurs made a lot of money. What happened next? We will recap the story at the end of this chapter, when we have some more elements with which to understand it.

The example of statistical arbitrage we focus on is a different one, and is older than the cap-swaption arbitrage. We are speaking of *capital-structure arbitrage*. A capital-structure arbitrageur seeks opportunities created by differential pricing of various instruments in regard to one corporation, such as stocks and bonds issued by the corporation, or options and credit derivatives having the corporation as an underlying, or convertible bonds. Their value should be the value of the traditional bonds plus the extra value of the option feature.[1] If the spread between the market price of the convertible bond and its synthetic price grows excessively, then the capital-structure arbitrageur will bet that it will converge.

The credit structural models we saw in 2.2.2 are typical tools for capital-structure arbitrage. Their forefather, the Merton model, was devised as a model for pricing the liabilities of a company, namely their stocks and bonds.[2] Since in this model the stock price is given by interpreting stocks as options on the value of a firm, also the price of equity options is given, by interpreting them as *compound options* (options on options). Thus this model is able to price both equity options and CDS or bonds with the same, very parsimonious set of parameters. The Merton model has, however, many shortcomings. The main one is that it assumes one single maturity T when the company is liquidated and the its value is distributed to bond-holders and equity-holders. This assumption allows us to have an endogenous expression for equity value. This also allows us to have an endogenous expression for default probability, since when at T the value of the firm is lower than the bonds' total notional the company will default. In this way, however, we have that default can only happen at T or never, and credit spreads will be the same for all maturities higher than T, and will be null for lower maturity.

This shortcoming is solved by first-passage models, where default happens whenever the value of the firm falls below that of a default threshold or barrier. Yet these models keep two main shortcomings: they exhibit little flexibility for calibration because as soon as parameters are time-dependent they become intractable, and they do not have an endogenous expression for equity and equity options. Among the different attempts made to overcome these residual model problems, I am very familiar with that given in Brigo and Morini (2009). This model claims to price consistently both the CDS market and the equity option market. And in fact we show in the following that in most market situations it can calibrate both markets with efficient and simple formulas. In other cases, however, this exercise does not work and the same model fails to calibrate. Considering that all the examples we found of this failure relate to rather special periods of crisis and turmoil for companies, should we deduce that in these cases there is an inconsistency between the CDS and the option markets, and bet on them to go back to consistency?

This is the suggestion that many arbitrageurs would give you. And yet I do not agree with this way of describing the situation, although I may in some cases agree with the trading strategy put in place by the arbitrageur.

[1] Capital-structure arbitrage is the most popular and 'heroic' example of statistical arbitrage. All idols of the statistical arbitrage and hedge fund world, such as Ed Thorpe, founder of 'the first market-neutral derivatives hedge fund', or Citadel's founder Kenneth C. Griffin, have made billions out of convertible trading and have told fantastic stories on how they made them. The account we give in the following is far less exciting; but it will contain a good deal of precise numerical and mathematical detail, something often missing from the stories of great investors.

[2] There is a reminder of this in the title of the seminal Black and Scholes (1976) paper, which actually included the Merton (1974) and is called 'The pricing of options and corporate liabilities'.

Model risk is inherent in any exercise of model arbitrage, and the trader is clearly aware that this is the main or only risk that he is facing. In the perfect arbitrage trade, as we will see, you make money in different ways – by appreciation of one security and depreciation of the other, and also if exactly the opposite happens – but only as long as the market moves in line with your model; and you only lose money when the discrepancy between model and market grows. Model risk is so crucial to these trades that I think it is important in this book to probe a bit deeper into the role that models really can play in designing these trades by analyzing some practical examples. You will see that the simple introduction of uncertainty on one single model parameter previously assumed to be deterministic makes 'arbitrage' disappear. It is somehow unnatural to use our no-arbitrage models to detect and exploit arbitrage. This does not eliminate the usefulness of models for cross-asset trades, but it does show that rather than arbitrage trades they could be seen as directional trades on the level of market uncertainty. Let us see in detail how we reached this conclusion.

11.2 CAPITAL STRUCTURE ARBITRAGE

In the following we describe a joint model for equity and credit based on a structural first-passage model with time-dependent parameters and a realistic default barrier. We start from the credit model, that is described in detail in the reference literature indicated (mainly Brigo and Tarenghi (2004) and Brigo and Morini (2006)) and then we see how simple but reasonable economic assumptions can lead from this representation of credit risk to a model that can endogenously give us also the value of equity and equity options, explained in more detail in Brigo and Morini (2009).

11.2.1 The Credit Model

We assume that the Firm Value process V_t evolves under the risk neutral pricing measure as

$$dV(t) = V(t)(r(t) - q(t))\,dt + V(t)\sigma(t)\,dW_t \tag{11.1}$$

where $r(t)$ is the risk free rate, $q(t)$ is the payout ratio and $\sigma(t)$ is the instantaneous volatility. This is the same firm value process considered in most structural models, but here the parameters are time-varying, increasing realism and flexibility of the model in calibrating real market data.

In Brigo and Morini (2006) the default barrier $H(t)$ also varies in time, as follows:

$$\begin{aligned} H(t) &= H \exp\left(-\int_0^t q(u) - r(u)du\right) \\ &= \boxed{\frac{H}{V(0)} E^{\mathbb{Q}}[V(t)]}. \end{aligned} \tag{11.2}$$

The behaviour of $H(t)$ has a simple economic interpretation. The backbone of the default barrier at t is a proportion, controlled by the parameter H, of the expected value of the company assets at t. H may depend on the value of liabilities, on safety covenants and in general on the characteristics of the capital structure of the company. This barrier is in line with observations in Giesecke (2004), pointing out that first passage models with flat barriers lead to an unrealistic decrease of credit spreads as maturity increases. In fact the firm value is expected to grow at a rate $r(t) - q(t)$, and so credit spreads will decrease with maturity if the default barrier is instead flat. As pointed out in Collin-Dufresne and Goldstein (2001), firms aim to maintain a stable leverage rather than a stable level of debt, so that the debt will also increase when the value of the assets increases, and the default barrier should follow the behaviour of the debt. Consistently, in the model above the default barrier remains a proportion $\frac{H}{V(0)}$ of the expected value of the firm.

Brigo and Tarenghi (2004) show for the first time how in a structural model of this kind we can have analytic formulas for default probabilities even with time-dependent parameters. The default time τ is defined as the first time where $V(t)$ hits $H(t)$ from above, starting from $V(0) > H$: $\tau = \inf\{t \geq 0 : V(t) \leq H(t)\}$. The probability of not touching the barrier before T, namely the survival probability until T, is

$$\Pr\{\tau > T\} = \left[\Phi\left(\frac{\log\frac{V_0}{H} - \frac{1}{2}\int_0^T \sigma(t)^2 dt}{\sqrt{\int_0^T \sigma(t)^2 dt}}\right) - \left(\frac{V_0}{H}\right)\Phi\left(\frac{\log\frac{H}{V_0} - \frac{1}{2}\int_0^T \sigma(t)^2 dt}{\sqrt{\int_0^T \sigma(t)^2 dt}}\right)\right] \tag{11.3}$$

so we write

$$\Pr\{\tau > T\} = \Pr(T, V_0, H, \sigma[0; T]).$$

where by $\sigma[0; T]$ we indicate the function $\sigma(t)$ for $0 \leq t \leq T$. A similar notation will be applied also in the following, if possible, when the input of a formula is a function of time.

In Brigo and Morini (2006) the model given by (11.1) and (11.2) is calibrated to Parmalat credit data in different days associated with the events that in 2003 led the market to discover that Parmalat's balance sheets were unreliable due to an accounting fraud, and eventually led to Parmalat's default on 24 December 2003. The goal of the exercise is to explore the capability of this model to explain stressed credit data. They find that the model has the same high calibration flexibility of a reduced-form or intensity model, and is able to calibrate Parmalat CDS market quotes until the very day of Parmalat default. However, in this model calibration is usually obtained by very high values in the short term for the volatility $\sigma(t)$, which then decreases quite dramatically on the long term. This could depend on a feature typical of first passage models based on a diffusion processes with a deterministic barrier. As Duffie and Singleton (2003) point out, in such models 'the likelihood of default within a short time horizon is extremely small because the asset process has continuous paths that take time to cross the default boundary'. Thus, when the barrier is deterministic, it is hard for models to calibrate a considerable probability of default in a very short horizon without supposing particularly high short-term volatility.

The model assumption that the default barrier is a deterministic, known function of time corresponds to assuming that accounting data are fully reliable. This was not the case for Parmalat because of an accounting fraud, neither was it for Lehman. In the latter case it was due mainly to lack of transparency in the accounting of credit derivatives and deep uncertainty about the correct valuation of such products (see Brigo, Morini and Tarenghi (2010) for tests on Lehman's default case). It seems that in many of the most painful actual defaults there was uncertainty about the financial situation of a company so that the assumption of a deterministic default barrier was unrealistic.

In order to take market uncertainty into account in a simple but reasonable manner, in the above model H can be replaced by a random variable assuming different values in different scenarios, each scenario having a different probability. This leads to replacing (11.2) with

$$H(t) = H^I \exp\left(-\int_0^t q(u) - r(u)du\right) \tag{11.4}$$

where $\Pr(I = i) = p_i$, $p_i \in [0, 1]$, $i = 1, 2, \ldots, N$, and $\sum_{i=1}^N p_i = 1$, so

$$H^I = \begin{cases} H^1 & \text{with probability } p_1 \\ \vdots & \vdots \\ H^N & \text{with probability } p_N \end{cases}.$$

If we are to price a default-sensitive discounted payoff Π, by iterated expectation we have

$$\mathbb{E}[\Pi] = \mathbb{E}\left[\mathbb{E}\left[\Pi|H^I\right]\right] = \sum_{i=1}^{N} p_i \mathbb{E}\left[\Pi|H^I = H^i\right],$$

so that the price of a security is a weighted average of the prices of the security in the different scenarios, with weights equal to the probabilities of the different scenarios. For example the survival probability is given by a weighted average of probabilities computed as in (11.3). With this different model, assuming $N = 2$ which means two possible scenarios, in Brigo and Morini (2006) the credit data are calibrated with no need of a discontinuity in volatility between short and long term, and the distribution of the barrier they obtain represents the unfolding of the Parmalat crisis in a very meaningful way. In fact, in the Brigo and Morini (2006) calibration exercise the probability of the most pessimistic scenario increases as evidence of the accounting fraud emerges, and the associated default barrier becomes closer and closer to the value of the firm as the news reveals that the true situation of Parmalat is much worse than what was revealed in official accounting.

In the following we will extend to equity pricing the model with deterministic barrier given by (11.1) and (11.2); we will resort to the model with uncertain barrier (11.4) only when this is required by the market situation we are analyzing.

11.2.2 The Equity Model

A model for the value of equity and the price of equity options is derived from the above credit model in Brigo and Morini (2009). In the standard Merton model, to infer an expression for the value of equity $E(t)$ from the credit model one needs to assume that there exists a terminal time T for the company, when the value of the firm $V(T)$ is distributed to bondholders and stockholders. Equity at T is then just what remains of firm value (if positive) when all debt has been paid

$$E(T) = (V(T) - D(T))^+,$$

where $D(T)$ is the value of debt at time T. In the Merton model T is the only possible terminal time for the life of a company, since default cannot happen earlier, thus equity value corresponds to the value of a European call option

$$E(t) = \mathbb{E}_t\left[e^{-\int_t^T r(s)-q(s)ds}(V(T) - D(T))^+\right].$$

The reason why the discounting is done at rate $r(s) - q(s)$ is the following. Discounting at rate $r(s)$ is correct when the interest rate to pay for financing the equity asset is $r(s)$, as shown in Piterbarg (2010). Thus a discounting rate $r(s)$ is correct only if the asset pays no dividends. If the asset pays a continuous dividend yield $q(s)$, the actual cost of financing is $r(s) - q(s)$ and this is the rate we have to use for discounting if we want to have an arbitrage-free model, following Piterbarg.

One can consider $D(t)$ as a default threshold or barrier $H(t)$ such that default happens at T when $V(T) < H(T)$, so with a change of notation we write

$$E(t) = \mathbb{E}_t\left[e^{-\int_t^T r(s)-q(s)ds}(V(T) - H(T))^+\right].$$

Now we want to move to a first-passage model, where default can also happen before T, and we want to keep a model that implies an expression for the value of equity $E(t)$. We still have to assume, at least at the beginning, that there exists a terminal time T for the company when the value of the firm $V(T)$ is distributed to bondholders and stockholders if default has not happened earlier. Additionally we now have to consider the possibility that default happens before T, due to $V(t)$ falling lower than $H(t)$, in which case there will be nothing left for stockholders. Thus in the structural model equity at T is

$$E(t) = 1_{\{V(s)>H(s),0\leq s<T\}}(V(T) - H(T))^+.$$

and its value at a generic time $0 \leq t \leq T$ is

$$E(t) = 1_{\{V(s)>H(s),0\leq s\leq t\}}\mathbb{E}_t\left[1_{\{V(s)>H(s),t<s<T\}}e^{-\int_t^T r(s)-q(s)ds}(V(T) - H(T))^+\right],$$

thus the equity value corresponds to the value of a barrier option of the type Down and Out Call. We write

$$E(t) = 1_{\{\tau>t\}}\mathbb{E}_t\left[1_{\{V(s)>H(s),t<s<T\}}e^{-\int_t^T r(s)-q(s)ds}(V(T) - H(T))^+\right],$$

where we have indicated by $1_{\{\tau>t\}}$ the indicator $1_{\{V(s)>H(s),0\leq s\leq t\}}$, since the latter simply corresponds to a survival indicator guaranteeing that the company is alive at the valuation time t.

Remark 16. *In Merton-style models, T is usually interpreted as the unique maturity of the company debt, so that $H(T) = D(T)$, which must be equal to the value of the debt, also equals the notional of the debt. This simplified assumption is not strictly necessary here. In fact, for the above model setting to be realistic we just need $D(T) = H(T)$ to be the market value of the debt at T: if T is not the debt maturity a company whose value of the firm is higher than the market value of this debt can close down its operations at T just by buying back its own debt at market value, without defaulting and giving the rest to equity holders. This way it is possible to have $H(T)$ lower than the debt notional, for example, if T happens to be in a moment of crisis $H(T)$ can be even closer to the expected recovery level. We point this out because in all first-passage models the barrier must be close to the recovery debtors receive at default τ, since $H(\tau) = V(\tau)$ and*

$$V(\tau) \approx R(\tau)DebtNotional(\tau).$$

If T was treated as the debt maturity and therefore $H(T)$ was associated with the notional of the debt, this would imply a recovery close to the entire notional at least at T, which is unrealistic and inconsistent with subsequent tests where we assume lower recovery. This is avoided since we avoid associating T with the maturity of the debt. We have highlighted this *remark to help the reader think about the meaning of a structural model; but in practice the assumptions made on this fictive terminal date* T *will not influence the results, since this fictive maturity* T *will disappear completely from the model in subsequent computations. This is an important point in support of the reasonableness of the approach taken in Morini and Brigo (2009).*

11.2.3 From Barrier Options to Equity Pricing

Since the above equity model has a structure similar to a barrier option, Brigo and Morini (2009) look for an analytic formula for this barrier option when parameters are time-dependent. They look at the results in Rapisarda (2003) and Lo et al. (2003) that were used in Brigo and Tarenghi (2004) to derive (11.3) and which relate to barriers that, after some adjustments, can be adapted to the shape of our default barrier. We recall these computations in the following.

Pricing formulas for a barrier option

According to Rapisarda (2003) and Lo et al. (2003), when the underlying is $X(s)$ and the barrier is $H_x(s)$, with the following dynamics

$$dX(s) = X(s)(r(s) - q_x(s))dt + X(s)\sigma_x(s)dW(s), \tag{11.5}$$

$$H_x(s) = H_x \exp\left(-\int_s^T (r(u) - q_x(u))du\right), \tag{11.6}$$

the price of a down and out call option with strike K and maturity T,

$$\mathbb{E}_t\left[1_{\{X(s)>H_x(s), t\le s\le T\}} e^{-\int_t^T r(s)ds}(X(T)-K)^+\right],$$

can be computed analytically as

$$\begin{aligned}
&DO_t(T, X(t), H_x, K, r[t,T], q_x[t,T], \sigma_x[t,T]) = e^{-\int_t^T r(s)ds} \\
&* \left\{ X(t)e^{\int_t^T v(s)+\frac{\sigma_x(s)^2}{2}ds}\,\Phi\left(\frac{\ln\left(\frac{X(t)}{H_x}\right) - \ln\left(\frac{K}{H_x}\right) + \int_t^T v(s)+\sigma_x(s)^2 ds}{\Sigma}\right)\right. \\
&- K\Phi\left(\frac{\ln\left(\frac{X(t)}{H_x}\right) - \ln\left(\frac{K}{H_x}\right) + \int_t^T v(s)ds}{\Sigma}\right) - H_x(t) \\
&* e^{\int_t^T v(s)+\frac{\sigma_x(s)^2}{2}ds}\,\Phi\left(\frac{\ln\left(\frac{H_x(t)^2}{X(t)H_x}\right) - \ln\left(\frac{K}{H_x}\right) + \int_t^T v(s)+\sigma_x(s)^2 ds}{\Sigma}\right) \\
&\left. + K\left(\frac{X(t)}{H_x(t)}\right)\Phi\left(\frac{\ln\left(\frac{H_x(t)^2}{X(t)H_x}\right) - \ln\left(\frac{K}{H_x}\right) + \int_t^T v(s)ds}{\Sigma}\right)\right\},
\end{aligned} \tag{11.7}$$

having indicated $v(s) = r(s) - q_x(s) - \frac{\sigma_x(s)^2}{2}$ and $\Sigma = \sqrt{\int_t^T \sigma_x(s)^2 ds}$.

Adapting the Barrier Option to the First Passage Model

The main difference between the assumptions (11.1) and (11.2) of the credit model and the assumptions (11.5) and (11.6) underlying the option pricing formula relate to the barrier dynamics. The barrier depends on time-to-maturity in the option formula, while it depends on time in the model. To close this gap we can set

$$q_x(s) = r(s), \tag{11.8}$$

so that the barrier $H_x(s)$ is flat at the level H_x. Now for pricing equity at a generic time t we additionally set

$$\begin{aligned} X(t) &= V(t), \\ \sigma_x(s) &= \sigma(s),\ s > t. \\ H_x &= H(t) \end{aligned} \tag{11.9}$$

We have a process very similar to $V(t)$ (apart from $q(t) \neq q_x(t)$) and associated with the flat barrier $H_x = H(t)$. We can price with the analytic formula (11.7) the barrier option problem (with strike equal to the flat barrier, $K = H_x$)

$$1_{\{X(t)>H_x\}}\mathbb{E}_t\left[1_{\{X(s)>H_x, t<s<T\}}e^{-\int_t^T r(s)ds}\left(X(T)-H_x\right)^+\right].$$

To compute the equity value, instead we need to compute

$$E(t) = 1_{\{\tau>t\}}e^{\int_t^T q(s)ds}\mathbb{E}_t\left[1_{\{V(s)>H(s), t<s<T\}}e^{-\int_t^T r(s)ds}(V(T)-H(T))^+\right].$$

We notice that, for $s \geq t$

$$V(s) = X(s)\exp\left(\int_t^s -q(u)+r(u)du\right),$$

$$H(s) = H_x \exp\left(\int_t^s -q(u)+r(u)du\right)$$

therefore, for $t < s < T$,

$$\begin{aligned} &X(s) > H_x \Rightarrow V(s) > H(s), \\ &1_{\{X(s)>H_x, t<s\leq<T\}} = 1_{\{V(s)>H(s), t<s<T\}} \end{aligned}$$

and we can write

$$\begin{aligned} &\mathbb{E}_t\left[1_{\{V(s)>H(s), t<s<T\}}e^{-\int_t^T r(s)ds}(V(T)-H(T))^+\right] \\ &= \exp\left(\int_t^T -q(u)+r(u)du\right) \\ &\quad \times \mathbb{E}_t\left[1_{\{X(s)>H_x, t<s<T\}}e^{-\int_t^T r(s)ds}\left(X(T)-H_x\right)^+\right]. \end{aligned}$$

We have (11.7) for the latter expectations, so that

$$\begin{aligned}
E(t) &= 1_{\{\tau>t\}} e^{\int_t^T q(s)ds} \mathbb{E}_t \left[1_{\{V(s)>H(s), t<s<T\}} e^{-\int_t^T r(s)ds} (V(T) - H(T))^+ \right] \\
&= 1_{\{\tau>t\}} e^{\int_t^T q(s)ds} \exp\left(\int_t^T -q(u) + r(u)du \right) \\
&\quad \times DO_t \left(T, V(t), H(t), H(t), r[t,T], \left[r(s) - (1+2\beta)\frac{\sigma(s)^2}{2} \right]_{t\le s\le T}, \sigma[t,T] \right) \\
&= 1\{\tau > t\} \exp\left(\int_t^T r(u)du \right) \times DO_t(\ldots).
\end{aligned} \tag{11.10}$$

Now we compute explicitly the formula starting from the general one (11.7) and recalling (11.8) and (11.9). This gives an analytic expression for equity in the model.

$$\begin{aligned}
& DO_t\left(T, V(t), H(t), H(t), r[t,T], r[t,T], \sigma[t,T]\right) \\
&= e^{-\int_t^T r(s)ds} \left\{ V(t)\Phi\left(\left(\ln\left(\frac{V(t)}{H(t)}\right) + \frac{1}{2}\int_t^T \sigma(s)^2 ds \right) \Big/ \Sigma \right) \right. \\
&\quad - H(t)\Phi\left(\left(\ln\left(\frac{V(t)}{H(t)}\right) - \frac{1}{2}\int_t^T \sigma(s)^2 ds \right) \Big/ \Sigma \right) \\
&\quad - H(t)\Phi\left(\left(\ln\left(\frac{H(t)}{V(t)}\right) + \frac{1}{2}\int_t^T \sigma^2(s) ds \right) \Big/ \Sigma \right) \\
&\quad \left. + V(t)\Phi\left(\left(\ln\left(\frac{H(t)}{V(t)}\right) - \frac{1}{2}\int_t^T \sigma(s)^2 ds \right) \Big/ \Sigma \right) \right\} \\
&= e^{-\int_t^T r(s)ds} (V(t) - H(t)).
\end{aligned} \tag{11.11}$$

We have reached a surprising result according to which, under the hypotheses of this work, the value of the down and out call barrier option is the same as a forward contract on the underlying. We can understand and verify this result in three ways, using three different model specifications: when $V(t)$ is just a driftless arithmetic Brownian motion, we can intuitively use the method of images; in the restriction of the model where parameters are flat, we can use standard formulas from Hull (2006); for the general case, we can use the results in Carr and Chou (1997). This is done in Brigo and Morini (2009).

Equity and Equity Options

From (11.10) and the subsequent computations, we have found that

$$\begin{aligned}
E(t) &= 1_{\{\tau>t\}} e^{\int_t^T r(u)du} e^{-\int_t^T r(u)du} (V(t) - H(t)) \\
&= 1_{\{V(s)>H(s), 0\le s<t\}} (V(t) - H(t)).
\end{aligned} \tag{11.12}$$

Thus we have an expression for equity in terms of firm value and default barrier which is simple and tractable. Notice that the value of equity no longer depends on the arbitrary expiry date of the company which was introduced in order to represent equity as an option on the value of the firm. Although this value was derived based on this assumption, whatever arbitrary expiry date one assumes the result does not change.

The equity has a dynamics similar to a shifted lognormal process with time-dependent drift and, more importantly, time-dependent shift. This dynamics, however, allows us to price equity options with an analytic formula. An equity option with maturity $\hat{T}$ has price

$$
\begin{aligned}
&Call_t(\hat{T}, K, E(t)) \\
&= \mathbb{E}_t\left[e^{-\int_t^{\hat{T}} r(u)du}(E(\hat{T}) - K)^+\right] \\
&= \mathbb{E}_t\left[e^{-\int_t^{\hat{T}} r(u)du}\left(1_{\{V(s)>H(s),0\leq s<\hat{T}\}}\left[V(\hat{T}) - H(\hat{T})\right] - K\right)^+\right] \\
&= 1_{\{\tau>t\}}\mathbb{E}_t\left[e^{-\int_t^{\hat{T}} r(u)du}1_{\{V(s)>H(s),t<s<\hat{T}\}}\left(\left[V(\hat{T}) - H(\hat{T})\right] - K\right)^+\right].
\end{aligned}
$$

Indicating

$$
\hat{K} = H(t) + e^{-\int_t^{\hat{T}} r(u)-q(u)du}K
$$

we have

$$
\begin{aligned}
&Call_t(\hat{T}, K, E(t)) \\
&= 1_{\{\tau>t\}}e^{\int_t^{\hat{T}} -q(u)+r(u)du}\mathbb{E}_t\left[e^{-\int_t^{\hat{T}} r(u)du}1_{\{X(s)>H(t),t\leq s<\hat{T}\}}\left(X\left(\hat{T}\right) - \hat{K}\right)^+\right] \\
&= 1_{\{\tau>t\}}e^{-\int_t^{\hat{T}} q(u)-r(u)du}\mathbb{E}_t\left[e^{-\int_t^{\hat{T}} r(u)du}1_{\{X(s)>H(t),t\leq s<\hat{T}\}}\left(X\left(\hat{T}\right) - \hat{K}\right)^+\right] \\
&= 1_{\{\tau>t\}}e^{-\int_t^{\hat{T}} q(u)-r(u)du} \times DO_t\left(\hat{T}, V(t), H(t), \hat{K}, r\left[t,\hat{T}\right], r\left[t,\hat{T}\right], \sigma\left[t,\hat{T}\right]\right), \quad (11.13)
\end{aligned}
$$

where

$$
\begin{aligned}
&DO_t\left(\hat{T}, V(t), H(t), \hat{K}, r\left[t,\hat{T}\right], r\left[t,\hat{T}\right], \sigma\left[t,\hat{T}\right]\right) \\
&= e^{-\int_t^{\hat{T}} r(s)ds}\left\{V(t)\Phi\left(\left(\ln\left(\frac{V(t)}{\hat{K}}\right) + \int_t^{\hat{T}}\frac{\sigma_X(s)^2}{2}ds\right)/\Sigma\right)\right. \\
&\quad -\hat{K}N\left(\left(\ln\left(\frac{V(t)}{\hat{K}}\right) - \int_t^{\hat{T}}\frac{\sigma_X(s)^2}{2}ds\right)/\Sigma\right) \\
&\quad -H(t)\Phi\left(\left(\ln\left(\frac{H(t)^2}{V(t)\hat{K}}\right) + \int_t^{\hat{T}}\frac{\sigma_X(s)^2}{2}ds\right)/\Sigma\right) \\
&\quad \left.+\hat{K}\left(\frac{V(t)}{H(t)}\right)\Phi\left(\left(\ln\left(\frac{H(t)^2}{V(t)\hat{K}}\right) - \int_t^{\hat{T}}\frac{\sigma_X(s)^2}{2}ds\right)/\Sigma\right)\right\}.
\end{aligned}
$$

This also provides an analytic pricing for equity options. In the next section we are going to test whether this system of expressions is consistent with the real prices of equity, equity options, and credit default swaps.

11.2.4 Capital-structure Arbitrage and Uncertainty

Now let us see how we can calibrate this model. In the dynamics of the value of the firm (11.1),

$$dV(s) = V(s)(r(s) - q(s))\,dt + V(s)\sigma(s)\,dW_s,$$

the market provides directly $r[t,T], q[t,T]$ while the remaining parameters are $V(0), \sigma\,[t,T]$. In the barrier dynamics

$$H(s) = H \exp\left(-\int_0^s (q(u) - r(u))\,du\right)$$

the only remaining parameter is H. These parameters need to be calibrated to credit and equity quotes. If we make the volatility a piecewise constant structure that can take M different values,

$t \in [T_0, T_1]$	$t \in [T_1, T_2]$	$\ldots$	$t \in [T_{M-1}, T_M = T]$	(11.14)
$\sigma(t) = \sigma_1$	$\sigma(t) = \sigma_2$	$\ldots$	$\sigma(t) = \sigma_M$	

we have $M + 2$ unknown parameters to calibrate. If volatility is flat, there are only three parameters

$$V(0) \quad H \quad \sigma.$$

How many liquid products do we have in the market that depend on these parameters and at the same time can be priced in the model with analytic formulas, so that it is reasonable to use them in calibration? We have CDS for different maturities, we have the equity price, and we have European options for different maturities and different strikes. The approach we will follow is to calibrate $V(0), H, \sigma$ by solving the following system:

1. $\Pr(T; V(0), H, \sigma)$, the model default probability, is used to calibrate market CDS.
2. $E(0) = (V(0) - H)$, the model value for market equity, is a constraint to write $V(0)$ as a function of H.
3. $Call\,(0, K_i, T; V(0), H, \sigma)$, the model option price, is used to calibrate a set of equity call options with different strikes K_i, $i = 1, 2, \ldots, n$.

We want to test how the model can be calibrated jointly to equity and credit. The most liquid equity options usually have a short maturity, so we will test the model behaviour when fit to credit and equity using a set of European options with maturity around 1y, and the 1y CDS. Credit and equity data jointly can fix all model parameters. For this test we keep volatility flat at σ. If we are interested in calibrating different maturities, we can make volatility time-dependent as in (11.14) to increase our degrees of freedom.

We consider two companies with different characteristics. The first company is British Petroleum (BP), an example of a company that went through the credit crunch remaining financially solid and with good growth perspectives, only later to encounter an unexpected and deep crisis following an oil spill, an ecological disaster that hit in 2010. The other company is Fiat Spa, which expanded during the years of the credit crunch, most notably by the acquisition of Chrysler. The market sentiment about Fiat seemed to change dramatically after Lehman's default, when market investors appeared to think that the crisis in the auto sector was going to take a heavy toll on the Italian carmaker, also considering that the group was increasing its leverage in an acquisition campaign.

BP and Fiat in 2009

We show calibration results for different days. We start from 6 April 2009. For BP we have the following market data:

BP, 6 April 2009					
Equity:					
Equity price: 458.25					
Dividend yield=6%					
9m expiry option:					
Strike	420	440	460	480	500
Implied Vol	42.7%	40.6%	39%	38.7%	37.5%
Credit:					
Recovery: 40%					
1y CDS spread: 64.7 bps					

Both equity and credit data are those of a healthy company compared to the general market situation in spring 2009. We use the equity price to write $V(0) = E^{Mkt}(0) - H$, so that we are left with two parameters H and σ. These two parameters are used to calibrate the above set of 6 market data (CDS spread and 5 equity options) obtaining the results shown in the next table and in Figure 11.1.

Calibration Results

CDS Spread Error (Market spread minus Model spread): 0 bp

Errors (Market Vol minus Model Vol) on 9m expiry option:					
Strike	420	440	460	480	500
Implied Vol	0.48%	0.18%	−0.1%	0.17%	−0.23%

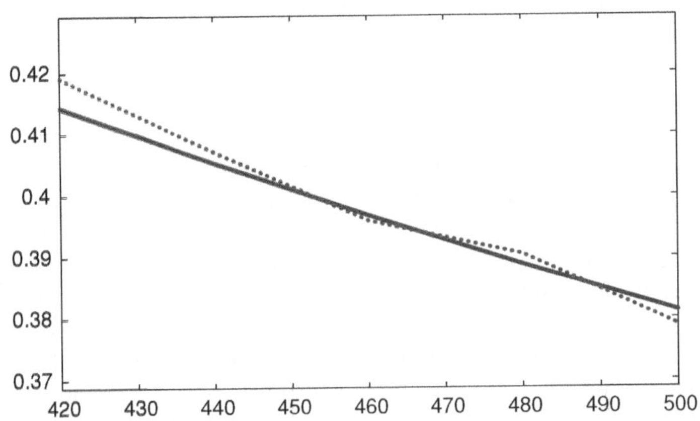

Figure 11.1 BP 06/04/09 – Equity options implied volatility (Dot: Market – Continuous: Model)

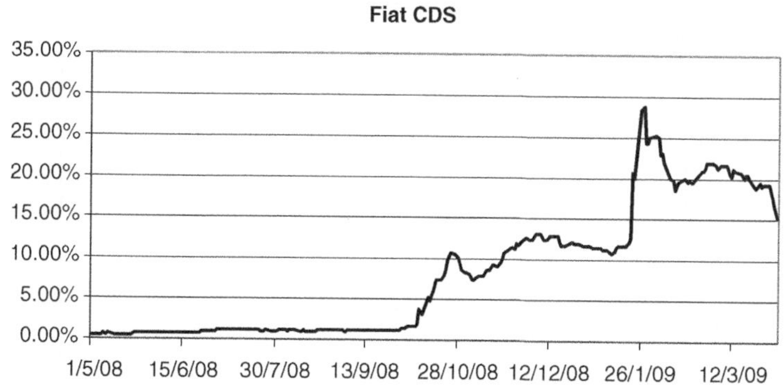

Figure 11.2 Fiat historical data

Considering that the credit spread is fit exactly and the implied volatility error is within the bid-ask spread, this calibration is satisfactory and would suggest that the consistency relationship between equity and credit that we derived is reasonable and consistent with market data.

Let us now consider Fiat on the same day. The market data are:

Fiat, 6 April 2009					
Equity:					
Equity price: 7.215					
Dividend yield=0%					
9m expiry option:					
Strike	6.8	7	7.2	7.4	7.6
Implied Vol	72.9%	71.5%	70.5%	69.5%	68.6%
Credit:					
Recovery: 40%					
1y CDS spread: 1211 bps					

Both markets clearly reveal a more stressed situation, particularly the credit market. One can see when this dramatic worsening of Fiat credit spread started by looking at Figure 11.2.

Results of the calibration are as follows:

Calibration Results

CDS Spread Error (Market-Model): 305bp

Errors (Market-Model) on 9m expiry option:					
Strike	6.8	7	7.2	7.4	7.6
Implied Vol	−7.7%	−7.6%	−37.2%	−6.8%	−6.5%

The errors are now not negligible, as can be seen in Figure 11.3 for the equity option market. In particular, the model underestimates credit spreads and overestimates implied volatility.

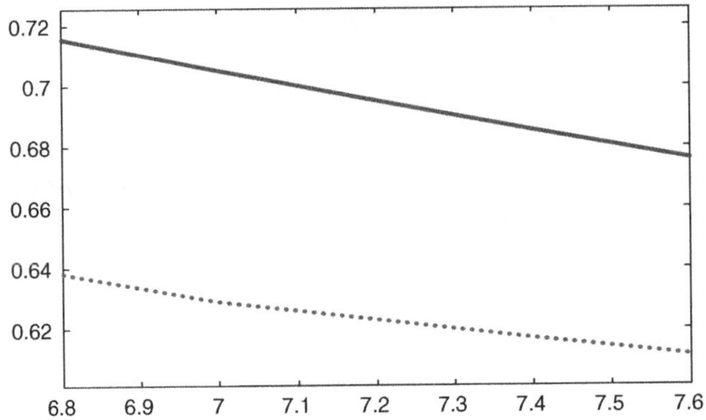

Figure 11.3 Fiat – Calibration to equity and credit – Equity options implied volatility (Dot: Market – Continuous: Model)

Statistical Arbitrage?

It becomes interesting to see which level of implied volatility the model predicts if we force good fit to the CDS spread leaving equity volatilities to be determined by credit calibration. This is what we see in the next table and in Figure 11.4:

Calibration Results

CDS Spread Error (Market-Model): 5bp

Errors (Market-Model) on 9m expiry option:					
Strike	6.8	7	7.2	7.4	7.6
Implied Vol	−15.4%	−15%	−14.6%	−14.2%	−13.7%

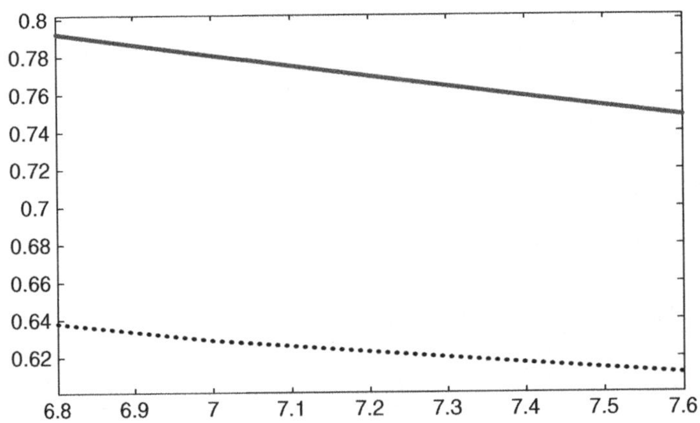

Figure 11.4 Fiat – Calibration focused on Credit – Equity Options implied volatility (Dot: Market – Continuous: Model)

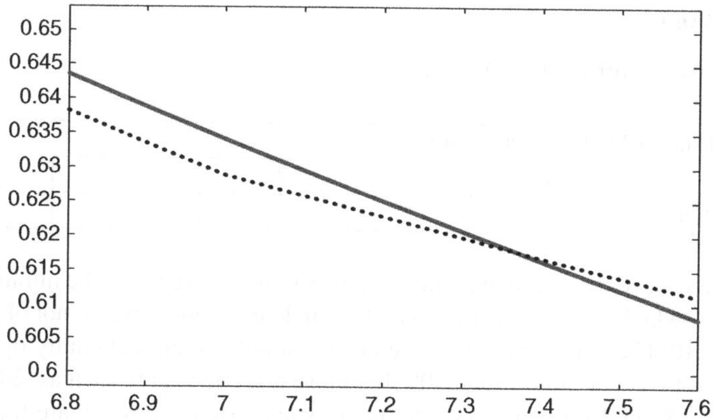

Figure 11.5 Fiat – Calibration focused on Equity – Equity Options implied volatility (Dot: Market – Continuous: Model)

This confirms that credit data seem to imply an equity volatility much higher, and a steeper skew, than we have in the equity market. Now let us see what happens if we force good fit to equity options leaving the credit spread to be determined by equity calibration.

Calibration Results

CDS Spread Error (Market-Model): 567bp

Errors (Market-Model) on 9m expiry option:					
Strike	6.8	7	7.2	7.4	7.6
Implied Vol	−0.5%	−0.5%	−0.2%	−0.04%	−0.3%

Consistently with the results of the previous calibration, but now reversing the approach, we see that a good fit to equity options, evidenced in Figure 11.5, implies a CDS which is 567 bp lower than the actual market CDS spread.

What can we deduce from these results? A player with a strong faith in all the assumptions of the model we are using will think that this is a typical case of 'capital structure arbitrage'. This means that there is an inconsistency between what the credit market and the equity market say about this company. This inconsistency is revealed by the very same model that for BP explained both markets with negligible errors. We may think that this inconsistency cannot last; as soon as the market realizes this inconsistency, it will go back to a situation where the model can calibrate well the two markets. This means that either CDS spreads are going to decrease, or the equity volatility skew is going to get higher and steeper. In fact it is known that a number of banks were involved in a Fiat CDS-Equity arbitrage trading, by betting exactly on such a market move.

However, there are different ways to explain the situation. First, notice that our pricing assumes a recovery of 40%. Although this was the quote by Markit CDS data both for Fiat and BP, one may think that an implied recovery of 40% was too high for Fiat in a time of crisis. That is reasonable. However, even if we set recovery equal to 0%, we are not able to fit the market with the precision we saw for BP. See the results below.

Calibration Results

CDS Spread Error (Market-Model): 45bp

Errors (Market-Model) on 9m expiry option:					
Strike	6.8	7	7.2	7.4	7.6
Implied Vol	−2.1%	−2%	−1.8%	−1.5%	−1.2%

Lowering the recovery seems a step in the right direction, but even with the minimum possible recovery of 0%, which is certainly a conservative underestimation, we do not obtain the good fit we had for BP. There are still noticeable errors on both credit and equity options. And if we use a value of recovery lower than 40% but more realistic than 0, such as 20%, the errors are even bigger. Should we now conclude that to some extent we really are facing a capital structure arbitrage? However, there is something important to consider first.

Uncertainty in market expectations

Recall that, as we explained in Section 11.2.1, Brigo and Morini (2006) and Brigo, Morini and Tarenghi (2010) notice that better results are obtained in first-passage models when one takes into account that the default barrier is not perfectly known to market players, since actual liabilities are not perfectly known and it is oversimplified to take the barrier as a deterministic parameter as in the above model. The uncertainty on the barrier can be due to the risk of an accounting fraud as in the Parmalat or Enron case, or to accounting opacity and illiquidity in the market of CDO's as in the case of Lehman. Market investors may have been in a situation of similar uncertainty in respect of Fiat in April 2009, since the company was increasing its leverage for considerable investments compared to its size, and the outcome of such investments was still unclear, particularly after Lehman's default. The issue can be addressed in our modelling framework by assuming that the barrier is uncertain. In particular, we assume that the barrier can take two different values, one higher (higher default risk) and one lower (lower default risk), so that the deterministic barrier (11.2) is replaced by (11.4) with

$$H^I = \begin{cases} H^1 & \text{with probability } p_1 \\ H^2 & \text{with probability } p_2 \end{cases}.$$

Let us first apply this model to the first company we tested. Are we able to improve the already good results we obtained for BP by introducing uncertainty in the default barrier, which appears in any case a realistic feature? The results of the application of this new model to the BP data on April 6 that we have already used is as follows:

CDS Spread Error (Market spread minus Model spread): 0bp

Errors (Market Vol minus Model Vol) on 9m expiry option:					
Strike	420	440	460	480	500
Implied Vol	0.48%	0.18%	−0.1%	0.17%	−0.23%

Compare these to the results we obtained with the model having deterministic barrier. The addition of two parameters (one level of the barrier H^2 and its probability p_2) does not improve the situation at all. In fact, looking at the details of the calibration results, we have obtained $H^1 \cong H^2$. Uncertainty in the company liabilities does not appear to be necessary to fit jointly BP equity and credit data, since this is done easily in the more parsimonious model where the default barrier is deterministic. The calibration returns two barrier values which are the same, which confirms that we do not need any uncertainty in the balance sheet to explain BP market data: this is done very well by the deterministic model. The model, for the little it is able to say, says that the market was not uncertain about BP's financial situation on 6 April 2009.

Now let us test this new model with barrier uncertainty on the Fiat market data, again for 6 April 2009, and keeping the initial recovery of 40%. The results for the barrier scenarios and the scenario probabilities are as follows:

$H^1/V_1 = 0.98$	$p_1 = 0.35$
$H^2/V_2 = 0.0001$	$p_2 = 0.65$

We no longer have $H^1 \cong H^2$. On the contrary, the barrier under the two scenarios is extremely different, giving a very pessimistic scenario (1) less likely, and a more likely very optimistic scenario (2).

With this model, the calibration results are as in the following table and in Figure 11.6.

Calibration Results

CDS Spread Error (Market-Model): 0.2bp

Errors (Market-Model) on 9m expiry option:					
Strike	6.8	7	7.2	7.4	7.6
Implied Vol	−0.18%	−0.36%	−0.17%	−0.07%	0.4%

It is a dramatic improvement compared to the previous results we obtained with the deterministic barrier. Although, due to uncertainty on the default barrier, this model has 4 rather than 2 parameters, the model is still parsimonious since we are fitting 6 market quotes (CDS spread and 5 equity options). But the fit is now perfect from a financial point of view. Since perfect fit has been obtained by introducing an element of realism into the model that does not make the

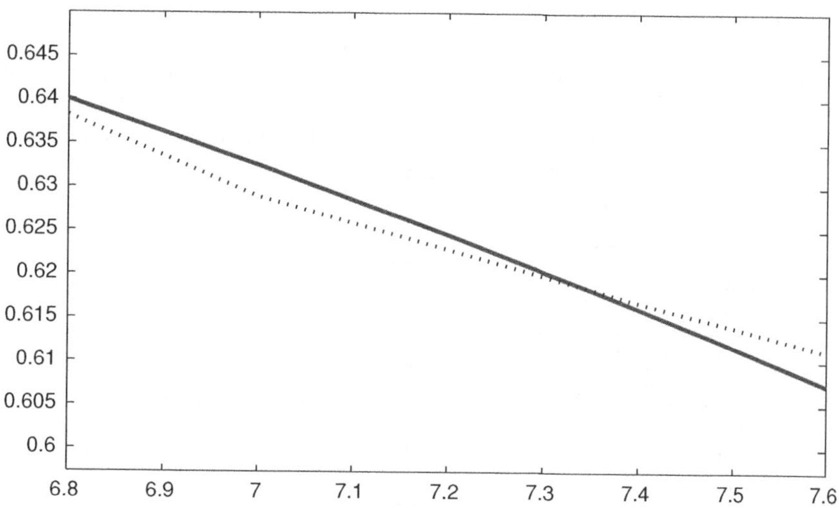

Figure 11.6 Fiat – Calibration to equity and credit – Equity options implied volatility. Model with barrier uncertainty (Dot: Market – Continuous: Model)

model overly complex, we do not think there is any ground to claim we are facing a capital structure arbitrage. One simpler answer is available: additional uncertainty on the financial situation of the company.

This answer is not necessarily less attractive for a trader than the idea of a 'capital structure arbitrage'. When the arbitrageur sees an arbitrage, he bets the market will go back to a no-arbitrage situation as soon as the market itself realizes the presence of arbitrage. In our case, this means lower CDS or higher and steeper equity volatility skew, namely a situation where the deterministic barrier model can calibrate well equity and credit jointly. If the trader, instead, accepts the indications of the above model that the market is just pricing in uncertainty about the financial situation of Fiat, he can also in this case see a trading opportunity. The trader may find it reasonable to suppose that uncertainty will be resolved sooner or later; this also means lower CDS or higher and steeper equity volatility skew, and lower uncertainty means the possibility of calibrating the deterministic barrier model. The same directional trade can be justified by saying 'there is an arbitrage, the market will eliminate it *as soon as* it realizes it, and I want to bet on it' or by saying, 'there is uncertainty about the market situation of this company; *sooner or later* this uncertainty will be resolved, and I want to bet on it'.

From the point of view of a financial modeller, the results we have obtained with the above quantitative models justify the second approach and not the first one. The first one can be justified only by an operator which has a personal belief that market uncertainty on company books is impossible, even for a short period of time. Notice also that the two approaches can justify the same trade, but pay attention to the fact that some relevant details are different in the two cases. The mechanisms and the timing that can lead the trade to be a success or a failure are different. In the first case you claim you have found an 'inconsistency' and you expect the market to eliminate it. In the second case you claim you are giving a description of the market and then you take a view on what will happen in the future.

Further Results. Fiat in 2008 and BP in 2010

In the following we investigate further whether this model can actually provide a simplified but reasonable interpretation of reality. For example, the above results suggest that uncertainty on the default barrier is important when some event suddenly confounds market expectations about a company, as the Lehman's default may have generated worries about a company involved in a risky expansion such as Fiat. Otherwise uncertainty in the barrier seems less important – or not important at all, as with the BP case in April 2009. To see if this interpretation is reasonable, we will try to calibrate the simpler model without uncertainty to Fiat data from before Lehman's default. We see below market data for 11 March 2008:

Fiat, 11 March 2008				
Equity:				
Equity price: 12.588				
Dividend yield=0%				
6m expiry option:				
Strike	11.33	12.27	12.9	13.85
Implied Vol	44.6%	43.2%	42.8%	41.8%
Credit:				
Recovery: 40%				
1y CDS spread: 173 bps				

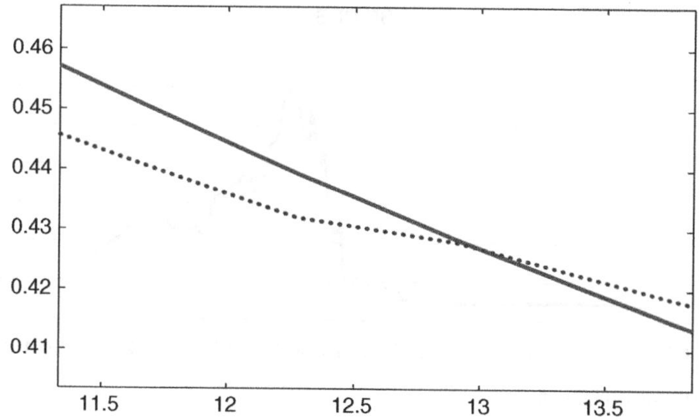

Figure 11.7 Fiat – Calibration to equity and credit – Equity options implied volatility. Model without barrier uncertainty on 11 March 2008 (Dot: Market – Continuous: Model)

The market views on the credit quality of the company appear much better. Calibrating the model with deterministic barrier we obtain:

Calibration Results

CDS Spread Error (Market-Model): 0bp

Errors (Market-Model) on 6m expiry options:				
6m expiry option:				
Strike	11.33	12.27	12.9	13.85
Implied Vol	−1.1%	−0.7%	−0.05%	0.4%

In difference to what happened after Lehman's default, on these earlier data the simpler model with deterministic barrier can fit the credit spread exactly while still implying errors around the bid-ask spread on equity options, as we see in Figure 11.7 similarly to the results obtained for the healthy company BP. This confirms our initial interpretation.

There is an additional test of our conclusion that we can perform. The other company we considered, BP, entered into an unexpected crisis when on 20 April 2010, the BP's Deepwater Horizon drilling rig exploded, killing 11 employees and starting an oil spill that immediately appeared one of the worst environmental disasters of the past decades. This created a real upheaval in market views about BP's perspectives. BP could be considered responsible for dozens of billions of damage to the environment; but BP may also prove to have followed best practice and due diligence, reducing its responsibilities. From being one of the most solid international companies in the world it turned into one with a troubled future. The value of its assets was certainly high and probably not so difficult to evaluate for market investors, but the value of its liabilities had become very difficult to assess, making BP a typical example of a company affected by high uncertainty.[3] The crisis that hit BP is clearly visible in Figure 11.8

[3] It should be pointed out that we chose BP as a benchmark for our tests at the beginning of 2009, well before the rig explosion in 2010. Thus the possibility of testing our hypotheses given by this subsequent event had not been planned in advance. In spite of the confirmation of the initial hypothesis that we reached from the test we present below, we strongly regret the occurrence of this disaster which gave us the opportunity to perform this test. We would very much have preferred clearer waters in the Gulf of Mexico rather than clearer ideas on any financial problem.

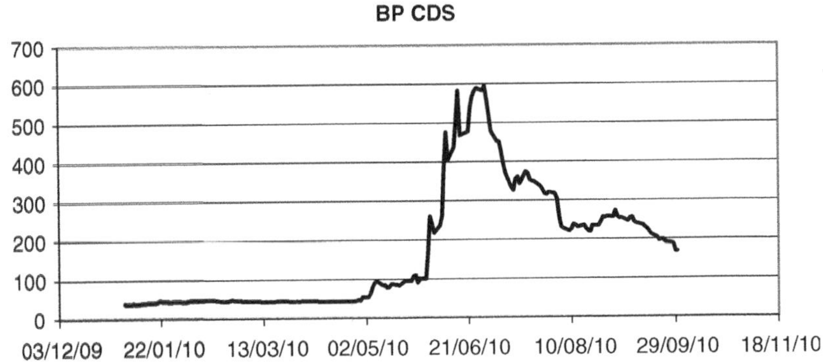

Figure 11.8 BP historical data

where we report its CDS spread, and from the market data of CDS and equity options that we report below for the day 17 June 2010, just after BP agreed to pay an initial 20 bn dollars to the US government as reparations for the damage created by the oil spill.

BP, 17 June 2010					
Equity:					
Equity price: 337					
Dividend yield=0%					
9m expiry option:					
Strike	280	320	360	400	440
Implied Vol	53%	49.7%	46.8%	45.7%	44%
Credit:					
Recovery: 40%					
1y CDS spread: 635bps					

If the interpretation we gave above is correct, after this event it should be very difficult to calibrate jointly to BP CDS and equity option with the basic model that assumes a deterministic default barrier. In fact, the results we obtain are as follows:

Calibration Results

CDS Spread Error (Market spread minus Model spread): 244 bp

Errors (Market Vol minus Model Vol) on 9m expiry option:					
Strike	280	320	360	400	440
Implied Vol	−7.2%	−6.6%	−6.3%	−5.2%	−3.7%

In such a situation, a model with explicit uncertainty on the level of liabilities (default barrier) should work better. We have tried this, obtaining the following results.

Calibration Results

CDS Spread Error (Market spread minus Model spread): 3bp

Errors (Market Vol minus Model Vol) on 9m expiry option:					
Strike	280	320	360	400	440
Implied Vol	−0.4%	−0.9%	−1.3%	−0.6%	0.8%

This has been obtained with the following parameters for the uncertain barrier

$H^1/V_1 = 0.92$	$p_1 = 0.52$
$H^2/V_2 = 0.6$	$p_2 = 0.48$

which show uncertainty between a higher level of BP's liabilities and a lower one, with almost the same probability. In confirmation of the above interpretation, only with these two scenarios are we able to calibrate market data for BP at the peak of the Deepwater Horizon's oil spill crisis. We comment further on what this suggests about model arbitrage in the Conclusions at 11.4.

11.3 THE CAP-SWAPTION ARBITRAGE

Another popular example of model arbitrage was the cap-swaption arbitrage. As we recalled in the introduction to this chapter, it is based on the fact that the payoffs of caps and swaptions can be seen as functions of exactly the same rates. As we saw in Chapters 6 and 9 both the payoff of caps and of swaptions can be seen as functions of Libor forward rates, with Libor rate correlations that control the relation between these two sets of quotes since they enter swaption prices without affecting cap prices.

There is one case where the relation between caps and swaptions simplifies in particular. It is the relation between one-period swaptions and the corresponding caplets. A one-period swaption is an option on a degenerate swap where one single Libor forward rate is paid by the swap-floating leg. Thus this swaption is an option on an individual Libor rate, like a caplet. The reason why there is no perfect overlapping of swaptions and caplets even in this case is that swaptions and caplets usually refer to Libor rates with different tenors. In the Euro market swaptions refer to annual forward rates,[4] where caplets refer to 3-month or 6-month forward rates (specifically, we consider 6-month caplets in the following).

A 1-year-tenor annual swaption is a quoted option, with exercise date T, that pays the Libor rate fixing in T and paying in $T + 1Y$,

$$F(t) = F(t; T, T + 1Y) = \left(\frac{P(t, T)}{P(t, T + 1Y)} - 1 \right),$$

observed at the moment of its fixing, $t = T$, minus a strike, if the difference is positive. The representation of the rate in terms of bond prices in the classic context of one single term structure has been explained in 6.2.1. It is the rate indicated with F in Figure 11.9.

[4] Notice that before the explosion of basis swaps in the credit crunch it was the frequency of the fixed leg that was crucial for defining the features of swaps.

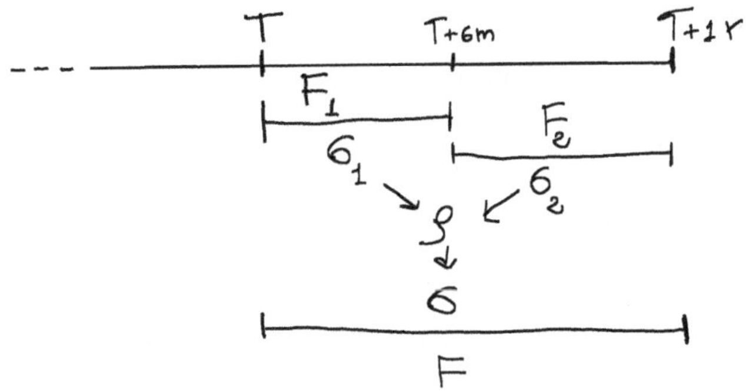

Figure 11.9 One-period annual swaption and nested caplets. Underlying rates

The corresponding 6-month caplets are two options, this time quoted in the caplet market, on two 6-month tenor Libor forward rates: one is the rate fixing in T and paying in $T + 6m$,

$$F_1(t) = F(t; T, T + 6m) = \frac{1}{0.5}\left(\frac{P(t, T)}{P(t, T + 6m)} - 1\right),$$

observed at the moment of its fixing $t = T$, and the other is the rate fixing in $T + 6m$ and paying in $T + 1Y$,

$$F_2(t) = F(t; T + 6m, T + 1Y) = \frac{1}{0.5}\left(\frac{P(t, T + 6m)}{P(t, T + 1Y)} - 1\right),$$

observed at the moment of its fixing $t = T + 6m$. These are the rates indicated with F_1 and F_2 in Figure 11.9 where it is clear that the rate F and the couple F_1 and F_2 span exactly the same 'area' of the term structure. Notice that

$$1 + F(t; T, T + 1Y) = [1 + F(t; T, T + 6m)0.5][1 + F(t; T + 6m, T + 1Y)0.5] \tag{11.15}$$

Thus the yearly rate underlying the swaption is just a deterministic function of the two rates underlying the caplets. Taking the Libor Market Model with lognormal dynamics, that is also the typical caplet 'market quotation' assumption, we can take $F_1(t)$ and $F_2(t)$ as lognormal rates with flat volatilities σ_1 and σ_2,

$$dF_i(t) = \sigma_i F_i(t) dW_i(t), \; i = 1, 2.$$

Knowing these two dynamics *and the instantaneous correlation* ρ between dW_1 and dW_2, the implied dynamics of rate $F(t)$ can be computed by (11.15) and Ito's Lemma. The resulting dynamics of $F(t)$ is not lognormal but is rather close to a lognormal dynamics, and if we project it onto a lognormal one with flat volatility σ we are consistent with the swaption 'market quotation' assumption and we can compute, via approximations similar to those used in Section 6.2.4, that

$$\sigma = \sqrt{u_1^2(0)\sigma_1^2 + u_2^2(0)\sigma_2^2 + 2\rho u_1(0)u_2(0)\sigma_1\sigma_2},$$
$$u_i(t) = \frac{1}{F(t)}\left(\frac{F_i(t)}{2} + \frac{F_1(t)F_2(t)}{4}\right), \; i = 1, 2. \tag{11.16}$$

See also Brigo and Mercurio (2006) and Brigo and Morini (2006) for the derivation of this formula.

We can fix σ_1 and σ_2 based on the quotations for these parameter provided by the cap market

$$\sigma_1 = \sigma_1^{cap}, \sigma_2 = \sigma_2^{cap}.$$

From the swaption market, we can get the quotation σ^{swap} for parameter σ and set

$$\sigma = \sigma^{swap}.$$

Using (11.16) we can compute a market implied value for the correlation,

$$\rho = \rho^{cap/swap},$$

that ensures our model will be calibrated exactly to the swaption and the corresponding caplet.

Once we have this correlation, we can find out different things, as happened to me in the analysis partially reported in Brigo and Morini (2006). Suppose that, repeating this exercise for a number of subsequent days, one finds reasonable values for these correlations, maybe even in line with the instantaneous correlation between $F_1(t)$ and $F_2(t)$ that one may compute through historical estimation. In this case a trader can convince himself that the cap and swaption market are fundamentally consistent, and this consistency is controlled by ρ. One following day, this implied correlation $\rho^{cap/swap}$ turns out to be an *impossible value*, for example $\rho^{cap/swap} > 1$, which is outside the mathematical boundaries for a correlation. An enthusiastic arbitrageur could see in this an immediate opportunity to trade: there is a dramatic inconsistency between the two markets, this cannot last for long so the market will move in such a way that $\rho^{cap/swap}$ goes back to values < 1. Even without such an extreme case, one can find that $\rho^{cap/swap}$ has gone far from its historical values, so that it can be a value as low as 0.44 that we found once in Brigo and Morini (2006). This is definitely too low for the correlation between two adjacent rates. In this case the enthusiastic arbitrageur would bet that the market will move in such a way that the infracorrelation $\rho^{cap/swap}$ increases.

According to rumours circulating among experienced market traders, and from the comments of Rebonato (2002a) and Pelsser (2000), it seems that there were such enthusiastic arbitrageurs in many banks and hedge funds just before the Russian crisis of 1998. For the first time advanced traders had the possibility of computing relations such as (11.16) and had a way to monitor the consistency between caps and swaptions. It seems that a stable relationship was detected in the first years of use of this framework. In the simplified representation we have given here, you can think of this stable relation as a stable value ρ^* for $\rho^{cap/swap}$, confirmed by historical analysis. Large deviations from ρ^* turned out to be temporary, allowing traders to perform very profitable trades. The game broke down in 1998, when the Russian crisis and the subsequent default of LTCM brought about such dislocations in the implied volatility surfaces for interest rate derivatives that the deviation from historical long term equilibrium became massive, leading to increasing mark-to-market losses for those traders betting for a return to the historical equilibrium. These trades had to be unwound at a large loss. No matter whether or not the long term equilibrium was going to come back, the market had gone too far from it for too long for a bank or a fund with a risk management unit to stand it. See also the next section.

11.4 CONCLUSION: CAN WE USE NO-ARBITRAGE MODELS TO MAKE ARBITRAGE?

From the perspective of a quant, and from the results on capital structure arbitrage and the examples about cap swaption arbitrage, model arbitrage appears to be one of those areas of trading where traders can become more enthusiastic about models than modellers themselves. This is always a symptom of some problems . . .

In this section I do not want to take a position about the markets being arbitrage-free or not, which we can rephrase by saying that I do not know if different markets are consistent with each other. I do not know what an arbitrageur wants to know: if two markets have a long-standing relation that we can capture by a model, and then these markets have temporary variations from it that we can exploit as trading opportunities. It may actually be so, as proven by the money that people made in this kind of trade, or it may be that nothing like that is possible, as proven by the money that people lost in this kind of trade. The important point I want to make is that no-arbitrage models like those used for pricing derivatives usually do not allow us to make such claims. We have seen in the detailed example about capital structure arbitrage that an apparently obvious arbitrage disappears immediately if we move to a model which is actually *more realistic* than the previous one (and incidentally it is still a quite unrealistic model, with single-point-in-time uncertainty in the barrier rather than real dynamic stochasticity). This model explains the different patterns of BP and Fiat quotes not by saying that there is an arbitrage in the pricing of the different parts of Fiat's capital structure, but simply by saying that there is more uncertainty. One can bet on how and when this uncertainty is going to diminish or grow. This is still a trading opportunity, but it is not *an arbitrage*. Which implies, by the way, that you cannot expect the patterns of Fiat quotations to come closer to those of BP *soon*, but, in the best case, just *sooner or later*. It is difficult for me to figure out market configurations that cannot be explained by some model; maybe it will be a much more complex model, but there is always the possibility to find one model, perhaps unreasonable but perhaps very reasonable, that explains any configuration. It is the trader with their knowledge of the market who at some point can say: no, this is not possible, reality has a simpler representation, and if quotes do not fit with this representation we have found an imbalance that will disappear soon. But this is the trader's choice not the model's choice.

In the second example about caplet-swaption arbitrage we have not proposed any model solutions to the inconsistencies that can appear from the application of the simple relation (11.16). This is a good thing, so you can try yourself to see how many possibilities there are that could explain reasonably any value for $\rho^{cap/swap}$ without requiring a breech of the no-arbitrage principle.[5] For example, we have assumed that rates are lognormal, but this is consistent with a market without a smile. Rebonato (2002a) says that a very evident smile was born in the interest rate market just after the Russian crisis. So it may be that the sudden strange values of $\rho^{cap/swap}$ after the Russian crisis simply means that after this crisis (11.16) is no longer valid because from now on interest rates must be unavoidably modelled with stochastic volatility, as confirmed by the appearance of the smile. Or think of the case in which the correct representation of ρ was as a stochastic parameter. Now $\rho^{cap/swap}$ takes a completely different meaning. The idea of stochastic correlations during interest rate crises is not at all illogical, as confirmed by the patterns of interest rate movements during the credit

[5] More recently, Rebonato (2011) makes an interesting analysis of the topic, showing that, even when standard models do not explain the relations between caps and swaptions, the no-arbitrage conditions that can be reasonably considered 'model independent' are still verified.

crunch seen in Section 6.3. And the credit crunch can teach us something more, something we have already analyzed in Section 4. A relation such as (11.16) can be wrong in some market situations, because in some market situations (11.15) is wrong: when the credit spreads of Libor banks get high, a basis can enter the relation between 1-year Libor rates and 6-month Libor rates. And the period of the Russian crisis was characterized by surprisingly high swap spreads. There may have been a third item involved in the 1-year/6-month Libor relation, the basis, with its own volatility, jumps and correlations, making any value for the dull number $\rho^{cap/swap}$ possible.[6] Apparent arbitrage opportunities can disappear with the introduction of more reasonable models, which can reveal trading opportunities other than arbitrage trades. A no-arbitrage model cannot, by definition, decide if an inconsistency it detects is a problem in the market (arbitrage) or in the model itself. This is a trader's job, and the model offers no alibi.

[6] This also applies to the relation (6.11) between swap rates and forward rates which is used to derive the swaption approximation in Section 6.2. And this is the answer to the question I posed at the end of that section.

"Other evils there are that may come . . . Yet it is not our part to master all the tides of the world, but to do what is in us for the succour of those years wherein we are set, uprooting the evil in the fields that we know, so that those who live after may have clean earth to till. What weather they shall have is not ours to rule."

Gandalf in 'The Lord of the Rings', by J.R.R Tolkien

"Learn from science that you must doubt the experts. As a matter of fact, I can also define science another way: Science is the belief in the ignorance of experts."

Richard Feynman, from 'The Pleasure of Finding Things Out'

12
Appendix

Here I provide a summary of some basic results in probability, stochastic calculus and mathematical finance that are used in this book. I have tried to report here all and only those results which are really crucial for understanding the models and the examples in the book. For a more general treatment of the foundations of financial modelling the reader has plenty of choice. One easy but rigorous and complete introduction is Björk (2004).

12.1 RANDOM VARIABLES

Random variables are the fundamental building-block of any computation in finance. I have assumed a basic knowledge of concepts such as probability density, expectation and variance of a random variable. Such concepts can be easily refreshed by reference to classic texts like Mood et al. (1974). However, there are a few concepts which I prefer to recall. We first recall how all random variables can be generated, for example by a computer, and then we present copulas, which have been mentioned so often when speaking of quantitative finance over the past years. Finally, we revisit a few useful formulas about Gaussian and lognormal distributions, which are ubiquitous in finance.

12.1.1 Generating Variables from Uniform Draws

Given a random variable X with cumulative distribution function

$$F_X(x) = \Pr(X \leq x)$$

we can build a variable $Y = g(X)$, where $g(\cdot)$ is an increasing function. What is the distribution of Y?

$$F_Y(y) = \Pr(Y \leq y) = \Pr\left(g(x) \leq y\right) = \Pr\left(X \leq g^{-1}(y)\right) = F_X\left(g^{-1}(y)\right). \tag{12.1}$$

Thus if we take a uniform random variable $U \sim \textit{Uniform}[0,1]$ we can build a variable

$$Y = F_X^{-1}(U)$$

such that

$$F_Y(y) = F_{\textit{Uniform}}(F_X(y)) = F_X(y).$$

This is how random variables can be generated starting from uniform random variables.

12.1.2 Copulas

Consider the stochastic vector $X = [X_1, \ldots, X_n]$ with joint distribution

$$F_{X_1,\ldots,X_n}(x_1, \ldots, x_n) = \Pr(X_1 \leq x_1, \ldots, X_n \leq x_n).$$

We set $u_i = F_{X_i}(x_i)$, where $F_{X_i}(x_i)$ is the marginal (individual) distribution of X_i. Now the joint distribution $F_{X_1,\dots,X_n}$ can be written as:

$$F_{X_1,\dots,X_n}(x_1,\dots,x_n) = F_{X_1,\dots,X_n}(F_{X_1}^{-1}(u_1),\dots,F_{X_n}^{-1}(u_n))$$
$$=: C_{X_1,\dots,X_n}(u_1,\dots,u_n). \tag{12.2}$$

The function $C_{X_1,\dots,X_n}$ is *the copula of the vector* X. Notice that with this function $C_{X_1,\dots,X_n}$ together with the marginal distributions F_{X_i} we can go back to the joint distribution:

$$C_{X_1,\dots,X_n}(F_{X_1}(x_1),\dots,F_{X_n}(x_n)) = F_{X_1,\dots,X_n}(x_1,\dots,x_n). \tag{12.3}$$

Remark 17. ***Copula as a Uniform Distribution.*** *We can see the copula as the joint distribution of* $[F_{X_1}(X_1),\dots,F_{X_n}(X_n)]$

$$\begin{aligned}C_{X_1,\dots,X_n}(u_1,\dots,u_n) &= F_{X_1,\dots,X_n}(F_{X_1}^{-1}(u_1),\dots,F_{X_n}^{-1}(u_n))\\ &= \Pr\left(X_1 \le F_{X_1}^{-1}(u_1),\dots,X_n \le F_{X_1}^{-1}(u_n)\right)\\ &= \Pr\left(F_{X_1}(X_1) \le u_1,\dots,F_{X_n}(X_n) \le u_n,\right).\end{aligned} \tag{12.4}$$

Recalling that, as we have shown in (12.1), when Y = g(X) then

$$F_Y(y) = F_X(g^{-1}(y))$$

it is clear that when $Y = F_X(X)$ *then*

$$F_Y(y) = F_X(F_X^{-1}(y)) = y, \tag{12.5}$$

thus the cumulative distribution of a random variable X always has a uniform $[0, 1]$ *distribution when seen as a function of X. Thus* $F_{X_i}(X_i)$ *is a uniform and the copula is the joint distribution of uniform random variables* $U = \left[U_1 = F_{X_i}(X_1),\dots,F_{X_i}(X_n) = U_n\right]$

$$C_{X_1,\dots,X_n}(u_1,\dots,u_n) = \Pr\left(U_1 \le u_1,\dots,U_n \le u_n,\right).$$

The random vector U has a copula which is also $C_{X_1,\dots,X_n}$*. This result explains the sense in which someone says that a copula contains the information on the dependent structure of a joint distribution without containing information on the marginals.*

12.1.3 Normal and Lognormal

The most common distribution is the Gaussian or Normal distribution. The variable X is Normal $\mathbb{N}(M; V^2)$, where M is the expectation or mean and V^2 is the variance, when the probability density is

$$f_X(x) = \frac{1}{\sqrt{2\pi}V} e^{-\frac{(x-M)^2}{2V^2}}.$$

The Moment Generating Function (MGF) of a continuous random variable X, when it exists, is the result of

$$\mathbb{E}[e^{tX}],$$

and for the for Gaussian X it reads

$$\mathbb{E}\left[e^{tX}\right] = e^{Mt+\frac{1}{2}V^2t^2}.$$

A random variable Y that can be written as e^X, where $X \sim \mathbb{N}(M; V^2)$, is called Lognormal. From the Gaussian MGF we can compute the expectation and the variance of a lognormal random variable,

$$\mathbb{E}(y) = e^{M+\frac{1}{2}V^2},$$
$$\mathbb{V}(y) = e^{2M+2V^2} - e^{2M+V^2} \tag{12.6}$$

12.2 STOCHASTIC PROCESSES

Section 1.2.1 presented the standard probability space of mathematical finance,

$$(\Omega, \mathcal{F}, Q). \tag{12.7}$$

This is the typical representation of information and randomness of a financial problem in a single point in time, where $\mathcal{F}$ is the σ-algebra, set of all possible events to which we can give a probability. When we consider stochastic processes, we also consider that information and randomness evolve in time, and add to the probability space the filtration $\mathbb{F} = (\mathcal{F}_t)_{t\geq 0}$, a family of σ-algebras that represents the flow of information in time. In fact $\mathcal{F}_t$ represents information up to t and we have

$$\mathcal{F}_t \subseteq \mathcal{F}_s \subseteq \mathcal{F}, \qquad s \geq t,$$

so that we move from (12.7) to

$$(\Omega, \mathcal{F}, \mathbb{F}, Q). \tag{12.8}$$

A stochastic process X is usually intended as a family of random variables $(X_t)_{t\geq 0}$. A process X is *adapted* to the filtration $\mathbb{F}$ if, roughly speaking, for each t the information contained in $\mathcal{F}_t$ determines the path of X until t. On the other hand, the flow of information generated by the observation of the trajectory of a process X_t in time is called the *filtration generated by* X_t. The classic references on stochastic calculus are Øksendal (1998) and Karatzas and Shreve (1991).

12.2.1 The Law of Iterated Expectation

It is now time to introduce a result of probability theory that turns out to be particularly useful in finance, and in particular when dealing with stochastic processes. It is the *Law of Iterated Expectation*, which says that, when $\mathcal{F}_{Big}$ represents a set of information larger than $\mathcal{F}_{Small}$, we have

$$\mathbb{E}\left[\mathbb{E}\left[X \mid \mathcal{F}_{Big}\right] \mid \mathcal{F}_{Small}\right] = \mathbb{E}\left[X \mid \mathcal{F}_{Small}\right],$$

which in the context of a filtration (information through time) reads

$$\mathbb{E}\left[\mathbb{E}\left[X_T \mid \mathcal{F}_S\right] \mid \mathcal{F}_s\right] = \mathbb{E}\left[X_T \mid \mathcal{F}_s\right], \quad s < S < T.$$

See, for example, Williams (1991) for a general proof and a deep analysis of the properties of conditional expectation. Intuitively, on the left-hand side of the above equations we are only pretending to have a larger set of information $\mathcal{F}_{Big}$ or $\mathcal{F}_S$, because then we take expectation of this expectation using only smaller sets of information $\mathcal{F}_{Small}$ or $\mathcal{F}_s$. It is the smaller set of information that matters in the end, leading to the right-hand side. This formula is extremely useful in finance, at times used from left to right to simplify a nested expectation, but more often from right to left, to break an expectation $\mathbb{E}[X \mid \mathcal{F}]$ into two expectations based on two different sets of information that can be easier to compute than the original $\mathbb{E}[X \mid \mathcal{F}]$.

12.2.2 Diffusions, Brownian Motions and Martingales

Let us look at the classic stochastic process in continuous time: the Brownian motion. A Standard Brownian Motion or Wiener Process is indicated as $W(t)$ and enjoys the following properties.

1. $W(0) = 0$.
2. $W(t)$ has independent increments, namely $t_1 < t_2 \leq t_3 < t_4 \Rightarrow [W(t_2) - W(t_1)] \perp [W(t_4) - W(t_3)]$.
3. For $s < t$, $[W(t) - W(s)] \sim \mathbb{N}(0, t - s)$ (so increments are also stationary, namely their distribution depends only on $(t-s)$)
4. W has continuous trajectories, $t \to W(t)$ is continuous for all $\omega \in \Omega$ (*almost certainly* continuous would be more precise, but the difference has no impact on any of our results).

This implies:

$$Cov(W_t, W_s) = E(W_t W_s) = \min(s, t), \; s, t \geq 0.$$

From the Wiener process we can build processes like

$$dZ(t) = U(\cdot)dt + DC(\cdot)dW(t), \tag{12.9}$$

that are called *diffusions*, since they have only a deterministic driver of instantanous changes, dt, and a stochastic driver which is the instantaneous change $dW(t)$ of a Wiener process, leading to a continuous path for $Z(t)$. What multiplies dt, namely $U(\cdot)$, is called the *drift*, while what multiplies $dW(t)$, namely $DC(\cdot)$, is called the *diffusion coefficient*.

When a diffusion has null drift, it is called a *martingale*. For $Z(t)$ above this means

$$dZ(t) = DC(\cdot)dW(t).$$

More generally, a martingale is a process $Y(t)$ which is adapted and non-exploding, and such that, for $t \leq s$

$$E[Y(s) | \mathcal{F}_t] = Y(t).$$

Given information up to t, the best prediction of future $Y(s)$ is current $Y(t)$.

The most popular diffusion is the Geometric Brownian Motion, used by Black and Scholes (1973). It is a process with dynamics

$$dX(t) = \mu(t)X(t)dt + \sigma(t)X(t)dW(t) \tag{12.10}$$

where $\mu(t)$ and $\sigma(t)$ are deterministic functions of time. To understand the meaning of the stochastic differential equations written in (12.9) and (12.10) we need to recall a few more results.

Stochastic integral

The dynamics (12.9) and (12.10) are of dubious definition, since $W(t)$ has paths which are not differentiable and therefore it is hard to define rigorously $dW(t)$. What happens in practice is that $dW(t)$ and the differential representations (12.9) and (12.10) are also used universally for complex computations, but in principle they should be intended as a shorthand for the integral version of the process,

$$Z(t) = Z(0) + \int_0^T U(\cdot)dt + \int_0^T DC(\cdot)dW(t) \tag{12.11}$$

and

$$X(t) = X(0) + \int_0^T \mu(t)X(t)\,dt + \int_0^T \sigma(t)X(t)dW(t) \tag{12.12}$$

which can be defined more precisely thanks to the definition of a *stochastic integral.* If the function $g(t)$ is square integrable and adapted to the filtration generated by $W(t)$, then the stochastic integral

$$\int_a^b g(t)\,dW(t)$$

exists and has the following properties

$$\mathbb{E}\left[\int_a^b g(t)\,dW(t)\right] = 0,$$

$$\mathbb{E}\left[\left(\int_a^b g(t)\,dW(t)\right)^2\right] = \mathbb{E}\int_a^b \left[g^2(t)\right]\,dt.$$

We have now seen that, for example, the dynamics (12.10) for the geometric Brownian motion should be interpreted as a shorthand for (12.12). Then there are conditions to guarantee that it *represents a stochastic differential equation* with a unique solution. This is different, however, from having an analytic solution which is easy to use. In order to get this for (12.12) we need to look at a few more results.

The rules of the street when dealing with Brownian Motions

One typical use of the differential notation in stochastic calculus is what follows. Let us simplify such concepts as *quadratic variation* and *covariation* to reduce them to the operative results that we need. Define dt as a real positive number such that $(dt)^\alpha$ is negligible when $\alpha > 1$. Set $dW(t) = [W(t+dt) - W(t)] \sim \mathbb{N}(0, dt)$. Notice that

- $E[dW(t)] = 0;$
- $E[dW(t)\,dt] = 0;$
- $E[(dW(t))^2] = dt,$

and

- $Var[(dW(t))^2] = 2(dt)^2 = 0$
- $E[(dW(t)\,dt)^2] = E[(dW(t))^2](dt)^2 = 0$
- $Var[dW(t)\,dt] = E[(dW(t)\,dt)^2] - E[(dW(t)\,dt)]^2 = 0.$

This provides an intutitive justification for the following 'rules of the street' of stochastic calculus

$$(dW(t))^2 = dt, \tag{12.13}$$

and

$$dW(t)dt = 0. \tag{12.14}$$

Also notice that if

$$dY = \sigma_y dW^Y, dX = \sigma_x dW^X, \; Corr\left(dW^Y, dW^X\right) = \rho$$

then

$$dYdX = \sigma_y \sigma_x \rho dt.$$

Ito's Lemma

The other result that we need is the famous Ito's Lemma, useful for computing the dynamics of a stochastic process defined as the function of another process with a known dynamics. Consider the stochastic process

$$X(t) = x_0 + \int_0^t U ds + \int_0^t DC dW(s),$$

where the functions U and DC are such that the integrals exist. In differential form it reads

$$dX(t) = U dt + DC dW(t).$$

Now the stochastic process

$$F\left(t, X(t)\right),$$

where F is a function of class $C^{1,2}$, namely with continuous first derivative with respect to t and continuous first and second derivatives with respect to $X(t)$, has dynamics

$$\begin{aligned}
dF &= \frac{\partial F}{\partial t} dt + \frac{\partial F}{\partial X} dX + \frac{1}{2}\frac{\partial^2 F}{\partial X^2} dX^2, \\
&= \frac{\partial F}{\partial t} dt + U\frac{\partial F}{\partial X} dt + DC\frac{\partial F}{\partial X} dW(t) + \frac{1}{2}\frac{\partial^2 F}{\partial X^2} dX^2 \\
&= \left[\frac{\partial F}{\partial t} + U\frac{\partial F}{\partial X} + \frac{1}{2}DC^2\frac{\partial^2 F}{\partial X^2}\right] dt + \left[DC\frac{\partial F}{\partial X}\right] dW(t).
\end{aligned}$$

This stochastic differential reminds us of the deterministic differential, or chain rule. But while in a deterministic differential there are only first order terms, here second order terms also appear. We can say, intuitively, that the stochasticity of $X(t)$ requires us to consider also the second order terms, and then from (12.13) and (12.14) we see that only one second order term is non-negligible.

Solving the Geometric Brownian Motion

Now we can solve the geometric Brownian motion equation

$$dX(t) = \mu(t)X(t)dt + \sigma(t)X(t)dW(t), \; X(0) = x_0.$$

The first step is to compute the dynamics of $\ln(X(t))$. This can be done by Ito's Lemma, setting $F(t, X(t)) = \ln(X(t))$, which requires first the computation of

$$\frac{\partial F}{\partial t} = 0, \quad \frac{\partial F}{\partial X} = \frac{1}{X(t)}(\text{assuming } X(t) \text{ always positive}), \quad \frac{\partial^2 F}{\partial X^2} = -\frac{1}{X(t)^2}.$$

Notice, by the rules of the street, that

$$dX(t)^2 = \sigma(t)^2 X(t)^2 dt.$$

Hence

$$d\ln(X(t)) = \mu(t)dt - \frac{1}{2}\sigma(t)^2 dt + \sigma(t)\,dW(t).$$

Going back to integral notation,

$$\ln(X(t)) = \ln(X(0)) + \int_0^t \mu(s)\,ds - \int_0^t \frac{1}{2}\sigma(s)^2\,ds + \int_0^t \sigma(s)\,dW(s),$$

so that

$$X(t) = X(0)\,e^{Y(t)}$$

where $Y(t)$ is normally distributed with mean $M = \int_0^t \mu(s)\,ds - \int_0^t \frac{1}{2}\sigma(s)^2 ds$ and variance $V^2 = \int_0^t \sigma(s)^2 ds$. This is a useful form for the solution of the above equation because it shows that $X(t)$ has a lognormal distribution with moments that can be computed following (12.6).

12.2.3 Poisson Process

While the Brownian motion is the prototypical continuous stochastic process, the prototypical stochastic process based on jumps is the Poisson process, which we define below.

Constant intensity

The Poisson process is a model for rare events based on the following three assumptions, which relate to the likelihood of events in a very short time interval Δt:

A the probability of 1 event in Δt is λ proportional to Δt.
B Δt is so small that there cannot be 2 events in Δt.
C the number of events in a period is independent of the number of events in any distant period.

The parameter λ is called intensity. To derive the properties of the process in continuous time from these assumptions, we focus on the period between two dates t and T, which we divide into m intervals of size Δt, so that

$$T - t = m \times \Delta t \text{ and } \Delta t = \frac{T - t}{m}.$$

We call $N(t)$ the number of events at t. We have the following results:

1. Applying assumption A, we get

$$Pr\left[N(t + \Delta t) - N(t) = 1\right] = \lambda \Delta t = \lambda\left(\frac{T - t}{m}\right).$$

2. Applying also B, we have

$$Pr\left[N\left(t+\Delta t\right)-N(t)=0\right]=1-\lambda\Delta t=1-\lambda\left(\frac{T-t}{m}\right).$$

3. Then, applying C, we can compute

$$\begin{aligned}&Pr\left[N(T)-N(t)=0\right]\\&=Pr\left[N\left(t+m\times\Delta t\right)-N(t)=0\right]\\&=\left(1-\frac{\lambda(T-t)}{m}\right)^{m}.\end{aligned}$$

Now let Δt tend to 0 (equivalent to m tending to infinity). Since

$$\lim_{n\to\infty}\left(1+\frac{x}{n}\right)^{n}\longrightarrow e^{x},$$

we have

$$Pr\left[N(t)-N(t)=0\right]=e^{-\lambda(T-t)}.$$

12.2.4 Time-dependent Intensity

Poisson processes with time-dependent intensity start from a set of hypotheses similar to A, B and C above, but A is replaced by

$$Pr\left[N\left(t+\Delta t\right)-N(t)=1\right]=\lambda(t)\Delta t,$$

which implies

$$Pr\left[N\left(t+\Delta t\right)-N(t)=0\right]=1-\lambda(t)\Delta t.$$

With $T-t=m\times\Delta t$ and $\Delta t=\frac{T-t}{m}$

$$Pr\left[N(T)-N(t)=0\right]=\prod_{i=0}^{m-1}\left(1-\lambda\left(t+i\Delta t\right)\Delta t\right)$$

$$\begin{aligned}\ln\left\{Pr\left[N(T)-N(t)=0\right]\right\}&=\sum_{i=0}^{m-1}\ln\left(1-\lambda\left(t+i\Delta t\right)\Delta t\right)\\&=\sum_{i=0}^{m-1}-\lambda\left(t+i\Delta t\right)\Delta t+o\left(\Delta t\right)\end{aligned}$$

where $o\left(\Delta t\right)$ is a quantity infinitesimal with respect to Δt. The last passage comes from a simple first order expansion

$$\ln\left(1-x\right)=\ln(1-0)-\frac{1}{(1-0)}\left(x-0\right)+o\left(\left(x-0\right)\right)=-x+o(x).$$

Then we let Δt go to zero, obtaining

$$\lim_{\Delta t \longrightarrow 0} \ln Pr\left[N(T) - N(t) = 0\right] = \lim_{\Delta t \longrightarrow 0} \sum_{i=0}^{m-1} -\lambda\left(t + i\Delta t\right)\Delta t + o\left(\Delta t\right)$$

$$= -\int_t^T \lambda\left(s\right) ds,$$

so that here we have

$$Pr\left[N(T) - N(t) = 0\right] = e^{-\int_t^T \lambda(s)ds}$$

rather than $e^{-\lambda(T-t)}$, which is the special case when $\lambda(t) = \lambda$.

12.3 USEFUL RESULTS FROM QUANTITATIVE FINANCE

12.3.1 Black and Scholes (1973) and Black (1976)

Black and Scholes (1973) assume that a stock price $S(t)$, paying no dividends, has a dynamics given by a geometric Brownian motion such as (12.10), so that under the real-world probability measure it evolves according to

$$dS(t) = \mu S(t)dt + \sigma S(t)dW(t).$$

Then, according to the reasoning in Section 1.2.1, we know that under the risk neutral pricing measure Q the dynamics becomes

$$dS(t) = rS(t)dt + \sigma S(t)dW(t). \tag{12.15}$$

Pricing a call option means computing

$$ECall\left(S\left(0\right), K, r, T, \sigma\right) = \mathbb{E}^Q\left[D\left(0, T\right)\max\left(S(T) - K, 0\right)\right]$$

$$= \mathbb{E}^Q\left[D\left(0, T\right)\left(S(T) - K\right)^+\right]$$

$$= e^{-rT}\mathbb{E}^Q\left[\left(S(T) - K\right)^+\right]$$

where the last equality comes from assuming a flat deterministic short rate r. Since we know that S_T has a lognormal distribution such as we have seen in Section 12.2.2, we can compute that

$$ECall\left(S\left(0\right), K, r, T, \sigma\right) = B\&S\left(S\left(0\right), K, rT, \sigma^2 T\right),$$

where we have used the following definition:

- **The Black and Scholes formula:**

$$B\&S\left(F, K, rT, v\right) = F\,\Phi(d_1) - Ke^{-rT}\,\Phi(d_2)$$

$$d_1 = \frac{\ln(\frac{F}{K}) + rT + \frac{1}{2}v}{\sqrt{v}}, \qquad d_2 = \frac{\ln(\frac{F}{K}) + rT - \frac{1}{2}v}{\sqrt{v}}.$$

When Black (1976) had to price call options on commodity prices, with payoff at T

$$\left(C(T) - K\right)^+,$$

where $C(t)$ is a spot commodity price at t, he found that commodity traders would not assume for $dC(t)$ a dynamics similar to the one assumed for $dS(t)$. In fact, the assumption made for equity appeared too simple for commodity prices, which are characterized by strong seasonality: for example, agricultural goods have prices that rise before harvest and fall afterwards. The idea Black had to overcome this difficulty was a change of variable: he pointed out that if we call $C^f(t, T)$ the *forward* price with delivery T then $C^f(T, T) = C(T)$ and the option payoff can be rewritten as

$$\left(C^f(T,T) - K\right)^+.$$

What's the difference now that we see the option written on the forward price $C^f(t, T)$? The difference is that $C^f(t, T)$ is not subject to seasonalities because it has a fixed delivery time. Thus it is acceptable to give it a simple dynamics. However, there will be differences from dynamics (12.15): forward prices have a different volatility σ_f and they are martingales under the risk-neutral measure. This can be easily proven for the equity world where forward contracts can be replicated by holding the spot so that

$$S^f(t,T) = S(t)e^{r(T-t)}$$

and we can compute $dS^f(t, T)$ by (12.15) and Ito's Lemma, but it holds also when, as in the commodity world, there is no spot dynamics as simple as (12.15) and, more importantly, there is no replication with the spot since holding the spot has a storage cost, it alters the nature of the product and has an opportunity cost since it involves not exploiting the seasonalities.

The martingale property of forward prices can in fact be more generally obtained by recalling that $C^f(t, T)$ is the equibrium price P of a forward contract with value

$$e^{-r(T-t)}\mathbb{E}_t^Q\left[(C(T) - P)\right],$$

so that setting this to zero and solving in P we get

$$C^f(t,T) = \mathbb{E}_t^Q\left[C(T)\right].$$

We can prove that such a price is a martingale by means of the Law of Iterated Expectation

$$\mathbb{E}_t^Q\left[C^f(t+h,T)\right] \overset{by\ def}{=} \mathbb{E}_t^Q\left[\mathbb{E}_{t+h}^Q\left[C(T)\right]\right] \overset{by\ LIE}{=} \mathbb{E}_t^Q\left[C(t)\right] \overset{by\ def}{=} C^f(t,T).$$

Now we can compute the price of the commodity option as

$$\begin{aligned} CCall\left(C^f(0,T), K, r, T, \sigma_f\right) &= \mathbb{E}_t^Q\left[e^{-r(T-t)}\left(C^f(T,T) - K\right)^+\right] \\ &= e^{-r(T-t)} \underbrace{\mathbb{E}_t^Q\left[\left(C^f(T,T) - K\right)^+\right]}_{B\&S \text{ when } r=0} \\ &= e^{-r(T-t)} Black\left(C^f(0,T), K, \sigma_f^2 T\right) \qquad (12.16) \end{aligned}$$

where we have used the following definition:

- **The Black formula**

$$Black(F, K, v) = F\ \Phi(d_1) - K\ \Phi(d_2)$$

$$d_1 = \frac{\ln(\frac{F}{K}) + \frac{1}{2}v}{\sqrt{v}}, \qquad d_2 = \frac{\ln(\frac{F}{K}) - \frac{1}{2}v}{\sqrt{v}}.$$

This formula is often recalled as a special case of the Black and Scholes one, but it is in reality a generalization: if one applies (12.16) to an equity option, where $S^f(0, T) = S(0)e^{rT}$, one gets the Black and Scholes formula. But the Black formula also holds when the spot has a complex dynamics and there is no replication of the forward with the spot.

12.3.2 Change of Numeraire

A numeraire is some traded asset, with a price in terms of which the prices of all securities are expressed. Or, with a definition that helps to understand the applications, it is the asset one uses for 'discounting'. Since it must be used as a 'denominator' in a ratio, it must be strictly positive. We have these fundamental requirements: the numeraire asset must be *traded* with *positive price*, and one requires it to pay no dividends. These conditions can be generalized as, for example in Morini (2009) or in Morini and Brigo (2009).

In Section 1.2.1 we introduced the money market account,

$$B(t) = e^{\int_0^t r(s)ds} = 1/D(0, t).$$

The standard asset pricing theory is based on taking $B(t)$ as numeraire. This is the numeraire used to discount in the Black and Scholes formula. The risk neutral measure Q used for pricing is the measure under which the drift of traded securities is r, so that under this measure prices discounted using $B(t)$ follow a martingale. We can say that *the risk neutral martingale Q measure is the probability measure associated with $B(t)$*. What do we mean by probability measure *associated with* a numeraire?

Definition 18. *Given a probability measure Q^{N1} equivalent*[1] *to the real-world probability measure, and a numeraire $N1_t$, Q^{N1} is the* **measure associated with** *$N1_t$ if the price of any tradable asset X_t expressed in terms of $N1_t$ is a martingale under Q^{N1}, i.e.*

$$\frac{X_t}{N1_t} = \mathbb{E}^{N1}\left[\frac{X_T}{N1_T}\middle|\mathcal{F}_t\right].$$

And now comes the useful part. The classic numeraire $B(t)$ is not the only numeraire that can be used for pricing.

Theorem 20. *(Geman-Eikaroui-Rochet. 1995 Theorem): if Q^{N1} is a probability measure associated with the numeraire $N1_t$, given a different numeraire $N2_t$ there exists a measure Q^{N2} equivalent to Q^{N1} such that Q^{N2} is the measure associated with $N2_t$.*

So one can move from a measure to a different one according to

$$X_t = \mathbb{E}^{N1}\left[\frac{N1_t}{N1_T}X_T\middle|\mathcal{F}_t\right] = \mathbb{E}^{N2}\left[\frac{N2_t}{N2_T}X_T\middle|\mathcal{F}_t\right]. \tag{12.17}$$

[1]

Definition 19. *Given two measures P and Q defined on the same σ-algebra $\mathcal{F}$, we say that Q is absolutely continuous w.r.t. P, $Q \ll P$, if*

$$P(A) = 0 \Rightarrow Q(A) = 0, \quad \forall A \in \mathcal{F}.$$

If $P \ll Q$ and $Q \ll P$ they are said to be **equivalent**, *$P \sim Q$. In this case $Q(A) = 0 \Longleftrightarrow P(A) = 0$, namely they have the same null sets. Taking negation, they have the same positive sets, taking complements they have the same a.s. sets (sets with probability 1).*

The measures we use in finance are usually equivalent to the real world probability measure. We may wish to modify the rate of return, for example to take risk into account as in the intuition about the risk-neutral probability measure we gave in Section 1.2.1. But it is rare that we would want to make possible events that are impossible in reality, or vice versa, nor do we want to alter events which have probability 1.

Notice that from (12.17) we can get a relation between expectation under Q^{N1} and expectation Q^{N2} where the process giving the relation is the so-called *Radon-Nikodym derivative* for the change of measure. In fact setting $t = 0$ and defining $Y_T := X_T / N1_T$,

$$\mathbb{E}^{N1}\left[Y_T\right] = \mathbb{E}^{N2}\left[\frac{N1_T N2_0}{N1_0 N2_T} Y_T\right]. \tag{12.18}$$

More importantly we have in (12.17) two expressions for the price which are absolutely equivalent, although one may be much easier to compute. In fact, change of numeraire is used most often to get computational simplification.

So, setting $Q^{N1} = Q$, all prices computed as expected values under Q with numeraire B can be obtained as expected values under a different probability measure Q^{N2}. Assume the claim I want to price is $\Pi(X_T)$, the price can be written

$$\begin{aligned}\Pi_t &= E^Q\left[e^{-\int_t^T r(s)ds}\Pi(X_T)\middle|\mathcal{F}_t\right] = B(t)E^Q\left[\frac{1}{B(t)}\Pi(X_T)\middle|\mathcal{F}_t\right]\\ &= N2_t\mathbb{E}^{N2}\left[\frac{1}{N2_T}\Pi(X_T)\middle|\mathcal{F}_t\right].\end{aligned}$$

Why in some situations may we be interested in operating a change of numeraire, and the corresponding change of probability measure? We can have two goals:

1. We want $\frac{\Pi(X_T)}{N2_T}$ to be a simple quantity, since pricing amounts to computing its expected value.
2. We want to express X_t as $\frac{TradableAsset_t}{N2_t}$, because in this case, by definition of Q^{N2}, we know that our underlying X_t is a martingale.

For European payoffs with maturity T a numeraire satisfying condition 1 is the risk-free bond price $P(t, T)$, to be seen as a function of t with T fixed. We know by the Geman Theorem that there exists a probability measure associated with $P(t, T)$. Such a measure is called T-forward measure and indicated by Q^T. In this case

$$\begin{aligned}\Pi_t &= E^Q\left[D(t,T)\Pi(X_T)|\mathcal{F}_t\right] \overset{D(t,T)\ definition}{=} B(t)E^Q\left[\frac{1}{B(t)}\Pi(X_T)\middle|\mathcal{F}_t\right] \overset{by\ CoN}{=}\\ &\overset{by\ CoN}{=} P(t,T)\mathbb{E}^T\left[\frac{1}{P(T,T)}\Pi(X_T)\middle|\mathcal{F}_t\right] = P(t,T)\mathbb{E}^T\left[\Pi(X_T)|\mathcal{F}_t\right].\end{aligned} \tag{12.19}$$

As we desired, we have simplified $\frac{\Pi(X_T)}{N2_T}$, which reduces to $\Pi(X_T)$ thanks to the fact that with this choice of numeraire $N2_T = P(T, T) = 1$.

If then the underlying was for example a forward rate, defined earlier as

$$F(t; T', T) = \frac{P(t, T') - P(t, T)}{P(t, T)}\frac{1}{T - T'},$$

as when we are pricing forward rate agreements or caplets in the classic risk-free interest rate framework, then condition 2 is also satisfied since $P(t, T') - P(t, T)$ is a tradable asset (portfolio of bonds) while $P(t, T)$ is the numeraire we are using in pricing.*

* This book expresses the views of its authors and does not represent the opinion of its employers, who are not responsible for any use which may be made of its contents.

Bibliography

Acerbi, C. and Scandolo, G. (2008). Liquidity Risk Theory and Coherent Measures of Risk, available at *http://papers.ssrn.com/sol3/papers.cfm?abstract_id=1048322.*

Alexander, C. (2002). Common Correlation Structures for Calibrating the Libor Model, University of Reading. ISMA Center Preprint.

Algorithmics (2009). Credit Value Adjustment and the changing environment for pricing and managing counterparty risk. http://www.algorithmics.com/EN/media/pdfs/Algo-WP1209-CVASurvey.pdf

Ametrano, F. and Bianchetti, M. (2009). Bootstrapping the Illiquidity, in *Modelling Interest Rates: Advances for Derivatives Pricing*, edited by F. Mercurio, Risk Books.

Andersen, L. (2006). Efficient Simulation of the Heston Stochastic Volatility Model, working paper available at *papers.ssrn.com/sol3/papers.cfm?abstract_id=946405.*

Andersen, L. and Andreasen, J. (2001). Factor dependence of Bermudan swaptions: fact or fiction? *Journal of Financial Economics*, 62(1), 3–37.

Andersen, L. and Piterbarg, V. (2006). Moment explosions in stochastic volatility models. *Finance and Stochastics*.

Andersen, L. and Piterbarg, V. (2008). Moment explosions in stochastic volatility models. *Finance and Stochastics*, 2006.

Andersen, L. and Sidenius, J. (2005). Extensions to the Gaussian copula: random recovery and random factor loadings. *Journal of Credit Risk* 1 (1), Winter 2004/05.

Andersen, L., Andreasen, J. and Sidenius, J. (2000). Jump-Diffusion Processes: Volatility Smile Fitting and Numerical Methods for Option Pricing. *Review of Derivatives Research*, 4, 231–262.

Aragones, J.R., Blanco, C. and Dowd, K. (2001). Incorporating Stress Testing Into Market Risk Modelling, *Institutional Investor*.

Avellaneda, M., Levy, A. and Paras, A. (1995). Pricing and Hedging Derivative Securities in Markets with Uncertain Volatilities, *Appl. Math. Finance* 2, 73–88.

Avellaneda, M. and Newman, J. (1998). Positive Interest Rates and Nonlinear TermStructure Models. Preprint, Courant Institute of Mathematical Sciences, New York University.

Avellaneda, M. and Paras, A. (1996). Managing the Volatility Risk of Portfolios of Derivative Securities: The Lagrangian Uncertain Volatility Model, *App. Math. Finance* 3, 31–52.

Baheti P. and Morgan, S. (2007). Base correlation Mapping, *Quantitative Credit Research Quarterly*, vol 2007-Q1, Lehman Brothers.

Barden P. (2009). Equity forward prices in the presence of funding spreads. ICBI Conference, Rome.

Bartlett, B. (2006). Hedging under the SABR Model. *Wilmott Magazine*.

Barucci, E. and Morini, M. (2009). What did not work in securitization, in *After the Shock*, Bocconi University Ed.

Bergomi L. (2004). Smile Dynamics, *Risk Magazine*, September.

Bergomi L. (2005). Smile Dynamics 2, *Risk Magazine*, October.

Bergomi L. (2008). Smile Dynamics 3, *Risk Magazine*, October.

Berkowitz, J. (1999). A Coherent Framework for Stress-Testing, *Journal of Risk*, 2, (Winter 1999/2000), 5–15.

Berrahoui, M. (2005). Pricing CMS Spread Options and Digital CMS Spread Options with Smile. The best of Wilmott 2, Wiley.

Bianchetti, M. (2009). Two Curves, One Price. Available at: *http://papers.ssrn.com/sol3/papers.cfm?abstract_id=1334356.*

Bielecki T. and Rutkowski, M. (2001). Credit risk: Modeling, Valuation and Hedging. Springer Verlag.

Björk, T. (2004). *Arbitrage Theory in Continuous Time*, 2nd ed. Oxford University Press.

Black, F. (1976). The Pricing of commodity contracts, *Journal of Financial Economics*, 3, 167–179.

Black F. and Cox, J.C. (1976). Valuing corporate securities: Some effects of bond indenture provisions. *Journal of Finance*, 31, 351–367.

Black, F., Derman, E. and Toy, W. (1990). A One-Factor Model of Interest Rates and its Application to Treasury Bond Options. *Financial Analysts Journal*, 46, 33–39.

Black, F. and Scholes, M. (1973). The pricing of options and corporate liabilities. *Journal of Political Economy*, 81, 637–654.

Brace, A., Gatarek, D. and Musiela, M. (1997). The market model of interest rate dynamics. *Mathematical Finance*, 7, 127–154.

Breeden, J. (2008). Validation of Stress Testing Models, in *The Analytics of Risk Model Validation*, pp. 13–26.

Breeden, D.T. and Litzenberger, R.H. (1978). Prices of state-contingent claims implicit in option prices. *Journal of Business* 51, 621–651.

Brigo, D. (2005). Market models for CDS options and callable floaters, *Risk Magazine*, January.

Brigo, D. and Alfonsi, A. (2005). Credit default swap calibration and derivatives pricing with the SSRD stochastic intensity model. *Finance and Stochastics*, 9 (1).

Brigo, D. and Capponi, A. (2009). Bilateral counterparty risk valuation with stochastic dynamical models and application to credit default swaps. SSRN: http://ssrn.com/abstract=1318024.

Brigo, D. and Chourdakis, K. (2008). Counterparty risk for credit default swaps: impact of spread volatility and default correlation. To appear in *International Journal of Theoretical and Applied Finance*.

Brigo, D. and Masetti, M. (2005). Risk neutral pricing of counterparty risk. In: Pykhtin, M. (Editor), *Counterparty Credit Risk Modeling: Risk Management, Pricing and Regulation*. Risk Books, London. Forthcoming.

Brigo, D. and Mercurio, F. (2001). *Interest Rate Models Theory and Practice*, Springer Finance.

Brigo, D. and Mercurio, F. (2006). *Interest-Rate Models: Theory and Practice. With Smile, Inflation and Credit.* Springer Finance.

Brigo, D., Mercurio, F. and Morini, M. (2005). The Libor Model dynamics: approximations, calibration and diagnostics. *European Journal of Operation Research*, 163, 30–41.

Brigo, D., Mercurio, F. and Rapisarda F. (2004). Smile at the Uncertainty, *Risk*, May.

Brigo D. and Morini M. (2003). An Empirically Efficient Analytical Cascade Calibration of the LIBOR Market Model Based Only on Directly Quoted Swaptions Data, working paper available at http://papers.ssrn.com/sol3/papers.cfm?abstract_id=552581.

Brigo, D. and Morini, M. (2005). CDS Market Models and Formulas, Proceedings of the 18th Annual Warwick Option Conference.

Brigo, D. and Morini, M. (2006). Structural credit calibration. *Risk Magazine,* February.

Brigo, D. and Morini, M. (2006). Efficient analytical cascade calibration of the LIBOR Market Model with endogenous interpolation, *The Journal of Derivatives*, Fall.

Brigo, D., and Morini, M. (2010). Dangers of Bilateral Counterparty Risk: the Fundamental Impact of Closeout Conventions. Working paper available at: *papers.ssrn.com/sol3/papers.cfm?abstract id=1709370 or at arxiv.org/pdf/1011.3355v1.*

Brigo, D., Morini, M. and Tarenghi, M. (2010). Credit calibration with structural models and equity return swap valuation under counterparty risk. The Lehman case. In *Recent advancements in theory and practice of credit derivatives*, Bloomberg Press, 2010.

Brigo, D., Pallavicini, A., and Papatheodorou, V. (2010). Bilateral Counterparty Risk Valuation for Interest-rate Products: Impact of Volatilities and Correlations. Working paper available at: *http://papers.ssrn.com/sol3/papers.cfm?abstractid=1507845.*

Brigo, D., Pallavicini, A. and Torresetti, R. (2007). Calibration of CDO Tranches with the dynamical Generalized-Poisson loss model, *Risk Magazine*, May issue.

Brigo, D., Pallavicini, A. and Torresetti, R. (2010). *Credit Models and the Crisis*, Wiley.
Brigo, D. and Tarenghi, M. (2004). Credit Default Swap Calibration and Equity Swap Valuation under Counterparty Risk with a Tractable Structural Model, In Proceedings of the FEA 2004 Conference at MIT, Cambridge, Mass, 8–10 November. Extended version available at www.damianobrigo.it.
British Bank Association (2009a). 'BBALibor Panels'. Available at http://www.bbalibor.com.
British Bank Association (2009b). 'BBALibor Explained'. Available at http://www.bbalibor.com.
Brunnermeier, M. (2009). Deciphering the Liquidity and Credit Crunch 2007–2008, *Journal of Economic Perspectives*, 23 (1), 77–100.
Bouyé, E., Durrleman, V., Nikeghbali, A., Riboulet, C. and Roncalli, T. (2000). Copulas for finance. A reading guide and some applications. Proceedings of the First World Congress of the Bachelier Finance Society.
Buraschi, A. and Corielli, F. (2005). Risk management implications of time-inconsistency: model updating and recalibration of no-arbitrage models. *Journal of Banking and Finance*, 29, 2883–2907.
Carr, P. and Chou, A. (1997). Breaking Barriers: Static Hedging of Barrier Securities, *Risk Magazine*, October.
Carr, P. and Madan, D. (1998). Option valuation using the fast Fourier Transform. Working paper, Morgan Stanley and University of Maryland.
Cherubini, U., Luciano, E. and Vecchiato, W. (2004). *Copula Methods in Finance*. John Wiley.
Cheyette, O. (1996). Markov Representation of the Heath–Jarrow–Morton Model. Working paper available at http://papers.ssrn.com/sol3/papers.cfm?abstract_id=6073.
Cho, M. and Rosemberg, J. (2008). Cross product debt research, Bank of America, April.
Collin-Dufresne, P. and Goldstein, R. (2001). Do credit spreads reflect stationary leverage ratios? *Journal of Finance* 56, 1929–1958.
Collin-Dufresne, P. and Solnik, B. (2001). On the term Structure of default premia in the swap and LIbro Markets., *Journal of Finance*, 56 (3), 1095–1115.
Cont, R. (2006). Model uncertainty and its impact on the pricing of derivative instruments. *Mathematical Finance*, 16 (3) July, 519–547.
Cont, R. and Tankov, P. (2004). *Financial Modelling with Jump Processes*. Chapman & Hall.
Cont, R. and Tankov, P. (2007). Calibration of jump-diffusion option pricing models: a robust non-parametric approach. *Journal of Computational Finance*, 7 (3), 1–49.
Cox, J.C., Ingersoll, J.E. and Ross, S.A. (1985). A theory of the term structure of interest rates. *Econometrica* 53, 385–407.
Dellacherie, C. (1972). *Capacité s et processus stochastiques*, Springer.
Derman, E. (1996). Model Risk. *Risk*, 9 (5), May, 139–145, 34–37.
Derman, E. (2001). Markets and Models, *Risk*, 14 (7), July, 48–59
Derman, E. and Kani, I. (1994). Riding on a smile. *Risk Magazine*, February, 32–39.
Duffie, D. (1996). *Dynamic Asset Pricing Theory*, 2nd. edn. Princeton University Press.
Duffie, D. and Garleanu, N. (2001). Risk and valuation of collateralized debt obligations. *Financial Analysts Journal*, 57 (1), 41–59
Duffie, D. and Huang, M. (1996). Swap rates and credit quality, *Journal of Finance*, 51 (4), 921–949.
Duffie, D. and Singleton, K. (1997). An econometric model of the term structure of interest-rate swap yields, *Journal of Finance*, 52 (4), 1287–1321.
Duffie, D. and Singleton, K. (1999). Modeling term structures of defaultable bonds, *Review of Financial Studies*, 12, 687–720.
Duffie, D. and Singleton, K. (2003). *Credit Risk: Pricing, Measurement, and Management*, Princeton University Press.
Dumas, B., Fleming, J. and Whaley, R.E. (1998). Implied Volatility Functions: Empirical Tests. *Journal of Finance* 53, 6.
Duminuco, C. and Morini, M. (2008). Correlation parameterizations for calibrating the market skew. Banca IMI internal report.
Dupire, B. (1994). Pricing with a smile. *Risk Magazine*, January, 18–20.
Dupire, B. (1997). *Pricing and Hedging with Smiles. Mathematics of Derivative Securities*, ed. M.A.H. Dempster and S.R. Pliska, Cambridge University Press, Cambridge, 103–111.

Dupire, B. (2006). Skew modelling. Talk at the ICBI Global Derivatives conference.
Elizalde, A. (2005). Credit Risk Models II: Structural Models, CEMFI and UPNA Working Paper.
Embrechts, P., Lindskog, F. and McNeil, A. (2001). Modelling Dependence with Copulas and Applications to Risk Management. Working Paper.
Embrechts, P. McNeil, A. and Strauman, D. (1999). Correlation and dependence in risk management: properties and pitfalls. Working Paper.
Facchinetti, G. and Morini M. (2007). *Modelling Correlations for Forward Exchange Rates*. Working paper.
Facchinetti, G. and Morini M. (2009). *Case study on Model Validation: dissecting and comparing the most popular credit models*. Working paper.
Fan, R., Gupta, A. and Ritchken, H. (2007). On Pricing and Hedging in the Swapton Market. *The Journal of Derivatives*, Fall.
Fermi L., Moreni N. and Morini M. (2007). The evolution of the term structure of volatility in IR smile models. Working paper, Banca IMI.
Flesaker, B. and Hughston, L. (1997). *Dynamic Models for Yield Curve Evolution. Mathematics of Derivative Securities*, Eds M.A.H. Dempster and S.R. Pliska, Cambridge University Press, Cambridge, pp. 294–314.
Fries, C. (2010). Discounting revisited: valuation under funding, counterparty risk and collateralization. http://papers.ssrn.com/sol3/papers.cfm?abstract_id=1609587.
Gatheral J. (2002). Stochastic Volatility and Local Volatility, Courant Institute of Mathematical Sciences, Fall Term.
Geman, H., ElKaroui, N. and Rochet, J.C. (1995). Changes of numeraire, changes of probability measure and pricing of options, *Journal of Applied Probability* 32, 443–458.
Giesecke, K. (2002). Correlated default with incomplete information, *Journal of Banking and Finance*, forthcoming.
Giesecke K. (2004). Credit Modelling and Valuation. An Introduction, to appear in *Credit Risk: Models and Management*, Vol. 2, Risk Books.
Gilboa, I., and Schmeidler, D. (1989). Maxmin Expected Utility with Non-Unique Prior, *J. Math. Econ.* 18, 141–153.
Glasserman, P., Kang, W. and Shahabuddin, P. (2007). Large deviations in multifactor portfolio credit risk, *Mathematical Finance*, 17 (3), July, 345–379
Glasserman, P. and Kim, K. (2008). Gamma expansion of the Heston stochastic volatility model. *Columbia Business School working paper*.
Gregory, J.K. (2008). A trick of the credit tail, *Risk Magazine*, March, 88–92.
Gregory, J.K. (2009). Being two faced over counterparty credit risk, *Risk Magazine*, 22 (2), 86–90.
Grinblatt, M. (2001). An analytic solution for interest rate swap spreads. UCLA Working Paper published in *International Review of Finance*, 2 (3), 3, 113–149.
Hagan, P.S. (2003). Convexity conundrums: pricing CMS swaps, caps, and floors, *Wilmott Magazine*, March, 38–44
Hagan, P.S., Kumar, D., Lesniewski, A.S. and Woodward, D.E. (2002). Managing Smile Risk. *Wilmott Magazine*, September, 84–108.
Harrison, J.M. and Kreps, D. (1979). Martingales and arbitrage in multi-period securities markets, *Journal of Economic Theory*, 20, 381–408.
Harrison, J.M. and Pliska, S. (1981). Martingales and stochastic integrals in the theory of continuous trading, *Stochastic Processes and their Applications*, 11, 215–260.
Heath, D., Jarrow, R. and Morton, A. (1990a). Bond pricing and the term structure of interest rates: a discrete time approximation. *Journal of Financial Quantitative Analysis*, 25, 419–440.
Heath D., Jarrow, R.A. and Morton, A. (1992). Bond Pricing and the Term Structure of Interest Rates: A New Methodology for Contingent Claim Valuation, *Econometrica*, 60, 77–105.
Henrard, M. (2007). The irony in the derivatives discounting. *Wilmott Magazine*, July, 92–98.
Henrard, M. (2009). The irony in the derivatives discounting Part II: The crisis. Preprint, Dexia Bank.
Heston, S.L. (1993). A closed-form solution for options with stochastic volatility with applications to bond and currency options. *Review of Financial Studies*, 6, 327–343.
Hoeting, J. A., Madigan, D., Referty, A. E., and Volinsky, C. T. (1999). Bayesian Model Averaging: A Tutorial, *Stat. Sci.* 14(4), 382–417.
Hull, J.C. (2006). *Options, futures, and other derivatives*. 6th edn, Prentice Hall.

Hull, J.C. and Suo, W. (2002). A methodology for assessing model risk and its applications to the implied volatility function model. *Journal of Financial and Quantitative Analysis*, 37, 297–318.

Hull, J. and White, A. (1990). Pricing interest-rate derivative securities. *Review of Financial Studies*, 3 (4), 573–592.

Hull J. and White A. (1994). Numerical Procedures for Implementing Term Structure Models II: two-factor models, *Journal of Derivatives*, Winter, 37–49.

Hull, J. and White, A. (1999). Forward rate volatilities, swap rate volatilities, and the implementation of the Libor Market Model. Preprint.

Hull, J. and White, A. (2005). The Perfect Copula: The Valuation of Correlation-Dependent Derivatives Using the Hazard Rate Path Approach. Working paper.

Hull, J. and White, A. (2006). Valuing credit derivatives using an implied copula approach. *Journal of Derivatives*, 14 (2), 8–28, Winter.

Hull, J. and White, A. (2008). Dynamic models of credit risk: a simplified approach. *Journal of Derivatives*, 15 (4), 9–28, Summer.

Hull, J. and White, A. (2010). An Improved Implied Copula Model and its Application to the Valuation of Bespoke CDO Tranches, *Journal of Investment Management*, 8 (3), 11–31.

ISDA – International Swaps and Derivatives Association, Inc. (2009). 'ISDA CLOSE-OUT AMOUNT', available at www.isda.org/isdacloseoutamtprot/docs/isdacloseoutprot-text.pdf

ISDA – International Swaps and Derivatives Association, Inc. (2010). Market review of OTC derivative bilateral collateralization practices, March 1.

Jäckel, P. and Rebonato, R. (2000). Linking caplet and swaption volatilities in a BGM/J framework: approximate solutions, *QUARC* preprint, available at www.rebonato.com.

James, J. and Webber, N. (2000). *Interest Rate Modelling*, John Wiley.

Jamshidian, F. (1997). Libor and swap market models and measures. *Finance and Stochastics*, 4, 293–330.

Jamshidian, F. (2004). Valuation of credit default swaps and swaptions. *Finance and Stochastics*, 8, 343–371.

Jarrow and Turnbull (1995). Pricing derivatives on financial securities subject to credit risk. *Journal of Finance*, 50, 53–85.

Jeanblanc, M. and Rutkowski, M. (2000). Default risk and hazard process. In Geman, Madan, Pliska and Vorst (eds), *Mathematical Finance Bachelier Congress 2000*, Springer.

Jouanin, J., Rapuch, G., Riboulet, G. and Roncall, T. (2001). Modelling dependence for credit derivatives with copulas, *Groupe de Recherche Operationnelle*, Credit Lyonnais.

Karatzas, I. and Shreve, S. (1991). *Brownian motion and stochastic calculus,* Springer.

Knight, F. (1921). *Risk, Uncertainty and Profit*. Boston: Houghton Mifflin.

Lando, D. (1998). On Cox processes and credit risky securities, *Derivatives Research*, 2, 99–120.

Li, A. (2006). Model calibration, risk measurement and the hedging of derivatives, http://papers.ssrn.com/sol3/papers.cfm?abstract_id=899081.

Li, D.X. (2000). On default correlation. A copula function approach. Working Paper 99–07, Risk Metrics Group, April.

Lo, C.F., Lee, H.C. and Hui, C.H. (2003). A simple approach for pricing barrier options with time-dependent parameters. *Journal of Financial Quantitative Analysis*, 3.

Longstaff, F.L. and Rajan, A. (2008). An Empirical Analysis of the Pricing of Collateralized Debt Obligations, *Journal of Finance*, February issue 2008.

Longstaff, F.A., Santa-Clara, P. and Schwartz, E.S. (2000). Throwing away a billion dollars: the cost of sub-optimal exercise strategies in the swaptions markets, Working Paper, UCLA, presented at the ICBI Risk Conference, Geneva.

Longstaff, F.A. and Schwartz, E.S. (2001). Valuing American options by simulation: a simple least-squares approach. *Review of Financial Studies*, 14, 113–147.

Lord, R., Koekkoek, R. and van Dijk, D. (2006). A comparison of biased simulation schemes for stochastic volatility models. Working Paper, Tinbergen Institute.

Marris, D. (1999). *Financial option pricing and skewed volatility*. M. Phil thesis, Statistical Laboratory, University of Cambridge.

Marshall, A.W. and Olkin, I. (1967). A multivariate exponential distribution. *Journal of the American Statistics Association*, 2, 84–98.

Mercurio, F. (2008). Interest rates and the credit crunch: new formulas and market models, available at http://papers.ssrn.com/sol3/papers.cfm?abstract_id=1332205.

Mercurio, F. (2009). Libor Market Model with Stochastic Basis, available at http://ssrn.com/abstract=1563685.

Mercurio, F. and Morini, M. (2007). A note on correlation in stochastic volatility term structure models, working paper available at SSRN.com.

Mercurio, F. and Morini, M. (2009a). A note on hedging with local and stochastic volatility model, in Modelling Interest Rates: Latest Advances for Derivatives Pricing, Risk Books.

Mercurio, F. and Morini, M. (2009b). Joining the SABR and Libor models together, *Risk Magazine*, March.

Mercurio, F. and Pallavicini, A. (2006). Smiling at convexity: bridging swaption skews and cms adjustments. *Risk Magazine*, 64–69, August.

Merton (1974). On the pricing of corporate debt: the risk structure of interest rates, *Journal of Finance*, 29 (2).

Michaud, F. and Upper, C. (2008). What drives interbank rates? Evidence from the Libor panel. *BIS Quarterly Review*, March.

Minucci, F. (2010). Gaussian Copula and Joint Default Probability Estimation. MSc Thesis, Politecnico di Milano.

Miron, P. and Swannell, P. (1991). *Pricing and hedging swaps*. Euromoney.

Mood, A.M., Graybill, F.A. and Boes, D.C. (1974). *Introduction to the Theory of Statistics*, 3rd edn McGraw Hill.

Morini, M. (2007). Modelling for Credit Derivatives. *Marcus Evans Workshop Material.*

Morini, M. (2008). Credit modelling after the subprime crisis. Fixed Income Conference, WBS, Budapest, September.

Morini, M. (2009a). Solving the puzzle in the interest rate market (Part 1 & 2). SSRN: http://ssrn.com/abstract=1506046

Morini, M. (2009b). One more model risk when using Gaussian copula for Risk Management. Available at http://ssrn.com/abstract=1520670, April.

Morini, M. (2010). Can the default of a bank cause the default of its debtors? The destabilizing consequences of the standard definition of bilateral counterparty risk. Working paper, March.

Morini, M. and Brigo, D. (2009). Last Option before the Armageddon, *Risk Magazine*, September.

Morini, M. and Brigo, D. (2010). Arbitrage-free equivalent measure for index options in a credit crisis, *Mathematical Finance.*

Morini, M. and Brigo, D. (2010). A structural model for investigating the relation between Equity and Credit and the possibility of Model Arbitrage. Working paper.

Morini, M. and Prampolini, A. (2011). Risky funding: a unified framework for counterparty and liquidity charges, *Risk Magazine*, March.

Morini, M. and Webber, N. (2006). An EZI method to reduce the rank of a correlation matrix, *Applied Mathematical Finance.*

Muliere, P. and Scarsini, M. (1987). Characterization of a Marshall-Olkin type class of distributions. *Annals of the Institute of Statistical Mathematics*, 39, 429–441.

Musiela, M. and Rutkowski, M. (1997). *Martingale Methods In Financial Modelling*, Springer.

Nawalkha, S. and Rebonato, R. (2011). What interest rate models to use? Buy side versus Sell side. Working paper.

O'Kane and Turnbull (2003). Valuation of Credit Default Swaps, Lehman Brothers, April 2003.

Øksendal, B. (1998). *Stochastic differential equations: an introduction with applications*, Springer.

Oyama, S. (2010). *Post-crisis Risk Management*. John Wiley.

Parcell, E. and Wood, J. (2007). Wiping the smile off your base (correlation curve). Derivatives Fitch working paper.

Pedersen, C.M. (2003). Valuation of Portfolio Credit Default Swaptions, *Lehman Brothers Quantitative Credit Research*, Vol. 2003.

Pelsser, A. (2000). Efficient Methods for Valuing Interest Rate Derivatives, *Springer Finance.*

Peng, S., Gandhi, C. and Tyo, A. (2008). Is Libor broken? Citi Fixed Income Strategy, Citigroup, April.

Picoult, E. (2005). Calculating and hedging exposure, credit value adjustment and economic capital for counterparty credit risk. In *Counterparty Credit Risk Modelling*, (ed. Pykhtin, M.), Risk Books.

Piterbarg, V. (2004). Risk sensitivities of Bermuda swaptions. *International Journal of Theoretical and Applied Finance*, 7 (4), 465–510.

Piterbarg, V. (2005). Stochastic volatility model with time-dependent skew. *Applied Mathematical Finance*, 12 (2), 147–185, June.
Piterbarg, V. (2007). Markovian projection for volatility calibration, *Risk Magazine*, 20 (4), 84–89, April.
Piterbarg V. (2010). Funding beyond discounting: collateral agreements and derivatives pricing. *Risk Magazine*, February.
Rapisarda F. (2003). *Pricing Barriers on Underlyings with Time-dependent Parameters.* Working Paper.
Rebonato, R. (1998). *Interest Rate Option Models.* 2nd edn, John Wiley.
Rebonato, R. (2001). On the simultaneous calibration of multifactor lognormal interest rate models to Black volatilities and to the correlation matrix. *The Journal of Computational Finance*, 2, 5–27.
Rebonato, R. (2002a). Term-structure models: a review. *Quarc working paper.*
Rebonato, R. (2002b). *Modern Pricing of Interest-Rate Derivatives. The Libor Market Model and Beyond.* Princeton University Press.
Rebonato, R. (2003). Theory and practice of model risk management. In *Modern Risk Management: A History*, 223–248, RiskWaters Group.
Rebonato R. (2010). *Coherent Stress Testing: A Bayesian Approach to the Analysis of Financial Stress*, Wiley.
Rebonato, R. (2011). Is it possible to reconcile the cap and swaption markets? presentation, Global Derivatives.
Rebonato, R. and Jäckel, P. (2000). The most general methodology to create a valid correlation matrix, *Journal of Risk*, 2 (2), Winter, 1–16.
Rubinstein, M. (1983). Displaced diffusion option pricing. *Journal of Finance* 38 (1), 213–217.
Sardo, M. (2010). Bespoke CDOs pricing: the deficiencies of standard mapping methods, Bocconi Univestity Master Thesis.
Schiavi, S. (2009). Capital management group, Banca IMI. Personal communication.
Schlogl, E. (2002). A multicurrency extension of the lognormal interest rate market models, *Finance and Stochastics*, 6 (2).
Schoenmakers, J. and Coffey, C. (2003). Systematic generation of correlation structures for the libor market model. *International Journal of Theoretical and Applied Finance*, 6 (4), 1–13.
Schönbucher, P. (2004). A measure of survival, *Risk*, January issue.
Shleifer, A. (2000). *Inefficient Markets: an Introduction to Behavioural Finance*, Oxford University Press.
Sorensen, E. and Bollier, T. (1994), Pricing Swap default risk, *Financial Anayst Journal*, May-June, 23–33.
Taleb, N. (2001). *Fooled by Randomness: The Hidden Role of Chance in the Markets and in Life*, Random House and Penguin.
Taleb, N. (2007). *The Black Swan: The Impact of the Highly Improbable.* Random House and Penguin.
Tuckman, B. and Porfirio, P. (2003). Interest rate parity, money market basis swaps, and cross-currency basis swaps. Fixed income research, Lehman Brothers.
Turc, J., Benhamou, D., Herzog, B. and Teyssier, M. (2006). Pricing bespoke CDOs: latest developments. Société Generale Credit Research.
Turc, J., Very, P. and Benhamou, D. (2005). Pricing CDO with a Smile. Société Generale Credit Research.
Vasicek, O. (1977). An equilibrium characterisation of the term structure. *Journal of Financial Economics*, 5, 177–188
Williams, D. (1991). *Probability with Martingales.* Cambridge University Press.
Wilmott, P. (2006). *Paul Wilmott On Quantitative Finance*, John Wiley.
Wilmott, P. (2007). *Paul Wilmott Introduces Quantitative Finance*, John Wiley.
Wood, D. (2009). The reality of risk-free. *Risk Magazine*, July.
Wu, L. and Zhang, F. (2006). Libor market model with stochastic volatility. *Journal of Industrial and Management Optimization*, 2 (2), May.

Index

Printed and bound by CPI Group (UK) Ltd, Croydon, CR0 4YY
16/09/2026
14963385-0001